Fifth Edition

WRITER'S GUIDE AND INDEX TO ENGLISH

Contributors

Benjamin DeMott, Amherst College

Wayne Harsh, University of California — Davis

Jarold Ramsey, University of Rochester

Jay Robinson, University of Michigan

Theodore Solotaroff, *New American Review*

Joseph M. Williams, University of Chicago

Fifth Edition

WRITER'S GUIDE AND INDEX TO ENGLISH

PORTER G. PERRIN

revised by
WILMA R. EBBITT

Scott, Foresman and Company
Glenview, Illinois   London

Acknowledgments

Acknowledgment is made to the following publishers and copyright holders for permission to use their material in *Writer's Guide and Index to English.*

The American Scholar: Excerpts from "On the Fashionable Idea of National Guilt" by K. R. Minogue and "If Not Reason, What?" by Kingman Brewster, Jr. Reprinted from *The American Scholar,* Volume 39, Number 2, Spring 1970. Copyright © 1970 by the United Chapters of Phi Beta Kappa. By permission of the publishers.

American Heritage Publishing Company, Inc.: Entry "style" from *The American Heritage Dictionary of the English Language.* © 1969, 1970, 1971 by American Heritage Publishing Co., Inc.

Atheneum Publishers: Excerpt from "The Busy Hand of Burgess" by Theodore Solotaroff from *The Red Hot Vacuum* by Theodore Solotaroff. Copyright © 1968 by Theodore Solotaroff. Reprinted by permission of Atheneum Publishers. Excerpt from *Language and Silence: Essays on Language, Literature and the Inhuman* by George Steiner. Copyright © 1961, 1963 by George Steiner. Reprinted by permission of the author, Atheneum Publishers, and Faber and Faber, Ltd.

The Atlantic Monthly: Excerpt from "Reports: Washington" by Elizabeth Drew, *The Atlantic Monthly,* June 1970. Copyright © 1970, by The Atlantic Monthly Company, Boston, Mass.

Barnard Alumnae: Excerpt from "Because I Am Black" by Deborah

Preface

Since its first edition, Perrin's *Writer's Guide and Index to English* has been an established source of information about current written English, in continuous use both as a text for writing courses and as a reference manual in and out of the classroom. Those coming to the *Guide and Index* for the first time will find a unique combination of rhetoric, guide to usage, and comprehensive reference book. Those familiar with earlier editions will discover that the Fifth—in keeping with the Perrin tradition—introduces new emphases as well as fresh material.

Chapters on organization and style have been added to the *Guide*. Some of the old chapters have been combined and some split up; all have been rewritten or extensively revised. More stress has been put on prewriting; and throughout the *Guide* there is steady insistence that at the heart of the composing process must lie a sense of personal commitment, personal engagement, personal responsibility. At the same time, most attention continues to be given to problems of execution—problems that recur in drafting and redrafting essays, in revising and rewriting. Like the earlier editions, the Fifth proceeds on the assumption that writing can be most satisfactorily practiced and studied in the context of a range of choices—rhetorical, syntactic, and lexical.

Few, if any, of the really interesting problems in writing can be solved by rule or formula, for each one arises in a new rhetorical situation and requires for its solution thoughtful appraisal of the writer-subject-reader relations that give it its special character. What can be done is to help students become alert to the varying pressures of the rhetorical situation and inventive in responding to them. And that is what this edition of the *Guide* undertakes to do.

The two strands of the writing process — its inside and outside, its private and public aspects — are introduced in Part One. The opening chapters distinguish the varieties of English, establish the criterion of appropriateness, outline the dimensions of the rhetorical situation, and deal with the agonizing uncertainties of getting started.

The next three sections of the *Guide* are given over to the content and organization of the larger rhetorical units. Part Two (Chapters Three, Four, and Five) investigates the traditional methods of development, considering what kinds of questions a writer can ask of his subject (and so generate ideas for his essay) and how he can sharpen his control over the strategies and techniques of presenting ideas in expository prose. Part Three (Chapters Six and Seven) discusses more fully the writer-subject-reader relations touched on in Part One, shows how arguments take shape, and examines the logical underpinnings of argument and the related fallacies. Part Four (Chapters Eight and Nine) treats structure — the structure of the whole essay, of the paragraph sequence, of the paragraph — and the different effects that result from different modes of organization.

Style becomes the main concern of Part Five. Chapters Ten through Thirteen move from a study of sentences and words to discussions by two professional writers of what style is and what makes a good style. In the chapters on sentences and words, the emphasis is largely on the range of choices and the different rhetorical effects that various choices produce. The essays in Chapter Thirteen make a more comprehensive approach, stressing the dynamics of the writer's situation and interpreting writing as process, as movement, as means to discovery, including self-discovery.

The final section of the *Guide* takes up the special problems of writing research papers (Chapter Fourteen) and critical essays (Postscript).

The exercises are an integral part of the text, designed to help students develop powers of criticism and, more important, of self-criticism. In this edition, instead of being clustered at the ends of chapters, they are interspersed within chapters, placed at points where they can contribute to one main purpose of the *Guide* — to help students develop criteria for judging their own work and so become self-reliant in their writing. Additional exercises, as well as suggestions for using the *Guide* in various kinds of courses, will be found in the Instructor's Manual, available from the publishers.

Because the alphabetical arrangement of the *Index* has been found practical and efficient by several generations of students and teachers, it remains unchanged. But the content has been largely rewritten. Articles with little bearing on expository writing have been dropped. Dated topics have been replaced with topics of current interest and usefulness.

On usage items, citations have been drawn from a much wider variety of sources.

In dealing with usage, the *Index* remains pragmatic in approach and inductive in method. It presents evidence about the status of a locution and invites the student to decide whether the locution is appropriate to the subject, the purpose, and the tone of *his* essay. Again, the aim is to make the student responsible for his choices and so to encourage self-reliance.

Several teachers and scholars have made major contributions to the Fifth Edition. The transformational analysis of sentences in Chapter Ten was drafted by Wayne Harsh and revised by Joseph M. Williams. The essays on style in Chapter Thirteen were written by Benjamin DeMott and Theodore Solotaroff. Jarold Ramsey drafted Chapter Fourteen (The Research Paper), and Mr. DeMott wrote the Postscript.

Joseph M. Williams reviewed and revised many of the articles on grammar in the *Index* and wrote several new articles. Jay Robinson wrote the article on the English language. The revision of the rest of the *Index* has drawn heavily on a work in progress, *Index of American Usage* by Porter G. Perrin and Ethel G. Strainchamps, particularly on the valuable contributions to that project made by James Sledd and James Fitzpatrick.

In planning this edition, the publishers solicited criticism of the Fourth Edition and advice about the Fifth from many teachers. Among those whose recommendations influenced the direction the revision took are Donald Craver, Donald C. Freeman, Arra M. Garab, Robert Kiely, William T. Lenehan, Raven I. McDavid, Jr., and Paul C. Rodgers, Jr.

All of the chapters of the *Guide* were read by Richard Daigle, Delmar Kehl, Glen A. Love, and William Powers; and one or more were read by Ronald Berman, E. Fred Carlisle, James McConkey, Louis T. Milic, and Joseph M. Williams. The final draft of the manuscript took into account many of their comments, and it is a pleasure to acknowledge their help.

Paula Fitzpatrick and Helen Scott of the Scott, Foresman staff were cheerfully competent in gathering up the manuscript and seeing it through the press.

Finally, the Fifth Edition of Perrin's *Writer's Guide and Index to English* owes much more than can be acknowledged here to the editorial talents and the good judgment of David R. Ebbitt. From first to last, his share in the project amounted to virtual collaboration.

Wilma R. Ebbitt

Contents

WRITER'S GUIDE

SPECIAL PROJECTS 393

Contents

INDEX TO ENGLISH

The *Index*, pp. 455–752, contains articles in alphabetical arrangement that fall roughly into four categories:

Articles on particular words and constructions, such as *continual(ly), continuous(ly); *get, got; *like, as; *plenty; *shall, will; *who, whom.

Articles for correction and revision of papers, indicated by longhand abbreviations.

Articles on English grammar, offering definitions and discussions of such matters as *case, *plurals of nouns, *principal parts of verbs.

Articles about language and language study, such as *American and British usage, *Analogy in language, *Foreign words in English, *Linguistics.

WRITING: A PREVIEW

Chapter One

THE WRITER'S RESOURCES

What do I want to accomplish with this essay? Who are my readers? What are their interests, doubts, fears, prejudices? How can I persuade them that my judgment is sound? What reasons can I give in support of my interpretation? What is the best order for these points? What kind of evidence will make this assertion more convincing? How can I make my audience share my feeling about the situation? What changes should I make in this sentence so that it will say exactly what I have in mind?

Questions like these—questions of rhetoric—are your real concerns in writing. They indicate that the choices you face go far beyond selecting one word or one grammatical form or one punctuation mark rather than another. But sometimes you find yourself puzzling longest over these less important decisions. And this is a pity; for while punctuation and mechanics, spelling and usage can influence a reader's response to what you write, nothing kills creativity and spontaneity more surely than an excessive concern with these matters in the early stages of composing.

In fact, a good many of these apparent difficulties become less troublesome once you recognize that correctness lies not in avoiding a list of *don'ts* but rather in choosing wisely from among the variety of forms English makes available. But because questions of wording—Is it *different from* or *different than?* Should I use *slow* or *slowly? finalize* or *finish?*—sometimes loom large and ominous, it may be useful to begin by discussing usage, the social bases on which experienced writers choose to say something in one way rather than another.

Questions about usage arise because there are different

varieties of English and because these varieties do not fit equally well into every social or rhetorical situation. What is appropriate in casual talk is not always appropriate on the lecture platform; what sounds natural to an audience of teenagers baffles a Golden Age club; what amuses readers in one context alienates them in another. For English is not just a single set of words and forms. Like every other language, it makes available a range of choices appropriate to different situations. Knowing what the alternatives are and recognizing how and why they differ puts you in a position to suit your language to your subject and to your audience and to the occasion. When you speak and write English that is appropriate to the rhetorical situation, you are making the right use of the language. Good English is not just arbitrarily "good"; it is good under certain conditions.

CAUSES OF VARIATION IN ENGLISH

The three principal causes of the differences between one kind of English and another are the time, the place, and the circumstances in which the language is used.[1]

The Time

Like every other living language, English has changed over the centuries. A reader today has to be supplied with notes if he is to understand what some of the words in Shakespeare's plays meant to the author and to his contemporaries. Further back, English looks like a foreign language. (See *Change in language and *English language and the references cited in those *Index* articles. Here and throughout this book, asterisks mark the titles of articles to be found in the *Index*.)

Words, forms, and constructions no longer in use are called obsolete. No one today refers to a *bottle* of hay, or

---

[1]H. L. Mencken, *The American Language*, abridged 4th ed., ed. Raven I. McDavid, Jr. (New York, Knopf, 1963); William Labov, *The Social Stratification of English in New York City* (Washington, D.C.: Center for Applied Linguistics, 1966); Walter Wolfram, *A Sociolinguistic Description of Detroit Negro Speech* (Washington, D.C.: Center for Applied Linguistics, 1969); Roger Shuy, ed., *Social Dialects and Language Learning* (Champaign, Ill.: National Council of Teachers of English, 1965); Martin Joos, *The Five Clocks* (New York: Harcourt, 1961). For some results of work on the *Linguistic Atlas*, see Hans Kurath, *Handbook of the Linguistic Geography of New England* (Washington, D.C.: American Council of Learned Societies, 1939) and *A Word Geography of the Eastern United States* (Ann Arbor: Univ. of Michigan Press, 1949); E. Bagby Atwood, *Survey of Verb Forms in the Eastern United States* (Ann Arbor: Univ. of Michigan Press, 1953); Hans Kurath and Raven I. McDavid, Jr., *The Pronunciation of English in the Atlantic States* (Ann Arbor: Univ. of Michigan Press, 1961); Raven I. McDavid, Jr., "The Dialects of American English," in W. Nelson Francis, *The Structure of American English* (New York: Ronald, 1958); and Carroll Reed, *Dialects of American English* (Cleveland: World, 1967).

uses *can* in the sense of "know," or *coy* in the sense of "quiet." Old usages now in the process of disappearing from the language are called archaic: *anon* for *at once* or *soon*, *betimes* for *quickly*, *doth* for *does*. Some archaic words survive in special situations, like the *thou* and *saith* of church services, and in set phrases, like *kith* in *kith and kin*.

Differences in usage make themselves felt in relatively short time spans as well as in long ones, from generation to generation as well as from century to century. Some expressions in current use are old-fashioned: *icebox* for *refrigerator*, for example. Though young people may pick up some old-fashioned usages from their parents or grandparents (many who say *icebox* have never seen one), they are more likely to be attracted by innovation than by nostalgia. Slang flourishes among the young.

Slang is only one category of the new words that keep coming into the language, giving evidence that the language is still changing. The journal *American Speech* treats many new words as they appear, and the supplements to the principal encyclopedias list new words. Inventions and discoveries spawn their own special terms—the space program produced a considerable vocabulary—and political and social developments regularly give new meanings to old words: *grass, heavy, freak, hawk, impacted, pad, renewal, rock, straight, transplant.* Computers generate trade names. The computer industry itself has created new words and new meanings for words: *bit, baud, nanosecond.*

Shifts in grammatical construction come about more slowly, partly because they meet with more resistance than additions to vocabulary. Many of the disputes about usage arise because of the gradual collapse of distinctions, real or imagined—between *who* and *whom*, *like* and *as*, and so on.

If you write naturally, choosing among the different Englishes created by historical change—the English of Shakespeare, of Joseph Conrad, of your own parents, of the 1970's—will present no real problem. Because you learn your language chiefly by imitating what you hear and read, you will use current English, and you will not be tempted to flavor it with terms that are obsolete or archaic or old-fashioned. But current English is not just one English, nor are all its words and phrases appropriate in every writing situation. A usage that is new to your audience can frustrate communication. An up-to-date usage that is on everyone's tongue is likely to become an out-of-date usage very quickly. A usage that appears regularly in statements from Capitol Hill (*massive*) or from the offices of university administrators (*meaningful*) can be almost meaningless. No word should be used merely because it is new or popular or prestigious; it should be used because it fits the situation better than any other word does.

The Place

No language is spoken in exactly the same way every-where. We can spot an Englishman (or a Canadian, if we listen closely) because some of his pronunciations and expressions are different from ours. (See *American and British usage.) We can also tell what part of the United States a person comes from by listening to him talk. Differences in vocabulary, pronunciation, and grammatical habits that are characteristic of fairly definite regions set off *regional dialects*. Put another way, a regional dialect is speech that does not attract attention to itself in the region where it is used but does outside that area. A pronunciation, a word or meaning of a word, or a grammatical form that is current in one region and not in others is called a *localism.

Dialects are not peculiar to backwoods areas. The "Oxford accent" distinguishes a minor British dialect; both Bostonians and New Yorkers have characteristic speechways. Nor are dialects the result of lack of education or social standing. An educated Westerner will speak somewhat differently from a Southerner or a New Englander who has had a comparable education.

An American dialect may retain traits of the various British dialects spoken by early settlers or show the influence of foreign languages spoken by large numbers of people in the region, as in the German sections of Pennsylvania and the Scandinavian parts of the Middle West. It may show traits of a neighboring language or of the language of an earlier settlement: the dialect of the Southwest has Spanish elements; the dialect of New Orleans, French. But there are fewer differences among the dialects of the United States than would be expected in a country of such size—many fewer than exist among the dialects in much smaller Great Britain. Thanks to the relative freedom of movement of the American people, the educational system, the circulation of books and national magazines, and the omnipresence of radio and television, people living thousands of miles apart speak substantially the same language.

Three major speech areas have traditionally been recognized in the United States: *Eastern* (New England and a strip of eastern New York), *Southern* (south of Pennsylvania and the Ohio River, extending west of the Mississippi into Texas), and *Western* (extending from New Jersey on the Atlantic, through the Middle West and along the whole of our Pacific Coast), sometimes called *Northern*. As a result of the work being done on *The Linguistic Atlas of the United States and Canada*, the boundaries are being more exactly drawn, subdivisions indicated, and lines of influence between areas shown. The major speech divisions have been renamed *Northern*, *Midland*, and *Southern*, but their boundaries have not yet been carried far enough westward so that they can take the place of the traditional areas in amateur discussion. Regional varieties exist within each of the three main areas, as in the Ozarks or in New York City, but the differences between the speech of California and Illinois are fewer than the differences between either of these and, say, Georgia or Massachusetts. Roughly one twelfth of the population speaks Eastern, one sixth Southern, and three fourths Western.

While the layman might miss many differences a professional student of American English hears, we are all aware of some of them. Some New Englanders use broad *a*, as in /äsk/, /gräss/, /päst/, where most Americans have short *a*, and they do not pronounce a postvocalic *r*, as in /bän/ for *barn*.[2] A Westerner has a distinct, even a prolonged, *r* after vowels as well as before. Like many Americans he rounds the *o* in *hog, frog, log*. Beginning in New York State, most speakers of the Western type do not distinguish *hoarse* and *horse, mourning* and *morning*, pronouncing them all with a sound like the word *ore*. A Southerner from the lowlands (as distinguished from the hill country) does not sound *r* after vowels (for example, *suh* for *sir*, /dōä/ or /dō/ for *door*). The long *i* both in the lowlands and in the hills may suggest a broad *a*, as in the spelling *Ah* for *I*. Southerners from the hills usually pronounce *r* after vowels, as all fanciers of country music know. Each region—Eastern, Southern, Western—also has its characteristic intonation and speech rhythm.

Different regions have different words for many common objects: *bag, sack, poke; overshoe, rubber; piazza, porch, stoop, veranda; seesaw, teeter-totter, teeterboard; doughnut, fried cake, cruller*. Each region also has special words for local features of the landscape and for occupations that are more or less local: *coulee, hogback, sierra, mesa; mesquite, piñon; mule skinner, selectman*. And there are local idioms like the Southern "I would *like for* you to do it" and like different ways of telling time—"quarter *of* four," "quarter *till* four," "quarter *to* four."

People differ in their attitudes toward localisms. Some believe that they should be weeded out; others believe that a person should retain as much as possible of the flavor of his native dialect. Those who move away from where they were born may have little occasion to use purely local words and, unless they settle among other migrants from the same area, are likely to shed their more conspicuous local words and pronunciations except when talking to family and old friends. But when someone consciously tries to change his speech to a different pattern, he often ends with an unhappy mixture of the native and the acquired.

---

[2]See the *Index* article *Pronunciation for a key to phonemic transcription.

Dialect differences and the prejudice that attaches to them assume special importance when society is changing rapidly. Members of minorities who have risen on the scale of social power and prestige may be particularly intent on eradicating the dialect that middle-class prejudice made an obstacle to their ambitions. On the other hand, their more self-confident colleagues may keep their regional speechways as a badge of independence.

Localisms are less appropriate in writing than in speech. If they come naturally, they can give a note of freshness and authenticity to accounts of personal experience; and regional terms may be desirable, if not essential, in writing about regional occupations or activities. But when the topic has no regional associations and the material is not being given personal treatment, localisms are at best quaint and should normally be replaced with words of more general currency.

The Circumstances

Differences in the language that stem from historical change or from geographical region normally present fewer problems than those that relate to the immediate circumstances in which the language is being used.

Many words of similar meaning, though in current use and without regional associations, are not always interchangeable. *Depart, leave,* and *split* have the same meaning, but they are not used in the same social situations. Nor are *surrender, give in,* and *quit: give in* is less casual than *quit* but less formal than *surrender.* Consider these groups:

spent, fatigued, weary, exhausted, tired, worn-out, played out, used up, all in, pooped

stripling, youth, lad, boy, youngster, kid, punk

Tired and *boy* certainly belong to the central stream of the language and might be used by anyone in any circumstances. The same is true of the words and phrases near them in the lists. But as we move away from these central expressions, the words become more limited in use, until at the ends of each series there are items that we expect to find only in distinctly formal situations or in distinctly informal ones. Unless we were aiming for a special kind of humor, most of us would not use *spent* or *stripling;* they have an old-fashioned, bookish flavor. Among friends we would use *all in* and *kid,* but in some other situations we would probably choose less casual terms.

The differences between *fatigued* and *all in, indigent* and *broke* stem not from any variation in their central meanings but from the circumstances in which they are customarily used. Words pick up associations from their contexts, carrying traces of the situations in which they are most often spoken or written. If a word strikes us as bookish, it is because we have come upon it only in bookish contexts. If a phrase strikes us as noticeably casual, it is because we are used to hearing it only in informal situations. When we write, we need to be alert to the shades of meaning in the words we use and aware of the attitudes these shades of meaning convey and evoke. (Connotation, the associations of words, is discussed on pp. 357 – 59.)

EXERCISE

Examine the introductory material in your dictionary to find out what labels it uses to record variations due to time, to place, and to circumstances. When a word is not labeled, do you feel free to use it in any writing you are doing? Why or why not?

THE VARIETIES OF ENGLISH

There are several ways of classifying the many Englishes we hear and read and speak. In this book we recognize two cultural varieties, Standard and Nonstandard, a division based on a fairly small number of pronunciations and grammatical constructions that speakers of different educational and social standing habitually use. We subdivide Standard into Formal, General, and Informal — labels that broadly correspond to the social and rhetorical situations in which the varieties commonly occur. Recent research has shown that Nonstandard English also has its subdivisions. Both educated and uneducated speakers adapt their speech to situations requiring different degrees of formality.

Nonstandard English

The everyday speech of many Americans relatively untouched by school instruction or by the traditions of printed English makes up Nonstandard. This speech variety (which carries over into writing) has developed from the same language stock as Standard but represents a selection of sounds, words, and forms made under different social conditions. Although Nonstandard works well in carrying on the affairs and occupations of millions of Americans, for social reasons it is generally avoided in business, government, and literature and in middle- and upper-class society generally.

To speakers of other kinds of English, the most conspicuous trait of Nonstandard speech is its use of variants not heard in Standard — a instead of an before some words beginning with vowels, pronouns like *hisself* and *youse*, plurals like *foots*, and, in particular, some verb forms. Where Standard has narrowed choice to *saw* and to *drank* or *drunk*, Nonstandard has *saw, see, seed*, or *seen* and *drank, drunk, drink*, or *drinked*. Nonstandard reduction in forms, on the other hand, gives unchanging negatives like *ain't* and *don't*, *was* throughout the past of *be*, and adverbs without *-ly* (*real* for *really*).

Studies in recent years indicate that "Black English," one of the numerous Nonstandard dialects, has its own structure and organization and a grammar as logical and regular as the grammar of Standard. Sentences like "They be here in a minute," "They gone now," "He seen that" have traditionally been described as illiterate, grammarless — mere corruptions of "good" English. But it has recently been shown that they correspond to Standard English in a very regular way. Wherever Standard English speakers contract a *be* or *have* ("They'll be here"; "They've gone"), typical speakers of Black English delete. Judged solely on the basis of regularity or logic, the two Englishes are equally good. (See *Subject and verb §4.)

The division of English into Nonstandard and Standard does not mean that the users of the language are necessarily so divided. Some speakers have considerable command of both Standard English and a Nonstandard dialect, using now one and now the other as circumstances dictate. And what is regarded as Nonstandard in one region may be accepted as Standard Informal in another.

Though deviations from Standard may be scarcely noticeable when spoken rapidly and without emphasis, they are always conspicuous in writing. Chiefly for this reason, Nonstandard is inappropriate in the writing college students normally do. (For *Index* articles on Nonstandard words and forms, see the cross-references in *Nonstandard English.)

Standard English

A regional dialect calls attention to itself except among those who customarily speak it. The same can be said of Nonstandard, which encompasses a variety of dialects, both

Summary of Principal Social Varieties of English

STANDARD ENGLISH

INFORMAL ENGLISH

More often spoken than written

The speaking and writing of educated people in informal situations

Typical uses: casual conversation; letters between people who know each other well, diaries, personal writing; fiction and nonfiction that simulates ordinary speech

GENERAL ENGLISH

Both spoken and written

The speaking and writing of educated people in most situations

Typical uses: conversation; talks to general audiences; most correspondence, most college papers, and most newspapers, magazines, and books

FORMAL ENGLISH

More often written than spoken

The speaking and writing of the educated for largely intellectual audiences in formal situations

Typical uses: ceremonial addresses; lectures to professional audiences; certain types of correspondence; some academic writing, such as dissertations and some term papers; scientific reports; articles and books addressed to scholars and cognoscenti

NONSTANDARD ENGLISH

Chiefly spoken

The everyday language of people not much influenced by school instruction

Typical uses: conversation at home, with friends, on the job

COMMENTS

1. Standard English is here divided into Informal, General, and Formal. Analogous divisions could be made of Nonstandard.

2. The varieties are not to be thought of as sharply defined and mutually exclusive but as shading into each other. A passage may be described as Informal or as Formal if it has several traits characteristic of that variety, even though most of it is in General English.

3. The varieties are characterized by some differences in pronunciation, spelling, vocabulary, grammatical forms, and sentence structure.

4. Labeling a usage Formal, Informal, or General indicates that it is characteristically used in Formal, Informal, or General English, that its connotation comes from this use, and that it is not characteristic of either of the other varieties. In many cases, however, classification of a word—and judgment of its appropriateness—depends entirely on context.

5. Usage is said to be divided when two or more choices are in good standing in General English—for example, *catalog* or *catalogue, dived* or *dove* as the past tense of *dive*, a comma or no comma after the item followed by *and* in a series of three or more items (a, b [,] and c).

rural and urban, geographical and social. Standard English is also a dialect, but because it is used, and therefore approved, by the dominant middle class, it has become the standard. And because it is the dialect of those who have access to control of the schools, of newspaper, magazine, and book publishing, and of radio and television, its speakers have the most opportunity to display its resources, range, and flexibility.

The labels for the varieties of Standard described below should not be rigidly interpreted or rigidly applied. Though certain contrasts are unmistakable, the categories are not mutually exclusive. They shade into each other with a large area of overlap. While some words and phrases are distinctively Formal or Informal, others can be so labeled only when they are examined in context. A word that stands out as inappropriately Formal in one context might, in a different one, pass unnoticed — that is, might pass as General. And the boundaries between varieties are constantly shifting, for even short periods of time bring changes in the status of individual items. A phrase that is Informal this year may be General next year. Further, to say that a passage is Formal does not mean that the word choice and phrasing are Formal without exception. It means that there are enough of the traits usually associated with that variety to give the passage a Formal feel or tone even though the language of most of it is General.

Formal English.   Formal English can still be heard in some political oratory, some sermons, some academic addresses, and even in some conversations — particularly among foreign-born intellectuals of an older generation — but it is far more characteristic of writing than of speaking. And it is appropriate chiefly in books and articles dealing with serious, specialized topics and addressed to audiences with general or specialized intellectual interests.

The vocabulary of Formal English tends to be literary, scholarly, and abstract. It includes words seldom used in ordinary conversation (*desultory, ubiquitous, redoubtable*) and a rather high proportion of nouns like *distinction, concept,* and *hiatus,* which summarize experience rather than present it directly. For those familiar with them, the literary words are rich in suggestion (*omen, luminous, transcend*) and often have some special appeal of sound or rhythm (*immemorial, quintessence*), while the abstract nouns and technical terms permit the exact and concise statement of ideas.

Though Formal English uses short, compact sentences for emphasis, its typical sentence is fairly long, and the elements in it are ordered with care. In the interests of precision, it may place modifiers between subject and verb or between verb and object, and it may make other departures from normal word order. Clauses are often built to show parallelism and balance. Formal takes few syntactic shortcuts. It avoids contractions, rarely deletes relative pronouns, and usually repeats prepositions and conjunctions in parallel constructions. Deliberate, studied choice of sentence patterns as well as words characterizes Formal writing, making its impact quite different from the more casual styles of most General and all Informal English.

Informal English. In everyday use, Informal English is spontaneous rather than studied, casual rather than careful. It is the variety of Standard that most of us ordinarily talk or write to our family and to close friends. Informal is also used—sometimes appropriately, sometimes not—when a writer or speaker who shares no intimacy with his audience tries to give an impression of breezy spontaneity.

Informal English swings over a wide range, sometimes including distinctly Formal traits for contrast and Nonstandard forms for accuracy or novelty. It makes free use of slang and of coinages for common things or situations; it draws on the shoptalk that develops in every occupation and the ingroup vocabulary that attaches to every sport. Since the speaker-writer usually has a good deal in common with the listener-reader, he can take much for granted—in material, in allusions to shared experiences, and in the special connotations of words. He can also take a good many syntactic shortcuts, omitting nonessential relative pronouns, conjunctions, and prepositions and using contractions freely. Some of the sentences of Informal are short and elliptical; others are unusually long, with asides and afterthoughts keeping the structure loose and relaxed.

General English. Occupying the great middle ground between Formal and Informal is General English. It is the variety of Standard that educated people most often read, that they hear in talks for general audiences, that they themselves most often write, and that they use when they speak with some care. The words in the General vocabulary are of wide currency (*roomy* rather than *spacious, rainfall* rather than *precipitation*). They are likely to be concrete, close to experience, referring to things, people, actions, and events more than to abstractions. The turns of phrase reflect those of speech (*look into, give up, take over*); coordinating conjunctions like *and* and *so* are often preferred to conjunctive adverbs like *furthermore* and *consequently*. The sentences are of moderate length, without interrupting phrases or involved movement.

General is much less restrictive than Formal, more so than Informal. Though it is more likely than Informal to follow subject-verb agreement by form, it does not do so as consistently as Formal does. It often ignores Formal distinctions—as between *can* and *may, raise* and *rear.* Yet it is slower than Informal to accept slang and shoptalk. General has a wide range, overlapping to some extent the other two varieties. Because it is the most versatile and serviceable of the three varieties of Standard, and because it has such wide currency and can reach so many, it is the variety you will use in most of your writing.

EXERCISES

1. How would you describe the tone or style of each of the passages that follow? What words, phrases, and sentence patterns depart from General? Are the departures marked enough to move the passage into either Formal or Informal, or do such borderline labels as General-to-Informal seem more accurate? Explain why you find the style appropriate or inappropriate to the subject.

a. Visitors to our place, instead of being barked at by dogs rushing from under the porch, are squalled at by peacocks whose blue necks and crested heads pop up from behind tufts of grass, peer out of bushes and crane downward from the roof of the house, where the bird has flown, perhaps for the view. One of mine stepped from under the shrubbery one day and came forward to inspect a carful of people who had driven up to buy a calf. An old man and five or six white-haired, barefooted children were piling out of the back of the automobile as the bird approached. Catching sight of him, the children stopped in their tracks and stared, plainly hacked to find this superior figure blocking their path. There was silence as the bird regarded them, his head drawn back at its most majestic angle, his folded train glittering behind him in the sunlight.

"Whut is thet thang?" one of the small boys asked finally in a sullen voice.

The old man had got out of the car and was gazing at the peacock with an astounded look of recognition. "I ain't seen one of them since my granddaddy's day," he said, respectfully removing his hat. "Folks used to have 'em, but they don't no more."

"Whut is it?" the child asked again in the same tone he had used before.

"Churren," the old man said, "that's the king of the birds!"
—Flannery O'Connor, *Holiday,* Sept. 1961

b. The most difficult task for a writer is to get the right "voice" for his material; by voice I mean the overall impression one has of the creator behind what he creates. Now I've always liked the ironic voice that the line of great nineteenth-century novelists, from Austen through to Conrad, all used so naturally. We tend today to remember the failures of that tone—the satirical overkill in Dickens, the facetiousness of Thackeray, the strained sarcasm of Mark Twain, the priggishness in George Eliot—rather than its virtues. The reason is clear enough: irony needs the assumption of superiority in the ironist. Such an assumption must be anathema to a democratic, egalitarian century like our own. We suspect people who pretend to be omniscient; and that is why so many of us twentieth-century novelists feel driven into first-person narration.—John Fowles, *Harper's*, July 1969

c. The word alone is limited in function. It can be an expletive, a curse, an answer or key of some sort, but its main business is to relate to others, to be part of a sequence, to help carry an idea toward its fulfillment. For this we have rhetoric, and if words themselves are miracles of human achievement, the whole resultant operation is a much greater miracle. Rhetoric has made civilization possible, and any notion of wringing its neck is childish. Certain forms and costumes of rhetoric may be suffocating to free spirits; tradition of any sort grows ritualistic and must be attacked and liberated; academies in France or elsewhere which seek to fix tradition in perpetual stasis lead us into cultural stagnation. Change, or mutability, as the old poets called it, or perhaps simply the illusion of change, is necessary to the health and happiness of thinking men. And the making of words into sentences, and sentences into paragraphs and compositions, and the achieving of viable and communicable Idea, is almost comparable to the mysterious process of birth itself: the word *conception* is used for both.—Gerald Warner Brace, *The Stuff of Fiction*

d. How many of you saw the Frank Sinatra special? Let's have a show of hands. That many, huh? Then you know what I mean. The man sang lyrics as if they meant something to him, and we could understand and feel every word.

Talk about anti-Establishment! Here I came to the TV set, loaded down with the usual Excedrin, Dramamine, assorted meprobamates, and earplugs, waiting for The Beat to begin and drown out the lyrics, and this fellow sings words I can hear set to music that touched the soul. The nerve of the guy!

He grooved so that I climbed walls. Not only was there not obeisance to the folk and rock singers, but he gave not even a nod of recognition to The Beat. As far as he was concerned The Beat could have been China. Oh, the beat was there all right, but in lower case, and so sublimated that the lyrics came through crystal-clear. Not with The Beat that rattles around in the heads of the young these days.—Goodman Ace, *Saturday Review*, Dec. 13, 1969

e. The drama of this landscape is in the sky, pouring with light and always moving. The earth is passive. And yet the beauty I am struck by, both as present fact and as revived memory, is a fusion: this sky would not be so spectacular without this earth to change and glow and darken under it. And whatever the sky may do, however the earth is shaken or darkened, the Euclidean perfection abides. The very scale, the hugeness of simple forms, emphasizes stability. It is not hills and mountains which we should call eternal. Nature abhors an elevation as much as it abhors a vacuum; a hill is no sooner elevated than the forces of erosion begin tearing it down. These prairies are quiescent, close to static; looked at for any length of time, they begin to impose their awful perfection on the observer's mind. Eternity is a peneplain. — Wallace Stegner, *Wolf Willow*

f. Cynical disparagement of objectivity as a "myth" seems to me both naive and irresponsible. Any claim of novelty to the observation that men are fallible at best, corruptible at worst, is naive. Its irresponsibility lies in the conclusion that, since the ideal is unattainable, it should not be held up as a standard to both practitioners and critics.

Precisely because the unknown truth defies conclusive verification; precisely because the intellectual promise is not easily assayed; precisely because reasonable men will differ about the quality of another's work, it is all the more important that differences be articulated in terms of reason. The difficulty of judgment should not be used as an excuse for bias. Due process in academic affairs, as in legal affairs, is even more important for hard cases than for easy ones.

The apparatus and practices designed to assure as much objectivity as possible will vary from institution to institution. The common denominator that cannot vary, however, is a good faith attempt, at least, to assess the merits of the work or of the man — be he student or colleague — by a reasoned elaboration of a common understanding of these qualities related to the academic mission. Primary among these, surely, are the honesty and rigor of a man's thought and craftsmanship; and his ability to contribute to the understanding of those who listen to him, or argue with him, or read or view or listen to his works.

I say "reasoned elaboration" because there is no room for the notion that some unarticulated hunch, some subjective, unreasoned assertion should be allowed to substitute for evidence made pertinent by reasoned elaboration of the university's purpose. Abuse of academic power, like abuse of judicial power, can be held in check not so much by the independence of the judge as by the requirement that reasons must be given for the opinion. These reasons, in turn, must wash in terms of general principles and propositions embraced by the institution. The judge is disciplined by the realization that the reasons he gives in any one case would have to be applied to similar cases involving other people. — Kingman Brewster, Jr., *American Scholar*, Spring 1970

2. Choose one of the passages in Exercise 1. Keep the basic ideas, but rewrite the passage in a different style and tone. (If it is mainly Formal, try rewriting it in Informal; if General, make it Formal or Informal.) Select an audience for whom the shift in style would make sense and keep that audience in mind as you rewrite the passage. Evaluate your rewrite. Does it have its own consistency of style and tone? What has been gained or lost in your adaptation of the original passage?

3. Explain how the author of the following passage makes his criticism of the general style and tone of Henry Kissinger's prose. In his "rough translation," what variety of English does TRB use, and why? Does his rough translation adequately represent Kissinger's thought? Do you agree with TRB's criticism of Kissinger's language as quoted, or do you think there are circumstances in which the language would be appropriate?

Mr. Kissinger rejects the architectonic approach to political multipolarity. Yes, sir! In an essay written a couple of months before taking office he explains that "military bipolarity is a source of rigidity in foreign policy" because "a bipolar world loses the perspective for nuance." He says we should "avoid an American-Soviet hegemonial position in Eastern Europe." What the poor man is evidently trying to say is (and it makes a good deal of sense) that the two superpowers can now bomb the hell out of each other, and it presents quite a problem for frightened lesser nations who don't want nuclear war but who also don't want the giants to be too palsy-walsy (rough translation). — TRB, *New Republic*, Feb. 22, 1969

4. Group the following words according to the varieties of English in which they are typically used. Refer to the table on pp. 10–11 and consult a dictionary if necessary. (It won't follow the classification outlined here, but it will give you some hints.) For words not typical of General English, give an equivalent General word or phrase.

abrogate	drownded	nonage	therein
blurt	freak out	OK (verb)	this-here
boughten	give up	plethora	thrombosis
con (verb)	groove	rev (verb)	uptight
condign	hiccup	risky	viewpoint
disparate	mire	smog	whence

5. Sometimes the sense in which a word is used determines how it should be classified. In this pair of sentences, *stoned* is Informal in the first, General in the second:

He was really stoned.

The police were stoned by the advancing mob.

For each of the following words, write sentences illustrating at least two varieties of English (Nonstandard, General, Informal, Formal): *jazz, pad, rap, level, best, sack, hustle.*

The division of Standard into Formal, General, and Informal gives us a simple, practicable scheme for describing the varieties of English that we commonly hear and read. More refined classifications have been worked out, taking into account age, economic and social class, and geographical location, as well as the circumstances in which the language is used. Whatever the scheme, the important point to recognize is the need for discriminating among the varieties of English in talking, writing, and reading. To a student of language, all the varieties are equally deserving of careful study. But they differ considerably in the impression they make—the essential objection to Nonstandard, Raven Mc-David has said, is that people disapprove of it. Just as we behave differently in different social situations, so we should talk and write differently in different rhetorical situations. To be understood and listened to in our society generally—not just in the classroom or in the gym or in the laboratory or in the garage but in all these places and many more—the speaker-writer needs to develop skill in using many different Englishes.

Primarily, people want to be able to speak and write their language so that they will be understood and given a fair hearing. Some want much more—to be able to persuade, impress, command, delight. But first they must reach their audience; they must be understood. Of course, a writer may play with the language or manipulate it with the intention of puzzling or deceiving an audience. But the ordinary and principal function of language is effective communication, making someone understand, intellectually or emotionally, what you want him to understand or getting him to do what you want him to do.

This fundamental purpose sets limits to the deviations from established usage that we can permit ourselves. To communicate satisfactorily we have to use words in the meanings they have acquired and to make our statements in understandable verbal patterns. This fundamental purpose also gives us a basis for judging our success in using language. C. C. Fries puts it this way:

. . . language is a means to an end, and that end is specifically to grasp, to possess, to communicate experience. Accordingly, that is good language, good English, which, on the one hand, most fully realizes one's own impressions, and, on the other, is most completely adapted to the purposes of any particular communication. — C. C. Fries, *What Is Good English?*

In other words, so far as the language used furthers the intended effect, it is good; so far as it fails to further that effect, it is bad, no matter how "correct" it may be. Clearly this definition is a functional one, not an ethical one. (Some of the moral aspects of using language will be discussed in Chapter Six.) And clearly it offers much more flexible criteria for judging writing than those afforded by "correctness" in mechanics and usage.

THE RHETORICAL SITUATION

Since good English is English that does what you want it to do, you can test the appropriateness of what you are saying and how you are saying it only in *a particular rhetorical situation.* In conversation you adjust easily and automatically to the group you are in. Among nature lovers, you compare notes on hikes and trails, wildlife and ecology; among sports-car buffs, you talk of makes and models, mileages and speeds. And just as you choose appropriate subjects, so you adjust your language to your listeners. Though you may make precisely the same judgment about a college course when talking to an academic dean, to your parents, and to your roommate, you will certainly use different language to express that judgment.

You need to make comparable adjustments when you write. If this is sometimes difficult, it is mainly because your sense of the rhetorical situation is seldom as keen when you are writing as when you are talking. In particular, you may lack the sense of an audience. To ward off the feeling that you are writing in a vacuum, it is always a good idea to visualize a specific audience for what you write—the board of trustees for an essay on student participation, the director of the movie you saw last night for an essay on the film-rating system, the president of General Motors for an essay on pollution. For other topics, other audiences will seem plausible—the brightest person in your class, say, or a childhood friend, or a group of sixth-graders, or a militant campus organization, or a typical reader of the *Atlantic* or of *Playboy.* Only when you have an audience, real or assumed, are you operating in a rhetorical situation, and only then can you judge realistically how to say what you want to say.

But there is more to the rhetorical situation than your conception of your readers—their tastes, their interests, their views on the subject you are discussing. There is the subject itself. There is your purpose in dealing with the subject—to amuse, to inform, to persuade, or whatever. There is your conception of yourself in relation to your subject and the audience you are trying to reach. Finally, there is the kind of essay you are trying to produce. Is it a satire for the college literary magazine, a critical essay for the *New York Review of Books*, a term paper for a sociology seminar? This element in the rhetorical situation is closely related to the audience but at times serves to specify the writing job more narrowly. Though many of the same people read the *New York Review of Books* and the book section of their Sunday newspaper, they bring to their reading of the two publications quite different expectations. They know the essays in *NYRB* will be more detailed, more scholarly, more critical than the newspaper reviews.

As we shall see in later chapters, these elements of the rhetorical situation influence all aspects of writing, including the selection of the basic content, the choice of illustrative material, and the structure and style of an essay. The criterion of *appropriateness* will be central to our discussion of all these matters. Here we will speak mainly of appropriateness of style or tone in the most general sense and of how it is affected by the variety of English you use.

Finding the right style is one sign of a sensitive, experienced writer. The basic precept is simple—aim for a style that matches your intention in the particular rhetorical situation. The informality appropriate in a newsy letter to a younger brother is incongruous in a letter applying for a scholarship grant. The formality suitable to an investigation into the origins of mercantilism to be published by a university press is out of place in a review of a rock concert for the campus newspaper. But many decisions about appropriateness of style are harder to arrive at. The contrasts are not so obvious, and the interaction of the elements of the rhetorical situation creates complications.

Does subject determine style? Serious subjects can be treated lightly and light subjects seriously; abstruse material can be given simple treatment, and trivia can be handled in complex and subtle detail. For a more reliable index to the general style to aim for, you must consider subject in relation to your purpose. And for a more reliable index still you must take your audience into account.

The interaction of these three—subject, purpose, and audience—should influence not only the general tenor of the vocabulary in an essay but also the treatment of whatever special vocabulary attaches to the subject. Not all subjects have special vocabularies or registers, but a surprising number do—from surfing to surgery and from stamp collecting to art criticism. Not only do they have their unique technical terms, but they often give special meanings to familiar words.

Gig, for example, has totally different meanings for the boatman, the horseman, the fisherman, the jazz man, and the military man. For the writer, these special vocabularies create problems.

How you use the special vocabulary of your subject should be determined by your readers' knowledge, interests, and needs. Will they understand what the technical terms mean with no help from you? Or should you define each new term you introduce? Or have you reason to believe that they will be confused, or intimidated, or antagonized, or bored by any esoteric word, no matter how clearly defined, and should you therefore substitute synonyms or paraphrases from the general vocabulary?

Both Formal and Informal English make use of special, ingroup vocabularies — the former, the dignified technical vocabularies of scholarship, the arts, the professions; the latter, shoptalk, which includes the workaday words of the laboratory as well as of the repair shop. Using a special vocabulary can shift your style toward either the Formal or the Informal end of the continuum. If the nature of your audience leads you to avoid specialized terms altogether, using equivalents or near-equivalents in their place, the net effect will be to keep your style General.

While shoptalk is Informal, it often fits comfortably into an essay written in General English. Terms from the special vocabularies of sports and of many hobbies may be the most natural choices and the best choices in discussing the subjects. (An essay about a day at the races might include as many special terms as an essay on schizophrenia.) But unless you are treating your subject lightly and have a very close relationship with your audience, an Informal style is not a wise choice. It can cheapen a serious subject. It may be used for humorous effect — to express satirical irreverence and so on — but being funny on paper is a difficult undertaking, and when the attempt fails, Informal becomes tiresome or objectionable. Ordinarily, the style appropriate for dealing with a light subject or for treating any subject playfully is in the Informal-to-General range.

Syntax, like vocabulary, is affected by the subject-purpose-audience interaction. If you are on intimate terms with your audience and want to have your "speaking voice" come through your prose, your sentences will probably show a good deal of variety: some will be long and loosely constructed, others short and elliptical, omitting connections that you count on your audience to supply. When you are aware that your audience is only casually attentive, you should not risk using involved, complicated syntax; read-as-you-run material has to be written in simple sentence patterns if it is to be read at all. Utilitarian directions and instructions should be given in simple, straightforward sentences that leave no room for misinterpretation. (The rhetorical effects of different sentence patterns are examined in Chapter Eleven.)

In discussions of ideas, the sentences lengthen and the syntax tightens. This is not to say that serious subjects intended to inform serious audiences should always be treated in complicated sentences. As a general rule style should be no more complex than honest exposition requires; and some good Formal prose uses a high proportion of short, direct sentences. But in other cases the need for precision may result in sentence patterns so elaborate that they must be thoroughly digested rather than simply inhaled. Readers of scientific journals and literary quarterlies are accustomed to finding that syntax as well as vocabulary requires their close attention.

Roles and Voices

So far we have focused on appropriateness in terms of the subject-purpose-audience relationship. But your choice of words and syntax — and, more generally, your choice of the variety of English you will use — is governed in large part by your own relation to your subject and your audience. The final test of appropriateness is that the language fit the writer.

Whenever you launch into an essay, you should ask yourself who is writing. Naturally, the writer is you; but which you is writing this particular essay? The you who argues about the curriculum is not the same you who reminisces about a grandfather in small-town Nebraska or in westside Chicago. The you who tells how to build a bird feeder is different from the you who criticizes a television program. And in addition to these real selves, there are imagined ones: the strategist, advising a political candidate; the reformer, pointing out ways to improve society; the dropout, explaining why he left. As a writer, you speak in many different voices, play many different roles.

You also assume different relationships. You may be an expert addressing experts, an expert addressing laymen, a layman addressing experts, or a layman addressing laymen. And your relationship with an audience may be characterized by any one of an infinite number of degrees of formality or familiarity, antagonism or congeniality. Each different relationship calls for adjustments in vocabulary and syntax as well as in what you say.

The audience-writer relationship determines a great deal about your general approach. It gives a rough indication of where your writing should fall in the Informal-General-Formal continuum, where it should fall in the range from simple to complex. And it suggests the degree of intimacy you should assume or seek to establish. The language offers choices for registering close proximity, remoteness, and every degree of distance in between.

Some students tend to write formally even when the subject is a simple one of general interest and there is nothing in the audience-writer relationship to call for a Formal style. Perhaps they doubt that what they are saying has much value and so turn to Formal style as a means of making it sound impressive. Or perhaps they were pushed too hard toward Formal either at home or at school. Remembering pressure of this sort, they tighten up as soon as they begin to write, adopting a self-conscious, artificial manner of expression that they have come to think of as the only appropriate writing style.

Formal English can have great dignity and nobility, marvelous clarity and precision. Every college student should be able to read it with understanding and appreciation and, when the occasion demands, to write it, too. Handled well, it can be effective in dealing with topics of general interest — just as General English can be effective in dealing with specialized topics. But Formal English is unsuitable for many topics, and when it does not come naturally, there is the danger of exaggeration and excess. The degree of formality expected in college writing can ordinarily be achieved in the stylistic area where General and Formal overlap — where the tone is serious but not stuffy or pompous, where the words are chosen with care but chosen for the most part from the central, General vocabulary, and where the sentences express the necessary logical relationships but remain readily comprehensible to a reader of ordinary intelligence and patience.

The Informal end of the language continuum also presents risks. Writing that is inappropriately Informal may result from laziness, from deliberate rejection of convention, or from a mistaken notion that chumminess will disarm the reader and perhaps mask a failure in intellectual rigor. Informal English is incongruous in critical or analytical essays. Discussing ideas in college papers is not the same thing as rapping in the student union, and adopting a style that implies intimacy where no real intimacy can or should exist is as offensive in the writer as it is in the huckster.

Like Formal English, Informal can be good or bad. Good written Informal is lively and interesting, creating the effect of good conversation. Bad Informal is loose, vague, tiresome. Like Formal, Informal can be appropriate or inappropriate. In college writing, the Informal end of the General range is probably informal enough for even the most relaxed assignment.

Though there will certainly be occasions when the relationship you assume with your readers makes a consistently Formal or a consistently Informal style the right choice, General English, with its breadth and flexibility, will ordinarily meet your needs. Interaction of the elements in the rhetorical situation will guide you to the appropriate segment of the wide verbal and syntactic range General English offers.

EXERCISE

In a letter to a close friend, describe a campus custom or current fad. Then write an account of the same custom or fad for a national magazine whose readers are mainly middle-aged college graduates. For each paper, consider what role you want to play. Are you writing as a participant or as an observer? Are you defending the practice or attacking it or simply reporting it? The two essays should probably differ somewhat in content and should certainly differ in style.

Stylistic Consistency

Having settled on the appropriate variety of English, you should normally stick to it unless you have good reason for departing from it. Given the wide range of General English, this is hardly restrictive advice: we can use "stick to it" without introducing a jarringly Informal note and "departing from" without being noticeably Formal. But stylistic inconsistency does call attention to itself in the following passage, where the beginning of the second sentence marks an abrupt shift from the tone of the first:

However clear his conceptions and however strong his motivation, the writer who has not yet committed a word to paper still has much to do. To get on the ball, he should. . . .

Unintended shifts of this kind often occur when the writer is hurrying to meet a deadline. An Informal expression pops into his head, and he writes it down. Or he is laboring over a passage that doesn't seem very impressive, and he finds a good, big Formal synonym for a word he has used; so in it goes. You can catch and correct such unconscious inconsistencies by careful editing. The word that pops into your head or that you pluck from a dictionary is likely to jump out at you when you read what you've written — particularly if you read it aloud.

Current writing shows considerable mixing of styles. But a good writer mixes deliberately; when he makes a marked shift, it is for a purpose. He may wish to express an attitude toward his readers: by dropping a mockingly Informal expression into a serious discussion, he can shock or delight them. Or he may wish to underline his own attitude toward his subject, as in this sentence from a movie review:

Ray, played by Tony LoBianco, is an oily con man, a misogynist, and a generally hung-up kiddo who marries and preys upon lonely old maids. — *Newsweek*, Feb. 16, 1970

Would you call Hamlet a "generally hung-up kiddo" — not in a broad burlesque but in a serious paper? The "kiddo" would certainly be a doubtful choice, but, given its recent vogue, "hung-up" might well occur to you. So far as meaning is concerned, it's a possible choice. But is it the right choice for the rhetorical situation — right for your purpose in dealing with *this* subject for *this* audience? Is it consistent with the prevailing tone of the paper, and, if not, is there a sound reason for deviating from that tone?

At times a writer will deliberately range over several varieties of English in a single sentence:

What an intriguing thought — for a man to take his new riches and free time and his machines and *split* from *communitas* and start his own league. — Tom Wolfe, *The Pump House Gang*

Wolfe's shifting of verbal gears seems appropriate to his subject (Hugh Hefner), and there is nothing in the writing situation that makes it inappropriate (as it might have been if he had been writing Hefner's obituary). The strong and amusing contrast between "split" and "communitas" is itself his way of making a social comment.

The Writer's Responsibility

However many roles you play, however many voices you speak in as a writer, it is you — the actual you — who must make the rhetorical decisions. Your judgment, your sense of fitness, controls the relationship between you and your reader. And no matter which real or imagined you does the writing, what you write represents you as a person. You are responsible for the language you use. In meeting this responsibility, you should find out as much as you can about the resources of English. The less you know about them, the more restricted will be your use of the language and the more limited and distorted the representation of yourself in your writing. The more you know about them, the more chance there is that you will be able to say exactly what you want to say in the way you want to say it.

SOURCES AND RESOURCES

The spoken language is one of the two major resources of any writer. The other is the language as it appears in published form. If we are ever to write with real ease, we need to read a good deal, as well as listen, and so learn the ways of our language by direct experience.

Reading and Writing

Constant reading of excellent prose does not guarantee that you will become a good writer, any more than constant exposure to fine paintings means that you will become a good painter. But reading is probably the most valuable formative influence on a writer. Sometimes the influence is direct, as when there is conscious, deliberate imitation of an admired author. More often it is indirect, casual, cumulative. Just as we unconsciously pick up expressions and modes of expression from those we talk to, so we absorb rhythms, turns of phrase, and syntactic patterns from our reading.

What you read, then, is important to you as a writer. Constant reading of nothing but the sports pages will leave one mark on your prose; constant reading of nothing but *Commentary* magazine or *Psychology Today* will leave another. If you immerse yourself in medical journals or in economic reports or in Elizabethan literature, your style will probably reflect that fact.

Most college students need to make a special effort to read widely. Course work normally requires intensive use of textbooks, reference works, and the documents and literature of various disciplines. However valuable it may be educationally, such material may not have much stylistic variety; it should be supplemented by reading in current magazines and books, fiction and nonfiction. Wide reading helps you separate good writing from bad and discriminate among various kinds of good writing. Reading current literature keeps you close to the idiom of your own time.

If you read a good deal, you are likely to be more comfortable writing yourself; you will write more easily and confidently. And you will be a better judge of what you write. The ability to be your own reader, critic, and editor is an essential part of the writing process; and it is developed largely through reading. Understanding and appreciating good prose makes you more sensitive to both the strengths and the weaknesses of your own writing.

Aids to Writers

In addition to the general benefits offered by reading, you can get direct help on various aspects of writing from certain textbooks, reference works, scholarly journals, and popular magazines. A good dictionary is indispensable, and some writers find a thesaurus useful. (Dictionaries are discussed on pp. 350–54.) Handbooks give information and advice on grammar and mechanics. Books on language trace the history of English, discuss its vocabulary, and analyze its structure; rhetorics set forth the principles of good writing; and style manuals deal particularly with such matters as punctuation, capitalization, spelling, abbreviation, and documentation. Books on usage discuss the status of locutions and may help you decide whether or not a word is appropriate or inappropriate in a particular context. (See *Usage.)

This book is accurately described by its title: it is a guide to planning and writing essays; and it is an index to specific items of English usage, grammar, and mechanics. Many of the *Index* entries give advice on troublesome individual problems you will encounter in your writing. The *Guide* offers a way of looking at language that provides a rationale for this advice; and it offers instruction in creating rhetorical contexts in which the advice can be applied.

Personal Resources

The resources we have discussed so far are public ones, available to all. Besides these, there are the personal resources that vary from one individual to another—the interests, the experiences, the abilities, and the mental and emotional characteristics that make each one of us unique. Your personal resources are a combination of your native talents and all that you learn, in school and out.

Though public resources yield information and ideas, a writer has to depend on himself for his major sources of material. Essays are made up of facts, feelings, impressions, assumptions, beliefs, details, generalizations, causal relations, comparisons, definitions, interpretations, judgments, illustrations, anecdotes, quotations, and summaries. This substance comes from experiencing and observing and remembering, from talking and reading and studying, from reasoning and analyzing and reflecting. All of us perform these activities; all of us need to learn to exploit our particular set of sources as efficiently as possible.

Memory is an invaluable source of details, the stuff of life in most kinds of writing. Besides their obvious usefulness in autobiographical essays, the personal experiences you recall can provide bases for your opinions, give authority to your explanations, bring an abstract discussion down to earth, add conviction to an argument. While memory seems to be the source least amenable to conscious cultivation, it can be coaxed. When it offers you only blurred impressions, work on it till the fog clears. Often you will find your memory expanding and sharpening under pressure.

Accurate and adequate information is the core of a good essay, and the best means for getting the facts straight, for knowing what you are talking about, is through observation. By observing the world around you with open eyes and an open mind, you can stock your memory with the images that make it a major resource for writing of every kind. For the most part, you see only what you want to see or what you have been brought up to see, but with conscious effort you can expand the circle of your awareness — you can literally see more. Train yourself to be a good observer. Instead of settling for a general impression, look for parts and interrelationships. Single out the specifics which, translated into exact images, will make your writing concrete. The kind of observation — examination and reexamination — that turns up good material is purposeful, directed, deliberate. Open your eyes. Observe. Perceive. Become aware.

Ideas for essays come from listening, reading, and studying — from what you talk about with your friends, from what you read about in newspapers, magazines, and books, listen to on radio, and watch on television, from what you hear in lectures and class discussions and study in course assignments. This is as it should be. Use your papers as testing grounds for the ideas you are incubating — ideas you have formed in response to what others have said or written.

Material for short papers will come chiefly from your experiences, past and current, and from your thinking about topics that are making news. Longer, more comprehensive papers may call for the kind of authoritative information provided by your courses or by research in the library. Sometimes information from a course can be combined with personal experience: perhaps you can illustrate (or challenge) a sociological theory about urban or suburban life from your own experience. In other cases, what you have learned in a course equips you to deal with topics remote from your experience: a physics course may help you make sense of a new proposal for space exploration; a course in economics will help you argue for or against the monetary policy being pursued by the Federal Reserve Board.

Lack of personal experience does not—and should not—mean lack of personal involvement. Granted you have never ridden in a space capsule or controlled the money supply, but you can have strong convictions about the relative importance of the space program and the antipollution program, and you can be personally concerned about the cost of tuition.

Of all your sources the most important are reasoning and reflecting. Until your mind begins to analyze data, reflect on it, reason about it, it remains data and nothing more. Whether you are drawing on past experience, observation, discussion, or reading, you need to keep thinking. Sift and sort, selecting what is pertinent, questioning what is peripheral, discarding what is irrelevant. Evaluate your data. Decide which information is most reliable, which authorities are most trustworthy. Decide what you, in fact, believe—and why.

Your mind is your resource, its activity your source, every time you draw an inference, point out an unexpected likeness, establish a distinction, form a new grouping, or shape a generalization. Your mind is the personal resource that sets you apart from everyone else and gives your writing its individuality.

Chapter Two

GETTING STARTED

An experienced writer works partly by habit, partly by improvising. Habits vary. The testimony in the three volumes of *Writers at Work* (New York: Viking) shows a surprising diversity in the ways professional writers incubate ideas. Some can't write at all until they have a clear, strong conception of what they want to say; others have to write in order to find an idea or a plot. Some make elaborate plans before they begin to write; others work out the structure as they go along. Some write a first draft at top speed, paying no conscious attention to matters of sentence structure, word choice, or punctuation. Others proceed with the greatest care and deliberation, intent on perfecting one sentence before going to the next.

Evidently there is no one method for writing well. What works for one writer doesn't work for another; the good route for one is another's dead end. But everyone has to find a route, and it is altogether likely that for you one way will prove easier going than another. So experiment. Try out different approaches. Settle on the habits of composing that you find most congenial, that seem to work best for you most of the time. All the evidence suggests that finding your own characteristic way of handling writing projects will increase both your confidence and your competence. And however successful you are in finding *your* way, you will still have plenty of scope for improvising, for no two writing projects are exactly alike.

 ## THE PROCESS OF WRITING

Looked at from the outside, writing is the act of joining words into sentences and recording the sentences on paper. But what words? What sentences? Clearly, a large part of composing must take place in the mind. Some of this initial activity we are scarcely aware of; if not below the threshold of consciousness, it is scarcely above it.

But if writing is not just exercising the fingers, neither is it necessarily the act of finding words to match conceptions that exist fully formed and definite in the mind. For some writers, it is: they "think the whole thing out" before they put words on paper. For others, the physical act of writing is itself a means of exploration and discovery that stimulates their thinking and gives them ideas. Like E. M. Forster, they ask, "How can I know what I think till I see what I say?"

The initial stage in composing may be called prewriting. Without sustained and inventive prewriting, a good essay can only be a lucky accident.

Prewriting

Prewriting is discovering what you think and feel about your subject; it is finding the perspective from which you will treat it. It includes whatever goes on before you make a deliberate, purposeful effort to produce a first draft. Depending on the subject and your habits of work, prewriting may be a quiet period of brooding and meditation. Or it may involve talking, reading, taking notes, making more or less systematic outlines. Or it may mean endless scribbling in an effort to get at a hazy notion that, you feel, may turn out to be the core of your essay. Some people think on paper.

Whether your hands are busy or still, prewriting is the process of discovering your ideas — where you stand in relation to your subject, what meaning it has for you, what you want to say about it. From this it follows that a central requirement of prewriting is, in the words of Gordon Rohman and Albert Wlecke, an "absolute willingness to think one's own thoughts, feel one's own feelings." Only by involving yourself completely with the subject will you make it your own.

Making the subject your own does not mean that all your writing will be personal; it means that all your writing will be motivated by personal concern. Writing that lacks personal concern — intellectual commitment or emotional commitment or both — is likely to be dull and perfunctory; the thoughts are clichés, the feelings conventions. Essays that grow out of personal concern sound as though they were written by someone who believes in the ideas he is expressing and accepts their consequences. And whether the style is smooth or rough, the voice of a living person comes through. Certainly personal concern need not and should not manifest itself in ego trips or self-conscious mannerisms. In a research project it may involve nothing more *and nothing less* than the determination to give a faithful and coherent account of the truths scholars have discovered. That may be as much a commitment as the commitment to self-expression in uninhibited autobiography.

EXERCISE

Take any activity that interests you — singing, surfing, cooking, courting, crashing, or whatever — and keep turning it over in your mind until you know how you feel about it and what you want to say about it. There is no best way to do this, but you might try the method of comparison. See how many resemblances, even accidental and partial ones, occur to you when you think of the activity in terms of another that seems somehow related to it. What new perspectives on your subject are gained if you think of surfing as flying, of courting as fencing, of cooking as composing poetry, of walking as attending a religious service? Thinking in terms of metaphors and analogies may give you a controlling image, a root idea for further thought, that will help you discover how you really feel about your subject.

Or try treating the activity as unique. Ask yourself what qualities it has that make it — at least for you — different from everything else. You may find this approach just as effective in opening up the subject.

Now write an essay, saying in one or two pages what the activity means to you.

What the preceding exercise is intended to suggest is that if you are to write well, you must work to make each subject you write about your own. Composing is the product of creative thought; so to a considerable degree it is a private activity. A textbook like this one necessarily deals mainly with the public aspects of writing — with the problems that writers have in common. But in addition to carrying out the tasks all writers share — finding material, organizing it, presenting it to a specific audience — you must yourself become personally engaged with your subject. Personal engagement, involvement, commitment, is at the heart of the prewriting process.

Ordinarily the heaviest demands on your private resources and on your prewriting activity are made by an assignment that is wide open—a "free choice"—or by one that invites you to stake out a topic for yourself from a very broad area like education or politics. For a free choice, don't spend too much time trying to decide what to write about. Indecision can be fruitful so long as you are genuinely considering options, but at some point it becomes unproductive, and eventually it is paralyzing. You can keep it from reaching that stage if you recognize the simple truths that you are a person of many experiences, interests, and talents, and that there are certainly a dozen topics you can write on with more authority than anyone else in the classroom, including your instructor. Without wasting time waiting for the ideal topic to suggest itself, you should be able to find a subject that is not only good but good for *you*.

The subject you settle on should be close enough to your own experience so that you can feel comfortable with it. You will only flounder if you launch into something like "The Impact of Existential Thought on American Society." At the same time, don't limit yourself to a trivial, unchallenging topic. Unless your subject stirs your imagination and stretches your mind, you are not likely to say much that will interest the reader.

Often you will arrive at a good topic by building up and out from a particular incident—something that has amused or stirred you, given you pleasure or caused you pain. If you keep a journal, you will find that entries in it can serve as excellent starters for topics, reminding you of half-forgotten impressions and emotions associated with certain experiences. When you are faced with a broad, general subject like education, you have to find ways of making it manageable. Perhaps the best way is to cut in on the subject where you have some personal experience with it. Last summer you tutored some teen-agers? Then don't write about education, or high-school education, or the problem of dropouts, or teaching disadvantaged children. Write about tutoring your tenth-graders. Move from that experience, if you like, to some provisional generalizations about reaching unmotivated tenth-graders, but let the generalizations develop out of your summer's work.

Once you have moved in on your topic and become fully engaged with it, you will find it helpful to frame a tentative statement of your purpose—what your essay is to describe or demonstrate or prove. True, your purpose may change as you gather material or start writing or even when you are well along with your first draft. But to give your thinking some direction, to have some criterion to help you sort out the relevant impressions and seize on the leads worth following up, you need to commit yourself to a thesis.

An assertion is always more useful than a title. If the paper is to support an idea or advance a position, make the assertion a *thesis statement:*

College students have every right to be represented in faculty councils.

Our school paper should concentrate on campus affairs and not try to cover the national or international scene.

A professional army is morally and practically preferable to an army of draftees.

Or, if the paper is not to develop a thesis or recommend a course of action, make it a *statement of intention:*

This essay will give an account of student-faculty relations on this campus.

I want to explain how I developed my ideas about the present working of the draft system.

I will tell about my experiences with Operation Head Start.

What I want to do is describe a current style-setter (in music, fashion, sports).

Once you have made a commitment to a thesis or phrased a statement of intention, you are launched into the phase of writing that classical rhetoricians called *invention*. You are ready to set about discovering specific things to say. Depending on what you are writing about, this may or may not involve reading and research to collect facts and assemble evidence. It should mean settling on strategies for developing the root idea in your thesis statement. It will certainly mean digging into your own background and experience for relevant details and images, ideas and opinions.

All the while, your mind has to be active. It has to confront and master the material you are assembling, make something new of it, something that is the product of *your* thinking and bears the mark of your individuality. When you are reading and taking notes, remind yourself of the function the notes are to serve. When you are figuring out how to present and develop the material, ask yourself what the audience needs in the way of illustration and definition. Think *through* your topic. Don't just think about it. (And don't be afraid to modify your thesis statement. It's no sin to change your mind.)

Prewriting—finding out what you think and feel about the subject and what you want to say about it—should be neither ignored nor hurried. Careless, hasty, superficial thinking will leave your field of operations cluttered with obstacles that can trip you when you reach the writing stage.

Writing

Prewriting and writing overlap. Preparing an essay is not a mechanical, linear process in which each operation is wrapped up before the next one is begun. It is more like the growth of a living thing, in which all the vital activities continue even though the organism has passed from one stage to another. As has already been pointed out, some authors prewrite well into the stage of putting sentences on paper. Even so, "writing" proper brings in a whole new dimension of creative activity, for you have to juggle and weigh varying (and sometimes conflicting) demands: you must do justice to your material and at the same time reach your audience, say what you mean but say it so that it will interest and persuade others.

Find the way in that suits you best. Will you begin by making a detailed plan for your paper, or will you let the plan develop as you write? Some professional writers like to build the structure before they have much to put into it. They start with a few phrases or sentences, push them into the pattern of an outline, formal or informal, and keep working until they have a series of statements representing the main points they want to make. Only then do they start writing consecutive sentences. Others like to coax the structure out of the material. They find that the actual process of composing keeps suggesting new possibilities for developing ideas and new ways of arranging them.

Use an outline or not, as you see fit, but above all, get started. Students are not the only ones to inflict the self-punishment of putting off the job. Commenting on the habits of professionals, Malcolm Cowley has said, "Apparently the hardest problem for almost any writer, whatever his medium, is getting to work in the morning (or in the afternoon, if he is a late riser . . . or even at night)." Recognize rationalizing and procrastinating for what they are, plunge in, and keep going. Don't waste time trying to dream up the perfect opening. Chances are that when you have finished the paper, you'll have a much better notion of what will make a good first paragraph.

Once started, give yourself enough time to write several pages — if possible, a complete draft. Writing done in one sitting is likely to have better continuity, more consistency, more life than writing that is repeatedly interrupted. Most professional writers find it good practice to make the first draft full rather than skimpy. If you are in doubt about some of your material, include it. When you have finished, you will be in a better position to decide whether or not a particular passage is relevant. Make your paragraphs full-bodied, with plenty of details. In revising, it is easier to shrink an out-size paragraph than to fatten up an undernourished one.

Unless you are the most careful and deliberate kind of writer, your first draft will be rough and uneven. If some of the sentences are sharp and clear, others will be rambling, clumsy, even unintelligible. All the paragraphs may be more or less related to the thesis statement, but they may show little relation to each other. Even so, writing the first draft should have helped enormously to clarify your thinking, to give you some notion of the real shape the paper ought to take, and to show you what needs to be done to produce a strong, unified essay. Possibly you need hard evidence to replace vague speculation; possibly you should build up what is now a subsidiary point into a major one. Certainly you should give attention to linking paragraphs in order to show the connection of ideas, revising sentences to make the thought come clear, finding the words and images that will sharpen and freshen your meaning. One of the main objectives of this text, both *Guide* and *Index*, is to help you rework early drafts.

As you revise and rewrite, keep your mind open to new ideas. If the process of setting down your thoughts has made you realize that some of them contradict each other or that some are foolish, it should also have generated sounder, more consistent ones. Keep your mind open to new ways of expressing your ideas. The biggest obstacle to improvement in writing is the feeling that once a sentence is written, it is frozen forever. Take the attitude that nothing you write is sacred, that anything you write can be improved.

Even with the most careful job of prewriting, an essay should go through several drafts. Good writing is rewritten writing. Rework your papers — and the emphasis is on *work* — until you are satisfied that the content and organization represent the best you can do with the topic in the time you have and that you have said what you want to say to your audience.

Revising

In the final stage of composition, get outside your essay. Look at it from the perspective of a critical reader. Become objective about your work. You can hardly be detached enough unless you let a day or two pass between writing the last draft and doing the final editing.

Taking a fresh look at your essay may persuade you to make substantial changes in content. A new idea may suddenly hit you. For the first time you may see that dropping paragraph 5 and merging paragraphs 4 and 6 will make the structure tighter and more economical. But if you have given enough thought to composing and if you have gone through enough drafts to produce a version that satisfies you, most of the job of revising will consist of reworking sentences and checking mechanics. Slash the unnecessary phrases, the ones you wrote just to get your thinking started or just to fill up space. Pare and prune. Try to pack more meaning into fewer words.

As you give your paper this final editing, read it aloud once or twice. Your ear will catch some weaknesses your eye has missed. A shapeless sentence may betray itself by the fact that you stumble over it as you read aloud. Clichés, flabby phrases, even errors in spelling and punctuation sometimes call attention to themselves if you are listening hard. Keep your dictionary and the *Index* section of this book open. Check anything that raises doubt in your mind.

Finally, type a clean draft, following the instructions in *Manuscript form. Before submitting your essay, give it a careful proofreading to get rid of typographical errors.

A Checklist

Before they have established their own habits of composing and developed skill in sizing up the requirements of an assignment, some students find it helpful to have a list of steps to follow in producing a paper. Any division of the writing process into steps is bound to be somewhat artificial and arbitrary; but making due allowance for the telescoping of some steps in certain projects and the overlapping of others, and for the varying weight given to each because of differences among writers, we may take these seven steps to be the important ones in most college writing. Depending on the writer's habits of composition, prewriting may merge into writing as early as the first step or as late as the fifth.

1. Focusing on a subject, locating a topic in the subject, and phrasing a tentative thesis statement or statement of intention.

2. Gathering material, sifting it, and evaluating it—whether the material comes from memory or reflection or from reading or study.

3. Deciding on ways of developing the material.

4. Organizing the material, using an outline or some other method to project the structure of the essay.

5. Writing drafts of the essay, rewriting until the thought comes clear within a sound structure. (During this stage, every careful writ-

er is prepared to reconsider the decisions he has made up to this point.)

6. Revising the paper.

7. Preparing and proofreading the manuscript.

Self-Analysis and Evaluation

We have not yet discussed specific techniques of developing, organizing, testing, and expressing ideas; these topics will be taken up later. Our main concern in this section has been to make clear that good writing springs initially not from formulas but from creative activity, from the desire and need to express thoughts and feelings, from the wise exploitation of personal resources. Even when it is not at all personal in the sense of being about you, your writing always deserves a personal commitment — not only to the subject but to the actual job of composing. If you are to take full responsibility for what you write, you need to develop habits that work for you (though not necessarily for anyone else), and you need to learn to appraise the strengths and weaknesses of your own essays. Commitment to writing requires both genuine involvement and candid self-criticism.

As a means of self-appraisal, you should find it helpful now and then to keep a running account of how you go about preparing an essay. Try to adopt a double vision: watch yourself as you work, and jot down notes on how you go about the job. Identify the trouble spots at every stage from prewriting to revision. Note how you try to solve (or sidestep) each problem. When you have finished the paper, write an account of what you did, and make an honest attempt to evaluate your essay.

EXERCISE

The following essay and the accompanying analysis were produced at the end of the first week of a composition course in response to a broad assignment — "Write a two-to-three-page essay describing a personal experience of some significance to you. With the essay, submit a brief account of how you went about writing it."

As you read the essay and the analysis, ask yourself these questions: So far as you can tell, did the writer make a wise choice of subject? Has she successfully solved the problems of thinking and composing discussed in the analysis? Has she found a satisfactory perspective on her subject? Can you visualize the scene? Does the writing re-create the experience clearly and vividly enough for you to share her feelings?

Has the writer made a sound evaluation of the essay? Do you think it went through enough drafts? What are its strengths and weaknesses? Can you make specific suggestions for improvements in organization, in paragraph development, in sentence structure, in word choice?

An Island Perspective

I suppose everyone on the island had a favorite spot. Mine was a little cove about a quarter of the way around the coast from the hotel. If none of the guests were around—we had to preserve a conservative image for them—I would take off my shift and, in my swim suit, test the freedom of my limbs against the stability of the rocks, running and leaping from one to another. It was simple happiness then, but here at college I wonder that it didn't approach the ecstasy I know I would feel now if somehow I could be back at Star Island.

I would arrive at the cove breathless, quickly dive in, and then in one continuous movement slide from the water to a prone position on the rocks. For the first few moments I could do nothing more than lie there, still breathing hard, and feel the rays from the omnipresent sun weave their way through the cool ocean breeze. The regularity of the waves as they broke against the rocks was nothing short of a lullaby for me after the frantic business of serving breakfast to two hundred guests. I would let the sound gradually replace the echo of banging dishes, chattering girls, and shouted orders, until my mind was blank except for the rhythmical song of the sea.

It must have been an ambitious nature that made me plan reading and letter writing each time I went to the cove. Whatever it was, it fought a losing battle all summer, never giving up the hope that maybe *today* would be the day I would finally accomplish something "productive." But I was in the sea world, and the most productive thing I could do was to become a part of that world. That meant, at first, letting the sounds of gulls and waves override my mind's activities, and allowing the sun, air, and spray to relax my tense body. It meant giving in to the hypnotic power of the sea.

Later, though, after I'd become like a mussel on the rocks—part of the rocks, yet not a rock—my mind would begin to respond to the sea. Thoughts flowed in and out, short, almost wordless impressions as quickly gone as they had come. Gently they came, yet more and more pervasively, like the rising tide, and I'd begin to play with them, holding them a little longer, asking a little more of them. Thoughts that had been troublesome and seemed complex drifted to their natural place and, feeling at home there, could relax and stop demanding attention by pretending they were more important than they were.

I don't know if I was experiencing Contemplation, Meditation, or just Peaceful Solitude as I lay there on the rocks in the cove. Now that I'm back on the mainland, it seems impossible to find time to be alone, to empty myself as I did by the sea, and then to explore my thoughts with such curious, sometimes amusing, sometimes startling objectivity. If I miss the sea, it's because it expected nothing of me, yet gave me its perspective on my often confused thinking, a perspective of simplicity and naturalness.

Comment

At first mention of writing about a personal experience, I thought of Star Island, one of my most recent and more unusual experiences. But I hesitated a few days, considering topics not quite so immediate that I could perhaps handle more objectively. There was also the fear that anything I wrote about Star would lose something in the telling and fail to communicate to the reader the experience that had meant so much to me. I finally decided that the topic must be Star, because I rejected all other ideas as less interesting. Besides, it was a good justification for thinking about Star as much as I wanted to without feeling that I was shirking school responsibilities.

I started several times, the first a light description of some of the more amusing aspects of living on an island for ten weeks. Now I think perhaps I should have continued with that idea, rather than switching to a more serious topic. It's easier to convey the humor in incidents than it is to convey feelings. I began the submitted essay on Monday. I wrote two paragraphs after reliving the experience I wanted to re-create several times earlier that day. I rejected a first paragraph about how I got the job as irrelevant and made the second paragraph the opening one. At the point where I mention feeling like a mussel on a rock, I was stuck for a transition to describe the gradually increasing activity of my mind. I was also bothered that my feelings sounded too "romantic" and unreal. My problem—that of describing a situation that at the time wasn't analyzed or "metaphorized" (I can't think of any other word for it), yet now, in retrospect, doing both. I did not solve that problem, so I am not accurately describing to the reader my feelings of the moment, but rather the significance they have taken in my memory—my feelings *now*, at college, about *then*, at Star.

My ideas grew more complex, thus harder to express, and further away from the simplicity I wanted to convey. Tuesday I did quite a bit of piecemeal composition. I went to bed Tuesday night wanting to change topics but forced by the schedule to stay with the one I had chosen. Wednesday morning I reread what I had written, crossed out one whole paragraph, and gave up on a transition I had been trying to make from the experience on Star to the problem of re-creating the situation here. Wednesday afternoon I rearranged a few sentences, reworded several phrases, and bought paper for the final typescript. I have to admit that the essay falls short of my expectations by a more than usual distance. However, I am satisfied with several of the sentences and out of necessity must for the present consider the essay finished.

BUILDING CONTENT

Faced with the job of writing an essay, students often complain that they are short of ideas ("I've got nothing to write about") or that they don't have the knack of saying what they mean ("I know what I want to say, but I don't know how to say it"). In fact, students are never totally bankrupt of material; no matter what the subject, they can always get a few ideas down on paper. But they sometimes have great difficulty in settling on a fruitful approach to the subject, in fleshing out the topic, in bringing their ideas into some sensible relation to one another. (Fleshing out doesn't mean padding. It means putting meat on the bones, not clothes on the body—developing ideas, not just adding words.)

The way to solve the problem of inadequate substance is to call on your personal resources in prewriting—remembering, observing, reasoning, reflecting—and to use these resources, as well as your reading, intelligently and systematically. This section will make some suggestions about how you can generate content as you think and write your way through an essay. First, though, a word about various types of essays. You can reduce some of the waste motion in writing by recognizing what kind of essay you are trying to produce.

Types of Essays

Whether a topic is specified or you are asked to discover or invent your own subject matter, most of your college writing will be analytical and critical, not wholly personal. Occasionally you may have the opportunity to write purely autobiographical accounts of the kind discussed on pp. 49–61. More often, when you draw on your personal experience—and you should, whenever the topic permits—it will be in papers that are primarily expository or argumentative. Sometimes the same experience will provide material for all three kinds of essays. Your part in a show put on by the senior class at your high school might produce a good personal narrative. Handled differently, the experience could be used in a general, objective analysis of the problems of presenting an original musical. And the same experience could be used as evidence if you chose to argue that school administrators should adopt a hands-off policy toward the theatrical productions of student organizations.

What is the difference between an explanatory essay and a persuasive essay? Clearly, not the source of the material. Either may draw on a personal experience; either may be based largely or entirely on reading and research. And not the nature of the material. Wildlife conservation has been the subject of countless explanatory essays as well as countless persuasive essays. The only sound basis for differentiating the two types of essays is the use to which the material is put; and use is determined by purpose. In an explanatory essay, your purpose is to *inform* your reader, to clarify the subject for him, to increase his understanding of it. In a persuasive essay, your purpose is to *influence* your reader to think or act in a certain way. Naturally, one of these purposes does not rule out the other: informing may be the first step toward influencing. But in a good essay one purpose usually dominates, and that broad purpose guides you in searching for material and deciding how to develop it.

Details and Generalizations

To develop material means, among other things, to establish a cooperative relationship between the details you use in dealing with your subject and the generalizations you make about it.

Details in writing represent truths in experience — statements of fact ("President Pompidou, who owns a pinball machine, . . ."); images that carry sense impressions ("The heavy downpour beat the crops into the ground"); and indeed all the descriptive words and phrases that stand for attributes ("*ice-cold* wind") or parts ("the *red* and *yellow markings* of the waxwings"). Details like these are the product of observation and perception and are essential in writing about physical objects and experiences. But details are just as necessary in dealing with ideas, abstractions, and works of the imagination. A critique of a novel calls for specific statements about plot, characters, and style; and a discussion of the abstraction *virtue* might use as details the individual virtues honesty, charity, and so on. Every subject has its details — its particulars.

Though necessarily based on particulars, generalizations go beyond them to show patterns in experience. By means of generalizations, we set up groupings, establish relationships, advance interpretations, draw conclusions. A generalization may sum up a number of experiences ("Growing up black means growing up angry"); it may bring out the meaning of particular experiences ("There are times when mere survival is enough"); or it may express an opinion or judgment about an occurrence or a course of action ("The administration's policy is suicidal").

Generalizations are indispensable in dealing with ideas. Predictions, hypotheses, speculations are all dependent on the power to generalize; and generalizations are of central importance whenever the writer's purpose is to interpret, to criticize, to evaluate. Whole sections of essays will spin from or build toward a single generalization. And the right generalization, adequately supported, will set the reader's mind in motion and open up new perspectives. Notice how much is implied in Irving Howe's remark, "The day *Native Son* appeared, American culture was changed forever."

But without the support of relevant details, generalizations may seem empty or pretentious or simply false. Much weak writing comes from parroting generalizations that are no more than platitudes. While in many contexts the reader can expect no great novelty in the conclusions, he has a right to hope that even if the generalizations are well-worn, they will be renewed by fresh details, the authentic product of the writer's own perception.

Some types of writing—description and narration immediately come to mind—are packed with details. Later in this chapter (pp. 54–55) we shall see the function and value of details in personal narrative. Other types of writing rely heavily on generalizations. The nature of the subject, the writer's purpose, his relation to his audience—all these have a bearing on the right proportioning of details to generalizations. In most college essays, there should be a regular interplay between them—generalizations bringing out the significance of the details, details providing the concrete particulars without which the generalizations would be unclear or unconvincing. As you go about developing your essays, many of your tactical decisions will have to do with this relationship. Ordinarily you will use details either to clarify or to support the generalization you are advancing. Beyond that, details can serve either explanation or persuasion by supplying reasons, filling out comparisons, providing a basis for causal connections. In short, details give your writing substance; generalizations interpret the complex of details and capture their significance.

EXERCISES

1. For each of the following passages, identify the main generalizations and explain why you think the writer's use of supporting detail is or is not satisfactory. Has he used enough details? The right details? Relate your discussion to the subject treated in the passage.

a. The entire journey down [Bright Angel Trail] is through scenes indescribably grandiose, often between colorful hillocks and buttes but always austere and sometimes, especially within the inner gorge, somber almost to the point of gloominess. Vegetation is sparse and obviously just surviving; animal life extremely scanty. One is constantly reminded of terrific forces, vast stretches of time, and the death of whole races of once flourishing living creatures now reduced to a few mineralized skeletons or a few impressions in the hardened mud, and it is easy to realize how desolate and terrifying it all was to those earlier explorers who were completely alone in a forbidding, seemingly accursed land where nature was many things but certainly not kindly.

Here now at the bottom she smiles again. Water brings life, and wherever there is life, there is beauty and a sense of joy. Bright Angel Creek makes a kind of oasis. Birds again inhabit the trees; along the stream bank for miles scarlet monkey flowers and Cardinal flowers draw, even in mid-October, a curving red line. The sense of being almost perilously cut off from the rest of the world which one ought perhaps to feel is reduced to no more than an agreeable feeling of peaceful retirement. The little oasis one has come to rest in is snug and cozy, and though surrounded by buttes and cliffs, they so cut off the view in most places that had one been taken here blindfolded one would never guess how deep he was below all the surrounding country except the channel of the river. — Joseph Wood Krutch, *The Best Nature Writing of Joseph Wood Krutch*

b. Blue is rare in nature. Sky and sea have most of it. True blue is hard to find on earth. Most of what's called blue runs off into the purple. But there's the bluebird, a piece of sky. The indigo bunting of unearthly dark vibration. No color like it. No mineral, no jewel. There's the bluejay, whose big bold blue is muted by the black leading which holds his panes of sapphire glass in place. There are the dark-blue seeds of wild grape, almost black. The big round balls of moonseed vines, dark blue and shiny. There are the hanging blue balls of the Solomon's seal in autumn, dark as wild grape. Blue seeds of sassafras trees held in scarlet cups. Once I saw a cerulean warbler. So high up, so far away, that only once the blue shone through the opening of green leaves. But I'm positive of it. There are the blue eyes of chalky blue-green dragonflies. And in summer mornings, drifts of blue along the road from chicory flowers. But here we start creeping into the lavender, the true blue fading; the wild hyacinths aren't really blue, we start calling violets blue, pale wild pansies rising to purple, rich, shining purple in the wild larkspur flowers. And the whole field of purple broadens out and carries one away. — Josephine Johnson, *The Inland Island*

c.   Language, the most versatile and indispensable of all symbolisms, has put its stamp on all our mental functions, so that I think they always differ from even our closest analogues in animal life. Language has invaded our feeling and dreaming and action, as well as our reasoning, which is really a product of it. The greatest change wrought by language is the increased scope of awareness in speech-gifted beings. An animal's awareness is always of things in its own place and life. In human awareness, the present, actual situation is often the least part. We have not only memories and expectations; we have a *past* in which we locate our memories, and a *future* that vastly overreaches our own anticipations. Our past is a story, our future a piece of imagination. Likewise our ambient is a place in a wider, symbolically conceived place, the universe. We live in a *world*. — Susanne K. Langer, *Man and Animal: The City and the Hive*

2.   Take a generalization — one of those below or one of your own — and support it with sensory details.

a.   What I saw from the top of the hill startled me.

b.   Red is rare in nature.

c.   When I came to, all I felt was pain.

Developing Generalizations

The various means we use to develop generalizations can be discussed both in terms of the conscious thought that goes into them and in terms of what they are meant to produce — a stretch of prose that communicates what the writer wants to communicate. Ordinarily a writer aims not simply to convey his opinion or attitude but to have the reader share in the thought process that led him to believe or feel as he does. In his essay he will not reproduce the actual course of his thinking, which is rapid, helter-skelter, full of false starts, digressions, and dead ends. Instead, he will prune, arrange, and edit to give the flow of his thought sufficient coherence so that it can be grasped by the reader. But what he writes will in some degree represent the *process* of his thinking and not merely the product of it.

What we call methods of development offer one way of discussing some aspects of that process. Although the approaches and techniques are familiar—you use them constantly yourself and encounter them regularly in what you hear and read—you may not realize how generally useful they are. In the early stages of composing, the half-random, half-purposeful mulling over of ideas and strategies that constitutes prewriting, your awareness of the methods will often open up channels of exploration and help you settle on a statement of intention. As you plan and write, they will continue to generate ideas for the essay, pointing you in the right direction in your search for material. For these methods of developing ideas are themselves a resource, if not a source of material. Though they do not yield data for an essay, they suggest the kind of thinking and investigating that will turn up data. As guides to discovery and invention, they have been analogized to direction markers and to pump primers: they point the writer in the direction he should go in search of material; they start the flow of thought. An example will show how.

Suppose you have been given the broad assignment of writing about your hometown (or suburb or urban neighborhood). You can't think of a thing to say. (Oddly enough, it is the simple assignment on familiar material that most often results in glazed eyes and empty minds.) After turning the subject over for a while, you decide that all you can say about Mazenod is that it is a dull place. That's hardly a rich, juicy generalization. Still, the kernel of an essay is here, an impression or judgment that opens the door to prewriting. What you need to do now is find ways of expanding the generalization, supporting it, justifying it, perhaps proving it. Reminding yourself of typical methods of developing a generalization will open up possibilities for you, help you discover the right perspective on your subject, lead you to a definite statement of intention, and suggest what kind of material you need in order to follow through on that intention.

How can you expand on your generalization, sharpen it, give it substance?

One thing you can do is pile up descriptive details that will make the reader see, hear, smell, taste, touch, and ultimately absorb the flavor of Mazenod as you have experienced it. You may want to start your essay with one striking detail, say the broken clock in Market Square, and use that as a clue to life in Mazenod. At any rate, whatever details you give about setting, climate, buildings, people, community affairs should all contribute to the general impression you want to get across, an impression that you might phrase for yourself as "Growing up in a gray world."

Or try supporting your generalization by telling about an

incident ("The time the hippie hitchhiker almost turned Mazenod on") or a series of incidents. The narrative can be personal, your own reactions and interpretations serving as the center of interest; or it can be impersonal, presenting without comment the round of activities that make up the daily lives of the residents ("If you think weekdays are deadly, try our weekends").

Or you might contrast Mazenod, detail for detail, with a town that seems to you to be alive and exciting — "Ettington is the kind of town Mazenod could be and should be." You might use comparison to make other distinctions — "Mazenod is a fine place to grow up in, until you grow up." Or you might develop a figurative comparison in which you draw an analogy between living in Mazenod and being trapped in a stuffy classroom while a dull lecturer drones on and on.

As one chief means of supporting your thesis, you can classify the townspeople according to their interests and activities, their economic and educational backgrounds, or their political and social views. In your essay you might lead with a thesis like "The citizens of Mazenod are vociferous patriots who oppose the Bill of Rights" or "The liveliest place in my town is the Senior Citizens' Club."

To find other topics for discussion, you may want to divide or analyze your subject into whatever aspects of the town seem relevant to your main idea — what the town offers (or fails to offer) in the way of satisfying work, intellectual stimulation, entertainment, variety of people, and so on — and discuss each aspect in turn.

After establishing the *fact* of Mazenod's dullness through description, comparison, or other methods, you might explore the causes of it. Is the dullness to be attributed to the location of the town, the main industry, the absence of entertainment, the habits and attitudes of the citizens? Examining reasons might lead to the conclusion that the dullness of the town is unavoidable — "Outlying shopping centers drained the life out of Mazenod." Or you might argue that some enterprise and imagination — radical changes in present policies — could put some life into Mazenod. You might develop the implications of a figurative statement like "For some conditions, blood transfusions are the only hope."

Mazenod could serve as a springboard for an essay defining small-town life. The aim of the definition might be simple explanation, with Mazenod emerging as a typical example of small towns everywhere. Or the aim might be to persuade the reader that life in a small town is bound to be dull. What else could it be, you ask, given the built-in limitations of small towns?

In a paper aiming at definition, Mazenod itself would serve as the example. In the other approaches suggested here, you would use concrete illustrations and details to support or prove a generalization about Mazenod. Gathering a dozen for-instances will translate abstract dullness into audible, individual yawns. And that presumably is the intention you had when you started.

It may not be the intention you end with. By the time you have thought through your material, you should have refined, modified, narrowed, or expanded your original "Mazenod is a dull place" into a proposition that indicates more precisely what your paper will do. Awareness of the methods in the prewriting stage will have pointed you in the direction of a specific, manageable central idea for your essay. And it may have led you to change your original intention rather drastically. Perhaps you will decide to settle on a thesis like "Living in Mazenod offers the disadvantages—and the advantages—of living in any small town" or "Dullness is in the eye of the beholder." Serious prewriting effort may lead to the discovery that the initial generalization won't stand up—that it must be revised or even replaced. Whether it does or not, this kind of effort will refine your perspective, helping you decide whether you are going to analyze and explain, or criticize and evaluate, or simply reminisce—and whether your treatment of the subject is to be personal or detached.

EXERCISES

1. Review the possibilities for an essay on Mazenod, pp. 46–48. Write three beginnings for a paper on the community where you grew up—the town, the urban neighborhood, the suburb, or the rural area. Each beginning should be at least 150 words, and each should signal a different method of developing your main generalization about the community. Then, in an essay of about a thousand words, complete the beginning that interests you most. Address your essay to a friend you would like to have along on your next trip home.

2. Choose three of the general subjects below. After turning them over in your mind, narrow each subject to two topics, one for a short paper (400–700 words), one for a longer one (800–1200 words). For each topic, phrase a thesis statement or statement of intention that makes clear whether your purpose is to explain, to persuade, or to narrate a personal experience. Write on any of these your instructor assigns. In planning your paper, review the possible approaches outlined in the preceding section, "Developing Generalizations."

learning a new language	movies	student power
admission to college	national defense	rock
television	religious training	architecture
life in the suburbs	prestige symbols	sports fans
group therapy	race relations	comic strips

PERSONAL NARRATIVES

The opening assignment of a writing course may invite you to draw material entirely from your own experience—to prepare a brief autobiography or narrate an episode or describe a place you know well. Assignments like these give your instructor a chance to learn something about you, as well as about your writing skill, and they give you a chance to write about a subject on which you are certainly the chief authority.

This section will offer suggestions for writing a personal narrative and will introduce some matters that will be taken up in more detail in the chapters that follow. As you work through the section, adapt the material to your own use. This is a good time to experiment with taking notes on how you go about writing an essay. (See pp. 38–41.) Analysis of your methods of composing comes most naturally when you are writing about yourself. Anyone who keeps a journal finds himself reflecting on his successes and failures in recording his own feelings and perceptions.

What to write about? As you mull over the possibilities, memories of a good many experiences may surface—memories of big experiences, perhaps, like a trip to Africa or a skydive or an escape from a near-fatal accident. Or the incidents that come to mind may seem embarrassingly trivial: "I've never done anything—nothing's ever happened to me." In either case, you will be better off if you base your decision not so much on what the experience was as on your reaction to it. If you are to write convincingly, the experience should have made its mark on you. Choose one that caught your imagination, made an impression, possibly taught you something. Perhaps visiting Africa or jumping out of a plane or surviving a smash-up on the highway *should* have had meaning for you; but did it? Be honest with yourself. Examine your feelings. Maybe, whether you've had an assortment of big experiences or "never done anything," the memory that keeps tugging at your mind concerns an event that is very small when judged by objective standards. No matter. Objective standards don't apply. This is your experience, with meaning for *you.*

What are you going to say about the experience? That depends on what you actually feel about it. To find out what you feel—what the true meaning of the experience has been—you need to relive the event in your imagination, perhaps in the process learning something about yourself. It may turn out that what the experience means to you now is not at all what it meant then. Intervening events as well as insights gained from reading and reflection may have given you a new perspective on it. If so, you will need to decide whether you want to re-create the experience as it was or present it as you now interpret it.

In trying to clarify your reaction to the experience, you will be groping toward a statement of intention. If you can, build into the statement a suggestion of the significance of the experience—not "I will describe my best friend's wedding day" but "I will tell how my friend's wedding altered my ideas about marriage"; not "I will tell about my first experience with politics" but "I want to explain how my father's campaign for city councilman changed my attitude toward both politics and my father." That hint will help give a focus to your account of the experience.

But the experience is primary. You want the reader to share what you have seen and done and felt, to live the experience as you lived it. Only when he believes in the experience will he be in a position to accept your interpretation of it. So you have to make the experience real. Plumb your memory. Straighten out the sequence of incidents. Bring the images into focus, one after another. Hunt up reminders of the past: snapshots, letters, diaries, old phonograph records will often stir half-forgotten sense impressions. Do everything you can to recapture the details that alone can give your reader a sense of participating in the event. And start thinking about how you are going to present the material you are assembling—what narrative method you will adopt.

Narrative Method

Narratives fall into three broad types—*dramatized, generalized, summarized*—depending on how time is handled and how close the reader is brought to the action. Dramatized narrative presents individual scenes in which the action, including dialog, is given in full ("'Wait,' he said, stooping to adjust his pack"). Generalized narrative uses repeated actions and representative events ("We *used to* . . ."; "My grandfather *always* . . ."; "The cowboys *would* hit town . . ."). Summarized narrative ("The winds *rose* during the afternoon"; "We *left* Portland that summer") is more specific than generalized narrative; and though it may lack the vividness of dramatized narrative, it is more economical and more flexible, allowing the writer to vary pace and emphasis by compressing—that is, summarizing—some stretches while treating significant episodes in appropriate detail.

Summarized narrative is the characteristic method for an account of something that took place over a period of time, and it will probably be your natural choice. Even so, you may incorporate a stretch of dramatized narrative—for the climax, perhaps—or use generalized narrative in setting your scene, particularly if you are writing a nostalgic reminiscence. (Why is generalized narrative the best choice for the material in "An Island Perspective," pp. 39–40?

The basic structure for a narrative is the temporal sequence of the events; and the simplest pattern is straight chronology, in which one action follows another as it did in the original experience. Occasionally you may want to shift temporarily to an earlier time, as the cutback or flashback does in movies, plays, and fiction, signaling the shift with a phrase like "Six months before" or "I remembered an earlier climb, when. . . ." Unless you are introducing unusual complexity into the time sequence, a formal outline won't be necessary. Jot down the order of events for reference, but don't spend time working out an elaborate pattern of heads and subheads. Instead, start writing, and, as you write, pay particular attention to maintaining a consistent point of view and to keeping the narrative moving.

Point of View and Distance

You are writing a personal narrative, not an objective report. Keep yourself in the story. Use *I, me, my, mine*—no such awkward disguises as *we, one,* or *this writer. I* is simpler, clearer, more natural. It gives you your best chance of controlling your reader's reactions. How the reader views the event you narrate will depend largely on the *distance* you establish between yourself and what you are writing about (and sometimes the distance between the reader and what you are writing about). Distance may be temporal, spatial, or psychological.

Temporal distance becomes a significant element in the narrative whenever you want to establish a contrast between past and present—how you felt about an incident *then*, say, and how you feel about it *now*. In a retrospective account, temporal distance can help create nostalgia and other special effects. But for most purposes the writer of narrative prefers to wipe out temporal distance—to give immediacy to the event whether it occurred yesterday or twenty years ago.

Spatial distance locates you in relation to the action. Perhaps you will want to eliminate it entirely: you are there, *in* the action, as participant or observer. To produce a sense of personal physical involvement, you will probably find it most natural to adopt a restricted point of view, "seeing" for the reader only as much as you could actually see and know about in that position. ("As I ran out of the dorm, I could hear shouts and the crash of breaking glass in the next block.") When, as narrator, you change your physical location in relation to the action, keep the reader informed so that he can continue to share your view of it: "I turned the corner of the Ad building just as the fire trucks pulled up." To bring in information about events taking place outside your immediate range, use explanatory phrases like "as I later learned."

When you assume a restricted point of view, you commit yourself to the natural order of events as seen from that physical location. If you take illogical liberties with chronology or geography, you destroy the great advantage of the restricted point of view—the illusion of direct participation.

While spatial distance has a direct bearing on what the reader sees, psychological distance has a direct bearing on how he interprets what he sees. Physical and psychological points of view are separate, or at least separable. As a first-person narrator, you may be involved in the action emotionally as well as physically. Or you may be psychologically an observer and nothing more, reporting what happened but not registering any personal responses to it. Or you may occupy a middle ground psychologically—amused, perhaps, or mildly approving or disapproving but essentially detached. The attitude you express should be the one you want your reader to share. If the event filled you with excitement or terror or disgust, reduce the psychological distance so that he feels it as you did. If the action left you emotionally and intellectually untouched, hold it out for him to see, and to see why.

EXERCISES

1. Examine this entry from a journal:

June 28, Tuesday
We were karooming down the unfinished road last night toward the highway camp on what was to be another business visit for Bob Henderson. Going about fifty, we went into a skid, then another worse skid, and hit an embankment, luckily at such a slant that much of the force of the truck was expended in spinning around to point in the opposite direction

and in flipping over onto the roof. Neither of us was injured badly, Bob not at all. I found myself lying on the roof, which was now the floor, looking up at him, in his driver's seat, upside down. He asked how I was, extricated himself quickly, and got out through the back door, which had popped open (it's a delivery-type truck). Off he went, I thought into the woods to recover his temper, since he was near tears. Instead, with the presence that marks him, he was going for help. Like most people in an accident who have broken their glasses, I immediately began to search for the parts, only later looking for the exit, thinking of fire. The air was bristlingly dusty. Sand from the road, powdered eggs, tire chains, Bull Durham tobacco, leaking oil and paper money were strewn or spattered everywhere. The last skid had been one of those slowly unrolling, inevitable-seeming emergencies. Having considered the likelihood of a smashup several times lately, I drew up my knees in order not to go through the windshield, and after denting the dashboard with them, rose out of my seat like a ball and fell on my head halfway back in the truck. My arms drew in to protect themselves rather than protecting my head. We would have faced a twenty-mile walk in either direction except that the highway company foreman had been out fishing. Bob brought him back. I was wandering up and down, coughing and chuckling in shock. A long time was spent in transit and in righting the truck with a winch and chain.

Today I'm shaky, limping, a band of pressure around my head. — Edward Hoagland, *Notes from the Century Before*

Explain why you think the writer has been successful or unsuccessful in presenting:

    a. the initial account of the accident itself. Is it clear? Vivid?

    b. the sequence of events immediately following the accident. Is the sequence clear? Is the information that Bob was going for help brought in smoothly and convincingly?

    c. the passage that fills the reader in on precisely what had occurred during the accident. Would it have been better or worse to have included details like "I drew up my knees" in the initial account? Would the time sequence be clearer if "I drew up" were changed to "I had drawn up," and so on?

    2. Rewrite the passage, converting it from a journal entry to an account intended for publication. In your rewrite, consider the possibility of making several paragraphs of Hoagland's one.

In writing your narrative, you should keep the action moving, let the story unwind. At the same time, you must supply enough descriptive details of character, motivation, and scene to explain the action and make the account a coherent whole. While long passages of static description destroy the unity of a narrative by drawing attention away from the action, failure to supply details where they are needed will impair clarity and coherence. The trick is to find the right tempo or pace for the narrative and to introduce necessary descriptive details without impeding the forward movement.

Descriptive Details

With details, you can give your narrative individuality, immediacy, concreteness. During an actual experience — say a trip to the dentist — sense impressions predominate. In telling about your experience, you should try to convey those sense impressions, not just the reflections that come after any experience is over. Don't talk about having felt pain; make the pain real. Abstractly, pain is "a distressing sensation of a part of the body"; concretely, it is the throbbing of an abscessed molar or the shocking twinge when the drill touches a nerve.

It is concreteness that individualizes an experience. Abstractly, one automobile race is similar to all other automobile races; concretely, every race is unique. To catch the special flavor of an experience, strip away the everyday details that apply to whole classes of people and places — the high voices of small children, the bustle of shopping centers — and concentrate on the qualities or attributes that alone make the particular person or place distinctive.

Sensory details show the reader an action instead of merely telling him that it happened. From a statement like "Frank's leg twitched, and he chewed on his thumbnail," the reader can visualize the scene and deduce that Frank was nervous or distraught. But he cannot convert a general, abstract statement like "Frank acted nervous" into the image that was in the writer's mind. If he visualizes anything at all, it is likely to be different from what the writer intended.

Details can be organized so that they build to a generalization, or the generalization can be stated first and made to serve as a unifying theme for the specific details that follow. Perhaps the most common weakness in descriptive writing is to rely on general statements to do all the work of describing. Left to itself, this generalization would strike most readers as pleasant but too bland, too inert, to be convincing: "Summer evenings here on the river have a quietness and a feeling of completion about them that I have never known in any other place, and I have kept in mind the evenings of that summer."

When the same generalization is supported by the details that made it true for the writer, it becomes true for the reader too:

Summer evenings here on the river have a quietness and a feeling of completion about them that I have never known in any other place, and I have kept in mind the evenings of that summer. The wind dies about sundown, and the surface of the river grows smooth. The reflections of the trees lie inverted and perfect on it. Occasionally a fish will jump, or a kingfisher hurry, skreaking, along the fringe of willows. In the clearing around the house the phoebes and pewees call from their lookout perches, circling out and back in their hunting flights as long as the light lasts. Out over the water the swallows silently pass and return, dipping and looping, climbing and dipping and looping, sometimes skimming the surface to drink or bathe as they fly. The air seems to come alive with the weaving of their paths. As I sat there watching from the porch those evenings, sometimes a profound peacefulness would come to me, as it had at other times, but now it came of an awareness not only of the place, but of my marriage, a completeness I had not felt before. I was there not only because I wanted to be, as always before, but now because Tanya was there too. — Wendell Berry, *The Long-Legged House*

To make sure that you have not relied too heavily on generalizations in a descriptive passage, read the passage through, skipping all the general statements. If the details alone don't make you feel that you are in the presence of what you meant to describe, you need more facts, more images, more sense impressions. And you need to substitute specific, concrete diction for some of your general statements.

Reading a passage aloud will also bring to your attention details that are repetitive or extraneous or misleading. Although reliving the experience and recapturing sense impressions are essential in the prewriting stage, not everything you relive and recapture should appear in your completed essay. The bad storyteller is always bogging down in unnecessary or irrelevant detail. His buildup seems aimless; he keeps getting sidetracked; he often leaves his listener wondering what the point of the story was. Written narrative is susceptible to the same weaknesses. Whether for you the process of discarding the tangential incident and weeding out the superfluous details comes most naturally in the prewriting stage or after you have written a rough draft, it must come; and the more discriminating you are, the stronger your narrative will be.

EXERCISE

Discuss these passages from personal narratives. (Here and elsewhere, exercise passages that are not documented are from essays by students.) Among the questions worth considering are these: Have enough concrete details been supplied for the reader to share the experience? Do the details feed into one another to produce a unified impact? Is the description sharp and clear, or has the writer relied too heavily on generalizations? Is the point of view consistent, or, if it shifts, is the shift reasonable? Are the style and tone appropriate to the material?

a. The stifling subway ride from Port Authority was finally over. I was sustained only by the mental picture created by the name Forest Hills. As I dragged myself up the last flight of stairs, my nose was the first to detect something was amiss. The "clear forest air" was delicately perfumed by car exhaust and soot. The last step completed my disillusionment. I found myself confronted by a ten-lane monster of screeching, misdirected chromium and steel. Amidst this mangle was a distraught, heavily perspiring young officer. This giant, called Queens Boulevard, plows its way through Queens, and connects with the 59th Street Bridge to Manhattan. Clutching harder all the paraphernalia I had just brought back from camp, I asked a reddish-pink-headed lady where I could get the 108th street bus that would take me to my new home. I waited an hour for the bus (guaranteed to run every fifteen minutes) with my hair sticking to my face, and my grimy camp yearbook forever sliding from under my arm. When the bus finally arrived, I was propelled onto it by about forty other dripping riders. As I boarded it, I couldn't help thinking of the grotesque sense of humor of whoever named Forest Hills.

b. I remember the smells most of all in that Indian summer — the musty smell of a large vacant house; the poignant scents of the old fruit cellar — plums, peaches, apples, pears; the pleasant odor of walnuts drying row upon row on the damp cellar floor. Upstairs I found the funny, small kitchen with, of all things, a smaller room adjacent to it filled with rows of shelves and cupboards. The dining room and living room were completely bare, so that the reddish-brown mahogany woodwork framing the doorways and running along the lower walls asserted its permanence; then up the wooden staircase to the second floor. A glance into each of the three large bedrooms assured me that there would be sufficient lodging for the family. (Moisture underneath the wallpaper on the ceiling had produced shapeless patterns of light and dark. I stood there for several moments forming mental pictures of phantom stallions and western cowpunchers.) Then I was downstairs again, meeting myself in the huge wall mirror suspended at the bottom of the stairway; and pushing the screened-door open, I went outside to inspect the exterior. (The sprawling front porch held eye-hooks overhead for an old fashioned seat swing.) Down the steps and turning around for a full view of the large but modest two-story frame structure. In front, a flowering pine tree and a drooping willow contrasted east and west: towering above one side-yard, a top-heavy elm; in the other, a healthy pear twenty feet high. Running now to the backyard, I perceived an apple tree, a cherry tree, and behind the simple garage, two leafless walnut trees. Tripping uneasily over the fallen fruit, I surveyed the remaining landscape of my new home. That immense lot east of the house—was that ours too? I felt young pride for the withering rows of brown corn stalks, piles of decaying matter which had produced beans, peas, and tomatoes for the family before; and the very thin stems of drying zinnias and snapdragons. All this was my new home—and it looked darn big to a boy six years of age.

c. The camp counselors would occasionally take us to a riding stable, where the horses would try to rub us off against fence posts, or to a monster swimming pool, where the sun never shone and the wind always blew. One day I remember as a series of particularly grotesque experiences. It was very hot and we started a forced march down an interminable road, ankle deep in dust. Eventually we arrived at a large deserted quarry, where the rock had been extensively exposed, but not deeply excavated. I wandered off from the group and found myself confronted by two dogs that had apparently died at each other's throats. Their seams had burst and I suppose they would have looked horrible to some, but to me they somehow looked natural in that jumbled rock setting. When I returned to the group I said nothing. Everybody was gathered around a green pond, and a boy named Charlie had just hit a small fish with a large rock. "What a shot!" The fish fluttered down into the reeds, smoking dark brown.

The road back to the shelter was all uphill. Looking back on the day, I see it as a basic lesson in surrealism.

The Point of the Narrative

The last sentence of the passage just quoted—"Looking back on the day, I see it as a basic lesson in surrealism"— gives the meaning the experience had for the writer. Although a personal narrative is not expected to develop an abstract idea, it should have some central meaning. It should make a point; it should have an impact.

If you build some hint of that meaning into your statement of purpose, it will help give direction to your planning and writing. Your point of view, narrative method, and descriptive details—all these affect the reader's understanding of the significance of the event. All these should be selected, therefore, to the end of bringing out that significance. But you still have the problem, in writing the paper, of how to get the meaning across. Will you tell the reader how you felt, what conclusions you came to as a result of the experience? Or will you let the experience speak for itself?

When the meaning of the experience is stated explicitly, it often comes at the end of the essay, usually in the form of a comment or reflection on what took place. It may, however, serve as a starting point for the paper, as in this opening paragraph of a personal narrative:

I cannot imagine how anyone could be so foolish as to assert that childhood is a time of bliss in which one's lack of maturity and knowledge keep him from real suffering. I certainly would not support such a statement, for I can think of not one but many incidents from my own limited experience which caused me to suffer as a child with a pain keener than any I feel now. My twelfth summer was just such a time. I was at camp, not for the first time nor the last.

The paper goes on to narrate an incident at camp which supports the generalization in the opening paragraph. The meaning of the event is made clear enough, and little further comment is required. The paper concludes:

At length I convinced my mother to come for me, though by the time she agreed to do so I had recovered sufficiently to be ashamed of my ever having been homesick. After all, it was not my first summer away. It was, however, my first contact with the real world, and remembering it now, I feel like crying still.

Comment like this is not obtrusive and is justified if it is made to seem proportionate to the experience. There is always the danger, however, of being too talky or of making an experience of modest personal significance assume cosmic importance. "My First Date" should have sufficient point to be worth writing, but no reader expects it to carry a profound philosophical message. Though universals can lend great interest to an essay, few readers will tolerate the moralizing tone that sometimes creeps into retrospective comment. To avoid crossing the line that separates interpreting from moralizing, a writer often goes to great effort to select just those details that will invite—even compel—the reader to make the comment for him. In writing about accidentally killing a bird, a student chose to avoid making any explicit statement about his emotional reaction. Instead, he made his point through a series of contrasts. Before the incident, everywhere he looked he saw beauty; after it, everywhere he looked he saw ugliness. Not that he used the abstract nouns *beauty* and *ugliness*. He relied on contrasting images—the colors of fallen leaves, the taste of an apple, the glance of a girl; later, slime and rubbish in the streets, a drunk lurching by, dirty words scrawled on the side of a freight car.

One way or another, directly or indirectly, a personal narrative should carry its own meaning. Whether that meaning is clear to you in the prewriting stage or whether it comes clear only as you write the paper, it should be in the forefront of your consciousness as you revise. Weed out incidents and details that contradict or blur the impressions that you want to get across; keep only incidents and details that reinforce that impression.

There are other things to look for in revising. Does the draft carry out your intention? Does it hang together? Has it unity and direction? Will a reader be able to follow the succession of events to their conclusion without becoming lost or confused? And if he can understand, will he also enjoy? Have you provided enough details? Are they all relevant, or should some be replaced? Have you droned, or have you given your prose some life and movement? Is there enough of *you* in the paper—your voice, your experience—to justify calling your essay a *personal* narrative?

Rewrite, and rewrite again until the words on paper come as close as you can make them to matching the conception in your mind. Finally, on the basis of the notes you have kept, write an account of how you went about producing the essay, and assess both your methods and the paper you have written.

EXERCISES

1. Write a brief essay (500–750 words) on one of the following topics:

a. Tell about a single episode (or a series of related incidents) in such a way that the reader will understand the significance it had for you.

b. Describe a scene of violence you have witnessed or been involved in.

c. Write a chapter of your autobiography that represents an important stage in your development.

d. Give an account of an incident that reflects a sharp disagreement you have had with a friend, a parent, or someone in a position of authority.

e. Describe a person you know well, using only concrete details of physical appearance, mannerisms, habitual actions to convey something about his personality or character.

f. Describe one of your favorite activities as a child.

g. Evoke the special qualities of a place that has emotional associations for you.

Before you begin to write, specify a reader for your paper—someone you want to share the experience with, someone you can count on being a sympathetic audience. In a note at the beginning of the paper, name the reader you have in mind and, in a phrase or two, say what your relationship to him is.

2. Study the paper reprinted below. What function is served by ¶2? By ¶3? How successful is ¶5 in its handling of the time sequence? In its handling of point of view? Explain why you find the paper successful or unsuccessful in conveying the meaning of the experience.

Spectators

¶1 One Friday last fall I was coming home after a trip downtown. After a twenty-minute ride on a horribly crowded train, I was waiting for a bus on the corner of Wentworth and 59th. It was about 5:30, and it was already getting dark. Along with about twenty other people, I waited for the bus that would take me home. Most of them were probably downtown office workers; stenographers, receptionists, and salesgirls. Also, there were several men dressed like laborers, probably a street repair crew. There was no talk. We just stood waiting.

¶2 We stood facing the street, directly in front of a small dingy beer tavern. Across from us also was a tavern. On the diagonal corner was a drug store, and on the fourth corner was another tavern.

¶3 I was getting tired from standing, so I walked back to the wall of the tavern and leaned against it. I watched the crowd of people in front of me and thought about them. Somehow all these silent figures in their cool-weather coats seemed to me to be devoid of sense or feeling. I wondered if they would have reacted at all if someone had stuck pins in them. Anonymous people huddled in a crowd often make that impression on me. They seem to be just blobs of life, not concerned about anything outside of themselves.

¶4 I sighed with relief when I saw the bus coming. I thought that it would be good to get home. Out of merely existing, and into my home, where there was food and warmth and rest and life.

¶5   The bus was coming to a stop. At this time, I pushed my way into the crowd to get on before some of the others. The doors opened. I felt pushing people behind me and resistance from those in front. Suddenly, I sensed something was wrong, or maybe I heard something. I glanced over my shoulder. I saw an old man (perhaps sixty) with an expression of horror on his face. I was shocked and looked more closely. Behind him was poised a tall, nondescript man. His hands were under the old man's long coat. His right had found the old man's right hip pocket; his left hand, the left pocket. As if lightning had hit me, I froze. My heart beat furiously. After a moment, I realized what the situation was. Suddenly, I felt superhuman. I felt as though I could have run a mile in three minutes; I felt as though I could have defended myself against anyone. I realized the old man was only five feet from me. If some man would help me. . . . But then I was nauseated as I saw the old man struggling futilely. He reached behind him to grasp the robber's hand. He wheezed. His tortured, plump face was deathly pale. His cap fell off, his white hair was mussed. The robber still did not have the wallet. They struggled. I heard the bus driver shout, "Somebody help. . . . That man is being robbed!" Several women said, "Why doesn't somebody do something?" Still they struggled.

¶6   The last person got on the bus, and the driver closed the doors. I watched from the window. Still they struggled. The robber spun around, throwing the old man down. He hit him hard, I do not know where but I think near the head. The old man gave up the struggle. The robber turned the old man over, reached into his pocket, and pulled out the wallet. As the bus pulled away, I saw the robber running north, up Wentworth. I also saw the old man, lying face down in the gutter, in the spit, and dirt, and rain water, and cold darkness, alone.

¶7   We are scum. We are sheep.

Chapter Three

NARRATING, DESCRIBING, ILLUSTRATING

Narrating, describing, illustrating, comparing, dividing, classifying, defining, investigating causes and effects—as we saw in Chapter Two, these are the chief ways of supporting generalizations. Though not always conscious of the methods as formal categories, every writer is bound to make use of them, for they are simply extensions of the ways he sees and thinks and reasons, the natural and necessary means of saying what he wants to say.

In this chapter and the next two, we will see what questions you can profitably ask yourself about these techniques as you put them to work in essays of various kinds. Keep in mind that they seldom occur in isolation except as practice exercises; normally you will find yourself drawing on several, not just one. Keep in mind, too, that they are not mutually exclusive: a narrative can serve as an example; a cause-effect analysis may provide the background for a definition. But though they are constantly forming alliances and interacting, they can be separated for purposes of analysis; and taking them up one by one makes it easier to single out the special problems in planning and writing that they entail. What is said about each method applies whether the method develops just part of a paragraph, a whole paragraph, a sequence of paragraphs, or (more rarely) a whole essay. As the cross-references indicate, many of the topics introduced here are discussed further in other chapters.

 ## NARRATION AND DESCRIPTION

Narration and description have a natural affinity, mixing freely in all kinds of papers. Taken together, their purpose is to make the reader visualize particular entities and events. They are central to autobiographical essays (see pp. 49–61) and to all accounts in which people, things, or happenings are presented for their own sakes—the dean, your uncle, a dolphin, an oil well, a mountain range, a flood, a battle, a concert, a career.

Narration and description also lie at the heart of many essays that explain or analyze. Narration is the characteristic method for historical reports—reports that trace the development of a scientific theory, a philosophical concept, a movement in art or literature, a political party, or a sociological trend. How-to-do-its (how to start skiing, how to stop crabgrass, how to set up a particular experiment) typically combine directions that are ordered chronologically with descriptions of equipment. An account of a process—whether human or nonhuman, organic or mechanical—is basically an explanation cast in a narrative framework.

While pure narrative tells what *did* happen ("Once upon a time . . ."), the process essay tells what always does happen and always will happen under a given set of circumstances ("Whenever the temperature drops below freezing, . . ."). Roughly similar distinctions can be made between pure description (my brother, my basset hound) and the kind of description that contributes heavily to definition (what man is, what a mammoth was). In writing the one, you try to capture the features that are unique; in writing the other, you present details that apply to the whole class.

Brief passages of description and narration have a place in many critical and persuasive essays. An argument for slum clearance may open with a description of life in the slums, an evaluation of a novel with a summary of the plot or a description of the central character, a proposal for a change in policy with an anecdote. Such passages should be kept functional and made to bear directly on the thesis. Although a pertinent paragraph or page of good narrative-description will enliven as well as advance the discussion, storytelling or scene painting that is included just for the sake of variety will mislead or distract the reader.

Whether the narrative-descriptive material is central or subordinate, you need to discover for yourself a perspective on it. Only by finding your own "angle of vision" can you control your reader's response to what you show him.

Narrating

To begin with, what kind of narrative are you writing? A pure narrative of an event—an account made for its own sake—differs substantially from an explanatory account of the same event. A narrative of a related sequence of incidents differs from an account of the same sequence viewed as process.

EXERCISES

1. Write two narratives of the same event, one with the chief purpose of re-creating the event, the other with the chief purpose of explaining it. (Notice the emphasis on *chief*. Naturally, one purpose does not exclude the other.) Example: Write an account of your part in an incident (the meeting of an encounter group, perhaps, or a homecoming or a street crime), telling what you did, what you saw, what you felt; then write a report of the incident with the aim of making the reader understand what happened and why. Though both accounts are rooted in your own experience, there should be noticeable differences in approach and content. The first will concentrate on actions and sensations, the second on causes and significance. Details that are crucial in the first will be subordinated or even omitted in the second; generalizations that are valuable in the second might seem an unjustifiable intrusion in the first.

2. Write two essays on similar subjects, one with the chief purpose of presenting a particular scene or action to the reader, the other with the chief purpose of explaining a phenomenon. Example: Tell about the hurricane that hit Cape Cod (or the Florida coast) when you were vacationing there; then write a "process" essay on hurricanes. In the first essay, try to convey what was distinctive and unique in experiencing *that* hurricane at that time in that place; in the second, tell what meteorological conditions typically breed hurricanes, how they develop, what course they follow, and what effects they have on the land and sea areas they pass over. (The first essay should be based on your own experience; for the second you may have to do some reading.) Other examples: (a) An incident (perhaps an accident) that took place when you were riding a motorcycle; how to ride a motorcycle. (b) Experiencing a beautiful garden; making a garden beautiful.

In preparing to write these and other essays in narration and description, you may find it helpful to refer to pp. 183–88 on organizing essays, pp. 255–59 on connecting sentences in paragraphs, and pp. 328–31 on the cumulative sentence, a type of sentence that is especially useful in giving details of action and appearance. See also *Absolute phrases, *Adjectives §6, and *Adverbs §4.

Finding a Perspective. Chapter Two outlined some of the choices available in narrative method and technique. Of the three types of narrative described on pp. 50–51, the most common in expository writing is summarized narrative, for it permits full development of an attitude or situation—the growth of opposition to a government policy, say—and wide coverage of time and place—an account of the westward movement, for example. Dramatized narrative may be used to give a close look at a striking incident or to throw an issue into sharp perspective. Passages of generalized narrative are sometimes incorporated into summarized narrative to characterize habitual attitudes or to describe a way of life.

Decisions about distance and point of view (see pp. 51–52) are more complicated. The real problem of narrative distance is to establish simultaneously your relation to the action you are recounting and your relation to your reader. Are you trying to produce an exact record of what happened—nothing more, nothing less—in order to enlighten and inform him? Or do you want to involve him in the action? And if so, what feeling do you want him to have toward it?

Just as the restricted point of view is the natural choice for a personal narrative, the unrestricted point of view is the likelier choice for a comprehensive account of an event. It is the typical approach whenever you need to jump-cut from one incident to another in order to present the complete picture ("Meanwhile, across the Atlantic . . . ."). It gives you freedom to maneuver, both temporally and physically, and offers you more options than the restricted point of view in structuring your paper. In a process essay it permits you to coordinate stages of the process that have been going on simultaneously ("During this time, the welder has been heating the iron"). For some processes, however, you may find advantages in the restricted point of view, identifying yourself with your reader and watching (or going through) the process with him step by step, sharing with him the discovery of what comes next. If you are teaching him a swimming stroke, your exposition may be clearer and more interesting if you swim with him.

EXERCISES

1. Examine the narrative method and technique in each of the four excerpts below. Consider such questions as these: Does the writer use summarized narrative, dramatized, or generalized—or a combination? Can you justify this choice in terms of his subject and what he does with it? What is the

distance—temporal, spatial, psychological—between him and his subject? Does he indicate, explicitly or implicitly, what his physical location is? Does he express an attitude, either overtly or through his use of details? In which action do you feel most involved? In which least involved? Do you attribute your sense of involvement to the nature of the action, to the writer's choice of descriptive details, or to some other cause?

a.   On the third lap of the Italian Grand Prix at Monza last week, just as the cars were approaching the wrenching curve known as *La Parabolica*, a rabbit darted out of the infield grass and ended its life under the wheels of Jackie Stewart's Matra. Sixty-five laps later, with the rabbit little more than a blur of fur on the line through that treacherous corner, Stewart swept under the flag to win both Monza and the world driving championship. The only casualty of the day, if you discount a few thousand pinched bottoms in victory lane, was the unfortunate rabbit. Nobody mourned him, but let's try to imagine his last impressions: the sudden approach of the pack—15 cars flat-out, black dots emerging from the Ascari curve and magnifying almost instantly into giant torpedoes of blue and red and marigold orange. The noise ripping upward from a moan through a snarl to a steady explosion. The drivers barely visible within their bonedomes. Stewart's close-set, sensitive, mud-colored eyes, with one drooping lid masked behind the smoky visor of his helmet, the eyes of a hunter flicking down and seeing the rabbit sprint and freeze on the track, widening, holding firm on the line ahead. The broad reach of the Dunlop tire blurring into treadlessness, rising above the doomed animal. Thump.

Arrivederci, rabbit.—Robert F. Jones, *Sports Illustrated*, Sept. 22, 1969

b.   The lawns [at Wimbledon] are mowed every day in the springtime—with hand mowers, of course. Power mowers frog and rib the courts—"frog" and "rib" being terms for various unkempt results—and, moreover, power mowers cannot be as finely adjusted as hand mowers. The height of the grass at Wimbledon is three-sixteenths of an inch. The mower that keeps it at that level is a sixteen-inch Ransome Certes, which has a high-speed, precision-ground ten-knife cylinder, makes a hundred cuts every thirty-six inches, costs forty-one pounds twelve and six, and hums with the high sound of a vacuum cleaner while it moves. It throws its cuttings forward into a hooded catching device, the design of which causes the over-all machine to look very much like an infant's perambulator and the crewman who pushes it to look like a grandfather in St. James's Park. In the early spring, the courts are cut diagonally. In mid-spring, they are cut from side to side; and as the Fortnight approaches, the cuts are made the long way, end to end. Cutting the long way, the lawnmower is always pushed in the exact swaths that were cut the day before, and it always moves on each alternating swath in the same direction that was followed in earlier cuttings.

The effect of this, to an observer at one end of the court, is that the lawn appears to be made of an enormous bolt of green seersucker, the alternating stripes being light and dark. If, in making the cut, the mower was going away from the observer's point of view, the cut appears light. If the mower was moving in the observer's direction, the cut appears dark. The light cuts and dark cuts have no influence on the bounce of the ball, but they follow the line of play and thus remind the players of the direction in which the ball is supposed to be hit. — John McPhee, *A Roomful of Hovings and Other Profiles*

c.   Khesanh was a very bad place then, but the airstrip there was the worst place in the world. It was what Khesanh had instead of a V-ring, the exact, predictable object of the mortars and rockets hidden in the surrounding hills, the sure target of the big Russian and Chinese guns lodged in the side of CoRoc Ridge, eleven kilometers away from the Laotian border. There was nothing random about the shelling there, and no one wanted anything to do with it. If the wind was right, you could hear the N.V.A. .50 calibers starting far up the valley whenever a plane made its approach to the strip, and the first incoming artillery would precede the landing by seconds. If you were waiting there to be taken out, there was nothing you could do but curl up in the trench and try to make yourself small, and if you were coming in on the plane, there was nothing you could do, nothing at all. — Michael Herr, *Esquire*, Sept. 1969

d.   Jim Jensen did most of the rock digging, chopping, and splitting that Colbert would have done under kinder circumstances. Jensen worked with bare palm-mitts, holding bits of bone in place with three fingers so they would not pop off into the air and down the cliffside while he chiseled them loose. Overwhelmed by awareness of the evolutionary history that was unraveling in his hands, he stayed on the job until his entire nose and one cheek of his face were in a state of frostbite comparable to lacerated boils, with a scab that gave him a top-heavy feeling. He feared to risk glancing into the chasm below him as he pried out bone after bone, wrapped them in toilet tissue along with penciled identification, and stuffed them into a bone bag lashed to his back beside his parka, ice ax, and crampons.

In the midst of this automaton-like procedure, he came upon a tooth measuring two or three inches long and three-eighths of an inch thick. It once had occupied the right side of some animal's jaw. Jensen could see the root of the tooth as well as the tooth itself, for the rock containing the fossil split like a hot-dog bun cut lengthwise. . . . He was too numb to do more than register the fact that he had picked up fossils like this before, at the feet of the Andes in Argentina.

Jensen marked the tooth for special attention, and when he got back to base camp gave it to Colbert before going into the mess hall to try to thaw his frostbitten face. The thawing had reached an excruciating stage when Colbert ran into the hall crying, "Jim! This looks like a lystrosaurus I found in Africa." —John Lear, *Saturday Review*, Feb. 7, 1970

2.   Review the four excerpts above to see what words or phrases mark the passage of time. Which has the most need of time indicators? Which the least? Why?

Chronology and Causality.   Even in essays aimed primarily at reconstructing an event, simply reporting the many incidents that comprised it is seldom satisfactory. Links do not make a chain until they are joined: the reader has to understand the action as well as know its parts. An account of an event will be coherent—will make sense—only if the incidents in it are related to one another. An analysis of a process will be coherent—will make sense—only if it is clear how and why one stage follows another. The writer has to show the connections and relationships.

Every good narrative—personal or impersonal, an account of a specific event or an analysis of a process—achieves coherence through chronology (what happened next) and causality (why it happened next). Because what happened goes on in a temporal sequence, a narrative finds its chief organizing principle and its momentum in *then* and all the related indicators of time (*later, next, after that, meanwhile, the following day, finally*, and so on). Why it happened is signaled by such cause-effect indicators as *because, since, for, thus, therefore*, and *consequently* and such phrases as *gives rise to, leads to, results in*. (See pp. 257–58 and *Transition.)

Though both pure narrative and process deal in *what, how*, and *why*, narrative is usually stronger on *what*, process on *how* and *why*. So far as possible, causality, like chronology, should be embedded in the narrative. In pure narrative, the action should to a large extent explain itself. In expository narrative and process, however, it is often necessary and appropriate to supplement both causality and chronology with explicit comment. You may need to speculate about motives, weigh conflicting reports, point up significance, or otherwise generalize about the action—either in your own person ("I") or using the "we" that clearly means writer-and-reader ("We may question the wisdom of their tactics, but . . ."). The nature and tone of your comment will depend on your purpose. If you are assuming the role of historian and analyst—uninvolved psychologically—you will want to speak with objectivity, impartiality, detachment. If you are an advocate rather than a strict historian, you will advance a thesis about the event, arguing issues and responsibility; in short, you will enlist narrative in the service of argument.

In the account of a process, explicit running commentary is often necessary to make causality plain. You may want to point out the significance of each stage and the procedure by which one stage merges into the next. Or you may decide to first give an overview of the process, emphasizing function or usefulness and so directing the reader's attention to the whole scheme before dealing with its separate stages. Similar comment is useful and may be essential in studies of historical process, for these usually attempt to explain the recurrence of actions or patterns. Any detailed study of a political movement would probably include a good deal of explicit analysis of motives and causes.

Describing

While narrative moves through time, description either moves through space or is static. Because it consists essentially of a list or series of attributes, straight description can rarely be sustained successfully for long. Page after page of it becomes tiresome. But brief patches of description are essential in virtually all kinds of writing, for they satisfy the reader's need to visualize a scene or to know the truth about the subject through sensory experience.

Description feeds on the concrete. Because only details can convey the look and feel of things, success in describing lies chiefly in the right choice and arrangement of details. (Details and generalizations are discussed on pp. 42–43.)

Selecting Details. The basis of all good description is close observation. To start with, you need a store of particulars to draw on, many more than you can use. From these, you want to select just those details that suit your purpose. If your intention is to make a specific, literal description, the details should supply definite information about dimensions and attributes—color, shape, sound. To give a suggestive, impressionistic picture of the same thing, you might use different details or, if you used the same ones, you would alter them through your choice of modifiers and metaphors, perhaps blurring and shading, perhaps heightening and sharpening. The objective "navy blue" of the literal description could become a "drab" or a "depressing" or a "sturdy" or a "comforting" blue, depending on the impression you were trying to create.

Some writing situations call for description that is primarily objective, others for description that is primarily subjective. Objective description offers the reader what any impartial observer could see; in its purest form it tries to put into words the image a camera would record. Subjective description presents reality as it appears to *one* observer — the writer. The physical facts are filtered through his perception, colored by his attitude; and what emerges is not the subject as recorded on film but the subject as reported through the writer's mind and emotions. A "Wanted" bulletin in the post office gives an objective description of a person, a catalog of physical data. Its sole aim is to permit accurate identification. A description of the same person by his mother would be very different. So would a description by someone he had robbed or assaulted.

Though accurate representation is the aim of objective description, the means used need not be — and should not be — commonplace phrases and clichés. When John McPhee says that the lawn at Wimbledon "appears to be made of an enormous bolt of green seersucker" (p. 69), any reader who tests his perception against McPhee's recognizes that the description is the product of fresh, honest observation — what any man could see if his eyes and mind were really open.

In selecting details, be guided not only by your intention but also by your audience's probable knowledge of your subject. If you are describing your basset for an audience that can't tell a basset from a beagle, concentrate on details that describe all bassets. If your audience already knows what bassets look like and what their habits are, concentrate on the characteristics that make your dog an individual among bassets.

EXERCISES

1. Study the use of detail in each of the following passages. Is it the writer's purpose to show you what *he* saw or to show you what any attentive observer would see? Define as precisely as you can the writer's attitude toward what he is describing.

a. Ice-blue rain beats against the windows and peppers Park Avenue below as Ava Gardner stalks her pink malted-milk cage like an elegant cheetah. She wears a baby-blue cashmere turtleneck sweater pushed up to her Ava elbows and a little plaid mini-skirt and enormous black horn-rimmed glasses and she is gloriously divinely barefoot. — Rex Reed, *Do You Sleep in the Nude?*

b. In the walnut grove, whose leaves are gold in the evening light, the blue bellflowers are beginning to bloom, tall and delicate spires along the path. And the small blues, the butterflies, open their mini-wings that alternate blue and grey like dusty jewels. A bit of fudge hops in the path, a toad traveling. The path is a delight. Broad and covered with small leaves, second growth of thimbleweed and clover, close to the ground. Each leaf like a flower, so that one walks on a delicate carpet, winding through the grove under the thin trees bordered with bellflowers, and emerges into the sunlight of the pasture. — Josephine Johnson, *The Inland Island*

c. The careful observer will see a good deal when he looks at a stamp. Besides its central theme, the name of the issuing country, and its face value in the currency of that country, the stamp will usually offer other bits of information. These may include the year issued, the printer's name, the artist's name, the common name of the organism shown, and frequently the Latinized generic and specific names. Changes in currency from one year to another may also appear on the stamp, as in the case of New Zealand, which recently changed to a decimal currency. Occasionally, stamps are overprinted with a short phrase or sentence that honors or commemorates some noteworthy event, person, or cause. Some may even be surcharged, which means altering or restating the face value. This is frequently done in lieu of issuing an entirely new stamp. — Arnold Ross, *Natural History*, Jan. 1968

2. Over a period of several days, describe the same natural object—a tree, a lake, a cat—four or five times. Describe it at different times of day. Each time try to see it afresh, and in each description try to give a sharp image of *that* object at *that* time. After a week or so, review your descriptions. If you find no differences between them, you were not looking hard enough.

3. Write two descriptions of the same thing, aiming for two different effects. Examples: (a) Describe the fall foliage in your area. Write one account for a prospective visitor who wants to know what to look for. Point out features that will help him identify trees and shrubs; use precise details about colors and shapes of leaves; *show* him the scene. In the second paper, *give* the reader the scene. Try to make a nature lover experience the foliage as you have experienced it, possess it as you have possessed it. (b) Describe your desk. Make one account a "For Sale" paragraph to be posted on a bulletin board. Give particulars that will identify your desk and tell a prospective buyer what he needs to know. Write the other account for a close friend. Describe your desk in such a way

that he will know how you feel about it, about studying, about intellectual activity in general. In the first passage your desk remains an object; in the second make it a symbol.

Arranging Details.　　　Though the first requirement in writing good description is to have an adequate supply of details to draw on, simply having enough details doesn't solve the problem. You must arrange the details so that they create a coherent image. A photograph presents the details and the whole simultaneously; writing has to build the whole part by part. If the reader is to relate the parts to each other and grasp the subject as a whole, he must be fed the details in some systematic order.

When the object described is relatively small and stable, neither writer nor reader pays physical point of view any special heed. But it may be a useful organizing device in describing a sizable object (a cathedral), a place (a town), or a changing scene. Even then, you may prefer not to make your physical location explicit, but having it clear in your own mind will help you settle on a logical progression of details and keep the *scale* of the description right—the relation of large elements to small, of more important to less important.

Whenever the physical point of view is explicit, you are likely to impose a spatial organization on the details. The movement may proceed systematically (left to right, say, or top to bottom, or inside to outside); or it may reflect your sense of the relative importance of the details (beginning with the most striking feature, perhaps, and moving to more commonplace ones, or reversing that order). But sometimes, to achieve the effect you want, you may choose to forego spatial organization and instead select and arrange details so as to create a dominant impression. In much good description, the details cluster around a controlling image (the broken clock in Market Square) or a generalization. The dominant impression may be the most striking feature of the object itself; or it may be your attitude toward the object (admiration, fear, affection, boredom); or it may be a combination of the two (your impatience is caused by the stagnation the broken clock symbolizes).

The more you emphasize a dominant impression, the less likely you are to make a systematic inventory of parts and to map out spatial relations. As the following description of sea elephants shows, however, exact details about physical appearance can be coordinated with both a dominant impression ("immense") and a psychological reaction ("fabulous and ridiculous," "grotesque and revolting," "alarming").

Even a photograph cannot give a true picture of these fabulous and ridiculous creatures. Not only are they immense, males growing to eighteen feet in length and as much as fifteen feet in girth, but this sex is adorned with an eighteen-inch trunk that normally flops down over the mouth but which is also connected with the nasal passages and can be inflated and raised almost straight up. Worse still, these animals are clothed in very short sparse greyish brown hair, which they moult once a year and in doing so not only lose their fur but also their whole outer skin; they are then bright pink and present the most grotesque and revolting appearance, especially when they lounge around on shore in great misshapen, heaving masses under a hot sun, moaning, groaning, gurgling and roaring. They live on cuttlefish, seaweed, and shellfish and are fairly agile in the water but spend a lot of time on land. The great bulls heave their immense bulk up gently sloping beaches and into the tussocky tall grass of the islands they most prefer and then go to sleep. Nothing is quite so alarming as to stumble up against one of these animals at such a time since they come "unstuck" with a veritable explosion and rise to full height, blowing and snorting. —Ivan T. Sanderson, Living Mammals of the World

EXERCISES

1. Describe an object or scene of your choice. Experiment to see what arrangement of details will show it off to best advantage. If you are describing the exterior of a church, should you start with the front doors, with the spire, or with the windows? If you are describing a landscape, should you begin with the most striking feature and then fill in the more commonplace details, or should you reverse that order? If your scene is a political convention, should your viewing point be fixed (the gallery of the hall) or moving (advancing up the center aisle) or roving (scanning the hall and zooming in on people and events as a television camera does)? Should you present the subject twice, the first time giving the reader a general impression, the second time focusing on the details you want him to remember?

For most subjects, many different progressions are possible. Find one that is logical, feasible, and appropriate to your subject and to your purpose. Do you want to render the object or the scene without involving the reader? Or do you want him to respond to it and perhaps form a value judgment about it? (For further discussion of organizing description, see pp. 183–88.)

2. Review Sanderson's description of sea elephants. Write a description of a person or an animal in which precise physical details are coordinated with a dominant impression.

EXAMPLE

If they are chosen wisely and developed adequately, examples, like descriptive details, will give your writing concreteness and authority.

Because they perform similar functions, an example is often considered a special type of detail. Both examples and details supply the particulars of a subject; both may make it lively and interesting. But they differ in one respect. Details are parts or fragments of larger wholes; examples are cases or instances, complete in themselves, that illustrate generalizations. "The *webbed toes* of the Labrador . . ." is a detail. "Retrievers, among them *the Labrador*, . . ." is an example.

Material for Illustration

Citing a member of the class is the typical way of illustrating, but almost any kind of material can serve the same purpose. Anecdotes (or small-scale narratives) are often used to illustrate. An account of an experience you had when you were five might lead to a generalization about the impressionability of children. Or instead of an actual case you might offer a hypothetical one, as on p. 46 of this text: "Suppose you have been given the broad assignment of writing about your home town. . . ." Comparisons can serve as examples: a comparison between social dancing in 1940 and social dancing in 1970 might support a generalization about the cultures of the two periods.

What turns an anecdote or a comparison into an example is its connection with a general statement. Most examples stand in a close and obvious relationship to their generalizations—illustrating, confirming, or proving them—and often they wear a label, as in this use of a single example to support a generalization:

Normal infants are born fully equipped to learn any human language spoken anywhere in the world, and all normal children go through more or less the same stages of learning language, with no language appearing to be more difficult to learn than any other. For example, if an American child were adopted as a baby by an Arab family in Saudi Arabia and were raised by them in their homeland, he would come to speak their Arab language as fluently as he would have learned American English if he had remained in the United States. — Roderick A. Jacobs and Peter S. Rosenbaum, *English Transformational Grammar*

Illustrations can often be run into the text smoothly, without introductory tags like *for example* or *for instance:*

Many slang words pass into standard use and once they do, of course, they don't sound slangy at all. Among such now-sturdy-re-spectables are *club* (social), *dwindle, flout, foppish, freshman, fretful, glib, hubbub, nice, ribaldry, scoundrel, simper, swagger, tidy, tantrums, tarpaulin* and *trip* (journey).

Even more interesting is that many slang words stay in the language for centuries, but remain slang. *Booze,* once standard, became dialectal and then slang and has remained slang for centuries, spawning recently, in British slang, *boozer* (a pub). *Brass* (impudence) is also centuries old. So is *to chisel* (to use trickery), and so are *frisk* (to search a person for weapons), *corporation* (large belly), *leery, pad* (bed), *mum, blab, gag* (joke), *pigeon* (dupe), *hick* (rustic), *grub* (food) and hundreds of others.

A word can remain slang and undergo a semantic change just as if it were standard. Forty years ago a *nut* was a ludicrous eccentric; today he is one who is dangerously deranged. Like so many other things in the world, the word has acquired a menace. — Bergen Evans, *New York Times Magazine,* March 22, 1964

It takes a shrewd assessment of the rhetorical situation to decide how many examples you need. How familiar is your reader with the subject? How willing is he to accept your generalization? Too few examples will leave him uninformed or unconvinced; too many will bore him. The number needed depends also on the nature of the illustrative material. If the instances have a high degree of uniformity, as in the passage by Jacobs and Rosenbaum ("all normal children"), one will do. If the instances are heterogeneous, each unlike the next, several may be required. In the passage by Evans, a generous supply of examples is needed to support the statement about "many" slang words. The subject is specialized, and for most readers — the *New York Times Magazine* audience — the examples are separate and discrete (the example *club* doesn't readily call to mind the example *dwindle*). By contrast, the third paragraph obviously does not require a long list.

Example   77

Developing an Example

The Evans passage points up another question about the use of illustration: Can the examples stand alone (those in Evans' first two paragraphs can), or do they need to be commented on, clarified, developed (as in his third paragraph)? Familiar examples need only be mentioned—"Freestanding sculpture may be small enough to hold in one's hand or huge, like the Statue of Liberty" or "The Wobblies, like most labor movements, produced some splendid songs, among them the old railroad ballad 'Casey Jones.'" But referring to an object or citing a title may be only the first step in using an example; often, if it is to convince, it must be developed and explained. In the following passage, simply offering "my mother's house" as an example to prove that a drab life affects taste would be meaningless. What is needed—and what the author supplies—are details that *develop* the example and so make it convincing.

The drabness of real life seems to affect taste. If your life is exciting you are likely to decorate in stark Danish and wear simple unadorned black classics. But in my mother's house there is glitter—a dazzling wall clock that bongs every half-hour, an oversized, wood-inlaid painting of Chinese dancers (à la Coney Island), painted figurines of bongo players, and a giant Buddha perched atop the TV. In her clothes my mother prefers bright reds to black. She will choose the flashy fakes over subdued pearls, big beads over smaller ones, and three strands over one. Size, quantity, and glitter always count. Her car is an orange and white Mercury (now in its declining years), and her hair is of rather similar hues—it all seems somehow gayer that way.—Patricia Cayo Sexton, *Harper's*, Oct. 1962

Functions of Examples

Clarifying general statements in expository prose is probably the commonest function of examples. Another function, of particular relevance to argument, is justifying generalizations, showing them to be sound or compelling or at least feasible. The method of proof known as *induction* consists of offering clusters of examples or instances designed to lead up to or support an assertion about *all* or *most* members of a class. (See pp. 148–53.) Since some arguments stand or fall on the number and nature of the examples, both writers and readers need to be on guard against showing bias in choosing examples and against misrepresenting their significance. Sometimes the authority of the writer guarantees that the examples will be accepted by the particular audience; but if the writer's credentials are not well established, he may need to argue that his instances are both typical and cogent — an adequate basis for the inference he is drawing from them or the generalization he intends them to support.

Sometimes an example is sustained through an entire essay and so becomes its chief method of development: an account of the polluting of Lake Erie can substantiate a generalization about water pollution. More often, the role of illustrations is a supporting one, giving meaning to abstract statements and strengthening shaky generalizations. As you write, examine your general statements to see whether they need to be bolstered or clarified by examples. If they do, ask yourself whether a string of examples, or a simple list, would be more or less useful than one or two instances developed in some detail. Decide whether the examples should precede the generalization, leading up to it, or whether they might better stand as supporting witnesses immediately following it. Finally, determine whether in the particular context you can safely let them speak for themselves or whether you have to speak for them and demonstrate their relevance.

Example   79

Chapter Four

MAKING COMPARISONS, FINDING CAUSES

You can often generate ideas for your essays by asking how your subject is like another or why it is the way it is. In conversation we are constantly making comparisons—of books, movies, teams, life-styles, and so on. And we are constantly looking for causal explanations of events that puzzle or otherwise interest us: Why did Don enlist? Why did the team lose? In writing we go through the same procedures more thoroughly and systematically in order to inform or to persuade an audience.

 ## COMPARISON AND CONTRAST

To compare and contrast is to set forth points of resemblance and points of difference between two or more entities—objects, places, institutions, people, groups, ideas. Strictly, *comparison* implies likeness, and *contrast* implies difference; but ordinarily the term *comparison* is applied to the whole operation of discovering and presenting both similarities and differences.

Whenever a writer's main intention in an essay is to bring out the similarities and differences between poems, paintings, historians' interpretations, novelists' techniques, economists' analyses, or any other related entities, comparison is central. It is subsidiary, but often essential, in essays with other aims. A good way of explaining how a new mechanism works is to compare it with a familiar one, using a "known" as a point of reference to shed light on an "unknown." To establish a generalization about the tastes of television audiences, you might compare shows that have proved popular with shows that have failed. The technique of comparing is useful in argument — inevitable, in fact, in controversies about which policy should be adopted or which candidate elected.

Points of Comparison

Your interest or purpose dictates the basis for your comparison, and the basis for your comparison influences your choice of material. If you are comparing two men as political thinkers, you will develop certain points of comparison; if you are comparing them as prose stylists, you will develop different ones. A point of comparison implies a question that you can profitably ask of each of your subjects. If you inquire whether they agree or disagree in their view of human nature, then *view of human nature* is a point of comparison, a topic that you will discuss in connection with your two subjects.

You are scarcely ever interested in bringing out *all* the possible resemblances and differences; many are trivial or obvious or simply irrelevant to your purpose. What you want is a manageable number of points of comparison that, when applied to particulars, will yield significant likenesses and differences — significant for your purpose in bringing the subjects together. You are most likely to discover relevant points of comparison if you begin by experiencing your subjects as fully as possible. Investigate each one, jotting down all the details and aspects of it that occur to you. Keep turning it over in your mind; keep asking questions of it. Once you have two full lists, review them, looking for points of contact that suggest relationships worth exploring. As you examine these relationships more closely, you will begin to make finer distinctions, asking yourself whether the likenesses you are uncovering are fundamental or superficial and whether the differences are differences in degree or differences in kind.

A difference in degree is expressed in terms of more or less, or better or worse, or stronger or weaker: "Both *A* and *B* are enjoyable, but *A* gives more lasting pleasure than *B*." Differences in kind are illustrated in this excerpt:

A true critic is not necessarily a reviewer; a reviewer is not necessarily a critic — in fact, rarely is. Each has his rightful place, but they are really quite different breeds of cat. The reviewer is fundamentally a newsman, and the review is basically a piece of news, what the French would call an intellectual *fait divers*. He is temperamentally very different from the critic, who is really a kind of garden-variety philosopher. The reviewer's strong points are speed, topicality, wit, and fact. The critic publishes several months after the reviewer has forgotten what the movie was even about; his virtues are long meditation, a firm historical sense, profound insight, truth—even truth with a capital T.—Stephen Koch, *Saturday Review*, Dec. 26, 1970

Once you have discovered the points of comparison that have a bearing on your purpose, you have the criteria you need to screen from your lists just those characteristics and qualities and details of your subjects that have a bearing on what you want to demonstrate or prove. Then you are ready to consider how you can best organize your comparison.

EXERCISE

Speed, comfort, freedom of movement, and opportunities for relaxation are points of comparison that might be used in deciding whether to cross an ocean by plane or by freighter. What points of comparison would you use to bring out significant similarities and differences between two musicians or groups of musicians (you name them), two courses that you are now taking (you select them), two methods of learning a skill (a skill you are qualified to teach)? In each case, state what interest you have in making the comparison—what you are trying to demonstrate or to prove—and what audience you are addressing. (Shipboard peace and quiet would not be presented as a profreighter argument to an audience mostly concerned about action and excitement.)

Structuring a Comparison

Essentially, a passage of comparison consists of several points of comparison filled out with details, examples, facts. How you arrange the points and the supporting information will depend on the material itself, on your audience's familiarity with it, and on your purpose. The following exercise brings out the basic ways of structuring a comparison.

EXERCISE

Make an outline of each of these three passages.

A

Thomas Jefferson grew up among the landed gentry of Virginia, and he remained a confirmed Virginian throughout his life. He was a thoughtful man, a scholar and a philosopher, always eager to add to his knowledge of the arts and sciences and to explore the mysteries of the universe and of the human spirit. Though reluctant to take part in the clamor and conflict of politics, he became a powerful political leader, working for the welfare of his nation. A patriot and statesman, he devoted his life to the development of the Republic he had helped to create. His writings reflect a hopeful view of human nature, a belief that under the right conditions men will improve. That faith is implicit in the great Declaration of Independence, of which he was the author. It is the basis of his dream of a happy land of free men, living together in natural harmony. And that faith is, of course, the root of his objection to any kind of government that would stifle individual liberty and hamper individual growth. Both his faith and his dream became permanent parts of American democracy.

Alexander Hamilton came from a background very unlike Jefferson's. He was born into a poor family on an island in the Lesser Antilles. He became a New Yorker, joining a society of men as competitive and aggressive as himself. A gifted organizer and administrator, he used his brilliant mind as a weapon with which to fight not only for personal success but also for the practical policies he supported. His patriotism was as great as Jefferson's, but his view of the future of the nation was dictated by a very different reading of human nature. He believed that men will act upon the same selfish motives whatever the form of government and that therefore a government with sufficient authority to impose order and stability is always essential. Only through a strong central government, he thought, could America achieve peace, progress, and prosperity. This idea, powerfully expressed in his *Federalist* papers, had great influence upon the organization of the new republic and upon its subsequent history.

B

Thomas Jefferson and Alexander Hamilton were two of America's most influential statesmen in the early period of the Republic. Jefferson grew up among the landed gentry of Virginia; Hamilton was born into a poor family on an island in the Lesser Antilles. Only with great reluctance did Jefferson accept a political career, with its accompanying clamor and conflict. A thoughtful man, he would have preferred to spend his life in his native state, free to add to his scholarly knowledge of the arts and sciences and to explore the mysteries of the universe and of the human spirit. Hamilton, on the other hand, found his natural milieu in New York City, in a society of men who shared his competitive, aggressive spirit, and he entered politics with the enthusiasm and efficiency of the born organizer and administrator. His brilliant mind served him admirably in his fight for personal success and for the political policies he supported. His *Federalist* papers are among the greatest documents of the period, ranking in historical importance with Jefferson's Declaration of Independence. Both are the works of great patriots.

Jefferson's political philosophy was optimistic; he believed that, given the right conditions, men would improve. By contrast, Hamilton was convinced that, regardless of environment, human nature does not change. Accordingly, while Jefferson dreamed of a happy land of free men, living together in natural harmony, Hamilton worked for order and stability, for system and organization. The Virginian feared that the machinery of a strong central government would stifle individual liberty and hamper individual growth; the New Yorker believed that government must have authority in order to ensure peace, progress, and prosperity. Regardless of the differences in their views, both men devoted their lives to the welfare of the new nation, which both had helped to create and which both helped to survive. And their different views had permanent influence upon the history of America.

C

Thomas Jefferson and Alexander Hamilton were fellow patriots and fellow statesmen. Men of true brilliance, the powerful influence that they exerted upon the Republic at the beginning of its history had an effect that has persisted to the present day. To them we owe some of our greatest historical documents — to Jefferson the Declaration of Independence and to Hamilton a number of the famous *Federalist* papers. Both were powerful political leaders, working for the welfare of the new nation which they had helped to create and which they helped to survive.

At the same time, their differences were numerous and profound. They were unlike in background, in temperament, in habit of mind, and in political philosophy. Jefferson grew up among the landed gentry of old Virginia; Hamilton was born into a poor family on an island in the Lesser Antilles. Throughout his life, Jefferson remained a confirmed Virginian, but Hamilton became a New Yorker, flourishing in a society of men as competitive and aggressive as himself. Jefferson shrank from the clamor and conflict of politics; Hamilton had the zeal of a born organizer and administrator. Jefferson was a thoughtful man, a scholar and a philosopher, always eager to add to his knowledge of the arts and sciences and to explore the mysteries of the universe and of the human spirit. Hamilton used his mind as a keen weapon with which he fought not only for personal success but also for the practical policies he supported.

They differed markedly in their views of human nature. An optimist, Jefferson believed that, under the right conditions, men would improve; Hamilton was convinced that, regardless of environment, human nature would never change. Because of their different readings of human nature, they had different views about the role of government. Since he could not believe that a new type of government would result in a new type of citizenry, Hamilton worked for the old objectives—order and stability, system and organization; he sought to build a government with traditional authority, which he considered essential to peace, progress, and prosperity. Just as naturally, considering his philosophy, Jefferson fought against a strong central government, fearing that it would stifle individual liberty and hamper individual growth, seeing it as a threat to his dream of a happy land of free men, living together in natural harmony.

a. Do your outlines show any significant differences in content between *A, B,* and *C*? If not, what is the main difference between *A* and *B, B* and *C, A* and *C*?

b. What are the points of comparison in *A*? In *B*? In *C*? That is, in what respects are the men shown to be either similar or different?

c. Why do none of the selections mention the historically important fact that Jefferson founded the University of Virginia? Why do none mention the dramatic fact that Hamilton was killed in a duel?

d. What changes would be necessary in *A* if Hamilton were discussed first? Would it be possible to shift the first paragraph of *C* to the end of that passage if minor adjustments were made at the start of the second paragraph?

e. In the three passages, is comparison being done for its own sake, simply to show the points of similarity and the points of difference between the two men, or is it being done to prove a thesis (for instance, that one of the men made a greater contribution than the other)?

f. Construct diagrams that represent *A, B,* and *C* as abstract patterns.

The exercise you have just completed brings out the main features of three patterns commonly used to build balanced comparisons—comparisons in which roughly the same attention is given to each of the entities. Passage *A* we call whole-to-whole, Passage *B* part-to-part, Passage *C* likeness-difference. The passages are designed to show that the same material can be arranged in three ways, each giving the reader a slightly different view. The first, in which the writer has his say about one of the subjects before turning to the other, presents each subject as a whole rather than focusing on precise similarities or differences. The part-to-part scheme, with its perfect symmetry, highlights specific points of comparison, leaving the reader with a sharp impression of how the subjects relate to each other on each point. (Notice how the symmetry extends even to the individual sentences. Many of them are balanced, the two halves built just alike. See pp. 324–25.) The third pattern begins with similarities but emphasizes differences; what is given most space and placed last is remembered longest.

Actual comparisons seldom fall into patterns as neat as these, with such a careful balancing of points. In the whole-to-whole pattern illustrated here, the writer has returned faithfully in the second half to the points of comparison that he introduced in the first half; but the correspondence is seldom so precise or so complete. Nor should it be. If you were comparing the British and American political systems in order to explain the British system to an American audience, you would naturally give the American "whole" short shrift. A few generalizations would be enough to remind readers of what they already knew and to open the way for the contrast. The same lopsidedness would be apparent if you used the part-to-part structure: whenever a point of comparison was introduced, you would touch on its application to the American political system only briefly, giving much more space to the corresponding details about the British system.

There are other rhetorical situations in which it will suit your purpose to emphasize certain features of one or both of your subjects. If you are arguing the merits of a political candidate, you will naturally give most attention to his strong points, least to those on which he compares unfavorably with his opponent. If your intention is to bring out hidden likenesses between two things normally thought of as strikingly different, there would be no point in reviewing the differences; you would acknowledge these very briefly and move on to what you are really interested in—the similarities.

There are valid reasons, then, for giving one of your subjects more attention than the other or for otherwise modifying the basic patterns. But if you do so inadvertently or through carelessness when you have committed yourself to giving a full, balanced comparison, your essay will be poorly proportioned and the comparison incomplete or unfair. Each of the patterns presents hazards in this respect. In the whole-to-whole the two halves of your essay will drift apart if, in dealing with the second whole, you lose sight of the points you made about the first. Part-to-part has the advantage of keeping the topics in view, but unless they are smoothly related, the essay will seem choppy and disjointed. And if the third pattern is less common than the other two, it is probably because many subjects yield such a random collection of either likenesses or differences that half the comparison turns out to be weak and uninteresting.

In choosing among the patterns, try to decide which best suits your material, your purpose, and the needs of your audience. Suppose you are writing an article for a popular magazine about the pollution of waterways and you use as evidence a comparison of the Concord and Merrimack rivers as they are today with the rivers as Henry David Thoreau knew them in 1839. Doing a part-to-part comparison will probably not suit your purpose. You will be more likely to offer a brief sketch of the rivers as Thoreau knew them and then move to a detailed account of their present deplorable state. Your overriding pattern will be unbalanced whole-to-whole.

When you write an extended, analytical comparison for an audience that is knowledgeable about your subjects, you will probably use the part-to-part pattern. Close analysis of separate points can be sustained longer in that scheme than in the whole-to-whole. A detailed comparison of the techniques and contributions of two film directors, supported by examples of their work, would be easier to follow in the part-to-part scheme than in whole-to-whole, and relationships could be stated with greater precision than in the likeness-difference pattern.

Sometimes you will combine methods. A lengthy comparison that begins with either whole-to-whole or part-to-part may conclude with a section on similarities (or differences) to pull together what has gone before. In making a choice of methods, ask yourself questions like these: Will my purpose be best served (and my audience best informed) if I present a general view of each whole? Or should I set certain aspects of each side by side to sharpen the contrast? Or will it be more effective to talk entirely in terms of *like* and *unlike?* Do *like* and *unlike* need equal attention, or should I pass over the likenesses quickly and get on to what really counts — the differences?

Though the structure of a comparison must be clear, mechanical symmetry does not guarantee a good essay. Organization is only a means of focusing attention on the similarities and differences. To convince the reader they are real ones, you must present the details, the examples, the facts that make your subjects alike or different in respects that you consider important and interesting.

EXERCISES

1. Review the three methods of organizing a comparison, and then write an essay of about a thousand words on one of the following topics.

   a. For a sympathetic audience, such as an old friend or a school counselor, compare and contrast your views and attitudes with those of your parents on matters that are especially important to you. (Suggestions: political, religious, or moral views; social activities; dress; education; money.)

   b. For the sports section in a newspaper or magazine, compare and contrast the physical skills required for filling two different positions on a team or for engaging in two different sports.

   c. For a campus newspaper, bring out the similarities and differences between two kinds of music you know well (for example, rock and jazz, folk and country, Renaissance and Baroque).

   d. For an audience of your choice, compare the aims and methods of two campus or community groups or two national organizations (the National Rifle Association, the NAACP, the DAR, the Black Panthers, the American Legion, and so on).

2. Write an essay comparing and contrasting the ways in which various ethnic or religious groups celebrate their holidays. Assume a reader who belongs to one of the groups whose holiday rituals you are discussing.

3. For a theater magazine, write a comparison of the styles of two comedians or two serious actors with a view to demonstrating that one is more talented or more entertaining than the other.

Analogy

To compare is to bring out actual, specific likenesses and differences between two acknowledged members of the same class (two statesmen, Jefferson and Hamilton; two wars, Korea and Vietnam). To draw an analogy is to uncover resemblances between entities not ordinarily thought of as similar. In order to describe the forest, Marston Bates drew an analogy between the forest and the sea. As a means of dramatizing the place in society of the typical American adolescent, Edgar Z. Friedenberg drew an analogy between him and the native inhabitant of a nineteenth-century colony.

In offering an analogy, the writer does not claim that the two entities are alike in all respects or even in most. (Probably everyone would agree that the differences between the colonial native and the American adolescent far outnumber the similarities.) He says only that the two are similar in some respect that is pertinent to the point at issue. (According to Friedenberg, the treatment of adolescents by adults in our time is comparable to the treatment of native peoples by colonial administrators in the last century.) Normally the writer makes an inference on the basis of his analogy. He may suggest that because two entities are known to be similar in a certain respect, they are likely to be similar in a further respect about which we can't be sure. Or, to arouse interest or strong feeling in his audience, he may call attention to a general metaphorical likeness between wholes that can scarcely be supported by any precise, literal similarity: "Our solar system has become a cluttered junkyard."

Even though it is too frail to carry the entire burden of proof, a good analogy brings the point home and often induces strong emotional conviction. It is especially useful in giving tangible form to abstractions, as in this passage:

If the word Ethics has any meaning, then we must agree with Wittgenstein, "Ethics does not treat of the world. Ethics must be a condition of the world, like logic." The law of ethics, that is to say, must be like the laws of physics and chemistry, laws we can, out of ignorance or willfulness, defy but cannot break, any more than I can break the laws of biochemistry by getting drunk or the law of gravity by jumping out of the window, and the consequence of defying them must be as inevitable and as intrinsically linked to their nature as a hangover or a broken leg. —W. H. Auden, *New York Times Magazine*, Aug. 1, 1965

The use of analogy in persuasion is discussed further on pp. 142–43 and 152–53. Whether it is used for persuasion or for clarification, an analogy is of great value in stimulating thought. To perceive resemblances between two things normally regarded as unlike generates new ideas and points the way to new understandings. It is analogy, after all, that permits us to form classes and make groupings. When things are similar in certain respects, we are justified in relating them even though in many respects they are unlike. Seeing class relationships is essential if we are to think at all. Seeing relationships that others have overlooked opens the door to a fresh, inventive, creative approach to a subject.

A comment by Marston Bates gives a clue to the real difficulty with analogies: "The analogy, once thought of, was easily developed." *Once thought of*. The imaginative insight that uncovers hidden similarities can't be called up at will. Good analogies often seem to be lucky accidents. Or perhaps they come to minds accustomed to looking for similarities between things that, on the face of it, are altogether different.

EXERCISES

1. Compare the uses of analogy in the two passages that follow. What seems to be the purpose—to give the reader a new insight into the subject or to prove something about the subject? How does each writer develop his analogy? The first passage illustrates what is sometimes called a *literal* analogy, the second a *figurative* analogy. What is the essential difference between the two types?

a. Most of the Black Panthers I have known are naive, malleable ghetto kids, angry and despairing, but not vicious, mean-spirited men and women. Watching their haphazard close-formation drill on a makeshift parade ground in Oakland, listening to their banal, adolescent chatter as they bundle copies of the obscene and race-baiting *Black Panther* weekly, even shuddering as they go through precisely coordinated public demonstrations of ferocity with clearly implied goals of assassination and guerrilla warfare, one catches the bizarre mirror image of Boy Scouts. Like Tenderfeet, new to the troop (their party, after all, is less than four years old, and most of them are teen-agers, quite a few not yet halfway through adolescence), they seem both awed and securely warmed by the first good feelings of fraternity and solidarity that inevitably accompany mild military or quasimilitary discipline. I'm sure that Hitler's Brown Shirts felt it; so did Mao's Fourth Route Army, the original American Minutemen, the present-day nuts of the same name, the Kerensky revolutionaries, the Bolsheviks, the officers of the Bolivian General Staff, the Pathet Lao and the Viet Cong, among others. The analogy may seem ludicrous, but it is not inept, because while the goals of good Scouts and Black Panthers are appallingly disparate, the raw material in which they are implanted is not: little kids, for the most part, indoctrinated in the flush of fraternity and solidarity to suspend critical judgment in areas that are vital to the greater organization and the ideals of its leaders. . . .

Both groups indoctrinate their young members in the classic military virtues of *unquestioning* duty, loyalty, and physical courage, and the chief difference may only be that from one, as any army commander will tell you, you get excellent battlefield soldiers, while from the other you get unpredictable urban guerrilla fighters whose willingness to commit suicide scares hell out of their immediate opponents, the cops.

That's quite a difference. Most Scouts get over their boyish gullibility and adopt a pragmatic regard for self-preservation that doesn't always include doing their duty for God and their country (Jerry Rubin was a Boy Scout). I doubt whether many Panthers will develop self-serving critical minds, because to the everlasting regret of the white society that made them what they are, the kids who become Black Panthers have been motivated by life, as well as indoctrinated by their party, to emulate Samson, whose historical first act of suicidal blind rage they can understand better than Boy Scouts understand patriotism. Unhappily, it probably won't occur to many of them that Samson didn't accomplish much beyond the immortality of his own name when he brought the Philistines' building down on his unshorn head. — Don A. Schanche, *Atlantic*, May 1970

b. One basic cause [of the students' revolt] arises from the fact that the leaders of revolt see clearly something that most of their elders simply cannot admit. They see that the accepted and entrenched educational, economic, and political systems have produced a world with more warfare, bigger massacres, more powerful criminals, and more overall violence than at any other time since the Age of Enlightenment began. Yet many of the leaders of these systems are still spouting platitudes which, to the young people, are patent expressions either of ignorance, self-delusion, or pure hypocrisy. Moreover, not only do these elderly folk refuse to admit any incompetence; they actually boast of the eminence that they have achieved — utterly unaware that to youth *this* is proof of incompetence. When one is part of a system that has brought a whole world to disaster, only a fool boasts that he is an *important part*. Yet these are the people, say our youth, who have the unmitigated gall to expect that we will gladly accept them as fit to train us for *any* kind of leadership.

Youth's first reaction to all of the foregoing is one of frustration, rage, and desire to destroy. The situation is similar to a man trying to learn to ride a bicycle with such crooked handle bars that he always finds himself in the ditch. He tries to fix it; he can't; no one helps him; in a rage he kicks the whole thing to pieces. He must then pick up the pieces and build a new bicycle — or perhaps a motorcycle, or even a machine never before seen. Can he do it? — John F. Wharton, *Saturday Review*, July 12, 1969

2. Explain why you do or do not find each of the passages in Exercise 1 illuminating or convincing. If you are dissatisfied with

the analogies, try constructing new ones that will throw a truer light on the subjects.

3. Find analogies that will express your attitude toward each of the following:

April	the F.B.I.	hitchhiking
traffic	racial conflict	marriage
guilt	loneliness	hair

CAUSES AND EFFECTS

Cause-effect connections are conveyed not only by explicit statements (*A* is the cause of *B; B* is the effect of *A*) but by such common transitional words and phrases as *because, so, therefore, consequently, in order that, as a result*, and, in some of their uses, *for, since, then*, and *thus*. Sometimes the parts of a sentence are linked so that they suggest a causal relation ("The higher the tuition, the better the school"), and sometimes the simple juxtaposition of statements implies one:

On April 6, Lincoln sent word to the governor of South Carolina that supplies would be shipped to Fort Sumter. On April 12, Confederate guns began to bombard the fort.

Causal connections contribute to coherence in material that is organized chronologically—sets of instructions and descriptions of processes as well as narratives told for their own sake. In recipes the causal statements are usually spare and undeveloped: "Don't overcook, or the eggs will curdle." In more elaborate instructions (how to refinish a piece of furniture or how to swim the butterfly stroke) statements of cause and effect may be introduced both to explain each step and to justify the order in which the steps are presented. In an explanation of a natural process like soil drifting, causal statements show how one stage relates to another and so help the reader understand *why* what happens does happen.

In other essays cause-effect analysis is the dominant method of development. The writer probes the causes of (or reasons for) an event or situation or policy. He traces the effects (or results) it has had or will have. Or he conducts both inquiries in the same essay—first setting forth the events that led to a particular state of affairs, then revealing what developments have ensued or predicting what developments will ensue. In an essay on the *causes* of political apathy or the psychological *effects* of abortion, the writer's interest is centered not so much on the situation itself as on what led to it or on what it led to or will lead to. His main concern is to present—and perhaps argue for—the relationships and connections he has arrived at by *reasoning about* origins and results.

Reasoning in terms of cause and effect, like any other kind of reasoning, can be done well or badly. A writer who approaches a cause-effect analysis too blithely or too timidly can easily make a fool of himself. Typically, he oversimplifies: bureaucracy is to blame for high taxes; slavery caused the Civil War; campus unrest is the result of subversive activities; coed housing will put an end to campus unrest. He matches one cause to one effect, often without providing any evidence that his one cause is, in fact, a cause at all, and so turns what should be a reasoned discussion into a dogmatic statement of opinion.

Or, convinced that only an omniscient being can assign causes or attribute results, he refuses to commit himself. He loads his discussion with cautious qualifications, presents an endless list of "possible" causes, or traces the "possible" immediate causes back to such remote and virtually meaningless causes as "civilization," "chance," or "human nature"—thus World War II (or World War I or the Trojan War or the Vietnam War) was caused by human nature. Whether his tendency is to oversimplify or to overqualify, he needs to develop a realistic notion of how to go about answering *why* questions.

Discovering Causes

Why questions are asked in many different contexts. Why did the automobile accident occur? Why did the student fail the course? Why do birds migrate? Why is the crime rate rising? Why do I have insomnia? Why does Hamlet decide to feign madness? Why did the president resign? What you are seeking when you try to answer a *why* question may be a cause, a reason, a motive, a description, a process, a justification, an analysis of a situation. Though the subjects under examination differ, the procedure in answering a *why* question always involves investigating the facts and reasoning from the facts to a causal explanation. This procedure—inductive inquiry—is discussed on pp. 150–52.

Anyone accustomed to thinking of cause-effect relations in the context of scientific experiments knows that two phenomena are causally related only if the existence of one *requires* the existence of the other. A causal relation between A and B can be established with certainty only if it can be demonstrated that whenever *B* occurs, *A* is present; that *B* never occurs in the absence of *A*; that the presence of *A* is always accompanied by the occurrence of *B*. A laboratory worker tries to isolate all variables and then puts strict controls on one variable after another until eventually he determines what conditions or set of conditions operates as a cause. He can run experiments again and again until he either verifies or disproves his hypothesis—his hunch or guess that *A* is the cause of *B*. The following paragraph makes clear that observation under controlled conditions was necessary to prove that the causal factor in the flying behavior of bats is an "internal timing device" or biological clock—not, as was formerly supposed, the coming on of evening.

Those who are familiar with the habits of bats will know that each day these animals begin to fly in the early evening just when the insects they feed on are most abundant. The inference that this flying behavior is controlled by some internal timing device is based in part on measurements which have been made on caged bats in controlled conditions. The activity of bats, even when confined to a cage, shows a pattern of active periods followed by rest periods, and this pattern is repeated periodically with a well-defined rhythm. Even in complete darkness at a constant temperature this rhythm persists indefinitely. Of course, in such conditions the rhythm no longer has exactly a twenty-four-hour period, but at regular intervals of perhaps 23 or 23½ hours (depending on the individual bat) the cycle of activity repeats itself. —Victor G. Bruce, *Frontiers of Modern Biology*

In interpreting the results of his experiments, the laboratory worker needs to apply some such rules as those formulated by John Stuart Mill (*Cause). Mill's canons survey systematically the procedures for testing causal hypotheses. Outside of the laboratory, they have practical limitations, for they assume that all the possible circumstances can be known, that controlled experiments can be repeated, and that only a single cause is operating. Even so, they are valuable in stressing the need for rigor in any causal inquiry, for distinguishing between necessary and sufficient causes, and for distinguishing between certainty and probability in attributing causes.

In many of the things that matter most to us, probability is all that we can hope for. We cannot set up controlled laboratory experiments that will nail down cause-effect relationships; we cannot call into existence the actual circumstances in which a crime was committed or an election lost or a battle won. And even if we could rerun such episodes, we would rarely be able to isolate a single cause that inevitably led to the given effect. "In the world of reality," a logician observes, "there is no such thing as *the* cause of anything.

There are many causes, or necessary antecedents, for everything that happens." The simplest event may have unexpected complexities. An investigation into a collision of two cars may have to take into account weather, traffic, and road conditions, the mechanical condition of the cars, and the competence of the drivers. The investigator may find that no one "cause" can be isolated. If his job is to assess responsibility, he will try to demonstrate that one of the many contributory causes had a more immediate connection with the accident than the others, was in itself sufficient to have caused the accident, and therefore can be treated as *the* cause. But he may have to content himself with listing three or four contributory causes, none of which can be said to be decisive.

Social and moral problems are infinitely more complex than street-corner accidents. When you are writing about drug addiction, the divorce rate, nakedness on the stage, student unrest, or similar issues, you will probably want to adduce several causes or antecedents, not just one, and to distinguish immediate causes from causes several times removed. In a thoroughgoing causal analysis you may need to examine the evidence for conflicting hypotheses, show that a commonly accepted cause is insufficient or implausible, distinguish between antecedent conditions that made the outcome likely and those that actually triggered an event, perhaps rank contributory causes in order of decisiveness — any or all of these.

In any case, your reader will be interested not just in the list of causes you offer but in your demonstration that the relationship between each cause you postulate and the effect is indeed a probable one. Merely asserting causal connections is not enough: you need to mass enough details to join "cause" to "effect." For causal analysis usually has an argumentative edge. (See pp. 137–39 and 150–52.) There is no point in writing about cause-effect relations that are obvious to everyone (touching a hot stove causes pain). There *is* some point in exploring those relationships which, even though they can't be pinned down with absolute certainty, can, when shown to be probable, increase the reader's understanding of the subject. And it is demonstration, not mere assertion, that establishes probability — demonstration in the form of concrete, relevant details and facts knitting cause to effect.

EXERCISES

1. For an audience of your choice, state clearly and give reasons for your political convictions, your religious beliefs, or your moral code. To make your causal explanation convincing, you will probably need to tell something about your background and experiences.

2. Review the excerpt by John F. Wharton, p. 91. In a brief essay, explain why you do or do not agree with his analysis of a basic cause of student unrest. If you agree, supply supporting evidence from your own reading and observation. If you disagree, offer one or more causes that seem to you to be more probable than Wharton's.

Attributing Effects

Attributing effects requires as much discriminating thought as identifying causes, for what you assume to be the effects of one antecedent may in fact result from the agency of another antecedent, so far unknown. But despite its uncertainties, speculating about effects is often the only guide we have to future action. Policies are made and altered on the basis of probable effects. When you work from a current policy (instituting coed housing, say, or a black studies program, or abolishing ROTC) to the effects, it is ordinarily with the purpose of arguing that since the effects have been desirable (or undesirable) the policy should be continued or changed. The basic method is contrast: you present details that show how the situation is different (and better or worse) than it was before the policy (the cause) was instituted.

Frequently you *predict* effects as part of your argument for accepting or rejecting a proposed policy. The procedure is the same, but the element of prediction imposes on the responsible writer the need to bring in all the evidence he can to show that the results he projects are likely to occur. All of us are familiar with predictions, based on unqualified and unsupported generalizations, about the bad consequences that will flow from courses of action or habits that the speakers disapprove of—continued attempts to integrate public schools will destroy the American educational system; rock concerts will deafen a whole generation; the expansion of anti-pollution measures will bring on an economic depression; grass will grow in the streets; and so on. The political candidate's routine prediction of horrendous consequences for the country if his opponent is elected is not taken seriously by many intelligent voters. To make sure that your analysis of effects *is* taken seriously, you should make every effort to proportion effects to the causes and to establish, through detailed evidence, reasonable links between the event or situation and the results you say it will bring about.

EXERCISES

1. Examine the following passage of causal analysis, noting especially the methods the authors use to present their findings and the style in which they write.

In addition to the various subjective effects of the hallucinogens there are a number of observable changes in physiological function and in performance that one can measure or at least describe objectively. The basic physiological effects are those typical of a mild excitement of the sympathetic nervous system. The hallucinogens usually dilate the pupils, constrict the peripheral arterioles and raise the systolic blood pressure; they may also increase the excitability of such spinal reflexes as the knee jerk. Electroencephalograms show that the effect on electrical brain waves is usually of a fairly nonspecific "arousal" nature: the pattern is similar to that of a normally alert, attentive and problem-oriented subject, and if rhythms characteristic of drowsiness or sleep have been present, they disappear when the drug is administered. (Insomnia is common the first night after one of the drugs has been taken.) Animal experiments suggest that LSD produces these effects by stimulating the reticular formation of the mid-brain, not directly but by stepping up the sensory input. — Frank Barren, Murray E. Jarvik, and Sterling Bunnell, Jr., *Scientific American*, April 1964

Write an essay on either the psychological or the social consequences of the hallucinogens. Choose an audience for your essay, and adapt your style to that audience. (Would a *Scientific American* style be appropriate in discussing the social consequences of drug taking with a junior-high-school audience?)

2. To support his contention that the side effects of technical innovation may be more influential than the direct effects in transforming the behavior, outlook, and moral ethic of a civilization, Jacob Bronowski uses this illustration:

Who would have thought that the unfortunate character who invented photographic film would have been responsible for the California film industry? And thus, indirectly, for contracts that would prevent film stars from having affairs that might give rise to gossip and scandal? That consequently stars would lead their love life in public, by repeated divorce and marriage? That therefore the beautiful pin-ups of film would, in time, become the models of the divorce business? And the climax, that one-third of all marriages contracted this year in California are going to end in divorce—all because somebody invented the process of printing pictures on a celluloid strip?—Jacob Bronowski, *Saturday Review*, July 5, 1969

Write an essay—serious or humorous—showing the unanticipated side effects of a recent discovery or policy.

3. Discuss the probable social consequences of any scientific breakthrough you think is feasible within the next twenty years—the ability to control the sex of an unborn child, perhaps, or to convert sea water into fresh water at nominal cost, or to produce a cheaper, more efficient, pollution-free substitute for the internal combustion engine. Give reasons why you predict the effects and side effects that you do.

Chapter Five

DIVIDING, CLASSIFYING, AND DEFINING

Whenever you are investigating a subject thoroughly, you will want to explore it in terms of class relationships—to see it as a member of a class (either a well-established class or one that you have invented), to distinguish it from other members of that class, and to discern its subclasses or parts. Whether or not the results of these inquiries find a place in your essay, classifying and defining and dividing are the basic procedures by which, consciously or unconsciously, you identify your precise subject and grasp its internal and external relationships. This chapter will deal less with the pump-priming function the procedures perform in prewriting than with the questions you can profitably ask of the analyses and definitions you use in your essays.

DIVISION AND CLASSIFICATION

Division—sometimes called partition or analysis—is the process of separating a single object (an automobile) or institution (a university) or concept (democracy) into its parts. Classification is the process of bringing together related objects or institutions or concepts: automobiles, universities, and theories of government can be sorted into groups on the basis of their resemblances. Division reveals internal structures; classification shows how a thing relates to other things. When you divide, the movement is from the whole to its parts—a downward, slicing action. When you classify, the movement is from individual items to families or classes—an upward, piling action. You *analyze* the fugue as a musical form; you *classify* rock musicians. You analyze the Republican party platform; you classify Republicans.

Logicians offer two hard-and-fast rules for making a division or classification. First, in dividing or classifying, apply only one principle at a time. Second, continue dividing until all the parts of the entity have been accounted for, or continue classifying until every entity has been placed in one of the groups. The first rule warns against inconsistency and overlapping, the second against incompleteness. An analysis will be logically sound if the basis for dividing or classifying is followed consistently, if no part or group overlaps another, and if no essential part or group is omitted. Taken together, the rules are indispensable in rigorous scientific procedures, and they provide an excellent guide to clear thinking in any circumstances. But the degree to which the requirements can be or need be satisfied in empirical inquiries depends both on the nature of the subject and on the writer's purpose.

Dividing

Criteria for completeness and consistency are easiest to apply when the subject is an object like an automobile. An elementary division of a car might yield three main parts: the chassis, the engine and the parts it drives, and the body. Many other divisions are possible, and certainly further subdividing would be necessary to explain how a car works; but as far as it goes, this simple, three-part division is consistent and complete. By contrast, a division into chassis, engine and driving parts, and fenders would strike anyone as incomplete. And a division into chassis, body, and inexpensive transportation is both incomplete and inconsistent: the third "part" has been arrived at by introducing a completely new basis or principle of division — expense.

Criteria of completeness and consistency are harder to apply when no natural or mechanical principle of division suggests itself or when the subject does not have parts that can be pointed to and separated in a physical sense. How do you go about analyzing an institution? Are the essential parts of a college the people who make it up — students, faculty, nonacademic staff, administrators, trustees or regents? Or the buildings that stand on the campus — libraries, laboratories, classrooms, dormitories? Or the courses that are offered? Or the activities, both curricular and extracurricular, that faculty and students engage in? Or the functions that society has delegated to colleges? All of these are elements in a college — and there are more, too — but which are the *essential* elements, and how do they relate to each other? Even more difficult questions have to be asked when the subject is a concept (or intellectual whole) like patriotism or communism or love or goodness, or when it is a process like the course of a love affair or waking up in the morning or listening to music.

When the subject is an institution or a concept or an activity or a process, the writer has to find a principle of division that will reflect his interest, his way of looking at the subject; he must estimate what line of division will be most productive in carrying out his intention. In general, division will serve its purpose if it singles out those aspects of the subject that, discussed separately, will increase the reader's understanding of the essential parts and, taken together, will enable the writer to come to a significant generalization about the whole. In the following paragraph, the author makes a division of the highly complex activity of listening to music, admits that the division is somewhat arbitrary, and then points out its usefulness for his purpose:

We all listen to music according to our separate capacities. But, for the sake of analysis, the whole listening process may become clearer if we break it up into its component parts, so to speak. In a certain sense we all listen to music on three separate planes. For lack of a better terminology, one might name these: (1) the sensuous plane, (2) the expressive plane, (3) the sheerly musical plane. The only advantage to be gained from mechanically splitting up the listening process into these hypothetical planes is the clearer view to be had of the way in which we listen.—Aaron Copland, *What to Listen for in Music*

The passage illustrates how the act of making a division forecasts the topics to be taken up and so virtually outlines the discussion. Division affords a scheme for organizing an essay as well as a method of exploring a subject or investigating a problem.

The dichotomy, a division into two parts, is often used in argument to pose questions or to offer choices. Is a certain course of action wise or unwise? Is the action wise or foolish? In a strict dichotomy the parts are mutually exclusive—*A* or *not-A* (wise or unwise)—but frequently the question is posed in the rhetorically more interesting though logically less sound form *A* or *B* (wise or foolish). The uses and abuses of *either-or* reasoning are discussed on pp. 161–62.

EXERCISES

1. Identify the parts of a mechanism—a can opener, a pencil sharpener, a mower, an automobile engine—that are related to the *use* or *function* of the mechanism. In an essay intended for

junior-high-school students, give an accurate description of each part, tell how the parts interact, and explain how each part functions in the working of the mechanism.

2. For a campus magazine, analyze the sources of humor in a comic strip, a television comedy program, a movie, or any recent happening.

3. Describe the structure of a college organization or the activities of a club, showing how structure or activities relate to purpose.

4. Propose three different ways of analyzing your neighborhood. Write an essay developing the one that would be most useful to someone who is organizing a political campaign in the area.

Classifying

Though in classifying you are working with a collection of items instead of a single entity, the procedure you follow is much like that in dividing. First find a principle of classification, derived from a study of the characteristics of the subject that you regard as most significant for your purpose; then apply it to all the items, sorting them into groups or classes. The general rule is that only one principle of grouping should be applied at any one time. Once a principle has been applied to all the items, a second principle may be applied to produce subgroups, then a third, and so on.

How rigorous and complete a classification should be depends on the nature of the data and the purpose the classification is intended to serve. A formal classification in a textbook or scientific journal usually undertakes to organize all the available data into a comprehensive scheme. The grouping is intended to be objectively sound—that is, the same classes should emerge if other investigators examined the same data with the same purpose in mind. A deliberately alogical grouping—"male chauvinists, female liberationists, men, and women"—may be used to startle, to enlighten, or just to amuse. Many informal classifications have a personal flavor: in offering a new way of looking at a situation, they reveal something about the classifier as well as about his subject. Often they make no claim to completeness.

EXERCISES

1. The same material can be classified in different ways. Which way you choose depends on what purpose you want the classification to serve. For what purposes and for what audiences would it be useful to classify hockey players on the basis of aggressiveness, boats on the basis of social prestige, a city's residents on the basis of race, sports on the basis of seasons played, marriages on the basis of duration, acquaintances on the basis of their favorite topics of conversation? Choose one of your subject-purpose-audience combinations and write a brief essay.

2. Who would find the following classification useful and for what purpose? What are some other ways of classifying reference works? For what purposes would they be more useful than Glixon's?

There are just four types of reference books: a) the kind you buy for somebody else — and decide you really should have a copy of for your own use, too —, b) the kind you know are precisely what Don or Winnie needs — but how do they stand it? —, c) the kind you've just got to have for yourself — and to hell with everybody else —, and d) the kind you can't afford to buy but if your public library doesn't get it you'll resign your membership. — David M. Glixon, *Saturday Review*, Dec. 6, 1969

If a grouping is to be reasonably sound, the classes must emerge as separate and distinct. This means that you must apply the principle of classification consistently to all the data. When you are classifying heterogeneous items (people, for instance), the basis of the classification may shift in mid-essay without your being aware of it. In a paper describing his own experiences in the Air Force, a student identified four groups of transport pilots: nervous pilots, old pilots, ex-fighter pilots, and reliable pilots. As a descriptive classification, this is obviously unsatisfactory. The classes overlap: both old pilots and ex-fighter pilots might be nervous, either or both might be reliable, an ex-fighter pilot might be old, and an old pilot might have flown fighters. The writer was using several different principles of classification simultaneously. What he needed to do was to apply a single criterion at a time — age *or* reliability *or* experience — and then go on to establish subgroups by using either or both of the other principles of classification.

What probably happened is that, in thinking through his material, the student kept his attention focused on individuals. As a result, his classification emerged as a series of character sketches. But the classifier must concentrate on the type, not the individual. His primary concern is not the idiosyncrasies and complexities that make any two people different but the characteristics that they share when they are looked at from a particular perspective. What the classifier says, in effect, is that *for the purpose he has in mind* some people can be grouped with some other people because, despite their many differences, they are alike in terms of the single principle of classification he is applying.

Members of the black movement could be classified in a dozen different ways. In 1970 one observer identified three groups in sharp disagreement over aims and methods: traditional integrationists, symbolized by the late Martin Luther King, Jr., and Roy Wilkins of the NAACP; black nationalists, represented by Roy Innis of CORE and Ron Karenga of US; and Marxist-oriented revolutionaries like the Black Panthers. The grouping indicates that the principles of classification were applied successively, not simultaneously. The first principle—method—yielded two groups: passive protesters and activists. Then, on the basis of aim, the passive group was identified with integration and the activists with anti-integration; and the activists were subdivided into nationalists and revolutionaries. Note that in this analysis individuals are used illustratively: they are treated not for their own sake but to illuminate ideology. In another context there might be good reason to put Innis and Karenga in separate categories (classes); in this one they belong together.

The classifier's interest in the type rather than the individual often makes necessary some relaxation of the logician's rule that every member of the group must be included. A too-conscientious effort to make sure that a niche is found for every member may result in an extreme clutter in which the significant major groupings get lost among minor divisions and catchalls with labels like "borderline," "miscellaneous," and "other." For most purposes the rule can be modified to something like this: a classification should be as complete as the material allows and as the writer's purpose requires. In classifying a large, heterogeneous group of people, there is no necessity for pigeonholing every last individual. The essayist who states that there are four types of students or five types of statesmen or three types of black protesters is not saying that *every* student or statesman or protester fits comfortably into one of the groups. What he is saying is that four (or five or three) discernible classes can be differentiated in ways that are significant for the purpose he has in mind. If the classification is relatively inclusive, if each class is substantiated by enough details to make it a real one, and if the classes are adequately differentiated from each other, the reader will be satisfied.

EXERCISES

1. Classify a group of students you know well on the basis of their motives in attending college, the ways they spend their leisure time, their political views, their moral code, or some other principle. In developing your paper, use contrasts that will keep the groups distinct and descriptive details that will make them real.

2. Examine the following groupings. Explain why you think each grouping is or is not logically sound (or as sound as the material permits). If you find a grouping satisfactory, indicate the kind of essay in which it might be appropriately used. If you find a grouping unsatisfactory, propose a better one.

a. Student protesters: those who want to make things happen and those who want to stop things from happening

b. Crime-and-detection TV programs or movies: criminal-centered, police-centered, private-detective-centered

c. Cars: those that look good and those that give good service

d. Churchgoers: the devout, the psychologically insecure, the socialites

e. Political extremists: the ultraconservatives, the ultraliberals, the know-nothings

f. College students: loners and joiners

g. Courses of action: Red, dead, or heroic

Sometimes you will be interested not in setting up a comprehensive classification but in fitting your subject into a classification that already exists. When you want to make a judgment about a movie, you often start by placing it in its category — comedy, satire, melodrama, or whatever. Then you go on to make further distinctions by comparing it with other members of the same class. Sometimes you can draw some interesting conclusions about your subject by demonstrating that it doesn't fit into existing categories. In the passage below, the author reflects on the problem of classifying his subject and in the process finds it necessary to propose a new category, analogous to Britain's "landed civilized gentleman type":

It is difficult to appraise Fulbright justly because he does not fit the easy stereotypes of American politics. He is not a rebel, a dissenter, a crusader, or a fighting liberal. He is not a liberal at all. In Britain this young heir of Fayetteville, Arkansas's First Family would have been easily placed. There he would have been recognized at once as a well-educated young country squire of minor but inherited and ample wealth, with a taste not so much for politics as for public life. There he would naturally have joined the Conservative party, and soon found himself on its rebel wing among those who wanted a more thoughtful foreign policy. He would also have been allied with those Tories who have a feeling for social reform as long as it is neither too sweeping nor too hasty. This is the landed civilized gentleman type, not unknown even today in New England and the South but foreign to the American egalitarian tradition. We are willing to extend equal treatment in politics even to Rockefellers — after all they are only trying to make a bigger bang with a bigger buck — but the country gentleman is as alien to our tastes as hereditary monarchy. (We prefer *elected* Caesars.) In England Fulbright might conveniently be described as an American Anthony Eden. Here the average American would be puzzled by the comparison. None of us finds it easy to place J. William Fulbright in our rather rough-and-ready political categories — I. F. Stone, *New York Review of Books,* Dec. 29, 1966

Observers with a discriminating eye for new trends and new variations on old themes are constantly creating classifications or making fresh applications of existing ones. The category *black humor* offers an insight into one variety of the humor of the sixties. To classify jokes as clean or dirty is thoroughly conventional; Saul Bellow made a fresh application when he divided contemporary novelists into the Cleans and the Dirties. In the prewriting stage, when you are mulling over possible approaches to a subject, you can often generate good ideas by putting the subject into as many different classes as you can think of. So long as things are in the process of changing — and they always will be — there are endless opportunities for giving a fresh reading of experience and creating new classifications.

EXERCISES

1. Propose five different bases for classifying each of the following subjects:

notions of physical beauty humorists clothes
liberation movements   vegetables poems

Not every basis need be serious. Use your imagination. Once you have your five bases, state the classes each basis yields. Then choose one of the classifications and use it in an essay.

2. Write an essay explaining why, in classifying movies, you would or would not set up the Western as a category in its own right; or why, in classifying poems, you would or would not treat the limerick as a separate class; or why, in classifying novels, you would or would not include a class of epistolary novels—novels in which the story is told entirely through letters.

3. What does I. F. Stone mean by "the easy stereotypes" of American politics (p. 106)? What is the difference between stereotyping and the kind of inquiry that Stone makes as he tries to classify his subject? List several easy stereotypes of each of the following: college students, City Hall politicians, fatherhood, masculinity. Then write a brief paper about a person who does not fit the stereotypes for his general category. Sketch a new class—not a stereotype—that accounts for him.

DEFINITION

Whatever your subject, definitions provide the groundwork for your discussion by explaining unfamiliar terms or giving new meanings to familiar ones or indicating the precise sense in which a word is to be understood. These are incidental, though essential, uses of definition. In some essays, definition becomes central—the chief means of explaining a subject or persuading an audience to respond to it in a particular way. Many interesting questions about the counter-culture, for instance, or obscenity or alienation or psycholinguistics can be answered only by extended definition.

Clarifying Definitions

The need for brief clarifying definitions, usually no longer than a phrase or sentence, depends chiefly on the writer-reader relation. Technical terms and the special vocabulary of a subject are perhaps the most conspicuous barrier to communication between expert and layman, a problem touched on in pp. 20–21; but everyday terms often need defining too. Some words of wide currency — *rhetoric, liberal, dissent* — are used in so many different ways that it may be prudent to specify the meaning you intend. On some occasions you may need to distinguish between the popular and the scholarly sense of a term.

At the beginning of *The American Myth of Success*, Richard Weiss writes:

I do not use the word "myth" to imply something entirely false. Rather, I mean it to connote a complex of profoundly held attitudes and values which condition the way men view the world and understand their experience.

A definition like this one — a *stipulative* definition — establishes common ground for the discussion and so makes communication easier. (Communication is not made easier if the meaning stipulated is one never before given to a word. Nobody will pay much attention to a writer who in a serious discussion decides, like Humpty Dumpty in *Alice in Wonderland*, that *glory* is to mean "a nice knock-down argument.")

In other situations it takes some tact to know when you need to define. If you neglect to supply a definition when understanding is at stake, you will lose touch with your audience; if you keep pausing to define when there is no reason to, you may lose your audience altogether. Newspaper columnists and others who address heterogeneous audiences often use the device of speaking to both the informed and the uninformed at once:

Dave Henry is a Weatherman and, on the unlikely chance that you've never heard of the Weathermen, I should explain that most people look on them as the lunatic fringe of the protest movement. — Bob Bossin, *Maclean's*, March 1970

Phrasing a clarifying definition requires some tact, too. Don't confuse a general audience by defining a technical term in terms that are equally technical; don't insult a learned one by oversimplifying at the expense of precision and subtlety. So far as you can, harmonize the definition with its immediate context. Using zoological terminology to define *bush baby* is appropriate for a course paper in Zoology 101 but pretentious in a paper describing the attractions of the zoo.

Though occasionally you may want to introduce a key term with a little pomp and ceremony to make sure that the reader fixes his attention on it long enough to assimilate the meaning, usually the explanation can be slipped in casually and unobtrusively, without delaying the forward movement of the discussion. There are many ways of working a brief defining statement into a sentence:

If our universities were interested in education, which is to say in helping the young grow in self-awareness, it would follow that they would be deeply interested in teaching. — Martin Duberman, *New Republic*, June 22, 1968

From the start, book publishing has been a prime instance of what Max Weber called the Protestant ethic: to serve God by making money. — Stanley Kauffmann, *New Republic*, Nov. 5, 1966

Dr. King was a radical in the truest sense: he insisted at the same time upon the terrible reality of our problems and upon their solubility, and he rejected everything that was irrelevant to their solution. — *New Yorker*, April 13, 1968

By "Vietnamization" — substituting Vietnamese infantry for American infantry — the bulk of the American ground combat forces will be withdrawn. — Stewart Alsop, *Newsweek*, Sept. 15, 1969

Extended Definitions

Defining as a method of developing a subject includes, but goes beyond, defining that functions solely as an aid to clarity. The primary impetus for extended or comprehensive definition is not the need of the reader but the intention of the writer. He may find that the question he is raising about his subject can best be answered by explaining what a term means or by asserting what it ought to mean. Is electronic music really music? That depends on your definition of music. Is violence a legitimate form of dissent? That depends on your conception of both violence and dissent. Should universities take official positions on political issues? The question can scarcely be answered without defining the proper function of a university.

To answer questions like these, you will not simply report on how a term is used — though you may need to do that, too. You will engage in a searching examination of the *class* of events or objects designated by the term — music, violence, dissent, universities. (Definitions are concerned with classes, not with individuals. If a thing is unique, all you can do is describe it; you cannot define it.) Once you have isolated the distinctive characteristics, properties, qualities, or functions of the class, you will have a sound basis for answering the question you posed. (Arguments grounded in definition are discussed on pp. 131 – 34.)

EXERCISES

1. State the problem that each of these passages deals with:

a. Words, like trees, bend with the prevailing winds. In the climate of opinion of the past few years, the word dissent has undergone a decided transformation. For most of U.S. history, it clearly meant speech — the unorthodox opinion, the challenging idea. Then, during the 1960's, civil rights protesters took to the streets to fight segregation, and the word became associated with demonstrations as much as with speech. As protests have continued to broaden and increase, dissent has come to be used to describe and defend a wide variety of physical acts, including violence toward property and even toward people.

The explanation many protesters offer for their switch from verbal to physical dissent is that no one pays attention to words alone any longer. However eloquent it has been, however imaginative its uses, language has not succeeded in eliminating racial discrimination or ending the war in Indochina. So the protesters have resorted to what Social Psychologist Franklyn Haiman of Northwestern University calls "body rhetoric" — sit-ins, lie-ins, marches — and more and more bodies have started colliding. Such public confrontations are an expression of gathering frustration over a society that no longer seems to respond to more traditional forms of dissent. — *Time*, May 18, 1970

b. "Aggression" can mean different things to different people. In politics a "treaty of non-aggression" clearly refers to moral decision; it is optional, not "instinctive." But in the new pseudo-sciences aggression becomes a basic drive, the quintessential relationship between paired individuals. For psychoanalysts it is quite explicitly hydra-headed, embracing in the first instance both physical violence and sexual love and then extending, by sublimated derivation, into every imaginable variety of human interaction. [Anthony] Storr, for example, cites one analyst as saying that: "at origin, aggressiveness is almost synonymous with activity" and another for the view that "aggression springs from an innate tendency to grow and master life which seems to be characteristic of all living matter. Only when this life-force is obstructed in its development do ingredients of anger, hate, or rage become connected with it." Ethnologists say much the same thing in their own special language: the outcome of evolution is that each individual animal is endowed with an innate tendency to act aggressively against its neighbors, whatever their species, in order to preserve its living space. This drive is not self-destructive because the sequence of stimulus and response that would ordinarily lead to violence can be modified by superimposed mechanisms ("ritualization") which allows for courtship and friendliness. — Edmund Leach, *New York Review of Books*, Oct. 10, 1968

2. If a term means one thing to a politician and another to a psychoanalyst and if a term means something different in 1970 from what it meant in 1960, is it ever possible to pin down one fixed, unchanging meaning of a term?

3. Are the passages concerned with defining words or with defining classes of events or objects? Or both? Lexical or "dictionary" definitions describe how a word is generally used — what a word means or expresses. (Dictionary definitions are discussed on pp. 350–53.) "Real" definitions describe the essential nature of a class of things — what the class is. Why is it important for a writer to make clear which kind of definition he intends?

When you write an extended definition, you usually want to make several different approaches to your subject. There are many ways of defining. Each can give you a purchase on your subject, some a more secure purchase than others.

Etymology. One method is to trace the word back to an earlier form and perhaps show the changes it has undergone. Etymologies do not, as some people think, get us any closer to the "real" meaning of a word, and they are of very uneven value in developing extended definitions. To point out that the word *car* goes back to the Latin *carrus*, a word of Celtic origin that meant a four-wheeled wagon, hardly provides a promising start for a definition of the class of objects we call cars. But etymologies do have some force in some rhetorical situations. A good many persuasive accounts of current problems have begun by reminding readers that the word *radical* comes from the Latin *radix*, meaning "root." And the etymologies of *charisma* and *integration* have provided imaginative ways of opening up those subjects. When you are analyzing something new, it may be helpful — if only to clear up mysteries—to explain the origin of the label it goes by. The article cited on p. 108 went on to note that the name "Weathermen" comes from Bob Dylan's line, "You don't need a weatherman to know which way the wind blows." While this fact does not go far in explaining the Weathermen group, it could provide a starting point for an analysis.

Synonyms.   Synonyms are more generally useful than etymologies as a means of defining. Though no two words mean exactly the same thing, several words may mean roughly the same thing; and the value of synonyms is in indicating the general area of meaning. To define *perfidy* by *treachery* or *disloyalty* or *faithlessness* helps launch a writer into full definition, for it creates a context in which further distinctions can be made.

Examples.   In making such distinctions, examples are useful—illustrations that bring out the differences between a perfidious and a disloyal act, say. To cite a single example or to equate an instance (having breakfast in bed on Sunday morning) with the word that is being defined (*contentment*) does not constitute complete definition but often stimulates the imagination and can be effective in relaxed writing situations. Generalized examples are perfectly adequate in defining some terms, as in " 'body rhetoric'—sit-ins, lie-ins, marches." But as a rule specific examples offer a better path to definition: a detailed examination of one member of a school of poetry (Wordsworth) can contribute a good deal to a definition of the school (Romanticism).

When the class is generally well understood, examples—including hypothetical examples—can do the entire work of defining:

To me, there are two kinds of liberals: the type of fellow who would take his coat off in a snowstorm and put it around my shoulders, and the type of fellow who would caution me to wear a coat against the snow. And I prefer the latter to the former simply because he is real and may be genuinely concerned over my keeping warm, whereas the former is concerned with suffering from the cold himself for my benefit.—James Alan McPherson, *Atlantic*, April 1970

Connotation.   Sometimes you define to extend the range of associations a word has—its connotative meaning—as a way of ensuring that your audience will share your emotional response to the subject. *America* is scarcely ever defined except in terms of connotations. Or you may want to expose and reject the connotations of a word as a preliminary to setting forth its denotation. (Connotation and denotation are discussed on pp. 357–59.)

Genus and Differentiae. The traditional way of establishing the denotative meaning—of pointing to the objects or events named by a term—is first to specify the genus or set to which the class designated by the term belongs and then to differentiate it from other classes in the set. "A ballad is a song that tells a story" puts the class of ballads into the larger class or genus (song) and then selects the quality (storytelling) that differentiates it from other songs. You can see the same pattern in "Dialectic is a method of investigation whose object is the establishment of truth about doubtful propositions" (Richard M. Weaver, *The Ethics of Rhetoric*). For some terms, one differentiating characteristic is sufficient; for others, several may be required to isolate the precise combination of qualities that characterizes the class.

EXERCISE

Compose a one-sentence genus+differentia(e) definition for each of the following terms: *history, rage, power, salt, skunk cabbage, weed.* Test your definitions against the following traditional requirements for definitions built on the pattern of genus+differentia(e):

a. The definition must be neither too broad nor too narrow. In "A bachelor is an unmarried person," the genus *person* is too broad; it should be limited to *man.* In "A shoe is a leather covering for the human foot," the definition is too narrow; the differentia *leather* excludes shoes made of other materials.

b. Unless privation or negation is the distinguishing characteristic (as in bachelor, *not* married; orphan, *without* parents), the definition should be positive, not negative. "Liberty is the state of not being restrained" violates this rule.

c. The definition should not be circular, as in "A linguist is one who specializes in linguistics." This rule frowns on some dictionary definitions.

d. The definition should not be expressed in figurative language. This rule excludes Karl Marx's metaphor, "Religion is the opiate of the people."

Framing sound definitions on the genus+differentiae pattern gives excellent training in precise, literal statement, for much discriminating thought has to go into the selection of both genus and differentiae. (Which is the most real or the most useful of the many different genuses available? Which of the many qualities that characterize any class of things really mark the class and not just individual members of it?) A genus+differentiae definition is often at the heart of an extended definition, with the genus and each of the differentiae being discussed in detail. But for some purposes the pattern seems too confining or smacks too much of textbook-encyclopedia style. At any rate, not all our definitions require the rigor of formal logic. A metaphorical definition can give fresh insight or can powerfully shape an attitude. And negative definitions have their uses, too.

Negation.   When you are aiming for compact statement, you will certainly want to concentrate on telling what your class *is*, but in discursive discussion much can be gained from telling what it is *not*, as well. In the following passage, the concept of protest gains clarity from being contrasted with revolution.

How does protest differ from revolution? The word "revolution" is often used for any radical change in an aspect of government or society, but in its strict and more correct historical usage revolution is the great exception, whereas protest is the norm. Protest is an attack on the prevailing system in an intellectual or organized way. Revolution is a sickness in society, a breakdown of the social order, the kind of general demoralization and civil war that the ancient Greek philosophers called *stasis*. Protest uses violence, but it is strictly controlled and specific in its purposes—the seizure of a building, a riot, a political assassination—designed to shock and bewilder the elite and to advertise a grievance. Revolution is unchecked violence in which social groups war against one another for dominance, although violence usually becomes an end in itself and the groups often lose sight of their original purposes.

Revolution occurs only when an old regime defends itself against protest by becoming more reactionary and oppressive but, once having radicalized the middle class and stirred the workers and the poor to involvement, is too inefficient or guilt-ridden to carry out the necessary slaughter and imprisonment of protesters. The political and legal system then splinters, and uncontrolled violence takes over. Finally, some army or police leader takes advantage of middle-class fear of extermination and working-class hunger and establishes a new tyranny. Protest in the twentieth-century has led to social change and, more often than not, to social melioration; revolution has been the road to chaos, civil war, and new tyranny.
—Norman F. Cantor, *The Age of Protest*

To gain a hearing, you may need to take up current misconceptions, sweeping away fuzzy or wrong notions before offering more accurate ones. Or you may begin with a single explicit negative like "A composition text is not a book of etiquette" or "Loyalty is not conformity." Defining by negation can be a risky technique — you may become so wound up in telling what the subject is *not* that you never get around to telling what it is — but the method is justifiable when you have to dislodge connotations that your audience stubbornly clings to — for example, *youth* equals *irresponsibility*. In such a situation, no one who is committed to his thesis can afford to sidestep either the job of attacking the entrenched definition or the obligation to create a more accurate one.

The Center of the Definition

Even when you do not need to get rid of misconceptions or false notions, negating is inherent in the thinking process by which you arrive at a positive definition. To define is to limit and to exclude — to narrow down to the characteristics or properties that set the class off from other classes. This is the process that brings you to the real center of your essay in definition. One helpful means of finding that center has already been suggested and illustrated in the discussion of the formal, genus+differentiae definition. Weaknesses in definition essays often stem from failure to give serious thought to the class the thing belongs to and to the characteristics that differentiate it from other members of the class. "A campus radical is a long-haired student who should have left school and had a haircut years ago" is a trivial definition, for it does not concern itself with central identifying characteristics.

Naturally, the elements that are central to any particular definition depend on what is being defined. They may relate to the origin of the subject or its history or what it is made of or what it looks like or what it is used for or what effects it produces. A physical object like a lathe will be defined in different ways from a concept like patriotism, and a concept will be defined in different ways from a school of economic thought. Hence there are *genetic* definitions, which give the origin of a thing; *analytic* definitions, which detail the parts that it is made of; *constructive* definitions, which tell how it is made. *Enumerative* definitions list all the members of a class (the Big Three), and *ostensive* definitions list representative members (Wordsworth and Coleridge as representative of the Romantic poets). You can define by function or by typical behavior. What the central elements in your definition are will also depend on where your interest in your subject lies. "Man is a talking animal" is a good definition for some purposes; "Man is a laughing animal" is a good one for others. Will you define creativity primarily as a process or as the outcome of a process?

Once you have decided on the center of your definition, you will find yourself drawing on the other methods of development. These summaries of what some students have done in writing definition essays suggest a range of possibilities:

The center of a paper defining a stapler was a statement of its use. From there the student went on to tell what a stapler looks like, what its parts are, what materials it is made of, and how it operates. The essay was developed mainly by division and objective description.

A definition of Cubism first placed the movement in time, giving a narrative account of how and why it arose, explaining the theory on which it was based, and showing how it differed from other contemporary philosophies of art. By using examples of major Cubist artists and describing some of their chief works, the student arrived at the characteristics of form, color, and handling of subject that make a painting representative of Cubism.

A definition of brainwashing centered on the purpose, contrasted the methods and effects of brainwashing with those used in psychiatric treatment, and drew examples and details from a factual study of American captives in the Korean War and the novels *1984* and *The Manchurian Candidate*.

An essay on electronic music compared it with traditional music in terms of method of production, role of composer, range of sounds used, and kind of appeal. It reviewed various definitions of music in order to see whether they would admit electronically produced sounds as a legitimate class. Finally, it proposed a definition of music broad enough to include electronic music.

These summaries are not intended to represent the only ways of developing definitions or the best ways; in each case you should be able to think of other good approaches. They simply suggest the great variety of resources at hand when you set about the task of defining—not only etymologies, synonyms, examples, and connotative and denotative meanings but also description, narration, comparison and contrast, classification, division, analysis of causes and effects. Choosing wisely among these techniques of defining will help you make clear the properties or characteristics of your subject— those distinctive features that set it off from everything else. And this is the purpose of definition.

EXERCISES

1. Choose a term from current slang, illustrate its use, and offer some reasons for its popularity.

2. Explain the meaning of sin, pain, tolerance, courage, or prejudice — or any other concept that appears to have different meanings for different people.

3. Define a political *ism* like conservatism or liberalism or radicalism.

4. Through examples and personal anecdotes, show how a term like *love* or *fear* has come to have a new meaning for you.

5. Write a paper on some group you are familiar with, one which can be identified by its habitual activities; its moral or social standards; its dress, language, or ceremonies. Make clear through concrete details the distinguishing traits of the group, its typical behavior, and the shared attitudes that give it unity and explain its actions. Your audience is a class in sociology.

6. Compare the meanings given the term *rhetoric* (or *rhetorical*) in the passages below. Which uses are favorable? Which neutral? Which pejorative, or unfavorable?

a. There are extremes of exaggeration here that I must suppose to be rhetorical if I am to avoid attributing an implausible degree of ignorance to those of my interlocutors who indulge in them. — Louis J. Halle, *New Republic*, Nov. 23, 1968

b. When the action is hot, keep the rhetoric cool. — President Richard M. Nixon in a television address, May 1970

c. The reformers would save the university by stimulating needed changes both in administration and curriculum, but their rhetoric is often so strident and their actions so violent that it is difficult to distinguish them from the revolutionaries who believe that society's institutions must be destroyed before they can be reshaped to serve humanity's ends. — James Cass, *Saturday Review*, June 21, 1969

d. But to those devoted to other concepts of science, Erikson often seems inexact, elusive, rhetorical, and even mystical. — Kenneth Keniston, *Science*, July 19, 1968

e. Rhetoric, therefore, is the method, the strategy, the organon of the principles for deciding best the undecidable questions, for arriving at solutions of the unsolvable problems, for instituting method in those vital phases of human activity where no method is inherent in the total subject-matter of decision. — Donald C. Bryant, *Quarterly Journal of Speech*, Dec. 1953

f.   ". . . do you think back on the fight?"

"Not as much as I thought I would," Ali answered. "Fighting is more of a business now than the glory of who won. After all, when all the praise is over," and he shifted into the low singsong voice that he uses for rhetoric and poetry, "when all the fanfare is done, all that counts is what you have to show for. All the bleeding; the world still turns." — George Plimpton, *Sports Illustrated*, April 5, 1971

g.   The problems of focusing human energies in common endeavors are not solved by mere analysis, mere dialectic: "Reason by itself moves nothing." The communicated vision that moves, moves not only or even essentially in the physical sense but by engaging the interests, the emotions, and the basic aspirations of men. It is characteristic of Churchill's rhetoric, perhaps especially in his later years, to strike those deep chords which can serve to bind men together in broader communities than those generated by the shared interests of classes, parties, and even nations. In large part this quality derived from his ability to communicate his own sense of the grandeur of the human struggle, the greatness of the deeds of which men are capable, the size of the roles which an individual, a nation, or a generation may play in the history of man's fate. Is not the persuasive communication of such a possibility itself the realization of it? — Charles Wegener, *Ethics*, Jan. 1967

h.   Rhetoric, we argued, is concerned primarily with a creative process that includes all the choices a writer makes from his earliest tentative explorations of a problem in what has been called the "prewriting" stage of the writing process, through choices in arrangement and strategy for a particular audience, to the final editing of the final draft. — Richard E. Young, Alton L. Becker, and Kenneth Pike, *Rhetoric: Discovery and Change*

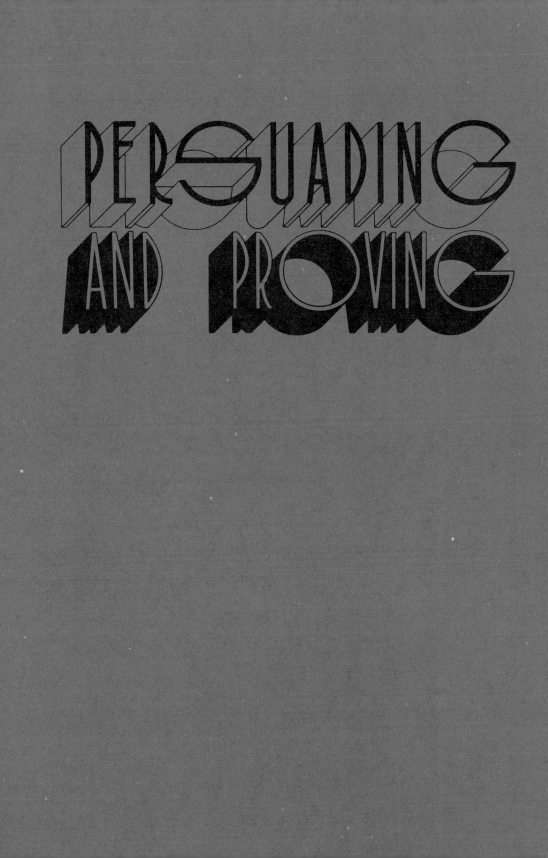

PERSUADING AND PROVING

Chapter Six

PERSUASION

In the broad sense, any piece of writing that makes the reader see what the writer wants him to see may be called persuasive. In a narrower sense — the sense used in this book — *persuasion* refers to prose in which the writer sets out to influence the convictions or attitudes or actions of his audience. A persuasive essay has a thesis that is sure to arouse differences of opinion among reasonable men. There is virtually no difference of opinion in many situations that elicit both diatribes and eulogies. Political speakers at $100-a-plate dinners for the party regulars ordinarily engage in ritual, not persuasion, for those they are exhorting are already persuaded. Persuasion occurs when the speaker (or writer) tries to win over an audience from a position of either neutrality or opposition.

Persuasion has a range of purposes and a range of means. Most openly designed to persuade are speeches and essays and advertisements that call for out-and-out action — voting for a candidate, changing a policy, buying a product. But though the contexts of politics and advertising have accustomed us to think of action as the desired outcome of persuasion, many sharply argumentative essays ask something different of us — intellectual conviction, perhaps, or moral assent, or judgment, favorable or unfavorable, about the issue under debate. And in attempting to influence our attitudes or shape our values, writers make their appeals with varying degrees of force and explicitness: both the hard sell and the subtle techniques of advertising have their counterparts in arguments on all kinds of subjects. An interpretation of a poem may be totally analytical, severely objective, and consistently impersonal in presentation; yet its ultimate purpose is to convince the reader that what is offered is not just plausible but more plausible than any competing interpretation. Though the ends in view are different—action in the one case, intellectual assent in the other—both the campaign speech and the essay in literary analysis attempt to influence the audience. Both are exercises in persuasion.

In some rhetorical situations conviction alone is rightly the goal. In others the proper goal is a two-stage response—conviction followed by action. For a variety of reasons, this two-stage response may be short-circuited to *either* conviction *or* action (assuming, of course, that the audience responds at all). That is, the audience may be convinced in the sense of agreeing with the argument advanced yet may feel no impulse to act. (Possibly the speaker has not succeeded in making the action seem necessary; possibly the audience does not have the courage to act on its convictions.) Or members of the audience may be persuaded to take action before they have taken thought—before they have any sound reason for acting. Some men set out to deceive; they knowingly manipulate their audiences for purely selfish ends, aiming straight for action and bypassing the stage of convincing the audience. And some audiences are compliant because they are naive or intellectually lazy or corrupt.

What this means is that persuasion can be used for dishonest as well as for honest ends. Good arguments may fail in their immediate purposes, and bad ones may succeed. We should not, however, regard persuasion with fear or hostility or cynicism simply because it can be turned to bad uses or because, in certain cases, honest persuasion does not work. Few of us are consistently reasonable, temperate, unprejudiced, and emotionally balanced. We are not always persuasive in the right way nor open to the right kind of persuasion. But since our personal happiness, as well as our political survival, depends to a very great extent on persuasion, we must learn to reckon with it and to use it well.

Part of the responsibility of using persuasion fairly and reacting to it intelligently is being alert to *fallacies*—factual errors, mistakes in reasoning, unsound judgments. Familiarity with the fallacies does not give a writer the resources he needs to build a convincing positive argument, and in any case their random, miscellaneous character makes undertaking a systematic study of them scarcely feasible. Still, some acquaintance with them is useful. For one thing, skill in detecting fallacies keeps the reader-writer from being taken in by a clever deceptive argument; and that is all to the good. For another, probing an argument for soft spots and identifying the fallacies is a necessary first step in refuting or attacking it. Finally, knowledge of the common fallacies guides a conscientious writer in checking his own work for inadvertent errors or lapses in logical sequences. In this chapter and the next the treatment of the fallacies is geared mainly to these practical ends.

THE MEANS OF PERSUASION

Whenever a writer asks anything of his reader—assent or belief or action—he is within the province of rhetoric. Rhetoric in Aristotle's definition is the art of discovering the available means of persuasion with respect to any subject whatever. *Means* → The means of persuasion are three—the way the material is organized, the style of the discourse, and the nature of the arguments advanced. This chapter and the next will give primary attention to the arguments themselves—both tangible proofs (arguments for and against propositions) and other appeals which, though less tangible, nevertheless exert a potent influence on the audience.

A word first on the term *argument*. Aside from its everyday meaning of "disagreement" or "dispute," *argument* is used in various ways. Sometimes it refers to the entire speech or essay that is designed to induce conviction in an audience. Or it refers to the line of thinking, the string of key propositions that runs through a piece: we speak of "the argument" of a book or an essay or a poem. It is also regularly used to designate a reason for believing what might otherwise seem doubtful; in this sense "an argument" can be a very small part of an essay, perhaps just a sentence. Thus in presenting his argument (first sense) to Congress, a legislator may use as his argument (second sense) the thesis that wiretapping should be discontinued, and he may offer as one of his arguments (third sense) the view that wiretapping is an illegal invasion of privacy.

Arguments in the sense of reasons for holding a position may be of many different kinds. It is customary to make a basic distinction between *logical* proofs, addressed to the intellect, and *emotional* appeals, addressed to the passions. Logical appeals, it is said, convince; emotional appeals get action. Though the distinction has some value, it oversimplifies the psychology of persuasion; and if it implies that the two types of appeals are opposed or that emotional appeals are inherently inferior, it is unacceptable. In most of the world's great arguments, appeals of both kinds work cooperatively, reinforcing each other. Neither type of appeal is immune from misuse. In bad arguments as well as in good ones, the logic can be impeccable; deliberate appeals to the emotions are made in good arguments as well as in bad ones. To avoid misinterpretation, it is better to label some appeals *logical* and others *nonlogical* or *alogical*—not illogical but simply outside the province of logic. (The term *illogical* refers primarily to mistakes in reasoning.)

Before we examine types of arguments in more detail, we need to look briefly at the context in which persuasion operates. We have convictions, beliefs, solutions to problems. How do we go about persuading others to assent to our views, to share our beliefs, to act in ways we think right? We need first to remind ourselves that an argument is made by a particular person to a particular audience at a particular place and time. Admittedly, some arguments (in philosophy, for instance) seem to be addressed to mankind through the ages, but as a rule even the least topical argument assumes a certain psychological, political, social, or moral context as well as readers of certain habits and attitudes. It exhibits, in short, adaptation *by* a writer *to* an audience *of* an argument on a specific subject. The whole art of persuading consists in discovering and maintaining the right balance among these three elements—the rhetorical balance or, as Wayne Booth has called it, the rhetorical stance.

The "I" of Argument

"Who am I," you need to ask yourself, "in *this* particular rhetorical situation? How do I want to appear to my audience?" You are always yourself, of course; but a self is made up of many selves, and in any particular writing situation one of them dominates. That's natural. After all, the way you think about, talk about, and argue about love is different from the way you think about, talk about, and argue about politics. And (leaving aside love) you shape your argument on a political issue one way when you're talking to a neutral but receptive listener, another when you're having a dispute with a heels-dug-in dogmatist. To be persuasive in both situations requires a good deal of flexibility.

Flexibility doesn't mean fakery. If you try to assume a pose that is totally alien to you, the strain will probably make itself felt. A professional writer can sometimes successfully wear the mask of bland, humble inquiry when he is actually in a rage. Worn by someone less experienced, the mask usually slips, and the deception publishes itself. Nothing so quickly destroys a sympathetic relation with the reader as evidence of insincerity.

Then why not sidestep this problem of the "I"? Wouldn't it be smart to conceal yourself altogether, to cancel yourself out of the writer-reader-subject equation? No. For in situations that require judgment, the qualifications of the person who is judging constitute the most powerful of the alogical arguments in favor of that judgment. Intrinsically, the worth of an idea has nothing to do with the character of the person advancing it; but in areas where differences of opinion exist among men of good will, it *is* a matter of importance for the audience to have confidence in the speaker. Indeed, it has such weight that some students of rhetoric (following Aristotle) give a separate label to this dimension of the rhetorical situation: they use the term *ethical proof* (from *ethos*) for all those appeals that relate directly to the character and authority of the speaker. If you are inclined to accept a thesis solely or principally because it has been urged on you by someone you admire, then you are being persuaded by ethical proof. (In the Aristotelian system, appeals to the emotions of the audience are called *pathetic proofs* and arguments on the issue itself are called *logical proofs*.)

The ethical dimension in argument is inescapable. Because your own presence in the discussion is necessarily one main argument for your case, you should try to make that argument a strong one. By creating a favorable impression, you make the audience want to identify with you, and identification paves the way for assent. In general, what wins confidence is a discussion conducted with intellectual vigor by a person who evidently knows his subject, has a good grasp of the issue under debate, is fair in examining alternatives, but at the same time shows a strong commitment to the solution he is convinced is right. Intelligence, good sense, and integrity are the primary virtues in any rhetorical situation. Beyond that, different circumstances call for different strategies. In one situation crisp, incisive, confident argument seems right; in another, a tentative searching out of the truth works better. Some situations require zealous advocacy of a cause; in others, the audience may be more responsive to cool, detached counsel.

On the face of it, adapting an argument to the reader might seem to mean that you start by telling him what he wants to hear. At times it does; at other times it means telling him at the outset what he *doesn't* want to hear. Tough talk sometimes succeeds where sweet talk does not. The reader may be moved to grudging admiration for the writer who is not afraid to assert an unpopular principle boldly. Grudging admiration may make him receptive to arguments on the issue itself. But if you do come out swinging, in the course of the argument you must find ways to bring yourself and your reader around to the same side. The prickly individualist may command respect but win few converts.

In recent times some speakers have sought a reversal of roles; refusing to accommodate themselves to their audiences, they have relied on shrieks and sneers, threats and insults — one aspect of what Edward P. J. Corbett calls "the rhetoric of the closed fist" — and have expected audiences to do the accommodating. And, perhaps because of feelings of guilt, some members of some audiences have. But other listeners who were originally sympathetic have responded to abuse with resentment; and it seems doubtful that those who were neutral or hostile to begin with have been won over by invective and intimidation. Emotional blackmail or other forms of coercion may affect an audience temporarily. Lasting conviction results from reasoned argument.

You should be able to make your presence felt rhetorically without either abusing your audience or harping on your own tastes, feelings, and attitudes and relating all your arguments to your own ego. Glib assumption of authority is potentially irritating; you need to earn the respect and trust of your audience. The "I" dimension of persuading is one more of the rhetorical matters that call for just the right balance between too much and too little.

The "You" of Argument

The more sharply you can characterize your readers, the more likely you are to speak directly to them. (A presidential address to the nation sometimes misses everybody.) In accommodating your argument, you need to take into account the general state of their knowledge as well as their grasp of the particular issue. Are they, on the whole, naive or sophisticated? Are they, compared with you, novices or experts? What basic attitudes, values, and prejudices can you expect of them? What is their probable initial response to your thesis —hostile, critical, skeptical, open-minded, tolerant, sympathetic? Is there apathy to be overcome, tension to be relieved, fear to be allayed?

If you can accurately assess your readers' acquaintance with the issue, you will know how much background information is needed, how much specialized or technical data is called for, and, perhaps, how the issue can be related to other issues in which your readers have a stake. If you know what your readers' values and prejudices are, you will be less likely to insult them inadvertently. Insolence sometimes works (witty insolence, that is); but in general it is prudent to show respect for entrenched positions and basic prejudices even as you are urging the need for change and the need for taking an *un*prejudiced stand on the particular issue. There are times when you will have to appeal directly to self-interest (as in persuading purchasers to pay an extra 30 percent for optional safety equipment on a new car); there are other times when you will need to urge an audience to rise above self-interest (as in persuading the elderly and childless to vote for higher taxes to improve schools). In either case it is necessary to know what *they* construe to be to their own advantage.

Direct appeals to the audience usually entail alogical proofs. It goes without saying that these should support the rational appeals, not supplant them. Don't substitute emotion for reason when the proposition requires logical proof. On the other hand, when circumstances call for action as well as for intellectual conviction, don't hesitate to supplement logical proof with honest appeals to your readers' hopes and fears, their sense of what is right and just, their sentiments of love and pity. Visceral responses are bad if they block out rational ones, but rational responses alone, and rational commitment alone, may stop short of any action. In some situations moral exhortation has its place; readers may need to be told not only that they *can* embark on a certain course of action but that they *should* embark on it.

Your sense of your audience's mood and convictions will help you decide how much space you should give to refutation—to attacking opposing views. Other men of good will, remember, have lined up in support of the counter-proposition. If they have made a strong case for it, you will need to give that case your serious attention. Whether you want to make refutation a major part of your paper or an incidental one will depend, in part, on how much your audience has been swayed by the views of the opposition. Anticipating and dealing with objections your audience is likely to raise is an excellent rhetorical technique. (Refutation is discussed on pp. 173–77.)

Taking into account the special characteristics of your audience will help you hone the edge of your positive argument. Every appeal for funds to support the university library gives primary attention to the library's need; but an appeal to one alumnus may emphasize school pride, and an appeal to another may stress the financial advantage of a tax write-off. Both appeals are legitimate attempts to accommodate an argument to a particular audience.

The Limits of Accommodation

Though we have temporarily separated the "I" and the "you" of the rhetorical situation from the substance of the argument, accommodation is by no means a separate dimension to be superimposed on an existing full-fledged argument. It involves the content of the argument itself—the use of evidence, the choice of logical and alogical appeals, and the explicitness with which those appeals are made. It affects the order in which the separate arguments are set forth and the weight and emphasis given them. It determines many features of the style.

If accommodation is not just adornment, neither is it the con man's bag of tricks. Accommodation is a necessary dimension of argument. The need for it begins as soon as you undertake to argue at all. What is the distance, you ask yourself, between the views your readers hold and the views you want them to hold? If it is great, how can you go about reducing it so that you will get a fair hearing? Finding common ground, however limited, is a necessary first step in persuading.

Finding common ground does not mean that you should

start by buttering up your readers—flattering them, cajoling them, feigning a comradeship that doesn't exist, or telling a round of jokes just to get them in a good mood. A joke may be the way in, particularly when there is something special in the relationship between you and your audience; but the technique of the after-dinner speaker rarely succeeds in print. Nor does accommodation mean putting your virtues on display in an effort to persuade your audience to accept your position just because you're you—good fellow that you are. Everyone is familiar with such transparent attempts to curry favor, to subordinate issues to personalities, to win friends *to* influence people. The devices are used, and sometimes they work. But they do not represent accommodation at its best.

Accommodation in a deeper sense means finding ways to bring your readers to feel the force of the reasons that have led you to believe in your thesis. In persuading, you are not selling a piece of merchandise that can be returned tomorrow through the "complaints" department; you are contributing to the responsible discussion of ideas that educated people are expected to engage in. Probably the best protection against the shoddier devices of accommodation is to remind yourself that whether you "win" the argument or not, you are trying to lead your audience to see the truth as you see it. The right procedure is to find good reasons for supporting the position you have taken and then to use all the resources of *responsible* communication to persuade your reader to assent to it.

The criterion of responsible communication put limits both on what you say and how you say it. In accommodating your argument to your audience, don't compromise either your best self or your best arguments. Spellbinding aside, we give our serious attention to the speaker or writer who, as we say, knows his subject (meaning that he knows more about it than we do) and who gives cogent reasons for the position he is taking. That position may be the minority one; his views may be extremely unpopular. But we listen to him if we have the impression that he is testifying to the truth as he sees it. In honest persuasion, the speaker adjusts neither his thesis nor his evidence to his notion of what his audience wants to hear. He arrives at his thesis on the basis of a detached, impersonal examination of the evidence and what can justifiably be inferred from it. Though he adapts his arguments to a particular audience, he does not alter his basic beliefs. He does not speak in support of wiretapping to an audience favorably disposed to the practice and then speak against it when he knows his audience is highly critical of it. Accommodate your argument to the audience, yes; but don't accommodate it out of existence.

EXERCISES

1. Though the same basic material can often be channeled into either explanation or argument, a persuasive essay is not just an exploration of the topic. It affirms something about the topic; it sets forth and supports a proposition. Your essay on a college club may be simple explanation, designed to show how the organizational structure or activities relate to the club's purpose. Or the essay may be shaped into an argument that because the club performs valuable functions, it deserves to be subsidized by the college administration (*or* that because of certain activities, it should be censured, *or* that because its membership rules are discriminatory, it should be disbanded). In selecting a topic for a persuasive paper, the primary requirement is that you see an *issue* in it—something you regard as desirable or undesirable, beneficial or harmful, wise or unwise. The best topic is one about which you have not only adequate information but convictions and beliefs that you want to express.

From the subject areas of education, politics, social reform, art, popular culture, draw up a list of propositions that you are prepared to support—for example, that students should have a voice in promoting and firing faculty members, that voting rights should be restricted to property owners, that adults should be made legally responsible for the welfare of their aged parents, that transistor radios should be banned from public transportation, parks, and beaches. (The propositions can be much more specific—that the management of the cafeteria or the bookstore should be replaced, that Instructor X was treated unjustly because of her sex.) Settle on one that your instructor approves. Write two essays (about eight hundred words each) on the same topic, one addressed to a neutral audience, one to an audience that is at least mildly opposed to the action you propose or the judgment you make.

2. What is the thesis of the passage below? What arguments are used in support of the thesis? Do you regard these appeals as logical or as alogical? Why? What can you infer about the writer's conception of his audience?

I hope that the cynicism that pervades so much of modern life has not yet grown to exclude the demands of common morality. The black man was brought to these shores in chains, enslaved for 250 years, kept in peonage for most of the past hundred years, and now suffers disproportionately in all areas of life. Common decency demands that this situation be changed. The growing anger of the black masses, especially among the younger people who see through the hypocrisy of this society, will not lessen unless such a national commitment is swiftly implemented. Countering such protest with increased repression can only fan the flames of anger and eventually lead to the kind of police-state that will enslave all Americans.

Those in this morally underdeveloped nation who do not readily respond to the demands of conscience may be more responsive to self-interest. The black minority, disproportionately disadvantaged as it is, constitutes a huge market that cannot be ignored. Negroes earn about $30-billion, form up to 50 per cent of the total consumer market for certain goods, and will be in the majority in about a dozen major cities well before 1980. Economic equality would mean enlarging this market by about $25-billion, and it would also mean the creation of a stable urban middle class.

Our economy can ignore this huge market and the implications of equality only at its peril. The question really becomes: Does a society dominated by white-run institutions have any kind of future in a world that is three-fourths non-white? And can a business-oriented society survive when its major centers of power and commerce are populated by poverty-stricken, angry black majorities? — Whitney M. Young, Jr., *Saturday Review*, Aug. 23, 1969

THE SUBSTANCE OF ARGUMENT

The two essential elements in a persuasive essay are the *thesis* and the *proof*. The thesis, or the central proposition, is the belief or conviction or recommendation for action that represents your stand on the issue. The proof is the evidence you offer in support of it. Thesis and proof make up the *what* and the *why* of argument.

Proof in persuasive papers is not the same as scientific demonstration. If we could settle a disputed point with absolute certainty, presumably one demonstration would be sufficient to end debate. But the things we argue about from week to week and from generation to generation are precisely those that are *not* subject to indisputable demonstration. When sensible men of good will honestly disagree about whether a course of action is just or a work of art good, it is because the evidence brought to bear on issues like these can never be conclusive and irrefutable.

Absolute proof may be hard to come by in factual matters as well as in questions of judgment. Even when the facts are available, they may be open to interpretation. When the evidence itself is inaccessible or irrecoverable, proof as ordinarily understood is unattainable. But we can still talk in terms of proof, as this passage illustrates and demonstrates:

It is sometimes asserted that speech cannot be "proved" to be older than writing. But this is true only if the term "proof" is made to bear a far greater load than we generally require it to bear in questions of historical fact. We know of no system of writing with a history of more than some six or seven thousand years. On the other hand, there is no group of people known to exist or to have existed without the capacity of speech; and many hundreds of languages have never been associated with a writing-system until they were committed to writing by missionaries or linguists in our own day. It seems reasonable to suppose therefore that speech goes back to the origins of human society. —John Lyons, *Introduction to Theoretical Linguistics*

As Lyons implies, proof is best defined as what any *reasonable* man would feel obliged to accept as evidence in support of the thesis.

From the point of view of the writer, proving means giving reasons for holding a belief or advocating a policy—reasons of sufficient force, he hopes, to lead his audience to share his belief or agree that the policy is wise. Discovering proof is a dynamic—even a strenuous—activity. You don't stumble upon arguments ready-made. You need to hunt for compelling reasons, to search out promising lines of argument, to construct logical chains of reasoning. The finding and creating of arguments is treated in classical rhetorics under the concept of *invention*, a procedure for engaging in a systematic search for arguments instead of relying on inspiration alone.

Where do you find your arguments? Some are firsthand observations of incidents or situations or characteristics; some are reflections about relationships and inferences from data; and some stem from the investigations or observations or judgments of other people. A writer who is "looking for an argument" finds his reasons both in the subject itself—the internal sources of argument—and in external sources, those that lie outside the subject.

Internal Sources of Argument

A lively issue will yield any number of particular arguments. You can put yourself on the track of generating some of them by studying the nature of what you are arguing about, by investigating its causes and effects, and by finding out what it is like and unlike. In other words, you can raise questions of *being, cause,* and *relation.* Carefully thought-out answers to these fundamental questions will suggest fruitful premises or starting points for individual arguments. To see how, we will refer again to some of the methods of developing ideas discussed in Chapters Three, Four, and Five. Definition, example, classification, division, causal analysis, and

Persuasion will not work if "I" or "you" is unreasonable.

comparison can all be given an argumentative thrust that shapes them into support for a belief or a proposal.

← Generally Accepted Truths and Assumptions

2. **Argument from the Nature of the Thing.** If you take the position that college students should have certain privileges and if you offer as a reason the assertions that college students are mature and that mature people should be granted these privileges, you are drawing your argument from the nature of the thing—the subject—here, the nature of college students. A vital part of the argument is the case you make for putting students into the class of mature people. (Naturally, asserting their maturity is not enough; you need to give evidence about their habits, activities, and so on. For the moment we are not concerned with the details of the proof but only with the general lines of the argument.)

Making a similar approach to a different issue, you might argue against the practice of wiretapping on the grounds that it is an invasion of the individual's privacy, a fundamental right that must not be infringed on. Or, on still a different issue, you might argue that a particular war should be halted because war is immoral—the argument of the pacifist. In each instance, you are saying that something—the "something" that occurs as a subject term in the thesis you are supporting—exists as a member of a class. It follows that any assertion you can make about the class as a whole, you can make with equal confidence about your "something"—so long as you have persuaded your audience that your "something" is indeed a member of that class. The essential rhetorical task is to select a class or *genus* that your audience will be responsive to. *Maturity* (in connection with privileges), *privacy* (in connection with the rights of free citizens), *morality* (in connection with human values)—terms such as these permit you to relate your particular case to propositions that are generally accepted or that you can make acceptable.

In building your argument, give your main effort to supporting the proposition that is more vulnerable—the one your audience is less likely to find acceptable. In most rhetorical situations, though perhaps not in all, arguing that college students are mature is more to the point than arguing that mature people deserve specific privileges. It is usually more telling to argue that wiretapping is an invasion of privacy than to argue that citizens are entitled to privacy. It is usually more pertinent to argue that war is immoral than to argue that a specific military conflict is a war. Occasionally, however, the debate hinges on the proposition that would ordinarily be taken for granted. Take the last example. You might find general agreement that war is immoral but disagreement about the specific case: your audience may have accepted a current interpretation of the conflict as not really a war at all but "a police action" or "a defense of the right of self-determination" or "a protective reaction." Any such labeling tactic is really an attempt to dislodge a thing from its commonly accepted *genus*, to take it out of the class in which it is normally found. If you were committed to arguing the issue on the grounds that any war is immoral, you would in this case first need to persuade your audience that the conflict under discussion was indeed a war.

It is well to remember that the defining and classifying inherent in arguments based on the nature of the subject are geared not to the purpose of explaining but to the purpose of proving that a belief is sound or a policy wise. Often in arguing you need to engage in explanatory defining, too, in order to make clear exactly what the issue is. Anyone defending or attacking civil disobedience as a legitimate type of protest would be well advised to begin by making clear his understanding of what the term means—to stipulate the meaning *civil disobedience* is to have in his discussion. But the real issue lies elsewhere. It has to do with the relation of individual morality to the law, and the writer's chief obligation is to try to prove that his conception of that relation is right and sound and just. The heart of the argument is about the nature of things, not about what terms mean.

Though arguments from the nature of things can often be stated concisely, they are thoroughgoing, and they always have implications for the other arguments adduced in support of the thesis. If you hold the view that men are motivated largely by irrational and primitive urges, whatever action you propose with respect to a specific policy is bound to be different from what it would be if you viewed man as essentially reasonable and altruistic. If you hold the view that human nature never changes, the reasons you give for advocating certain social reforms will be different from those you would give if you viewed man as capable of radical change for the better.

Your basic beliefs about human nature and politics and religion and ethics and aesthetics are so much a part of your thinking that you may scarcely be aware of them. Nevertheless, they shape your convictions on a vast number of issues, and they stand as silent *assumptions* in the background, if not in the foreground, of every serious argument you engage in. The thoughtful writer takes pains to recognize his own assumptions, whether or not he intends to invite his audience to examine them. In some rhetorical situations, they can remain implicit. In others, they had better be stated openly. Though initially hostile to your position on a specific issue, an audience that shares your basic assumptions can sometimes be led to see that position as a logical consequence of those assumptions and so be won over. And even when you know that your audience does not share your assumptions, making them explicit may prevent confusion and misunderstanding.

The bare statement of a shared assumption can carry great rhetorical weight. Consider this assertion by John T. Rule: "To punish all to prevent the transgressions of the few is, on the face of it, unjust." The words "on the face of it" indicate that the writer believes it unnecessary to offer proof. Any reasonable man, he says in effect, will accept as an axiom, or at least as a tenable assumption, that punishing all to prevent the transgressions of the few is unjust. Another unstated assumption lurks behind this one: no unjust policy should be pursued. Again he takes it for granted that any reasonable man would accept that assumption.

Though many assumptions are too remote from experience to be subject to empirical proof, they can be made to seem more or less probable, more or less reasonable, by appeals to both tangible and intangible evidence. To the degree that evidence is offered in support of them, assumptions take on the character of definitions or statements about class relationships.

Typically, when you base an argument on class relationships, you refer the specific issue to a larger context. A question about university policy will be discussed in the context of what a university should be. A question about the value of a particular dictionary will be referred to the question of the nature and function of dictionaries. Once the larger question of definition has been dealt with, you can turn to the particular instance with confidence that your argument is solidly grounded.

Working in terms of definitions and class relationships is one way, but not the only way, of conducting an argument based on the nature of the subject. Examples (see pp. 76–79 and 148–50) have great persuasive value when they can be shown to be representative of the whole. And division (see pp. 99–101) opens the way to two common ways of arguing. One is to make inferences about part-whole relationships — to argue that what is true of a part is true of the whole or that what is true of the whole is true of a part. The other is to examine each part in turn and come to some judgment. The parts may be constituent elements, as plot, character, and theme are constituent elements of a novel. Or they may be alternative courses of action, in which case the typical procedure is to show that since one course of action is impracticable or unwise or impossible, the other should be adopted.

When arguments go wrong, it is because of false premises or faulty reasoning or both. Fallacies relating to the nature of the subject can be traced to an imperfect conception of the whole, to the use of inadequate or unrepresentative examples, or to incomplete or illogical analysis. Some of the potential trouble spots were identified in Chapter Five, and more will be taken up in Chapter Seven. To summarize and anticipate: Arguments based on the nature of the subject, like all arguments, are susceptible to faulty generalizations (pp. 149–50) and such fallacies as question-begging (pp. 171–72) and irrelevant emotional appeals (pp. 172–73). They are especially susceptible to the use of stereotypes and of classes or *genera* that can be counted on to stir deep but irrational feelings, either unexamined "God-terms" (*democracy, free enterprise, law and order*) or unexamined "devil-terms" (*communism, lawlessness, revolution*). A responsible argument deals not with words but with what words stand for. The groundwork for sound argument is fair and accurate analysis of the subject. Faulty analysis leads to fallacious *either-or* arguments (pp. 161–62). Mistakes in inference about part-whole relationships are related to the fallacy of equivocation (p. 166).

EXERCISES

1. From the following passage, what can you infer about the speaker-audience relationship? What techniques does the speaker use to accommodate his audience? Explain how Bettelheim's concept of the university determines his attitude toward student revolt. If you disagree with Bettelheim's position, explain why. Is it because you do not accept his conception of a university, or is there some other reason?

All of us have heard of the so-called "student revolt." Some who have taken part claim they learned more from their participation than from all their classes. If this was so, their time in college was ill spent, and both they and the university they revolted against would have been better off if they had never enrolled.

If your years as students are not to be a period of intense living, if you are going to sit in your classes like inert bodies, if what you study and what it does to you are not going to change your whole life — in short, if you close yourself to intellectual discoveries — even the best instructors will bore you. But then you should not have come. There is no greater abdication of self than when a student says he did not learn about life from the intellectual venture that a university *is*. If he did not learn about life from his studies, why did he study — to evade the draft, to find a marriage partner, to enjoy a paid vacation without working for it?

This is not to say that one cannot learn about life through political activities, or that you should not participate in them. Of course you should. But the university is not the ground on which to carry on politics, nor does the learning that can be gained from political action belong in a university. Certainly *something* can be learned about life through taking part in a revolt. That's the wonderful thing about life—there is practically no human situation from which we cannot learn a great deal about ourselves and our world. But this happens only if the setting is germane to the type of learning we are after.

There is only one purpose for which a university exists: to enable you to live the sometimes disappointing, often strenuous, but always exciting life of the intellect. The only true gains to be won on a campus are the intellectual virtues. The purpose of a university is to *study* political revolt, not to engage in it; to *examine* how peace might be won and maintained, not to crusade against war; to *investigate* and *plan* for social reforms in the university and outside it, not to carry them out. Thus, the sole objective of a university is to study every possible question, but to fight for only one cause: *freedom of inquiry and thought.*

For example, if one wishes to demonstrate for or against the draft or the war in Viet Nam, there are appropriate places to do so—but they are not the university. Here one should study objectively whether there should be a draft and what alternatives exist. Demonstrations interfere with such unbiased, in-depth investigation, which requires research, quiet concentration, and a careful weighing of all arguments.

All of us are familiar with Camus and his conviction that one ought to live an engaged and committed life. I could not agree more. But what, exactly, the engagement should consist of depends on what, at the moment, forms the center of our lives. If it is politics, then *that* should engage us. But the life of action is not that of carefully examining all sides of an issue; revolt is the opposite of contemplation. If you opt for a life of violent action, you may find in it self-realization. But the university is the least suitable place for this way of finding yourself. Indeed, if at this moment, strife *is* your way of finding yourself, you have no business being here because it is a way that only destroys what a university is for *without* adding to the general weal.—Bruno Bettelheim, *Rochester Review*, Fall 1968

2. What evidence is there in the following passage that the definition is being used for argumentative purposes, not just for explanation? Is the definition one that Bettelheim would find acceptable? Do you?

Turning back to the fifties, I will assert that we were right on one absolutely vital point: we knew what the university was for: learning. The university is for learning—not for politics, not for growing up, not for virtue, except as these things cut in and out of learning, and except also as they are necessary elements of all good human activity. The university is for learning as an airplane is for flying. This is its elemental and defining purpose. There is both affirmative and negative reason for this purpose: no other institution has this mission, and no other mission justifies the university.

One word is not a philosophy of academic life, but to begin with the right word is crucial. I choose "learning" rather than "scholarship" or "education" because "scholarship" puts too much emphasis on faculty alone, and "education" too much on students. Moreover, "scholarship" suggests what the scholar does to knowledge, and "education" suggests what someone does to a student. "Learning" suggests what professors and students do with knowledge, with thought, and with one another. Whitehead had it right and I repeat him: "uniting the young and the old in the imaginative consideration of learning." What helps with that is good for the university. What hinders it, hurts. For the academy this is the first and great commandment. — McGeorge Bundy, *Daedalus*, Summer 1970

3.   What are the essential points of difference between the views expressed in the passage below and those expressed by Bettelheim and Bundy? How does the issue of student power relate to the purpose of a university? What can you infer that Bettelheim and Bundy would say about the specific issues that Schwartz discusses — the rules governing dormitory hours, and so on?

The educational premise behind demands for student power reflects the notion that people learn through living, through the process of integrating their thoughts with their actions, through testing their values against those of a community, through a capacity to act. Education which tells students that they must prepare to live tells infants that they learn to walk by crawling. College presidents who invoke legal authority to prove educational theory — "if you don't like it, leave. It's our decision to make" — assume that growth is the ability to accept what the past has created. Student power is a medium through which people integrate their own experience with a slice of the past which seems appropriate, with their efforts to intensify the relationships between the community within the university.

Let this principle apply — he who must obey the rule should make it.

Students should make the rules governing dormitory hours, boy-girl visitation, student unions, student fees, clubs, newspapers, and the like. Faculty and administrators should advise — attempt to persuade, even. Yet the student should bear the burden of choice. They should demand the burden.

Students and faculty should co-decide curricular policy.

Students and faculty and administration should co-decide admissions policy (they did it at Swarthmore), overall college policy affecting the community, even areas like university investments.

Student power brings those changes, and in the latter cases, it means that the student view will be taken seriously — that it will be treated as a view, subject to rational criticism or acceptance, not simply as "the student opinion which must be considered as the student opinion — *i.e.*, the opinion of those lesser beings in the university."

Student power brings change in the relationships between groups within the university, as well as change in attitudes between the groups of a university. It renders irrelevant the power of factions outside a university who impose external standards on an internal community — Trustees, alumni.

Student power should not be argued on legal grounds. It is not a legal principle. It is an educational principle. — Edward Schwartz, quoted in Immanuel Wallerstein and Paul Starr, eds., *The University Crisis Reader*, I

4. What is the purpose of a university [Bible College]? Is it for learning, for politics, for growing up, for virtue, or for something else? Write a persuasive essay in which you make the best case you can for *your* view of the purpose of a university. Adapt your argument to a particular audience and state what that audience is.

Argument from Causal Relations. A second fruitful line of argument opens up when you inquire into the causes or the effects of a situation or a policy. Here the main emphasis is not on the nature of the thing but on its origins and its consequences — how it came about and what it will lead to and, often, what should be done about it. An argument from causal relations (or argument from consequences, as it is also called) is the natural approach whenever you are urging that a new policy be initiated or an old one changed.

Many social issues are debated largely in medical terms of diagnosis and prognosis or diagnosis, prognosis, and prescription. Typically the argument moves through four stages: an analysis of conditions ("Among the slum-dwellers in our central city, unemployment has reached 60 percent . . ."); an investigation of causes ("With no incentive to stay in school, these young people enter the job market lacking any real qualifications . . ."); a proposal designed to correct, control, or improve the conditions ("What is needed are tax adjustments that will enable companies to provide job training . . ."); and a call for action to put the proposal into effect ("So write your representative in the legislature, urging him to support immediate revision of the tax structure so that . . .").

An argument based on cause-effect relations may lead you in any of several directions. If you can pinpoint the probable cause of a bad situation, the way is clear to arguing that the situation will be improved if the cause is eradicated. But as our earlier discussion of causes indicated (pp. 92 – 95), it may be impossible to isolate *the* cause. And even if it can be isolated, removing it may be difficult or dangerous, if not impossible. In these circumstances you may find yourself arguing that the only feasible course of action is to treat the symptoms — that is, to alleviate the effects. Or you may reject conservative efforts at amelioration or containment, taking instead the radical position that anything short of uprooting the fundamental causes is futile. Often the crux of the argument is not what the cause of the situation is but what should be done to correct it.

In the following passage the argument against wage and price controls is made in terms of the bad effects such controls have:

When excess demand is pulling prices up, wage and price controls work against the basic forces. If firms and unions in some sector of industry are induced or compelled to hold prices or wages down, that is like pinching one corner of a large balloon. The lucky buyers of the goods pay less and have more left to spend elsewhere — driving other prices up still higher and not reducing over-all inflation at all. Jobs in the industry become unattractive, so it will be short of labor. The amount produced will be less than the amount demanded, so buyers will have to be rationed somehow. Distortion of output, black markets, government controls, inefficiency — these are the clearly predictable results. Repressed inflation rolls merrily on, doing far more harm than open inflation. — Milton Friedman, *Newsweek*, June 15, 1970

There is one form of argument from causal relations that may neglect causes completely and that denies the existence of any real choice among cures. In the argument from circumstances the writer's energy is devoted to establishing that a current situation dictates a particular course of action. He hammers away at the point that the circumstances are overpowering — that pollutants from the internal-combustion engine are killing us *now*, that the strike has brought the corporation to the very brink of bankruptcy, that the occupation of buildings and disruption of classes by campus revolutionaries is intolerable. Essentially he tells his audience, "Given this situation, there is only one thing we can do." Not because it is a good or wise or happy action but because the only alternative is death or ruin or some other inconceivable choice.

The following excerpts show a typical use of the argument from circumstances — first the situation, then the solution, then the call for action.

Ten percent of the human beings ever born are now alive and breeding like bacteria under optimum conditions. As a result, millions live at famine level. Yet even with the fullest exploitation of the planet's arable land—and a fair system of distribution—it will not be possible to feed the descendants of those now alive. Meanwhile, man-made waste is poisoning rivers and lakes, air and soil; the megalopolis continues to engulf the earth, as unplanned as a melanoma and ultimately as fatal to the host organism. Overcrowding in the cities is producing a collective madness in which irrational violence flourishes because man needs more space in which to *be* than the modern city allows. . . .

To preserve the human race, it is now necessary to reorganize society. To this end, an Authority must be created with the power to control human population, to redistribute food, to purify air, water, soil, to repattern the cities. . . .

These, then, are the things which must now be done if the race is to continue. Needless to say, every political and economic interest will oppose the setting up of such an Authority. Worse, those elements which delight in destroying human institutions will be morbidly drawn to a movement as radical as this one. But it cannot be helped. The alternative to a planned society is no society. If we do not act now, we shall perish through sheer numbers, like laboratory rats confined to too small a cage. — Gore Vidal, *Esquire*, Oct. 1968

> The fallacies that arguments based on causal relations are vulnerable to are discussed on pp. 150–52. The argument from circumstances shares the risk of the variety of *either-or* argument known as the dilemma (p. 162). It is also susceptible to the *prodigious* fallacy—gross exaggeration or hysterical overstatement.

Argument from Likenesses and Differences.   Conceptions about what a thing is like and what it is unlike can provide a lead-in to productive argument. As we have noted, the pacifist argues for the abandonment of a particular war on the grounds that all wars are immoral. Some Americans used a different approach in arguing for the cessation of hostilities in Vietnam. *That* war, they declared, was uniquely immoral. Though both arguments lead to the same conclusion, they are different in substance, they require different supporting evidence, and they are likely to elicit different reactions from any one audience.

In arguing that all wars are immoral, the pacifist proceeds largely on the basis of definition, emphasizing the immorality of taking life under any circumstances. To be persuasive, he needs to secure assent to certain basic assumptions about human values. In his argument *war* remains an undifferentiated term: all wars are the same. By contrast, the other approach requires the making of distinctions among wars, for it entails establishing two categories of wars—some moral (at least relatively), some immoral. Whether the argument succeeds or not depends on whether the contrasts between the Vietnam War and other wars are made convincing.

Much sophisticated argument (and some sophistic argument, too) proceeds by making distinctions where similarities have been taken for granted. The following passage is part of an argument in which the writer is challenging the view that "America and Americans" must accept responsibility for the shooting of civilians by some American soldiers in Vietnam. The question of causation (and therefore responsibility) is altered, he says, depending on whether it is treated in moral or in scientific terms. To confuse the two is to destroy moral judgment altogether.

The argument I am presenting depends upon making a very clear distinction between moral and scientific discourse. In the moral world, we recognize good people and bad, right acts and wrong ones. The good people are generally innocent and the bad ones are guilty, and in each case these words are used because of the choices that have been made. A good person is one who refrains from acting nastily even though he might have justification; he respects the integrity of other people and is capable of dealing with his own tendencies toward aggression and self-aggrandizement. Someone who is bad, by contrast, chooses to hurt or steal or lie when it suits his own purposes or passions. And although we may explain these choices up to a point, we can never regard them as *nothing else but* the outcome of external forces. The moment we do that, we have given up moral judgment in favor of some kind of intellectual construction.

So much for the moral world. If we are trying to be scientific, on the other hand, we treat whatever is to be explained as the effect of precedent conditions, and we believe that if we can discover both the relevant preconditions, and the laws of their combination, then we shall have a complete explanation of the act that puzzled us.

Now there are problems about thinking of human behavior in either of these ways. To interpret people morally is to judge behavior in terms of choices, and this involves us in the difficult problem of whether the concept of choice does not rest, when analyzed sufficiently far, upon a mysterious judgment whose only basis is our ignorance of what goes on in the human mind. And when we try to be scientific about human behavior, we are forced to construe choices as being nothing but stages in the emergence of the conditions of an act. Neither way is, then, entirely satisfactory: What is quite fatal is to confuse them. Nor does it matter, in logic, whether we are dealing with "good" or "bad" science. A great deal of inquiry into "the social system" would be regarded by natural scientists as being too woolly to qualify as science at all. The point is that the *mode* of description is scientific, and the logical point applies.

To import moral terms into scientific description is intellectually fatal because it leads to an infinite regress. If I regard Americans who may have shot civilians in Vietnam as guilty, then I may try to explain their behavior as the outcome of tendencies in American society. In doing this, I have switched from a moral judgment to a scientific one, transferring the guilt across the ledger from the moral column to the scientific. But having discovered the "guilty elements" of American life, I must now seek to explain these; and if I discover *their* causes, I must go on to find the further causes, and so on. Having moved the guilt from the few American soldiers involved, I shall find no place to terminate my attribution of guilt until I come to—what? The apes? The missing link? The regrettable events in the Garden of Eden? It becomes very easy to see why the doctrine of original sin has been so attractive to generation after generation of men.

To confuse moral with scientific judgments constitutes, then, a clear fallacy, which underlies a great deal of the more tedious breast beating that passes for social criticism throughout the Western world today.—K. R. Minogue, *American Scholar*, Spring 1970

EXERCISE

Examine these excerpts from arguments against Minogue's position, both published in *The American Scholar*, Autumn 1970. Then write a persuasive essay, intended for publication in the same journal, arguing your view on the issue of the individual citizen's responsibility for the actions and policies of his government.

a. Minogue lives in a very simple world, where morality involves only a few clear-cut decisions between absolute good and absolute evil. In real life, those who make evil inevitable must share responsibility with those who do the dirty work. In America, all those who pay taxes that make war possible, who elect Presidents who make war without necessity, who elect representatives who demand war, and who belong to organizations that endorse war share responsibility to varying degrees for the results of war. Anyone who does not protest is an accomplice.—William Palmer Taylor

b. I live in a country whose elected leaders consistently and characteristically commit various kinds of its national resources to actions I find morally appalling. It is a country where many millions of people consistently and characteristically make moral choices (in their political relations to their government and in their social relations with each other) of which I generally disapprove. It makes sense to me, then, to speak of the nation's moral failure or guilt even though not every American participates in that guilt. (Some men are in jail.) There are of course differences in moral response among the national citizenry. A small minority seem to me innocent; among the others there are differing degrees of guilt and complicity — of failed responsibility. — David Weber

The main function of *difference* arguments is to make distinctions among things normally thought to be the same. And the main function of *likeness* arguments is to persuade the reader that things not normally thought of as alike are, in fact, alike in important respects that bear directly on the point at issue. A typical use of likeness arguments is to urge that a program or policy be adopted — or rejected — because the same program or policy, or a similar one, has — or has not — been successful in a comparable situation. One argument for some universal form of health insurance in the United States is that socialized medicine functions well in Great Britain. For those who attribute criminal behavior to a disorder of the individual personality, it is reasonable to argue that it be treated medically, as other physical and psychological ailments are. Some members of the women's liberation movement see the position of women as analogous to that of an exploited racial or ethnic group and call for a program of action like that pursued by black militants.

In other instances, little or no literal resemblance is apparent, but one or more significant points of similarity lend probability to an argument from likeness. The analysis of the strategies used in games, war, politics, and economics according to mathematical "game theory" implies an argument that these seemingly disparate entities are alike in significant ways.

The use of analogy in argument entails risks. Critics point out that no matter how many similarities have been uncovered, no two situations are identical and therefore a solution that is viable in one may be worthless in another. And it is true that many analogies fail at a point that is crucial to the argument. Nevertheless, analogies have great persuasive force and are extremely useful so long as they are not expected to carry the entire weight of proof. (Could Friedman, in the quotation on p. 138, have successfully extended his pinched-balloon analogy?) An analogy is not fallacious because it ignores differences; it is fallacious when the differences it ignores bear directly on the issue.

Likeness and difference relations enter into a great many arguments where the aim is not to establish absolutes but to make a comparative judgment: to prove that one novel is better than another, to show that the choice is between a greater and a lesser evil, and so on. Whether in critical essays or in practical politics, judgments involving *more* and *less*, *better* and *worse*, are grounded in likeness and difference.

Faulty analogies are discussed on pp. 152–53.

External Sources of Argument

Internal arguments grow out of the issue itself or, rather, out of the writer's elaboration and development of his views on the issue. The case is decided on its merits: a product should be used because it is well-made and serviceable; a policy should be adopted because it is wise and humane. External arguments do not relate directly to the issue or the writer's analysis of it but to evidence brought to bear from outside—the testimony afforded by documents or by statistics or, most commonly, by other people: a certain type of tennis racket should be used because the Wimbledon champion uses it; a certain foreign-aid bill should be enacted because the Secretary of State has spoken in its favor.

In structure, the argument from authority could hardly be simpler: it asks for the reader's assent or belief on the basis of the recommendation of somebody (or a number of somebodies) presumed to be better informed or wiser than either the writer or his audience. To use this kind of argument responsibly, you must first of all be sure that your authority *is* an expert. If you ask your readers to take his word on a factual matter, they have the right to assume that he has access to the relevant information and that his integrity guarantees honest reporting. If you ask them to accept his opinion, they should be able to count on his ability to form sound judgments. Thus the ethical dimension of argument bears as strongly on the external sources a writer uses as it does on the writer himself. He must choose authorities whose integrity and competence on the particular issue are unquestioned.

When equally respected authorities offer testimony supporting different sides of the same issue, the writer has to go beyond the simple use of authority. He needs to make clear to his readers why he finds his expert's view more convincing than the opposing view, why he has chosen this expert rather than that one.

Argument from authority is so frequently abused that it must be handled with special care. It is misused when it is substituted for reasoned discussion: "Dr. Rogers says so, and that settles the matter." Authority and issue must be precisely matched: not only can a television star's opinion of toothpaste or an evangelist's opinion of fiscal policy be inexpert and irrelevant, but a literary scholar may lack authority in linguistics, and a historian who specializes in medieval France may have no expert knowledge of Victorian England. And the right authority must not be used in the wrong way: obviously, an authority should never be misrepresented by selective quotation or other distortion.

One of the common abuses of argument from authority is to appeal not to any identifiable individual but to a vague, general class: "Scholars tell us . . . ," "Scientists say . . . ," even "Everybody knows. . . ." The next step—the fallacy known as *hypostatization* or reification—is the appeal to an abstraction: "Science tells us . . . ," "History says . . . ," "Democracy teaches. . . ."

Sometimes you may want to present testimony from a respected or revered document like the Bible or the Constitution. The effectiveness of such testimony will depend on the predisposition of your audience, but it is well to remind yourself that the Constitution is open to conflicting interpretations on many points and that "the devil can cite Scripture for his purpose."

Which brings up the use of quotations, maxims, proverbs, platitudes—miniature testimonials that are supposed to distill the wisdom of the ages but must be classified as nonauthoritative. As premises for arguments, they are unreliable. An alert reader can usually find another bit of wisdom that directly contradicts the one whose truth he has been asked to accept: "Look before you leap," but remember that "He who hesitates is lost."

The testimony of statistics is used so widely that it deserves special consideration. The basis for its persuasive appeal is the maxim that figures don't lie. But of course they do lie when opinion polls are not representative, when rating systems have biases built into them, when the figures are irrelevant, or when they are dishonestly used (as when a count of the dead, on a highway or a battlefield, is preceded by "only"). Like your authorities among men, your statistical authorities must be carefully selected and responsibly presented. Announcing that 274 students signed a petition may help your argument, but if you hide the fact that 742 explicitly refused to sign it, you are grossly distorting the situation.

Even when statistics are accurate and honestly presented, an argument based on them is not necessarily sound. Establishing the fact that a sizable majority agrees with you proves only that a sizable majority agrees with you—not that your audience should therefore agree. Use of the *bandwagon* fallacy—vote for the candidate who's going to win, buy the product that "everyone" buys, read the best seller, join the crowd—is an appeal not to authority but to the herd instinct.

So far as everyday matters go, it is advisable to restrict the use of authority and testimony to *supporting* evidence. As such, it can strengthen an essay whose main substance has been developed through the internal sources of argument. In research projects of all kinds, the use of authority and testimony is essential, and wise and scrupulous use is of first importance not only in doing justice to the subject but in establishing your own credentials as a scholar (see pp. 418–26).

Some acquaintance with the sources of argument, both internal and external, will help you size up realistically the job of proving your thesis. In its skeleton form, proof consists of a chain of related propositions, one anchored to another and all giving support, direct or indirect, to the thesis. Once you have visualized your argument as a series of key assertions moving from *here* (the problem) to *there* (the solution), you can turn to the question of proof in the particular context, asking which of the assertions can stand unsupported and which, without support, are likely to strike your readers as arbitrary or shaky or unreliable. Making wise decisions at this point is the essential rhetorical task. Belaboring the obvious will bore your readers. Asserting as uncontrovertible truths what they regard as debatable issues will outrage them.

For each of your key assertions, then, ask yourself: Is this a basic assumption I can count on my audience to subscribe to, or does it need support? If it needs support, what route will I take in developing the particular point? What possibilities open up when I try to support the assertion by analyzing the nature of the thing? By investigating causal relations? By making comparisons? And what concrete evidence will convince my readers that the definition is reasonable? The causal analysis sound? The comparison legitimate? For what instances, what particulars, can I draw on my own knowledge and experience? What kind of support can I find in the speeches and writings of others? If authorities disagree, how shall I choose among them?

Good answers to these questions will generate the substance of your essay.

EXERCISES

1. From each of two newspapers or magazines that are known to have basically different political viewpoints (*The National Review* and *The New Republic*, for instance), copy out or Xerox an

editorial or column dealing with a topic of social or political importance. (If possible, choose articles on the *same* topic.) Submit them with an essay in which you compare and contrast the two articles. Give the best explanation you can for the similarities and differences you find in the views stated in the articles, in the assumptions underlying these views, in the kinds of arguments used, and in the style and tone. Be objective; do not express your own opinion on the issue.

2. Select a campus issue that interests you and use it as the basis for two papers, about 750 words each, in which you attempt to persuade two distinctly different audiences to share your judgment or support your recommendation. (An illustration—but only an illustration: Write to the curriculum committee asking that specific changes be made in a course. Write to a friend urging him not to sign up for the course until these changes have been made.)

Though your two papers will present the same general views about the issue, they should differ in the space you give to each reason, the order in which you present your reasons, the way you open and close, and the general style and tone. Your task is to accommodate the same argument to two very different audiences and to lead them both to the same conclusion.

3. From the subjects below, choose one that interests you. Define a problem related to it, and when you have committed yourself to a thesis, write a persuasive essay for an audience of your choice. For some of the subjects you may want to support your thesis by offering the testimony of experts. If you do, give some attention to establishing their credentials.

wiretapping	psychiatry
drug taking	abortion
the draft	work and the workweek

Keep asking questions about your subject until you can see a problem in it. For example, about work and the workweek: What are the psychological effects of working? Of not working? If you found you could meet expenses by working only ten hours a week, would you choose to work only ten hours? Would a three-day workweek be desirable? What should a person do whose job brings him a good paycheck (which he wants and needs) but no satisfaction? What should a person do whose job brings him great satisfaction but not enough money to live on?

4. Review the passage by Schwartz, Exercise 3, pp. 136–37. Write a persuasive essay expressing your views about student power in one of the areas he refers to—fees, admissions policy, and so on. Your audience is the faculty.

Chapter Seven

TESTING LOGICAL RELATIONSHIPS

Chapter Six sketched some general lines of inquiry that can profitably be pursued in building the content of any persuasive essay. We turn now to the logical underpinnings of particular arguments. To gain assent to your thesis, you must, to begin with, convince your readers that you have made a good case for it. In writing your essay—and especially in revising it—you need to anticipate at every stage the questions a skeptical reader will raise: Is this assertion accurate? Is this generalization convincing? Does this statement follow from that one?

In answering these questions, you can rely to a considerable extent on your own good sense, but you will also find some helpful cues in the procedures of logic. There are, to be sure, distinct limits to the applicability of formal logic to persuasive prose. Formal logic deals in certainties, rhetoric in probabilities. The neat paradigms of logic texts bear little resemblance to the shape that actual arguments take. Still, logic offers help in investigating some of the main concerns of persuasion—methods of proceeding from hypothesis to probability and methods of drawing out probable inferences from statements that are believed to be true even though they cannot be conclusively proved. In particular, logic affords criteria for testing the reliability (or probability) of certain statements and the validity of inferences made from them.

Traditionally, the terms *induction* and *deduction* identify two ways of reaching conclusions. In argumentative prose, inductive reasoning and deductive inference mix freely; but because different methods are used to test the conclusions they lead to, we will discuss them separately. Tests for reliability—tests relating to induction—are easy to grasp but often hard to apply. Tests for validity—tests relating to deductive inference—are more complicated but, once understood, are easy to apply.

As we discuss the tests, we will identify the main fallacies that the tests can expose—both the formal fallacies that result from incorrect inference and the informal fallacies that originate in the content itself or in the language in which the argument is presented.

TESTING INDUCTION

An inductive inquiry is grounded in particulars. It moves from the observation and analysis of facts, characteristics, attitudes, or circumstances to an inclusive statement or generalization. It has its origin in a puzzle or a question (What is Bergman trying to do in his films? What makes his films distinctive?) and is essentially a search for a pattern or an explanation. The inquiry is set in motion by a hunch or guess—a hypothesis—that is then tested by further investigation.

The generalization that is the outcome of an inductive inquiry may describe and classify, or express a causal relation, or make a comparison. Induction is the typical procedure you use when you approach your subject from the various perspectives we have discussed as the internal sources of argument (pp. 130–43); it is the characteristic procedure for amassing the evidence that will make your particular assertions convincing. When you are basing your argument on external sources, the inductive investigations are one step removed: you accept, and you ask your readers to accept, the results of the inductive investigations carried out by the authorities you cite (pp. 143–45).

Class Relationships

What makes a sound induction? That depends, to begin with, on what is being asserted. Criteria for reliability are easy to state, and reliability is easy to assess, when the generalization is a statement of verifiable fact. If the assertion "All the members of the freshman class were in the upper third of their high-school classes" is based on an examination of the grade records of all the freshmen, and if the calculations are accurate, the statement is true. (Actually this is nose counting rather than rhetorical induction.) But only rarely do significant arguments rest exclusively on factual statements that can be definitely confirmed or contradicted. The evidence is less certain, less "hard," and altogether more difficult to weigh when you are generalizing, say, about the quality of the imagery in Theodore Roethke's poems or about the contribution Godard has made to a new conception of realism in films or about the nature and degree of political activism on campus. Even when you can examine all the data (study all the poems of Roethke, for example), inspection alone will not produce a sound generalization. You need to interpret and judge.

For the vast majority of the generalizations that figure in persuasive prose, not all the data have been examined or can be examined. The distinguishing feature of most inductive inquiries is the *inductive leap*, the insight or conviction that a characteristic or relationship that has been observed again and again probably holds true for all data of the same kind. The inquiry may have been extremely thorough, covering case after case; but at some point the investigator makes a shift from a descriptive or statistical statement about *this* member, *that* one, and the *next* one to a confident assertion about the whole class, including those members not available for inspection. Typically, an inductive generalization pertains to the future as well as to the present and the past. ("All men are mortal" includes those not yet born.)

Whenever unexamined data are included in a generalization—and no one has ever examined all men or all lyrics or all planets or all VW's—the logician insists that the inference (in contrast to a nose count) is not certain, however high its degree of probability. Although this principle may strike you as excessively cautious, it is a reminder that inductive generalizations need the best support you can give them. Support comes from examples, the prime instrument of rhetorical induction. You do yourself and your argument an injustice if you simply assert the generalization or if the examples you use show that your investigation has been superficial or biased. An inductive generalization stands or falls on the amount and kind of evidence that backs it up.

> *Hasty generalizations* are based on inadequate, scanty evidence. *Faulty generalizations* are based on weak, unrepresentative, or irrelevant evidence, or on emotion rather than evidence. Generalizations that do not stand up represent one of the most common fallacies in argument.

Take a relatively simple generalization: "Students on this campus have practically no interest in national politics." Unsupported, it does not convince. Backed up by well-chosen examples, it may be highly persuasive. But how many examples, and what kind? Probably no reader would be persuaded by one instance—"My roommate never reads the editorials in the newspaper" or "The Young Democrats had to disband this year because of lack of members" or "Only a handful turned out to hear Senator Patch." On the other hand, the reader will resist sheer quantity of evidence if he has reason to believe that the instances you cite are unrepresentative. To decide that students are politically apathetic on the basis of the indifference shown by your roommate would be premature: the sample is too small and the generalization hasty. To base the judgment on the indifference shown by all students majoring in music would be unwise: because the sample is unrepresentative, the generalization is faulty.

Naturally, when you are gathering evidence for your persuasive papers, you haven't time to conduct comprehensive polls, nor do you have at your command the complicated statistical systems that make some polls reliable. But with care and thought you can strengthen the key generalizations your argument depends on.

You run the risk of producing an unsound generalization whenever you brush aside contradictory evidence. Your inductive inquiry has its origin in a hunch that your roommate's attitude toward politics is not a personal idiosyncrasy but a characteristic shared by a great many other students. On the basis of that hunch you start to investigate. The hypothesis is necessary; without it you could hardly launch an inquiry. But if investigation proves that the hypothesis is incorrect, abandon it. Sticking to it in the face of contradictory evidence is foolish, and suppressing or disguising contradictory evidence is dishonest.

> Deliberately slanting evidence by suppressing or disguising contradictory data is a variety of faulty generalizing known as *card-stacking, special pleading,* or *dealing in half-truths.*

Remembering that inductive generalizations yield only probability should make you more generous in admitting the existence of negative evidence. Acknowledging exceptions will damage your case less than ignoring them. As a matter of fact, you can often make your generalizations sturdier by offering plausible reasons for the exceptions.

> Citing numerous examples and recognizing contradictory evidence will protect you from *stereotyping*—applying group labels that ignore individual differences and may also ignore the significant characteristics of the group. There are popular stereotypes for almost any group—scientists, schoolteachers, Swedes, redheads, Baptists, bird watchers, Rotarians, Texans, "the enemy," and so on—including college students and young people generally. Stereotypes in your own thinking, or nonthinking, may reflect unexamined assumptions that weaken your entire argument.

Causal Relations

So far we have been concerned with the making of an inductive generalization that describes or classifies, that makes an assertion about the nature of the thing. (College students are asserted to be in the *class* of people who are uninterested in national politics.) Inductive inquiries undertaken to establish causal relations need to be handled with special care, particularly when they are given predictive value as guides to future action. Some causal relations are indisputable: anyone who puts a plastic dishpan on a very hot burner will not do it a second time. But in other situations causal connections are much harder to establish. A college admissions officer is struck by the fact that the last ten students admitted from Monitor High School have had disastrous college careers. He wonders if any student from M.H.S. could succeed in college. He forms, however tentatively, a causal connection between *students-from-M.H.S.* and *failure-in-college.*

Is he right? Probably everyone would agree that the causal connection is less sure than the one established between the hot burner and the ruined dishpan. The capacity to withstand heat is not likely to vary much from one plastic dishpan to another. But the admissions officer cannot count on such a principle of uniformity when he is dealing with the quality of instruction in a high school from year to year or with the capacity of individual students to succeed in spite of poor instruction.

> Logicians give the label *post hoc, ergo propter hoc* ("after this, therefore because of this") to the fallacy of assuming that whatever comes after an event is necessarily a result of it. The mere fact of temporal succession—one event following another in time—does not necessarily indicate any causal relationship. *Post hoc* is the most common fallacy of causal relations.

Did the ten students fail *because* they came from Monitor High? The evidence at hand might be compelling enough to suggest this as a hypothesis, but a thoughtful admissions officer would do no more than use it as a starting point for further inductive inquiries about the students who failed, the school they came from, and so on. These inquiries might enable him to confirm the hypothesis; on the other hand, they might force him to alter it or reject it altogether. Determining causes is the most rigorous stage of any inductive inquiry, for only a good deal of analytical skill can distinguish coincidental circumstances from genuine causes. (See pp. 93 – 95 and *Cause.)

> *False cause* embraces all the fallacies relating to causal reasoning—*post hoc,* mistaking an antecedent circumstance for a cause, failure to recognize multiple causes.

Most of the issues you will debate—social and political and educational questions—are too complex to be argued on the basis of a single overriding cause. You can acknowledge the complexity by ranking causes in terms of probability, by classifying different kinds of causes, and by proposing solutions that take a variety of causes into account.

Analogies

Inductive procedures enter into those generalizations that express comparative judgments—this policy is better than that one, this system of learning a foreign language better than that. Though the judgments are arrived at deductively, by referring to other generalizations about values and ends to be achieved, it is inductive inquiry that yields the points of similarity and difference. If they are to have persuasive value, the points of similarity and difference must be made relevant to the issue.

The logical form of analogy (see pp. 82–90 and p. 142) is a partial induction: two things alike in certain respects are presumed to be alike in another respect. Induction establishes a general conclusion; analogy moves from similarities (sometimes few, sometimes many) to an inference about still another similarity.

> _Faulty analogy_ results from selecting similarities that are not relevant to the issue, from pressing an analogy beyond legitimate similarities, from treating a figurative analogy as a literal one, or from insisting that analogical resemblances constitute adequate proof. The fallacy of the _perfect analogy_ results from reasoning from a partial resemblance to an entire and exact correspondence.

Reasoning by analogy is extremely common; though always vulnerable, it is often our only guide to action. We argue from analogy when we say that because the period we are living in is strikingly similar to some period in the past, we should adopt a policy now that proved successful then. We argue from analogy when we say that the methods used to solve an economic or social problem in Detroit can be successfully applied in Milan, or that blacks can work their way out of the slums as white ethnic minorities have done. These are literal analogies, in which things of the same class are compared—historical periods, economic or social problems, people. The argument will be persuasive if the similarities between the two cases have a direct bearing on the point at issue.

In a figurative analogy, the writer sees a relationship that involves members of different classes—countries and dominoes, for instance; and he may argue that adjacent countries will behave like adjacent dominoes (see pp. 175–76). Figurative analogies are of value in throwing a new light on a subject, in opening up an avenue of speculation, in giving colorful support to an argument; but they do not have logical validity, and any conclusions drawn from them are only suggestive. Though they may have great persuasive value in leading the audience to entertain a thesis (about the expediency of a foreign policy, say), in themselves they do not prove it. A frank admission of precisely where an analogy breaks down — where the similarities run out — is rhetorically far more effective than pressing it to the point where it becomes absurd.

In sum, the two chief features of the inductive procedure are the framing of the hypothesis and the inductive leap. The three chief fallacies, or sources of error, are (1) hasty or faulty generalizing, (2) mistaken causal relationships, and (3) faulty comparisons and analogies. Knowing the possible sources of error can guide you in testing the reliability of the generalizations that run through your persuasive papers.

SUMMARY

EXERCISES

1. Xerox eight or ten typical advertisements in current magazines, and submit them with an essay in which you generalize about the techniques used in the ads. Then, on the basis of your inductive investigation, make an inference about the nature of the audience aimed at — age, sex, economic bracket, and so forth. (Notice that for this part of the paper you are engaging in a complicated process of reasoning that relies on many inductions you have performed and assumptions you have formed in the past.)

2. Explain how analogy functions in the advertiser's plea to the public to use a product because a man of athletic skill or a woman of charm testifies to its excellence.

3. If you were the college admissions officer referred to on p. 151, how would you go about testing the hypothesis that no students from M.H.S. will succeed in college? How much evidence and what kind of evidence would persuade you that the hypothesis could safely be treated as a sound generalization? How much evidence and what kind of evidence would persuade you to abandon the hypothesis?

4. In the following excerpts identify the generalizations, both explicit and implicit, that seem to have been arrived at by induction or by partial induction (analogy), and explain why

you do or do not find them reliable. In your own words, reproduce the train of reasoning in each excerpt and explain why you do or do not find it convincing. Then try composing a different argument to prove the point made in each excerpt.

a. When mosquitoes are a problem, it is standard practice to get rid of stagnant water and to cover windows with screens. Nobody calls that coddling mosquitoes. But when somebody proposes spending money to clean up slums, and to screen society from crime by building humane jails and by hiring many more honest, well-trained cops, the outcry against coddling criminals always kills the budget. — Robert Sherrill, *Life*, Nov. 13, 1970

b. My psychoanalytic experience has made me dubious as to whether rational explanations ever quiet anxiety anyway; something else happens, namely, the explanation becomes the vehicle for a more profound mythos that does grasp people on levels deeper than rationality. The explanation, for example, becomes part of the mythos that I, the one doing the explaining, care for you, that you and I can trust and communicate with each other. This implication may be, as it surely is in psychoanalysis, a good deal more important than whether my "explanation" or interpretation is, in itself, entirely accurate or "brilliant" or whatever. I often notice, when I give an interpretation to a patient in a psychoanalytic session, that what impresses him most at the moment is not the theoretical truth or falsehood of what I say, but the fact that my saying it shows my belief that he can change and that his behavior has meaning. These are aspects of a positive myth. The deeper myth in such explanations may be that we can trust the meaning of our interpersonal universe, and that human consciousness can, in principle, be in touch with that meaning. — Rollo May, *Love and Will*

[Elsewhere in his book May has remarked, "I use the term 'myth' not in its deteriorated popular sense of 'falsehood,' but in its historically accurate sense of a psychobiological pattern which gives meaning and direction to experience."]

c. Everyone would agree that poetry needs rhythm, but some people still cling to the notion that a poem is not a poem unless it has rhyme as well. In connection with this, one is reminded of a woman wearing an extraordinary diamond necklace. The necklace enhances her costume, but whether or not she *needs* it is questionable. The jewelry may be so distracting that perhaps we will not notice the fact that she is not attractive. If she is really beautiful, the necklace will serve only as a charming incidental. Similarly with poetry. If the work is a piece of great writing, rhyme acts only as an incidental. If, however, the work is poor, the rhyme may serve to distract us from that fact.

5. Though naming a fallacy is not so important as seeing

precisely what is wrong with the reasoning, try your hand at identifying in the following list examples of (1) stereotypes and other hasty or faulty generalizations; (2) card-stacking, or misuse of evidence; (3) *post hoc* reasoning and other mistakes in assigning causes; (4) misused analogies.

a.   The Democrats are warmongers. Every time this country gets involved in a war, it's when they're in power.

b.   *Times* book review: "Mr. Shaw's novel might have brought us the fresh insights and bubbling energy of youth; instead, it is hackneyed and dull." Publisher's blurb: "' . . . fresh insights and bubbling energy,' says *Times!*"

c.   America has won every war it ever engaged in.

d.   And the reason for all the trouble in our universities is easy enough to identify: permissive parents.

e.   Peckham was a New Englander through and through — cold, narrow, tight-fisted, self-righteous, and smug as a Persian cat.

f.   Like a skyrocket, he has made a colorful ascent in our political skies; but no skyrocket can climb forever. In the end, it must return to earth — with a resounding thud. We can predict the same fate for Candidate Kent.

g.   All I know is, every time I carry that rabbit's foot, my luck is just great.

h.   Franklin Roosevelt's Communist connections are a matter of record: he allied himself with Joseph Stalin, supplied the Soviet Union with weapons of every variety, and traveled half way round the world to confer with Communist leaders.

i.   Training and practice? Forget it. A musician like that is born, not made.

j.   Returning from his three-day inspection trip, Congressman Flood reported that both civilian and military morale was high, that the enemy's strength had been shattered, and that victory was being rapidly achieved.

k.   Parents have no right to criticize the public schools. After all, they don't tell their surgeons how to operate.

l.   America today has adopted the repressive tactics of Nazi Germany; and just as Nazi Germany went up in flames, so will America.

m.   I oppose the registration of firearms. History shows that registration leads to confiscation.

TESTING DEDUCTION

In reasoning inductively, we pull particulars into an inclusive generalization that describes or explains them; in reasoning deductively, we draw a conclusion from propositions that we accept as true or that we have already proved to be true, or probable, by inductive procedures. We reason deductively when we say, "If this is true, that *must* be true." If Jack is a National Merit finalist, he must be smart. Why *must*? Because we take it for granted, or perhaps are convinced on the basis of our own inductive inquiries, that all National Merit finalists are smart. The essence of the deductive process is the *must*—drawing an inevitable conclusion from propositions known or assumed to be true.

Some assertions—though by no means all—can be proved both deductively and inductively. A cluster of examples, each giving evidence of Jack's braininess, would lead to the same conclusion as the deductive inference. For sound induction you would have to know a lot about Jack. For sound deduction you would need to know only the one fact about him so long as you could get agreement on your general principle about *all* National Merit finalists.

To test conclusions arrived at deductively, you need to ask two questions: Are the premises true? Is the reasoning valid? Only if you can answer both affirmatively is your argument sound.

Though logic offers some rules of thumb for testing the reliability of inductive generalizations, it does not tell you whether a specific generalization is true or untrue, probable or improbable. This you can determine only by examining the material—the facts or instances that have gone into the making of the induction. Similarly, logic cannot tell you whether the premises you are working from in deduction—many of them inductive generalizations—are true or false. (Are all National Merit finalists smart? Is the generalization unquestionably true, or is it only highly probable? The question is a complex one, involving among other things the meaning of *smart*.) What logic can do is provide rules for testing the validity of the conclusions you draw from your premises.

To begin with, you need to uncover the chain of reasoning in your essay—reduce complex propositions to simple ones, sort out premises from conclusions, and bring into view whatever generalizations are not stated but simply implied in the argument (in the example above, "All National Merit finalists are smart"). In this preliminary analysis, your aim is to reduce your reasoning to a skeletal pattern that will conform to the three-part structure of assertions known as the *syllogism*. Once your reasoning is laid out in syllogistic form, you can begin testing your premises for reliability and your conclusion for validity.

The three parts of the syllogism are the *major premise*, the *minor premise*, and the *conclusion*. The phrasing of the major premise allows us to distinguish three common patterns: the hypothetical syllogism (If P, then Q), the *either-or* syllogism (Either P or Q), and the categorical syllogism (All P is Q). An argument can often be reduced to more than one of these patterns, but ordinarily one will seem more natural and easier to deal with than the others.

Hypothetical Syllogisms

The pattern is familiar from mathematics:

Major premise	If P, then Q		If P, then Q
Minor premise	P	*or*	Not Q
Conclusion	Therefore Q		Therefore not P

The major premise asserts that if the antecedent P is true, the consequent Q is true. The minor premise asserts that P is true, and the conclusion drawn is that Q must be true. Or the minor premise denies that Q is true, leading to the conclusion that P is not true. These are the two valid forms of inference in a hypothetical syllogism.

Consider the reasoning of the admissions officer who decides to reject a candidate from Monitor High School. He says, "Better not admit this one. He's from Monitor High. Chances are he'll never get through college." Put more formally, his reasoning is:

If an applicant is from Monitor High, he will not succeed in college (If P, then Q)

This applicant is from Monitor High (P)

Therefore this applicant will not succeed in college (Therefore Q)

Another chain of reasoning, based on the premise that no college should admit students that it knows will fail, leads to the decision "Better not admit this one." But first it is necessary to establish the fact (or the probability) that the candidate will fail. The admissions officer has followed a valid pattern of inference. After asserting the minor premise, he can move confidently to his conclusion. As we have already seen, the major premise ("If an applicant . . .") asserts a causal relation based on induction. If the causal relation is sound, the conclusion is true as well as valid.

Using the same major premise, the admissions officer

could infer from a student's success in college that he was *not* from Monitor High:

If a student is a graduate of Monitor High, he will not succeed (If P, then Q)

Bob Burns is succeeding in college (Not Q)

Therefore Bob Burns is not a graduate of Monitor High (Therefore not P)

The minor premise has denied the consequent Q; from this it follows that the antecedent P can be denied.

But look at these two inferences:

Jane Smith is not from Monitor High, so she will succeed in college

Steve Johnson is flunking out of college; he must be from Monitor High

Both inferences are incorrect. The *if . . . then* relationship is not reversible. The major premise has asserted that P implies Q, but it has not ruled out the possibility of other antecedents for Q. Nor has it asserted that Q implies P—that every case of failure in college can be attributed to attendance at Monitor High.

To summarize, the two patterns of valid inference are these: affirming the antecedent entails affirming the consequent (P, therefore Q), and denying the consequent entails denying the antecedent (not Q, therefore not P).

> In the hypothetical syllogism, it is fallacious to move from denying the antecedent (not P) to denying the consequent (therefore not Q) or from affirming the consequent (Q) to affirming the antecedent (therefore P). The argument will also be unsound, of course, if the implication stated in the major premise is untrue.

Look again at the conclusions that are labeled invalid: "Jane Smith will succeed in college" and "Steve Johnson must be from Monitor High." It may turn out on further investigation that Jane *does* succeed in college and that Steve *is* from Monitor High—that is, we may discover that both conclusions are true. They are true, however, for reasons *other than* those given in the premises we were working with. Unpalatable as the idea seems, invalid inference may yield a conclusion that happens to be true, just as valid inference may yield a conclusion that happens to be false. Validity means only that the stated conclusion follows from the premises that have been supplied. For a *sound* argument, you need valid inference from true premises.

Although the *if . . . then* pattern is peculiarly appropriate for expressing causal relations, it is not limited to them. The senator who says, "I oppose this bill because it is unconstitutional" could put his reasoning into the *if . . . then* framework:

If this bill is unconstitutional, then I oppose it

This bill is unconstitutional

Therefore I oppose it

In his argument he gives little attention to establishing the necessary relation between the unconstitutionality of a bill and his opposition to it. For him, that is a *given*, an assumption. His real job is to prove the minor premise, and this requires making a careful analysis of the bill to show that it is unconstitutional. Definition and classification, not causal relations, lie at the heart of this syllogism.

If . . . then is central to many problem-solution arguments. Two thirds of an essay by Derek Wright (*Life*, Nov. 6, 1970) analyzes "the new tyranny of sexual 'liberation.'" The last third opens with an *if* (actually several *if*'s) summarizing the problem and a *then* that opens the way to the solution:

If we are to be truly liberated, if we are to understand and explore the contribution sexual arousal can make to relationships, if we are to make it possible once again for this activity to kindle the imagination and intellect, and if we are to do justice to the fact that man has a single nervous system whose functions are integrated and interdependent, then we must evolve a way of thinking about sex which sees it as embedded in a personal context.

Wright counts on his audience to agree with him that the *if*'s are desirable and that the consequent can therefore be affirmed. In the rest of his essay he develops the consequent, outlining the steps that must be taken to achieve the new way of thinking about sex. (Once again, note that if the argument is to be sound as well as valid, the major premise must be true—the consequent must *necessarily* follow from the antecedent. Does it? Or can you offer another *then* clause that is equally convincing?)

Reasoning in *if . . . then* terms can sharpen an issue, making an audience face up to the implications of a widely held but perhaps unexamined view. The following assertion brings out the logical consequence of the notion that the price consumers are willing to pay provides an adequate and accurate index to the value of goods and services:

If price were the only criterion of value, we should really have to accept the phrase *de gustibus non disputandum*, and concede that the desire for heroin was to be regarded by society as equal in every regard to the desire for education. — Eugene V. Rostow, *California Management Review*, Spring 1963

Rejecting the consequent (which, it can be assumed, any reasonable man would do) entails rejecting the antecedent, and this in turn paves the way for reconsidering what criteria should be used in determining the value of goods and services.

EXERCISES

1. Keeping Rostow's antecedent in the passage quoted above, substitute a number of other consequents; for example, "If price were the only criterion of value, everyone would agree that owning a huge diamond is preferable to having adequate housing." Then, keeping Rostow's consequent, substitute a number of other antecedents; for example, "If heroin addicts have made valuable contributions to society, the desire for heroin should be regarded by society as equal in every regard to the desire for education." Use your list of assertions to demonstrate why it is possible to move from affirming the antecedent to affirming the consequent, but not the reverse, and from denying the consequent to denying the antecedent, but not the reverse.

2. What is meant by "failure of logic" in this assertion?

It is a serious failure of logic to argue that because we are in Vietnam or Negroes are poor or policemen are brutal, classrooms should be disrupted, buildings occupied, and libraries destroyed. — Nathan Glazer, *American Scholar*, Summer 1970

In a brief essay, support or attack Glazer's position.

⌐ 3. Support or attack this assertion:

The much-vaunted sexual freedom that the sex researchers and their disciples insist we share is turning out to be a new bondage. — Derek Wright, *Life*, Nov. 6, 1970

Either-Or Syllogisms

The *either-or* pattern offers a natural way of formulating those arguments that weigh possibilities — courses of action, judgments, points of view. The two forms are

	Disjunctive	Alternative
Major premise	Either A or B but not both	Either A or B
Minor premise	A	Not A
Conclusion	Therefore not B	Therefore B

The major premise in the disjunctive syllogism is exclusive — *but not both*. The major premise in the alternative syllogism is not exclusive: both A and B can be true. The minor premise of the disjunctive affirms. But to be valid, an alternative syllogism must have a negative minor premise that excludes one of the possibilities.

> An alternative syllogism with a positive minor premise can have no valid conclusion. If we read, "The senator could either run for reelection this year or try for the presidency two years from now, and he's decided to run for reelection," we cannot assume that the senator is no longer a possible candidate in the next presidential election. He could return to the Senate and then seek the presidency.

In fact, disjunctive syllogisms usually appear as simple *either-or* arguments, with "but not both" implied but not stated: "The senator must either win reelection this year or return to his law practice." Then the assertion that the senator has campaigned successfully means that he is not returning to his practice, and the assertion that he is returning to his practice means that he has lost his bid for reelection.

The simplest form of *either-or* reasoning is the strict dichotomy: Either A or not-A (the senator will either win reelection or not win reelection). Affirming the minor premise automatically denies the conclusion; negating the minor premise automatically affirms the conclusion. In ordinary discourse, not-A is usually transformed into a positive choice, like the defeated senator's return to his law practice.

> The most common *either-or* fallacy is an error in content, not in inference: it results from a major premise that poses incorrect alternatives (*false dichotomy*) or that fails to offer all the alternatives (*incomplete enumeration*). The untrue claim or implication that there are two and only two alternatives is extremely common. The cigarette advertiser asked, "What do you want — good grammar or good taste?" as if he were setting up mutually exclusive alternatives. The militant says, "You're either with me or against me," canceling out neutrality. Both the claim that "We must destroy communism or be destroyed

by it" and the resigned "Better Red than dead" ignore coexistence. In the late 1960's the American people were told that they had to choose between inflation and recession. They got both.

A choice between inflation and recession is a mild example of the dilemma, the form of either-or argument in which both alternatives are unpleasant. The fight against pollution frequently creates true dilemmas—for example, either permit a lake to continue being polluted by industrial wastes or close down the industry and so create unemployment.

Either-or arguments are inviting because they are simple, dramatic, direct. But the real world is complex, not simple like the world of either-or. Often there is another alternative, or there are a dozen more. Whenever you find yourself writing, "We must make this change or accept defeat," or "We must choose either law or justice," or posing alternatives like "He is on our side, or he is an enemy," stop and ask yourself, "Really?" Perhaps if no change is made, the situation will remain about the same. Law with justice is a possibility. He may be neither ally nor enemy. Between black and white there are many shades of gray.

The fundamental test of an either-or argument is less often a matter of logic than of truth—the truth of the major premise. That premise always reflects a classification or division of the material under consideration; it will be true only if it proceeds from rigorous and accurate analysis. (See pp. 99–105.) If other alternatives can be shown to be feasible, the argument is unsound. A systematic consideration of genuine alternatives offers an excellent way of structuring and developing a persuasive essay. But a shrill insistence on an either-or premise that stems from a faulty analysis of the material can be very damaging to the case you are trying to make.

EXERCISE

Thermal pollution of the environment is a major ecological problem. We could eliminate it by shutting down power plants. But that would mean cutting off our supply of electricity. What to do?
Write a "Letter to the Editor" offering your solution.

Categorical Syllogisms

A categorical syllogism asserts a series of class relationships. "All actors are egotists, and Van is an actor; so Van is an egotist." The major premise makes an assertion about all members of a class (actors), the minor premise relates the subject of discussion (Van) to that class, and the conclusion states what necessarily follows.

Each of the three assertions in the categorical syllogism contains two terms. The major term (P) is the predicate of the conclusion, the minor term (S) is the subject of the conclusion, and the middle term (M) appears in both the premises but—naturally—not in the conclusion. Diagrams show the relationships among the terms: the class M falls within the larger class P, and so on.

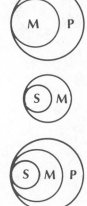

Major premise   All actors are egotists

Minor premise   Van is an actor

Conclusion   Therefore Van is an egotist

In ordinary prose the categorical syllogism is sometimes hard to recognize, for the assertions may occur in any order and one of them may be omitted altogether:

Van is an actor [Minor premise], so he must be an egotist [Conclusion].

Van must be an egotist [Conclusion]: he's an actor [Minor premise].

All actors are egotists [Major premise]; so naturally Van's an egotist [Conclusion].

Van is an actor [Minor premise], and actors are egotists [Major premise].

Here are some other everyday prose statements sorted into premises and conclusions:

We should give this plan serious consideration because it offers a possible solution to the deadlock.

All plans that offer possible solutions to the deadlock are plans that should be given serious consideration. (All M is P)

This plan is a plan that offers a possible solution to the deadlock. (S is M)

This plan is a plan that should be given serious consideration. (S is P)

I know some of my friends oppose the administration; they wouldn't have taken part in the protests if they didn't.

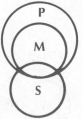

All participants in the protests are opponents of the administration. (All M is P)

Some of my friends have been participants in the protests. (Some S is M)

Some of my friends are opponents of the administration. (Some S is P)

It's unreasonable to suppose that Laux, a staunch Republican, voted for a Democratic governor.

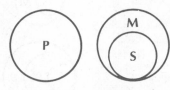

No staunch Republican is a person who votes for a Democratic governor. (No M is P)

Laux is a staunch Republican. (S is M)

Laux is not a person who votes for a Democratic governor. (S is not P)

The tests for the categorical syllogism are precisely the same as for the other types of syllogisms: the conclusion must make a valid inference from true premises. Once again, truth and validity must be examined separately, but in any case the first step is to reconstruct the syllogism so that you can see exactly what is being asserted as true and what inference is being made. In everyday argument it is often the suppressed premise that contains an error. In "All fish have gills, so whales must," the concealed minor premise, "Whales are fish," is false, and so the conclusion is unsound. In "Jack must be a Democrat; he's in favor of socialized medicine," the concealed major premise, "Anybody who favors socialized medicine is a Democrat," is false, and so it is unsound to conclude that Jack is a Democrat. In both instances, as we shall see, the inferences are valid. But validity does not imply truth.

To test the validity of an inference, you often need to rephrase an assertion as well as to expand an elliptical statement into a full syllogism. The terms in the premises of a formal categorical syllogism are qualified in only three ways:

all, no, some. Few and *most* are always translated into *some,* *every* and *any* into *all.* The trickiest qualifiers are *the only* and *only.* "The only people in favor of socialized medicine are Democrats" is clearly the equivalent of "All the people in favor of socialized medicine are Democrats." But "Only Democrats are in favor of socialized medicine," when rephrased as an *all* assertion, must have the term following *only* transferred to the predicate: "All who are in favor of socialized medicine are Democrats."

Diagramming offers a visual test for the validity of deductive inference. An inference will be valid only if the premises yield enough information to locate each circle (representing a class) in relation to the other two. "Jack must be a Democrat; he's in favor of socialized medicine" is valid because the premises tell us where M is in relation to P and where S is in relation to M.

But "Jack is in favor of socialized medicine so he must be a Democrat" is invalid. Though we are told that Democrats (M) are in favor of socialized medicine (P), we cannot tell from the fact that Jack (S) is in favor of socialized medicine whether the S circle falls inside the M circle or in the part of the P circle that lies outside of M. For valid inference you must know whether one circle lies entirely inside another, lies entirely outside it, or intersects with it. A circle without a fixed location indicates that the inference is invalid.

— Diagramming will tell you that an inference is valid or invalid, but to know exactly why it is invalid you need to apply the rules for inference. Two of the rules rely on the concept of *distribution.* A term is said to be distributed when the proposition in which it appears affirms or denies something about the entire class for which the term stands. Propositions are of four kinds:

Universal affirmative	All men are mortal
Particular affirmative	Some men are liars
Universal negative	No men are four-legged
Particular negative	Some men are not liars

In the universal affirmative "All men are mortal" (Fig. 1), the subject term *men* is distributed; mortality is said to be an attribute of the whole of the class. The predicate term *mortal* is undistributed, for no assertion is made about the whole of the class. In the particular affirmative "Some men are liars" (Fig. 2), both terms are undistributed: some men (not all) are in the class of liars, a class whose limits are not specified. In the universal negative "No men are four-legged" (Fig. 3), both terms are distributed: the class of men is excluded from the entire class of four-legged things. In the particular negative "Some men are not liars" (Fig. 4), the subject term is undistributed; an assertion is made about some members of the class but not about all of them. The predicate term is distributed, however, for something *is* asserted about the entire class of liars — that some men are not in the class.

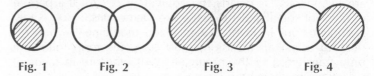

| Fig. 1 | Fig. 2 | Fig. 3 | Fig. 4 |

The shaded circles represent the distributed terms.

Knowing how the terms are distributed provides one quick test for validity. We can now move to the rules for valid inference in the categorical syllogism.

1. A syllogism contains three terms, and the meaning of these terms is the same every time they appear.

> The *fallacy of four terms* is illustrated in this sequence of statements: All intellectuals are aesthetes, and Pete is an incessant reader; so Pete is an aesthete. If you try to diagram the sequence, you will find that there is no way to relate Pete to aesthetes. The most common variant of the fallacy of four terms is *equivocation*, which results from a shift in the meaning of one of the three terms in the syllogism:

All other democratic republics are acceptable as allies of the United States

East Germany is the German Democratic Republic

Therefore East Germany is acceptable as an ally of the United States

> A sly or inadvertent shift in the meaning of a term (as in "democratic republic" here) results in invalid inference. A related error occurs in inferences whenever it is incorrectly assumed that what holds for a class collectively holds for every member of the class. Though Americans *as a whole* may have the highest standard of living in the world, it does not follow that every American lives well. Nor does the truth of the part guarantee the truth of the whole: the malnutrition and wretched housing of American migrant workers do not mean that the American people are ill-fed and ill-housed.

2. The middle term must be distributed at least once in the premises.

> The *fallacy of the undistributed middle* is the most common of the formal fallacies. It is illustrated in this pattern:

American flags are red, white, and blue

This flag is red, white, and blue

Therefore this flag is an American flag

No inference about "this flag" can be drawn because neither premise has supplied any information about the whole class of red, white, and blue flags. In a diagram, "this flag" would fall somewhere within the circle of red, white, and blue flags, but there would be no way of knowing whether it would fall inside or outside the smaller circle of American flags.

3. No term can be distributed in the conclusion unless it was distributed in at least one of the premises.

Illicit process results from distributing in the conclusion a term that was not distributed either in the major premise (the *fallacy of the illicit major*) or in the minor premise (the *fallacy of the illicit minor*). In this syllogism

All good citizens are nature lovers

No hippie is a good citizen

Therefore no hippie is a nature lover

"nature lover," distributed in the conclusion, is undistributed in the major premise. The inference is invalid because, even though hippies are excluded from the smaller circle of good citizens, they may still fall within the larger circle of nature lovers. Do they? We can't tell.

Four other rules will help you spot invalid inference without going through the analysis of terms and their distribution:

4. From two particular premises (assertions about some—not all—members of a class), no conclusion can be drawn. (From "Some men are honest" and "Most thieves are men" we can infer nothing about the honesty of thieves.)

5. From two negative premises, no conclusion can be drawn. (From "No thieves are honest" and "Some men are not thieves" we cannot infer that some men are honest.)

6. If one premise is negative, the conclusion must be negative.

7. If one premise is particular, the conclusion must be particular.

Non sequitur (does not follow) is a comprehensive category covering all those errors of reasoning in which the stated conclusion does not follow from the premises that have been supplied—the fallacies of undistributed middle terms, denial of the antecedent, and so on. But often what looks like a *non sequitur* to the reader is simply a lapse in continuity, a failure to make the relationship clear. It can occur whenever you skip a step in the argument and so leave the reader confused about how one assertion connects with another. Take the statement,

"If you really love Lake Baikal, boycott Gogol's products."
The reader who knows that the Gogol Company has been responsible for polluting Lake Baikal will grasp the relationship between antecedent and consequent. The reader who does not know will be puzzled. In this case, the impression of a *non sequitur* can be avoided by supplying the missing link in the reasoning. In other cases, where the error lies in the reasoning itself and not in the phrasing of it, the relation of the premises must be reexamined and strictly logical tests applied.

The criteria for valid inference in the categorical syllogism apply, with appropriate modification, to other types of deductive reasoning that are variations on the basic three-statement pattern. In a chain argument the inferential process is extended through four or more premises, with any two successive ones sharing a common term: "India was poor; it was ruled by Britain; British interests took goods and money out of India to Britain; therefore India's poverty was caused by British rule." (For the context, see pp. 195–96.) Still other trains of deductive reasoning are grounded not in class relationships but in generally understood relationships such as better-worse, stronger-weaker, older-younger, parent-child, and so on: "If their new release is better than 'Shriek,' it must be better than 'Groan,' because 'Shriek' was the best thing they'd done."

Logical inference offers general guidance but no sure criteria for the arguments we use most commonly in persuasion. By following the rules for valid inference, we could achieve certainty (not just probability) if we knew we were arguing from statements that were incontrovertibly true. But for the most part our reasoning is not grounded in universals (*all* or *none*) and does not yield—or claim to yield—certainty. More often we argue and act on the basis of probability: "The Corner Bookstore carries a good stock of new novels, so I'll probably find Roth's latest there." To say that you will certainly find the novel you want is to commit the fallacy of the undistributed middle; to say that you will probably find it is a reasonable inference. Weighing the probabilities is the crucial test for a good many of the deductive inferences we make, as well as for our inductive generalizations.

EXERCISES

1. Examine these brief bits of deductive reasoning. Sort out premises from conclusions; where necessary, uncover and examine concealed premises; and decide whether or not the

conclusions are sound. If a conclusion is unsound, identify the fallacy.

a. If the Constitution was wisely conceived, the United States was destined to become a great and powerful country. The United States has become a great and powerful country. Therefore, the Constitution was wisely conceived.

b. Why study logic? It certainly has no bearing on the things that matter most to us — love, faith, and so on.

c. He must be either very foolish or very stupid; he's left all his money to charity.

d. He's a radical, all right. Birds of a feather flock together.

e. More students go to college every year. Unfortunately, our mental institutions are getting more crowded all the time. There's obviously something wrong with the education our colleges are giving.

f. Studying logic improves reasoning power. Literature is not logic, so studying literature does not improve reasoning power.

g. Style is choice. Choice reflects personality. Writers differ in their personalities. Therefore writers differ in their styles.

h. No wonder the book is a best seller. Look at the sex in it.

i. He doesn't really believe that human life is sacred. He drives his car every day.

j. He's a distinguished atomic scientist, so the President should seek his advice on this international problem.

k. No sentimentalists are tough-minded; some businessmen are tough-minded; therefore some businessmen are not sentimentalists.

l. All underdeveloped countries are countries where the standard of living is low. All countries where the standard of living is low are countries susceptible to Communist influence. So all countries susceptible to Communist influence are underdeveloped countries.

m. The notion that college students are unconcerned about national politics is absurd. Millions of them have participated in marches and demonstrations.

n. I can't understand why he spends so much time in Europe. He must be un-American.

o. You believe in free enterprise in business, so why won't you support competition in the postal service?

2. Do you agree or disagree that the reasoning as outlined in the second paragraph of the following excerpt should be labeled a

"shoddy" syllogism? If you agree, is it because the inference is invalid or because the premises are unreliable?

What, then, is the danger confronting the American university? It is, simply and seriously, this: that force and violence will become the governing rule on the campus, and that independent criticism, learning, and reflection will fall as the first casualties. This can happen, not only because of Deans, Faculties, and Trustees who may have narrow visions or who may be stodgy and selfish, but also because of a student radicalism whose slogans are premised on shoddy syllogisms and whose impatience becomes an intolerance for all those who have the temerity to dissent from their vision of the true, the good, and the beautiful.

On the matter of shoddy syllogisms, consider one of the favorite rationales that is often heard. It goes something like this, and it will justify any and every action you might wish to take: America is a rotten society resting on and addicted to force, as in its brutal destruction of Viet Nam; the university is a part of American society and thus it, too, rests on force; therefore, it is reasonable to go after universities with whatever techniques and force seem most efficacious, for that is all that universities respect and understand. — C. Peter Magrath, *Brown Alumni Monthly*, July 1968

3. Analyze the train of reasoning in each of the following excerpts and explain why you find it sound or unsound. If it is unsound, identify the fallacy.

a. I see no reason in morality (or in aesthetic theory) why literature should not have as one of its intentions the arousing of thoughts of lust. It is one of the effects, perhaps one of the functions, of literature to arouse desire, and I can discover no ground for saying that sexual pleasure should not be among the objects of desire which literature presents to us, along with heroism, virtue, peace, death, food, wisdom, God, etc. — Lionel Trilling, quoted in Kenneth Tynan, *Esquire*, Oct. 1968

b. The remaking of American education will not be possible without a new kind of synergistic relationship between the colleges and universities and the public schools. The schools cannot be transformed unless the colleges and universities turn out a new breed of teachers educated to think about purpose, teachers who are themselves, in Dewey's phrase, students of teaching. But the colleges and universities will be unable to train the kinds of teachers we need unless they, working with the schools, create classrooms that afford their students models of what teaching can and should be like. — Charles Silberman, *Atlantic*, Aug. 1970

c. Nothing, absolutely nothing, could give more joy to the Kremlin men than to have a university throw out the ROTC and nothing is better for America's fundamental security than to have a university take it on. — Henry J. Taylor, syndicated columnist, July 6, 1970 *d.* All life and property are now in jeopardy because the foreign policies of the national sovereignties produce total anarchy. It is necessary, therefore, for people to stretch their minds, their concepts, and their demands in order to bring about a government over governments. Anything else is irrelevant to their safety and indeed to their destiny. — N[orman] C[ousins], *Saturday Review*, June 27, 1970

e. [Billy Graham] made patriotism an exercise in religion, for patriotism is a form of religion. As the Apostle Paul said, dedication to God and country, that is patriotism of the highest form. It has upheld this nation for 194 years. — *Newport Daily News* editorial, July 10, 1970

f. Sheer literary talent is not enough to make a great writer. A great writer must feel deeply enough about great issues to subdue his talent and to attempt heroic feats. So long as Updike's imagination remains chained to those who fiddle while America burns, as a writer he will remain a supertalented square. — C. W. Griffin, Jr., *Reporter*, May 30, 1968

g. The newspaper should stop reporting local incidents of rape and assault. Such reports arouse fear in our citizens and do harm to the image of our town as a safe, pleasant place to live. The ill effects of such news items certainly outweighs any benefits. — Letter to the Editor

4. From the excerpts in Exercise 3, select any assertion that interests you and write an argument supporting or attacking it. For example, "Literature should [not] have as one of its intentions the arousing of thoughts of lust."

GENERAL FALLACIES

In discussing the tests for reliability and validity and the related fallacies, we have so far been concerned with the process of reasoning that arrives at single propositions — the assertions that result from inductive inquiries or the conclusions following from deductive inference. We turn now to other fallacies relevant to both deduction and induction and applicable either to the logical structure of an argument as a whole or to its distinctly alogical aspects.

> *Begging the question* means assuming the truth of a proposition that actually needs to be proved. "This unfair method of voting must be changed" assumes that the method *is* unfair.

arguing in a circle

("Unfair" is a question-begging epithet.) Though the writer hopes to take advantage of a general predisposition in favor of virtue over vice, in begging the question he is himself engaging in an unethical tactic. One common form of begging the question is *arguing in a circle*. At its simplest, the circular argument asserts that X is true because X is true: "In our society it is necessary to keep up with the latest styles because it is essential to be fashionably dressed." This evasion is often hard to recognize when it is buried in a long chain of argument; but in developing an argument, you should be sufficiently aware of the steps you take to avoid tripping over your own heels.

Another version of begging the question is the *false* or *complex question*. "When is the Administration going to stop leading the country into illegal wars?" begs the question of whether the Administration has led the country into wars and, if it has, whether the wars have been illegal.

Ignoring the question is a broad label for various kinds of irrelevant argument, including *argumentum ad hominem*, the straw man, the red herring, *argumentum ad populum*, and name-calling. It consists in shifting the grounds of the argument from the real issue to one that is not under consideration. In one characteristic form, *argumentum ad hominem*, the attack is not on the issue itself but on those who support the view that is being opposed: "It should be mentioned that this noble champion of academic freedom recently had his license suspended for driving while intoxicated." The trial lawyer's tactic of seeking to discredit hostile witnesses usually depends on *ad hominem* argument. Related to it is the tactic of *damning the source*—dismissing the opposing view because of its origin ("After all, that was Franco's line"), sometimes called *poisoning the well* (or *spring*).

To set up a *straw man* is to argue not against the opposing point of view but against a caricature of it which supports propositions it does not support and may even expressly condemn—that is, to attack an opposition that does not exist. To use a *red herring* is to introduce an issue that diverts the discussion from its proper course: "Before we permit this rock festival to be held in our town, let us remember that hundreds of long-haired young radicals went to Communist Cuba to help harvest the sugar cane."

Irrelevant emotional appeals can be subtle or blatant. Question-begging epithets may be slanted to arouse admiration, sympathy, anger, disgust. Vocabulary may be deliberately used to impress: sometimes a parade of technical terms will hoodwink an audience into accepting claptrap. The *argumentum ad populum* (which usually incorporates a variety of other fallacies) speaks to the jealousies, hatreds, fears, resentments, prejudices, and passions of audiences: "Are you going to continue to allow your hard-earned tax dollars to be handed over to a bunch of immoral bums who are too lazy to work?" Name-calling includes not only insulting racial epithets and crude slurs like *commie, fascist, bum,* and *pig* but labels chosen for their connotations for particular audiences: *liberal, effete, controversial, Eastern, Southern, conservative, intellectual.* Propaganda regularly substitutes diabolic abstractions for human beings.

In the fallacy known as *shifting the burden,* the writer asserts his case and dares the audience to prove him wrong. All manner of beliefs and superstitions fall into this category, from the Great Conspiracy theory of national and international affairs to the conviction that toads cause warts.

In testing your argument, you need to examine all the alogical appeals, as well as the logical appeals, that you have used to support your thesis. Appeals to emotions and ideals —to pride, to justice, to morality—can be powerful means to persuasion. They are properly used when they are brought to bear on the real issue. To use them to cloud or misrepresent or smother the issue is to pervert the nature of responsible argument.

REFUTING ARGUMENTS

Testing relationships and scrutinizing the argument for fallacies should be a regular part of revising every persuasive paper you write. It is also the first step in preparing a paper that sets out to correct a misinterpretation or to refute an opinion—but here you are probing logical relationships and searching for fallacies in the speeches or writings of others.

In the background of every piece of persuasion lurks the opposing thesis. And very often it looms in the foreground as well. In preparing any argument, find out what has been said on the other side or figure out what might be said. Even if you give no explicit recognition to the opposing view in your paper, knowing what arguments its proponents present will help you decide what kind and quantity of evidence you need, what reasons give strongest support to your thesis, and how they can best be ordered. In some of your essays you may limit yourself to constructive argument—affirmative support of your thesis—but in others you will probably want to meet objections, demolish misconceptions, and in general strengthen your own thesis by showing the weaknesses in the counter-thesis.

Especially when you have reason to believe that your readers lean to the opposing view, you may find it useful to open your paper by analyzing and attacking that view. Launching a brief and temperate offensive at the start can clear away obstacles to a sympathetic hearing for your own views. On the other hand, it is ordinarily a bad tactic to recognize and deal with the opposition at the very end of the paper, no matter how briefly; the conclusion should strongly reaffirm your own thesis.

Refutation is an attack on the evidence and the reasoning that make up the proof for the counter-thesis. It occurs when a writer challenges and opposes the position set forth in an editorial, speech, article, or book. In most cases, attack is not enough; the writer bolsters it by building an affirmative argument for the thesis he supports. The term *refutation*, however, properly belongs only to that part of the argument which proves the opponent wrong.

Refutation requires careful analysis of the substance of the argument and of the reasoning that leads to the conclusion. Possible lines of refutation are as numerous as the ways of building an argument. Four common ones are these:

1. The inductive generalizations may be shown to be based on evidence that is inaccurate or misleading—a sample of data that is incomplete or unrepresentative. Sometimes this involves challenging the opponent's powers of observation or his opportunities for finding out the real facts. Sometimes it can be shown that he has relied on unqualified or biased authorities or that he has misused statistics.

2. An attack may be launched on any of the premises on which the opponent has built his case, not only on the factual statements but on the definitions, the causal relationships, the analogies. And the attack may involve challenging basic assumptions that often lie far below the surface of the argument.

3. The refutation may uncover errors in deductive reasoning: unwarranted shifts from *some* in the premise to *all* in the conclusion, improper inferences stemming from an undistributed middle term, subtle changes in the meaning of a word.

4. Finally, the refutation may attack those techniques of persuasion that can be shown to be irrelevant to the issue or manifestly unfair—character assassination by *argumentum ad hominem*, question-begging, devious or overt appeals to prejudice, card-stacking, and so on.

Full-scale refutation, then, extends far beyond the correction of a small error; it goes to the roots of the argument. If it is to be convincing, it must attack premises, not merely conclusions; if it is to win respect, it must scrupulously avoid those tactics that it criticizes in the opponent.

Many editorials and articles in magazines and learned journals attack the views or proposals of specific individuals. Many others attack opinions or attitudes so widely held that they need not be attributed to any one person. In the following editorial, published in 1968, the theory under attack is stated succinctly in the fourth sentence. The containing argument is phrased in the first sentence as a hypothetical syllogism, with most of the space being given to denying the antecedent—that is, to refuting the view that countries and dominoes behave in analogous ways. Though some constructive argument occurs in the second paragraph, the editorial is primarily concerned with refuting, not with supporting a counter-thesis. As the final sentence makes clear, undermining the analogy is intended to cast serious doubt on any foreign policy based on it.

If countries were small, flat rectangular blocks, the domino theory might be a useful principle for the conduct of foreign affairs. However, not only do countries not look like dominoes, they don't behave like them, either. And the theory is not a theory at all but a rather seductive metaphor with almost no support in contemporary history. The idea, as it is viewed from Washington, is that a Communist seizure of power in one country will exert an almost irresistible compulsion on neighboring countries to topple because of insurrection, perhaps with some outside help. (This is to be distinguished from the more familiar truism that unopposed armies can conquer other nations. That is checkers and not dominoes.) Yet the clear lesson of the past few decades is that real countries refuse to act like their hypothetical wooden counterparts. After the Second World War, the Soviet Union was able to dominate the Eastern European nations to the precise extent that its invading armies gave it control, and the war-weakened nations of Western Europe did not succumb despite very large Communist Parties in France and Italy and a guerrilla effort in Greece. The United States supplied help but did not send armies to fight, and the dominoes remained erect. In 1949, the world's biggest domino, China, fell to Mao Tse-tung. Yet in almost twenty years no other Asian nation has established Communist rule, with the exception of North Vietnam — and that country began its struggle against French colonialism in 1945, four years before there was a successful Chinese example to follow. In fact, if it had not been for Communist China's restraining hand at Geneva, coupled with the fear that Mao's victory had bred among the Western powers, it is probable that Ho Chi Minh would today be the peaceful ruler of all Vietnam. On New Year's Day of 1959, Castro marched into Havana. Yet the dire prophecies of further Communist successes across the hemisphere have not materialized. In fact, its Communist Parties and would-be guerrilla movements are weaker today, especially on the crucial and symbolic battleground of Venezuela, than they were when the decade began. Even the minor and partial Communist triumphs in places such as the Central African Republic and Ghana not only failed to influence others but were themselves overturned. For that matter, the non-Communist empire-builders, such as Nasser, have found their neighbors resistant to their ambitions. One might, indeed, almost posit an anti-domino theory: that neighboring countries of similar ideology will tend to draw further apart. Thus Russia and China, China and North Korea, Russia and Eastern Europe.

Nor is the domino theory simply a contemporary fallacy. It has stirred wishful thoughts among revolutionaries throughout the modern age. Lenin and his colleagues expected the Bolshevik triumph to set off revolutions across Europe. They were especially confident of Germany—and Germany's Fascist armies invaded the Soviet Union within a quarter century. Similarly, many of those who helped lead the French Revolution believed they would soon be joined by much of Europe. Yet it took the armies of Napoleon to force other states into an unwilling and temporary association with France. Nor is a comparable, if more abstract, version of the domino theory absent from the rhetoric of our own revolution. Fortunately for the fearful and the apocalyptic, the domino theory directly conflicts with the one really powerful and successful ideological movement of the modern age: nationalism, and the desire to maintain national independence. Nor are countries—even new countries—fragile and tremulously vulnerable. Each of them consists of a people and a land with a history and a culture strengthened by nationalist hopes and ambitions. There is something of condescension as well as a misreading of history in the assumption that these countries will topple at the slightest push. Large powers will tend to influence nearby smaller states—though even this is not a rule, as Yugoslavia and Cuba have proved. Yet in the light of contemporary history the domino theory dissolves, reminding us again that in today's confrontations there are no final defeats, just as there are no final victories, and each battle must be fought on its own terms. The theory is just another abstract and unlikely exercise in historical prophecy—hardly a solid enough justification for sending real men to fight real wars.—*New Yorker*, Feb. 10, 1968

Refuting by analogy often involves *reductio ad absurdum*—pushing the thesis or the proposed course of action to an illogical extreme. The main argument for the control of guns is that guns are used to kill people. Opponents of gun control have argued that if the use of guns is to be regulated because they are sometimes used to kill people, then the use of knives, hammers, cars, and hands should also be regulated. The counter-argument (really counter-counter-argument) typically rejects the analogies by pointing out that whereas the other means of killing have various legitimate uses, the only function of a gun is to destroy. Or it may point out a difference in degree, relying on statistics to show that most murders are committed with guns. Or it may itself advance a *reductio ad absurdum* by inquiring whether the sale of atomic bombs should be unrestricted.

Drawing out the implications of a proposal is an effective technique in refutation and, if it is done fairly, a reputable one. If used unscrupulously, it will distort and misrepresent the original argument, creating a straw man.

Making a lucid, accurate statement of the view that is being refuted is the best protection against misrepresenting it. Caricaturing comes easy in refutation, because normally anyone who undertakes a rebuttal has been stirred—emotionally as well as intellectually—to disagree. But setting up a straw man, or distorting to any degree the position that is being opposed, means there will be no real joining of issues. Ask yourself: Have I represented my opponent's case in such a way that he would find it an acceptable statement of his position?

It is also easy, when feelings are strong, to berate and scold and ridicule. But no one who is seriously interested in dealing with the issue, as opposed to cowing the opposition, uses language as a club. A temperate tone in refutation is not incompatible with strong, incisive assertion of an opposing view. Most important, perhaps, for responsible refutation is to have respect for your opponent. Instead of seeing him as sly, stupid, and dogmatic, picture him as the kind of person you would like to think you are—open, intelligent, reasonable. And as you proceed with your refutation, remember that the purpose of argument is to get closer to the truth. Much sound refutation is devoted not to rejecting the opposing position out of hand but to refining and modifying it.

EXERCISES

1. Analyze the techniques of refutation used in each of the following passages and explain why you do or do not find the refutation convincing. Consider such questions as these: Exactly how does the writer go about the job of refuting? Is he mainly concerned with pointing out errors of fact or judgment or with uncovering mistakes in reasoning or with exposing weaknesses in alogical matters—emotional appeals and so on? Is he himself responsible in his use of evidence and his use of language, or is the refutation open to criticism on these counts?

a. There is a traditional metaphor which makes the critic the "judge" of literature. Such a metaphor may imply that Shakespeare and Milton and other impressive people are, relatively to the critic, in the role of prisoners or petitioners, a prospect so exhilarating that many critics wish to leap into a judicial role at once, on the Alice-in-Wonderland principle of sentence first, verdict afterward. I am aware of the weight and influence of critics today who insist that criticism is primarily evaluative, and my next sentence, whether right or wrong, has been carefully considered. The metaphor of the judge, and in fact the whole practice of judicial criticism, is entirely confined to reviewing, or surveying current literature or scholarship: all the metaphors transferred from it to academic criticism are misleading and all the practices derived from it are mistaken. The reviewer of a current book, whatever its content, is expected to lead up to a value-judgement, to give a clear indication of whether or not he thinks the book worth reading. But an academic critic, concerned with the scholarly organization of literature, is never in this judicial position. He is dealing with a body of literature which has all, whatever its merits, been accepted as a valid subject of scholarly study. For current literature there is an audience that wants to select its reading, but for Lydgate's poems or Heywood's plays there is no such audience—except students, and selecting for them is a function of teaching and not of criticism. Yeats, writing an essay on Swift, remarks that he is unable to check a remark made by a critic about Swift's letters to Vanessa, because those letters bore him. He is really saying that he does not wish to be a scholar, for no scholar can afford the luxury of being bored by anything that is in the least relevant to his area of study.—Northrop Frye, in *The Aims and Methods of Scholarship in Modern Languages and Literatures*, ed. James Thorpe

b. Robert F. Kennedy had a way of saying things loosely, and it may be that that is among the reasons why so many people invested so much idealism in him, it being in the idealistic (as distinguished from the analytical) mode to make large and good-sounding generalities, like the generality he spoke on April 5, after the assassination of Martin Luther King, two months exactly before his own assassination. *"What has violence ever accomplished?"* he asked—as if, one broods in retrospect, he were pleading with the assassin whose name neither he nor anyone else knew, but whose existence he had frequently conjectured—*"What has it ever created? No martyr's cause has ever been stilled by his assassin's bullet."* A martyr being someone who sacrifices his life, station, or what is of great value for the sake of principle or to sustain a cause, it is readily seen a) that not every assassin's victim can lay claim to martyrdom; violence is in fact frequently inflicted against persons qua persons, rather than against persons as representative of causes or principles; and b) some "causes" *have* in fact been stilled by assassins' bullets, it being, however, important to note that "causes" are not necessarily noble causes. The assassination of George Lincoln Rockwell put an end to the American Nazi Party, which was most clearly a "cause." The assassination of Imre Nagy and his followers certainly settled *that* problem. The assassination of Malcolm X accomplished the liquidation of the competition to Elijah Muhammad's hegemony. . . . [Buckley cites other assassinations—including those of Huey Long, Trotsky, Trujillo, civil-rights workers in the South, Presidents McKinley and Kennedy, and Robert Kennedy—and attributes effects to each.]

Indeed, assassinations more often than not *do* accomplish something—I think offhand only of the exception of Hendrik Verwoerd and maybe Diem in recent times. —William F. Buckley, Jr., *Esquire*, Oct. 1968

c. Reams of copy have been written about the strange apathy in the universities. "The kids," it seems, hardly ever trash buildings or badger elderly deans any more. What is the matter with them? The cant answer is that the arduous idealism of the young has been crushed by the tragic failure of "The System" to respond to their strivings for peace and justice, and they are therefore filled with despair.

The non-cant answer is that most students now know they won't get drafted or shot at. A majority of them have been dealt lottery numbers high enough to put them out of danger. Those with low numbers know that, given the increasingly fail-proof techniques of draft evasion, they can be almost sure of beating the draft, for anything from a bum knee to an attack of conscience. And since the U.S. ground combat role in Vietnam is scheduled to end in May, the very few who might get drafted into combat jobs (always a tiny minority of college men) are in virtually no danger at all of getting shot at.

It has always been perfectly obvious to those not bemused by kid worship (including most of the kids themselves) that the more violent manifestations of the arduous idealism of youth sprang largely from an arduous desire not to get drafted or shot at. And this, after all, is not very surprising.

Dr. Johnson once remarked that "Being in a ship is being in jail with the chance of being drowned." Being drafted is being in jail with the chance of being killed. Given a deeply unpopular war, what sensible young man would not resent and resist that prospect? But why must his pious elders interpret this perfectly natural reaction as springing solely from a disinterested idealism? —Stewart Alsop, *Newsweek*, March 8, 1971

d. When I read the works of men like Emerson, who are convinced of the fundamental goodness of man, I find it hard to suppress fits of uncontrollable laughter. Their concept of human nature, which assumes man to be normally motivated by a sort of fraternal benevolence, has, it seems to me, no foundation in fact. Are the bulk of the instances of human relations that we see carried on with consideration for others? I think not. And is there any evidence in nature of a kind of fundamental goodness and charity in the nonhuman world? Nature actually offers a spectacle of death and constant struggle in which the strong continually destroy the weak, where no quarter is asked and none given. I cannot imagine a tiger or lion having pangs of conscience for eating a helpless, harmless, friendly gazelle. This whole process in nature is neatly labeled *natural* selection, a term which implies that this process of dog-eat-dog is a trait inherent in all natural situations. If not from nature, then, from what source comes this most remarkable statement that men are basically good, kind, and full of love for their fellows? The inspiration for it is merely the wishful thinking of Emerson and the rest of the sunny-side-of-the-street gang.

2. Xerox a newspaper editorial or column or a magazine article that expresses an opinion or makes a recommendation that you challenge. Submit the copy with a "Letter to the Editor" or an essay in which you make clear your reasons for disagreeing. (If you prefer, refute an excerpt from the exercises in this chapter or in Chapter Six.)

Chapter Eight

ORGANIZING ESSAYS

Looked at from the outside, the structure of good prose seems frozen. We commonly speak of *the* organization of an essay, as if what lies before us on the page represents the one possible arrangement of the material. Experienced from the inside, however, the process of organizing is, at least up to a point, highly fluid. In the prewriting stage, it is scarcely more than an attempt to piece together a collection of facts and a jumble of ideas. Even in his early drafts the writer may still be searching for order, trying to discern patterns in his material and working to bring the particulars of his subject into a fruitful relation with his formed or half-formed thesis.

In his search for order, the writer is guided primarily by two considerations—what his subject yields to thoughtful analysis and what he wants to say about his subject to his particular audience. The structure he settles on is likely to be the result of a complicated process of reconciling the demands of his material, the needs and interests of his readers, and his own purpose. As he writes and rewrites, he compresses material here and expands it there, possibly transposing or otherwise shifting major blocks. Such juggling is to be expected, for no structure is inevitable. Every essay ever written could have had a different arrangement. The good writer makes the reader feel that the structure he settled on is a sound one. The great writer creates the illusion that it is the only possible one.

Initially we will treat the structure of an essay as the product of the interaction between the writer's material and his purpose in dealing with it. Later we will consider how the writer's sense of his audience will lead him, as he builds his essay, to select certain alternatives and reject others.

There are two basic types of order, *natural* and *logical*. To a large extent, natural order reflects an arrangement inherent in the material itself; logical order represents an abstract pattern imposed on the material by the writer.

Natural Order

Whenever you give a physical description of your subject or treat it in the framework of chronology, the structure of your essay is rooted in the space-time arrangement of the material. For some purposes, you will reproduce the space-time arrangement as accurately as you can; for others, you will alter it. Even when your prime obligation is fidelity to what is before you, you have some options. You can choose a spatial order, proceeding systematically from left to right, top to bottom, inside to outside, suburbs to the heart of town, and so on. Or you may find that you can give a clearer, more unified account by employing a chronological order based on the sequence of your own observation. Large-to-small is one such sequence—the major features first, visible from a distance perhaps, and then successively smaller details. Another is movement from the most striking feature (not necessarily the largest) to less dramatic elements.

Whenever you use description to support a thesis, the order you give your visual impressions will be strongly influenced by your thesis. Think, for instance, of the different ways you might describe a light show or registration day, depending on whether the impression you wanted to get across was purposeful activity or aimless, chaotic movement. But in either case, if your intention is to produce a factual account, the spatial arrangements indicated in your essay should be verifiable by anyone who looks at the same scene. He should be able to see what you have seen, even though it might be fundamentally more congenial to him to see it in a different way. The college registrar sees the light show as chaos, registration day as gratifying design. Your impressions may be the reverse.

For any material presented in a time sequence—an account of a process or a political campaign, a plot summary, a personal narrative—the typical movement is chronological (raw material to product, opening to closing, 1970 to 1973). But again you can modify the actual sequence in various ways. You can describe the finished product before giving instructions about making it. You can begin with the climax of a narrative and then work both backward and forward from it. You can start with the concluding episode and use flashbacks to fill in the action. Whatever the modifications, the order should make sense to your reader, except on those rare occasions when it is your purpose to suggest a chaotic situation. Ordinarily, temporal relationships should be made explicit enough so that the reader can, if he wishes, reconstruct the actual chronology. And whether or not the point of view is explicit, it should be consistent. Weaknesses in descriptive and narrative papers can often be traced to a physical point of view that falters or shifts unaccountably or to confusion or ambiguity in the psychological point of view — to situations in which the reader simply cannot tell where the writer stands, literally or metaphorically, in relation to his subject.

Loosely related to spatial and chronological ordering of material but less common, less useful, and altogether less amenable to analysis is associational order. As the label suggests, this type of organization has its origin not in the observed object or event but in the association the object or event creates in the writer's mind. Associational thinking is often very fruitful in pursuing an elusive word or idea in the prewriting stage, and some professional writers say that in their early drafts associational writing (a this-reminds-me-of-that connection) helps them perceive new relationships in their material. Occasionally, associational order is turned to good use in reminiscences and in published essays of a special type, particularly the light, humorous Sunday feature piece that says less about the subject itself than about the writer — his personality, his habits, his ways of thinking. When it is handled successfully, the strengths of associational order are this personal flavor, the unexpected relationships it reveals, and the artistry that links seemingly random images or ideas. But associational order has risks: the movement may seem illogical or eccentric and the essay as a whole rambling and pointless.

EXERCISES

1. Examine this complete essay, paying special attention to its organization.

So Much Going On

¶1 Because his air bubble nest wasn't ready, he attacked her savagely, his jaws clamping down on her tail fin. She wriggled free and like a gray bullet streaked to the other side of the aquarium, where she took refuge in a web of twisted underwater plants. Having defended his home, the male Siamese Fighting Fish returned to his secluded corner and continued to blow bubbles of air coated with saliva. Each pearl of air rose dizzily to the surface of the water, bobbed momentarily, and then adhered to the other bubbles. Within a week there were hundreds of these jewels of air floating in a mass. The nest was near completion. As each new bubble rose, the female, swollen with eggs, became more desperate. Finally she left her grove of protective vines and once again approached her future mate. This time his nest was ready and he could devote himself to the beautiful creature before him. In anticipation of a mating, her sides were no longer a dusty gray but boldly streaked with glistening blue.

¶2   The male put on his show. He fanned out his plumes of dark violet streaked with a lighter shade. He shook his body, and the sailing fins waved furiously. Gracefully he dropped to the rocks below, the female following his every move. Suddenly from below her abdomen, the eggs spewed. The male quickly passed over them several times, depositing a cloud of sperm. Now the female was hungrily eyeing her fertilized eggs. Her mate opened his mouth in a wide "O" and darted toward her. She had felt his wrath before, however, and was gone before he reached her wake. Because of her voracious appetite for her own young, the male would never again let her come near them. Scooping a cluster of fertilized eggs into his mouth, the male Fighting Fish transported them up to the floating air bubbles. Due to the care of their father, the new-born young would be assured of plenty of oxygen when they hatched.

¶3   Peering into the microscope, looking at the drop of pond water sandwiched between the slide and the lens, one feels that he's stealing his way into a fantastic subworld of nimble beasts a hundred times smaller than a speck of sand. They dart three-quarters across the field of vision, stop, then whirl about and cavort away. Here comes another tumbling about. One can only stare in awe at his enormous littleness. The seemingly playful antics often disguise their true nature. Give them half a chance and they will attack tissue and tear it to pieces like crazed, silent assassins.

¶4   But this new, mysterious world under the microscope can be inhabited by other things besides strange animals and plants. Under the glass a few slivers of hair are transformed into great rough logs. One steps back, awed at the outlandish perfection of the sting of a worker bee or the barbed leg of a mosquito or the thousand light receptors on the "eye" of a fly. What a thrill to see the orange, sun-shaped egg of a sea urchin bombarded by thousands of tiny, comet-like sperm. When one finally crashes through the membrane, a new organism is born under your eyes. With the right simple mixture under the lens, one can see a coacervate, the pre-cellular form that gave rise to life—and you don't have to go back millions of years to see it.

¶5 The other chicks have pecked their way out of their wonderfully protected shells. But one little fellow hasn't the strength to peck out more than a small window. The air circulates in, hardening the blood and membranes. The protective shell has been transformed into a suffocating, binding prison. Soon he will die unless you free him. Bit by bit you peel off the shell flakes. He peeps in pain when the dried membrane is stripped from his delicate feathers. Soon the exhausted chick lies prostrate on the paper. Propped up by your hand, he toddles on wobbly legs that quickly collapse. He lies flat, his legs bent crazily sideways. They punch outwards with astonishing vigor, but they never get under him. He gropes and fumbles, raising false hopes. But it is to no avail. He is a splay chicken. The tendons in his legs never took hold, and he will never walk. Humans like this are put in wheel chairs and fed. Not chickens. It's a sad paradox that you have to take this chick whose life you've saved and plunge him head first into a beaker of water. His mouth closes and opens frantically, gasping for air. But all that enters is heavy, suffocating water. Soon his lungs are filled, and he stops struggling. Your own face feels uncomfortably hot and your shirt is all sweaty.

¶6 Dissecting a shark's head, one is appalled by the vast subway system of olfactory organs that lies beneath the tough leather hide. The horseshoe-shaped canal, with turnstile plates that first sense the moving chemicals in the water, is fascinatingly intricate. As commuters on subway trains are moved from place to place, so the chemical sensations are transmitted from organ to organ until they reach the brain. A big-thumbed male frog jumps on a female frog ripe with eggs. He holds her in his powerful grip and punches her sides until the eggs come flowing out. At the same time his sperm mixes with the eggs. Why do the frogs fertilize externally rather than internally? In an hour the fertilized eggs divide once, then twice. Soon a cluster forms, then a hollow ball. Then a turning-in occurs, a neural plate arises from the buckling outer layer, an elongation slowly takes place, and soon a tadpole is swimming about. The pleasant, powerful aroma of the sea that still clings to seaweed is overwhelming. A paramecium bumbles upon a salty concentration of water and begins to shrink. Why? And to take it a step further, what can it tell a nurse who must prepare an intravenous feeding mixture? A decapitated frog still shows a scratch reflex—how come? A pregnant mouse toddles with the weight of twelve youngsters in her. Placing her little paws around her head, she bears the pain of dropping them out one by one. One tiny pink tike strays away from the nest. It's easy to pick him up by the tail and return him to his mother. And all the friendly, sour, grateful, crabby, shy, carefree, happy, apprehensive, funny, and serious classmates that come are just as fascinating as the marvellous things already there.

¶7 To think that some students say it's all in the book so there's no sense wasting one's time in the Biology lab!

a. Describe the organization of "So Much Going On." To begin with, what are its main parts or divisions? What is the writer's purpose? Is that purpose stated explicitly? If so, where? Do all the parts of the paper contribute to the chief point the writer is trying to make?

b. Now consider how the parts of the essay are related. Do you find an adequate connection between ¶2 and ¶3, between ¶4 and ¶5, between ¶5 and ¶6? Could the order of the paragraphs be changed without damaging what unity the essay has? That is, could ¶3 serve as the opening of the paper? Could ¶5?

c. Structure and unity are intimately related at the level of the paragraph as well as at the level of the whole paper. Examine the material in ¶6. Do you find a reasonable progression from one topic (or detail) to another—shark's head to male frog, for instance? Could the order of the details be changed, or would any change weaken the paragraph? What purpose is served by the questions the writer asks in this paragraph?

d. Has the writer made clear his psychological point of view, his attitude toward his material? Has he established a physical point of view (a viewing point) and maintained it consistently? Study his use of personal pronouns to see how he locates himself in relation to his material.

e. Now that you have described the organization, evaluate it. Is the material developed according to any plan you can discern? Is there a spatial movement that permits you to visualize the laboratory? Is there a chronological movement—events arranged in a time sequence or according to the order in which objects or activities are observed? Is there a progression that makes sense in terms of bringing out the significance of what is being observed? If not, should there be? Or is this kind of material suitable for an essay that is ordered largely on the basis of the writer's associations? If so, what are the associations that apparently govern the order of details?

f. If you judge the organization to be weak, try to identify the main source of the weakness. Is it the writer's uncertainty in handling point of view? Is it his uncertainty about what impression he wants to leave with the reader? Or what?

g. Sketch three plans for organizing the material in this paper, one relying mainly on spatial relations, one on temporal relations, and one on association. Which of these plans do you think would make the best paper? Are any or all of your plans superior to the one you assume the writer followed? If so, in what respects?

h. Try rewriting the paper, using the bulk of the material but rearranging it as you think best. Pay special attention to the beginnings and endings of your paragraphs.

i. Reread the essay, taking into account the content and style as well as the organization. What are its strengths? What are its weaknesses?

2. Paying special attention to selecting and maintaining your point of view, write an account of a high-school graduation, a memorial service, or some other ceremonial occasion.

Logical Order

Except in space-time progressions, the material itself rarely suggests and scarcely ever requires a definite order of discussion. There is no necessary order, for instance, in an analysis of communism or a criticism of a novel or an argument about Black Power. The structure of any essay that explains an idea or presents an argument is an outgrowth of the writer's purpose and his estimate of the rhetorical situation — what aspects of the subject to discuss, in what order, and with what emphasis. The structure is good if it does justice to the material and at the same time makes the writer's ideas and convictions about his subject clear and acceptable to his audience.

Applied to any order that is invented, created, or adapted by the writer, the term *logical* is descriptive, not evaluative. If the writer has done a bad job of organizing, the movement of his essay may be downright illogical.

Because logical order is always invented to accommodate specific material, it can be discussed thoroughly only in connection with a specific essay written to fulfill a specific purpose. The interaction of the writer's purpose and his material may call for a movement through prevalent misconceptions to the truth of the matter as he sees it. It may call for an examination of the many separate particulars of the subject, followed by a comprehensive statement about them. It may call for listing and supporting six reasons for holding a conviction — the six ordered from weak to strong, or from strong to weak, or from middling strong to strongest. It may call for an exploration of three proposed courses of action with a demonstration that one is not feasible, another feasible but not desirable, and the third both feasible and desirable. It may call for a systematic investigation into what the subject is like and unlike, what caused it, what effects it has, and perhaps what good it is.

There are other possibilities, more than can be listed here. Whatever the structure, it should result from the pressure of the writer's idea making itself felt. The good essay has direction and destination. The thought moves. It gets somewhere. Good organization reveals the relation between clusters of details or ideas and carries the reader smoothly from one stage of the discussion to another. Poor organization makes him puzzle over the relation of, say, the sixth paragraph to the fifth and makes him wonder why a topic is treated *here*, not *there* — or why it is treated at all.

Though many variations occur, the skeleton organization of an expository essay is likely to follow one of three basic schemes. In the *support* structure, the essay develops *from* the central idea — an assertion, a generalization, a thesis. In the *discovery* structure, the essay develops *toward* a generalization, a thesis, a solution. In the *pro-and-con* structure, a generalization, hypothesis, or thesis is examined from different points of view, perhaps undergoing qualification, correction, and refinement.

The support structure is sometimes called deductive and the discovery inductive — terms borrowed from logic (see p. 147). As convenient labels for organizational patterns, *deductive* and *inductive* do no harm so long as they are not taken to mean that deductive reasoning must always be presented in deductive order and inductive reasoning in inductive order. The order in which ideas are presented in an essay may be quite independent of the way the writer arrived at those ideas.

Support Structure.   Early in an essay that follows the support (or deductive) plan, the writer advances the idea or cluster of ideas that he intends to illustrate or develop in the rest of the essay. The assertion in the first sentence of the paragraph below (which begins an essay) and the related prediction in the last sentence represent the core of the subsequent discussion:

One of the most interesting changes taking place in our language today is the acceptance of an enormous amount of slang into standard English. Formerly it often took centuries for a piece of slang to gain such acceptance, if it ever gained it. Dr. Johnson, in 1755, insisted that words such as *frisky, gamble,* and *conundrum* "ought not to be admitted to the language." But times have changed. So rapid, indeed, has the process of absorption become that there is a possibility that slang, as a clearly delimitable form of language in America, may be on the way out. — Bergen Evans, *New York Times Magazine*, March 22, 1964

And this sentence, which comes in the second paragraph of an essay, makes the reader expect — rightly — that the writer will undertake to substantiate the five charges in the rest of the essay:

I am compelled to believe that Mrs. Lindbergh has written an offensively bad book — inept, jingling, slovenly, illiterate even, and puffed up with the foolish afflatus of a stereotyped high-seriousness, that species of aesthetic and human failure that will accept any shriek as a true high-C. — John Ciardi, *Dialogue with an Audience*

In essays on this pattern, what follows the initial generalization, assertion, or thesis may be roughly equal blocks of material (groups of paragraphs, sometimes called paragraph sequences), each developing one aspect of the lead-off idea or ideas. Or there may be a progressive narrowing from the initial inclusive statement to a particular application of it (an assertion about a civil-rights principle, followed by an examination of precedents, concluding with a recommendation for action in a here-and-now case). Or the writer may shift immediately from the initial assertion, drop down to the most specific aspect of his subject, and then build back up to the assertion, now giving it more complex or more decisive statement.

Discovery Structure. The typical procedure for an essay on the support pattern is analytic: the writer slices or divides his opening block of material. In the discovery pattern, the procedure is synthetic: he pulls together, gathers up, as he builds toward his thesis. Again, many variations are possible. The writer may begin with a particular aspect of the subject, move to a related one, then to another and another, unfolding his ideas step by step. Sometimes the essay shows a progressive enlargement, starting small and ending broad in inverted pyramid fashion. (A discussion of a campuswide or statewide or nationwide issue may be opened with an account of a single incident that the writer saw or took part in.) Sometimes it starts small, moves to a generalization, and from there, shifting to the deductive procedure, goes on to a new particular that can be inferred from it.

One very useful variation of the inductive pattern is the *problem-solution* (or *question-answer*) structure. The occasion for the essay lies in a problem that needs solving, an issue that needs settling, a phenomenon that needs explaining; and the essay comes to a close when the solution has been offered, the course of action shown to be wise, the explanation made. The writer may move directly from his analysis of the problem to his solution. Or he may explore alternative hypotheses or proposals, showing them to be inadequate and all the while piling up evidence for the solution he is going to embrace. Though the content of essays on this pattern may be complex and the analysis subtle, the bare structure can often be reduced to some such simple formula as:

> To solve *X*, we need to take steps *A*, *B*, and *C*.

or:

> What caused *X*? Not *A*. Not *B*. Not *C*. But *D*.

or:

> What is the right course of action? Not *A*. Not *B*. Not *C*. But *D*.

Because the sense of inquiry or investigation is strong in the problem-solution structure, the approach is particularly useful for persuasive essays, ranging from the mildly controversial to the sharply argumentative. It is also suitable for explanatory essays in which the writer canvasses techniques or methods before offering his own analysis.

EXERCISES

1. Describe the organization of each of the essays printed below. Consider these questions: What is the central idea, and how is it developed? Is the general approach a good one for accomplishing the writer's purpose? What alternative ways of organizing the material can you suggest? In what rhetorical situations might an alternative approach be preferable? Has the writer succeeded in making the movement from point to point smooth and clear? If not, suggest revisions that would improve the continuity.

a.   . . . Because I Am Black

During my first week as a Barnard freshman I was infused with a spirit of adventure, of anticipation at being in New York—that legendary metropolis where all things are possible. I had chosen Barnard because I was so enraptured by the thought of New York City, and the idea of a small college within a large university appealed to me. I would, I thought, be able to do all those things I'd dreamed about, and read about, and heard about—all the things that other girls in America were doing. Those "other" girls, however, happened to be white.

My goal, from junior high on, had been to go to a big college in a big city, major in English, and, presto—become a rich and famous writer. I was unaware at that time how utterly unrealistic these goals were, how childish—not simply because I was expecting success to come so easily, but because I am black, and these things that I dreamed about were white dreams. I did not admit it to myself, but I was saying, in effect: "Well, I may not be good enough for them (white people) now, but when I'm rich and famous, they can't help but respect me." The things that I wanted when I came to Barnard were products of the white-oriented books, movies, and television that I had been brought up on and the urgings of my white teachers in junior and senior high school, and, in fact, everyone else around me.

My background—black middle-class comfortable—dictated that I should strive for this kind of success. My parents thought, and still think, that a degree would open up all the doors that I wanted to open—and I agreed with them. I had very little contact with whites, except as teachers, and I staunchly supported the idea that only through integration and communication between the races could we ever have harmony. Still, I worried about assimilation and acceptance here at Barnard. From the very first, I had felt uncomfortable and uneasy with the white girls I met. I felt that I had nothing to say to them, and vice versa, but I ignored the feeling, chalking it up to "the period of adjustment." This feeling persisted, though, and I began to feel overwhelmed and surrounded. The social life—freshman orientation programs, floor parties, mixers, luncheons, teas—was geared to the incoming white freshman, completely ignoring the different needs of the black students. We were treated as whites too. This may sound fine and dandy, but it is a kind of racism in itself. The administration, the student sponsors, everyone was so willing to "overlook" the fact that we were black and to ignore the different cultural and social background that is black people's. Barnard's lily-white faculty and courses of study emphasized even more the lack of concern or interest on the part of the "powers that be" about the needs or interests of blacks. There were courses in the lives of Ancient Greeks and Romans, in Russian history, in Oriental Studies, but the contributions and considerations of black people in history, in literature, in everything that had to do with the shaping of this country, were skillfully omitted.

It has been put forth as an excuse that the white administration and students know nothing about us and therefore cannot possibly understand what it is that we want, or why we are dissatisfied; in other words, their treatment of us results from ignorance and is not their fault. I contend, however, that it is their fault. They have taken neither the time nor the initiative heretofore to learn anything about black people because the "subject" either did not interest them or did not seem important. Black people, on the other hand, know just about everything there is to know about white people.

At this particular point in history, when suddenly everyone and his brother wants to know what the black person is thinking and why, we have been accused of shutting off the communication lines. "How are we to know what you want us to do, unless you talk to us?" is the cry that I and other black students have heard time and again from administration, faculty, and students here. The answer is, I think, that we no longer want to have things done "for" us, we want to do them ourselves. We are willing to have dialogue, but to protect ourselves, we must dictate the terms. — Deborah L. Perry, *Barnard Alumnae*, Spring 1969

b.　　　　　　Appreciating Modern Art

A work of art is, in one sense, a theory; it is the creative, systematic organization of the artist's ideas. Like any theory, a work of art must be studied in order to be comprehended and appreciated. There are two ways of studying a work of art. When we look at a painting, we can focus on the image it conveys, the scene and the figures before us. Or we can try to see the meaning behind the scene and interpret its symbolic values. The first approach concentrates upon the iconographical elements of the work, the second on the iconological elements. In a good painting, the artist makes the iconographical elements create the meaning of the work, his message. It seems logical, therefore, that we should be most concerned about the iconological elements. Most laymen, though, are not. The lifelike figures and familiar subjects of traditional art have made works of art satisfying at the purely iconographical level. When they look for the same values in modern art, they are often disappointed. Perhaps they can appreciate Andrew Wyeth, but they do not know how to react to Jackson Pollock. What is hardest for them is to appreciate works of modern art that contain strange and distorted figures, iconographical elements that give them no aesthetic pleasure. They will not understand the work or enjoy it unless they make an iconological approach.

The impact of Picasso's "Guernica," for example, depends entirely on its iconological elements. The painting commemorates the bombing of Spanish civilians in the market place of Guernica during the Spanish Civil War. We would expect a realistic representation of the bombing to depict masses of people running in confusion and panic. But the iconographical elements bear little resemblance to our expectations. There are no planes in the painting and no soldiers. There are only eight figures. Three are animals, and the other five only vaguely resemble human forms. One woman, whose eyes penetrate the side of her uplifted face, holds a dead child and cries out. Another woman, whose body stretches like a rubber band, runs toward the left side of the painting, where the first woman stands. Another thrust to the left is produced by a third woman whose head and long, cloudlike arm shoot out of a window. She clutches a lantern. A fourth woman, the lower portion of her body missing, falls down into flames on the right side of the painting. The fifth human form is a decapitated statue of a soldier lying below the other figures.

At the center of the painting is a huge horse that stretches upward and seems to be crying out in pain. On a fence in the background is a small bird, also crying out. The only immobile figure in the work is a bull on the far left side. He stands calmly viewing the agonized activity of the others. He is the central figure, for all the others seem directed toward him through either their horizontal or their vertical thrusts.

The iconographical elements of the painting not only fail to depict a bombing scene but are disturbing for other reasons. There is an absence of males although there were as many men as women in the market place during the actual bombing. Moreover, the emphasis on animals is hard to understand.

To appreciate the painting, we have to see the scene as symbolic. The woman and her child represent all women and children. The woman who runs represents the fearful, the woman with the lantern the hopeful, the woman falling into the flames those who died in the bombing. The decapitated statue represents the destruction of Spain's ancestral honor by the Civil War. The huge horse is a symbol of Spain itself, mortally wounded, and the bull who stands so calmly among the imploring figures symbolizes Franco, who was responsible for the bombing.

From the iconological viewpoint, it is clear that Picasso is not attempting to reproduce the scene of the bombing of Guernica but to express an idea about it. The figures in the painting are distorted and unnatural to instill a feeling of shock in the viewer and to reinforce the idea that the Civil War was a terrible and unnatural occurrence. Picasso was much more interested in conveying this message to the viewer of "Guernica" than in creating a work that would give immediate iconographical pleasure. Other modern artists often similarly distort iconographical elements to force the viewer to search for the symbolic meaning. Unless the viewer looks beyond what is on the canvas he will not appreciate some of our great modern artists.

2. Write an explanatory or persuasive essay on any topic suggested to you by one of the essays in Exercise 1. If you like, respond directly to the central idea of the essay, either supporting it or refuting it. Indicate the audience you have in mind. In revising your essay, pay special attention to making the structure firm and clear.

Pro-and-Con Structure.   Instead of exhibiting a movement either from or toward a generalization, the pro-and-con pattern examines the same generalization from different points of view. Though less common than the deductive or the inductive structure, it is admirably suited to purposes that call for balanced appraisal of good features and bad, risks and opportunities, advantages and disadvantages. The basic movement is zigzag, signaled by terms of contrast, concession, and qualification like "on the one hand . . . ; on the other. . . ." The pattern is turned to persuasive purposes when the writer ends on a strong note of preference for his *pro*.

The opening of a discussion of British colonialism in India shows the use of the pro-and-con pattern to probe competing generalizations. The first paragraph states the opposing points of view:

The British Raj: imperialist aggressors, exploiters of the Indian sub-continent, repressive tyrants betraying the principles of their own civilization. Or the British Raj: benevolent despots, peacemakers in India, enlightened rulers bringing order and efficiency where chaos had reigned and training in the most precious element of the Western tradition, democracy. Two views: one couched in the rhetoric of Indian nationalism, the other in that of the British administrators of India.

In the four paragraphs that follow, the author turns to the Indian charge of economic oppression and finds it essentially unproved. He does not, however, dismiss the charge out of hand; his method is to moderate and refine the initial generalization rather than to reject it. Notice the repeated use of *but* in the paragraphs analyzing the nationalists' claim. The pro-and-con movement is well suited to the practice of making distinctions that qualify an initial generalization.

The theme of economic distress and oppression was a fundamental part of the rhetoric of Indian nationalism. Nationalists pointed to India's poverty and charged — but did not prove — that this poverty was the fault of the British Empire. The authors of this charge were themselves generally middle-class Indians enjoying at least fair economic security. Their argument was simple: India was poor; it was ruled by Britain; British interests took goods and money out of India to Britain; therefore India's poverty was caused by British rule.

To describe the source of the charge is not to prove it false, but the failings of British economic policy in India show evidence of negative rather than of positive harm. Nineteenth-century Indians spoke often of the "drain" on India caused by the British by which they meant that there was a steady flow of gold and goods out of the country which was not balanced by an equal influx of goods of any kind. This drain, they claimed, impoverished India and caused the rural poverty and periodic famines that plagued the country.

There had been an actual drain of goods from India during the latter part of the eighteenth century and probably extending into the nineteenth, but it resulted less from British actions than from failures to act. Tariffs are a good example. British economic policy, the famous laissez-faire, prevented the creation of protective tariffs on goods coming into India; emergent Indian industries were thus left to the mercies of general competition. Only once did the British government take positive action directly against Indian interests — and that was to establish a tariff on Indian cotton in order to protect the Lancashire wool industry. But this move was the exception. British economic failure in India was generally the result of the absence of any action at all.

Not that the British Empire in India did not operate in the long run against the interests of Indians. The destruction of village industries through European competition and the failure to establish modern industries are probable evidence of the destructive effects of British rule. It has been argued that the passion of the British governors for caution and economy kept them from undertaking programs that would have been beneficial to the country and policies that might have led to the eventual industrialization of India. But if India failed to progress, it seems fair to say that it was less because of the conscious policy of its rulers than because of the combination of current economic fashion and the unconscious, though consistent, British pursuit of imperial interests. British policy *may* have damaged the Indian economy, and India's poverty *may* have been a function of British rule. But twenty years after independence and partition, it is more difficult and less convincing to charge British imperialism alone with the responsibility. — Norman F. Cantor, *The Age Of Protest*

In the remainder of the passage, the author examines the British claim that imperialism brought enlightenment to India and gave training in democracy. Again he makes distinctions, demonstrating that while *political* oppression was sporadic, psychological oppression was chronic and its effects widespread. Again the pro-and-con structure affords the means of testing and refining the initial generalization. The upshot of the discussion is a new view of "the British Raj" — one different from either of those presented at the start.

The three movements outlined so far are best viewed as abstract patterns, radical simplifications of the actual structure of most essays. An essay often embraces several generalizations, roughly comparable in weight; instead of being lumped at either beginning or end, they are distributed in such a way that each is the nucleus for one section of the essay. Still, the progression within each section will roughly approximate one of the patterns. Thus a generalization may be either the departure point or the culminating point for a cluster of examples:

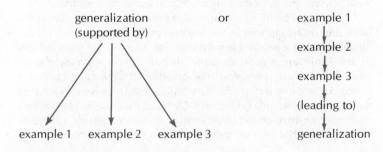

Or the initial generalization undergoes qualification as it is tested by examples arranged as lateral, contrasting pairs:

generalization
example 1   *but*   example 2
example 3   *but*   example 4
example 5   *but*   example 6
Therefore, generalization 1 emerges as generalization 2.

These are the basic movements. Of course, further choices have to be made. The examples themselves should be arranged in a sequence that makes sense—chronological, simple-to-complex, increasing importance, or whatever order suits the writer's purpose.

In the same way, you can organize a passage of causal analysis by first stating the causes (or effects) and then treating them one by one. Or you can present the causes one after another until the full scheme is revealed. If your aim is to weigh and judge several probable causes, you may use the pro-and-con movement ("The evidence points to this cause, but . . ."; "Still this is not entirely plausible, for . . ."; and so on). You have similar options when you are defining.

Division is typically treated in a support structure, the various parts or stages set forth at the outset and then taken up in turn. Classification uses either support or discovery. If you are classifying television commercials, you may say at the outset that your investigation has turned up four main kinds of appeals made in commercials, identify each in a sentence or two, and then proceed to discuss them in turn— moving from the least common to the most common, or through degrees of subtlety, or according to some other principle. Or you can start with a description of one commercial, gradually build up to the class that it represents, then move to a striking example of a different class, and so on. The first option gives stronger emphasis to the class; the second highlights individual examples.

Comparisons have their own built-in structures: whole-to-whole with its broad contrasts, part-to-part offering the opportunity for more searching analysis, and likeness-difference (or the reverse) carrying its own special emphasis and leaving the reader with a strong impression of either similarity or dissimilarity, depending on which is discussed last. (See pp. 82–87.) Choices among them depend on the complexity of the material and on the writer's purpose. All three can fit into the pro-and-con scheme. Or, if the writer chooses to summarize the upshot of the comparison before going into it in detail, the containing structure may be deductive.

As the list of options suggests, an essay need not display a single uninterrupted movement in one direction. It may be made up of half a dozen sections or paragraph sequences, each with a recognizable movement of its own—particular-to-general, general-to-particular, or pro-and-con. The key to the structure of an essay is the perception that each of these sections has its separate identity and makes its unique contribution to the overriding purpose of the writer yet falls into a necessary relation to the other sections.

EXERCISES

1. Describe the organization of "Exploring the Land of the Sticks," the essay beginning on p. 433. Is the general plan closer to the support structure, the pro-and-con structure, or the discovery structure? Explain why you think the structure is or is not the best choice for the subject.

2. From a book of readings or from current magazines, select half a dozen explanatory and persuasive essays. Describe the large-scale organization of each essay; consider alternative ways the material might have been presented. Taking into account the author's purpose in writing the essay and the audience he is writing for, explain why you think he did or did not find a good way of structuring his discussion.

For this exercise there is no need to make detailed outlines of the essays. Read an essay several times to get control of the content, and then prepare any kind of skeletal scheme that will help you indicate the large-scale features of the organization. The notes below are based on an essay by Benjamin DeMott in *Life*, April 17, 1970.

Problem	1	The root problems are not *A*, *B*, *C*
	2–3	One root problem is *D*—discussed in terms of two opposing groups
	4–5	The second root problem is *E*—analyzed in terms of two opposing attitudes
Solution	6	The first step toward the solution is *X*
	7–8	Another step toward the solution is *Y*—broken down into three recommendations
	9	Central problem restated and need for solution reaffirmed

3. How much influence should students have in deciding the content and the method of the courses they take? Think through the problem of the nature and degree of student participation in curriculum planning. Then write three essays sup-

porting your thesis—one addressed to a neutral audience, one to a sympathetic audience, and one to an audience hostile to your position. The three essays should differ somewhat in content—a sympathetic audience does not need precisely the same kind of evidence that a neutral one does—as well as in structure and in style. To each of your essays, attach a diagram or a few sentences identifying its basic organization.

STRATEGIES OF ORDERING

The nature of the material and the writer's purpose in dealing with it always have a strong influence on the structure of an essay. That influence is necessarily decisive when the audience is so heterogeneous, so remote, or so vaguely defined that the writer cannot even speculate about what strategies of ordering might be most successful in reaching it. But in most writing situations, the audience is and should be a third determinant of structure.

The two chief rhetorical strategies in ordering material are the strategy of _announcing_ and the strategy of _disclosing._

In announcing, the structure of the essay is made explicit, either in a fairly elaborate program paragraph early in the paper or in guidepost statements interspersed at key points throughout (or, sometimes, in both). A program paragraph previews the organization by indicating the divisions of the subject or by listing the topics to be treated; it may or may not include a direct statement of purpose of the "This-essay-will-attempt-to-show" sort. At any rate, the writer tells what he is going to do before he does it. When the function of announcing is performed by sentences interspersed through the essay, they often summarize as well as forecast, reminding the reader of what ground has already been covered besides orienting him to what lies ahead.

The strategy of announcing is evident in an essay that opens with the remark that the unexpected decline in the President's popularity needs looking into or (more pointedly) that news analysts are offering five reasons for the decline in the President's popularity or (more pointedly still) that the writer proposes to investigate reasons for the decline in the President's popularity. The writer who adheres to the policy of announcing keeps few organizational secrets from the reader. Structure is exposed or, at any rate, lies close to the surface of the essay.

In the strategy of disclosing, structure lies deeper. The

beginning does not forecast the end, and the discussion proceeds from stage to stage without overt signaling. When the strategy is used successfully, the subject seems to unfold according to its own inner pressure, and the climax sometimes brings with it an element of surprise. (In the good essay, the surprise is immediately tempered by a "Why, of course!" reaction, for in retrospect it shows itself to have been inevitable.)

At first glance, announcing would seem to be the likelier strategy for an essay that moves *from* a generalization, disclosing the likelier strategy for an essay that moves *toward* a generalization. But there is no necessary correlation. A problem-solution essay may proceed with the full panoply of announcing, including direct comment on the procedures being followed, the alternatives being excluded, and so on. Or the discussion may be handled in such a way that the reader is gradually brought to realize that a problem exists and then given a sense of sharing in a joint inquiry that leads to the solution.

For some of your papers it will seem natural to adopt one strategy rather than the other. But often material is amenable to either. In making your choice you should be guided by your estimate of the audience's needs, interests, and predispositions. If the material is inherently difficult or the organization complicated, you may decide that the reader will find the essay hard going unless you announce at some length, offering a blueprint to show how each topic or section fits into your whole scheme. Or you may decide that the blueprint approach is too formidable and that you should instead begin with the segment of material most familiar to the audience and gradually work up to the more complex aspects of the subject, disclosing the full scheme only toward the end of the essay. (You can find both approaches in the textbooks on your desk.)

If you can count on your reader having a strong initial interest in the subject, you may decide to plunge directly into the material without offering any guidance to structure. Or you may conclude that economy and clarity would be better served if you sketched the course of discussion in a program paragraph; that way, you may feel, the reader can move confidently through the essay, concentrating on the content. If you suspect that your reader's interest is so minimal that he will go woolgathering while you are expounding, you have an even harder decision to make. Can you announce in such a fashion that your promise of good things to come will counteract his indifference? Or does the strategy of disclosing hold more likelihood of capturing his interest? If you are writing an argument, size up the audience's probable attitude. Is it largely hostile to your position or sympathetic to it or indifferent? Will announcing harden hostility or dissolve it?

Answers are hard to come by and probably shouldn't be attempted except in individual writing situations. Few rhetorical problems are solved by formulas. Perhaps the most that can be said in a general discussion is that, when handled well, both strategies can result in strong, satisfying organization—though neither guarantees it.

In the long run, the justification for structure is internal. Announcing does not create good structure; it simply makes it manifest. Though announcing ensures that the reader knows where he's going, it may make the structure seem mechanical. The strategy of disclosing escapes this danger but has hazards of its own. Unless the parts of the essay have a tight, organic connection, making the logic of a shift from one part to another immediately clear, the reader may not see what direction the essay is taking. And if he has difficulty grasping the general drift, he will probably miss the significance of many of the details. A good writer always offers clues to structure, even if he seeds them deep.

One strategy does not necessarily rule out the other. In long papers you often have occasion to use both. In the first half you establish the universe of discourse, perhaps by giving a chronological sketch of the origins of the problem, analyzing its current dimensions, and offering a methodology for solving it—all this in a structure strong in announcing. In the second half you shift the technique, now organizing the discussion as an exploration in which you and the reader are carried forward by the logic of the inquiry.

Whether you choose to announce or to disclose (or to announce and disclose by turns) you should, in organizing your material, aim to involve the reader in your discussion as deeply as you are involved in it. You want him to understand what you have to say, to take an intelligent interest in it, and ultimately to accept it.

SIGNALS OF ORDER: TRANSITIONS

Strong organization demands that the parts of the essay be in the right order, the order that permits the writer to say what he wants to say to his particular audience. It also requires that the order be apparent to the reader and that it seem at least reasonable, at best inevitable. Though the essay of a writer who is in control of his material may meet the first requirement, it can fall short of the second simply because he hasn't bothered to provide connecting links. Knowing himself how the parts fit together, he forgets that the reader doesn't have his inside information.

Sometimes the connections are discernible in the material, and the movement seems as natural and necessary as the change from night to day. More often they have their origin in the writer's insight into his subject, his approach to it, his analysis of it. He *makes* the connections, and in composing his essay he must be sure they come clear to the reader. At the structural joints where one stage of the discussion ends and another begins, the writer—especially if he is given to announcing—will consider using explicit *transitions*, bridges that carry the reader from one topic to the next.

In themselves, explicit transitions seldom advance the discussion. They signal relationships; they establish connections. Often they comment directly on the structure of the essay, as in this passage, where the first paragraph looks back and the second ahead:

Such are the four basic processes by which air carries its moisture aloft. They can work alone or together to produce an infinite variety of cloud forms and combinations.

Now suppose we spend two or three days observing the sky during the approach and passage of a typical warm front. This means we start with a cold air mass around us. The air behind the front is comparatively warm. What kinds of clouds do we see as the boundary between cold and warm air approaches?—Richard M. Romin, *Natural History*, June-July 1968

The machinery of transition is also visible in the following key paragraph, which comes exactly in the middle of its essay. The first sentence summarizes the discussion to this point; the last forecasts what is to come:

These, then, are the negative effects of the scientific literature I have observed in the course of teaching scientific writing. I am glad to say that there are also definite positive findings. The most striking observation is that by teaching writing you can actually strengthen students' ability not only to write but also to read more attentively and to think more logically and rigorously.—F. Peter Woodford, *Science*, May 12, 1967

Paragraphs that announce their function as directly as these do are easy to identify as transitional even out of context. Other transitional paragraphs do their work less obtrusively; only in context are they seen to be gathering up and pushing on.

Transitional paragraphs are the most overt signals you can use in the body of an essay. They are usually brief—often only a sentence long—and because they normally have a strong imperative force, they should be reserved to mark major turns in the discussion. In short papers their function can be performed by transitional sentences, which differ from transitional paragraphs only in the quantity of the material they gather up and in the attention they ask of the reader.

The transitional sentence normally comes either at the

beginning or at the end of a paragraph—only occasionally in the middle. It signals a shift from one idea to another, indicates that the discussion is to take a new turn, or marks a digression from the main thread. In some cases a transitional sentence might just as well be set off as a separate paragraph (the first one below). In other cases (the second example) the connection with what follows is so close that the sentence needs to be run into the paragraph.

A word, finally, about the isolation of our colleges, particularly those not attached to great universities. Colleges tend to be ingrown, and this tendency is aggravated by geographic isolation. . . .—Henry Steele Commager, *Saturday Review*, Feb. 21, 1970

But this is only part of the truth. For broadcasters are not so much in thrall to sponsors as they claim to be.—Charles A. Siepman, *New York Times Magazine*, April 19, 1964

Raising a question is a common way of marking a new stage in the discussion:

In contrast, what are our hopes for the United States?—Alvin C. Eurich, *Reforming American Education*

The question has distinct merits as a transition. It structures the discussion very clearly. Although in introducing the new topic it does not disclose precisely what the writer's position is, it does promise an answer. Used sparingly, it is a good device. Overused, it quickly becomes tiresome. Misused—as when the question does not rise naturally out of the discussion—it is amateurish.

Tangential points and digressions are marked by transitions:

Before I try to look into the future, I would like to present a debit and credit sheet on mankind.—G. L. Stebbins, *Saturday Review*, March 7, 1970

While in no way central to his development as an artist, Tennessee Williams' career as a shoe salesman is worth recalling at this point.

Most transitional paragraphs and some transitional sentences are like road signs: they tell where you are going and perhaps where you have been. Other transitions prescribe routes, signaling connections that must be made if the reader is to understand the writer's thought accurately. A good many words and phrases perform this function, among them *however, moreover, likewise, on the contrary, consequently, incidentally, therefore, as a result, on the other hand, nevertheless, in the first place, in short.* These and other transitional words and phrases are discussed in detail on pp. 255–62 and in *Transition.

Explicit transitions serve the writer well when they point out connections that the reader would not otherwise perceive. But if too many are used, they can weigh writing down, slow its movement, and make the machinery of expression seem to take precedence over the thought. If the direction of the discussion is perfectly clear and the order predictable, announcing in the form of the authoritarian "First it is important to consider . . ." or the chatty "Now let's examine . . ." is wasteful and sometimes annoying; and *however*'s and *therefore*'s following too hard on each other create a thudding effect. But inadequate use of transitions results in disconnectedness; the reader may fail to see the relationship the writer intends. The skilled writer, though careful not to overload his prose with overt signals, uses explicit transitions where he needs them—especially to mark a turn in the discussion and to relate paragraphs in which the ideas are not obviously consecutive.

The skilled writer also knows the value of less obtrusive means of establishing continuity. Instead of standing outside his material and pointing the reader in the right direction, he tries to make the language of the discussion do the work for him. The phrase at the beginning of a paragraph may allude to a point he made three paragraphs earlier. Or, in moving from one paragraph to another, he may carry over a key word or synonym that echoes the idea. Here a slight variation ("undignified"—"lack of dignity") accomplishes the transition:

. . . And the statement becomes undignified—if not, indeed slanderous.

The lack of dignity in such statements is not in the words, nor in the dictionaries that list them, but in the hostility that deliberately seeks this tone of expression. — Bergen Evans, *Atlantic*, May 1962

Semantic connections that grow from within the material—*organic* transitions—bind the prose together without stopping the flow of the discussion. These as well as grammatical means of establishing continuity, such as the use of pronouns and parallel constructions, will be discussed in the next chapter.

EXERCISES

1. Identify the transitional paragraphs and sentences in three fairly long articles (two thousand words or more) in current magazines. If one article shows a much higher frequency of these overt signals than the other two, can you account for the difference in terms of the subject matter or the writer's purpose or his style of writing? Do you find any relation between the use of transitional paragraphs and sentences and the general strategy (announcing or disclosing)?

2. In one of the articles, identify the words and phrases that serve as explicit transitions from paragraph to paragraph. Look closely at the beginnings and ends of paragraphs to find out what devices other than explicit transitions are used to establish the continuity of the discussion.

3. Review the two essays in Exercise 1, pp. 191–94. Mark the transitional sentences and paragraphs. If you think the essays would profit by more explicit transitions, compose sentences or paragraphs to do the job.

BEGINNINGS AND ENDINGS

The beginning of an essay may be a paragraph, less than a paragraph, or several paragraphs. The same is true of endings. Although some good essays do not have identifiable sections that can be labeled "beginning" or "ending," how an essay opens and how it closes have a bearing on the reader's interest in and acceptance of the content.

Beginning

For the typical reader, "interest" and "understanding" have a bearing on each other. If he doesn't understand what the writer is up to, he won't be much interested. If the opening captures his interest, he will work harder to understand what follows; if it doesn't interest him, all the clarity in the world is largely wasted on him. The beginning should be clear, then—for "understanding"—and it should catch the reader's attention—for "interest."

An essay begins well when interest and clarity cooperate, each nourishing the other. If they are in conflict or if one dominates at the expense of the other, the opening is likely to be unsatisfactory.

The sure way to achieve clarity, it would seem, is through the technique of announcing. But the labored statement of purpose will kill off interest: "This paper is going to discuss. . . . The four chief topics to be treated are. . . . First in importance. . . ." This crystal-clear blueprinting works in some stereotyped situations, as in the impersonal, factual report where the only desiderata are accuracy and system; and in special circumstances it can be highly dramatic, as when a trial lawyer begins, "I am going to prove to you. . . . First, I will describe. . . . Second, I will trace. . . . Third, I will expose. . . . And, finally, I will demonstrate. . . ." But for most purposes the announcing should be more subtle. And it need not come in the first sentences, for the program paragraph—the announcing paragraph—is not necessarily the lead-off one. In a long essay it is often the last in the sequence of paragraphs that makes up the opening section, sometimes the first paragraph of the second section. In such cases, it is preceded by a stretch of material that contrives to bring the reader into the essay less formally and less abruptly—the short relevant anecdote; the passage of descriptive details (giving, say, the look of clouds in a summer sky as a way in to a careful, precise account of how clouds are classified and what causes cloud formations); the larger context that points up the significance of the issue being debated. And so on.

A dull opening, though regrettable, is less irritating than one that is either meretricious or misleading. Deliberate efforts to whip up interest are always objectionable. Sensational details, forced enthusiasm, and chitchat actually draw attention away from the subject, not toward it. One trouble with a wildly provocative opening is that the writer robs himself of the opportunity to build toward any sort of climax. The paper can only trail off. Another is that concentrating on "interesting" material often produces an opening that is tangential to the real subject of the paper and hence misleading: the short, dramatized narrative used as a standard opening for articles in popular magazines is sometimes germane to what follows, sometimes no more than a gimmick. In general, the beginning should offer clues not only to the subject of the essay but to the way it is to be treated, and the opening sentences should set the tone of the discussion. Compare these two beginnings, each of which is entirely in keeping with the discussion that follows it:

I have at least one qualification for writing about the generation gap. I have lived with two, if not three, of them during my lifetime.

To be sure, practice does not make perfect. But it does teach one to realize an important human truth. The movement of events is almost always a great deal faster than the movement of our own minds.

In my youth, for example. . . .—Walter Lippmann, *Harper's*, Oct. 1967

I've grown damned sick and tired of having the youth culture, whatever that is, rammed down my throat by members of my own generation. I am all, as I said here last month, for the self-determination of the old, or getting on for old, and I do not think that a mindless and guilt-ridden capitulation to the questionable values of the young will set my people free. Those of us who were born before, say, 1935, have some values and some virtues of our own, and I think it's high time one of us spoke up for them.

In the teeth of a perfect gale of mass-media propaganda to the contrary, I'd like to suggest that the middle generation possesses a greater share of skill, subtlety, discipline, and judgment than its juniors. . . .—L. E. Sissman, *Atlantic*, April 1971

Instructors and editors who have been swamped by openings that are phony or plodding or pointless sometimes advise throwing away all first paragraphs and letting second paragraphs stand as openings. It's true that a short essay scarcely needs a paragraph that can be identified as a separate, distinct "beginning." But both writer and reader must have a sense that the starting point is a logical or natural one, and throwing out the first paragraph doesn't guarantee that the next will make a strong start. The best course is to cut in on your material at a point that has caught your own interest. If this doesn't work, try writing the introduction last in order to gear it to the rest of the essay. A good beginning arouses expectations that the body of the essay satisfies.

Ending

Short papers seldom need identifiable conclusions. When the process has been described, the narrative completed, the problem solved, nothing more need be said—or nothing but a brisk sentence or two of comment, perhaps an allusion to something at the start of the paper to round out the discussion.

But essays that move through several stages need recognizable endings if they are not to give the impression of having been cut off too abruptly or of simply running down, and the good writer knows how to turn this necessity to his own uses. The ending is his last chance to bid for the acceptance of his ideas—to drive home the thesis or clinch the argument. A good conclusion manages to bring out the significance of the whole discussion. A mechanical summary on the order of "In this paper I have shown that . . ." is lifeless, but a restatement of the course of the discussion, drawing out implications, is appropriate in long papers and may be necessary when the material is difficult. When evidence has been built up throughout the paper, the ending can repeat as an authoritative statement what was presented at the start as a tentative hypothesis. Or the ending may recapitulate only the strongest of the arguments made in the essay. Even when it is little more than a summary, an ending can take on freshness from a slight change in style — a sharpening of the tone or a relaxation of tension or a touch of wit.

The good ending makes it clear that the essay has arrived at its destination; it strikes a note of finality and completeness. Whatever works against that sense of completeness weakens the paper. The ending is not the place for afterthoughts, for bringing in ideas that should have been treated in the body of the paper. Nor is it the place for apologies or confessions of inadequacy. It is the place for as much affirmation as is justified by the discussion that precedes it. It may also be the place for pointing to broader implications, for indicating the significance of the findings, or for throwing a challenge to the audience. An ending that brings an essay to a totally satisfying conclusion may at the same time open a door into another essay as yet unwritten.

EXERCISES

1. Here are the openings of two papers on the fluorescent lamp, the first prepared for beginning high-school students, the second for college students with some knowledge of physics. State in detail the differences between them and discuss their appropriateness to their intended audiences.

a. You turn the switch. For an instant, nothing happens. Then light flickers along the tube. And finally there is full, steady illumination. As contrasted with the ordinary bulb, which lights up as soon as its switch is turned, the fluorescent tube always provides a moment of dramatic uncertainty. Why the hesitation?

b. The fluorescent lamp is a device which utilizes a relatively low voltage electric current to provide artificial illumination. Unlike an incandescent light, it employs an electrical discharge through tenuous mercury vapor to convert electrical energy into light energy. The discharge produces invisible ultra-violet light. The long glass tube through which the discharge passes is coated on the inside with a substance that transforms the ultraviolet light into visible radiation. That the visible light comes from this coating rather than directly from the discharge differentiates the fluorescent lamp from other types of discharge lamps.

2. Describe and evaluate the beginning and ending in each set quoted below. What expectations does the beginning arouse? How do you know that the ending is an ending? In making your evaluation you may find it useful to take into account the publication in which the essay appears.

a. It was just after dawn on a chilly November morning, and the three surveyors were scratching about the barren earth southwest of Fort Stockton, Texas looking for the old cedar stakes that would give them their bearings. The men were members of a seismic team, jolting and bullying the earth out of its geologic secrets on behalf of a major petroleum company. One of them, 49-year-old Raymond Medford, reached down to tug at a gray pipe protruding from the chalky soil; as he did, there was a sharp report and something tore upward into the fleshy part of his hand. "What happened?" one of the other men shouted. Medford, confused and shocked, was running in circles. Then he calmed and said, "That thing went off! It had an explosion, whatever it was." A doctor in Fort Stockton looked at the bloody hand, administered first aid and sent the surveyor off to bed. An hour later Medford was dead.

Investigation showed that the pipe in the earth was a so-called "coyote-getter," a deadly device loaded and cocked and set to shoot a cyanide charge into the mouth of any animal that pulled at its aromatic wick.

. . . .

One comes away from a discussion with this plain-spoken biochemist—and other experts in the field—with the uneasy feeling that there are serious gaps in the toxicological profile of sodium fluoroacetate. Whole tables and booklets have been prepared on such practical matters as the exact amount of 1080 required to kill kangaroo rats, ferruginous rough-legged hawks, Rhode Island red hens and Columbian ground squirrels, but no one seems to have done much research into an equally practical matter: What is the total amount of 1080 and other poisons that the sodden soils and polluted waterways of the West can absorb without becoming lethal agents themselves? One asks, and one is told: "Nobody knows."

Someday we may be dying to find out. — Jack Olsen, *Sports Illustrated*, March 8, 1971

b. The course of Negro American literature has been high-lighted by a series of social and political crises over the Negro's position in America. The Abolition Movement, the Civil War, Reconstruction, and the riot-lynching periods both before and after World War I have all radically influenced Negro writing. Each crisis has brought in new themes, new motivations, new character-types, new viewpoints; and as each crisis has passed, the Negro writer has tended to drop most of the special attitudes which the crisis produced and to move toward the so-called main-stream of American literature.

Between, roughly, 1940 and 1965, two new crises occurred: the Integration Movement (which was climaxed by the 1954 Su-preme Court Decision) and the Civil Rights Revolution (which is still with us and which began to take on its present day characteris-tics around 1960). Each of these movements has affected Negro writing.

. . . .

Summing up again — these, then, are the trends I find in the lit-erature of the Black Revolt: a repudiation of American middle class values; a revival of interest in protest writing; the glorification of the black jazz musician; a "mixed" attitude towards whites, particular-ly white women; and a tendency to depict through the ghetto kid the evils of the inner city. In the works of the period which I have read, I have found two or three highly competent productions but none of the caliber and scope of *Invisible Man*, the finest fruit of the Integration Movement. Perhaps it is far too soon to expect that kind of synthesis.

What about the future? Where will these tendencies lead? When America grants full equality to the Negro (as it will), several of these current attitudes and themes will be dropped. The Negro American writer will do then what he has always done after each crisis in the past — continue on his trek to the mainstream of Ameri-can literature. — Arthur P. Davis, *The Promethean*, May 1967

c. The contemporary crisis of American confidence comes in great part from a growing sense of our inability to manage violence. The rise of violence at home has done more than anything else to create doubt about the internal prospects of American life; while, ironically, it has been the failure of violence to achieve our aims in Vietnam which has created equal doubt about the prospects of our foreign policy.

When President Johnson spoke to the nation about Vietnam on March 31, 1968, he did more than suspend military escalation, in-tensify the search for negotiation, and remove himself from the impending Presidential contest. Though he did not of course put it this way, he announced the collapse of a policy and even perhaps the end of an era. His speech implied a rejection, or at least a drastic modification, of the premises which have governed American foreign policy since the end of the second world war.

. . . .

The experience of Vietnam has shown that we cannot run two crusades at once—that we cannot wage even a small war against an underdeveloped country and at the same time move creatively to meet the problems of our own land. The policy of total involvement in the world is incompatible with the policy of social reconstruction at home. It would appear that in the years ahead America will exercise international influence less by trying to run the planet than by trying to solve the new problems of the high-technology state—the accelerating pace of technical change, the humanization of the city, the dilemmas of racial justice, the reform of education, the plight of the individual in a world of great organizations. In the years immediately to come, the world will follow us less because of our armed might than because of our capacity to heal the disruptions and fulfill the potentialities of the electronic society. If this is so, then we return to an earlier conception of the way America should seek to lead the world. "She will recommend the general cause by the countenance of her voice, and by the benignant sympathy of her example," said John Quincy Adams. ". . . But she goes not abroad in search of monsters to destroy." — Arthur Schlesinger, Jr., *Harper's*, March 1969

d. The nature of the United States government's attempts—and failure—to get sufficient relief to starving Biafrans at the end of the Nigerian civil war provides perhaps the first real view of how the carefully constructed foreign policy machinery of the Nixon Administration works in a crisis. A great many human lives were involved. No one can say how many, but a series of medical surveys within the former Biafran enclave in eastern Nigeria report the highest starvation rates recorded in human history, and no substantial alleviation since the end of the war in January.

. . . .

The debate continues over whether it would have made any difference if the United States government had tried earlier and harder to get more food to the Biafrans. There is of course the possibility that it would have made no difference; that this is another case of America as "Prometheus Bound." But that is not the point. Nor is it very relevant whether the doctors were right or wrong, whether the Biafran officials were responsible for the condition of their population or whether anyone was being "political."

The central issue is how this government responded in a crisis, when there was information available that indicated a human tragedy of substantial magnitude. It chose to ignore the unpalatable facts.

Its communication system failed. It was not ready to act. In a moment of uncertainty, when there were moral as well as practical reasons to anticipate the worst, the instinctive bureaucratic response was to defend what it was doing and hope everything would turn out all right. The President, who had the ultimate responsibility, did not choose to intervene in the bureaucratic struggle. A matter of life and death in another continent was transfigured into an issue of institutional rivalry in Washington. When a consensus finally developed in Washington, there was trouble in getting the policy executed in the field. And even now, there is a reluctance to face, or admit, the facts. It must be emphasized that all those involved in this particular issue approached it intending to do something about the starvation. In terms of the human lives involved, that is what makes what happened so hard to accept. — Elizabeth B. Drew, *Atlantic*, June 1970

3. Review the opening sections of the passages in Exercise 2. Which illustrate the strategy of announcing, which the strategy of disclosing? Does the strategy seem to be appropriate to the subject (so far as you can determine it) and to the general style?

 PROPORTION AND EMPHASIS

Some papers have such long introductions that they are more overture than opera. Some papers are all middle; the discussion has neither context nor justification. And some papers rush through the beginning and the middle and then hammer away at a conclusion as if reiteration were a satisfactory substitute for substance.

An essay needs to have shape as well as direction. A bulge occurs whenever the writer lets a minor point get out of control and take up more space than it deserves. Good proportions in a paper come from the writer's own sense of the relative significance of the separate ideas, modified by his sense of the needs of his audience. If his readers are unfamiliar with the subject, he will spend time breaking ground; if they are likely to find one of his ideas thoroughly uncongenial, he will pile up convincing evidence at that point; if the discussion has been complicated, he will devote space at the end to pulling things together.

Emphasis is related to proportion. What deserves most emphasis usually gets most space. Position can give emphasis, too: beginnings and endings offer major opportunities.

Beginnings can arouse curiosity and dispel doubt, and endings (of sentences and paragraphs as well as of essays) can serve as clinchers. A comparison that aims to prove the superiority of one product over another puts its strongest claim either at the beginning or at the end—the beginning if the writer senses initial resistance, otherwise the end for climax.

Failures in proportion and loss of emphasis often stem from the practice of writing by association and from the habit of qualifying. You may find that associational thinking is a fruitful technique in prewriting (writer-in-search-of-a-topic) and in early drafts. One idea reminds you of another, one image calls up another, one word leads to another. You stalk your subject, chasing it through related pictures in your mind or through the connotations of the words you are setting down (even through puns and other varieties of word play). You are hospitable to all ideas. But an essay is not a tote bag; you can't stuff everything into it. At some stage you need to make a more disciplined approach. Otherwise, the digressions will elbow out the central topic, or there will be a constant drift away from the line of argument. As your real topic shapes up, you will have to prune away the extraneous material that associational thinking has produced and distribute the relevant material with attention to both proportion and emphasis.

The habit of qualifying also has both dangers and strengths. Properly, every writer strives for accuracy and truth. This means he will need to qualify some of his generalizations, take note of exceptions, and ward off unwarranted inferences. In some rhetorical situations, he will want to establish himself as a man of moderation, not given to extremes either in the ideas he advances or in the tone of his discourse; and so he will qualify and temper his remarks. All this is reasonable, often admirable. But carried too far, the practice dissipates the force and interest of both ideas and expression. When the qualification takes space that should go to the assertion, timidity has undermined proportion. When the qualification swallows the assertion, timidity has destroyed emphasis.

TESTING ORGANIZATION: OUTLINING

Opinions differ sharply on the value of outlining in the prewriting stage. Some professionals never make outlines of any kind. Outlines inhibit them, they say, choking off their ideas instead of stimulating them. Or they find that the act of outlining, by satisfying the need for expression, kills the desire to write. Equally experienced writers have testified that they can't write without an outline. Some work from sketchy notes. Others draw up an extremely detailed plan before they begin, tinkering with it until they know it is right. Still others *think* the whole thing through, so that they have the complete structure in mind before they write a word.

What kind of writer are you? If your essays read as if you are mechanically ticking off points one, two, three, then perhaps you are being cramped by your outlines and should learn to use them more flexibly. If your essays are criticized for being scattered and disorganized, you probably need to try outlining—in your head or on paper—before you write. But never let an outline freeze an essay. As you write, you should always feel free to move away from your plan. The act of writing down one recollection may spark another that throws a different light on the event; a new example may cancel out an old one; a sequence of details may point toward a conclusion quite unlike the one that originally seemed logical. Whenever you have to choose between following an outline and following your ideas, go with your ideas. Change your outline. Keep your mind open.

Types of Outlines

The working outline (or scratch outline or informal outline) is a private affair—fluid, subject to constant revision, made without attention to form, and destined for the wastebasket. But enough working outlines have been retrieved from wastebaskets that something can be said about them.

A working outline usually begins with a few phrases and some descriptive details or examples. From them grow fragmentary statements, tentative generalizations, hypotheses. One or two of these take on prominence, shaping into the main ideas that seem worth developing. New examples bring to mind new ideas, and these find a place in the list of phrases, canceling out some of the original ones. The writer keeps adding and subtracting, juggling and shifting, until he has his key points in an order that makes sense to him. He scribbles a sentence, works in a transition, and adds examples.

Depending on his habits, he may discard his working outline as soon as it has served the purpose of getting the direction and shape of his essay clear to him. Or he may keep it beside him as he writes, checking off points as he covers them, rejecting those that prove unsatisfactory, taking out time to rethink and reorder before finishing the first draft. By then, if he has kept expanding and correcting it, his outline comes close to being a rough summary of the essay itself.

Here—minus crossings-out, arrows, and general untidiness—is a working outline prepared for an essay about the record album of the musical *Hair*. When it had reached this stage, the student was ready to begin writing.

What's with my generation? Listen to *Hair*—captures attitudes, language of many young people.

Songs use wit, sarcasm, anger, "brass-knuckle boldness."

Even the music is a put-on—parody of "Star-Spangled Banner"; mother's song. Exaggerated rhythm ("Black Boys/White Boys").

Down with intellectual, technological man. Seek truth in astrology ("Age of Aquarius"), meditation, drugs. "Where Do I Go?" Look to nature (though see what man's doing to it—"Air"), children. "Down to the gutter/Up to the glitter."

Down with racial prejudice ("Colored Spade"), down with *accepting* racism, down with old heroes ("Abie Baby"), old taboos.

Great appeal—"Let the sunshine in."

Full of savage attacks. Painful humor. Language intended to shock. To accomplish what? On the positive side: simplicity. (Simplemindedness?)

Immediate popularity of some catch lines. Big disputes about how good it is. On first hearing, POW! On fifth? Fiftieth?

Where the working outline is ragged, the formal outline is tidily schematic. Though not necessarily a public affair, it may be; and when it is intended for eyes other than the writer's, it should observe certain conventions. Some of these conventions make the formal outline more remote from the actual essay than the working outline is. Following the title, for instance, stands a thesis statement, which may or may not appear in the paper and, if it does, may not occur at the beginning. The outline itself passes over introductory and transitional material as well as most illustrations and restatements. In its final version, it reflects a process of logical analysis that has broken down the thesis into its parts, each represented by a main heading in the outline. These main heads are in turn analyzed into their parts, with subdivisions indented to show relationships of coordination and subordination. Theoretically, the subdividing can go on indefinitely; practically, it is rarely carried on beyond the third level. On the logical principle that division always produces at least two units, no single subdivision is permitted in the formal outline.

Following are two versions of the formal outline—the topic outline and the sentence outline—both based on parts of the paper we saw taking shape in the working outline above. Note that the topic outline uses phrases or words for heads; the sentence outline uses complete sentences. In both, logically parallel ideas are presented in matching grammatical structures. First, the topic outline:

The strength of the score of *Hair* is in its initial impact and appeal.

I. The *Hair* recording as a picture of today's youth
    A. Language
    B. Life style
    C. Philosophy

II. The music
    A. Parody
    B. Satire

III. The lyrics
    A. Philosophy of youth
        1. Rejection of science and materialism
        2. Search for meaning
    B. Social commentary
        1. Attack on status quo
        2. Racial attitudes
        3. Moral attitudes

The sentence outline:

III. The lyrics answer the question: "What's with the younger generation?"
    A. They express the philosophy of the alienated young.
        1. They reject intellectualism, science, technology.
        2. They propose seeking truth and love through meditation, drugs, and astrology, and in nature and children.

    B. They express youth's attitude toward contemporary society.
        1. They depict the status quo as dishonest, hypocritical, obscene.
        2. They speak for the embittered black.
        3. They demand complete frankness and openness in word and deed.

IV. The songs in *Hair* have great initial impact.
    A. Judged in context, the lyrics are effective.
        1. They should not be confused with poetry.
        2. They are strongest as satirical attacks, weakest as positive statements.

    B. Reaction to the vocabulary used in the lyrics involves the generation gap.
        1. For older listeners, the four-letter words are a serious obstacle to sympathetic communication.
        2. For many of the young, the language fits the situation.

The topic outline is the usual choice if you are preparing an outline to accompany a short or medium-long paper. For long papers, especially for reference papers, a sentence outline is often required, and it is always the best choice when you are asking for advice and criticism. Because the ideas are expressed in complete sentences, inconsistencies and lapses in logical progression will be more obvious in the sentence outline than in the topic outline or the working outline. Though preparing a sentence outline is sometimes as time-consuming as writing an essay from a working outline, the sentence outline may be worth the effort, for of all the outlines it remains the most informative for both writer and reader.

Testing Organization

Though professional writers disagree (often passionately) on the value of outlining in prewriting, probably everyone would agree that reducing a completed essay to an outline is an excellent way to expose its structure and test the progression of ideas. Making a detailed textual outline on the model of the sentence outline is the surest means of gaining control of any difficult reading you are assigned. And making an outline, however rough, of your own essays is the surest way to determine whether or not they have genuine progression. For this purpose, begin by making a paragraph-by-paragraph summary (a sentence for each paragraph is safe enough) and then, on the second round, bracket related sequences, and use indention to mark off subordinate points. Probably a two-level sentence outline will tell you all you need to know.

Once you have made this rough approximation of a sentence outline (including the formal statement of a thesis), you can move quickly to close gaps, improve sequences, and in general give your rewrite a stronger, firmer organization. Unquestionably, bad essays are sometimes written from good outlines, but accurate outlining does expose structural weaknesses, and simple exposure at least clears the ground for sound revision.

EXERCISE

Review the sentence outline, p. 216, examine the instructions in the *Index* article *Outline form, and then criticize the form and content of the following outline. Suggest specific ways of improving it.

American Opera: The First Hundred Years

Though opera in America was limited by circumstances, its gradual but sure development revealed the strong need for this art form among the American people.

I. The New Setting for Opera
    A. Limited by struggle to live
    B. Opera didn't fit present life

II. First Performance
    A. *Flora*
        1. February 18, 1735
        2. Charleston, South Carolina
        3. Quality of performance
           a. Singing
        4. Attendance
    B. *The Beggar's Opera*
    C. Audience
        1. Fashions
        2. Divided by classes

III. Types of Early Operas
    A. Ballad Operas
        1. Plots concerned with daily life
        2. Used popular tunes for music
    B. Folk Operas
        1. Plots based on folklore
        2. Music derived from traditional tunes

IV. How Presented
    A. Traveling stock companies
        1. Limited wardrobe and settings
        2. Limited number of artists

V. Expansion of American Opera
    A. French influence
        1. French popularity after Revolution
        2. French operas in New Orleans
    B. Italian influence
        1. Steamboat
        2. Visits by Italian touring companies
        3. Erection of first permanent opera house in New York by Lorenzo da Ponte

VI. Conclusion

Chapter Nine

PARAGRAPHS

Paragraphs in newspaper stories and in dialog are marked off mechanically; and paragraphs that fulfill special functions of transition, restatement, and emphasis may be so closely bound to the context that they have little if any independent character of their own. But in expository prose most of the content paragraphs — those that do the work of conveying the writer's ideas — are paragraphs by virtue of their internal organization.

A content paragraph is a group of related statements that a writer presents as a unit in developing his subject. It appears as a unit to the eye because it is physically set off from what precedes and what follows, either by indention of its first line or by spacing above and below. More fundamentally, it strikes the mind as a unit because of the connections that exist between the statements it contains. Each cluster of related statements — each paragraph — forms a stage in the flow of thought (as this paragraph defines the subject, and the next expands on the function of paragraphing).

If one function of paragraphing is to join related statements into a unit, another is to separate that unit from what precedes and what follows. Experience leads us to expect the statements in a paragraph to have a connection with one another. It also leads us to expect that every new paragraph will take a somewhat different tack. We read indention as a signal that the thought is going to shift, and we adjust our attention automatically. Paragraphing therefore offers indispensable clues to the movement of ideas in an essay. Careless paragraphing obscures that movement; careful paragraphing helps make it clear.

To gain some understanding of the various roles paragraphs can play, it is useful to approach them through an intermediate structural unit, larger than the paragraph but smaller than a full essay. This unit is given various labels—part, stage of discourse, paragraph group, paragraph sequence. We choose the last of these, even though on rare occasions the paragraph "sequence" is a single paragraph. Normally a sequence consists of several paragraphs, so related that an attentive reader recognizes that they perform one main function in the total scheme of the essay.

 ## PARAGRAPH SEQUENCES

Paragraph sequences are the main blocks of material you isolate when you are reading carefully, trying to grasp the organization of an essay. To find them, you look for structural joints and bridges. Joints are the breaks or pauses where a writer moves from his opening to the first point he discusses at length, where he turns from one main section to another, where he shifts into his conclusion. Often, but not always, these joints are indicated by bridges—transitional sentences and paragraphs designed to help a reader move easily from one section to the next. (See pp. 202–03.) When you have marked off the opening and closing sections (if any), labeled transitional elements, and bracketed as a sequence each stretch of paragraphs that makes up an identifiable section of the discussion, you have blocked out the main features of the organization.

On the next page are simple diagrams of the structure of four essays of moderate length (1200–2000 words). "Beg" stands for the opening, "End" for the conclusion, "S" for paragraph sequence, "Tr" for transitional paragraph or paragraphs. As the diagrams indicate, the divisions we call paragraphs may or may not correspond to the significant structural units of an essay. The beginning may be a paragraph (as in Essay One) or more than a paragraph (Essay Two), or the essay may lack any identifiable introduction (Essay Three). The same is true of the ending. A main part—our paragraph sequence—may be identical with a paragraph, as in the last paragraph of Essay Four, but usually consists of two, three, four, or more paragraphs. A transition from one paragraph sequence to another may be bridged by a sentence that is run into the beginning or end of a paragraph (not marked in the diagrams), by an entire paragraph (¶8 of Essay One), or occasionally by two or more paragraphs (¶s 4 and 5 of Essay Four).

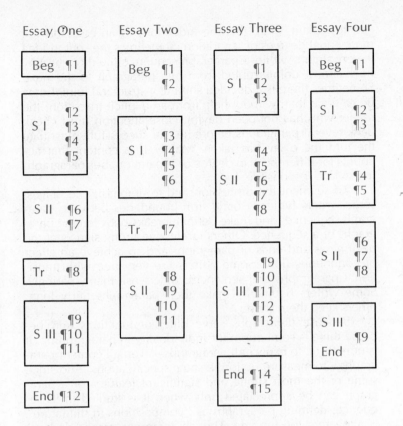

Essay One | Essay Two | Essay Three | Essay Four

Essay One:
Beg ¶1
S I ¶2 ¶3 ¶4 ¶5
S II ¶6 ¶7
Tr ¶8
S III ¶9 ¶10 ¶11
End ¶12

Essay Two:
Beg ¶1 ¶2
S I ¶3 ¶4 ¶5 ¶6
Tr ¶7
S II ¶8 ¶9 ¶10 ¶11

Essay Three:
S I ¶1 ¶2 ¶3
S II ¶4 ¶5 ¶6 ¶7 ¶8
S III ¶9 ¶10 ¶11 ¶12 ¶13
End ¶14 ¶15

Essay Four:
Beg ¶1
S I ¶2 ¶3
Tr ¶4 ¶5
S II ¶6 ¶7 ¶8
S III ¶9 End

Roles of Paragraphs

When you examine paragraphs in context, you see at once that they differ substantially in the roles they play in the whole discourse and in the way they relate to neighboring paragraphs. One paragraph is pivotal, laying the groundwork for and controlling the discussion carried on through a sequence. Another is a structural guide—a transitional paragraph. Still another is little more than a breathing space—a restatement of an abstruse or complicated part of the discussion. One paragraph depends heavily on its immediate environment; another does not. In a group of three linked paragraphs, the second and third may bear on the central point made in the first one, amplifying, illustrating, and proving the point but adding nothing that is not implied by the preliminary statement. In another sequence, the paragraphs may stand in a first-second-third relationship, each partially autonomous, all of roughly the same weight and importance. A pair of paragraphs may stand in a complementary relationship—one cause and the other effect, one positive and the other negative, one listing advantages, the other disadvantages.

It is plain, then, that the indentions in an essay do not mark equal degrees of separation. Sometimes the shift in idea is very slight: within a paragraph sequence the thought may flow almost uninterrupted from one paragraph to the next. Sometimes there is a decided shift: at a structural joint it may be so great that, without help from an explicit transition, the reader who has not been paying close attention must check back several paragraphs before he can successfully negotiate the turn the essay has taken. Mainly it is content that accounts for differences in degree of separation, but paragraphing style is responsible, too.

To segment the discussion and to emphasize its stages, some writers typically build firm boundaries between paragraph sequences and make definite breaks between the paragraphs of a sequence. Others rarely give strong signals at the beginnings and ends of paragraphs and so achieve an effect of continuous flow. Some writers are very free with transitional paragraphs and sentences; others use them sparingly. Some writers habitually make their paragraphs fairly long; others keep them short.

Because paragraphs serve different functions and because there is some room for individuality in paragraphing, it is unrealistic to expect all paragraphs—even all content paragraphs—to measure up to the same specifications. And since some of the most subtle and significant features of a paragraph can be appreciated only when it is studied in its sequence, defining paragraphs as "compositions in miniature" is altogether too limiting. Though some paragraphs do have a self-contained wholeness, most of those in tightly organized essays do not: when they are detached from context, they are manifestly incomplete. The beginning bears the marks of its uprooting, or the ending requires some further development, or the paragraph as a whole seems to lack point. Even when the paragraph makes perfectly good sense, it usually does not carry the full meaning or emphasis the writer intended; its justification comes from the larger movement of thought of which it is only a fragment. When that justification is missing, the paragraph does not say precisely what it says when it speaks in company with its neighbors.

EXERCISES

1. Examine the following passage:

¶1 A word is needed at this point to explain in fuller detail what is meant by the *structure* of a subject, for we shall have occasion to return to this idea often in later pages. Three simple examples—from biology, from mathematics, and from the learning of language—help to make the idea clearer. Take first a set of observations on an inchworm crossing a sheet of graph paper mounted on a board. The board is horizontal; the animal moves in a straight line. We tilt the board so that the inclined plane or upward grade is 30°. We observe that the animal does not go straight up, but travels at an angle of 45° from the line of maximum climb. We now tilt the board to 60°. At what angle does the animal travel with respect to the line of maximum climb? Now, say, he travels along a line of 75° off the straight-up line. From these two measures, we may infer that inchworms "prefer" to travel uphill, if uphill they must go, along an incline of 15°. We have discovered a tropism, as it is called, indeed a geotropism. It is not an isolated fact. We can go on to show that among simple organisms, such phenomena—regulation of locomotion according to a fixed or built-in standard—are the rule. There is a preferred level of illumination toward which lower organisms orient, a preferred level of salinity, of temperature, and so on. Once a student grasps this basic relation between external stimulation and locomotor action, he is well on his way toward being able to handle a good deal of seemingly new but, in fact, highly related information. The swarming of locusts where temperature determines the swarm density in which locusts are forced to travel, the species maintenance of insects at different altitudes on the side of a mountain where crossbreeding is prevented by the tendency of each species to travel in its preferred oxygen zone, and many other phenomena in biology can be understood in the light of tropisms. Grasping the structure of a subject is understanding it in a way that permits many other things to be related to it meaningfully. To learn structure, in short, is to learn how things are related.

¶2 Much more briefly, to take an example from mathematics, algebra is a way of arranging knowns and unknowns in equations so that the unknowns are made knowable. The three fundamentals involved in working with these equations are commutation, distribution, and association. Once a student grasps the ideas embodied by these three fundamentals, he is in a position to recognize wherein "new" equations to be solved are not new at all, but variants on a familiar theme. Whether the student knows the formal names of these operations is less important for transfer than whether he is able to use them.

¶3 The often unconscious nature of learning structures is perhaps best illustrated in learning one's native language. Having grasped the subtle structure of a sentence, the child very rapidly learns to generate many other sentences based on this model though different in content from the original sentence learned. And having mastered the rules for transforming sentences without altering their meaning—"The dog bit the man" and "The man was bitten by the dog" — the child is able to vary his sentences much more widely. Yet, while young children are able to *use* the structural rules of English, they are certainly not able to say what the rules are.

¶4   The scientists constructing curricula in physics and mathematics have been highly mindful of the problem of teaching the structure of their subjects, and it may be that their early successes have been due to this emphasis. . . . — Jerome S. Bruner, *The Process of Education*

a.   Note that the fourth paragraph is incomplete. What are the indications that the three complete paragraphs form a unit, a paragraph sequence?

b.   Could ¶1 stand alone as an explanation of structure? If so, how do you account for the presence of ¶s 2 and 3? If not, what essential additions are made by ¶s 2 and 3?

c.   Is the separation between ¶s 1 and 2 greater or less than that between ¶s 2 and 3 and that between ¶s 3 and 4?

d.   Which of the three paragraphs is most dependent on its context — that is, which loses most in meaning and general significance when it is detached from the others?

e.   If you were to divide ¶1, where would you make the break? Why? Why do you think the author chose not to divide the paragraph?

2.   Following the procedure outlined on p. 220, mark off the paragraph sequences in a magazine article of substantial length. Explain how the author has signaled the beginning and the end of each sequence. (In some magazines extra space separates paragraph sequences, reinforcing the author's structural clues. But don't assume this is always so. White space is often placed arbitrarily, separating paragraphs that are actually very closely related.)

3.   Type up two or three selections from a book of essays without making any paragraph indentions. Ask five or six members of the class to indicate where the paragraph breaks should come. Do the readers generally mark off paragraphs where the author did? Do they generally agree with each other? If not, how do you account for the differences?

(Normally in experiments like this one, the style of the original has a good deal to do with the results. If the passage is expository prose in which the organizational signals are strong, there is little disagreement — no more, say, than whether a transitional sentence belongs at the end of one paragraph or at the beginning of the next one. But if the movement of the unparagraphed material is associational rather than logical, readers usually report many disagreements, some not easily ironed out in discussion.)

What does your experiment tell you about our concept of a paragraph? How flexible is it?

Paragraph Length

A good paragraph—when judged in its context—satisfies logical requirements, rhetorical requirements, and usually conventional requirements as well. Logic asks that consecutive statements in a paragraph be related in a way that is intellectually sound; the paragraph itself should make sense as the reader moves from one statement to another. Indention should also make sense, signaling a pause or turn in the thought as one paragraph ends and another begins. Rhetoric insists that the paragraph as a whole have a unified impact and that it convey its meaning with the emphasis the writer's purpose requires. Convention stipulates that paragraphing be done at least partly to break up the page, to provide some visual relief from a succession of full lines of type, to divide the text into manageable bites. No doubt paragraphing would be a simpler, more satisfying procedure if length were controlled by logical and rhetorical considerations alone. But length is partly a matter of convention and the reader's convenience.

EXERCISES

1. Count the words in each of the three complete paragraphs in the passage by Bruner on pp. 222–24, and calculate the average number of words per paragraph. Determine the comparable word counts and average for three consecutive paragraphs (but not opening or closing paragraphs)

a. in this chapter

b. in two essays in a scholarly journal such as *PMLA, American Historical Review, Journal of Psychology, Science*

c. in two nonfiction articles, without dialog, in one or more of the following: *Atlantic, Harper's, Saturday Review, New York Review of Books, New Yorker, Esquire, Scientific American*

d. in *Newsweek, Time, National Review,* or *New Republic*

e. on the front page, the editorial page, and the sports pages of a newspaper

2. What tentative generalizations can you make about the relation between paragraph length and the nature of a publication? Do your findings in *b* and *c* suggest that writers for the

same publication use paragraphs of roughly the same length or of very different lengths? Through further sampling, try to set up a hypothesis as to the relative importance for paragraph length of content, expected audience, and the writer's individual style and taste.

3. Make a count for ¶s 2–4 in a recent essay of your own. Can you justify the average length as appropriate to the rhetorical situation?

If the passages you selected were reasonably typical, Exercise 1 revealed significant differences in the average length of paragraphs from publication to publication. The physical makeup of the page, the anticipated attention span of readers, and the general character of the subject all influence a writer's (or an editor's) decision to indent, and sometimes modify the more fundamental consideration of just how much space is needed to give adequate development to the particular stage in the flow of ideas.

In most newspapers and some magazines, paragraphing is done almost entirely for visual effect: indention comes regularly after any single long sentence or after two or three short ones, with scant attention to the meaning of the sentences on either side of the break. In the expository prose of serious magazines and books—and this should be true of college papers as well—logical and rhetorical considerations carry much more weight. To the extent that such considerations prevail, paragraphing becomes the writer's means of showing how he has sorted and organized his ideas and of indicating their relative importance. But he still has some options in marking off his paragraphs. He may break a long paragraph in two—if he can find a satisfactory dividing point—simply as an aid to the reader. Or, in revising, he may decide to combine two paragraphs to tighten the connection between related points. (The two paragraphs that follow this one could be combined.)

Short paragraphs can be read more easily than long ones. They demand less sustained concentration; the reader does not have to hold so much in his mind. But an essay made up of very brief paragraphs is often hard to read with full comprehension: the discussion can be chopped into segments so small that the reader loses his sense of the relative importance of the ideas and of the connections between them. On occasion, he may also feel that he is being short-changed on evidence, for a rapid succession of indentions often means that ideas are left underdeveloped.

By contrast, long paragraphs permit—even encourage—the complete unfolding of an idea or the close-knit development of several related ideas. But they too have their risks. Some readers find them forbidding; they assume that long paragraphs mean difficult reading. The main rhetorical objection to long paragraphs, especially several in succession, is that the writer who groups a number of ideas, no matter how closely related, may be robbing himself of a legitimate means of emphasis. Since a paragraph break signals a pause, moving up to or away from indention provides the opportunity to highlight an idea.

Because several considerations enter into a writer's decision to indent where he does, length is best considered in relation to other features of a paragraph or of the paragraph sequence it belongs to. Do the paragraph breaks make sense both logically and rhetorically? This is the important question. Whether short or long, a paragraph is the right length if it brings out the right relations among its statements and if it puts the emphasis in the right place. The habit of making paragraphs unusually short or unusually long is often a symptom of a fundamental problem—inadequate development (a weakness in content) if the paragraphs are consistently short, and lack of unity (a weakness in both content and structure) if they are consistently long.

PARAGRAPH DEVELOPMENT

As you write, it is helpful to visualize each paragraph—at any rate, each content paragraph—as an organic unit built around a nucleus, linked to what precedes and what follows but with its own center, a core of meaning that justifies including it in the essay. For every paragraph must *do* something for its sequence or for the essay as a whole or for both—make a point, convey an idea, create an impression. It *will* do something only if all the sentences that make it up contribute to its core of meaning and if that meaning is an integral part of the stream of ideas that runs through the essay.

Cores of meaning are what you look for whenever you outline or summarize something you have read. How do you get the key statements that go into your outline? Some you copy verbatim from the text. Others you produce by combining and condensing several of the author's sentences. Still others you compose yourself as the most economical way of setting down the gist of a paragraph; it's all there, but you have to pull it together.

In writing paragraphs, it is well to remind yourself of your experience in reading paragraphs. They make their points in different ways. The core of meaning may be explicitly stated in a single sentence (called the *topic sentence*), or it may be scattered through several sentences, or it may be the unstated idea underlying all the particulars of the paragraph—sometimes of the entire sequence the paragraph belongs to. But in any case, if the paragraph is to do its job, it needs a nucleus—a topic idea. And if it is to have an impact and not just make an assertion, this core of meaning must be developed.

Topic Sentences and Pointers

Every content paragraph you write should have a topic *idea*. Whether or not it contains a topic *sentence* is secondary; normally the question won't enter your mind. When you are intent on formulating and expressing ideas, you don't think in terms of topic-sentence-and-support-for-it any more than you consciously decide that the paragraph is to develop by definition or by causal analysis or whatever. You follow the flow of your ideas. But when the flow is down to a trickle, you will probably start trying to figure out what general point you want to make next. Hitting on a core idea gives you the sense of direction you need, and framing a sentence that expresses the idea gives you something to work toward or away from. Once you have a topic sentence—either in mind or on paper—you will find it easier to write a paragraph that is a meaningful unit, not just a collection of statements.

Whether in its final draft you give the paragraph a topic sentence or allow the central idea to emerge without one depends on the rhetorical situation—your subject and what you want to do with it, your relation to your reader, and so on. Certainly your reader is no more concerned with singling out topic sentences than you are with writing them. But if the material is difficult or if the topic calls for interpretation and judgment, he will probably be looking for explicit guidance. And most often guidance can best be provided by the companion devices of topic sentences and pointer statements.

The passage by Jerome Bruner (p. 222) opens with two pointers that together give the reader a good deal of guidance to what follows:

A word is needed at this point to explain in fuller detail what is meant by the *structure* of a subject, for we shall have occasion to return to this idea often in later pages. Three simple examples—from biology, from mathematics, and from the learning of language—help to make the idea clearer.

Though at this point the reader does not know the outcome of the discussion—what *structure* means—he does know, as he reads on, what purpose the example from biology is intended to serve. And at the close of the paragraph he finds the promised definition, a definition that is expressed in a topic sentence and then, for clarity and emphasis, restated:

Grasping the structure of a subject is understanding it in a way that permits many other things to be related to it meaningfully. To learn structure, in short, is to learn how things are related.

These twin topic sentences sum up the content of the paragraph just as the opening pointers predict it. (Do the second and third paragraphs of the Bruner passage have pointers and topic sentences comparable in scope and prominence to those in the first paragraph? If not, why not?)

Topic sentences and pointers use somewhat different means to characterize and control the content of a paragraph or paragraph sequence. A topic sentence gives the gist of the discussion or states the central proposition to be explained or defended:

Cynical disparagement of objectivity as a "myth" seems to me both naive and irresponsible. — Brewster, p. 16

Khesanh was a very bad place then, but the airstrip there was the worst place in the world. — Herr, p. 69

The drabness of real life seems to affect taste. — Sexton, p. 78

Though the topic sentence seldom represents the central idea in every detail or with every qualification the writer intends, it is the most explicit statement he can make (or cares to make) of the meaning that the paragraph as a whole is to convey. In rhetorical situations where clarity is of first importance, a topic sentence may be restated — sometimes with greater precision or greater fullness — either immediately, as in the Bruner passage, or after an intervening passage has offered illustration or proof.

Instead of telling the reader the central idea — what the paragraph says — a pointer statement tells him what the paragraph is to do. Pointers are therefore part of the strategy of announcing. They include some questions ("What of the future?") and many transitional sentences ("Before we examine types of arguments in more detail, we need to look briefly at the context in which persuasion operates"). In any case, they indicate the scope of the discussion. "There are just four types of reference books" (p. 103) signals precisely what is to come. "'Aggression' can mean different things to different people" (p. 110) tells the reader that he can expect an account of different meanings of the term. "Now there are problems about thinking of human behavior in either of these ways" (p. 140) forecasts the next stage of the discussion.

Their procedural function makes pointers extremely useful in organizing a passage; but because they sometimes have authoritarian overtones, they are not appropriate in all contexts.

EXERCISES

1. Identify topic sentences and pointers in the passages by Cantor, pp. 195–96, Bettelheim, pp. 134–35, and Minogue, pp. 140–41. If you find a paragraph that has neither, explain how the topic idea is conveyed.

2. Review the first ten paragraphs in this chapter, and locate the topic sentences. Where do they most often come—at the beginning of the paragraph? in the middle? at the end? Can you explain why the topic sentences in some of the paragraphs are in other positions than the most common one? If you find a paragraph that does not have a topic sentence, explain why it does or does not need one.

Wherever the topic sentence is placed, it usually stands out as the most general or comprehensive statement, serving as an anchor for the more particular, more specific statements that move from it or toward it or around it. But not always. Especially in argument, the real point of the paragraph—its core of meaning—may be an inference drawn from the generalization, not the generalization itself.

(1) The fatal mistake we have been making is to sacrifice every other form of transportation to the private motorcar—and to offer as the only long-distance alternative the airplane. (2) But the fact is that each type of transportation has its special use; and a good transportation policy must seek to improve each type and make the most of it. (3) This cannot be achieved by aiming at high speed or continuous flow alone. (4) If you wish casual opportunities for meeting your neighbors, and for profiting by chance contacts with acquaintances and colleagues, a stroll at two miles an hour in a relatively concentrated area, free from vehicles, will alone meet

your need.   (5) But if you wish to rush a surgeon to a patient a thousand miles away, the fastest motorway is too slow.   (6) And again, if you wish to be sure to keep a lecture engagement in winter, railroad transportation offers surer speed and better insurance against being held up than the airplane.   (7) There is no one ideal mode of speed: human purpose should govern the choice of the means of transporation.   (8) That is why we need a better transportation *system*, not just more highways.   (9) The projectors of our national highway program plainly had little interest in transportation.   (10) In their fanatical zeal to expand our highways, the very allocation of funds indicates that they are ready to liquidate all other forms of land and water transportation. — Lewis Mumford, *The Urban Prospect*

The broadest generalization, stated in sentence 2 and asserted again in 7, is given support by the particulars in sentences 4, 5, and 6. But the real point that Mumford wants to establish is made in sentence 1 and made again in the last three sentences.

Not every paragraph either has or needs a topic sentence or a pointer statement. (Only paragraphs that lead off sequences and paragraphs that are strong in announcing are likely to have both.) Sometimes the language of the discussion makes it plain that a paragraph without a topic sentence of its own is firmly attached to one several paragraphs back, at the beginning of the sequence. Or the central idea, which might otherwise have been expressed in a topic sentence, may be parceled out to two or three sentences. Or the inference to be drawn may be so unmistakable that to state it is superfluous: the paragraph as a whole performs the function that could have been assigned to a topic sentence. This is very often true of narrative and descriptive paragraphs, where the details imply the generalization, and it is sometimes true of expository paragraphs as well. Though the following paragraph certainly has a topic idea—a core of meaning—the idea is not fully expressed in any *one* sentence of the paragraph:

I have seldom met a businessman who was not persuaded that inflation is produced by rising wages—and rising wages, in turn, by strong labor unions—and many a nonbusinessman is of the same mind. This belief is false yet entirely understandable. To each businessman separately, inflation comes in the form of higher costs, mostly wages; yet for all businessmen combined, higher prices produce the higher costs. What is involved is a fallacy of composition. Any one person may be able to leave a crowded theater in two minutes without difficulty. Let everyone try to leave in two minutes and there may be utter chaos. What is true for each separately need not be true for all together. — Milton Friedman, *Newsweek*, Sept. 28, 1970

Expanding the Core

Whether or not the central idea of a paragraph has been given expression in a topic sentence, the real work of explaining and persuading remains to be done. Anemic paragraphs and unconvincing essays often result from failure to recognize the need to expand and clarify and support the key generalizations. The failure is natural enough, for in the very act of framing a general statement, you have assimilated, and so in a sense discarded, the particulars that led you to it. But bare assertions and propositions cannot convey anything like the fullness and complexity of thought processes, and if the reader is to share in your thinking and be led to the same conclusion, he must be taken over at least some of the same ground. A topic sentence may be the most inclusive but also the least interesting sentence in a paragraph. What convinces is not so much the leading idea expressed in a topic sentence as the enrichment and clarification offered by the other sentences in the paragraph—sentences that restate, refine, and qualify the central idea, sentences that illuminate and support it with anecdotes, descriptive details, and examples.

Recall the difference between an essay or a chapter you have read and the outline you have made of it. Reviewing the outline several times while the complete reading is fresh in your mind is an excellent way to get control of the reading. But if you go back to the outline a few weeks later, you are likely to find it opaque and uninformative. In the interval you will have forgotten all the particulars—the details, the examples, the evidence—that originally supported and clarified the key statements you assembled.

This paragraph is both abstract and undernourished:

Americans have more difficulty verbalizing their political ideology than many Europeans do. Historical reasons are mainly responsible for their comparative inarticulateness on both domestic and foreign policy.

Fleshed out as it was originally written, it is a good deal more interesting and convincing:

An educated Russian can give a coherent statement of his beliefs and can argue ideology effectively with persons from other nations; so can an educated Englishman. Even many who have not had university training can do quite well. But most Americans have difficulty explaining to foreigners what their fellow citizens believe in. This is one of the paradoxes that, as Kluckhohn has stated, characterizes the American culture. We talk much of "the American way of life," but we are almost incapable of telling others about it. Much of the political ideology we do have stems from an intellectual movement of the late eighteenth century, a development discussed in later chapters. It was beautifully expressed by the most "egghead" of American Presidents, Thomas Jefferson, but since his time we have had difficulty in organizing our changing thoughts about beliefs. The Jacksonian movement of a generation later, for example, never had a philosopher who could systematically state its beliefs. The credo of the American businessman, dating from the post-Civil War days, is also a haphazard set of ideas. Furthermore, America had little in the way of a systematic foreign policy until the time of World War II, and hence until recently we learned a political rhetoric that concentrated on domestic issues rather than on foreign policy. In contrast, the Englishman's basic ideology concerning relationships with other nations has been relatively clear and has not changed fundamentally in 400 years. For that reason alone, he is far more likely to be able to state his nation's position in international affairs. —Charles R. Adrian and Charles Press, *The American Political Process*

Expanding the core entails two main obligations. One is to keep the paragraph unified. Stuffing a paragraph with tangential ideas weakens the force of the central idea; if the paragraph is to have an impact, all the statements in it must have some bearing on its core of meaning. The second obligation is to expand the core adequately. A broad assertion may be a good starting point for a paragraph, but left alone it is unsatisfactory. What you need to do is figure out the *kind* of support the assertion needs to make it clear or convincing or memorable—specific details, examples, definitions, comparisons, and so on. The ways of substantiating a generalization have been outlined in Chapter Two (pp. 45−48) and discussed fully in Chapters Three, Four, and Five. Virtually everything said there is applicable to paragraphs and to parts of paragraphs as well as to paragraph sequences and whole essays.

EXERCISES

1. For each of the four paragraphs in this passage, pick out the topic sentence or pointer, or, if the paragraph has neither, compose a sentence that expresses the topic idea. Then state the chief method or methods used in developing the paragraph. (For a review of typical methods, see pp. 46−48.)

Whatever is different about the scientist must begin with the particular kind of intelligence such a man possesses. It is said that the scientist must have an inquiring mind—which is true; and that he must also be one of those people who take deep pleasure in learning—which is also true, and also superficial; because both these qualities are demanded also by any number of other disciplines. The particular kind of sensibilities required by a scientist are more complicated.

Begin with his intense awareness of words and their meanings. While the poet's affinity for words makes him sensitive to their sound, emotion, and rhythm, the scientist uses them as instruments of precision. He must be capable of inventing new words to express new physical concepts. He must be able to reason verbally by analogy—to explain "how this thing is like that thing," and to be able to fit the many resemblances into one single generalization that covers them all.

The scientist must also think graphically, in terms of dynamical models, three-dimensional arrangements in space. The dynamical model of a bacterial cell, for example, is a hollow rigid capsule that may be either spherical or tubular, containing an otherwise shapeless living cell enclosed within a soft sac, the plasma membrane. Niels Bohr's dynamical model of an atom is a miniature solar system with relatively enormous electrons orbiting about an almost inconceivably small sun—the atomic nucleus—a tremendous distance away. Scientists keep these three-dimensional pictures in mind as vividly as if they were actually seeing them. Formulas and equations printed on a two-dimensional page have three-dimensional meanings, and the scientist must be able to read in three dimensions to "see the picture" at once. There is nothing "abstract" about a scientist's thinking.

This visualization is so vivid that a scientist examining a theoretical problem is really like a jeweler peering through his loupe at a gem which he holds close to his eye, turning it over and over in his fingers. To Einstein, there was nothing abstract about his theory of relativity. Even the slightest apparent deviation from the hard world of physical reality made him intellectually uncomfortable. For more than a decade, meeting at international science conferences, he and Bohr, by then both in middle age, had monumental arguments over the meaning of the uncertainty principle, with Einstein the one who stuck stolidly to the basic mechanistic principle of cause and effect. "I cannot believe that God throws dice," he said.—Mitchell Wilson, *Atlantic*, Sept. 1970

2. Compose a generalization about yourself, about college life, about some issue that interests you—or, if you prefer, choose one from the list below. Treat it as the topic *idea* that you develop in a sequence of two or three or four paragraphs. After you have written the sequence, examine the paragraphs. Explain why each does or does not contain a topic sentence or pointer.

a. Owning a sports car can be an educational experience.

b. The child of divorced parents has no real sense of security.

c. To sell their products, advertisers make appeals that have nothing to do with the quality of the products themselves.

d. My family has some unusual traditions.

e. Tolerance and indifference are sometimes confused.

f. The first few weeks of college are a difficult time.

g. Clothes tell more than the wearer realizes.

h. Popular songs fall into several groups.

PARAGRAPH STRUCTURE

To worry about the structure of your paragraphs while you are writing a first draft is more inhibiting than helpful. It is when you turn to revising and rewriting that you should ask yourself whether the paragraph breaks come in the right place, whether each paragraph has a satisfactory internal structure, and whether the sentences in it track one another logically and smoothly.[1]

A good paragraph satisfies whatever expectations it arouses. Have you made a promise, explicitly or implicitly, to discuss the imagery of a poem, or its metrical structure, or its meaning? Have you committed yourself to giving examples, to justifying a position, to attacking or modifying a generalization? Does the opening of the paragraph forecast an account of an episode? Once you recognize what obligation you have assumed, you can visualize the underlying structure or "plot" the paragraph should have. Though paragraphs are not necessarily miniature essays, their most common

---

[1]Since 1965 a good deal of scholarly attention has been paid to paragraphs, much of it with a view to finding productive methods of analyzing their structure. *College Composition and Communication* has been a hospitable forum for debate. Francis Christensen, "A Generative Rhetoric of the Paragraph," *CCC*, Oct. 1965; A. L. Becker, "A Tagmemic Approach to Paragraph Analysis," *CCC*, Dec. 1965; Paul C. Rodgers, Jr., "A Discourse-Centered Rhetoric of the Paragraph," *CCC*, Feb. 1966; and "Symposium on the Paragraph," *CCC*, May 1966, with contributions by Christensen, Becker, Rodgers, Josephine Miles, and David H. Karrfalt, are reprinted in *The Sentence and the Paragraph* (Champaign, Ill.: National Council of Teachers of English, 1966). Other useful articles, all published in *CCC*, are: Richard L. Larson, "Sentences in Action: A Technique for Analyzing Paragraphs," Feb. 1967; Paul Rodgers, "The Stadium of Discourse," Oct. 1967; David H. Karrfalt, "The Generation of Paragraphs and Larger Units," Oct. 1968; Willis L. Pitkin, Jr., "Discourse Blocs," May 1969. In these and other articles, many avenues of analysis have been opened. Some hold great promise for the teaching of close, analytical reading. A few applications to writing have already been made, and undoubtedly more will be. Whether or not the new techniques help a writer compose paragraphs, there is no doubt that they can help him revise them.

structures are small-scale models of those we have already observed in whole essays (see pp. 183–96). A paragraph, like an essay, may reflect natural order (chronological, spatial, associational) or logical order (support, discovery, pro-and-con). Recognizing that in the opening sentence or two you have committed yourself to a certain order is the first step in repairing a broken-backed paragraph—one that heads one way at the start and midway through veers off in another direction.

EXERCISE

How do the two paragraphs below—the opening of an essay—fail to satisfy the reader's expectations? What suggestions can you make for improving the passage? Should the order of the sentences be changed? Should some of the sentences be dropped? New ones added? Try rewriting the passage to strengthen its organization and to make each paragraph better unified.

Last June I went to England for a summer of archaeology and travel. I was to work for three weeks at the site of Fishbourne, near the city of Chichester. I was to be a "voluntary labourer" in the trenches and to otherwise help in every possible way. I had gotten interested in archaeology in the eighth grade during an ancient history course and since then had continually read journals about Roman excavations, called "digs." From these magazines, I learned the language and something about the technology of the archaeologist. One very widely used method of dating material is the Carbon-14 test, in which the amount of carbon in some artifact is measured. Its date of manufacture can then be estimated within about fifty years. Another method of dating sites, or levels of sites, is by identifying particular styles and types of earthenware. Often it is possible to even tell the place of origin of pottery by marks on the bases of the pieces, or by the way the pottery has been made.

The Romans were very helpful to archaeologists because usually when they tore something down they left the foundation and would rebuild over it. The actual process of archaeology consists of digging rectangular trenches vertically downward at strict right angles (for dating and photographic purposes) with the soil taken off in layers so as to keep the trench and all the uncovered artifacts within the same period. Trench digging is sometimes done to sample an area and see if there is anything worth uncovering with an excavation. I got involved with the English dig through a teacher at my high school who went to England each year to work at different sites. Last year he invited me and some other classmates to accompany him to the Fishbourne excavation.

As you reread your paragraphs, check too on the movement between general statements and particular ones. In most good paragraphs there is an interplay; paragraphs that remain on one level of generality are likely to be monotonous. (See pp. 42 – 43, 54 – 55.) Besides giving life and interest to your prose, the practice of interweaving details and generalizations helps ensure that you will strike a reasonable balance between asserting and offering proof, between giving evidence and interpreting it.

EXERCISE

The paragraph below has a degree of unity but sticks so close to one level of generality that it is dull reading. Rewrite, keeping the main idea but using details and examples to make the paragraph more lively and convincing. You may want to use two paragraphs.

Both at home and at school, children should be encouraged to be fearless. This is an essential part of a good education because fear is a corroding influence that can harm the character. Everybody knows that the irrational fears of childhood can do permanent damage to the personality. They can, for instance, develop a tendency to cruelty. Fear in the intellectual sphere is just as insidious. Men who have not been liberated in their thinking cling to orthodoxy and conservatism. They are afraid to be creative. Parents and teachers should do everything they can to help a child become a free and fearless citizen of the universe.

Functional Units

To test the structure of a paragraph, you will naturally look closely at individual sentences, asking what role each plays in furthering the topic idea and, if the role of a sentence is not clear, asking whether you need to delete the sentence or shift its position or revise it to link it more closely with its neighbors. But as you work to strengthen the continuity of the paragraph, you will find it useful not just to look *at* sentences but to look *for* functional units. Thus you may see your paragraph as having a two-part structure that can be described as cause+effect or problem+solution or positive+negative or topic+illustration. Or you may see it as consisting of three parts, or four, or more, each relating in some significant way to the others and to the whole essay.

The paragraph below is made up of just two functional units—a topic sentence (the first) and illustration (the other seven):

(1) Frequently the colonists made an old word serve with slightly different meaning. (2) The American red-breasted thrush, for example, was called a *robin;* the European bird which they had called a *robin* in Old England is somewhat smaller and has a yellowish-red breast. (3) *Blackbird*, which in Europe denotes a wild bird allied to the thrushes, was applied in America to any of various birds having black plumage. (4) A number of different brightly colored birds not closely related to the orioles of Europe were nevertheless given that name in this country, for example, the *Baltimore oriole*. (5) Similarly, the European partridge is not the same as its American namesake, or rather namesakes, for in New England *partridge* designates the ruffed grouse and in Virginia the bobwhite quail. (6) *Corn* was applied here to an altogether different cereal and lost its older general meaning "grain." (7) *Huckleberry* is a variant of *hurtleberry*, which is in turn an older form of *whortleberry* "bilberry"; but the American huckleberry is quite a different fruit. (8) *Beech, hemlock, walnut*, and *laurel* also acquired new meanings in the colonies.—Thomas Pyles, *Words and Ways of American English*

The format of the preceding paragraph is open-ended, in the sense that illustrations could be put in or pulled out and the paragraph shortened or lengthened without altering its basic structure. Though the examples that validate the opening statement do not come in random order—we would be disturbed if, say, the last sentence broke into the cluster of examples in sentences 2–5—the four categories of examples could be shifted about, and other categories could be added.

When you write a paragraph like the one above, ask yourself questions like these: Do the examples really bear on the opening statement? Is each one interesting in its own right? Are they all of roughly the same significance, so that the order is of no great importance, or are some examples more telling than others? Should I leave the paragraph open-ended, or should I close it out by giving an example that is clearly climactic?

In the paragraph that follows, the abstract pattern—the underlying "plot"—also has a two-part structure. The "many illusions" of the first sentence are enumerated one by one. The paragraph has a climactic effect, however, because of the phrasing of the last sentence, which provides a lead-in to the paragraph that follows:

We have many illusions about the arts. We believe that they are a sort of gratuitous bonus that God grants to a prosperous society that works hard and is well integrated. We believe that they ought to be there when we want them—like taxis; that when we wish to concentrate on really serious things, like business, they should keep in the background—like children; that if they are worth their salt they should be self-supporting; and above all that they should entertain us. We ask of them that they should be a flattering reflection of the life we lead or think we lead; and we talk glibly and unwittingly of holding the mirror up to nature because we don't really know what that means. But our most persistent and most pernicious illusion about the arts is that they follow a pattern, that they have boom times and recession times which follow one another according to some unspecified law.

A boom time, we fondly imagine, is a period when. . . .—Brian Friel, *The Critic*, Aug.-Sept. 1967

The simple two-part structure of topic+illustration or topic+development can be extended by adding functional units. Thus a three-stage pattern will often consist of topic+restriction (or development)+illustration. The intermediate stage, which may consist of several sentences, modifies or restricts the topic idea, narrows and limits it, defines it, or extends it. The following paragraph is partitioned into three related units—topic (sentence 1), restriction or development (sentences 2 and 3), illustration (sentence 4):

(1) One of the recurrent problems for liberals in the United States is what their relationship with radicals should be. (2) If liberals are defined roughly as those who accept the basic characteristics of the existing political and economic systems and who believe that the government should be an active instrument for improving the lot of our citizenry and perhaps of mankind as a whole; and if radicals are defined as those who seek fundamental changes in the political, social, and economic systems—some adhering to democratic norms and some not—then it is obvious that the relationship between liberals and radicals will usually be strained and often nonexistent. (3) Only in periods of great stress and loss of confidence

will liberals be drawn toward radical prescriptions and personalities. (4) The 1930's are the classic example of how alluring this temptation can become at such times. — William P. Gerberding, *Reporter*, Feb. 8, 1968

A long, closely reasoned paragraph will have a good many functional units, and in a careful analysis you will want to subdivide units until you can account for parts of sentences as well as sentences and sequences of sentences. Whatever the general plan your paragraph follows, identifying the functional units in it permits you to see its structure in detail and to decide whether or not there is a consistent logical movement.

The General Plan

The paragraphs by Pyles, Friel, and Gerberding are all built on the support, or deductive, plan. This is the favorite plan in exposition and argument, for it offers the easiest way of keeping the reader informed about what is coming next; and probably most of the expository paragraphs you write will observe this order. The opening sentence (or the one following any transitional material) more or less establishes the dimensions of the discussion either by telling what the subject is (topic sentence) or what procedure will be followed (pointer). After this initial statement — top sentence, as Francis Christensen calls it — come other statements that illustrate, interpret, extend, explain, or refute it. The supporting statements may be roughly equivalent to each other, as in Pyles and Friel, or they may be built one upon another, reflecting a train of reasoning, as in Gerberding.

When a paragraph on the deductive plan moves clearly to a conclusion — a *therefore* — or when the opening has given definite clues to the scope of the discussion — "Three qualities make him one of our most distinguished novelists" — you have a sure sense of just where the paragraph will end. But often you need to decide whether to leave a paragraph open-ended — more could be added — or to round it out with a climactic particular or signal the end by restating the initial generalization. Restatement — perhaps with more emphasis, perhaps with qualifications — is a common practice when the material is complicated or the paragraph long. Even a fairly short paragraph can profit by a restatement that doesn't just repeat but gives fresh expression to the leading idea:

Whitman is more coordinate and parallel than anybody, is *the* poet of parallel present participles, of twenty verbs joined by a single subject: all this helps to give his work its feeling of raw hypnotic reality, of being that world which also streams over us joined only by *ands*, until we supply the subordinating conjunctions; and since as children we see the *ands* and not the *becauses*, this method helps to give Whitman some of the freshness of childhood. How inexhaustibly *interesting* the world is in Whitman! Arnold all his life kept wishing that we could see the world "with a plainness as near, as flashing" as that with which Moses and Rebekah and the Argonauts saw it. He asked with elegiac nostalgia, "Who can see the green earth any more/ As she was by the sources of Time?" — and all the time there was somebody alive who saw it so, as plain and near and flashing, and with a kind of calm, pastoral, biblical dignity and elegance as well, sometimes. The *thereness* and *suchness* of the world are incarnate in Whitman as they are in few other writers. — Randall Jarrell, *Poetry and the Age*

Whether or not the end of a deductive paragraph should be signaled by restatement or some other device can often be decided only by examining the context. The paragraph that concludes a sequence is likely to be closed out; the paragraph inside a sequence often is not.

We can treat more briefly the chief problems of organizing a paragraph on the discovery plan, which reverses the movement of the favorite support plan. A purely inductive movement, which leads the reader through a series of particulars to an inference or generalization, is rather rare; but it has distinct advantages in some rhetorical situations. The writer may have any one of several motives for withholding the topic idea until the end of the paragraph — to make the reader feel he is sharing in the process of discovery, to give easier access (through specific details) to a complicated or difficult generalization, to counteract the reader's initial hostility, to achieve dramatic impact. (The first two of these motives were probably decisive for Bruner, pp. 222–24.) In any case, when the movement is *toward* a generalization, it is especially important that the particulars feed logically into each other and so into the generalization. The reader does not know just what the discussion is leading to, but he should have a sense that every detail is making its contribution.

Many paragraphs that are not purely inductive gain their persuasiveness through the accumulation of evidence and so have an inductive thrust. In the paragraph below, the first sentence gives a clear enough indication of the drift of the paragraph. The key word ("paradoxical") is elaborated in the four fairly general statements and then in the specific example (sentences 6–8). But the real push of the paragraph comes in the last three sentences, especially the final forceful one.

(1) The position of the psychologically non-violent revolutionary in opposition to a violent world is paradoxical. (2) On the one

hand, he seeks to minimize violence, but, on the other, his efforts often elicit violence from others.   (3) He works toward a vague vision of a peaceful world, but he must confront more directly than most of his peers the warfare of the world.   (4) The frustrations of his work repetitively reawaken his rage, which must continually be redirected into peaceful paths.   (5) Combating destructiveness and exploitation in others, his own destructiveness and desire to exploit are inevitably aroused.   (6) Furthermore, he is a citizen of a nation whose international policies seem to him only slightly less barbarous than the policies of the Nazis toward the Jews.   (7) He has been recently reminded that, with the support of world opinion, the State of Israel executed Adolf Eichmann because of his complicity in the extermination of the Jews (despite his plea that he was only following orders).   (8) Rather than be an accomplice in a comparable enterprise, should the radical not move toward the violent resistance that the world would have preferred from Eichmann?   (9) For all his efforts to control violence, cataclysm, and sadism, the young radical continually runs the danger of identifying himself with what he seeks to control, and through a militant struggle against violence, creating more violence than he overcomes. (10) The issue of violence is not resolved for these young men and women.   (11) Nor can it be. — Kenneth Keniston, *Young Radicals: Notes on Committed Youth*

This paragraph shows the familiar problem-solution movement:

(1) At a time when a number of competing world views impinge upon literature, each radically in conflict with one another, there arise severe difficulties in trying to relate the tacit assumptions of the writer to those of the reader.   (2) The bonds of premise between the two are broken, and must now become a matter of inquiry, effort, conflict.   (3) We read the last novels of D. H. Lawrence or the cantos of Ezra Pound, aware that these are works of enormously gifted writers yet steadily troubled by the outpouring of authoritarian and Fascist ideas.   (4) We read Bertolt Brecht's "To Posterity," in which he offers an incomparable evocation of the travail of Europe in the period between wars yet also weaves in a justification of the Stalin dictatorship.   (5) How are we to respond to all this?   (6) The question is crucial in our experience of modernist literature.   (7) We may say that the doctrine is irrelevant, as many critics do say, and that would lead us to the impossible position that the commanding thought of a poem need not be seriously considered in forming a judgment of its value.   (8) Or we may say that the doctrine, being obnoxious, destroys our pleasure in the poem, as some critics do say, and that would lead us to the impossible position that our judgment of the work is determined by our opinion concerning the author's ideology.   (9) There is, I think, no satisfactory solution in the abstract, and we must learn to accept the fact that modernist literature is often — not in this way

alone!—"unacceptable." (10) It forces us into distance and dissociation; it denies us wholeness of response; it alienates us from its own powers of statement even when we feel that it is imaginatively transcending the malaise of alienation.—Irving Howe, *Decline of the New*

The problem-solution format gives the paragraph a firm, two-part structure, with a progression within each part. In the first half, the problem is stated (sentence 1), made more precise (sentence 2), and illustrated (sentences 3 and 4). Sentences 5 and 6, in raising a question and pointing out its significance, furnish another version of sentence 1. Following that, one solution is rejected, a second solution is rejected, and a third alternative is offered and given support. It is relatively easy to organize a paragraph on the problem-solution or question-answer plan. The real challenge comes in demonstrating that the proposed solution is adequate—and this is a matter of content rather than structure.

The paragraph below successfully combines the inductive and deductive patterns, moving through a series of negations to the topic sentence—"History is, in short, a problem-solving discipline"—and then moving deductively. The paragraph also illustrates the flexibility in paragraphing; some writers would have indented after the topic sentence.

The logic of historical thought is not a formal logic of deductive inference. It is not a symmetrical structure of Aristotelian syllogisms, or Ramean dialectics, or Boolean equations. Nor is it precisely an inductive logic, like that of Mill or Keynes or Carnap. It consists neither in inductive reasoning from the particular to the general, nor in deductive reasoning from the general to the particular. Instead, it is a process of *adductive* reasoning in the simple sense of adducing answers to specific questions, so that a satisfactory explanatory "fit" is obtained. The answers may be general or particular, as the questions may require. History is, in short, a problem-solving discipline. A historian is someone (anyone) who asks an open-ended question about past events and answers it with selected facts which are arranged in the form of an explanatory paradigm. These questions and answers are fitted to each other by a complex process of mutual adjustment. The resultant explanatory paradigm may take many different forms: a statistical generalization, or a narrative, or a causal model, or a motivational model, or a collectivized group-composition model, or maybe an analogy. Most commonly it consists not in any one of these components but in a combination of them. Always, it is articulated in the form of a reasoned argument. —David Hackett Fischer, *Historians' Fallacies*

The pro-and-con movement has a more complex structure than those illustrated so far. The paragraph opens with a generalization, which is given support; then it takes a turn in another (but related) direction, the new direction signaled by *but, still, however,* or some similar contrast. The two-stage movement is well suited to balancing a positive against a negative—advantages against disadvantages, say—and is a natural choice for the paragraph that makes a concession before going on to refute an argument. In the passage by Northrop Frye on pp. 177–78, the second half refutes the position set forth in the first half; the main assertion comes midway in the paragraph.

The pro-and-con movement is also useful for the purpose of refining and qualifying one's own generalization. In the paragraph that follows, the pro-and-con movement is repeated several times, and the regular alternation of negative and positive statements about the average man of Lincoln's generation permits the writer to move judiciously to a final generalization that is considerably stronger than the initial one.

The average Western American of Lincoln's generation was fundamentally a man who subordinated his intelligence to certain dominant practical interests and purposes. He was far from being a stupid or slow-witted man. On the contrary, his wits had been sharpened by the traffic of American politics and business, and his mind was shrewd, flexible, and alert. But he was wholly incapable either of disinterested or of concentrated intellectual exertion. His energies were bent in the conquest of certain stubborn external forces, and he used his intelligence almost exclusively to this end. The struggles, the hardships, and the necessary self-denial of pioneer life constituted an admirable training of the will. It developed a body of men with great resolution of purpose and with great ingenuity and fertility in adapting their insufficient means to the realization of their important business affairs. But their almost exclusive preoccupation with practical tasks and their failure to grant their intelligence any room for independent exercise bent them into exceedingly warped and one-sided human beings.—Herbert Croly, *The Promise of American Life*

Organizing a paragraph on the pro-and-con pattern enables the writer to indicate his awareness of conflicting opinions and of the need to modify and qualify his own generalizations. Handled well, it suggests a certain subtlety and depth of thinking about the material. Handled badly, it can communicate a sense of indecisiveness, as if the writer is merely sitting on the fence, evading the responsibility of making clear what his own ideas on the subject are. A pro-and-con paragraph usually needs to end with a forceful, positive statement that leaves no doubt in the reader's mind as to the writer's final judgment.

Not every content paragraph you write need conform to one of the patterns illustrated here, but every one should *have* a discernible pattern. A paragraph should be built in such a way that the reader senses the direction in which the thought is moving and, when he has finished reading, grasps the structure that underlies and unites the individual sentences. (When he finds a paragraph so organized that it *seems* disorganized, he will want to be able to assure himself that the lack of describable order serves a rhetorical purpose.) The writer's intention, his subject, his audience, his style—all these elements have a bearing on how a paragraph can best be organized. And it is both natural and desirable to vary the structure of paragraphs to accommodate the material.

EXERCISE

Describe and evaluate the structure of each of the paragraphs below. Consider these questions: What are the main functional units in the paragraph? Is the paragraph tightly unified in the sense that all the sentences in it bear directly on the core of meaning? Or do some of the sentences relate to the core only loosely or tangentially? Is the paragraph tightly structured in the sense that the order of the sentences could not be altered without damaging the unity of the paragraph, or could some of the sentences be interchanged? If you find that one paragraph is less unified than the others or looser in structure, can you justify the difference in terms of the subject and general style?

a. Fort Hood. Fort Bragg. Fort Leavenworth. Fort Benning. Fort Lewis. The big army bases in the United States are tight societies, forts in more ways than one. A man and his family need never leave the post, not for birth, marriage, or death, not for shelter, food, fuel, or clothing, not for golf, drinks, dinner, dancing, or movies. A man is encouraged to spend his money on the base—as who would not, considering the bargains? One hundred and fifty dollars for an AKAI tape recorder worth two hundred, fifty cents for a V.O. and soda at the NCO club. A man can worship a nondenominational God ("army God," a senior soldier described Him) and putt on an army green and have a tooth pulled by an army dentist, and all the time call it home. There is only one thing that the Army doesn't have. It doesn't have schools for the children, at least at the bases in the United States it doesn't.—Ward Just, *Atlantic*, Oct. 1970

b. For a number of reasons it is not easy to collect a body of valid and reliable information on American dialects. The wide spread of education, the virtual extinction of illiteracy, the extreme mobility of the population—both geographically and from one social class to another—and the tremendous development of a number of media of mass communication have all contributed to the recession of local speech forms. Moreover, the cultural insecurity of a large portion of the American people has caused them to feel apologetic about their language. Consequently, they seldom display the same degree of pride or affection that many an English or a European speaker has for his particular patois. Since all dialect research is essentially a sampling process, this means that the investigator must take particular pains to secure representative and comparable samples from the areas which are studied. Happily, the very care which this demands has had the result of developing the methodology of linguistic geography in this country to a very high level. — Albert H. Marckwardt, *American English*

c.   One of the myths we have to fight against is that *no* changes occur without student disorder. This is simply not so. The innovative new campuses of the University of California were planned before the onset of university disorder. The plan for Hampshire College, the experimental Monteith College at Wayne State University, and other new colleges preceded student disorders, as did the program of freshman seminars at Harvard, credit in many places for advanced work done as an undergraduate, and numerous other changes. Admittedly, considerably more change has occurred since the onset of student disorder, less because students demanded it than because this was the one area in which response was possible. The university could not end the war in Vietnam, but it could introduce educational changes and give a greater voice to students in making these changes. Many of these changes are valuable. Some of them conceivably would have been instituted without student disorders. There was already considerable discontent with undergraduate education, even though there was no major constituency, student or faculty, that could force change. But many other changes were made simply to facilitate political activity of students on the campus. Whether this is a necessary or desirable change in undergraduate education depends in part on one's judgment about the desirability of the political viewpoint that radical students propagate as a result of these changes. Other changes, to my mind, involve an adaptation to the reality that many students are not interested in intellectual discipline, in any field, and want in their college years experiences of a different sort—they may be more interested in political organization and social action, in sensitivity training and intense personal relations. To make such experiences possible may be a valuable and necessary change, if we are to accommodate many thousands of students who are now in colleges and universities, although I think we could more efficiently provide for these experiences in other kinds of institutions. But it is hardly likely that these changes would have taken place as rapidly and on the same scale without the student disturbances. — Nathan Glazer, *American Scholar*, Summer 1970

A paragraph is coherent if it hangs together as a whole and if the thought flows smoothly and consecutively from sentence to sentence. Coherence has, then, two dimensions—one rhetorical and one grammatical. The rhetorical dimension involves both content and structure; it has to do with the selection and arrangement of the topics or ideas. If they are only vaguely connected, the paragraph will naturally lack coherence:

Many good citizens find it hard to convince themselves that their vote will make any difference. Men of good will have been voting for generations with little effect. The same hacks and manipulators seem to get into office every time, and the same corrupt Establishment runs the show. When a young person becomes eligible to vote in a national election, he should either acquaint himself with the issues and the policies of the candidates or use the day to catch up on lost sleep. Voting Republican or Democratic because that's how your parents vote is irresponsible if not stupid. A thoughtless vote can cancel an intelligent one, and this country has no intelligent votes to spare.

Three sentences on one topic, three on another: the structural gap suggests that the writer made two different stabs at his subject. Instead of abandoning his first approach, however, he plunged on, ignoring the commitment he had made originally. Jamming together two topics as loosely connected as these produces an incoherent paragraph. And tinkering with it won't help. Before he can revise it sensibly, the writer needs to decide what he wants to talk about.

EXERCISES

1. Revise the paragraph quoted above ("Many good citizens find it hard to convince themselves . . .") so as to strengthen its structure and give it coherence. (Will you keep it a single paragraph, or will you make two paragraphs of it? In either case, how will you solve the problem of the structural gap?)

2. What is wrong with the continuity in the paragraphs below? How would you rewrite?

a. Although Farrell cannot resist any deviation from his narrative, any pause, subplot or digression, he writes with such assurance, with such an elegantly faded sensuality, that we bear with him, usually enthralled, through convolutions of plot beyond synopsis. It is easy to say what is wrong with this good novel, but harder to say what is right. It is grossly over-long. Too many of the expertly realized scenes merely reinforce what has been expertly established before. — *Newsweek,* Feb. 15, 1971

b. My first trip out as a Ranger was a lot better than my second. The boys were well disciplined and worked hard. After a day of orientation in camp, we went out on the trail. I instructed them in using an ax and saw, building fires, cooking, making and breaking camp, and general woodsmanship. We had good weather, good climbing, and no problems. On the fifth day we hiked back to camp. I had the rest of the day off and began to wonder what the next group would be like. Some of the Rangers had groups that were in poor physical condition. The boys were from twelve to sixteen, and each group had one adult advisor. Almost all of them were from the East Coast and had had no previous experience camping in high country. They weren't prepared for the beauty of the snow-peaked Rockies, and they weren't prepared for forty-mile hikes either. Some of them were jumpy about the proximity of wildlife, like bears.

Though unified content and orderly movement are necessary conditions for coherence, they are not sufficient. Even if each sentence in a paragraph can be seen to have a bearing on the central point, and even if the order of the sentences is sensible enough, the paragraph may fail to give the reader a sense of wholeness and an understanding of how one thought relates to the next. The grammatical aspect of coherence — the one we are mainly concerned with in this section — has to do with the writer's skill in making clear to the reader the connections he himself perceives in his material. The following paragraph is hard to read because the sentences seem to be sealed off from one another; the reader gets no help at all in trying to move from one statement to the next.

When Nixon was elected President, bringing the American people together was supposedly one of his primary goals. It can be argued that President Nixon made no attempt to unify America. There were no discernible gains in national unity during the Nixon administration; in fact, disunity increased. The trouble with a slogan like "Bring us together" is that it has no specific meaning. With a population as huge as ours, it is ridiculous to expect everyone to agree on such issues as the war in Vietnam, race relations, national and personal goals, and life styles. The American people have seldom been unified for long, and their unity has always been limited. World War II was supported by a large majority of Americans. Some of our parents hated Hitler; some feared Japan; some wanted to save Western civilization from barbarism; some got rich on defense contracts and black marketeering. After the collapse of the Axis and the death of Franklin Roosevelt, the public demanded the immediate disbanding of our military forces and the abandonment of wartime controls.

Probably the habit of thinking in single sentences is at least partially responsible for the lack of cohesiveness in this paragraph. The sentence-at-a-time procedure results in a series of independent units. Thinking in patterns like this-that-and-therefore is more likely to produce a sequence of *related* statements—a coherent paragraph. In the revision below, the words and phrases that have been added bring out the connections in the material and so guide the reader. Each sentence looks back to the one before it, and this interdependence makes the paragraph cohere. It strikes the mind as a unit, not simply as a collection of sentences.

When Nixon was elected President, bringing the American people together was supposedly one of his primary goals. Whether he made any attempt to achieve that goal is debatable; that he failed to do so is not. But could anyone have succeeded? Presumably success in bringing us together would have meant securing general agreement on issues and problems like the Vietnam War and race relations, on national goals, perhaps even on personal goals and life styles. But the fact is that the American people have never been "together" except on limited issues for limited periods of time. Even during World War II, a period frequently pointed to as one of maximum national unity, those who supported the war (and a sizable minority did not) supported it for divergent reasons—from the most noble and idealistic to the most crass and self-serving. The war—and Franklin Roosevelt—brought Americans together, but with the end of the war and Roosevelt's death, the temporary and superficial nature of that unity was quickly revealed.

Paragraphs are made coherent by a variety of grammatical and lexical means, chiefly by (1) continuing the same grammatical subject (or its equivalent) through successive sentences, (2) repeating key words other than the subject, (3) making sentences and parts of sentences parallel in construction, and (4) introducing transitional words and phrases to connect the sentences. Each offers a way of improving the sentence-by-sentence consecutiveness of your paragraphs. The first three will be discussed in the next section, the fourth in the section after that.

Lexical and Grammatical Repetition.

The chief means of achieving coherence—the repetition of key words and the use of consistent grammatical patterns—are illustrated in this brief paragraph:

If this trend continues, if this crisis of understanding endures, the very survival of the nation will be threatened. A nation driven to use the weapons of war upon its youth is a nation on the edge of chaos. A nation that has lost the allegiance of part of its youth is a nation that has lost part of its future. A nation whose young have become intolerant of diversity, intolerant of the rest of its citizenry, and intolerant of all traditional values simply because they are traditional has no generation worthy or capable of assuming leadership in the years to come.—*Report of the President's Commission on Campus Unrest* (1970)

Of the hundred or so words, *nation* occurs six times, *intolerant* three times, and *youth, part, traditional* twice each. In addition, *its* substitutes for *nation's* four times, and *young* comes close to duplicating *youth*. All told, the paragraph exhibits an astonishing amount of verbal repetition. How much the repetition contributes to ease of comprehension and to the impact of the paragraph can be seen when it is rewritten without repeating any of the *form-class words:

If this trend continues, if this crisis of understanding endures, the very survival of the nation will be threatened. A country driven to use weapons of war upon its youth is on the edge of chaos. A land that has not retained the allegiance of some of its young people has lost part of its future. A state whose junior citizens have become intolerant of diversity, uncooperative with the rest of the public, and hostile to all traditional values simply because they are long-established, has no generation worthy or capable of assuming leadership in the years to come.

In the original, repetition of grammatical structures cooperates with the repetition of words in making the thought easy to follow. The grammatical subjects—"survival of the nation" and "nation"—all point consistently to the same central idea. Changing the subject (say from "nation" to "allegiance" to "values") would have blurred the rhetorical focus. Coherence is reinforced by the insistent parallelism within and between sentences: phrase is balanced against phrase, clause against clause, sentence against sentence. Again, the contrast offered by a rewrite brings out the distinctive features of the original. Continuity is seriously weakened in this version, which, besides avoiding repetition of form-class words, gives each sentence a different subject and shuns parallelism:

If this trend continues and we do not resolve this crisis, there will be a threat to the very survival of this nation. A country that is driven to use the weapons of war upon its youth finds chaos imminent. Whenever a situation has arisen in which a land is deprived of the allegiance of some of its young people, then part of its future is lost. There will be no generation worthy of assuming leadership in the years to come (or even capable of it) if the junior citizens are intolerant of diversity in the state, refusing to cooperate with the rest and hostile to all traditional values simply because they are long established.

The original paragraph is clearly superior on all counts — ease of comprehension, style, emotional impact. But the practice of repeating identical words and grammatical patterns should not be imitated indiscriminately. For one thing, so much verbal repetition and parallelism would, if sustained through several more sentences, become tiresome, and in less heightened contexts even this much would seem distinctly artificial. For another, repetition can become a threat to cohesion. So-called complete repetition — "He praised the men for their courage" and "He praised the men for their loyalty" — has the effect of turning sentences into units with no fixed order. So far as the syntax goes, "He praised the men for their courage" could either precede or follow "He praised the men for their loyalty." If the facts or ideas in consecutive sentences are indeed coordinate, if no sense of progression is involved, then the interchangeability of the sentences presents no difficulties and may even be an asset. But in most paragraphs the writer is advancing his subject sentence by sentence; the order of the facts or ideas *does* matter, and he should make that order seem necessary to his reader.

When you feel that full repetition has distinct rhetorical advantages, you can avoid the effect of autonomous, relatively isolated sentences by introducing some principle of progression. In the original paragraph, the second, third, and fourth sentences are syntactically autonomous, but their order is not random. The hint of chronological ordering (present to future) and, more important, the definite sense of climax ensure that the sentences could not be interchanged without damaging both the logical sequence and the rhetorical effectiveness — the major test for a close-knit, cohesive paragraph.

Though complete repetition can be disadvantageous, some repetition is unavoidable. The frantic effort to avoid repeating a word or a grammatical pattern, as in the rewrite on p. 251, is often so distracting that it becomes a threat to coherence; the reader has to search out a connection that repetition would have made immediately apparent. Ordinarily continuity is maintained and the sentences kept interdependent by the device of partial repetition. The ways of accomplishing it are simple and familiar. Synonyms often do the work of repeating effectively. Pronouns and determiners — *it, he, his, this, these, some* — do it economically and unobtrusively. If the context demanded that the order of the sentences discussed earlier be firmly fixed, with "loyalty" before "courage," substituting "them" for "the men" in the second sentence would make the sentences irreversible: "He praised the men for their loyalty. He praised them for their courage."

The combination of a key word and its related pronouns, determiners, and synonyms — all the words and phrases that in the context have roughly the same meaning or that refer to the same thing — creates an *equivalence chain*. The simplest chain is a pronoun and its antecedent *(its, nation)* or a pair of words or phrases that are synonymous *(youth, young* or *future, years to come)*; sometimes a chain consists of a dozen variations on the central meaning of the key term. In this example the words in color show how a dominant equivalence chain can link all the sentences of a paragraph:

No other living writer has yielded himself so completely and recklessly as has Isaac Bashevis Singer to the claims of the human imagination. Singer writes in Yiddish, a language that no amount of energy and affection seems likely to save from extinction. He writes about a world that is gone, destroyed with a brutality beyond historical comparison. He writes within a culture, the remnant of Yiddish in the Western world, that is more than a little dubious about his purpose and stress. He seems to take entirely for granted his role as a traditional storyteller speaking to an audience attuned to his every hint and nuance, an audience that values storytelling both in its own right and as a binding communal action — but also, as it happens, an audience that keeps fading week by week, shrinking day by day. And he does all this without a sigh or an apology, without so much as a Jewish groan. It strikes one as a kind of inspired madness: here is a man living in New York City, a sophisticated and clever writer, who composes stories about Frampol, Bilgoray, Kreshev *as if they were still there.* His work is shot through with the bravado of a performer who enjoys making his listeners gasp, weep, laugh, and yearn for more. Above and beyond everything else he is a great performer, in ways that remind one of Twain, Dickens, Sholom Aleichem. — Irving Howe, *Decline of the New*

In the fifth sentence, "his role," one item in the dominant chain, initiates the sequence "storyteller," "his," "storytelling," "its," "all this," "composes stories." In the same way, "his work" introduces "performer." These words and phrases, all stemming from the key word "Singer," make a network of relations linking the ideas. The paragraph contains other equivalence chains, among them "audience," "listeners." Parallelism of verbs strengthens continuity not only by the repetition of "writes" in three successive sentences but also by the consistent use of the present tense: "seems," "does," and so on. And parallelism of other words and phrases plays a role in keeping the stress where the author wants it. But by far the strongest cohesive force in the paragraph is the recurrence of the same grammatical subject, or its equivalent, from sentence to sentence. A new subject is introduced only when it is necessary to mark a shift in the point of view ("It strikes one" in the third-to-last sentence).

What you should work to avoid is not *every* shift but only the shift that is erratic, unmotivated, illogical—the changes in person, voice, tense, and structural pattern classed as *shifted constructions. Consistency in these matters contributes to the grammatical cohesion of a paragraph; lack of consistency detracts from it and gives even a well-unified paragraph a general air of incoherence.

Though using similar grammatical subjects is a dependable means of maintaining continuity, it is not feasible in all writing contexts. The process of reasoning from premises to conclusion or of relating causes to effects calls for a different procedure. Instead of always returning to the one subject (or a related subject), a writer may knit his sentences together by having the subject of a sentence grow out of the predicate of the preceding sentence. In this paragraph the strongest links occur not between grammatical subject and grammatical subject but between the end of one sentence and the beginning of the next:

The problem posed by popular culture is finally, then, a problem of class distinction in a democratic society. What is at stake is the refusal of cultural equality by a large part of the population. It is misleading to think of popular culture as the product of a conspiracy of profiteers against the rest of us. This venerable notion of an eternally oppressed and deprived but innocent people is precisely what the rise of mass culture challenges. Much of what upper-class egalitarians dreamed for him, the ordinary man does not want—especially literacy. The situation is bewildering and complex, for the people have not rejected completely the notion of cultural equality; rather, they desire its symbol but not its fact. At the very moment when half of the population of the United States reads no *hardcovered* book in a year, more than half of all high-school graduates are entering universities and colleges; in twenty-five years almost all Americans will at least begin a higher education. It is clear that what is demanded is a B.A. for everyone, with the stipulation that no one be forced to read to get it. And this the colleges, with "objective tests" and "visual aids," are doing their reluctant best to satisfy. — Leslie A. Fiedler, *Encounter*, Aug. 1955

EXERCISES

1. Rewrite the following passage to improve its continuity. Pay special attention to getting rid of unnecessary shifts in grammatical subject.

Counselors often rely very heavily on test scores for an insight into a student's mental ability and interests. Children are subjected to I.Q. tests all through elementary school. The most important of these tests is taken in the eighth grade. Advisors use these results to determine what kind of program a student is capable of following. It may seem very reasonable, but test scores are not always an accurate measure of a person's mental ability. Another kind of test that is popular is the interest test. I remember taking one of these tests and scoring high in business. Business has always seemed loathesome to me. But when asked questions like, "What would you rather be, a garage mechanic, a termite exterminator, or a secretary?" I quickly answered, "A secretary." Such tests are clearly not only worthless as guides to ability but are also an absolute waste of time.

2. Describe the use of grammatical and lexical repetition in the following paragraph. Distinguish between complete and partial repetition. Explain how the repetition does or does not contribute to the cohesiveness of the paragraph.

In contemporary life, the forces at work to deprive man of his quality of human-ness are many, and will increase in number and intensity in the decades ahead. A list of such forces need not be exhaustive to be depressing, and in most cases they represent the dark underside of some remarkable human achievement. We have worked feverishly to bring the blessings of the technological society to the entire country, and in the process have poisoned our lands, our water, our air. As the population has exploded and people have crowded into our great cities, the urban areas have become nightmares of hopelessness and despair, degradation and violence. As television and jet transports have contracted and compressed the world, they have subtly diminished man's imaginative conception of

himself. As life has become more computerized and homogenized, more comfortable and affluent, its meaning has become
more trivial and elusive. Men today live closer together, but
exist further apart. They have less cause for labor, but more
cause for anguish. They have more of technocracy's abundance
and wealth, but they have fewer of nature's simple gifts. They
have gained in gewgaws and gadgetry, but they have lost in
compassion and humanity. — James E. Miller, Jr., *College English,*
Nov. 1970

Transitional Markers

The most overt signals of movement in and between
paragraphs are connecting words, phrases, and clauses that
explicitly state the relations between ideas and in doing so
help make the sentence, paragraph, paragraph sequence, or
essay coherent. Of these signals, the most common are the
coordinating conjunctions (*and, but, or, nor, for, so, yet*), the
conjunctive adverbs (*however, indeed, moreover,* and so
on), and many phrases, including *of course, for example, in
the first place.* In some of their uses, subordinating conjunctions (*because, since*) and simple adverbs (*then, here*) mark a
transition.

It is not possible to make a systematic inventory of transitional words and phrases. For one thing, the grammatical
categories overlap: *but* (coordinating conjunction) and *however* (conjunctive adverb) both express contrast and are often — though not always — interchangeable. For another, the
nature of the connection made by a transitional word sometimes depends on the context: *then* may indicate a causal
relationship, or it may indicate a relationship in time; *on
the other hand* sometimes points up a contrast and sometimes
points out an alternative.

In selecting a transitional marker, the first consideration
is its adequacy to convey the logical relationship intended.
When choices are available, style or emphasis may make
one word or phrase preferable. The *Index* article *Transition
lists some of the ways of indicating the common relationships.

What the scores of transitional words, phrases, and
clauses all have in common is the function of calling the
reader's attention to the role played by a statement in the
paragraph or by the whole paragraph. As such, they make for
cohesiveness, binding ideas together and bringing out

connections in the material. They can also be misused, as when an *and* papers over a break in continuity or when a *therefore* suggests the clinching of an argument that really begs the question.

Transitional words and phrases are in color in the passage below. Note that the favorite position for transitional markers is at or near the beginnings of their sentences. Putting a connector early in the sentence usually permits it to do its work most efficiently.

There should no longer be any question—indeed, there probably never should have been a question—that Poe is one of our major writers. Yet in the august company of Hawthorne, Melville, Emerson, Thoreau, and Whitman, he alone is likely to have his credentials repeatedly challenged, as if he might actually be an impostor. Whatever their deficiencies as writers, his great contemporaries inescapably possess the bearing of serious artists. Poe, however, although he grandiosely proclaimed a theory of pure art, betrays an air of pretentiousness, posturing, and even downright fraud. To be sure, he has his devoted followers who see him as he wished to be seen: the embodiment of the Romantic Artist as Victim. And he has the sturdy corps of academic specialists and defenders seeking to protect his honor and reputation. Finally, he has more than his share of psychoanalytically minded critics seeking to define the nature of his threatened ego. —James M. Cox, *Virginia Quarterly Review*, Winter 1968

On the face of it, transitional markers seem to be the simplest of the devices for achieving coherence, but to use them well requires care and discrimination. If you use too few overt connectors, the sentences may seem to be mutually repellent particles (as in the example on pp. 248–49), and the sequence of thought will be hard to follow. If you use too many, the style will be heavy-handed. *For example* is the typical marker for an inclusive relation, indicating that what follows illustrates what has come before or particularizes it in some way; but if you use *for example* to signal every instance, you may sound pedantic.

The need for overt signals of transition depends partly on the writer's subject and rhetorical purpose. When the thought drives straight on, they are unnecessary. (In the three paragraphs quoted on pp. 128–29, Whitney M. Young, Jr., uses no transitional markers between sentences.) When the difficulty of the material makes it imperative to have the path of thought clearly marked, explicit transitions will be more numerous than when the material is simple and straightforward. And they will be more numerous when the writer aims to inform or instruct than when it suits him to express himself elliptically or to suggest rather than state.

The need for overt signals of transition should also be

gauged in relation to the other means of achieving coherence. In a paragraph that displays consistent focus and skillful use of equivalence chains, connectors that state logical relationships are often superfluous. A reader does not need to be informed twice how one statement relates to another: when he gets his clues from the language of the discussion itself, he will prefer not to be elbowed from one sentence into the next by a *therefore* or an *as a result.* Some of the clues he responds to are wordless. A colon often does the work of *for example.* The simple juxtaposition of two statements may signal a relation of addition or, in other contexts, of contrast or causality or inclusiveness. Transitions can be implied as well as expressed.

EXERCISE

Identify and explain the function of the transitional words and phrases in the paragraph by Adrian and Press, pp. 232–33. Explain why these transitional markers are or are not necessary to the reader's comprehension of the ideas.

So far in this section the means of achieving continuity have been illustrated by expository paragraphs. Though the same verbal devices can be observed in all good paragraphs, the *chief* means to coherence in narration and description are understandably somewhat different from those in exposition.

When the fundamental relationship is chronological, the movement through time is marked mainly by the sequence of verbs and by the use of adverbs, conjunctions, and some phrases (*then, soon, when, after, in the morning*). As the following passage demonstrates, time indicators are more numerous in summarized narrative that records a specific incident than in generalized narrative that records repeated actions. It also demonstrates how repeating the grammatical subject keeps the point of view consistent and gives the narrative coherence. Other devices that further coherence are noted in the comments on the right.

Every summer, sometime in August four good friends of mine and I go for a week's fishing on the St. Regis chain of lakes in the Adirondacks. We rent the same shack each summer; we drift around in canoes, and sometimes we catch a few bass. The fishing isn't very good, but we play cards well together, and we cook out and generally relax. This summer past, I had some things to do that couldn't be put off. I arrived three days late, and the weather was so warm and even and beguiling that I decided to stay on by myself for a day or two after the others left. There was a small flat lawn in front of the shack, and I made up my mind to spend at least three or four hours at short putts. That was how I happened to have the putting iron next to my bed.

Repeated action is conveyed by "every summer" and by the consistent use of the present tense: "go," "rent," "drift," and so on. The shift into summarized narrative comes with "This summer past" and the use of the past tense. Movement in time is indicated by "arrived three days late," "decided," "made up my mind."

The first day I was alone, I opened a can of beans and a can of beer for my supper. Then I lay down in my bed with *Life on the Mississippi*, a pack of cigarettes, and an eight-ounce chocolate bar. There was nothing I had to do, no telephone, no demands and no newspapers. At that moment, I was about as contented as any man can be in these nervous times.

In ¶2, two adverbial phrases and an adverb make transitions and help define the chronological movement: "The first day," "then," "At that moment."

It was still light outside, and enough light came in through the window above my head for me to read by. I was just reaching for a fresh cigarette, when I looked up and saw it on the foot of my bed. The edge of my hand was touching the golf club, and with a single motion I swept the club over and down, struck it a savage and accurate blow, and killed it. That was what I referred to before. Whatever kind of a man I am, I react as a man does. I think that any man, black, white or yellow, in China, Africa or Russia, would have done the same thing. — Howard Fast, "The Large Ant"

Continuity is maintained by "still" and "just" and by the adverb clause "when I looked up." The actual sequence of events is represented by the successive verbs. Simultaneity is accomplished through sequence of tenses: "was reaching," "looked up"; "was touching," "swept," "struck," "killed." The last three sentences switch to interpretation, in which indications of time are unnecessary.

When the main ordering principle is spatial, verbs fade in importance, and the paragraph is signposted by words and phrases that indicate physical dimensions or location.

The cottage belonged to State Senator Leroy Johnson, one of the key figures in Muhammad Ali's return to the ring. He had donated it to the Ali contingent for its training headquarters, and on this, the day of the Jerry Quarry fight, the interior was a shambles. The bedrooms, three of them, were crowded with unmade cots and half-filled suitcases. In the main room, where the curtains were drawn to provide a permanent gloom for TV and film watching, a mounted kingfish had fallen off the wall and lay with its tail in the fireplace. Beside it floated a half-deflated balloon with an inscription on it that read SOUL BROTHER. Scattered about the floor were newspapers and boxing journals, along with strips of film, soiled socks, upturned ashtrays and various items of athletic equipment, including a shuttlecock (there was a sagging badminton net out in the backyard), sweat pants and boots. Above an unmade cot a bed sheet was tacked to the wall to be used as a motion picture screen. A long sofa was set along one wall, with a television console opposite. In the corner of the dining alcove stood a big trunk marked MUHAMMAD ALI—THE KING. On it lay a yellow pad on which some-one had written the words, "Joy to the whole wide wide world a champion was born at 1121 W. Oak Street Louisville Ky it was. . . ." An unfinished document in the handwriting, it turned out, of Cassius Clay Sr.—George Plimpton, *Sports Illustrated*, Nov. 23, 1970

The details are ordered according to a consistent point of view. In the first few sentences the movement is from outside to inside: from "cottage" to "interior" to "bedrooms" to "main room." The dominant impression is made explicit in "the interior was a shambles," and the details that follow bear out the generalization. As one detail follows another, sentence-to-sentence continuity is maintained largely through these words and phrases: "off the wall," "in the fireplace," "Beside it," "Scattered about the floor," "Above an unmade cot," "along one wall," "opposite," "In the corner of the dining alcove," "On it."

Coherence in Paragraph Sequences

The same devices that contribute to coherence in a paragraph help carry the thought through a sequence of paragraphs. In essays of some length, the transitional markers are sometimes supplemented by transitional sentences and transitional paragraphs, both of which give the reader explicit guidance in moving from section to section of an essay. The role of such sentences and paragraphs in structuring an essay has been discussed and illustrated on pp. 201 – 04.

The paragraphs below open an eleven-paragraph essay,

"The Busy Hand of Burgess." (The eight that follow this sequence deal in detail with Burgess' novel *Enderby*; the first sentence of the fourth paragraph is quoted to illustrate the use of a transitional sentence to begin a new sequence.) Comments on the development and structure of the paragraphs are given in the column at the left; comments on the main means of making the paragraphs cohesive are given in the right-hand column.

The second clause of sentence 1 is the main assertion of ¶1: Burgess could be Irish. 2 supports this provocative "classification" by enumerating qualities of B's prose. 3 particularizes the first clause of 1, interprets it, and reverts to the main assertion, which is supported further by the comparisons in 4 and by the interpretation in 5.

(1) Anthony Burgess isn't Irish, but he could be. (2) He writes with the lilt, and a good deal of the blarney, and the roving eye for earthy detail. (3) As it happens, Burgess is a lower-middle-class Catholic from Manchester, which is already two thirds of being Irish, and his garrulousness takes him almost the rest of the way. (4) Like Wilde, Shaw, Yeats, Synge, O'Casey, Joyce, O'Connor, Behan, he is a nonstop talker with temperament to burn, and whose language is rinsed clean of literary detritus. (5) He has also been playing the Irish role on the English literary scene, which is to pepper and stir the pot: to be amusing about the things London takes seriously, such as status, and serious about what London finds amusing, such as sin.

The dominant equivalence chain is "Burgess," "he," "his," "him." Continuity is maintained by the use of the same grammatical subject (or its pronoun) in every sentence. 1 and 2 are closely linked by meaning: 2 stands in an inclusive relation to 1. "As it happens" links 3 to 1, "nonstop" in 4 echoes "garrulousness" in 3, and "also" links 5 to both 4 and 1. Parallelism in 5 contributes to coherence.

¶2 narrows to a comparison that stresses similarities between B and Joyce. The particulars move from external to internal: from B's work on Joyce (1) to their shared capacities, traits, and background (2), to their shared literary talents (3), to similarities in point of view (4). In structure, this middle paragraph of the sequence is simpler than either of the others.

(1) The Irish note is also owing to Burgess' feeling for Joyce, about whom he has written a long commentary (*Re Joyce*) as well as an abridgment of *Finnegans Wake*. (2) Joyce has been the lion in the modern novelist's path, but Burgess, whom nothing much intimidates, meets him eye to eye: a fellow musician (Burgess was trained as a composer), a linguist, a renegade Catholic, a cultural aristocrat from the back streets and pubs of a hard city. (3) He shares Joyce's true sense of the pith and pitch of the spoken language, his uncommon touch for the common life of a man, a family, a community, that creates a thick social atmosphere in which characters move and breathe, rather than just a background against which they stand. (4) Finally, there are strong affinities in point of view: a sympathetic attitude toward men, tempered by the Catholic awareness of human presumption, and emerging as comedy.

"Irish note" and "also" tie ¶2 to ¶1. Consistent with the aim of comparing, the Joyce chain ("whom," "the lion," "him," "Joyce's") has equal prominence with the *Burgess* chain; and the four sentences have different subjects. What is stressed in this paragraph comes not in the subjects but in the predicates. The series in 2 and 3 work for coherence. "Finally," in 4, explicitly links and concludes; and "affinities" picks up the idea of "shares" from 3.

¶3 falls into four closely linked units. 1 and 2 complete the comparison with Joyce, and the difference initiates the aim of the paragraph: to describe, account for, and evaluate B's literary output. What is asserted in 2 is made more specific in 3. 4-7 adduce possible causes for B's great productivity. 8-11 mass evidence for the hypothesis in 7. 12, the key generalization of the paragraph, summarizes the descriptive statements and marks the turn to evaluation. The complex judgment — "almost cursed" — is supported both by the example in 13 and by the division in 14 and 15 that discriminates among B's novels. The final interpretation rounds out the paragraph by recalling the comparison with Joyce. It also rounds out the sequence: the ideas developed are to serve as the basis for the discussion of *Enderby*.

(1) Joyce's talents and vision, however, were poured into four books and little else. (2) Burgess' spill over in all directions, spawning creations rather than nurturing them. (3) Since he started writing seriously in the late Fifties, he has produced eleven novels, as well as enough literary journalism to keep another writer fully employed. (4) I wonder what makes Burgess run. (5) Perhaps it's money. (6) A good English writer still has to hack out a living under conditions that few American writers have any longer to accept. (7) But there is also a performer in Burgess who obviously likes to stand up and have his say, to try his hand at this and that. (8) He has written a novel of Shakespeare's love life in fine Elizabethan prose and a portrait of a future juvenile delinquent, sometime around 1984, in a slang that brilliantly assimilates Russian and English. (9) He has produced a spy novel with the dark, Jansenist overtones of Graham Greene and an anti-utopian fantasy on population control and atavism that takes off from Huxley's *Brave New World* and *Ape and Essence*. (10) His fiction has toured Russia and the Third World, suburban Manchester and Soho. (11) He can describe anything, animate the most farfetched material. (12) He is one of those writers who seem almost cursed by their facility. (13) His last novel, *Tremor of Intent*, begins with a fine, grave wit, heads off into James Bond land, and then slyly circles home to its "eschatological" theme. (14) Only *A Clockwork Orange* and *A Right to an Answer* seem fully written. (15) The rest are full of splendid mimicry and improvisation and froth, as though Burgess were some sort of cross between Joyce and Peter Sellers.

(1) If anything, his new novel, *Enderby*, bears out sharply this difference between the artist's hand and the entertainer's. . . . — Theodore Solotaroff, *The Red Hot Vacuum*

"However" makes a transition from ¶2 and knits sentences 1 and 2. 2 and 3 connect through grammatical subject. The turn at 4 brings a new set of subjects: the syllogistic reasoning in 4-7 results in strong predicate-to-subject continuity. 8-12 have the same or virtually the same grammatical subject, and the sentences are also linked by parallelism (strong in 8-9, less so in the others). The turn in 12 comes unobtrusively: "facility" pulls together virtually the whole paragraph, especially 2 ("spawning creations"), 7 ("try his hand"), and 11 ("can describe anything"); "almost cursed" starts a new consideration. "His last novel" (13), "Only" (14), and "The rest" (15) are related as parts of B's output. "Only" and "The rest" also stand in a complementary relation to each other.

At the beginning of the new paragraph sequence, "artist's hand" and "entertainer's" summarize the whole of ¶3 and so make a transition.

Initially, coherence is an intellectual matter. It has its origin in a writer's sure grasp of what he wants to say. To convey to the reader the relationships you perceive among your ideas, you can use a variety of techniques—repeating, partially repeating, or echoing key words and ideas, repeating grammatical patterns, introducing overt transitions like *but* and *therefore*, and, on occasion, telling the reader explicitly what the preceding paragraph (or paragraph sequence) has done and what the next one will do. But to use these various ways of linking sentences and paragraphs successfully, you must first know what it is you want to say.

EXERCISES

1. Describe the structure of each of the following paragraphs, and examine each paragraph for sentence-to-sentence consecutiveness. Which paragraph is more tightly structured, more cohesive? If you find decided differences, can you justify them in terms of the subject, purpose, or some other element of the rhetorical situation? Do you judge one paragraph to be superior to the other? If so, why?

a. Harvard is not what it used to be. Nothing is: Harvard or the single-wing or McGeorge Bundy's image or the taste of baked sweet potatoes. College kids, especially, are not what they used to be. Presidents who lovingly speak of peace while aggressively waging war no longer fool them. Old fossils who vote to send them to die for corrupt Asian governments in the name of obscure freedoms, while closing their eyes to acts of genocide against the Black Panthers are quickly recognized as frauds. Screwing is better than killing, to say nothing of being ever so much more moral, and the young know this where their fathers did not. Pot being no worse than alcohol, they know the insanity in an alcoholic judge's sending a pothead to jail on the word of a drinking prosecutor slowly murdering his own liver—while Washington subsidizes tobacco growers and cancer research from the same pocket. They know that Eisenhower lied about our U-2 spying missions, that LBJ lied about the Gulf of Tonkin and much to follow, that had the Pentagon told truths all these years about its "kill ratios"—seven-to-one; ten-to-one; more—then the Vietcong would be more severely damaged than we now find it. They know the wide gap existing between the claims of institutional advertising and institutional performance, as is proved in malignant forms when they attempt to place Manhattan telephone calls or when a black man can't secure a loan outside the lairs of loan sharks or when doorknobs fall off or basements leak in new $50,000 split-levels and when the rich architects of faulty automobiles assign private detectives to dig up dirt on Ralph Nader. They know that careless ecological crimes are committed by our industrial kings against the land they are supposed to inherit (provided they don't die in Asia, on the campus of their personal Kent State, or attending a Democratic National Convention) and that Dr. Billy Graham, the Nixon Administration's official moralist, has not provided leadership on a major social crisis in twenty years, if ever: let them eat platitudes. They know that John Wayne, Bob Hope, Mendel Rivers, and other patriots who most publicly proclaim the need for more efficient killing tools, and young men to enthusiastically employ them, have never served a military day in their comfortable fat old lives. They know that J. Edgar Hoover is a despot, a tyrant, a vainglorious bureaucrat who runs his G-man corps with all the daily democracy attending a banana republic—and that not a man in Congress, or the White House, has guts enough to say so.—Larry L. King, *Harper's*, Oct. 1970

b. It is worth looking into the reason for our curious reluctance to use locutions involving the word "whom," particularly in its interrogative sense. The only distinctively objective forms which we still possess in English are *me, him, her* (a little blurred because of its identity with the possessive *her*), *us, them,* and *whom.* In all other cases the objective has come to be identical with the subjective—that is, in outer form, for we are not now taking account of position in the sentence. We observe immediately in looking through the list of objective forms that *whom* is psychologically isolated. *Me, him, her, us,* and *them* form a solid, well-integrated group of objective personal pronouns parallel to the subjective series *I, he, she, we, they.* The forms *who* and *whom* are technically "pronouns" but they are not felt to be in the same box as the personal pronouns. *Whom* has clearly a weak position, an exposed flank, for words of a feather tend to flock together, and if one strays behind, it is likely to incur danger of life. Now the other interrogative and relative pronouns (*which, what, that*), with which *whom* should properly flock, do not distinguish the subjective and objective forms. It is psychologically unsound to draw the line of form cleavage between *whom* and the personal pronouns on the one side, the remaining interrogative and relative pronouns on the other. The form groups should be symmetrically related to, if not identical with, the function groups. Had *which, what,* and *that* objective forms parallel to *whom,* the position of this last would be more secure. As it is, there is something unesthetic about the word. It suggests a form pattern which is not filled out by its fellows. The only way to remedy the irregularity of form distribution is to abandon the *whom* altogether, for we have lost the power to create new objective forms and cannot remodel our *which-what-that* group so as to make it parallel with the smaller group *who-whom*. Once this is done, *who* joins its flock and our unconscious desire for form symmetry is satisfied. We do not secretly chafe at "Whom did you see?" without reason. — Edward Sapir, *Language*

2. Write three separate paragraphs on various aspects of roughly the same subject. In the first, enumerate the traits of your subject. In the second, compare your subject with something else. In the third, give a causal explanation for it. How has your purpose in each paragraph influenced its structure and your choice of methods to connect the sentences? Which paragraph is most cohesive?

3. When a paragraph is unsatisfactory, the trouble may be caused by (1) inadequate development — not enough relevant details; (2) lack of focus — no controlling idea; (3) lack of continuity — insufficient indication of the relationship between statements; (4) unwarranted shifts in the direction of thought; (5) inconsistency in point of view or tone.

Using this checklist as a guide, identify the weaknesses in the paragraphs below and rewrite.

a. After I had been working for the company for a couple of weeks, I was introduced to Joyce, the office secretary. I soon discovered that Joyce was quite easy to talk to, and in our conversations she would pour out all her family problems, her health problems, and even some of her personal problems. In one conversation she told me that she saved her money every day so that on Friday she could put on her best dress, go downtown, and eat at an expensive restaurant. Without this wild fling every Friday night she could not face her job Saturday morning. And yet she seemed happy and content with her daily routine. Why?

b. The first step in rebuilding a motorcycle is to dismantle the cycle and clean all the parts. All metal parts that aren't chromed should be cleaned with an oil solvent, making sure all build-up of dirt and foreign particles is removed. The parts are then soaked in gasoline, then wiped, dipped in an alcohol solution, then again wiped clean. Chromed parts are cleaned with a light oil solution, rubbed clean, then alcohol-dipped and dried. You should clean the painted parts with plain soap and water. When they are dry, they should be covered with a paint remover. After fifteen minutes, the paint is scraped and sandpapered off until only the bare metal is showing. The metal is then polished with 00 sandpaper until smooth. The only non-metal parts are the battery, lights, tires, and seat, all of which should probably be replaced. When I rebuilt my motorcycle I had a new seat made to my specifications.

c. In *Our Blind Children*, Berthold Lowenfeld discusses four criteria for deciding whether to send a blind child to public or residential school: the personality of the child; his home environment; the geographic relationship between the home and the public school where the special program is available; and the quality of the school. In regard to the first factor, Lowenfeld suggests that consideration be given to how well the blind child has interacted with sighted peers in nursery school experiences. His intelligence is also very important, as Eric T. Boulter points out, for the slow-learning blind child should definitely be placed in a school for the blind. Blind students need from 40% to 60% more time than sighted students to complete assignments. It is obvious, therefore, that blind students having a below-average I.Q. should be placed where the subject matter can be presented more slowly. A blind child's talents and abilities should also be considered. One of the students I interviewed for this project had belonged to her school orchestra. Most blind students could not join an orchestra, for they would have to memorize all their music before they could play. This girl had perfect pitch and could learn the music after hearing it only once or twice. This is more important than it may seem, for there are not many opportunities for a blind student to integrate with sighted students outside of classes. Another blind student, who seemed very timid, told me that she had never joined any organizations in school. The residential school would be a better placement for such students, unless their parents would encourage them to join clubs. In a school for the blind, I am certain this girl would have participated in many activities.

Chapter Ten

BUILDING AND PUNCTUATING SENTENCES

Though a writer chooses the particular structure of a given sentence, the general structure—the arrangement of the words that makes it syntactically and semantically meaningful—is determined by the underlying sets of rules that govern English sentence structure. These sets of rules, which a native speaker has acquired without conscious consideration, control the patterns of word arrangement by which English relates sound to meaning. Therefore, according to Noam Chomsky, a leading theorist of transformational, or generative-transformational, grammar, it is a description of such rules that makes up the grammar of a language (see *Grammar). And it is this type of grammar—rules showing precisely how language operates rather than rules prescribing usage (don't end a sentence with a preposition, and so on)—that is especially useful in demonstrating the almost unlimited variety of sentences in English.

By using the language of transformational grammar to describe the stylistic possibilities in English sentences, we can become more conscious of them and perhaps better able to choose among them. If we simplify its concepts and terminology, we can use this approach to analyze the multitude of sentence structures—both the simple basic structures upon which communication is built and the complicated derived sentence patterns that result when we rearrange and expand basic sentence patterns.

 THE STRUCTURE OF ENGLISH SENTENCES

In transformational theory, sentences are "generated" either from *basic* sentence structures—the patterns behind the simplest subject-verb-object-adverb sentences such as "Roosevelt led America through most of the war" — or from *derived* sentence structures — rearranged or expanded versions of basic patterns, such as the expanded, passive-voice version of that sentence: "America was led through most of the war by Roosevelt, the thirty-second President of the United States." The last phrase is part of another basic sentence structure that has been changed into an appositive — " . . . by Roosevelt, [Roosevelt was] the thirty-second President of the United States" — and then combined with the main sentence.

Basic Sentences

To explain how we can form and understand literally thousands of different sentences, transformational grammarians first define the basic structures upon which all sentences are built. We can use a set of algebraic-like formulas to describe the meaningful order of components in the basic sentence patterns. These formulas, designated variously as constituent-structure rules, phrase-structure rules, and rewrite rules, give both the required and the optional components of several types of basic sentence patterns. "To generate" is used in transformational theory with something close to the meaning it has in logic — to apply a rule of substitution to an element to specify its internal structure.

In one form of a transformational grammar, the first rule for the basic sentence structure is $S \rightarrow NP + VP$. This means that a sentence (S) can be rewritten as — the arrow means "rewrite as" — a noun phrase (NP) plus (+) a verb phrase (VP). The noun phrase, the subject in this case, can include everything from *I* to *The man* to *One of the boys in the house*. But to keep things simple, we will rewrite this noun phrase only as an optional article (A), like *a* or *the*, and a noun (N), like *cat, dog, man, idea*: $NP \rightarrow (A)\ N$. The parentheses around A in this rule mean it is optional: either *Boys* or *The boys*, for example.

The verb phrase (VP) is much more complicated. It can be made up of just a verb (V): *breathe, kneel, sleep, twinkle;* or a verb plus a noun phrase object: *see the man, find the money, break the window;* or a copula verb that will link its subject to a predicate describing the subject: *is, become, seem, appear,* followed in the predicate by an adjective phrase (AP) — *is very tired, appears weak, looked somewhat old* — or another noun phrase — *became a football player, was my friend* — or, if the copula is *be*, a prepositional phrase (PP) — *was in the house, am across the hall, are against the door*. We can generate a prepositional phrase with the rule $PP \rightarrow P\ NP$.

The rule for the verb phrase looks more complicated.

$$VP \rightarrow V \left(\begin{Bmatrix} NP \\ AP \\ PP \end{Bmatrix} \right)$$

Listing the elements vertically within braces means that we choose one and only one of them. The parentheses around the braces mean that we do not have to choose any of them, though we must choose a verb.

These rules generate structures for the three primary sentence types in English: (1) sentences with an intransitive verb ("The boy laughed"); (2) sentences with a direct object ("A man kicked the dog"); and (3) sentences with a copulative verb that may be followed by a noun phrase, an adjective phrase, or a prepositional phrase ("He became a teacher"; "They look tired"; "She was in the house").

A complete set of phrase-structure rules would provide more information about generating basic sentences than can be included in this abbreviated and greatly simplified discussion. For one thing, in addition to listing required components—the noun phrase and the three different types of verb phrases—phrase-structure rules list the optional elements, such as adverbs ("The pro football season has become *absurdly* long *in the last few years*"). For another, the rewrite rules for verbs illustrate the regular, repetitive patterning in English verb phrases. A single inclusive rule, in fact, would show that we may select as predicating verb a single word, "He *eats* snails," or two or more words giving detail and qualification: "He *is eating* snails," "He *has been eating* snails," "He *might have been eating* snails." As complete rewrite rules would indicate, we must always show verb tenses—*eats: ate*—and if we use *modal auxiliaries (like *can* and *may*) or *have* or *be* auxiliaries, we follow a structured order: modal + *have* + *be* + verb—"may [or might] have been eating." We can select a *be* auxiliary alone to indicate progression of action—"The volume *is becoming* amazing"—or we can select a modal auxiliary alone to indicate condition of action—"But you *must* apply right away."

This very brief statement of the rules for generating basic sentence structures gives us some insight into their major components, but it is only the first step in explaining how we arrange and rearrange and expand them to create the longer and more complicated sentences we ordinarily use in mature writing. Because the first noun phrase, the subject, usually identifies the topic of a discourse, we often have to revise basic sentences so that their subjects all point consistently to a common idea. And because a series of basic sentences without modification and expansion would fragment a complex idea into a series of equally emphasized parts, we have to combine sentences to emphasize what is important and deemphasize what is not. A description of *derived* sentences explains how we can modify and change basic sentences.

Derived Sentences

Most sentences we write are not simple but derived, generated by "transforming" the basic sentence patterns (hence generative-transformational grammar). We can rearrange their internal order, delete parts, and expand the main pattern by combining with it parts of other basic sentence patterns. For example, a passive-voice sentence like "America's entry into the war had been justified by Wilson" is formed by adding elements and rearranging the simple, active-voice structure of a declarative sentence: "Wilson had justified America's entry into the war." The original direct object is put into subject position and the original subject into a prepositional phrase with *by, be* is added to the verb phrase, and the verb is changed to the past participle form.

A second kind of rule, a transformation, can account for these changes. Remember that base rules of the form $S \rightarrow NP + VP$, sketched on pp. 269–70, generate the basic sentence structures in English. We will call each of these the *deep structure* of a sentence. Transformations may then change this deep structure into a *surface structure* — the sequence of grammatical elements that we could find in a written or spoken sentence. In a transformational grammar, these transformations are represented in what appears to be an algebraic form:

NP^1 V NP^2

$\Rightarrow$ NP^2 be V-ed   by NP^2

But since we are primarily interested in style rather than in formal grammar, our transformations will be shown by rewriting sentences that might be found in ordinary prose. For example, we can represent the passive transformation above with a complete sentence:

Tom   helps   Bill.

$\Rightarrow$ Bill is helped   by Tom.

The double arrow indicates "transformation."

Transformations reflect our sense of how one sentence relates to another. For example, "Someone knows that he left," "That he left was known," and "It was known that he left" all mean the same thing. Although they differ stylistically, each communicates the same message. A transformational grammar generates only one basic structure for these sentences. This structure is very close to the surface structure of "Someone knows that he left." (For a variety of reasons, every deep structure must undergo some transformations to reach a surface structure, but such details are irrelevant to a sketch like this.) If we optionally apply the passive transformation, we get a new structure:

> Someone knows that he left.

⇒ That he left is known by someone.

If we apply an "extra-position" transformation, we get yet another new structure:

> It is known by someone that he left.

We can then delete "by someone":

> It is known that he left.

The last string of words we generate, the string that undergoes no further transformations, is the surface structure. In other words, from one basic deep structure we now have five possible sentences, including (if we delete "by someone") "That he left is known."

Here are some other examples of rearranged sentence order:

Predicate switching:

> Several other examples of the same process are more important.

⇒ More important are several other examples of the same process.

Adverbial clause shifting:

> Many elections are lost because the electorate often chooses not to exercise its obligation to vote.

⇒ Because the electorate often chooses not to exercise its obligation to vote, many elections are lost.

Relative clause shifting:

> Some colleges which are less academically oriented can still perform valuable educational functions.

⇒ Some less academically oriented colleges can still perform valuable educational functions.

Cleft-sentence shifting:

> Every college student needs a place where he can get away by himself and think through his experiences.

⇒ What every college student needs is a place where he can get away by himself and think through his experiences.

There shifting:

In many countries, laws state that a man is assumed to be guilty until he proves himself innocent.

⇒ In many countries there are laws that state that a man is assumed to be guilty until he proves himself innocent.

It shifting:

Many students are now studying socially relevant subjects.

⇒ It is socially relevant subjects that many students are now studying.

In all such cases, the context and what you want to emphasize will determine whether or not you should shift elements.

Transformational grammars describe not only the regular, predictable ways in which we can rearrange sentences but the ways we combine sentence patterns into longer and more complex sentences. When these basic sentence patterns are combined, they change considerably, but the original relationships among the words and phrases are retained. In "The Marshall Plan was almost rejected by Congress," we know that underlying the word order is a more primary relationship: "Congress almost rejected the Marshall Plan." And even though "Congress" does not stand in the subject position in the transformed sentence, we know that it still performs the action. If we transformationally combine the sentence pattern behind this sentence with the one behind "The Marshall Plan made the most profound and lasting impression," this more complicated sentence pattern could result: "Although barely accepted by Congress, the Marshall Plan made the most profound and lasting impression." Though no subject word at all occurs in the phrase "Although barely accepted by Congress," we know that on one level the subject of the passive "accepted" is "the Marshall Plan." But on another, deeper level it is a direct object: "Congress barely accepted the Marshall Plan." The transformation combined the two patterns by deleting both the subject of the first sentence and "was," thus reducing the sentence to a participial phrase.

The most common ways that a transformational grammar combines sentence patterns is by *conjoining*, using various kinds of connectives, and by *embedding*, inserting parts of the constituent sentences into the matrix, or original sentence, as various kinds of phrases and clauses. When patterns are conjoined, they are usually linked by conjunctions and are often shortened:

Colleges are changing. High schools are changing, too.

⇒ Colleges and high schools are changing.

Another kind of conjoining transformation produces subordinate clauses:

Eighteen-year-olds have the vote. No one expects big changes.

⇒ Although eighteen-year-olds have the vote, no one expects big changes.

Embedded sentence patterns can function as subjects and objects, as modifiers of nouns, adjectives, and adverbs. These full sentence patterns can be reduced to a phrase or even to a word. Here are some examples.

Noun clause:

He went home. Everyone knows that.

⇒ Everyone knows *that he went home.*

Gerund:

My roommate studies all night. It is not good for him.

⇒ *My roommate's studying all night* is not good for him.

Nominalization:

We discussed the problem thoroughly. It helped the situation.

⇒ *Our thorough discussion of the problem* helped the situation.

Infinitive:

Industry must stop polluting our environment. We all want that.

⇒ We all want *industry to stop polluting our environment.*

Noun modifier (clause):

Our teacher told us to read a new book. It analyzes the history of Chinese-American relations.

⇒ Our teacher told us to read a new book *that analyzes the history of Chinese-American relations.*

Noun modifier (phrase):

The food was on the table. It looked very tempting.

⇒ The food *on the table* looked very tempting.

Noun modifier (single word):

I saw a movie last night. It was exciting.

⇒ I saw an *exciting* movie last night.

As mature readers we easily recognize the relationships expressed in sentences as complex as this one:

Each year, in the United States, the trash contains a smaller and smaller portion of organic residues, which gradually change into humus, and a bigger and bigger portion of change-resistant, man-made artifacts and potions: old machines and their parts, bits of cities knocked down or dug up to be discarded, plastic containers in which men delivered their goods to one another, useless when emptied, tubs of chemicals that have served their purpose and represent the now worthless distillate of vast quantities of raw materials extracted from the earth. — Roger Starr, *Horizon*, Winter 1970

A partial and simplified analysis of adjectives, adjective clauses, and noun clauses in apposition in this sentence indicates the underlying relationships of the embedded structures of modification. A paragraph in which some of the underlying structures were represented as independent sentences might look like this:

Each year in the United States, the trash contains portions of organic residues. They are smaller and smaller. They gradually change into humus. A bigger and bigger portion of residue is man-made artifacts and potions. They resist change. They are old machines and their parts. They are bits of cities someone has knocked down or dug up to be discarded. They are containers made of plastic. Men deliver their goods to one another in them. They are useless when emptied. There are tubs of chemicals that have served their purpose. They represent the distillate of vast quantities of raw material which someone has extracted from the earth. They are now worthless.

Even this version is far from representing the basic structures which transformational grammarians postulate. The sentence beginning "A bigger and bigger portion . . . ," for example, would be made up of more atomic elements combined and transformed:

Portions are artifacts.

A man made artifacts.

Portions are potions.

A man made potions.

Portions are bigger and bigger.

Portions are of residue.

Knowledge of the underlying rules we use to frame basic sentences and to rearrange and combine them into complex ones gives, with our large lexicon, a potentially infinite number of sentences. As transformational scholars point out, the only limits to the number of clauses (basic sentences, that is) that may be conjoined or embedded are the practical ones of sentence length and clarity—limits imposed by human memory.

SENTENCE TYPES AND VARIATIONS

When we analyze and discuss sentences, it is convenient to use some general system of classification. The traditional practice has been to classify sentences as simple, compound, complex, and compound-complex, according to the number and kind of clauses in them. *A simple sentence*, such as this one, *has* only one independent clause with a subject and a verb. A compound sentence, like this one, consists of two potentially separate sentences, *so* possibly these really depend more on punctuation than on grammar (compare: ". . . separate sentences. So possibly these . . ."). A complex sentence, like the one *that* you are now reading, has at least one subordinate clause *that* functions as an adjectival, relative, adverbial, or noun clause. *Since* "compound-complex sentence" virtually explains itself, we need not give any special examples, *for* this sentence illustrates one.

The traditional terms are slightly misleading. The only difference between "While I was waiting for a bus, I glanced through the paperbacks" and "While waiting for a bus, I glanced through the paperbacks" is that a deletion transformation has dropped the repeated subject and the form of *be* in the subordinate clause in the complex sentence. This change makes the clause a phrase, and the whole sentence a simple sentence. The terms are still useful, since they do reflect significant patterns in mature prose; but we must remember that they refer to grammatical components, not to semantic or rhetorical complexity: a simple sentence may have a long and rather complicated structure, and a complex sentence may have a short, relatively simple structure. The sentence you are reading is complex. The next sentence is simple.

All four types of sentences make use of various kinds of elaboration: compound subjects, compound verbs, compound objects, and compound modifiers; prepositional phrases; verbals and verbal phrases; adjectives, adjective series, and adjective phrases; and nouns and noun phrases used as appositives.

To show how we combine sentence patterns, we will discuss the simplest ways first and then look at some that are more complicated.

Compound Sentences

Compound sentences contain two or more independent clauses — that is, two or more subject-verb combinations that could be written as simple sentences. The clauses may be joined by a semicolon or, in some instances, by a comma alone or by connecting words with or without punctuation.

Connecting words used to join the clauses of compound sentences are of three kinds: coordinating conjunctions — *and, but, for, nor, or, yet, so;* correlative conjunctions — *both . . . and, either . . . or, neither . . . nor, not so . . . as, not only . . . but (also), whether . . . or;* and conjunctive adverbs (sometimes called *adverbial connectors*) — *accordingly, also, besides, consequently, hence, however, indeed, namely, nevertheless,* and other similar words. The first type, the coordinating conjunction, is by far the most commonly used:

The United States is basically a conservative country, *and* its working class is one of the anchors of its conservatism. — Richard Hofstadter, *Harper's,* April 1970

Compound sentences with no connective word between the clauses are conventionally punctuated with a semicolon:

Book reviewers (as opposed to critics) were another matter; from the first, they took Sinclair Lewis with considerable seriousness. — Mark Schorer, *Sinclair Lewis*

In much contemporary writing, connectives like *however, nevertheless, consequently,* and the coordinating conjunctions *and, but, yet,* and others are used between two separate sentences rather than between two clauses of the same sentence.

What has happened, I think, is something that has happened to avant-gardes in many fields, from William Morris and the Craftsmen to the Bauhaus group. *Namely,* their discoveries have been preempted by the Establishment and so thoroughly dissolved into the mainstream they no longer look original. — Tom Wolfe, *Esquire,* July 1967

Frequently, the only difference between a compound sentence and two independent sentences is punctuation. In good modern prose, few writers hesitate to begin a sentence — or a paragraph — with a coordinating conjunction.

Why does the patriarchal family persist through all recorded history? Because the social learning process trains us to accept it as a necessary given. *But* why does this learning process itself persist through history? Because it is needed for sustaining the patriarchal family. *And* what does Miss Millett spinning in circles illuminate here? Very little. — Irving Howe, *Harper's*, Dec. 1970

Complex Sentences

As we have seen, complex sentences (following the terminology of traditional grammar) differ from simple sentences in containing one independent clause and one or more dependent clauses. Keep in mind, however, that "simple" sentence patterns may derive transformationally from "complex" ones:

Although the plan was disliked, it was accepted by a majority of people who were there.

Although disliked, the plan was accepted by a majority of people there.

The dependent clauses are of two general types: adverbial modifiers introduced by words like *if, although*, and *when*, and clauses used either as nouns or as adjectival modifiers, usually introduced by the relative pronouns (*who, whose, whom, which*, and *that*, and *whoever, whomever, whatever*) or by *how, when, what, where*. The introductory or connecting words of noun and adjective clauses are sometimes omitted.

Dependent noun clauses may fill any sentence position a noun fills—subject, object, complement, or appositive. Here they are embedded as objects:

The pilgrims were on the road for many days and stopped at places for the night. Chaucer does not tell us how many or where.

⇒ *How many days the pilgrims were on the road and at what places they stopped for the night* Chaucer does not tell us. — Albert Baugh, *Chaucer's Major Poetry*

Science is almost as rich in metaphors and figurative language as the most imaginative literature. Few laymen realize this.

⇒ Few laymen realize that *science is almost as rich in metaphors and figurative language as the most imaginative literature.*

Adjective clauses modify nouns or pronouns. A repeated noun is changed to a relative pronoun, and the sentence it is in is embedded in the matrix sentence:

The copula figures prominently in traditional logic. Nowadays, it is often said that it is superfluous.

⇒ Nowadays, it is often said that the copula, *that figures so prominently in traditional logic,* is superfluous. — Max Black, *Models and Metaphors*

The most common subordinating conjunctions are the following:

after	as much as	how	since	until
although	because	if	so that	when
as	before	in order that	that	where
as if	even	once	though	while
as long as	even though	provided	unless	why

Dependent adverbial clauses, whether placed before or after the independent clause, begin with a subordinating conjunction.

Though Alger was an ordained clergyman, there is hardly a trace of religious feeling in his novels. — Malcolm Cowley, *Horizon,* Summer 1970

They needed to strike his imagination *before they could pierce his intelligence, or his heart.* — Sean O'Faolain, *Vive Moi!*

Compound-Complex Sentences

Compound-complex sentences, as the hyphenated term indicates, contain at least two independent clauses plus one or more dependent clauses.

The cathedral at Chartres, I have said, says something to the people of this village which it cannot say to me; but it is important to understand that this cathedral says something to me which it cannot say to them. — James Baldwin, *Notes of a Native Son*

The very people who yearned for a fresh start on North American soil had brought with them the heritage of the past; the very people who hoped to create a new Eden bore the marks and stains of the world they wished to leave behind. — Irving Howe, *The Literature of America: Nineteenth Century*

Transformed and Reduced Clauses

The most common ways we expand sentences do not depend on full clauses but on clauses transformed to create shorter modifying structures:

The parts of the world which are the most beautiful are becoming overrun with tourists.

$\Rightarrow$ The *most beautiful* parts of the world are becoming overrun with tourists.

Compound Subjects, Verbs, Objects.   Transformationally, compound subjects, verbs, and objects result from combining two or more sentences with the same structure and deleting repeated parts. Such compounds are economical in that they extend the range of ideas a sentence can cover at little cost in sentence length. In the following example, note the effect the author gains through using a compound subject and compound adjectives and adverbs as well:

Radio offers short programs, interrupted between and within by commercials. They are also often unrelated. TV does this too.

$\Rightarrow$ Both radio and TV offer short, unrelated programs, interrupted between and within by commercials. — Edmund Carpenter, *Explorations in Communication*

Verbals and Verbal Phrases.   Verbals, the nonfinite verb forms that cannot be used alone to express sentence predication ("He eats" expresses predication; "He eating" or "He eaten" does not), are of three types: gerunds, the *-ing* forms of verbs used as nouns; participles, the present *-ing* forms and the past participle forms (*-ed* forms or words like *sung, fallen, broken*) used as adjectival modifiers; and infinitives, the base forms of verbs, with or without *to*, used as nouns or as adjectival and adverbial modifiers. All three may be used either singly or in phrases.

Gerunds, since they perform a function identical with that of nouns, may be used either as subjects or as objects.

As subject:

I read the book. It was a lightning shock, a portent, a mystical experience.

$\Rightarrow$ *The reading of the book* was a lightning shock, a portent, a mystical experience. — Morris Bishop, *Horizon*, Spring 1970

As object:

In 1960 the United States was accused of sending a U2 spy plane into Russia, but we denied it.

$\Rightarrow$ In 1960 the United States denied sending a U2 spy plane into Russia.

Participles may be used singly, in series, or in phrases to modify nouns, pronouns, or noun clauses. In his version

of the following five sentences, the author effectively enhances his description by juxtaposing past participles ("frustrated," "distorted") with adjectives and using both present
and past participles ("living," "limited," "life-denying") to
modify other nouns:

The citizens of Winesburg are frustrated and distorted. They are
violent or passive. They are also aggressive or self-destructive.
They are the living dead. They are victims of truths which are
limited and which deny life, and they are guilty for having
chosen them.

⇒ *Frustrated, distorted, violent* or *passive, aggressive* or *self-
destructive,* the citizens of Winesburg are the *living* dead, victims of *limited, life-denying* truths and guilty for having chosen
them. — Brom Weber, *Sherwood Anderson*

Participial phrases can be equally effective in giving
details, adding to the basic sentence the equivalent of one or
more sentences, as the following transformation shows:

The plots are variations on a basic formula. They vary just
enough to provide some stimulation.

⇒ The plots are variations on a basic formula, *varying just enough
to provide some stimulation.* — Glenn E. Reddick, *Christian
Century,* Sept. 29, 1965

Infinitives and infinitive phrases (sometimes with the *to*
omitted) may be used in a variety of ways.

As a predicate:

This flood of rhetoric had an effect. It befuddled the outside
world with the view that China was indeed being aggressive,
as the West already assumed.

⇒ The effect of this flood of rhetoric was *to befuddle the outside
world with the view that China was indeed being aggressive,
as the West already assumed.* — John K. Fairbank, *New York
Review of Books,* April 22, 1971

As adjectival modifier:

As the fruits and vegetables reach maturity, you must harvest
them and close the garden for the winter. He explains the
best ways.

⇒ As the fruits and vegetables reach maturity, he explains the best
ways *to harvest, and to close the garden for the winter.* — Joan
Michaelson, *University Review* #15

As object:

> Green is the "opposite" of red in the same way that black is the opposite of white. This ordering mechanism of the brain is such that anyone who is not color blind can readily be taught to feel this.

⇒ This ordering mechanism of the brain is such that anyone who is not color blind can readily be taught *to feel that green is the "opposite" of red in the same way that black is the opposite of white.* — Edmund Leach, *Claude Lévi-Strauss*

As adverb:

> The poet helps us to understand and feel the world. He creates these new forms, new metaphors, and new myths.

⇒ *In order to help us understand and feel the world,* the poet creates these new forms, new metaphors, and new myths. —William Van O'Connor, *The Shaping Spirit*

Adjectives and Nouns. In the sentence below, the author uses both adjectives and nouns as modifiers, singly, in series, and in phrases. How would his effect have been different had he used relative clauses or separate sentences to say the same thing?

Sometimes in dreams I see *decent* people as a group of pilgrims (like Bosch's peddler) looking for a *better* place, a *safer, cleaner* place to live, but attacked and plagued by the devils of this world, *human* in face and *animal* in soul. — Gilbert Highet, *Horizon,* Spring 1970

Nouns, singly or in series or in phrases (sometimes referred to as *noun clusters*), are used in apposition—that is, immediately after another noun to rename and further identify or describe it. In the first sentence below, the appositive identifies the proper noun; in the second, it lists descriptive types; in the third, it interprets the noun phrase it follows. Again, how are these different from full relative clauses or independent sentences?

Beckford alone, *a millionaire dilettante,* showed the fiery touch of real genius. . . . Walpole's personages are all of them decorative dummies—*a haughty tyrant, a brace of innocent maidens, a mysterious knight, and an unacknowledged heir.* — Peter Quennel, *Horizon,* Summer 1969

The reasonableness of a John Stuart Mill—*the addition to the notion of ideas as contending forces in a free market*—has no place in Marcuse's scheme. — Edmund Stillman, *Horizon,* Summer 1969

A sentence by Ernest Hemingway illustrates how complex a "simple" sentence can become:

Swimming slowly, the four of them swam out in the green water, their bodies making shadows over the clear white sand, bodies forging along, shadows projected on the sand by the slight angle of the sun, the brown arms lifting and pushing forward, the hands slicing in, taking hold of the water and pulling it back, legs beating along steadily, heads turning for air, breathing easily and smoothly. — *Esquire*, Oct. 1970

This sentence embeds structures almost to the limit set by human memory. To modify his one main clause, "the four of them swam out in the green water," Hemingway uses two simple participial phrases ("swimming slowly" and "breathing easily and smoothly") and seven absolute participial phrases — (1) "their bodies making shadows over the clear white sand"; (2) "bodies forging along"; (3) "shadows projected on the sand by the slight angle of the sun"; (4) "the brown arms lifting and pushing forward"; (5) "the hands slicing in, taking hold of the water and pulling it back"; (6) "legs beating along steadily"; (7) "heads turning for air." Certainly this sentence, along with other examples by talented writers, reaffirms the thesis that "simple sentence" is a grammatical designation, not a description or evaluation of the style or content of a sentence.

Minor Sentence Types

Since most written English sentences contain at least one independent noun-phrase-plus-verb-phrase combination, they can be classified as simple, complex, compound, or compound-complex. But a few sentences used deliberately for special effect do not have an independent noun-phrase-plus-verb-phrase core. In print as in speech, these minor sentences give the effects of emphasis and sometimes of informality. They also allow the author to avoid colorless or repetitious noun phrases or verb phrases. In context, minor sentence types are clear and complete; they do not require an "understood" constituent.

One group of minor sentences is made up of exclamations — "Ouch," "Indeed," and others. A second group includes "Yes," "No," and "Please," words with numerous uses, particularly in spoken English where vocal inflection can help indicate meaning. Longer, more individual minor sentence patterns are the phrases or clauses used in particular contexts. Note the informal, colloquial style of the passage in which this partial sentence appears.

What about the Old Lady? She's gone: We threw her out of the book, finally. A little late you say. *Yes, perhaps a little late.* —Ernest Hemingway, *Death in the Afternoon*

And observe the underplaying of emphasis the writer gives to his description of a race driver with the short minor sentence, a phrase that would have had a slightly different effect if it had been included along with the complete sentence.

Gurney says he doesn't believe in bad luck. Or the other kind. — Ken W. Purdy, *Mainliner*, June 1970

Minor sentences can also be used to convey ironic criticism effectively.

Lindbergh was free enterprise. Apollo was the work of a crowd. No ape could have flown the *Spirit of St. Louis* from New York to Paris. But we could have sent an ape to the moon. *Or a robot. With a fake flag artificially distended for a dead place where there is no wind.* — Peter Schrag, *Harper's*, April 1970

Minor sentences often serve as bridges to provide quick transitions.

So much for sexual comedy. Nobody dies in the book but a lot of people would like to, or at least wouldn't mind. — Kurt Vonnegut, Jr., *Life*, July 17, 1970

And minor sentences may be used to create any number of stylistic effects.

EXERCISES

These exercises, based in part on the preceding sections of this chapter and in part on related *Index* articles, deal with some fundamental problems in constructing sentences. In each set of exercises, you are asked to decide whether the items listed are or are not satisfactory for college writing. Some of the items are from essays by students, some from published sources. Do not assume that anything in print must be satisfactory; every writer writes badly on occasion.

1. *Fragments.* See *Fragment. This exercise asks you to distinguish between minor sentences (pp. 283–84) and fragments.

Minor sentences are grammatically incomplete but rhetorically acceptable; fragments are both grammatically incomplete and rhetorically unacceptable.

Whenever you depart from the convention of building a sentence around an independent noun-phrase-plus-verb-phrase combination, you should be able to justify the departure as a minor sentence — at least as an acceptable alternative to a full sentence and at best as rhetorically superior to it *in the context.* Most readers would agree that "So much for sexual comedy" (p. 284) is more effective (because more brisk, more final) than "That is all that needs to be said about sexual comedy." Any reader would be puzzled or irritated to find the verbal phrase "Having disposed of sexual comedy" punctuated as a sentence.

Other pairs of sentences illustrate the difference and suggest the grounds on which minor sentences can be justified.

College differs from high school in several obvious ways. First, in the relation between teacher and students. In college classes. . . .

College differs from high school in several obvious ways. Chiefly in the relation between teacher and students. In college classes. . . .

Though the two versions are superficially alike, the first is acceptable in General writing, the second not. The minor sentence makes a concise and easy transition into the topic to be discussed; the fragment is simply an unattached phrase that should either be made a part of the preceding sentence or rewritten as a grammatically complete sentence.

Take this pair:

That most people dislike poetry is a reflection on our methods of teaching it. Not an eternal truth of human nature.

. . . how can the greater judicial success in reapportionment be explained, as compared with that in racial desegregation? Not, surely, on the basis of arguments about the abstract power of the Court. — Arthur Selwyn Miller, *Supreme Court Review,* 1968

In the first, the elements in contrast should be juxtaposed with a comma between them, not separated by a period; in the second, the minor sentence offers an emphatic and economical answer to the question.

The examples of phrases and clauses punctuated as sentences in the article *Fragment would be criticized by any reader. Grammatically incomplete sentences that begin with phrases like *for example, in short, namely, that is* are criticized by some readers, accepted by others. Or the same reader finds them acceptable in some contexts, not in others.

They have their own schools, stores, and amusements. In short, a Chinese island inside San Francisco.

He had a fine record as governor and was respected by everyone. That is, until he called out the National Guard.

These might be defended on the grounds that *in short* and *that is* occur regularly enough in contexts like these to be accorded the independent status of the fuller statements for which they substitute. Or they might be criticized on the grounds that the semantic relation of the two units is so close that a period makes an unduly sharp interruption. What could make all the difference is the context. General writing is more hospitable to most types of minor sentences than Formal is. And some casual General styles permit types that rarely appear in General-to-Formal.

In the following excerpts, identify the sentences that are not grammatically complete. Distinguish between minor sentences and fragments. Justify each minor sentence by showing that it serves a function the corresponding full sentence would not serve. Rewrite the excerpts containing fragments to make them acceptable in college writing. If you find an item that you consider debatable, distinguish between contexts in which it would be acceptable and those in which it would not.

a.   No, I distrust Great Men. . . . I believe in aristocracy, though—if that is the right word, and if a democrat may use it. Not an aristocracy of power, based upon rank and influence, but an aristocracy of the sensitive, the considerate and the plucky.—E. M. Forster, *Two Cheers for Democracy*

b.   Magnificent, but is it art? Certainly not. Art follows rules based on our tiny comprehension.—Jacques Barzun, *God's Country and Mine*

c.   One of my greatest pleasures is to walk alone in the country. To hear the splash of a frog diving into the pond, to listen to the cries of the geese overhead, to catch the scent of pines and moist loam, to watch the changing colors of the evening sky.

d.   So much for millennial hopes and fears.—Sheldon P. Zitner, *Shakespeare Quarterly*, Winter 1967

e.   One solution is to remove portions of the bottom of the bay for purposes of navigation, land fill, and mining. If the water is deepened only in selected areas, the bay bottom becomes irregular, and circulation of water through the deeper portions decreases. Thus cutting down the amount of available oxygen in the water and increasing anaerobic activity of harmful, pollution-causing bacteria.

f.   Under the American system, the civilians have to control the military because there is no mechanism for the military to control themselves.
Similarly, machines. The technological revolution affects the Army as it affects the rest of society.—Ward Just, *Atlantic*, Nov. 1970

g.   Suppose that the last step had been taken.—Ruth B. Ginsberg, *Harvard Law Review*, Feb. 1969 *h.* Many young people of college age automatically make two assumptions. One that all men are individuals. The other that in America every individual has a right to a good deal of freedom. They themselves have been brought up in a permissive atmosphere and have rarely been disciplined. Which means they have little fear of authority and even less respect for the traditions of the past.

i. The book treats the Revolution under three topics. First, the causes of the war; second, the events; third, the effects.

j. Then the story we all know: exile, first in Switzerland, where he saw the fever-chart of Europe continue to rise; then Princeton, then California, with always the exhausting necessity of trying to help those who hadn't got out, those who had got out with less than he had. Honors, testimonial banquets, speeches, Books of the Month, American citizenship; and absolutely uncompromising and energetic support of the war against Germany; refusal to return to Germany, after the war. — John Thompson, *Harper's*, Jan. 1971

k. Words have users, but as well, users have words. And it is the users that establish the world's realities. Realities being those fantasies that control your immediate span of life. Usually they are not your own fantasies, *i.e.*, they belong to governments, traditions, etc., which, it must be clear by now, can make for conflict with the singular human life all ways. The fantasy of America might not hurt you, but it is what should be meant when one talks of "reality." Not only the things you can touch or see, but the things that make such touching or seeing "normal." Then words, like their users, have a hegemony. Socially — which is final, right now. — LeRoi Jones, *Home: Social Essays*

l. In the final minutes of the discussion, he clenched his fist and shouted. Actions that showed how passionately concerned he was for the welfare of the children.

m. Incredible. Here I was on a summer evening reading for pleasure the writing of students not my own. — Ken Macrorie, *Uptaught*

n. "We were all a little mad that winter," wrote Ralph Waldo Emerson, recalling the emotional excitement of 1840. "Not a man of us that did not have a plan for some new Utopia in his pocket." As common as a handkerchief and as casually displayed. Today, pockets seem to be empty of anything so inspiring. — *Time*, Jan. 18, 1971

o. Most style is not honest enough. Easy to say, but hard to practice. — F. L. Lucas, *Holiday*, March 1960

p. Since the administration of government is performed through agencies, one advantage of military agencies is their ability to send highly qualified specialists into areas of civic action, especially education. This being most important because future administrative policies and programs must be geared to the people's thinking and acceptance of goals. The United States has proven the worth of this concept in many nations; why can't we do it for ourselves? — Letter to the Editor, *Providence Sunday Journal,* Feb. 21, 1971

q. Sainte-Beuve said the whole art of criticism lay in "just characterization," and if that is not the final word on the subject it is certainly the necessary first word. Which means it is impossible to justly characterize movies if you confine your vocabulary, as Mr. Simon does, to the language — I almost said the clichés — of formal criticism. . . .

Thus a beginning to the problem of just characterization. But hardly the end of it. . . .

To be sure, movies have shown — in the past decade or two — a commendable and even exciting ability to grow beyond these origins, but as anyone can plainly see, many of the best films, from silent days onward, while clinging to the outward appearance of these forms, have transcended them. Which is merely a way of saying that movies are movies, that they have a logic of their own that is only partially to be apprehended in traditional terms, and it seems both pointless and annoying to criticize them for being what they have every historical justification for being. — Richard Schickel, *Harper's,* March 1971

r. The movie was widely admired. Especially by servicemen who could testify to its realism.

s. The Director was permanent, the General was temporary. The General — when he cared enough to interrupt the FBI's rigid routines — could influence the present, but the Director had a lien on the future. Especially when it came to reputations — reputations of individuals and, by extension, reputations of whole Administrations. — Victor S. Navasky, *Atlantic,* Nov. 1970

2. *Comma faults.* See *Comma fault and *Contact clauses. This exercise asks you to distinguish between faulty and acceptable use of the comma to separate independent clauses not joined by a conjunction. The following sentences offer some clues to situations in which the comma is frequently used instead of the semicolon:

The Director was permanent, the General was temporary. — Victor S. Navasky (Exercise 1s above)

It is not merely a regulatory board, it is a board of censorship.

Some will gain, others will lose.

Tolerance understands, compassion warms, charity forgives.

The most obvious characteristic of these sentences is that the clauses are short and parallel in form. The semantic relation of the clauses is also very close, the second filling out or amplifying the meaning of the first. In the first two sentences there is a clear pattern of opposition, though the implied *but* is not stated. In the last two, the meaning is additive and, especially in the last one, climactic. Intonation gives another clue—though not a sure one—to the difference between sentences in which the comma is acceptable punctuation and sentences in which it is not (see those in *Comma fault). If you read the illustrative sentences aloud, you will probably discover that your voice does not drop as much at the comma as it normally does when you come to the end of a sentence.

When you use only a comma between independent clauses, you should do it for a purpose. It can give the effect of rapid movement; it can reveal relationships without stating them explicitly; it can make a style seem easy and relaxed. But since some readers are prejudiced against such punctuation, you should make sure that the comma alone achieves something that would not be achieved by more conventional punctuation.

Justify or criticize the punctuation in each of the items below. See *Comma fault for various methods of revising comma faults, and make at least one revision of each unsatisfactory sentence.

a. Capitalism and socialism are not political systems, they are economic.

b. Lawyers and doctors can assess their abilities and their chances, and can resolve on a course of action. Writers hardly decide anything at all; they simply find themselves at work, in solitude, almost in secret. No one tells them or directs them, no one knows what they are up to, the world goes on regardless.

But sooner or later they do take thought. The intellect gets busy, means and methods are studied, purposes are assessed.—Gerald Warner Brace, *The Stuff of Fiction*

c. It is the writer's job to persuade his readers that he knows what he is talking about, nearly all good writing rests on the solid ground of experience and knowledge.

d. The need is not really for more brains, the need is now for a gentler, a more tolerant people than those who won for us against the ice, the tiger, and the bear.—Loren Eiseley, *The Immense Journey*

e. To the east are the two lumber yards, between them you can see the Co-op Dairy Company and the Soo Line Railway depot, now closed.

f. Once again I knew the powerful excitement of a group experience. I belonged, I was myself and the others too.

g. No cars crossed the bridge, no policemen came to ask what we were doing.

h. I had arrived from West Point, Mississippi, after less than a year there as the one reporter on the smallest daily in the state. Mississippi is different now, it is going through its own amazing revolution, but then it had a special darkness; for a variety of reasons it lacked freedom of speech. — David Halberstam, *Harper's*, Jan. 1971

i. White, yellow, and grey are the colors most anglers prefer, however, color of the lure is actually of little importance.

j. Not only is the armadillo likely to be of some benefit to the neighborhood, both conversationally and as a pest remover, the animal also has reached high station as another sort of symbol, for it has a certain kind of status apart from that conferred on it by youth. — Edwin Shrake, *Sports Illustrated*, Jan. 4, 1971

k. Some of his habits are amusing, others are disgusting.

l. This was bad, admittedly this was bad. — Helen Bevington, *A Book and a Love Affair*

m. I feel my life take its place among the lives — the trees, the annual plants, the animals and birds, the living of all these and the dead — that go and have gone to make the life of the earth. I am less important than I thought, the human race is less important than I thought. — Wendell Berry, *The Long-Legged House*

n. When I was a child, the city meant glamor and the country boredom, now the reverse is true.

o. The critics raise their eyebrows, the audiences clap their hands.

p. Black audiences and white audiences feel distinguishably different. Black audiences feel warmer, there is almost a musical rhythm, for me, even in their silent response. — *The Autobiography of Malcolm X*

q. The city is so close to bankruptcy that in six months it will no longer be able to pay for essential services, therefore the property tax must be increased immediately.

3. *Dangling modifiers.* See *Dangling modifiers, *Absolute phrases, and *Participles §2 and §3. See also pp. 280–81. This exercise asks you to distinguish between phrases that dangle and phrases that have a clear and precise relation to the main structure of the sentence. Dangling phrases are rather common in Informal and in some General writing but are considered too loose and casual for most General and for all Formal writing. Examples:

Though now a published author, Greene's life is unchanged. — *Saturday Review*, Feb. 4, 1961

Revisions: Though Greene is now a published author, his life is unchanged. Or: Though now a published author, Greene finds that his life is unchanged.

Walking down the street, an out-of-state motorist asked me for directions.

Revisions: Walking down the street, I was asked for directions by an out-of-state motorist. Or: As I was walking down the street, an out-of-state motorist asked me for directions. (Is one revision better than the other?)

Looking far to the south, the dirty smoke from the steel mills tinges the sky.

Revisions: Looking far to the south, I [you? we?] see the dirty smoke from the steel mills tinging the sky. Or: Far to the south, the dirty smoke from the steel mills tinges the sky.

Some readers, but not all, would criticize the first example. All attentive readers would criticize the second and third, and most would find the third more objectionable—or more troublesome—than the second. Why?

Identify the dangling modifiers in the following sentences. Distinguish between the various types (see *Dangling modifiers*), and propose revisions that will make the items satisfactory in college writing.

a. Foraging in Central Park, he collected materials for a three-course dinner. . . .—John McPhee, *A Roomful of Hovings and Other Profiles*

b. Judging from his review, Amis thinks Dylan Thomas is vastly overrated.

c. Judging from his posthumous reputation, Dylan Thomas is a great poet.

d. Reaching sixteen, my parents agreed to let me drive.

e. Reaching sixteen, my interest shifted from sociology to psychology.

f. Reaching sixteen, society no longer seems predictable.

g. Settled at last in Greensboro, it is my understanding that he was loved or admired by everybody in the place. . . .—John Crowe Ransom, *Southern Review,* Spring 1967

h. To succeed in life, luck is as essential as brains.

i. Awakened by a heavy hand tugging at the blankets, his arduous day began long before dawn.

j. Exhibiting wit as well as brevity, acronyms like SMASH (special materials and special handling) are deservedly popular.

k. Coming into the open, he could see the tracks plainly.

l. Coming into the open, the tracks were plainly visible.

m. When at home, everybody treats me as if I were still a child.

n. Compared with previous years, reporters have had few opportunities to interview the President.

o. An indication of the mood of the nation was found in thumbing through Sunday's newspapers.

p. The average Corpsman, based on a national study of the first ten thousand men to enroll, is seventeen and a half years old and unmarried. — John Bainbridge, *New Yorker*, May 21, 1966

q. Granted business is slow in the country, and unemployment runs 6 per cent of the labor force, 9.3 per cent for blacks and minority races, along with a sharp jump in white collar joblessness. This sort of thing would get the attention of any president. . . .
Looking back over the politico-economic scene of the last two decades when top men in the White House have learned how to manipulate short-term economic developments to make their administrations look good, much has been done to enliven the economy here, curb it there. — George H. Arris, *Providence Sunday Journal*, Jan. 24, 1971

r. Having written Quentin Reynolds' Class Day address for him, West's own graduation in 1924 was the climax to a history of what appears to have been endless lighthearted chicanery. — Mark Schorer, *Atlantic*, Oct. 1970

s. Figuring roughly, the tax comes to ten per cent.

t. Having awakened early, a quick glance outdoors convinced me that it would be a fine day for a visit to Jackson Park. Arriving there before six, a brisk breeze was blowing across the Wooded Island.

u. The legislators should realize that by denying citizens the right to explore and advocate all sorts of views the American system is being put in jeopardy.

v. By never beginning a sentence with a *being* phrase ("being eager to leave"), you can reduce your chances of writing the sillier kind of dangling modifier without seriously limiting your stylistic resources.

4. Some, but not all, of the following items contain grammatical mistakes; some of the grammatical forms would be acceptable in Informal-to-General contexts but not in General-to-Formal. Make distinctions where you consider them appropriate, and revise the unsatisfactory passages to make them acceptable in college writing. In making your revisions, consult relevant *Index* articles such as *Subject and verb, *Reference of pronouns, *Collective nouns.

a. The major fault of the black powder were the dense clouds of black smoke that it generated.

b. I'll have to take the plane; neither train nor bus is fast enough.

c. Neither poll nor straw vote convince me.

d. In strict Puritan households, dancing, music, and the theater—indeed, all manner of entertainment—was condemned.

e. In general, I don't admire his acting, but I liked him playing Hamlet.

f. I spent the next two months in a house the roof of which leaked.

g. Since sponges are capable of consuming food, making cells, and reproducing its own kind, they are living organisms.

h. The club is sponsoring a dance, and it plans to give the proceeds to charity.

i. He passed the examination, which surprised nobody more than himself.

j. Women won the right to vote, which happened in 1920.

k. Many people take pills without a doctor's prescription. This is unwise. They begin by taking habit-forming sedatives only when they cannot sleep or when they are tense. But it is not long before they can't do without them, and they increase the dose until all it does is make them worse.

l. The only correct standard of English is that which is appropriate to the occasion and accepted by the people with whom you are.

m. He asked me who I thought would win the election.

n. From the attic window of our home, one can command a view of our entire neighborhood. Situated on the north-east corner of this quiet suburb, it is a perfect spot from which to observe the community.

o. Our entire airline industry, domestic and foreign alike, is fundamentally sick—far beyond rehabilitation by an upturn. Its total debts are now so staggering that I found no airline executive who knows how these can be paid on time even with the predicted upturn.
Our entire air-frame and aircraft engine industry—immense contributors to employment and vital in the free world's defense—are as fundamentally sick.—Henry J. Taylor, syndicated columnist, Dec. 12, 1970

p. Those people with whom you went to high school but who didn't go on to college now have very different interests than yours.

q. Hotels are booked solidly for the convention.

r. The Democratic organization, as many other organizations, are concerned about young people's disenchantment with politics.

s. Residents object to the cutting down of trees which the officials say is necessary.

PUNCTUATING SENTENCES

Punctuation marks separate sentences and indicate the relationships of words and word groups within sentences, joining them, separating them, or setting them off.[1] Because punctuation is closely related to sentence structure, you need to know a good deal about syntax in order to punctuate satisfactorily. Properly used, punctuation reflects and supplements the spoken signs of meaning. Misused, it distorts those signs and confuses the reader. Though accurate punctuation can't redeem a mixed-up sentence—one that requires rewriting—it may save a weak sentence from ambiguity, and it can make the meaning of a complicated sentence precise and clear.

Some punctuation marks are substitutes for, or reminders of, elements in speech for which we have no written equivalents: in some of their uses, the comma, semicolon, and period are visual indications of speech patterns of pitch and pause. But though a writer should listen to what he is writing and punctuating, the correspondence between punctuation and features of speech is by no means precise or complete: we cannot always hear the difference between paired commas, dashes, and parentheses, nor can we hear the apostrophe in a genitive. Some uses of punctuation marks must be learned as arbitrary conventions.

The conventions governing the apostrophe, capital letters, and some other matters of mechanics are so well established that every careful writer observes them. But he still has considerable range of choice. In deciding whether to use a particular mark of punctuation, he may be guided by the emphasis, tone, and movement in a sentence or perhaps by the intention of an entire paragraph. Some uses of punctuation marks are almost entirely stylistic.

One group of marks can illustrate the choices that are often possible. A comma, a semicolon, or a period may be used between words or word groups, depending on the degree of separation the writer wants to indicate. A comma separates slightly, a period completely. While its chief use is to link clauses that would otherwise be separated by a period, the semicolon can also separate more definitely than a comma. Look at these versions of the same passage:

Fort Hood. Fort Bragg. Fort Leavenworth. Fort Benning. Fort Lewis. The big army bases in the United States are tight societies. Forts in more ways than one.

---

[1] Harold Whitehall in *Structural Essentials of English* (New York: Harcourt, 1951), pp. 119–33, gives punctuation four functions: linking, separating, enclosing, and indicating omission.

Fort Hood; Fort Bragg; Fort Leavenworth; Fort Benning; Fort Lewis: the big army bases in the United States are tight societies, forts in more ways than one.

Fort Hood, Fort Bragg, Fort Leavenworth, Fort Benning, Fort Lewis—the big army bases in the United States are tight societies, forts in more ways than one.

The first version strongly emphasizes each element and—in isolation, at least—has a portentous tone. The second is less abrupt, but the pace is still measured; the combination of semicolons and colon suggests a Formal style. The third moves most rapidly and has the lightest touch. In the original (p. 245) the author uses periods in the list but a comma after "societies," tolling the names of the bases but then speeding up the movement.

Another group of marks that have much the same function consists of paired commas, paired dashes, and parentheses, all of which are used to enclose words and word groups that are not part of the main structure of the sentence. In many cases, which you use depends on the nature of what you are setting off: an ordinary nonrestrictive clause is enclosed in commas; an interjected independent clause is usually enclosed in parentheses.

Because the majority of the people (and "majority" includes *elites* as well as *masses*) has benefited from the economic structure of the nation, they have been conservative. . . .—Michael Wallace, *American Scholar*, Winter 1970-71

But there are occasions when the choice depends not so much on how the embedded element relates to the core of the sentence as on how prominent the writer wishes to make it. Take this sentence:

One thing that might seem to be a liability for a college athlete but actually turns out to be a help is the fact that he usually has less spare time than a nonathlete.

There is no internal punctuation, nor is any needed. But suppose you intend to follow this sentence with a paragraph sequence explaining why a lack of spare time helps a college athlete. Then you may enclose "but actually turns out to be a help" in commas, or even set it off with dashes, to call the reader's attention to it.

Or suppose that the advantage of not having spare time is to have no special significance in the paper, that you are simply making the point in passing. Then you can enclose "but actually turns out to be a help" in parentheses to signal the reader that this is no more than an aside.

THE PRINCIPAL MARKS AND THEIR MAIN FUNCTIONS

Period
to end statements

Comma
to separate words and word groups within sentences

Paired commas
to set off words and word groups that are not part of the main structure of the sentence

Semicolon
to link clauses that would otherwise be separated by a period

Colon
to link words and word groups to the sentence element that introduces them

OTHER PUNCTUATION MARKS

Question mark
to mark a direct or a directly quoted question

Exclamation mark
to mark an exclamation—a word or a word group or a sentence that is vigorously stressed

Dash
to link to a word group an example or a surprising addition

Paired dashes
to set off words and word groups that are less closely related to the main structure than would be set off by commas

Parentheses
to set off words and word groups that are less closely related to the main structure than would be set off by dashes

Quotation marks
to identify what is directly quoted

Brackets
to enclose insertions in quotations

Ellipses
to indicate omissions in quotations

Apostrophe
to indicate the genitive case

Hyphen
to link words and to link syllables

Besides such specific choices for specific reasons, you can choose between two general styles of punctuation — open and close. A few generations ago prose was weighed down with close punctuation; writers drew on the full stock of punctuation symbols to pepper every page. Today, with the virtual disappearance of heavily Formal English, close punctuation is much less assertive; but it continues to use all the marks, and when there is a choice between punctuating and not punctuating, it punctuates. Open punctuation, on the other hand, makes little use of the colon and semicolon. For internal punctuation it relies on the comma, and it uses no more commas than are absolutely necessary.

Close punctuation puts a comma before the conjunction in every compound sentence, a comma after an introductory clause or phrase, commas around interrupting words and word groups. Open punctuation uses none of these unless there is a specific reason for doing so. Close punctuation typically encloses interrupters like *however, of course, too.* Open punctuation seldom sets off *too,* often leaves *of course* unpunctuated, and may omit commas around other interrupters.

Although punctuation in general is more open than it was a generation ago, the practice of most writers probably falls somewhere between the open and the close style, and good writers adjust their punctuation to their subject matter and their audience. The difficult concept may not be expressed in such elaborate, heavily punctuated sentences as it would have been in 1900, but it still requires syntactical complexity with supporting punctuation. Casual General-to-Informal writing can usually get by with a minimum of punctuation, but the writer needs to keep his audience in mind. A sophisticated reader skims such writing rapidly, and if the punctuation is so open as to permit confusion or ambiguity, he may quit rapidly, too. An unsophisticated reader needs the help that conventional punctuation can provide.

Punctuation is a part of syntax and is controlled by it. Little if any reduction in punctuation is possible in this sentence:

The modern student of prose may quickly praise plainness and condemn the eloquent, which he often calls high or flowery, but after consideration may remember that purposes differ and that if he wishes to move, to enhance, to persuade, some language of flowers, some structure of suspense and excitement, may be valuable, in contrast to a plain naturalness. — Josephine Miles, *Language and Proportion*

Nor does any punctuation need to be added to this sentence:

The camera is forced to pan over meaningless stretches of roads and houses as background for expostulations on the betrayal of

Argentinian intellectuals or the failure of the academic community or the role of the Pentagon. — Paul D. Zimmerman, *Newsweek*, March 1, 1971

A good practice is to use no more punctuation than your writing needs for clarity and no more than *current* convention calls for. But punctuation marks can be more than necessary nuisances. You may come to use them in ways that, while not proscribed by convention, are not strictly functional. Perhaps for your stylistic purposes, for the rhythm you want in your prose, for the consistency you admire, phrases like *of course* should regularly be enclosed in commas. Or perhaps the linkages provided by colons sometimes suit your way of relating ideas better than the separations made by periods. Then use them. Punctuation marks that are too numerous or too heavy call attention to themselves just as pompous, inflated vocabulary does. But limiting yourself to an austerity budget of commas and periods is no more essential to good writing than sticking to one- and two-syllable words.

What follows is a review of some of the principal situations in which punctuation is used and misused. Full discussion and illustration of the individual marks will be found in the *Index.*

At Ends of Sentences

Most sentences are statements and end with a period. When one sentence is allowed to run into another with no punctuation in between, the cause is likely to be carelessness rather than ignorance. Sometimes when a comma is placed where a period belongs, the writer has failed to identify a sentence correctly, but such slips can usually be eliminated through careful editing. (See pp. 288–90 and *Comma fault.)

A question mark is used after a clear-cut question: "When does the balloon go up?" It should not be used after an indirect question: "We asked when the balloon would go up." A question mark is not generally used after a request phrased as a question: "Will you please give this matter your immediate attention."

The exclamation mark should be reserved for expression of strong emotion — outrage, incredulity, determination — or, in dialog, high volume. The single-word exclamations range from powerful ones like *Ouch*, which almost always call for an exclamation mark, to mild ones like *Oh*, which may deserve only a comma. Outside of dialog, exclamation marks should be used only when special emphasis is fully justified. Dialog that consists of an exchange of shouts belongs in the comic strips.

Between Main Elements

As a mark of separation, the comma does not belong between the main elements of a clause—between subject and verb or between verb and object or complement—or between a preposition and its object. Old-fashioned writing occasionally has a comma between a long subject and its verb, but this practice is very rare in current writing. If you feel the need for a comma, try instead to reduce the noun phrase. You will probably end up with a better sentence.

Although punctuation rules usually forbid the use of a comma to separate the verbs in a compound predicate, many accomplished writers of General-to-Formal prose use such punctuation—to point up a contrast, to prevent misreading, or simply to mark a pause in a long, involved sentence. But in most General styles separating predicates with a comma creates an unnecessary clutter.

Between Coordinate Clauses

Formal writing ordinarily has a comma between the clauses of a compound sentence connected by *and, nor, or, yet*. General writing may omit the comma unless the clauses are long or have different subjects. In both styles commas are usual when the clauses are connected by *but* or *for* or *so*. A comma is always advisable when the absence of one permits misreading.

A semicolon is used to link independent clauses when there is no connecting word or when the connecting word is a conjunctive adverb (*however, therefore, nevertheless* . . .). A colon (or, in less Formal writing, a dash) is used when the first clause introduces or points to the second:

Some of the supporting performances are rather odd: Dorothy Tutin is wooden and rather withdrawn as Charles's Catholic queen. . . .— David Denby, *Atlantic*, Jan. 1971

After Subordinate Elements

In Formal style a comma is ordinarily used to separate a subordinate clause from the main clause it precedes. In General writing the comma is often omitted if the clause is short and closely related to what follows, especially if the two clauses have the same subject. For consistency, some writers use a comma after all introductory clauses and after any introductory phrase that contains a verbal; but most writers now punctuate short introductory modifiers only when the comma is needed to prevent misreading or to provide special emphasis.

But and other coordinating conjunctions are a part of the clauses in which they appear and should not be followed by a comma either when they join coordinate clauses or when they begin a sentence. Placing a comma after initial *And* or *But* probably results from punctuating entirely by ear: the writer hears a pause after the conjunction.

Before Subordinate Elements

Whether we punctuate words, phrases, and clauses coming after the main clause depends on how close they are to the core of the sentence. The question can be treated in terms of *restrictive and nonrestrictive modifiers. A modifier that limits the meaning of its headword in the main clause is not separated from the main clause. The principal modifier of this type is the restrictive adjective clause: "Latecomers repeatedly disturbed the man *who had the aisle seat.*" Similarly, an adverbial clause that follows the main clause and restricts its meaning should not be separated from it: "He left *because he could stand no more of it.*"

A modifier that comes after the main clause and is not a part of the central structure of the sentence is separated from the main clause by a comma. One such modifier is the nonrestrictive adjective clause, which does not alter the meaning of its headword. (The clause "which does not alter the meaning of its headword" is an example. Note that here the same clause is restrictive.) Others are absolute phrases, appositives, and some verbal phrases.

Sometimes, as in the following sentence, failing to indicate that a modifier is nonrestrictive would be disastrous:

Ionesco's play *Exit the King* is about nothing, which we must take seriously, but also must not erroneously mistake for something. — Lionel Abel, *New American Review #3*

But in many cases only you, the writer, can decide whether a modifier is a part of the main structure. Omitting a comma indicates that it is; using a comma indicates that it is not. Compare:

I drove back to the campus hoping she was still waiting there.

I drove back to the campus, hoping she was still waiting there.

Around Interrupting Elements

Traditionally, a word, phrase, or clause that is introduced within the main structure of a sentence but is not a part of that main structure is enclosed in commas or, in some cases, in dashes or parentheses. As we have noted, however, usage is divided over enclosing single words like *incidentally* and short phrases like *of course*. Some writers consistently set them off; some do so only to prevent misreading; and some use them or omit them depending on the emphasis and tempo they are aiming for:

A mood of course depends on your perspective. — David Halberstam, *Harper's*, Jan. 1971

The question, of course, is how much a media campaign will hurt Albert. — Ibid.

Setting off short interrupting elements slows the pace of the sentence, giving it a more deliberate movement.

If a writer feels that an interrupting word or word group is more separate from the core of the sentence than commas would indicate, he can enclose it in dashes. And if he feels that the separation needs to be made still more definite, he can put parentheses around it. *Feel* is the right word here, for the choice is often a subjective one that cannot be reduced to a "rule."

If you doubt this, try substituting a lesser sin — say gossiping — for adultery in this passage. . . . — Wayne C. Booth, *English Journal*, March 1964

It is exactly the same claim that we teachers want to make about a book like *Catcher in the Rye* (though few of us would go as far as one theologian who has called it a piece of "modern Scripture"). — Ibid.

In Series

Commas separate the items in a series of words or word groups. (If the word groups contain commas, semicolons may provide the separation.) Usage is divided over using a comma after the series item that precedes the conjunction: literature, painting, sculpture, music [] and drama. Close style uses the comma consistently; open style omits it unless the omission could cause misreading. Switching styles in the course of an essay can confuse your readers.

Commas are used to separate a series of adjectives before a single noun: "When the long, cold, lonesome evenings came, we would gather around the old wood stove." In this sentence there are commas between "long — cold — lonesome" because each stands in the same relation to the noun "evenings." But there is no comma between "old" and "wood" because "old" modifies "wood stove" rather than just "stove." Stylistic considerations may also affect the punctuation of a series. Note the difference in emphasis in these two versions:

The room with its old-fashioned, cross-beamed ceiling and its gray, brick fireplace presented a colonial effect.

The room with its old-fashioned cross-beamed ceiling and its gray brick fireplace presented a colonial effect.

For Clarity

In punctuating as in writing generally, the claims of the reader should be given precedence over the dogmatism of rules and the subtleties of styles. You should use punctuation marks to help him understand what you have to say. This does *not* mean that you should insert marks at every possible opportunity: overpunctuation creates an obstacle course that encourages dropping out. Neither does it mean ignoring the conventions or making a fetish of minimum punctuation. Often a comma that is not essential can help a reader interpret a sentence and make it unnecessary for him to go back over it. A comma between clauses connected by *but* or *for* signals the reader that the word is being used as a conjunction and not as a preposition.

With Quotation Marks

The chief use of quotation marks is to enclose the spoken or written words of others, quoted directly. A comma ordinarily separates the quotation from the words that introduce it (He said, ". . ."; As Dickens wrote, ". . .") unless the quoted words are built into the structure of the sentence:

He said "So long" and headed for the door.

When the quoted word or words are followed by a comma or a period, the punctuation comes inside the closing quotation marks. A question mark or exclamation mark is placed inside if it is part of the quotation, outside if it belongs only to the enclosing sentence:

Collins looked around and said, "Have they gone?"

I insist that you say "I'm sorry"!

When the quotation is followed by a colon, semicolon, or dash, the punctuation comes outside the closing quotation marks:

They waited in line until the agent said, "That's it for today"; then the door closed, and they were left standing in the cold.

The following *Index* articles deal with punctuation and mechanics:

*Abbreviations	*Ellipsis	*Question mark
*Apostrophe	*End stop	*Quotation marks
*Brackets	*Exclamation mark	*Restrictive and
*Capital letters	*Hyphen	nonrestrictive
*Colon	*Italics	*Semicolon
*Comma	*Numbers	*Series
*Dash	*Parentheses	*Titles of books,
*Division of words	*Period	articles, etc.

EXERCISES

1. Copy the items below, supplying appropriate punctuation and mechanics. If a mark of punctuation is optional, bracket it. If you have chosen between acceptable alternatives, give reasons for your choice.

a. here is a letter that gives a clue to his mysterious behavior and perhaps explains his mona lisa smile

b. isnt this the letter the clue to the mystery

c. when the war ended the trials of the traitors began

d. when the war ended the general returned to the pentagon

e. the constitution guarantees us our civil rights but does not set up the machinery to investigate violations of these rights

f. the constitution guarantees us our civil rights unfortunately it does not set up machinery to investigate violations of them

g. we walked in the park at night as though we were in our own garden

h. he told us we could feel perfectly safe walking in the park at night as though we needed reassurance

i. we walked in the park at night as though we were in our own garden because the grounds were always well patrolled

j. the election of jackson brought one era of our history to a close it represented the triumph of the masses over the classes

k. an era ended with jacksons election the masses had triumphed over the classes

l. adamss administration ended one era jacksons election began another

m. it is the student who works diligently and steadfastly who succeeds

n. the office girls who have worked hard all year deserve a day off

o. its the worlds oldest profession he says

p. these were lincolns words four score and seven years ago in 1776 our fathers brought forth on this continent a new nation

q. hers is a happy life she trusts her parents she likes her work she has many friends and a grey cat

r. all of us have some beliefs we cannot prove by induction or deduction basic assumptions standards of value articles of faith

s. not all superstitious people are ignorant however superstition usually stems from ignorance its not only ignorant people though who are superstitious

t. the difference between man and mans is a matter of case

u. the difference between man and boy is hard to state

v. as we drove along we found that chile was just like the travel posters towering mountains winding roads wayside chapels and glimpses of the blue blue pacific

w. the storm was violent but freakish straws were driven into concrete posts feathers were blown off chickens trees were stripped of branches yet frail flowers remained undamaged

x. packed in his suitcase were a few clothes including a turtle neck sweater two pairs of socks and a handkerchief the bible a hymnal and a pocket dictionary and a loaded revolver

y. at laredo tex the flooding rio grande forced 2500 persons from their homes and about the same number fled from homes on the mexico side of the river in the worst inundation in ten years maybe even in twenty

z. the psychologist henry g wegrocki explains abnormal delusion in these words the patients delusion is an internal resolution of a problem it is his way of meeting the intolerable situation

2. Supply appropriate punctuation for the following passages, from which all marks have been removed. First, read the passage to get a general grasp of the content. Then copy it, inserting punctuation, mechanics, and paragraph symbols. Bracket punctuation that you consider to be optional.

a. at key west a few days before christmas i visited the turtle slaughterhouse it is one of the few tourist attractions on this spot of island north havana raised far out into the sea off the coast of florida visitors take their kiddies by the hand and lead them to see the nice turtles before being killed and canned the turtles swim in dense kraals bumping each other in the murky water armor clashing dully lurching against the high pens later trussed on a plank dock they lie unblinking in the sun their flippers pierced and tied the tough leather of their skin does not disguise their present helplessness and pain they wear thick sun hardened accumulations of blood at their wounds barbados turtles as large as children they belong to a species which has been eliminated locally by ardent harvesting of the waters near key west but the commercial tradition still brings them here to be slaughtered crucified like thieves they breathe in little sighs they gulp they wait at a further stage in the room where the actual slaughtering occurs the butchers stride through gore in heavy boots the visitor must proceed on a catwalk a misstep will plunge him into a slow river of entrails and blood because it was near christmastime the owners of the plant had installed a speaker system for musical divertissement of the butchers and while the turtles dried under the sun or lay exposed to the butchers knives christmas bells tolled out electronically amplified god rest ye merry gentlemen or the bing crosby recording of adeste fideles—Herbert Gold, *The Age of Happy Problems*

b. here is the most important inference to be drawn from our knowledge of word families that the life and death of words in large part depends on our need to economize to make what words really mean agree with what they seem to mean there is a connectedness in our experience of reality dogs are dogs but they also have four legs and so relate to cats they eat almost anything and so belong with other carnivores unflaggingly but not always successfully we seek the same connectedness in the imaging of reality our language to picture the word within the system of which it forms a part imagine an orb like the sun with gaseous satellites revolving about it the central body is the core of the words meaning what it is taken to signify under normal conditions by those who hear and use it the gasiform satellites are the aura of all its apparent meanings when the core is relatively hard the aura continues to haunt the fringes but does not move in upon the central meaning when the core is diffuse the aura may blend with it and alter it completely the aura is like an accumulation of cosmic dust given off by all the other orbs in the galaxy of the language with which the one in question is associated in meaning or use as our word drifts its way about the verbal universe in the daily converse and intercourse of speech it accumulates this billowy sort of envelope that presses in upon it hard or softly depending on circumstances our astrological picture is necessary to get the facts in focus the essential fact is that every word or combination of words lays the stamp of its form on the meaning that it conveys once we say onion and associate with a certain adjunct to culinary art onion is available to come to mind whenever anything that sounds like onion in either form or meaning is mentioned in form it may be a rhyming word like bunion in meaning it may be a kindred term like soup meaning is ultimately form for it comes by way of the actual use together of onion and soup until the connection is unusually close no threat is posed to the stability of the word once the bond is firmly set a reaction begins to take place—Dwight L. Bolinger, *American Scholar*

Chapter Eleven

SHAPING SENTENCES

Whether the sentences you write and rewrite turn out to be clear or fuzzy, limp or emphatic, rhythmical or stumbling depends on how skillful you are in putting them together. Chapter Ten outlined ways of combining and rearranging sentences and parts of sentences. In this chapter we will consider the rhetorical effects of some combinations and arrangements.

As Chapter Ten demonstrated, you can express substantially the same idea in many different ways. In choosing among them, you need to consider both the rhetorical situation and the immediate linguistic context. Are you reporting on a laboratory experiment or analyzing a dramatist's techniques? Are you writing for an audience that needs to be led step by step through an argument, or can you count on a mature, attentive reader with an eye and an ear for subtle distinctions and nuances? Do you want to achieve the intimacy of casual talk, or does the situation call for some formality and distance? Good writers gear the syntactic complexity of their prose to their subjects and to their expected audiences. Some combinations of writer-topic-reader call for relatively simple sentences—not grammatically "simple" necessarily but free of long or involved modifiers or interrupting elements. In other situations the topic justifies, and the audience permits, much more complicated structures. Saying exactly what you want to say sometimes calls for short, direct statements, sometimes requires elaborate arrangements of clause and phrase.

As you shape a particular sentence, you also have to take into account the sentences that precede and follow it. Should its structure contrast with the structure of the sentence before it, or should it repeat it? Should the emphasis fall at the beginning of the sentence or at its end, close to the succeeding sentence? Whether a sentence is long or short, straightforward or involved, it should do what you want it to do in its immediate context. The good sentence honors the claims made on it by the paragraph, just as the good paragraph honors the claims made on it by the essay.

SEPARATING AND COMBINING IDEAS

Often in revising you will combine some first-draft sentences and split others — not just to make them longer or shorter but to make them clearer. Length alone is the least important feature of a sentence. Yet it has a bearing on more fundamental qualities, and you frequently need to take it into account when you are trying to make a difficult sentence easier to read, a dull one more arresting, an ambiguous one precise.

Long and Short Sentences

At best, short sentences have a simplicity and directness that makes them easy to understand and a briskness and drive that carries the reader along. But they can become choppy and jerky, breaking ideas into units too small to be followed easily; and several in succession can become unemphatic and monotonous. Long sentences offer comparable risks and opportunities. They can be so convoluted or so rambling that the reader (if not the writer) loses track of the main idea. But handled well, a long sentence — even a very long one — can gather up and convey the full measure of a complex thought, with all its distinctions and refinements and qualifications.

If there is no special virtue in either long sentences or short ones, there is a virtue in making the length of your sentences appropriate to what they are saying. This paragraph from a newspaper column shows how short sentences can segregate details, keeping them apart so that each one gains significance and point:

He was a sudden and surprising person. He never did things when other men were doing them. He went to Congress and the White House earlier than most. He married much later than his contemporaries. His war record, his political record, and his personal life were marked by flashes of crisis and even by a vague premonition of tragedy. He always seemed to be striding through doors into the center of some startling triumph or disaster. He never reached his meridian: we saw him only as a rising sun. — James Reston, *New York Times*, Nov. 15, 1964

In the same brief column a long sentence — longer than the seven short sentences combined — brings together many details and at the same time interprets them:

We will have to know much more about that confrontation between Kennedy and Khrushchev, one now deprived of life and the other of power, before we can be sure, but Kennedy said just enough in that room in the embassy to convince me of the following: Khrushchev had studied the events of the Bay of Pigs; he would have understood if Kennedy had left Castro alone or destroyed him; but when Kennedy was rash enough to strike at Cuba but not bold enough to finish the job, Khrushchev decided he was dealing with an inexperienced young leader who could be intimidated and blackmailed.

Note that this sentence, like many other compound-complex sentences, is orthographically rather than grammatically long: changing the punctuation would turn it into five separate sentences. Compare the sentence by Sapir, p. 310, which is grammatically long.

A long sentence coming after a series of short ones can pull particulars together into an inclusive statement that summarizes or interprets or evaluates. A short sentence following a long one can have a powerful effect. These two sentences illustrate the value of contrast:

As hectically put together as the United States, Israel yet seemed invested with an extra dimension of nationhood that America finally did not have: a cohesion deriving from that protean circumstance of their common experience of Jewishness in exile, a fundamental identity arising not out of any real racial unity or the fact of having long abided in a single geographical setting, but out of a shared two-thousand-year historical condition. They know who they are. — Marshall Frady, *Harper's*, Jan. 1971

The sentences are effective as a pair because the second gives concrete expression to the relatively abstract statement in the first, because in each one length seems to match expression, and because the switch from long to short makes a healthy change of pace. A sequence of ten sentences as long as the first would make for slow, difficult reading; ten as short as the second would make for intolerably dull reading, at least on any topic that called for interpretation and judgment.

EXERCISES

1. Compare the original passage by Karl Shapiro with the version that follows it. Does the rewrite gain or lose in clarity? In emphasis?

The jazz put-on is a major form of cultural blackmail by the Movement. Anyone not "with" the jazz is a marked man. The hagiography of jazz is as immense as the Vatican Library. It is all phony, a conglomeration of the Music Corporation of America and the masses of delayed and permanent adolescents. Jazz is only a minor facet of modern music. — Karl Shapiro, *Esquire*, April 1968

The jazz put-on, the notion that anyone not "with" the jazz is a marked man, is a major form of cultural blackmail by the Movement, because though the hagiography of jazz is as immense as the Vatican Library, it is all phony, a conglomeration of the Music Corporation of America and the masses of delayed and permanent adolescents; jazz is only a minor facet of modern music.

2. What is gained or lost by breaking Sapir's long sentence into five short ones?

It is strange how long it has taken the European literatures to learn that style is not an absolute, a something that is to be imposed on the language from Greek or Latin models, but merely the language itself, running in its natural grooves, and with enough of an individual accent to allow the artist's personality to be felt as a presence, not as an acrobat. — Edward Sapir, *Language*

It is strange how long it has taken the European literatures to learn that style is not an absolute. It is not something that is to be imposed on the language from Greek or Latin models. It is merely the language itself. It is the language running in its natural grooves. It has enough of an individual accent to allow the artist's personality to be felt as a presence, not as an acrobat.

3. Discuss the contribution made by each sentence in the paragraph below. Explain why the length of each sentence is or is not a significant element in your discussion of how it functions and how well it functions.

Picture then this mass, bored for hours by speeches, now elated at the beginning of the March, now made irritable by delay, now compressed, all old latent pips of claustrophobia popping out of the crush, and picture them as they stepped out onto the bridge, monitors in the lead, hollow square behind, next the line of notables with tens, then hundreds of lines squeezing up behind, helicopters overhead, police gunning motorcycles, cameras spinning their gears like the winging of horseflies, TV car bursting seams with hysterically overworked technicians, sun beating overhead — this huge avalanche of people rumbled forward thirty feet and came to a stop in disorder, the lines behind breaking and warping and melding into themselves to make a crowd not a parade, and some jam-up at the front, just what no one knew, now they were moving again. Forty more feet. They stopped. At this rate it would take six hours to reach the Pentagon. And a murmur came up from behind of huge discontent, not huge yet, huge in the potential of its discontent. "Let's get going," people in the front lines were calling out. — Norman Mailer, *Harper's*, March 1968

As you revise, pay attention to the length of your sentences. But don't just add or subtract words and phrases. Concentrate on separating, combining, and regrouping *ideas*. The best reasons for altering the sentence boundaries of your early drafts are to iron out inconsistencies, to introduce needed qualifications, to correct misplaced emphasis, and, most of all, to bring out the right logical relations.

Breaking Up Sentences

The sentences that most urgently need to be broken up are those that lack unity, that join unrelated ideas. These two assertions belong in separate — and separated — sentences:

The desert country in New Mexico presents a striking contrast to the mountain beauty of Colorado, where the citizens are strongly opposed to any increase in the state income tax.

Less blatant but still troublesome is the sentence that brings together ideas that are related but not closely enough to be joined. The lead sentence of a review or news report is sometimes too overloaded for clarity:

The Merry Month of May, a title used ironically, is a novel of dissolution, the dissolution of a family of American expatriates at the time, and partly because, of the student riots in Paris in the spring of 1968, which when the unions and the apache joined in brought all France to a standstill. — Edward Weeks, *Atlantic*, March 1971

Mr. Nader's criticism of pollution caused by Union Carbide's Ferro Alloy Division here, which results in a 24-hour pall of black, yellow and orange smoke and soot that nearly blots out the sun and has forced the Roman Catholic Church to enclose an outdoor statue of St. Anthony in a transparent plastic case, was contained in a letter to . . . the Carbide board chairman in New York. —*New York Times*, Oct. 15, 1970

In the second example the details about pollution compete so actively for the reader's attention that he is distracted from the main point. Separating out some of the details about the pollution would improve sentence unity. But the main point is hard to grasp for still another reason: the grammatical subject is swamped by the prepositional phrases, the verbal phrases, and the dependent clauses that separate it from the verb. Reducing the *nominalization and reordering the main elements would make the sentence clearer and more direct: "In a letter to the Carbide board chairman . . . Mr. Nader criticized the pollution caused by. . . ."

A sentence should not be so long nor so complicated in structure that the reader loses his way in it. Separation is often the best remedy for a house-that-Jack-built sentence that stitches several dependent clauses together. This one, with its eight dependent clauses — six built one upon another in the sequence called tandem *subordination — leaves the reader with only a blurred impression of what the writer is up to:

As everyone knows, Chicago has a traffic problem that needs to be solved, because every day that we ignore it brings us closer to the time when the congestion of traffic will be so great that it will paralyze the city, which cannot function at all unless there is an uninterrupted flow of goods and people from one section to another.

The first step in revising is to break up the unwieldy passage into manageable units:

Chicago's traffic problem must be solved. Every day that we ignore it brings us closer to the time when the city will be paralyzed by the congestion of traffic. Yet the city cannot function at all unless there is an uninterrupted flow of goods and people from one section to another.

Rethinking and reordering would produce a smoother passage:

Chicago's traffic problem must be solved. Without an uninterrupted flow of goods and people from one section to another, the city cannot function, yet every day the increase in traffic brings paralysis closer.

The *and so* sentence (ersatz Hemingway, it has been called) strings together one independent clause after another, flattening out logical relations so that everything seems to have equal importance. Unless there is a rhetorical justification for this effect—and in ordinary exposition there seldom is—the stringy sentence is unemphatic, imprecise, and tiresome:

He found his eyes blurring and so he took his usual headache pills and after a couple of hours the pain subsided and his vision cleared and he could go on with his work.

In revising, look for signs of a natural breaking point (here, after the second clause) and then consider whether the sentences would be improved by using subordination to bring out chronological and causal relations: "When he found his eyes blurring. . . ."

Combining Sentences

You may find that you used too many sentences in your first draft, perhaps giving an entire sentence to a peripheral detail, perhaps saying the same thing twice, perhaps keeping apart ideas that belong together—an assertion and its qualification, a cause and its effect, a likeness and a difference. If your sentences are consistently short (say under eighteen words) and if they show a minimum of embedding, you are probably fragmenting your ideas too much. Doling them out in bits and pieces, sentence by sentence, produces a style that lunges and stalls, lunges and stalls:

Patriotism is loving your country. This isn't the same thing as believing it can do no wrong. I love my father, but I can see his faults. He is inclined to brag, and he can be very self-righteous at times. He is also a little careless with the truth. When he has had an extra drink, his stories are pretty fantastic. I would die for him if I had to. But there are things about him I would change if I could.

When the ideas are grouped in logical units, the eight sentences are reduced to three, and the passage has more flow and continuity:

Although patriotism means loving your country, it does not mean believing your country can do no wrong. I love my father, but I'm well aware that he is boastful and self-righteous and that he has a tendency to inflate the facts when he's had an extra drink. And while I'd die for him if I had to, I wish I could help him get rid of his faults.

Coordinating and Subordinating. Ordinarily, when you combine sentences by conjoining (p. 273), what you want to say will dictate the choice between coordinating and sub-ordinating. But often you can say what you mean in either a compound or a complex sentence, and then you choose one rather than the other in order to achieve a smoother transition, to break up a succession of structurally identical sentences, or for some similar reason. Though there may be slight differences in emphasis and degree of explicitness in the following pairs, in some contexts either could be chosen:

He shouted, *but* the crowd paid no attention.
Although he shouted, the crowd paid no attention.

You must enroll for the course, *or* you will not receive credit.
Unless you enroll for the course, you will not receive credit.

He appealed the decision, *for* everyone advised him to.
He appealed the decision *because* everyone advised him to.

Both coordinating and subordinating offer further choices. Take these two statements:

He kept making eloquent speeches against pollution.

The Council remained indifferent.

If you want to point up the contrast, you can coordinate them in any of these ways:

He kept making eloquent speeches against pollution; the Council remained indifferent.

He kept making eloquent speeches against pollution, but the Council remained indifferent.

He kept making eloquent speeches against pollution; however, the Council remained indifferent.

He kept making eloquent speeches against pollution; the Council, however, remained indifferent. Or: . . . . remained indifferent, however.

Or you might have reason to reverse the order of the clauses:

The Council remained indifferent, but he kept making eloquent speeches against pollution.

And so on. Instead of *but* or *however*, you might use any one of a number of other connectives that indicate contrast: *yet, still, nevertheless, in spite of that* are examples. (See pp. 255–57 and *Transition.)

If you want to point up the contrast by subordinating, you have to decide which should be the independent clause — where the emphasis in the sentence should fall — and also whether it should follow or precede the dependent clause. If you settle on *though* as the subordinating conjunction, you have these possibilities to choose from:

Though he kept making eloquent speeches against pollution, the Council remained indifferent.

He kept making eloquent speeches against pollution, though the Council remained indifferent.

Though the Council remained indifferent, he kept making eloquent speeches against pollution.

The Council remained indifferent though he kept making eloquent speeches against pollution.

The Council, though he kept making eloquent speeches against pollution, remained indifferent.

He kept making, though the Council remained indifferent, eloquent speeches against pollution.

Stylistic considerations alone would rule out the last, with its awkward interruption of verb and complement, and perhaps the second last as well. Choices among the others should be made largely on the basis of context — what the neighboring sentences call for, what emphasis is needed. Compare:

Though he kept making eloquent speeches against pollution, the Council remained indifferent. So he gave up. Indifference was the one response he could not tolerate.

Nobody else in town showed his persistence. Though the Council remained indifferent, he kept making eloquent speeches against pollution.

In subordinating, it is good stylistic practice to experiment with the position of the dependent clause. Sometimes the position of an adverbial clause makes no difference in meaning:

When he spoke in support of the bill, he was in Washington.

He was in Washington when he spoke in support of the bill.

He was, when he spoke in support of the bill, in Washington.

But in some sentences the placing of the adverbial clause does make a difference in meaning:

While he was in Washington, he argued that the bill should be passed.

He argued that the bill should be passed while he was in Washington.

Note, too, that the second of these sentences is open to at least three interpretations: Is there a contrast between his arguing for the bill in Washington and arguing against it in, say, Denver? Was he arguing that the passage of the bill should be accomplished during the time that he was in Washington, not after he had left? Or does the sentence mean that though he argued for the bill while he was in Washington, he soon had to return to his post in Berlin? Although context could probably be counted on to resolve the ambiguity, the adverbial clause should be placed so that the meaning is unmistakable. If that is impossible, the sentence should be rewritten.

Adjective clauses and noun clauses are less mobile than adverb clauses. When an adjective clause is placed near a headword that it cannot logically modify, there is not so much change in meaning as loss of sense:

The catcher was the star of the game with a double, two singles, and a walk *that drove in four runs.*

Of the possible revisions, perhaps the simplest is to switch from subordination to coordination.

The catcher was the star of the game; with a double, two singles, and a walk, he brought in four runs.

In other sentences, shifting the clause will resolve the possible ambiguity:

The stanza in the poem that I prefer is only two lines long.

The stanza [that] I prefer [in the poem] is only two lines long.

When a dependent clause can come first, last, or in the middle without altering meaning, you should weigh the advantages of one position against another. Putting the clause first usually produces a neater sentence; putting it last gives a looser, more casual style. When it is placed first, the reader has the qualification or concession or circumstance in mind while he is reading the main assertion, and this is often an advantage. But you may decide to put the clause last or in the middle so that you can make a smoother transition into or out of the sentence. What is important is to recognize the difference between a situation in which you have a choice and one in which you do not and, when you have a choice, to select the alternative that best helps you say what you want to say.

In either subordinating or coordinating, the choice of

connective is often automatic, but in revising your early drafts you should remain aware of the pressures of context. Out of context, *and* is clearly additive and *but* contrastive. Just as clearly, the *and* of the first passage below conveys a different meaning from the *and* of the second:

Yesterday I had news of the two Smith boys for the first time since they left home. John is a bank manager in New York, and James is a professor at Yale.

Although he slavishly imitated his brother for years, James finally showed some independence. Now John is a bank manager in New York, and James is a professor at Yale.

In conversation, the clause introduced by the second *and* would have something of a "what-do-you-know" effect, with the *and* close to the usual meaning conveyed by *but*.

Context, then, can give an overlay of meaning—even a new meaning—to the commonest of the conjunctions. What causes trouble is the indiscriminate use of *and* in contexts that call for decidedly different conjunctions. Here the second *and* is used where the context seems to require *but:*

It is clear where Larteguy's sympathies lie—they are clearly with Che and, to a lesser degree, with Cuban Premier Fidel Castro. This is perfectly acceptable, if one makes a good case for these sympathies, and a critical reader must too often feel that he does not. — Georgie Anne Geyer, *Boston Herald Traveler*, Dec. 6, 1970

And here *however* (equivalent to *but*) is decidedly illogical:

Admittedly, the cost of automobile liability insurance is so high that it is a real burden to some drivers. However, the protection it affords is so limited that the insured may still be stuck with tremendous bills.

In other passages, a conjunction, though not misleading, may be less precise than the context warrants. In this pair of sentences, *because* makes explicit what *and* can only imply:

The film upsets traditional notions about morality, and conservatives are agitating to have its audience restricted.

Because the film upsets traditional notions about morality, conservatives are agitating to have its audience restricted.

In some rhetorical situations it is effective to invite, to permit, or to require the reader to supply the connection between statements. Punctuation alone—the semicolon, the colon, occasionally the comma (see *Contact clauses)—offers a writer those options.

A writer must learn to be reticent; he must ask himself whether the semicolon will not fulfill all requirements of clarity in a given sentence. — Harold Whitehall, *Structural Essentials of English*

Packing the Simple Sentence.   Combining sentences need not involve either coordinating or subordinating. When one sentence is embedded as a word or phrase in another that is grammatically simple, the resulting sentence remains simple (see pp. 273–75 and 279–83).

Grammatically simple sentences are by no means restricted to the simple treatment of simple topics. Although the idea in the following paragraph is complicated, even difficult, eight of the eleven sentences contain just one clause. But partly because of the word choice and partly because of the significant amount of embedding, each sentence requires the reader's careful attention; each carries its own weight in the paragraph. Not one is expendable, and it is doubtful that any reader would want to have the sentence boundaries altered as a result of combining any two (or more) of the sentences.

Between verbal languages, however remote in setting and habits of syntax, there is always the possibility of equivalence, even if actual translation can only attain rough and approximate results. The Chinese ideogram can be transposed into English by paraphrase or lexical definition. But there are no dictionaries to relate the vocabulary and grammar of higher mathematics to those of verbal speech. One cannot "translate" the conventions and notations governing the operations of Lie groups or the properties of n-dimensional manifolds into any words or grammar outside mathematics. One cannot even paraphrase. A paraphrase of a good poem may turn out to be bad prose; but there is a discernible continuity between shadow and substance. The paraphrase of a complex theorem in topology can only be a grossly inadequate approximation or a transposal into another branch or "dialect" of the particular mathematical language. Many of the spaces, relations, and events that advanced mathematics deals with have no necessary correlation with sense-data; they are "realities" occurring within closed axiomatic systems. You can speak about them meaningfully and normatively only in the speech of mathematics. And that speech, beyond a fairly rudimentary plane, is not and cannot be verbal. I have watched topologists, knowing no syllable of each other's language, working effectively together at a blackboard in the silent speech common to their craft. — George Steiner, *Language and Silence*

EXERCISES

1. Read the *Index* articles *Coordination, *Subordination, *and, *but. Revise the items below according to the instructions.

a. Locally the bicycle is the most popular means of transportation but there are a few cars, but these are usually owned by government personnel. (Revise to eliminate one *but.*)

b. It began to rain and the golfers took cover, and that ended the day's play. (Make one of the clauses dependent.)

c. The main reason I began college in the summer term is that it will take me several years to complete my formal education. The sooner I start, the sooner I will be through. (Make the causal relation clear and logical.)

d. Scientists face many conflicts between their work and moral standards that seem insoluble. (Revise to eliminate the confusion about what "that" modifies.)

e. I am sorry that you cannot offer me the position though I very much hoped you would. (Rewrite to make better sense.)

f. Teachers who are interested in their subject do the best work. The same thing is true of students. (Make one sentence, first by conjoining and then by embedding.)

g. Many nations that have built up a military caste have lived to regret giving power to those with the skill and inclination to use it. A good many people fear the prospect of a professional volunteer army in this country. (Subordinate one of the independent clauses.)

h. With a bedroom, a kitchen, a living room, and a bathroom up the hall that rented for $75 a month, the apartment was a great bargain. (Make clear what rents for $75 a month.)

i. Poe's tales and poems are characterized by melancholy, his criticism by harsh spitefulness. Jealousy of the success of other writers seems to reveal itself in his criticism. The melancholy tone is a sign of his morbid personality. (Clarify the logical relations.)

j. The Stanley Steamer looked like one of those cars of the nineties in every way except for its wheels, and they were changed so as to use pneumatic tires. (Make the relation between the statements more precise.)

k. In arguing that the factor of circumstance could assume so much importance that in itself it could be regarded as justifying a "right," Burke effectively reconciled one apparent inconsistency in the very different attitudes he took toward the

American and the French revolutions, but at the same time he created another, this one resulting not so much from abandoning a previously held position as from the convenient refusal to accept the fact that, if his own terms were to be carried to their logical conclusion, the radically differing circumstances of France and America actually justified the quantitative difference of the one form of resistance compared with the other, especially the difference in degree and extent of violence which Burke singled out as the chief evil of the French Revolution. By accepting the American form of resistance partly because of its mild and intellectual nature and then condemning the French Revolution because of its violence and its destruction of traditional institutions, and by basing both these attitudes on the proposition that "circumstance gives in reality to every political principle its distinguishing color and discriminating effect," Burke is inexcusably guilty of the failure to take into account the full set of circumstances giving rise to such violence. (Rewrite these sentences to make them clearer and better unified. In doing so, consider the possibilities of breaking them up and reordering their parts.)

2.   Compose two different sentences to precede each of the following compound sentences. One of your sentences should make the coordination seem reasonable; the second should make it necessary to subordinate one of the clauses.

a.   The sun was coming up over the lake, but the car stalled.

b.   The mayor has a secretive air, and his wife has a very frank one.

3.   By conjoining and embedding, reduce each of these passages to one sentence:

a.   Because the Chinese mainland was convulsed in civil war, news of the massacre received little world attention. The news was reported by a few foreign journalists on the spot.

b.   I feel that the loyalty oath and disclaimer affidavit are an infringement upon our inherent rights as Americans in a free society. They are in direct contradiction to two of our basic freedoms as granted in the Bill of Rights. The freedoms of speech and thought. These are two of the primary rights in our society. Free speech and thought are part of the American way, part of our democratic way of life. Both the loyalty oath and the affidavit curtail free speech and thought.

c.   In both speaking and writing, the organizational unit of communication is the sentence. A sentence is a structured, or ordered, string of words. It is this structured string of words that provides the grammatical device by which we organize individual words into units that are semantically meaningful.

ORDER AND PATTERN IN SENTENCES

As you work to disentangle a confused first-draft sentence or to smooth a ragged second-draft one, you will often find that parallelism offers the best way to bring related ideas into line.

Parallelism

Parallelism is the arrangement of words, phrases, clauses, or sentences in grammatically equivalent structures. Simple parallel constructions are indispensable in all varieties of English and often take the form of an ordinary list — the *words, phrases, clauses,* and *sentences* of the preceding sentence. More elaborate and conscious parallelism becomes an element of style.

Grammatical Uses.   Parallelism operates on the principle that matching ideas belong in matching structures. Grammatical equivalence signals the reader that the items have a close semantic relation. Ideas put in similar structures may be alike, or they may be opposed, or they may stand in some other relation to each other, like cause to effect or literal to figurative. What matters is that the parallel items fit together in some significant way. Though all such relations can also be indicated by transitional words or phrases or by an explicit statement of what the relation is, the economy of parallelism is often a distinct advantage.

On the most elementary level, parallelism is a way of making a confused sentence coherent or of ordering the parts so that the meaning will be conveyed efficiently. First, second, and third drafts of the same sentence illustrate the point:

One group favors gradual desegregation, another demanding immediate integration, and from the third group, total opposition to integration.

One group favors gradual desegregation, while another demands that integration be brought about immediately, and a third group says that it is altogether opposed to integration.

One group favors gradual integration, another demands immediate integration, and a third opposes integration altogether.

The first version is extremely difficult to grasp because, though the sentence pattern implies a series (*one group, another, a third group*), the structures brought together are grammatically unlike — an independent clause, a participial phrase, a prepositional phrase. The reader's expectation that the three parts of the sentence will match is thwarted. While the second version is less chaotic, the shift in structural pattern between the second and third clauses produces a sentence more flabby and diffuse than the third, where parallelism of the clauses makes the idea immediately accessible and its expression smooth and economical.

EXERCISES

1. Since parallelism is a mode of coordination, blunders in parallelism may occur in pairs of any kind or in a series of three or more on the pattern a, b, [coordinating conjunction] c. Faulty parallelism is a variety of shifted construction; the failure to carry out an implied promise of matching structures results from choosing the wrong form to fill a specific position in the sentence. What goes with what is the key question. A gerund can pair with a noun—"Swimming and music were his hobbies"—but not with an infinitive—"Swimming and to play the piano. . . ." Other shifts in grammatical form are illustrated in the *Index* article *Shifted constructions. After reviewing that article, indicate which of the items below contain blunders in parallelism. For each unsatisfactory item, identify the nature of the shift, and rewrite the sentence to make it satisfactory.

a. The volunteers were inventive, tough, and risk-takers.— Elizabeth B. Drew, *Atlantic*, July 1970

b. The achievements of our government were particularly impressive in view of the comparative weakness, ineffectiveness, and mounting problems of the governments of France and Britain.

c. Three aspects of college work that make it so challenging are the lack of supervision, the high intellectual standards, and the volume of work.

d. Because he had failed the course and with graduation now impossible, he simply decided to drop out and leave town.

e. Because he had changed and being a different person myself, we were strangers to one another.

f. The resort was quiet. There was not much to do besides swimming or the local movie house.

g. Ideal and practice will only be brought together when the laws are enforced and until observing the laws becomes the accepted thing.

h. The law serves a double purpose; first, it protects the people, and second, the capture of criminals.

i. Newspaper readers are interested in people and their personalities more than world affairs or national politics.

j. *Offensive* is often a synonym for the unconventional.

k. Some men in office are totally unfit to be public servants but are well qualified to be public nuisances.

l. Cox unostentatiously drives an old Ford station wagon and dresses in what one student cynically calls "planned dishevelment": a well-worn tweed jacket, old sweaters, penny loafers. . . . Besides squash, tennis and skiing, he keeps in shape by running up the six flights to his apartment. — *Life*, Jan. 22, 1971

m. The university has grown so rapidly that it is short of facilities, instructors, and is faced with a discipline problem.

n. My proposal for a new society does not require all men to lay down their tools, jobs, and ways of life. Each member of society would still be self-supporting and would assume a share of public responsibility.

o. People have different ideas about what is amusing and the extent to which Cosby is a true comedian.

2. Identify the parallel structures in each of the following passages printed elsewhere in this book, and comment on what effects the parallelism has in addition to ensuring clarity.

a. Wallace Stegner, p. 16

b. Michael Herr, p. 69

c. I. F. Stone, p. 106

d. Bruno Bettelheim, pp. 134 – 35

e. James E. Miller, Jr., pp. 254 – 55

Rhetorical Uses. Besides keeping order in a sentence, parallelism contributes to economy: a series of two or three or more embedded structures gives density to prose, increasing the yield of ideas. In addition, parallelism can have distinct rhetorical effects. A skilled writer knows how to turn it to more than one use:

The Masters, though they would establish the huge impersonality of corporation rule, could claim a striking image, an appalling carnage, a robber-baron polity. They robbed the Indians, they cheated the white man, they chucked out the squatters, they squeezed out the farmers, they greased palms, they twisted arms, they knifed one another. — Louis Kronenberger, *Atlantic*, Jan. 1971

In the first sentence, parallelism is a means to clarity and economy: the three elements in series ("striking image," "appalling carnage," "robber-baron polity") cooperate to produce a major generalization. In the second, the seven short clauses, all built on the same pattern, set up a fast-moving rhythm that reinforces the meaning. Here and elsewhere, it is the *repetition* of grammatical structure that creates a stylistic effect.

Whether it is used to point to similar ideas or to distinguish closely related ideas or to set off mutually opposing views, parallelism can work so unobtrusively that the reader is barely aware of the structural similarity or so insistently that he can't ignore the symmetrical design.

Parallelism is the principal grammatical-rhetorical feature of many sentences, including all *balanced sentences*. Grammatically, the balanced sentence is made up of matching structures. Rhetorically, the play of one structure against another brings out a similarity or an opposition of ideas. Here, word offsets word, phrase offsets phrase, and clause offsets clause:

Those who are naturally proud and envious will learn from Thackeray to despise humanity; those who are naturally gentle, to pity it; those who are naturally shallow, to laugh at it. — John Ruskin, *Sesame and Lilies*

The alternative to life in the paradise of his dream is death in the hell of his banality. — Eric Voegelin, *Harvard Theological Review*, July 1967

Though still found occasionally in Formal styles, such perfect balancing of part against part is not common today. Except on occasions that call for high oratory — presidential inaugural addresses, for instance — modern writers are unlikely to sustain even a simple type of parallelism through as many sentences as Emerson does in this passage:

The theory of books is noble. The scholar of the first age received into him the world around; brooded thereon; gave it the new arrangement of his own mind, and uttered it again. It came into him life; it went out from him truth. It came to him short-lived actions; it went out from him immortal thoughts. It came to him business; it went from him poetry. It was dead fact; now, it is quick thought. It can stand, and it can go. It now endures, it now flies, it now inspires. Precisely in proportion to the depth of mind from which it issued, so high does it soar, so long does it sing. — Ralph Waldo Emerson, "The American Scholar"

Every sentence but the first exhibits marked parallelism, and most have the perfect symmetry that makes a sentence balanced. "It came into him life; it went out from him truth" and the three sentences that follow illustrate antithesis, the use of identical grammatical structures to express opposed ideas. "It can stand, and it can go" and the sentence that follows use identical grammatical structures to express similar ideas. The two concluding clauses also exhibit balance: "so high does it soar, so long does it sing."

Though such careful, sustained patterning may strike a modern reader as mechanical and contrived, balance and antithesis still perform valuable functions. Pairing similarly constructed sentences or clauses offers a precise and orderly way of setting up a comparison:

Grammar and rhetoric are complementary, but their procedures and goals are quite different. Grammar maps out the possible; rhetoric narrows the possible down to the desirable and effective. — Francis Christensen, *Notes Toward a New Rhetoric*

Balance can match a positive statement with a negative one, an analogical statement with its literal equivalent, an abstract statement with a concrete expression of the same idea. It can give an assertion a forthright, authoritative, or aphoristic tone:

They have been educated to achieve success; few of them have been educated to exercise power. — Walter Lippmann, *A Preface to Morals*

A neat antithesis can be a source of wit: "to be amusing about the things London takes seriously, such as status, and serious about what London finds amusing, such as sin" (p. 260). And within the framework of balance, a rejection of the expected is always possible:

In charitable terms, this is a good work. In literary terms, it is anything but. — *Time*, July 22, 1966

But the powerful rhetorical effect of fully developed parallelism may not always be desirable. As usual, context counts. Though balanced sentences are appropriate for delivering carefully thought-out pronouncements, in most casual styles parallelism should be lighter and altogether less obtrusive:

What made the house a home was the runaround porch, a screen that stuck or slammed, a wire basket of dead ferns, a swing that scuffed the paint off the clapboards, a rail to lean on when you threw up, a stoop to sit on when you watered the grass. — Wright Morris, *God's Country and My People*

There is enough parallelism here to hold the sentence together and give it an easy, casual rhythm but not so much that it becomes monotonous or seems contrived. (If you try attaching a *that* clause to each of the nouns in the complement — "porch," "screen," "basket," "swing," "rail," "stoop" — you will see how stiff and affected parallelism can make everyday material sound.) Even in less casual contexts, the modern writer often takes care not to press parallelism to the point of exact symmetry:

A mood of course depends on your perspective. Warsaw to many who arrive from Paris is drab and joyless; to those who arrive from Moscow it is colorful, joyous, swinging. — David Halberstam, *Harper's*, Jan. 1971

The incessant moralizing of the New England mind, the sententiousness of its intellectual manner, the consciousness of being God's elect, above all the overcharged and often mystical symbolism which so many Puritans attached to their experiences in primitive New England — these were turned into fanciful, elusive, symbolic elements of human nature. — Alfred Kazin, *New York Review of Books*, Oct. 24, 1968

In the four parallel structures that open the second passage, variation is provided by the presence or absence of adjectives ("incessant moralizing," "sententiousness," and so on) and by the shift from prepositional phrases to participial phrase to *which* clause. The parallelism is definite but not rigid.

Though parallelism can give strength to a limp sentence and coherence to a sequence of sentences, making a fetish of parallelism will have adverse effects on any style. "We need to know who is to censor and by what methods" is clear and acceptable; only an examination of the context would tell whether parallelism would be more effective. Regardless of context, the parallelism here is forced and overdone:

Although some were shouting, like the men and women on the pier, although some were hysterical, like the men and women crowding around the plank, although some were dazed, there was a difference between them and the persons who awaited them. — Leane Zugsmith, *Home Is Where You Hang Your Childhood*

Parallelism has created an expectation. The writer has failed to deliver. After all the careful structuring, the final clause is a dud.

Get in the habit of using parallelism for clarity. Use it for rhetorical effect when the ideas you are expressing justify the emphasis parallelism gives. But don't strive for a series of three parallel clauses when all you have to say can be put in one clause or two. If you do, you will probably give your sentence a dying fall.

EXERCISES

1. Discuss the use of parallelism, balance, and antithesis in these excerpts. Is there too much parallelism? Too little? The right amount? Try to judge the appropriateness of the sentence patterns to the subject, the publication or occasion, and the general tone of the passage.

a. Most Americans, when they rhapsodize about wanting to find an unspoiled paradise, are spouting poppycock. They want their drinks iced, their sheets clean, their water pure, their meat untainted. They want people to cook their food, take them fishing, show them where to dive, and exchange a bit of intelligent conversation. They want the sensation of being in the wilds, but also the security of knowing that the jungle animals have been driven back, the dangerous fish have been discouraged from the lagoon and the natives pacified. They really want only the illusion of primitiveness. — Peter Benchley, *Holiday*, Nov. 1970

b. I decline to accept the end of man. It is easy enough to say that man is immortal simply because he will endure: that when the last ding-dong of doom has clanged and faded from the last worthless rock hanging tideless in the last red and dying evening, that even then there will still be one more sound: that of his puny inexhaustible voice, still talking. I refuse to accept this. I believe that man will not merely endure: he will prevail. He is immortal, not because he alone among creatures has an inexhaustible voice, but because he has a soul, a spirit capable of compassion and sacrifice and endurance. The poet's, the writer's, duty is to write about these things. It is his privilege to help man endure by lifting his heart, by reminding him of the courage and honor and hope and pride and compassion and pity and sacrifice which have been the glory of his past. The poet's voice need not merely be the record of man, it can be one of the props, the pillars to help him endure and prevail. — William Faulkner, Nobel Prize Address

As you revise and reorder a sentence, you may choose to make your main assertion (your action statement) at or near the beginning of the sentence and then add explanatory details or reasons or qualifications. Or you may choose to so order the elements that the sentence is not grammatically complete nor the action statement fully disclosed until you have written the last few words. Especially when you are writing a long sentence, the rhetorical effects of these two patterns are distinctly different.

Traditionally, the first of these two types of sentence has been called *loose*, the second *periodic*. Francis Christensen renamed the first type the *cumulative* sentence, demonstrated the rhetorical effects it can produce, and argued that it is "the typical sentence of modern English."[1]

Cumulative Sentences

The most distinctive variety of the cumulative sentence — the one Christensen gave most of his attention to — is found in narrative and descriptive writing. It is exemplified in the sentence by Ernest Hemingway quoted and analyzed on p. 283 and, in less extreme form, in this passage:

. . . we walked up the beach. We kept on walking until we left the public part behind and started passing the houses of the rich people, houses so rich and elegant that they didn't have to look it but sat back almost inconspicuously there among the palms and sea grape, each with its own little flight of steps leading up from the sand to the green lawn, each with its low cement groin projecting out into the sea to keep the beach from washing away. — Frederick Buechner, *Lion Country*

The cumulative sentence opens with a base structure, usually a short independent clause. Added to it are loosely

[1] "A Generative Rhetoric of the Sentence" (*College Composition and Communication*, Oct. 1963, p. 156). The article has been reprinted widely and is included in Christensen's *Notes Toward a New Rhetoric* (New York: Harper, 1967). Several other essays in the book have a bearing on Christensen's research into the nature and significance of the cumulative sentence.

related, or free, modifiers—appositives, prepositional phrases, participial phrases, absolute phrases, and nonrestrictive clauses—built on what precedes ("each with its own little flight of steps") or made parallel to what precedes ("each with its low cement groin").

The cumulative sentence of description and narration relies heavily on appositives and phrases, sometimes piling up a very large number of them as in the Hemingway sentence; and it is often open-ended, giving the impression that more phrases could be added. The cumulative sentences of exposition and argument—our main concern here—contain fewer structures of modification, and of these a higher proportion are nonrestrictive clauses. The difference is to be expected: the modifiers in descriptive-narrative sentences typically add details; in expository sentences they typically extend, explain, justify, or exemplify the main assertion. But in any case, the base clause stands near the beginning of the sentence, and it is qualified by one or more free modifiers. Here are some moderate examples of the type as it is commonly found in discussions of ideas:

Fiedler begins as a philosopher of mythic American literature, defining the Indian myth as an idol of the European mind, establishing basic American mythopoeic categories, locating the origin and history of his subject—the European discovery and Gothicising of the geographic and mythic West.—Peter Michelson, *New Republic*, May 11, 1968

The main clause in Michelson's sentence is followed by three parallel participial phrases, with an appositive attached to the last one.

Stalin's occupation of Eastern Europe was a political blow to "democratic Socialists" in New York, as it would soon be a catastrophe for non-Communists in all territory controlled by the Red Army—not least in Russia itself, where Hitler's frightfulness united behind Stalin many Russians who after the war were imprisoned or shot.—Alfred Kazin, *Harper's*, Jan. 1971

In this sentence the nonrestrictive, or free, modifiers have several restrictive, or bound, modifiers built into them. For instance, the nonrestrictive clause "as it would soon be . . . Red Army" contains the bound modifiers "in all territory" and "controlled by the Red Army." The sentence also illustrates how the last part of a cumulative sentence can be rounded out and so given a sense of completion; the free modifier "after the war" stands before, not after, the final predication. On the whole, the cumulative sentences of exposition and argument are less open-ended than the cumulative sentences of description and narration.

Because at least one free modifier always follows the base structure, the cumulative sentence can be cut off after the initial assertion (and often at several points beyond that) and still remain intelligible. But though the sentence remains intelligible, detaching the free modifiers will alter the rhetorical effect and may lop off the most important idea as well. In the following sentence, much looser and more elaborate than those quoted above, the real thrust of meaning comes not in the two opening clauses that together constitute the base structure, nor even in the long series of noun clusters that follow, but in the looser structures of modification attached to the series — the two appositives and the two concluding dependent clauses:

Symptomatically one hears everything, and clinically one sees everything: fatigue; pains and spasms and cramps and itches; indigestion and vomiting, with the food often enough blood-streaked; headaches and backaches and a throbbing or pounding in the chest, or a sharp, piercing kind of hurt there; loss of appetite, loss of energy, loss of alertness, loss of ability to sleep and "just plain loss of everything," a nondescript and unscientific summary that usually can be heard spoken quietly rather than angrily, and tied to all sorts of concrete diseases, ones easy to document, were there doctors in Marengo County, Alabama, or Wolfe County, Kentucky, of a mind to do so, and were all those law-abiding, out-of-the-way, utterly penniless individuals to become patients. — Robert Coles, *American Scholar*, Winter 1970-71

The fact that the cumulative sentence can be cut off well before its close without a loss of sense is the source of its ·potential weakness as well as its potential strength. Because it observes the natural order of oral expression — main statement first, then qualifications and particulars — it can and often does give the impression of naturalness and spontaneity, of following the workings of the writer's mind. As modifier is added to modifier, the thought can grow, change, become more precise. But if the modifiers do not strengthen the initial assertion, the sentence may trail off into insignificant or irrelevant detail or anticlimax. Or the openness of the structure may encourage the writer to add on ideas more and more remote from the initial assertion. Or what follows the base structure may turn into a tangled succession of phrases and clauses, hard to read in relation to each other. The last example quoted above could scarcely survive further additions, and without parallelism it could not have survived the number of additions it has. (Parallelism, it is worth repeating, contributes to the coherence of many sentences that have none of the symmetry or near-symmetry of the balanced sentence.)

Though the good cumulative sentence gives an impression of ease and flexibility, writing one calls for control over both content and structure. This sentence drifts, as detail is added to detail:

It was a new experience for us, waking before sunrise, the wind quiet then, the countryside still except for the first bird calls, the blackbirds whistling in the bushes, the pale light streaking the windows on the east side of the cabin, facing the barn, empty now, unused for years, its doors nailed shut to keep out tramps, waiting for the day to begin.

When modifiers are stacked like this, their grammatical relations must be clear. Participial modifiers are most likely to cause trouble because they depend on close position for unambiguous relationships. The sentence above drifts grammatically with its final participial phrase, "waiting for the day to begin." The phrase belongs just after "waking before sunrise"; in any position after that, it dangles.

Periodic Sentences

The cut-off test provides a simple means of identifying the periodic sentence: to be intelligible, it must be read through to the end or very near the end, for the base structure stands last. The reader has to hold the elements of the sentence in mind as he goes along, instead of getting the central message and then adding to it, detail by detail, as he does with the typical cumulative sentence.

Not so long before he died, still receiving carloads of honors as he always had, and still receiving, as also he always had, from Right or Left in turn, fanatic attacks on his social views, Mann remarked that he was a "great, unloved name." — John Thompson, *Harper's*, Jan. 1971

The standardization of curricula, the packaging of courses, the attempt by remote control to make the social and cultural life of various campuses conform to some abstract, homogenized standard, the effort to govern academic communities from a distance — all of this is subversive of the educational process. — William M. Birenbaum, *Overlive*

Nervous, strewn with knotty or flashy phrases, impatient with transitions and other concessions to dullness, willfully calling attention to itself as a form or at least an outcry, fond of rapid twists, taking pleasure in dispute, dialectic, dazzle — such, at its best or most noticeable, was the essay cultivated by the New York writers. — Irving Howe, *Decline of the New*

Even out of context, these sentences suggest the various

effects that periodicity can achieve. In the first, the dependent clauses and verbal phrases give the circumstances of the action reported in the final clause. In the second, the parallel noun clusters summarize evidence. In the third—an inverted sentence—the force lies in the descriptive details presented in the adjectives, adjective clusters, and participial phrases. What counts rhetorically in Howe's sentence is not the final assertion so much as the details that lead up to it. Turning the sentence around alters the emphasis:

At its best and most noticeable the essay cultivated by the New York writers was nervous, strewn with knotty or flashy phrases. . . .

As a musical composition remains in suspension until the final chords provide resolution and release, a periodic sentence achieves its effect by withholding its full meaning until its last words. Sustained periodicity, therefore, can be a tour de force, with the reader kept in suspense about how the sentence is to come out, both structurally and semantically. But unless there is a rhetorical reason for withholding the full meaning, a long, complicated periodic sentence may seem decidedly artificial; and unless parallelism enforces order among the elements piled up before the final clause, the syntax may become tangled and the sentence top-heavy.

A succession of long periodic sentences creates a style too elaborate and contrived for everyday topics, just as, even for everyday topics, a succession of long cumulative sentences may seem too casual and careless; and in much good current prose, the sentences are not noticeably of either type. When additions to the base clause are few or when suspensions are brief, there is no great contrast between sentences that technically belong to the two types. (For an example, see the passage by George Steiner, p. 318). Further, some orthographically long sentences are cumulative in the first half, periodic in the second.

Cumulative and periodic sentences sometimes offer alternative ways of expressing an idea. As you revise an essay, you may decide to make some of your loose sentences periodic for reasons of emphasis or to make some of your periodic sentences cumulative so that your prose will have a more relaxed and open style. But you do not always have the choice. In some sentences the nature and the order of the modifiers make it inadvisable to change the position of the base clause. Putting the base clause last would make this sentence a good deal harder to understand:

"The Conformist" is a lyrical film of memory, structured and composed subjectively, moving easily back and forth in time, flashbacks interrupted by flash forwards and fantasy.—Stephen Farber, *New York Times*, April 11, 1971

There is another reason why you may not be free to choose between the two types. How a sentence begins and ends—the simplest aspect of periodicity or its absence—is largely determined by what possibilities there are for fitting it smoothly into the paragraph. A brief passage illustrates the point:

That the "historical materialism" of Marx and the "dialectical materialism" of Engels represent different *aspects* of what is conventionally known as "Marxism" would not nowadays be denied even by orthodox Marxist-Leninists. They would simply maintain that Engels systematized the philosophical hints thrown out by Marx. What Marx himself thought of Engels's philosophical writings (so far as he was aware of them) remains uncertain, and is in any case a matter for his biographers rather than for historians of philosophy.— George Lichtheim, *New York Review of Books*, April 11, 1968

Though these sentences scarcely have enough complexity of structure to warrant labeling them, one can say that the first sentence is faintly periodic and the third faintly cumulative. (The second is neither, for it consists only of a base structure with bound modifiers.) And one can guess that the writer was guided in arranging the sentences not by considerations of periodicity but by the desirability of knitting the sentences more closely than any other ordering would have permitted: ". . . orthodox Marxist-Leninists. They . . . by Marx. What Marx. . . ."

Ordinarily it is the long cumulative sentence or the long periodic sentence that calls attention to itself; and when any sentence calls attention to itself, it should do so for the right reason—because its form reinforces and enhances the idea it expresses.

The study of good cumulative and good periodic sentences suggests one practical rule: Keep your main assertion short and direct. Whether the modifiers come early or late or are spread through the sentence, your writing will be clearer if your main assertions—your action statements—are short clauses rather than long ones.

EXERCISE

From the passages by Brewster (p. 16), McPhee (pp. 68–69), Buckley (pp. 178–79), Bruner (pp. 222–24), and Mailer (pp. 310–11), pick out at least six cumulative and six periodic sentences. Rewrite them, making the cumulative sentences periodic and the periodic sentences cumulative. State as precisely as you can what is gained or lost by the rewrite. Is the meaning clearer or less clear? Is the sentence more emphatic or less emphatic? Is the style better or worse?

Interruption and Suspension

Probably most of the sentences you write are neither noticeably cumulative nor noticeably periodic. Instead of locating your main assertion first or last, you may put it in the middle (as in this sentence), with modifiers falling at the opening and the close. Or you can spread the main assertion through the sentence, letting subordinate elements cluster around its subject, verb, and complement:

When pushed too far, permissiveness, which encourages questioning more than the acceptance of authority, may cause the child, and later the adolescent or adult, to be unable to accept authority altogether, however much he unconsciously craves it. — Ernest van den Haag, *Modern Age*, Summer-Fall 1970

Springing open the subject-verb-complement unit allows you to make qualifications just at the point where they are most pertinent. But this desirable effect is counteracted when the embedded phrases and clauses are so long that they create a definite sense of delay and interrupt the sentence movement. Degrees of interruption are illustrated in this passage:

In my mind, the effort to become a great novelist simply involves attempting to tell as much of the truth as one can bear, and then a little more. It is an effort which, by its very nature — remembering that men write the books, that time passes and energy flags, and safety beckons — is obviously doomed to failure. Success is an American word which cannot conceivably, unless it is defined in an extremely severe, ironical and painful way, have any place in the vocabulary of any artist. — James Baldwin, *New York Times Book Review*, Jan. 14, 1962

In the first sentence, the infinitive phrase "to become a great novelist" is an essential part of the subject, and "simply" is a short modifier of the verb; both are so closely worked into the structure of the sentence that no sense of delay is felt between the simple subject "effort" and the verb "involves." By contrast, there is a distinct delay in the second sentence, where both a prepositional phrase and a long, loosely related verbal construction separate subject and verb, and in the third, where the adverb clause separates the two parts of the verb, "cannot" and "have."

Long modifiers that break into the basic structure of a clause—subject-verb-complement in an independent clause, subordinating conjunction-subject-verb-complement in an adverbial clause—can so interfere with the forward movement of the sentence that the reader loses track of the really important assertion:

If, as seems necessary for a generation so many members of which are unable to spell, punctuate, or put together a decent sentence in the English of their period (and this goes for many of its writers as well as those engaged in other vocations) the Bible, in order to be appreciated and enjoyed, must be streamlined, then by all means let us coax them into reading Job and the Psalms, Ecclesiastes and Isaiah, and the New Testament, by these means.—J. Donald Adams, *New York Times Book Review*, April 26, 1953

And when repeated embedding juxtaposes two verbal phrases, the reader has to go back over the sentence to match the right verb with the right subject:

All these forces, added to the other deterrents which combinations of Powers, great and small, ready to stand firm upon the front of law and for the ordered remedy of grievances, would have formed, might well have been effective.—Winston S. Churchill, "The Munich Agreement"

The last two examples show how lengthy interrupters can cripple a sentence. Even short interrupters can spoil a sentence if they are allowed to create an erratic, jerky movement:

American drama, it is generally agreed, continues, as it has over a long period, to be in a seriously bad way.—Nathan A. Scott, Jr., *The Broken Center*

If you find yourself writing sentences that contain several paired commas or dashes or parentheses, examine the elements they enclose to see, first, whether you are making necessary, useful qualifications. Repeated interruption by unnecessary qualifications can make you sound indecisive, evasive, prissy; and if the enclosed elements are no more than asides or extraneous details, they simply overload your sentences.

If you are convinced that all the phrases and clauses are necessary, then check their position. The function of interruption is to make meaning more exact by introducing qualifications at the point where they are most pertinent. But sometimes an interrupting element can be moved with no loss in precision:

His prize-winning second novel, a well constructed and psychologically convincing portrait of a social climber, earned, to the embarrassment of the committee on awards, far more praise abroad than in this country, demonstrating once again the lack of correlation between a critical success and a popular success.

Here, the phrase "to the embarrassment of the committee on awards" could just as well introduce the sentence, permitting the verb to join its object.

And there are times when the qualifications, while precisely placed, are just too numerous, making the reader strain to determine the basic structure—and the basic idea— of the sentence. (For examples, see pp. 311–12.) The solution then is not to sacrifice precision but to restore clarity by breaking your one sentence into two or more sentences, with the interrupting elements logically distributed among them.

The reader can also be seriously handicapped when a single long postmodifier to a subject keeps the meaning suspended. Sentences like these are hard to read:

Any citizen who is really concerned about the kind of urban environment his children are going to inherit and who is convinced that action needs to be taken now to improve the quality of life that environment will permit should begin immediately to support the plans recommended by the Council.

To make it easier for your reader to grasp your main assertion, it is a good idea to keep the "simple subject"—the head noun in the subject phrase—reasonably close to the first verbal element. Otherwise he will have to hold the suspended subject in mind while he unravels the modifier and then reintegrate subject and verb. Sentences that have long subject phrases are front-heavy, slow moving, and difficult to read. In revision, trim the subject element so that your action statements are expressed in short clauses.

Inversion

If interruption can make a statement more precise, inversion can make it more emphatic. Inversion (or *anastrophe*, as it is called in Greek rhetoric) is any departure from the normal subject-verb-complement order. The inversions in questions are purely grammatical, but in declarative sentences they are optional and therefore stylistic. The chief motive for inversion is to throw stress on a word or phrase that would not receive it if normal order were observed. In this remark about Dylan Thomas, inverting the complement makes the judgment stand out:

That he was a true poet I am still quite certain, despite the persistent attacks of Robert Graves, David Holbrook, George Steiner, Kingsley Amis, and Geoffrey Gregson. — Matthew Hodgart, *New York Review of Books*, Aug. 3, 1967

Even the simplest inversion, a shift in the position of an adverb ("down he came") can have a powerful rhetorical effect:

And then down he came, his belly towards me, with a crash that seemed to shake the ground even where I lay. — George Orwell, *Shooting an Elephant and Other Essays*

Used with a negative, inversion may create an effect of flippancy or irony, as in this comment on the novelist Anthony Powell:

A Marcel Proust he's not. — John Gross, *New York Review of Books*, May 18, 1967

It is used in journalism to lend a little sprightliness:

Came the spring of 1963, and the Administration was in the process of committing itself to a new, controversial, and "strong" civil rights bill. — Victor S. Navasky, *Atlantic*, Nov. 1970

Since inversion in a declarative sentence immediately calls attention to itself, it should be used only when it offers the best way of stressing what needs stress. When the element shifted does not need or deserve emphasis, inversion sounds unnatural:

Cooperative the Administration was in the first stages of the discussion.

Good writers use inversion very sparingly. When they do use it, they usually make it serve a double purpose — to emphasize what needs emphasis and to make a smoother, tighter transition from the preceding sentence or into the next one.

EMPHASIS AND ECONOMY

As you revise and rewrite, keep trying to make your sentences say what you want them to say with the emphasis you intend. For the most part, this means expressing yourself directly and economically, for indirect, wordy writing blurs meaning and diffuses emphasis. It should also mean giving attention to the sound and rhythm of your sentences. In ways that are hard to analyze but nonetheless real, these qualities have a bearing on the way your reader receives and responds to your ideas.

Emphasis

In reviewing your early drafts, examine your sentences to see that you have emphasized ideas that deserve emphasis and, conversely, that you have not emphasized peripheral ideas or minor details.

To keep statements separate or to combine them, to coordinate or to subordinate, to express ideas in parallel structures or to avoid parallelism, to make moderate or marked use of periodicity or inversion or interruption — decisions about matters like these determine what gets emphasis and what does not. A few additional remarks on using separation and position to control emphasis will supplement the discussion of sentence patterns and stress on pp. 271 – 76.

Separation. In speaking, a pause allows what has just been said to sink in, or, if the voice is suspended, it throws emphasis on what is to follow. In writing, something of the same effect can be gained by separation. Consider this sentence:

The trouble with modern English spelling is that it does not spell or even approximately spell modern English but instead spells the English of the Late Middle English period around 1470 A.D.

Here is the much more emphatic form in which it originally appeared, as three separate sentences:

The trouble with modern English spelling is that it does not spell modern English. It does not even approximately spell modern English. What it does spell is the English of the Late Middle English period around 1470 A.D. — Harold Whitehall, *Structural Essentials of English*

In the following sentence, the use of two clauses instead of one ("It promises and delivers . . .") and the choice of a semicolon to mark the separation give emphasis to the second assertion:

It promises a civilized, casual, and colorful account of a phenomenon unfamiliar to many of us but important to our time; and it delivers. — Dan Wakefield, *Atlantic*, June 1966

In smaller units, repeating the conjunction or preposition in a series of parallel items isolates and emphasizes each item:

In the English-speaking countries the rights acquired by the gentry, by the yeomanry, by the merchants, by these developing classes in the middle of the social structure were not predominantly urban. — John Lukacs, *American Scholar*, Autumn 1970

Pages 294–95 discuss the use of punctuation to separate elements and so control the emphasis in a sentence.

Position.   The natural points of emphasis in a sentence are the beginning and the end. You will waste them if you launch your sentences with empty introductions or let them run down into trivial detail.

The introductions "It is," "There is," "It was," "There were" may perform necessary functions in pointing to or asserting the existence of what follows:

There are seven types of ambiguity.

They may provide special emphasis by shifting a word from the position it would normally occupy:

It is silly to quarrel about words. (Instead of: Quarreling about words is silly.)

And the expletive "It is" beginning for one sentence often opens the way for a smoother transition into the next one:

It is hard to comprehend the enormity of the slaughter and torture that hunters perpetrate every year. Statistics on this subject are like excerpts from a book on astronomy. — Fred Myers, *Fact*, March–April 1967

But "It is" and "There are" are criticized — properly — as sentence openers when, instead of performing a useful function, they substitute for a strong subject-verb combination. "It is interesting to note that . . ." is usually only a pompous delaying action. In other sentences, "It is/There are" is an unnecessary filler:

[There are] some people [who] read history to raise their self-esteem.

Unless the writer's intention is to assert what he assumes is in question — that people actually do read to raise their self-esteem — the shorter version is preferable.

Ending a sentence with a minor detail weakens emphasis. Necessary qualifications of the main assertion should come early in the sentence, where they can give the right perspective on the action statement:

With very few exceptions, Congressmen rallied in support of the President.

The qualifying phrase should stand last only if the exceptions are to become the main point of the next sentence:

Congressmen rallied in support of the President with very few exceptions. But those who dissented included the senators from his home state.

Conclusions that undermine what has gone before call for rethinking as well as rewriting:

Proust's account of the madeleine and tea episode gave me an entirely new notion of the relation between sense perception and memory, or at least one that I hadn't given much thought to until then.

Revising sentences (or paragraphs) for emphasis often means putting the elements in an order of increasing value. The value may be physical length, with words or phrases or clauses building from shortest to longest in rhythmical progression. Or it may be complexity of meaning or force of emotion, or distinction or bluntness of phrasing. In any case, what comes last should usually be strongest:

Impatience characterizes much of American life in the second half of the twentieth century: impatience of the young with the old, and of the old with the young; impatience with due process of law; impatience with old ideas rooted in tradition, and with new ideas that lack the authority of tradition; impatience with those who are neutral, and those who are independent; impatience with the machinery of adjudication and arbitration; impatience with any solutions short of utopian. — Henry Steele Commager, *Saturday Review*, Nov. 9, 1968

Ordinarily, climax is the natural order, the expected order, for items in a series, though the reverse — an order of diminishing importance — is also possible. Listing without any discernible direction results in flat, boneless sentences or, if the last member of the series is conspicuously less important, in absurd anticlimax:

No degree will be conferred unless the applicant shall have sustained a good moral character, completed the necessary study, and paid all fines to the library.

In addition to the opportunities for emphasis offered by syntactic maneuvering, there are various other means of emphasizing, some better than others. As a general rule, the more mechanical and obvious the means, the less effective it is likely to be.

Orthography and Word Choice.   Mechanical devices include underlining, capitalizing, and using exclamation marks. There are, of course, legitimate uses for all three, but dependence on them results in forcible-feeble prose which suggests that the writer may be excited but arouses no excitement at all in the reader. If the content and the style of writing are strong, such devices are unnecessary. If content and style are weak, they are insufficient.

Slightly less obvious are the qualifiers commonly used to strengthen adjectives (*very* beautiful, *extremely* successful, *terrifically* loud), the once-powerful adjectives that overuse in conversation has turned into *counter words (a *terrible* exam, a *horrible* day, a *wonderful* girl), and the colloquial superlatives (the *wildest* time, the *greatest* game). Reliance on any of these in serious exposition weakens rather than strengthens what is said. Nouns that are themselves emphatic in meaning—*triumph, disaster, sensation, tragedy, monster, genius*—have their legitimate uses, but applied indiscriminately they make a writer sound like a fool or a fraud.

Successful emphasis—that is, emphasis that convinces the reader—is less likely to be achieved by straining for emphatic words than by making good use of words already at hand. And this may entail repeating words.

Repetition.   Thoughtless, accidental, or lazy repetition of the kind illustrated in the *Index* article *Repetition invariably weakens style. But repeating words and phrases that are genuinely significant relates and emphasizes ideas. (The function of lexical repetition in binding sentences together and making paragraphs cohere has been discussed on pp. 250–54.) Controlled repetition of the key terms of a discussion keeps the reader's attention focused and makes for clearer, more honest prose than shifting restlessly from synonym to synonym: the Supreme Court, the high court, the highest tribunal.

The first sentence of the passage that follows shows Baldwin making careful discriminations in word choice ("chilling," "cruel," "bitter"); the second shows him using repetition deliberately and purposefully:

He could be chilling in the pulpit and indescribably cruel in his personal life and he was certainly the most bitter man I have ever met; yet it must be said that there was something else in him, buried in him, which lent him his tremendous power and, even, a rather crushing charm. It had something to do with his blackness, I think — he was very black — with his blackness and his beauty, and with the fact that he knew that he was black but did not know that he was beautiful. — James Baldwin, *Notes of a Native Son*

Notice that both nouns ("blackness," "beauty") and adjectives ("black," "beautiful") are involved in the repetition.

Often, as here, the effect of verbal repetition is enhanced by the repetition of sounds. Together the two sentences offer many examples of *alliteration — in addition to the insistent *b*'s, the patterns of sound in "indescribably cruel," "crushing charm," and so on. But like aimless repetition of the same word, aimless repetition of the same sound can become obtrusive and distracting, as in the hiss and clatter of "excessively successful executives." So can unintentional rhymes and off-rhymes, as in "I treated the wound, but the pain remained the same." Generally, in prose, words that rhyme should not be allowed to come close enough together to create accidental doggerel.

Purposeful repetition of sounds can reinforce meaning and make it more compelling. On occasion, a writer may deliberately combine sounds that are harsh, not pleasant to the ear, just as through his choice and ordering of words, he may produce rhythms that jolt rather than glide. Reading your essay aloud, or having it read aloud to you, is the one way to find out how your prose sounds.

When a passage purposefully repeats key words, structural patterns, and sounds, as in the Commager quotation above and in the Stevenson passage that follows, it takes on an oratorical flavor:

Intolerant power respects power, not weakness. It is imperative therefore to build and better the balance of power. Conspiracy and incitement prosper in disunion and discontent. It is imperative therefore to build and better the unity and well-being of the free world. We cannot do it alone. It is imperative therefore to build and better the coalition. — Adlai Stevenson, *Call to Greatness*

Such sustained repetition can be highly effective when spoken — witness the power of the chant in public gatherings. But what is very stirring from the speaker's platform may be considerably less so on the page, and the carefully constructed repetitions and insistent parallelisms of the orator are seldom appropriate in current prose.

Repetition, whether of sound, meaning, or structure, must be controlled; for like other means of achieving emphasis, it can defeat itself. Emphases that come in clusters — like repeated drum beats or high notes or dramatic gestures — soon cease to impress. To be successfully emphatic, writing must use emphasis sparingly.

Directness and Economy

Most good factual writing is direct and economical. One source of indirect writing is frequent *nominalization, the practice of deriving a noun from a subject-verb-object statement ("his cancellation of the flight" from "he cancelled the flight") or from a subject-*be*-adjective statement ("the pioneers' hardihood" from "the pioneers were hardy"). A moderate amount of nominalization is found in mature prose, since it offers a way of embedding one sentence in another and so of reducing two statements to one:

He discovered the drugs accidentally. That clinched the State's case.

His accidental discovery of the drugs clinched the State's case.

But repeated nominalization makes writing heavy, abstract, pretentious, and even dishonest.

There was an affirmative decision in regard to the implementation of a policy concerning a reduction in employment levels on the part of management.

Compare that sentence with two other versions:

The Board of Directors has decided to employ fewer workers.

The bosses are going to fire some of you.

One might argue that the more abstract version serves its rhetorical purpose: it obscures, it hides, it muddies an unpleasant situation. Which version the writer chooses depends finally on what he wants the sentence to accomplish. But whatever reason leads him to choose one over the other, the important point is that he *choose*. The real problem lies with the writer who habitually and unthinkingly writes sentences like this one:

A state of excitement existed among the crowd after their learning of the presence of the Beatles.

There seems to be no possible reason to prefer that sentence to a more direct version:

The crowd became excited after they learned that the Beatles were there.

If you find yourself using a good many abstract nouns, especially nouns ending in -*ence*, -*ity*, -*ment*, -*tion* — if you find yourself using them, say, once every six or seven words—you may be weakening your style.

Repeated use of the passive voice and series of prepositional phrases are other clues to an indirect style. Just as nominalization can be useful, so can many statements be put more conveniently and more smoothly in the passive than in the active voice; and a certain number of prepositional phrases are indispensable—we couldn't write without them. But if you keep nominalizing, if you keep using the passive, if you keep stringing out prepositional phrases, your writing will lose directness and vigor.

Usually directness and economy go together. In the examples used above, the more direct phrasing is the shorter. But sometimes nominalization is shorter:

What we say is true depends more on what we believe is true than what is really true.

Truth depends more on belief than on reality.

The rhetorical situation should help you choose between the two versions. In some situations the more specific statement might be worth the extra words.

Economy then, like most rhetorical virtues, is relative. The fewest and simplest words are not always the most economical, for they may oversimplify your ideas, or they may limit the audience to those practiced in following a tight, compact style. An economical style can become too abrupt, too dense, or too packed to be read with ease or pleasure. Saying a thing twice often means saying it more clearly, and the impact of a main idea may be increased if it is repeated in more concrete or more imagistic terms.

But though economy must be judged in relation to intention and audience, it remains true that *unnecessary* words and *needlessly* complicated structures work against economy. If they also work against clarity and directness, the long-winded sentence is fuzzy and weak as well.

When you are revising your essays, four steps will help make your sentences more economical: (1) reduce predication; (2) when you have a choice between grammatical constructions, use the shorter form; (3) choose direct phrasing instead of circumlocution; and (4) prune the deadwood.

You can reduce predication by combining and embedding.

The snow covered the countryside. It lay like a blanket.

The snow, which lay like a blanket, covered the countryside.

Lying like a blanket, the snow covered the countryside.

The snow covered the countryside like a blanket.

The snow blanketed the countryside.

The first three versions contain two predications (two verb phrases); the last two contain one. Which is most appropriate would have to be decided in context. Solely from the point of view of economy, the last two versions are better.

You often have the choice between long and short grammatical constructions:

The man [whom] I spoke to is my counselor.

He knew [that] the cause was lost.

Political success was limited to those [who were] skilled in public debate.

We are as much at fault as they [are].

Formal style may fill out the constructions; General prefers short forms.

In a series of parallel structures, deletions are often possible:

A light rain was called a bird sweat, a sprinkle was a shirttail shower, a heavy rain a frog-strangler. — Helen Bevington, *The House Was Quiet and the World Was Calm*

"Was called" in the first clause is reduced to "was" in the second and omitted altogether in the third without loss of clarity.

Both directness and economy are harmed by circumlocution, the use of several words where fewer would be just as clear. "I have the idea that" instead of "I believe," "in short supply" instead of "scarce," "destroyed by fire" instead of "burned" — these are typical circumlocutions. In context, there may be a sound reason for choosing the longer expression over the more direct one, but as a characteristic of style circumlocutions inevitably create pomposity or flabbiness or both. And they may hide, or at least veil, the central subject-verb-complement idea. In each of these pairs, the action statement comes through less clearly in the first version, with its circumlocution, than in the second:

The way psychologists measure ability is by the use of tests.
Psychologists use tests to measure ability.

As far as the purpose of the mission is concerned, there is no question that it was a success.
The mission succeeded.

The answer is in the affirmative.
Yes.

Circumlocution uses five words where two would do. A related kind of wordiness is caused by *deadwood—words and phrases that add nothing to the sense. The bracketed words in these sentences can be omitted with no loss at all in meaning and with a gain in economy:

All thinking persons [these days would] probably agree [with the conception] that the world has gone mad.

Anyone familiar with violin-making knows that the better the wood is seasoned, the better [the result will be as far as] the tone [of the instrument is concerned].

In [the course of] an hour we reached [the spot where] the red flag [was situated].

Deadwood is particularly annoying when it is redundant, as when *size* is added to a word that can only mean size—*large in size*—or when an unnecessary adverb doubles the meaning of a verb—*continue on, repeat again, return back*. And it is especially wasteful when it takes the emphasis from more important words. Giving a sentence an empty introduction ("It seems to me that . . ." or "What I would like to say is that . . .") means losing the chance to make a firm assertion.

Pruning deadwood is part of the job of revising sentences. And it is not an easy one. We hear and read so much deadwood every day that we find ourselves using the meaningless phrases automatically. Obviously no one uses deadwood deliberately or recognizes it as he sets it down on paper. To eliminate it, test the words and phrases in your early drafts by asking what they contribute. If they can be omitted without loss or change of meaning, they probably should be. Occasionally, for rhythm or pace or emphasis, you may want to keep a locution that is not necessary to your meaning, but as a rule you will find that getting rid of deadwood results in stronger, cleaner prose.

Though writing can be made so compact that it is hard to follow, more writers need to work for economical expression than for the reverse. Length in an essay should come from working out ideas, not from piling up words. The right kind of economy results from using no more words than you need to say what you want to say in the way you want to say it.

EXERCISES

1. Rewrite each of these passages according to the instructions.

a. In college an exposure to many views of government, morality, and society is beneficial not only because weaknesses can be detected but also because strong points might also be discovered that can be borrowed and incorporated into the American way of life. (Begin the sentence with "College students" and turn passive verbs into active ones.)

b. A good indication that man is still a brute at heart is to be found in the fact that there is an endless stream of books and articles on manners and etiquette, in all of which the purpose is to urge on us the desirability of introducing into our lives some of the amenities of gracious living. (Condense and make the phrasing more direct.)

c. The central character is admirable; he is conscientious, he is marvelously sensitive and humane, and he is thoughtful to his associates. (Make the sentence more emphatic.)

d. The findings of the report of the Center for the Study of Responsive Law, one of the organizations set up by Mr. Nader, bear out in general the conclusions of a number of other authoritative studies of the quality of medical care published in the last few years. — Selig Greenberg, *Providence Sunday Journal*, Feb. 14, 1971 (Reduce the number of prepositional phrases.)

e. Thus the crowds that surged into the Marignan and Francais [theatres] on that fateful night anticipated Martine Carol's superspectacle in much the same mood of voluntary debasement exuded by the New York opinion-makers when they trotted off to see Liz Taylor in *Cleopatra* at those two disastrous screenings in the Summer of 1963, a few months actually before the relatively uncut, unmutilated *Lola Montes* made its New York debut at the first New York Film Festival at Lincoln Center, at which time I created a critical scandal of my own by calling *Lola* "the greatest film of all time," just like that, with no ifs, ands, or buts, but I am getting ahead of myself. — Andrew Sarris, *December*, Vol. 12, 1970 (Decide what the author's main point is, and rewrite the passage so that the point receives proper emphasis.)

f. In our discussion we will be enabled by a typical quotation from each of the authors to increase our understanding of an actual LSD experience. (Turn into the active voice.)

g. More completely adapted for life in the trees than are the other anthropoids, the gibbons move through the trees with great facility, swinging by their elongated arms and getting tremendous momentum by releasing their holds at the most advantageous instant. Leaps of 30 and 40 feet from branch to branch are easily accomplished in this way. On rare visits to the ground they walk upright and even run, sometimes with surprisingly good speed. The same method is used in walking along lofty branches. — Lee S. Crandall, *A Zoo Man's Notebook* (Turn the passive verbs into active verbs, and explain why you think the changes do or do not improve the style.)

2.   Rewrite this paragraph — the first of a student's essay — to make it a more economical and more effective beginning.

When I look back at high school, and particularly at the one I attended, I can see that high school guidance counselors play a crucial role in shaping a person's life. In the ninth grade a student has to choose one of two alternatives — either he will go to college after graduation or go to work. The decision he makes will affect him for the rest of his life. This decision is influenced mainly by his family's interests. Some families, especially those in the middle and upper classes, emphasize the necessity of going to college, while other families do not. But the family is not the only institution that has a strong influence over the student's decision. I have noticed that high school guidance departments exert at least as much influence as the family does. One of the purposes of these departments is to help students make this important choice. Often, however, in doing this, counselors unwittingly do more harm than good. The guidance counselors I knew were extremely uninformed and careless. Some of the mistakes they made had exceedingly far-reaching effects.

3.   Examine the passage below and try to decide what makes it difficult to understand. Is the fault in the sentence structure or in the choice of words? Rewrite to make the passage as clear and direct as you can.

Out of the interstimulation of conversation there emerges an interweaving of understanding and purpose leading to coindividual behavior. Of course the conversation may be divisive, as well as integrating. But even these divisions may be regarded as mere differentiations within the general synthesis of human behavior. Thus in conversation is found that mutual understanding and common purpose essential to effective and continuous cooperation.

Chapter Twelve

DICTION

Much of the craft of writing comes in choosing words that *in context* will mean to your reader exactly what you intend them to mean. The groundwork for our treatment of words in context was laid in Chapter One, with our discussion of the varieties of English and of the need for fitting language to the rhetorical situation. We turn now to the question of how to find words and how to choose among them. Because the *Index* treats scores of specific problems of word choice, our discussion here can be brief and general. Though we may at times seem to treat words in isolation, keep in mind that the most important qualities and powers of a word come alive only in context—the immediate context of the sentence, the larger context of the essay, and the still larger context of the rhetorical situation.

We begin with the assumption that a writer of exposition and argument wants to express his ideas as clearly and direct-ly as he can. There may be times when he will veil his real intention, times when he will write obliquely or with calcu-lated ambiguity—not to confuse the reader or to deceive him but to circumvent his prejudices, perhaps, or to respect his sensitivities. These are special situations which call for spe-cial measures, and they make the problem of choosing the right words extremely complicated. It is complicated enough when a writer is simply trying to communicate his ideas and feelings directly. Even then he must work hard to make sure that the words he uses communicate his meaning rather than obstruct it.

Some of your problems in selecting words stem from the difference between your recognition vocabulary, the words you understand when you read or hear them, and your active vocabulary, the words you speak and write with confidence and assurance. When a word is in your recognition vocabulary but not in your active vocabulary, it may come out sounding inept, off-key, not quite right—"the dominating cause," for instance, instead of "the dominant cause." Or it may come out sounding quite wrong—"his dominant parents" instead of "his domineering parents," or "part of her mysticism" when you intend "part of her mystique." To increase your control over these borderline words—to keep words moving from your recognition vocabulary into your active vocabulary—listen, read (and read and read), and get into the habit of using dictionaries. Own a good dictionary, and open it often.

USING DICTIONARIES

There is no such thing as *the* dictionary, one that can be quoted to settle every question about words. But there is a real difference between a dictionary that is newly compiled or kept up to date by experts working with a recent accumulation of recorded uses of words and a dictionary that is patched together from older word books. The following dictionaries, appropriate for the personal libraries of college students, are listed alphabetically: *American College Dictionary*, revised edition (Random); *American Heritage Dictionary of the English Language* (Houghton); *Funk & Wagnalls Standard College Dictionary*, text edition (Harcourt); *Random House Dictionary of the English Language*, college edition (Random); *Webster's New World Dictionary of the American Language*, second college edition (World); *Webster's Seventh New Collegiate Dictionary* (Merriam).

Entries

To make good use of your dictionary, you should first read the introductory material. Lexicographers—dictionary makers—have to resort to space-saving devices wherever possible. The shortcuts they have used, as well as their general purposes and policies, will be explained in the front matter. Here, too, you will probably find instructions for using the dictionary.

After you have read the introductory sections and acquainted yourself with the arrangement of material, read a page or two consecutively; look up a few words that you know and a few that are new to you to see how they are handled. Try pronouncing some words, familiar and unfamiliar ones, to see how the pronunciation key works. Examine a few entries in detail to see what information they give. The main features of a typical dictionary entry are these:

Spelling and Division of Words.   A word is entered in a dictionary under its most common spelling. When more than one spelling is given, both are in good use: *esthetic, aesthetic; judgment, judgement;* but often the first is preferred or more current. The entry shows where a word should be hyphenated at the end of a line, as in *mor ti fi ca tion, dis par ag ing ly.* It also shows whether the editors have found a compound word most often as two words, as one word, or with a hyphen.

> **gar·rote** (gərōt′, -rŏt′), *n., v.,* **-roted, -roting.** **—*n.*** **1.** a Spanish mode of capital punishment, orig. by means of an instrument causing death by strangulation, later by one injuring the spinal column at the base of the brain. **2.** the instrument used. **3.** strangulation or throttling, esp. for the purpose of robbery. **—*v.t.*** **4.** to execute by the garrote. **5.** to throttle, esp. for the purpose of robbery. Also, **garote, garotte, gar·rotte′.** [t. Sp.: orig. a stick (formerly used in drawing cord tight), t. Pr.: m. *garrot* cudgel, stick for tightening the cord about a pack, der. Celtic *garra* leg] **—gar·rot′er,** *n.*

From *American College Dictionary.* © 1965 by Random House, Inc.

Pronunciation.   Dictionaries respell words in specially marked letters to show their pronunciation. The sounds represented by the symbols are usually indicated at the bottom of the page and are further explained in a discussion of pronunciation in the front matter. If more than one pronunciation is given without qualification, each is acceptable.

> **bo·vine** (bō′vīn, -vin, -vēn), *adj.* **1.** of the ox family, *Bovidae.* **2.** oxlike. **3.** stolid; dull. **—*n.*** **4.** a bovine animal. [< LL *bovīn(us)* of, pertaining to oxen or cows = L *bov-* (s. of *bōs* ox) + *-īnus* -INE¹] **—bo′vine·ly,** *adv.* **—bo·vin·i·ty** (bō vin′i tē), *n.*

From *The Random House Dictionary of the English Language,* College Edition. © 1968 by Random House, Inc.

Linguistic Information.   A dictionary entry indicates the part or parts of speech a word is generally used in, the transitive or intransitive use of a verb, the principal parts of irregular verbs, plurals of irregular nouns, and any other distinctive form a word may assume. An entry may also give the history of the word—its etymology. Sometimes this is merely a statement of the language from which the word came into English; sometimes it traces a chain of sources and changes in form, as here:

> **sil·ly** \'sil-ē\ *adj* [ME *sely, silly* happy, innocent, pitiable, feeble, fr. (assumed) OE *sǣlig,* fr. OE *sǣl* happiness; akin to OHG *sālig* happy, L *solari* to console, Gk *hilaros* cheerful] **1** *archaic* : HELP-LESS, WEAK **2 a** : RUSTIC, PLAIN **b** *obs* : lowly in station : HUMBLE **3 a** : weak in intellect : FOOLISH **b** : contrary to reason : ABSURD **c** : TRIFLING, FRIVOLOUS **syn** see SIMPLE — **silly** *n or adv*

By permission. From *Webster's Seventh New Collegiate Dictionary.* © 1971 by G. & C. Merriam Co., Publishers of the Merriam-Webster Dictionaries.

Definitions.   The definitions of words take up the bulk of space in a dictionary. When you check an entry to find out what a word means or to sharpen your understanding of a word that is only in your recognition vocabulary, keep three points in mind. First, a dictionary does not require or forbid a particular sense of a word but records the uses that have been found for it. It reports facts about words, including perhaps the fact that a word is acquiring a new sense or altering its customary one. Second, the words of the definition are not the meaning of the word being defined; they, together with any examples or illustrations, are to help you understand what, in the world of objects or ideas, the word refers to—its denotation. Words "have" meanings only as they are used in particular statements. As recorded in a dictionary or considered in isolation, they have only potential meanings—senses in which they may be used in actual contexts. Third, as we shall see later, a dictionary definition can scarcely hint at the associations or overtones a word has—its connotations. Since it is just these overtones that can make a word strikingly appropriate in one context but disastrous in another, it is unwise to use a word solely on the basis of what you have learned about it from a dictionary. You should have heard it or read it in various contexts and so know it in part through experience.

The order in which dictionaries offer definitions of a word may be either oldest meaning first or oldest meaning last. In a third form of entry, the "kernel" meaning of the word comes first. The front matter of your dictionary will tell you which order is followed in the entries.

> **style** (stīl) *n.* **1.** The way in which something is said or done, as distinguished from its substance. **2.** The combination of distinctive features of literary or artistic expression, execution, or performance characterizing a particular person, people, school, or era. **3.** Sort; kind; type: *a style of furniture.* **4.** A quality of imagination and individuality expressed in one's actions and tastes. **5. a.** A comfortable and elegant mode of existence: *living in style.* **b.** A particular mode of living: *the style of a gentleman.* **6. a.** The fashion of the moment, especially of dress; vogue: *out of* (or *in*) *style.* **b.** A particular fashion. **7.** A customary manner of presenting printed material, including usage, punctuation, spelling, typography, and arrangement. **8.** *Rare.* A name, title, or descriptive term. **9.** A slender, pointed writing instrument used by the ancients on wax tablets. **10.** An implement used for etching or engraving. **11.** The needle of a phonograph. **12.** The gnomon of a sundial. **13.** *Botany.* The usually slender part of a pistil, rising from the ovary and tipped by the stigma. **14.** *Zoology.* Any slender, tubular, or bristlelike process. **15.** *Obsolete.* A pen. **16.** A surgical probing instrument; stylet. —See Synonyms at **fashion.** —*tr.v.* **styled, styling, styles. 1.** To call or name; designate: *"whatever is mine, you may style, and think, yours"* (Sterne). **2.** To make consistent with rules of style. **3.** To design; give style to: *style hair.* [Middle English, from Old French, from Latin *stilus†,* writing instrument, style.] —**styl′er** *n.*

From *The American Heritage Dictionary of the English Language.* © 1969, 1970, 1971 by American Heritage Publishing Co., Inc.

Labels. Words that are unlabeled in a dictionary are assumed to belong to the general vocabulary; other words may be labeled *dialectal, obsolete, archaic, foreign, informal,* colloquial, slang, British, or United States or referred to some field of activity—medicine, law, astronomy, baseball, printing, electronics, philosophy. Subject labels indicate that a word is restricted to one field or has a special meaning in that field. Because labels can be only rough guides to usage, you have to supplement the advice they offer with your own judgment of the appropriateness of a word in a particular rhetorical situation. Many words that carry no label are rarely used (pursy, lucubration) and would mar most writing. You will sometimes find that the dictionary editors' point of view is rather cautious: many words marked Dial. or Colloq. fit perfectly well not only in Informal writing but also in General. The labels themselves are descriptive and are not intended to prohibit or even discourage the use of the words so labeled. Colloq., for example, simply means that the word is characteristic of ordinary conversation and of General rather than Formal writing; but some dictionaries have abandoned the label because readers persist in thinking it derogatory. Because dictionaries vary in the labels they use and in the amount of labeling they do, you may find it useful to consult several dictionaries when you are trying to determine the status of a word.

> **push·er** (pōosh′ər) n. **1.** One who or that which pushes; especially, an active, energetic person. **2.** Aeron. An airplane with the propeller in the rear of the wings. **3.** U.S. Slang One who illegally sells narcotics to addicts.

From Standard College Dictionary Copyright © 1968, © 1963, 1966 by Funk & Wagnalls. Reprinted with permission of the publisher.

Synonyms.   Most dictionaries gather words of similar senses into a group and show in what ways they are alike and in what ways different, as in the following:

> *SYN.* —**discuss** implies a talking about something in a deliberative fashion, with varying opinions offered constructively and, usually amicably, so as to settle an issue, decide on a course of action, etc.; **argue** implies the citing of reasons or evidence to support or refute an assertion, belief, proposition, etc.; **debate** implies a formal argument, usually on public questions, in contests between opposing groups; **dispute** implies argument in which there is a clash of opposing opinions, often presented in an angry or heated manner

From Webster's New World Dictionary of the American Language, Second College Edition. Copyright © 1970 by The World Publishing Company, Cleveland and New York.

Unabridged and Specialized Dictionaries

When you do detailed work with words and advanced reading in special fields, you will need to supplement your desk dictionary.

Unabridged Dictionaries.   The most complete dictionaries of present-day English are called unabridged, meaning that they are not selections from larger works as, in effect, many desk dictionaries are. Two important but dated unabridged dictionaries available in most libraries are the *Century Dictionary and Cyclopedia* and *Funk & Wagnalls New Standard Dictionary of the English Language*. *Webster's Third New International Dictionary of the English Language* was published in 1961 and the unabridged edition of the *Random House Dictionary of the English Language* in 1966.

Historical Dictionaries.   The *Oxford English Dictionary*, twelve volumes and a supplement, is the great storehouse of information about English words. It traces the various forms of each word and its various senses, with dates of their first recorded appearances and quotations from writers to illustrate each sense. The *Supplement* gives material on new words and evidence on earlier words not found in the original work.

The *Dictionary of American English*, four volumes on the same plan as the *OED*, is especially useful in reading American literature, for it gives the histories of words as they have been used in the United States. An entry begins with the first use of the word by an American writer and continues, with quotations, to 1900. The more recent *Dictionary of Americanisms* presents only those words and word meanings that have entered the language in this country.

Dialect Dictionaries.   Two standard dialect dictionaries are Joseph Wright's *English Dialect Dictionary*, which gives words in the various dialects of England, and Harold Wentworth's *American Dialect Dictionary*. Wentworth and Stuart Flexner compiled the *Dictionary of American Slang*. Eric Partridge's *Dictionary of Slang and Unconventional English* is a historical dictionary of English slang.

Dictionaries in Special Subjects.   For the vocabularies of special fields, you can find dictionaries in education, law, business, medicine, philosophy, psychology, sociology, economics, mathematics, and so on.

EXERCISES

1. Examine your dictionary and write out answers to these questions: What is the title, the date of original copyright (on the back of the title page), the date of the latest copyright? Who is the publisher? Do the editors state what they consider

the function of a dictionary to be? What supplementary sections are included at the beginning and at the end? Approximately how many entries are there? Is there a supplement of new words? Where are biographical and geographical names listed? Where is the key that explains the symbols used in giving pronunciations? When several definitions of a word are given, in what order do they appear—in historical order, in order of frequency, or in some other order? What labels does your dictionary use, and what does each label mean? Is profanity labeled?

2. Look up the following words to see what usage labels, if any, your dictionary applies. Then see what labels are applied by other desk dictionaries in the library. How do you account for differences?

bobby	dead set	honeymoon	pester
boss	dead pan	honky-tonk	snide
clepe	enthuse	hush puppy	turn on
clime	fain	nobby	whiz

3. Does your dictionary include synonyms and antonyms? If so, where in the entry are they placed? Does your dictionary discriminate among synonyms, explaining the differences between words that have similar meanings? Does it help you distinguish between *argue, dispute,* and *contend*? Does it help you decide in what situations you would use *done in, tired*, and *fatigued*?

4. Choose the word in parentheses which is most closely synonymous with the underlined word. Then test your answer by checking with your dictionary. Does it permit you to say with assurance that you have selected the right word?

a. The speaker's remark was entirely *apposite* (foolish, fitting, irrelevant, unintelligible, to the point).

b. The date of the ceremony was left *tentative* (indefinite, undecided, provisional, uncertain, contingent).

c. The well-dressed guest seemed strangely *diffident* (indifferent, shy, fearful, evasive, embarrassed).

d. Many causes have been suggested to explain the *deterioration* of moral standards in Roman society (degeneration, decadence, lowering, decline, decay).

e. The essay was badly written, but it was *sincere* (candid, simple, honest, guileless, frank, plain).

f. The affairs of the nation have now reached a *crucial* stage (dangerous, decisive, critical, ticklish, difficult, delicate).

5. Would your dictionary help a writer who was trying to make a choice between each pair of words in parentheses?

He had the (temerity, timidity) to suggest that he alone could solve the (issue, problem). As it turned out, his solution was (ingenious, ingenuous) but showed no (perceptive, perceptible) difference from one that had (failed, faltered) last year. What he was counting on was the (affect, effect) of the special appeal he directed to the (new, novice) voters — the eighteen-year-olds.

Are the choices offered by these seven pairs all of the same kind? If not, how do they differ?

6. What is *sound* used to mean in each of the following sentences?

   a.   The sound came from next door.

   b.   Sound the horn.

   c.   That's a sound point.

   d.   She sounds unhappy.

   e.   Let's sound him out on your proposal.

   f.   He was sound asleep.

   g.   I don't like the sound of the doctor's latest report.

   h.   The surgeon picked up a sound and began probing.

   i.   The children got a sound scolding.

   j.   He sounds off on every subject under the sun.

   k.   The Sound rarely has ice in it.

7. Write at least six sentences using the word *dog* in different ways. Write six using *bug, run, horse,* or *cast*.

8. The linguist W. Nelson Francis has said, ". . . words do not have meanings; people have meanings for words." For an audience of junior-high students, support these assertions and explain what is meant by the convenient shorthand expression, "the meaning of a word."

9. Although *lucid* means "clear" in such contexts as "lucid instructions" and "a lucid speaker," we do not talk about "a lucid liquid" or "a lucid day." We say "humid day" but not "humid towel." Explain why a person who is not a native speaker could, or could not, avoid lapses like "lucid day" and "humid towel" by consulting a dictionary.

Your dictionary can keep you from using a "wrong" word — a word that doesn't convey your meaning. It can help you distinguish between look-alikes (*insidious, invidious; incredible, incredulous*) and sound-alikes (*write, right; born, borne; bridle, bridal*—see *Homonyms). It can give you some help in finding synonyms, which have such a large overlap of meaning that in at least one of their senses they are interchangeable in some contexts. But it cannot tell you all you need to know about choosing between words that are very similar in meaning.

Scarcely any words in the language duplicate each other to the extent of being interchangeable in all contexts. *Flush* (in the sense "turn red") and *blush* are very close and often can be substituted for each other, but the overlap of the two words is not complete. Though we say "He flushed with anger," we do not say "He blushed with anger." *Pail* and *bucket* are used in different parts of the country to refer to the same thing, but people who normally use *pail* find *bucket* old-fashioned.

The difference between each pair of words lies not in their denotation—they refer to the same thing in the nonlinguistic world—but in their connotation, in the associations they have for speakers and hearers, for writers and readers.

English is rich in words that carry slightly different nuances of meaning:

joke and *jest; average* and *mediocre; childish* and *childlike; flashy* and *striking*

obedient, dutiful, amenable, docile, yielding, compliant

old-fashioned, antiquated, passé, dated, out-of-date

What makes it difficult to discriminate among synonyms is that though the related words have a common core of meaning, they carry connotations that make it inappropriate to substitute one for another freely in all contexts. Though a dictionary may define *mediocre* as "average," *mediocre* is uniformly derogatory, not neutral, in its connotations. *Average* is sometimes derogatory, often neutral, sometimes favorable. So making the right choice between closely related words requires care and thought and information. A thesaurus may offer a dozen words with the same general denotation, but unless you know what their connotations are, you are not in sufficient control of the words to make a wise choice.

The context in which a word has been regularly used, the variety of usage to which it belongs, and the prevailing social attitude toward its referent and toward the people who generally use it (politicians, prizefighters, advertising men, teachers, children, seamen) — all contribute to its associations. And connotations change with changing attitudes. The associations of much slang and profanity have altered in recent years with their widening use by adults of high social and economic status and by respected publications. Historically, connotations change as their referents move up or down in social esteem: *Methodist* and *Quaker* started as words of dispraise but are now either simply denotative or approving. For the general public, *drugs* has acquired wholly new connotations in the last generation. And it goes without saying that the connotations of *drugs* differ from group to group.

Dictionaries give some attention to more or less permanent connotations of words, often indicating the publicly shared associations that differentiate, say, *house* and *home* and *residence*. But they cannot begin to suggest the full implications of many words. Consider what must be omitted in a compact standard definition of *brother, cancer, courage, cupidity, hurricane, ignorance, integration, justice, race, sex, sunshine, traitor, trust.* How do we respond to these words? For most of us, *brother, courage, justice, sunshine, trust* have favorable connotations. For most of us, *cancer, cupidity, hurricane, ignorance, traitor* have unfavorable connotations. But some of the words — *integration, race, sex* — may arouse very different responses in different people.

Words that are heavily connotative are sometimes referred to as emotive, evaluative, intentional, loaded, or slanted words. As these labels suggest, such words are often regarded with suspicion, and it is true that slanting — in headlines, advertisements, and political and social discussions — can range from inconsequential to deliberately deceptive and malicious. But connotation is rightly an element in our use of language; for we use words not only to give information about things but to express our attitudes toward them and our feelings about them and to influence the attitudes and feelings of others. It is natural for us to apply words that have favorable connotations to actions we honestly admire (*courageous*) and to apply words with unfavorable connotations to actions we deplore (*foolhardy*). To do so is irresponsible only if we assume that by giving a name to the action we have demonstrated that it is indeed courageous or foolhardy, or whatever. In any event, if we are to be persuasive, we need to cope with connotation, not to evade it by trying to find words that are as purely denotative as possible. To describe a family in desperate need, *penniless*, with its emotional connotations, may be a more responsible choice than the flatly factual *without funds*.

Words pick up associations not only from the way we regard their referents but from the contexts in which they are commonly used. As we saw in Chapter One, connotation provides much of the basis for classifying words as Standard and Nonstandard, as Formal, General, and Informal. The words *stasis* and *eschew* are so unfamiliar to most of us that we probably have only the faintest emotional response to them, but we do have a definite sense that they are Formal, and so we would find them out of place in casual contexts. Whenever you ignore the social side of connotation by using a Formal word where the rhetorical situation calls for a casual one, or the reverse, you distract your readers from what you are trying to say—amusing them, perhaps, or annoying them, but in any case creating a barrier to communication.

EXERCISES

1. Explain what these words have in common and how they differ: *slender, slim, thin, lean, skinny, scrawny, svelte.* Which of the words do you consider neutral? Compose sentences to show which you would use if you wanted to be complimentary and which you would use if you meant to be insulting. Do you think everyone would choose the same words you do to accomplish similar purposes?

2. Explain why the words in each pair are not interchangeable in all contexts: *fair, objective; polite, courteous; clamor, uproar; stubborn, obdurate.*

3. Make a list of pairs that have the same denotation but are not interchangeable. Example: *cow* and *mature female bovine animal.*

4. What connotations or associations does each of these words have for you: *soul, hippie, politics, bag, dropout, science?* Which of the connotations do you consider to be generally shared? Which are private associations of your own?

5. Select a current issue that has stirred up controversy. From your reading in newspapers and magazines, find two discussions of the issue—one in which words are (in your opinion) used irresponsibly, in a slanted fashion, and one in which words are used responsibly. Write a page or two comparing and contrasting the two passages. Consider the extent to which your judgment of the two discussions is influenced by your own attitude toward the issue.

6. Write three brief descriptive accounts—one of a person you have no strong feelings about, one of a person you distrust or dislike, one of a person you admire or love. In each, try to express your attitude without stating it explicitly.

7. Classify the following as abstract or concrete (see *Abstract and concrete words): *shoe, rage, honor, onion, motorcycle, symmetry, evil, mayor, tulip, flower.*

8. In each pair, identify the more specific word: *tulip, flower; machine, typewriter; migraine, feeling; cabin, building; onion, vegetable; rage, emotion; sandal, footwear; typewriter, my Olympia portable.*

 ## BARRIERS TO COMMUNICATION

No word, no type of word, is in itself good or bad, right or wrong. All kinds of words can be put to good use—abstract words, concrete words, general words, specific words, relatively neutral words, highly connotative words, Formal words, General words, Informal words. Whether a word actually is put to good use can be judged only in context, for good diction is diction appropriate to the rhetorical situation. But something can be said about ways of using words that are likely to weaken writing and handicap you in your attempts to communicate.

Pretentiousness

You throw up a barrier to communication when you try too hard—when you use language for display rather than to inform. Perhaps this means using five words where one would do (*prior to the time that* instead of *before*); perhaps it means choosing a Formal word where a General one is more suitable (*ameliorate* instead of *improve*); perhaps it means adopting the jargon of a subject when you are only partly in control of it.

Many of the words selected more to impress an audience than to express meaning are *big words—deem* for *think, attire* for *dress, domicile* for *house.* Though big words are often long, they need not be, and length alone does not make them objectionable. Long words are the only words for some things: *polynucleated* and *sphygmomanometer* have their place. Short or long, big words are words that do not fit, words that are too heavy for the subject or too pretentious for what the writer is saying.

Triteness

You throw up a barrier to communication by not trying hard enough—not working to find words that express your ideas and feelings. It is easy to slide into the ready-made expression, the phrase that is on everyone's lips. It takes less effort to use a trite expression, a cliché, than to find the words that are right for *you*.

A word or a combination of words is not *trite simply because it is familiar. Formulas like "Nice day" and "Excuse me" can be used again and again without attracting attention to themselves, and the names of things and acts and qualities do not wear out. Trite expressions fall in between: they have become formulas, but they continue to be used in contexts where substance is expected. "Father Time," "irony of fate," "crack of dawn," "view with alarm," "acid test," "tower of strength," and scores of similar expressions have been used so often that they have scarcely any meaning. Nor does a phrase have to be ancient and corny to be trite: thanks to the saturation made possible by the mass media, last year's vogue expressions can be as thoroughly depleted of substance as frayed quotations from Shakespeare or the Bible. *Confrontation* was so widely applied in the late 1960's that almost overnight it lost its power. There is often an inverse relation between the scope of a word—how widely it is applied—and its strength.

Though everyday *clichés may do no harm in conversation, though fancier ones are the staples of some ceremonial speeches, and though, for the partisan, slogans retain their power throughout endless repetitions, the frequent appearance of trite expressions in an essay that has been revised will convince the reader that the writer made no effort to find words that would express accurately what *he* thought. And if someone writes in all seriousness that "there are two sides to every question" or that "life is what you make it," there is reason to suspect that he is making no effort to think. Triteness is a matter not only of using worn-out words but of using worn-out ideas as well. When the word comes before the idea, the trite expression can lead to the trite thought. If you write in clichés, you will think in clichés. (See pp. 386–89.)

What is most troublesome about triteness is that often a writer is simply unaware that he is using stereotyped expressions. Possibly he has not read enough or listened carefully enough to know his imagery is stale; possibly to his eyes original ideas shine through the age-filmed diction. At any rate, the first step in replacing stock phrases and senile figures of speech is to recognize them for what they are. Compare these two descriptions:

A grey mist overhung Nature like a pall. The somber shroud wrapped in oblivion lifeless forms which had been so beautiful in their summer splendor. The branches of the trees, shorn of their green raiment, appeared like spectral fingers reaching up to the somber, low-hanging clouds. Stunted shrubs, less bold, groveled to the ground. Closer still to the earth huddled withered blades of grass, corpses of the gallant, green-clad knights of early May. The staunch little soldiers of spring and summer were no more; they had succumbed in the battle with wind and storm. Faded autumn leaves stirred restlessly with every puff of wind, but seemed unwilling to leave the protection of Mother Earth's embrace.

The oak trees on our street were honest and forthright. The bark was not just a grey skin but a solid dark coat. In the winter they stood heavy and black against the sky, while other trees threw up mere bundles of twigs. In the spring, they did not creep out in pale green mistiness, like the other trees; they waited until they were sure, and then they put out their leaves in great confident clots. When summer winds blew, the oaks never trembled. They surged mightily, sighing fiercely. And in the fall, their leaves felt like stiff wrapping paper, and their seeds, which were not of membrane and cotton but of wood, bounced smartly when they fell on the sidewalks, and popped loudly in the fires.

In the first passage the clichés — including much trite *personification — make the description both flat and pretentious. In the second the student has recorded his perceptions in images that are fresh and natural. He knows how to avoid triteness: to look squarely at what he is writing about and present it as *he* sees it.

Just as reporting what you see is one way to avoid triteness in descriptive writing, saying what you think and believe is the first step in freeing your expository and persuasive writing of clichés. A good deal can be accomplished by simply rejecting combinations that come to mind automatically: "godless communism," "capitalist imperialism," "male chauvinism," "the weaker sex." Often the phrase that comes to mind without active thought performs no function in the context; the "godlessness" of communism may have no relevance to the thought in the passage. But even if you want to express the idea the stock phrase stands for, you will do better to reword it so that, in fresher form, it can make some impression on your reader.

Jargon

You throw up a barrier to communication when you hide your meaning in jargon — language that combines the pretentiousness of big words and the deadliness of cliché with an unreal quality all its own:

One of the prominent factors in marital discord is economic.

This sentence is so pompous that it positively struts. If the writer stopped to ask himself what he really had to say, he might come up with "Many husbands and wives fight over money" — a sentence that gives a recognizable picture of people in action.

Abstract terms are essential in all kinds of writing, and language that is predominantly abstract is capable of great precision. But it is annoying when it is substituted unnecessarily for concrete expression, and it can cripple communication by forcing the reader to guess at the meaning. The literature of the social sciences often suffers from a lack of clarity because of its fondness for impersonal constructions ("It is generally agreed that . . .") and for abstract and general terms that deny the reader images of human activity:

Conflict within and between groups in a society can prevent accommodation and habitual relations from progressively impoverishing creativity.

Here is another example of jargon, followed by a "translation":

It has been observed that the offspring of familial units in the lower economic brackets demonstrate a frequent tendency to sublimate status-anxiety by means of organized aggression against societal mores, such aggression taking the form of vandalistic assaults upon institutional properties.

. . . the children of poor parents often try to smother their sense of inferiority by throwing rocks at the schoolroom windows. — Robert Gordon, AAUP *Bulletin*, Spring 1957

The original passage creates no images at all; it is only when the abstract terms are replaced by concrete ones and the general terms are made more specific that we can "see" what the writer is talking about. Notice that one abstraction remains, and properly so: the concept of insecurity. Yet here, too, there is improvement in the change from jargon — "status-anxiety" — to the normal English of "sense of inferiority."

Just as the use of cliché expressions can lead to cliché ideas, so the application of laboratory jargon to human affairs can lead to a kind of thinking that ignores people. The children of poor parents just about disappear in "the offspring of familial units in the lower economic brackets." Many other collectives hide the particulars they stand for. *Capital* usually means employers and investors collectively, and *labor* stands for working men and women; but the terms are more likely to suggest impersonal forces than actual people. *Personnel* may conceal the notion of living beings ("Excess personnel will be reduced") and so lead us to write, and perhaps think, as if we were dealing with inorganic matter.

Like clichés, jargon is hard to avoid; all of us are exposed to it constantly. Daily, on radio and television, in newspapers and magazines, we hear and read the big, pretentious words of politics and economics, the arts and sciences, the professions and the academic disciplines. During the Vietnam War, politics and the military combined to produce a whole lexicon of *vogue words that, in their applications, were variously pretentious, euphemistic, evasive, and opaque—words like *infrastructure, incursion, interdiction, defoliation, ordnance delivery*, and *protective reaction*. In every college classroom words are regularly used for which simpler, more direct, more concrete substitutes could be found.

But finding the right substitute is not always a workable solution. In reading over what you have written, you are likely to find some big words you can't translate. They sound right in the context; you have a general notion of what they mean; you think most readers will understand what you intend. But in fact you don't know exactly what you are saying. The honest thing to do in such a situation is to ask yourself, "What am I talking about, and what do I want to say?" Then, using words you can control, say it as clearly as you can, no matter how many simple ordinary words it takes. (See *Psychologese.)

Bureaucratic jargon is not alone to blame for breakdowns in communication. "Poor parents" is a marvel of clarity compared with "familial units in the lower economic brackets"; but in some contexts *poor* needs further specification. If it means not having enough money to buy what you want, then the man who can't afford a new yacht this year and the man who can't afford a cup of coffee are both poor. And the frustrated yachtsman may even think of himself as poor. The fact is that the word *poor* categorizes different things to different people. So while it may be the right word in a particular context, you may still need examples or specifying details to pin down its meaning there. Often the best way to achieve precision is not to replace a word but to make clear what facts or characteristics or qualities it stands for. No amount of tinkering with words can substitute for searching out the sensory details of your subject.

EXERCISE

Rewrite each of the following sentences to make it clearer and more direct. This may mean reducing nominalization (see pp. 343–44) as well as making the expression more concrete.

a. Among the many alterations in life-style that require adjustment on the part of the freshman the most important are environmental changes, which range from a lessening of restrictions in socializing to greatly extended opportunities for intellectual development.

b. The artificiality of the collective conscience has so dehumanized society that nobody has guilt feelings about the difference between his conduct and the principles he professes allegiance to.

c. Governmental mandatory regulation of wages and prices cannot be implemented without consequent disaffection of powerful voting interests.

d. The cost reduction campaign was the most prominent factor in the decision not to augment the work force.

Euphemism and Overkill

You throw up a barrier to communication when you use words to hide the truth—either pale euphemisms chosen to disguise injustice and brutality and stupidity, or invective intended to insult or incite without regard for fairness or reason.

*Euphemism substitutes a milder, less disturbing word for one that is direct and explicit—the *departed* for the *corpse*. The substitute is usually less precise, more neutral in connotation, perhaps less harsh in sound than the term it displaces. Many euphemisms have their origin in prudishness, as substitutes for the vigorous monosyllabic names of physical functions: *perspire* for *sweat*, *expectorate* for *spit*, *odor* for *stink* and *smell*, and so on. Others originate in a desire to gloss over social situations or facts of life that might be regarded as distressing. Old people are *senior citizens;* the mad are *mentally ill;* those out of work are the *unemployed;* the poor and oppressed are the *underprivileged*, the *culturally deprived* or *disadvantaged*. Some of these terms are now so firmly established in current usage that you will find it natural to incorporate them in your writing, but you should never lose sight of the reality behind the label. *Liquidate, neutralize*, and *pacify* have all been used as euphemisms for *kill*.

Euphemism, like the language it supplants, is a relative matter: whether a word sounds genteel or neutral or blunt depends on the ear that hears it. And people differ in their attitudes toward specific euphemisms. Though *senior citizens* is widely deplored by those who are not so labeled, many old people prefer it to *old people*. Deciding whether to use or to avoid euphemism therefore calls for attention to the rhetorical situation. In everyday life the motive for euphemism is usually tact or consideration for the feelings of others. Euphemism is also used in public situations (sometimes justifiably, sometimes not) to dilute the audience's emotional response to a potentially explosive situation—as when a riot is reported as a "disturbance." But it can backfire. Many people prefer *slum* or *ghetto* to the euphemistic *undesirable neighborhood*, especially if they think the euphemism is being used to mask an ugly reality. So there are two sides to the relation between euphemism and good taste: even a well-intentioned attempt to avoid giving offense can itself be offensive.

Because a responsible writer faces facts, he does not seek out euphemism in a deliberate attempt to hide the truth. Neither does he bludgeon his audience by verbal overkill, language that exaggerates where euphemism minimizes. The usual motive for overkill is to blind the audience to all but the emotional aspects of an issue. The recent tendency to verbal violence, which made those in authority (at the precinct house, on the campus, in Washington) "racist murderers" and worse, and which turned critics of those in authority into "radicals," "subversives," "revolutionists," "anarchists," and so on, was probably more damaging to reason, to the language, and to human relations than the genteel Victorian substitution of *limb* for *leg*. Besides being irrational, verbal violence, including the use of obscenities, is surprisingly ineffective—in writing if not in oratory, chants, and shouts. An overkill expression quickly becomes a cliché and, like every cliché, loses most of its original force.

Finally, you throw up a barrier to communication when you unthinkingly adopt a radically wrong tone, drifting into a loose, casual style when the occasion calls for some formality, or adopting the language of the lecture platform when your audience needs friendly persuasion. Though deliberate shifts from one style to another can be brilliantly effective when they match shifts in idea, blundering between styles will lose you the confidence of your reader. See pp. 24–25.

Word choice poses a dilemma. If you use words in just the way everyone is accustomed to seeing and hearing them used, you will sound like an echo. Yet if you strain for original turns of phrase, you will sound affected or odd. So you need to look for ways of expressing yourself that fall somewhere between the thoroughly conventional and the thoroughly idiosyncratic. You must try to make familiar words take on freshness.

Giving words new life is partly a matter of perception, of how the writer sees what he sees, and partly a matter of controlling the context so that a word is freed from its routine associations. Metaphor, word play, and allusion can be used to make a new reading of experience, to reinforce or sharpen meaning, or simply to give the reader the pleasure that comes from finding words used in fresh and distinctive ways.

Metaphor

Many words which originally had narrowly restricted meanings have greatly extended their reference through figurative use. *Head* still has its old literal denotation as part of the body, but it is also applied to the top or principal part of a wide variety of things — of a screw, nail, pin, bay, news story, stalk of grain, hammer, bed, golf club, beer, boil, barrel — not to mention parts of a number of machines, the leaders in all sorts of institutions and governments and movements, the users of addictive or nonaddictive drugs, and a ship's toilet. *Head* for the head of a nail has become one of the senses of *head*: there is no other word for it, and it is one of the regular definitions listed in dictionaries. The language is full of such petrified, or dead, figures of speech.

A live figure represents a fresh extension of a word to a new referent — calling a novel a blowfish, for instance, or comparing freshmen to puppies (as on p. 375). Traditionally, figures have been classified on the basis of how the transfer of meaning is made (see the definitions and illustrations in *Figures of speech). But since a writer is less interested in naming figures than in making them work, we will here use the term *metaphor* for any transfer of meaning, any nonliteral use of words.

Functions of Metaphor. Metaphor can be used to please or to persuade or to explain; it is also a way of learning new things. The simplest of its functions is to enliven style. Because most figures create images, they naturally make expression concrete and specific. "His anger flared" is more imagistic, more vivid, than "He became angry." Because it can relate an abstraction to the physical universe, metaphor may make a difficult concept easier to understand, as here:

Marshall McLuhan posits that Western civilization has entered, or is about to enter, an era of electro-magnetic technology. This technology will radically alter the milieu of human perception, the reality-coordinates within which we apprehend and order sense data. Experience will not present itself serially, in atomized or linear patterns of causal sequence, but in "fields" or simultaneous interaction. To offer a very crude analogy (and the process of analogy may itself be a vestige of an earlier logic), our categories of immediate perception will shift from those at work in an Ingres drawing to those we experience in a Jackson Pollock. — George Steiner, *Language and Silence*

Or metaphor may be made to do all the work of explaining a concept or process. In the passage below, the process of trying to recall or invent a word is described wholly in figurative language; the validity of the figures is demonstrated by the example that follows them:

The chooser or inventor of a word must grope his way in the organon of language exactly as a composer in search of an apt musical phrase gropes his way in the organon of music. There are no clearly formulated rules; success is determined by fitness.

Fishing in the subconscious, when we are coining or choosing, brings to light the wayward associations that attach themselves like lily pads and old shoes to the hook, along with an occasional catch. Dr. Willis Whitney of the General Research Laboratory wrote of trying to recapture the name of Senator Kilgore. Before laying it by the heels, he had dredged up the German *Blutgut*, the Latinized *Carney*, and the Anglicized *Gormley*. — Dwight L. Bolinger, *American Scholar*, Summer 1953

Metaphor can become the means of investigating a subject. Analogies to natural objects or processes are often used to trace movements or to analyze intangibles. Following out the implications of a metaphor — discussing the origins of revolution in terms of seeds, nodes, zygotes, for instance — may bring new insights into the subject. If using clichés can lead to thinking trite thoughts, using original metaphors can lead to making intellectual discoveries. A metaphor that is a tool of investigation may be prolonged through an entire essay. The following passage outlines an analogy that is to provide the basis for the author's subsequent discussion:

There are, as I see it, three stages in the development of art. Let us pause to examine them a little more closely. I should call them first, the self-enclosed or infantile stage, the stage of self-identification; second, the social or adolescent stage, when exhibitionism passes into communication, with an effort not merely to attract attention but to create something worthy of approval; and finally, a personal or mature stage, when art, transcending the immediate needs of the person or the community, becomes capable of begetting fresh forms of life. . . . — Lewis Mumford, *Art and Technics*

Metaphor is a way of expressing what would otherwise be inexpressible — not only subjective feelings but ideas and concepts. The wave theory of light in physics and the concept of the watershed in the history of ideas — these represent not only ways of talking about a subject or ways of investigating it but ways of knowing it. Good metaphors open doors to perception and understanding.

Controlling Metaphor.   Though a good metaphor is a joy to both writer and reader, plain, literal language is preferable to figures that are stale, inconsistent, or incongruous. The figures you use should represent *your* way of perceiving your subject. If a borrowed figure fits the context, it is usually so general and time-worn that it contributes little. Now and then General writing can use effectively the homely similes of everyday life — "fresh as a daisy," "clean as a hound's tooth," "cold as ice" — but only now and then. The effectiveness of metaphor lies in its power to evoke images and emotions, to make the reader experience and not just apprehend. And a stale or trite figure simple doesn't stir the reader's imagination.

Even less evocative (and much more conspicuous) than commonplace similes are pseudo-literary clichés. Clouds that sail like graceful galleons, waves that charge like white-maned steeds, trees that stand like gaunt sentinels — these images come from the pages of books, not from direct observation of clouds, waves, and trees. Galleons, white-maned horses, and sentinels are no longer part of our experience.

The risks in using metaphor are greatest when you are working too hard at enlivening your prose. If the figure is not integral to your way of thinking about your subject, you may lose control of it and produce a mixed metaphor. Probably the most common variety results from the meeting of two figurative expressions that have lost most of their metaphorical power. In one context a worn-out figure may remain decently embalmed:

The voters made it clear they didn't want to switch horses in midstream.

In another it will show just enough life to clash with a similarly enfeebled neighbor:

If we switch horses in the middle of the stream, we'll find ourselves out on a limb.

"Her face froze into a mask of indifference" is conventionally trite. When fire is joined with the ice, the effect in ordinary prose is ludicrous:

Once seated, her face froze into a mask of smoldering irritability as photographers swarmed around the witness stand snapping pictures. —*Chicago Sun-Times*, Feb. 27, 1964

Other mixed metaphors result from a clash between live figures. Instead of elaborating a basic metaphor, the writer may move rapidly from one figure to another. Here simile and metaphor take turns:

Flashing their delightfully tawdry show tricks, they worked the Met as if it were a grind house in Liverpool. Roger Daltrey, a Greek god in chamois hip-huggers, pranced and shouted ecstatically, whirling a mike around his head like an aborigine's bull-roarer. Pete Townshend pogoed across the stage like Bugs Bunny riding an electric broom. Keith Moon, rock's greatest drummer, sat like an idiot prince bouncing a stick twenty feet into the air off a drumhead and catching it like a grandstanding center fielder. Only John Entwhistle, the Who's powerful bass player, contained himself, standing stalwartly in the stage-left shadows like a barrel-chested, bare-fisted pugilist. —Albert Goldman, *Freakshow*

Though some readers might feel that these figures follow one another too rapidly, they would probably recognize that the sense of frenetic busyness fits the scene being described. And they would also recognize that the writer has taken care not to let his figures mix. He keeps them separate. Trouble arises not from using several live metaphors in sequence but from picking up a second one before you have dropped the first. Here two metaphors that relate to the same referent are permitted to collide:

She was more sheepdog than chaperone, herding us onto the bus. When, at last, all her chicks were counted, she clucked contentedly.

And here, as the reader goes through the process of unpacking the thickly clustered metaphors, he is likely to raise questions about the relation between pastoral societies, boy scouts, and music boxes, between hospital lights and armored tanks:

The padded values and euphemisms of a more leisurely time have been ruthlessly stripped away under the hospital light of today's world; honesty, integrity, truthfulness, seem sentimental hangovers from a pastoral age, boy-scout ideals trying to cope with an armored tank of actuality that is crumpling the music-box values of the past like matchsticks. — Seymour Krim, *Views of a Nearsighted Cannoneer*

Readers vary in their sensitivity to mixed metaphors, just as they vary in their sensitivity to clichés. Some readers, though not all, would be troubled by the proximity of "flows" and "bleeding":

One day my writing just flows; the next day the page I grind out leaves me bruised and bleeding.

Some readers would find "grass-roots" and "roots" illogically combined:

We cannot think of organizing the grass-roots in America unless we sink our roots in it. — Paul Starr, in *The University Crisis Reader*, II

Some readers would be disturbed (or amused) by the combination of the literal with the figurative in the second sentence of this passage:

In areas of culture not regulated by law, such as music, haircuts, clothes, and, to some extent, life-styles, the students have swept all before them. Long hair, for example, has crossed all barriers. — Charles A. Reich, *The Greening of America*

To avoid slips like these, a writer has to be alert to all the meanings of a word. Behind every figure of speech, including petrified ones, is a literal referent, capable of making him look foolish. To keep the reader's attention where it belongs — on *what* he is saying — he must make sure the reader is not distracted by unintended images or meanings.

Figures should be appropriate. Both the degree and kind of figuration should be in keeping with the subject and the style. Since perception is such an individual matter and since words can always be turned to new uses, it is difficult to say flatly that any particular joining of literal and metaphorical meaning would be inappropriate. But on the face of it, some relationships are suspect: a snake and a lovable child, for instance, or a flash of lightning and the slow mastery of a skill, or reading and the behavior of a carnivorous animal. Metaphors like the following seem much too violent to suggest even voracious reading:

He sank his teeth into the throat of the book, shook it fiercely until it was subdued, then lapped up its blood, devoured its flesh, and crunched its bones.

The appropriateness of a figure depends in part on the rhetorical situation. The better you know your audience, the less likely you will be to stumble into an inappropriate metaphor. You need to be aware of all of the connotations of the term being used metaphorically. "Game plans," with connotations of sport, might be acceptable when used in connection with political campaigning but objectionable in the context of the nation's military or economic policy. During the Vietnam War the verb *zap* was just a word to most Americans—a funny word to some, including some comedians—but for others it had connotations of brutality that reflected on the speakers and writers who used it.

The problem of controlling the reader's response to metaphor is particularly acute when you are using irony. Though overstatement, understatement, and irony represent discrepancies between the situation and the language used to describe it, irony is less explicit than the other two and so requires more participation from the reader. If the writer cannot count on the rhetorical situation to make plain that his real meaning is the opposite of what it seems to be, he must plant clues so that the reader will not be misled. In this passage the effect of irony is safeguarded both by the rhetorical situation—the nature of the speaker—and by the language he uses—"impoliteness," "in good season," "fine":

A revolution is always distinguished by impoliteness, probably because the ruling class did not take the trouble in good season to teach the people fine manners.—Leon Trotsky, quoted in H. J. Muller, *The Uses of the Past*

Word Play

Occasionally it is fun to try experiments with words, either by making old words do new tricks or by inventing new words. The results are often disastrous—in fact usually so—but now and then an experiment is successful. The commonest form of word play is the pun: "Don't learn traffic laws by accident"; "A girl's best friend is her mutter." The temptation is sometimes irresistible:

Boston's Andrew Dexter got hold of a bank and its banknote plates, ran off bills for himself which he had his cashier sign after work and which he then sold. Getting hold of a second bank, he andrewdextrously fed each with the other. . . .—Louis Kronenberger, *Atlantic*, Jan. 1971

Word play is risky because the failures are conspicuous, but a full use of language calls for taking some chances.

You should, of course, make sure that what looks like

word play in your writing is, in fact, deliberate. The unconscious pun—obvious to the reader but not to the writer—usually results from a petrified figure unexpectedly taking on vitality. In this context, "outskirts" remains inert:

On the outskirts of the town was a fine antique shop where I found some hand-made wooden egg cups.

But here the figure comes alive, and the unconscious pun (outskirts—woman's dress) either irritates or amuses:

In some tribes of American Plains Indians, men who prefer to play women's roles have a respected place in the social structure. Instead of being cast to the outskirts of the group, they dress like women and do women's work.

Related to the unconscious pun is the unintentional use of words that sound very much alike and the unintentional use of the same word in different senses. Here, "indefinite" and "definite" trip over each other:

The indefinite pronoun *one* has a definite connotation of stiffness and formality.

And here "color" changes meaning:

America has traditionally welcomed people from all lands, regardless of race, creed, or color; many have retained their own folkways, lending variety and color to our national life.

You should be on the alert for slips like these when you revise your essays.

Allusion

Sometimes a writer adds interest or clarity or emphasis to what he is discussing by alluding, explicitly or subtly, to something extrinsic to the topic. A brief reference to literature, to history, to a public figure can contribute to the meaning and also have a distinct stylistic effect.

An allusion leaves the reader some work to do. Instead of referring to an event, the writer refers to the place where it occurred. Instead of quoting and acknowledging the source of his quotation, he refers to his source in an indirect way. Sometimes he incorporates phrases from a literary work, as in the following sentence, with its deliberate echoes of *Hamlet* and *Macbeth:*

There is nothing new in heaven or hell not dreamt of in our laboratories; and we should be amazed indeed if tomorrow and tomorrow and tomorrow failed to offer us something new to challenge our capacity for readjustment. —Carl L. Becker, *The Heavenly City of the Eighteenth Century Philosophers*

But a literary or historical allusion may be no more than a word or two (*summer soldier, honorable men*), a place name (*Hiroshima, Kent State, Gethsemane*), or a name (*Ahab, Dillinger, Canute*). By summoning up the context in which the phrase or name originally appeared, an allusion of this kind can add a new level of meaning to the discussion. This reference to Diogenes makes a very strong claim for the function of news analysts:

We are not in the business of winning popularity, and we are not in the entertainment business. It is not our job to please anyone except Diogenes. —Walter Cronkite, *Saturday Review*, Dec. 12, 1970

General English often draws its allusions from advertising slogans, popular songs, gag lines. A well-chosen topical allusion may convince the reader that the writer knows what's going on; but the topical allusion quickly becomes a cliché. On the other hand, the obscure, esoteric allusion may be taken as a sign of the show-off. Allusions, then, should be appropriate to the rhetorical situation, giving the reader the pleasure of recognition and at the same time adding richness to the idea.

Some allusions have made themselves so much at home in the language of every day that we no longer think of them as allusive; but recalling that what hangs over the head is the sword of Damocles can give a little more zest to both writing the phrase and reading it:

Drawing a daily comic strip is not unlike having an English theme hanging over your head every day for the rest of your life. —Charles M. Schulz, *Saturday Review*, April 12, 1969

EXERCISES

1. Make a list of things, experiences, and activities that interest, amuse, please, or annoy you. Then write a brief figurative passage that shows how you perceive each item in the list and (perhaps) how you feel about it. Sample list: walking, skiing, sunrises, beagles, birthday celebrations, word play, Chinese food.

2. Write a brief paper on religion, morality, justice, or some other abstraction. Single out one aspect of the subject to discuss, and organize your discussion at least partly in terms of a metaphor.

3. Examine each of these excerpts (those unidentified are by students) and explain why you do or do not find it an effective expression of the idea. Try your hand at rewriting the figurative passages that you consider weak, incongruous, overdone, or otherwise unsatisfactory.

a. This is a blowfish of a novel. It tries to swim the depths, only to puff itself up with false vanity and empty rhetoric, rising pathetically to the shallows to show itself off as the bloated creature it is. — *Newsweek*, Aug. 18, 1969

b. I loved the freshmen dearly, as one loves a docile child who takes all one's time and love. They were like puppies. They swirled and barked around me like the hellhounds of remorse. — Helen Bevington, *The House Was Quiet and the World Was Calm*

c. Last night I sang like an angel for three hours. You don't even hear yourself when it really gets going. Only the sensation of rushing vibration all through the head and chest everywhere. As if the body were a jet engine taking in air at supersonic speeds then filtering the air into melody. The pitch isn't heard; it's felt.

d. Away from the cities and their parroted chatter of Christmas, which would fail to fool any self-regarding child, the world rolls to the brink of the solstice, where life lives banked in burrows and the earth is a surface of storm tracks: wide miss, near miss, direct hit, and snowbound. — L. E. Sissman, *Atlantic*, Feb. 1971

e. Man at his best is a sort of caricature of himself, and even when we are eulogizing him for his finer attributes, there has to be a minor theme of depreciation, much as a vein of comedy weaves in and out of a great tragedy. — Richard M. Weaver, *The Ethics of Rhetoric*

f. The lurid, greenish glow of the streetlight showed a woman covered with blood. Thick, ropy blood oozed slowly from angry abrasions on the side of her head, and a stream of bright gore spouted like a geyser from a cut on the bridge of her nose.

g. The island, shielded from the throb of Kowloon by the harbor and Victoria Peak, is necklaced by a road that vistas down over fishing villages like Aberdeen, with its famed double-decker floating restaurants — sweet and sour upstairs, mahjong below decks — and shifting water carpets of sampans. — Carol Wright, *Providence Journal*, Jan. 10, 1971 *h.*   Children have a tendency to take adult pronouncements as true merely because they are uttered by a source cloaked with mysterious power.

i.   The noise, like an enthusiastic roar from a distant sports stadium, yet as insistent as the surge of distant surf, grew till it was galloping up the quadrangle in massive waves.

j.   Hemingway thought that as long as anything scares us away from seeing the truth, the emptiness of incomplete vision will cripple our ability to live.

k.   I oppose the plan for reorganizing the college because its sponsors have not given enough thought to the effects it will have. We are told by architects that form should follow function. We need to know what functions, what needs, what ends, what values we should be pursuing before we form new structures. We have too often erected buildings and created organizational structures without making a careful analysis of educational goals and ends. Once created, they tend to freeze existing value orientations and severely limit flexibility.

l.   In his first few years with the Bureau, he climbed right to the top of the pecking order. His colleagues, all busy in their own affluent ant hills, scarcely realized what was happening.

m.   The only opium available to him is that hallucinogenic agent the layman calls "memory"—a drug of the most awful and powerful properties, one that may ravish the psyche even while nurturing the soul. Stiff penalties should be affixed to its possession, for its dangerous components include disappointing inventories, blocked punts, lumpy batters, and iron buckets of burden. It is habit-forming, near-to-maddening in large doses, and may even grow hair on the palms.—Larry L. King, *Harper's*, April 1971

n.   The film studios want to have one foot in the door should home pay-TV become a reality tomorrow. It is a situation which puts the film people in a particularly awkward position. They let TV have their movies but at the same time they object when they find that most stations regard a movie as simply the thread on which to string as many profitable beads as possible. The more commercials, the more money. The movies and TV are, it seems, destined for a shotgun marriage—two spheres locked in combat, yet each realizing in the other the fattening of its pocketbook.

o.   The ultimatum was issued in the wake of a rash of outbreaks of violence.

p.   A beacon of hope has been lighted in our cradle of independence.

q.   To call out the National Guard at the first hint of trouble means inflicting a permanent wound on the fabric of our national life.

r.   The huge building—with its bigger-than-life statues of the lawgivers of history, its columns, friezes, bronze horses and monumental staircases—looks like the the puffy oratory of a prolix lawyer translated into stone.—Paul Hofmann, *New York Times,* May 10, 1970

s.   The semester break was so short that it was no more than a bite for a starving man.

t.   Most students seem to feel, as I did, that the selection of a major field of study is a miraculous phenomenon similar to falling in love. This expectation accounts for the feelings of guilt and anxiety that many of us experience when we realize we have made a wrong choice. It's like feeling unfaithful. In choosing a career it would be better to consider some fields more appropriate than others but no field supernaturally perfect.

u.   The rewriter is as one who packs his thought for a long journey. Having packed the garment, he does not merely straighten out the folds and close the paragraph. Instead, he unpacks completely and repacks again. And again; and again and again. Each time, he tucks just one more thought into this or that pocket. When he quits, there are more of them than of words. So many labors of love on a single sentence, that many rewards for the rereader. On the surface, one teasing half-reward; others at successively greater and greater depths, so that each reading finds one more. . . .
Conceivably those successive depths might be achieved in one writing; but more probably the genius is simply the man who can do the repacking inside his skull. In any case, there must be repacking with more ideas insinuated into the wording. The rewards will lie at successive depths only if they were packed into the text in successive repackings. That is simply the kind of wits we have.—Martin Joos, *The Five Clocks*

4.   Review the preceding passages. For each, try to decide whether the metaphors were used chiefly for vividness, or for greater clarity, or as the only way the writer could say what he wanted to say. Evaluate each figure, explaining why you think it is or is not successful.

Chapter Thirteen

STYLE: TWO ESSAYS

In the essays that make up this chapter, two professional writers discuss what style is and what makes a good style. Benjamin DeMott, a novelist and essayist, teaches English at Amherst College. Theodore Solotaroff is a critic and the editor of New American Review.

ON STYLE

By Benjamin DeMott

Best to be blunt: worrying about "style" in the usual ways is, for most writers, bad business. It weakens a person's grip on a tricky but unarguable truth, namely that style is a function of character: no changing the former without changing the latter. Worry about yourself, aim to be brainier, work for breadth and generosity of understanding, value the experience that seeks you out even when it's harsh or tormenting — do all this and you're in process of "improving your style." Worry about increasing your vocabulary or varying your sentence patterns, and you remain in the world of mechanics — a world it's possible to master without effect upon your style.

    The reason this is so is, of course, that fancy synonyms and sentence patterns come from the top of the head, whereas the shape and method of attack of a piece of writing — the primary influences on any reader's response, and the major constituents of a style—grow from the center of your being, are as much a part of you as your face. (Schopenhauer said style is "a safer index to character than a face.") Wise to keep this in mind when sitting around your room planning a line of argument for a paper in a course, deciding what ought to come first, what the middle will be, and where the thing is going to come out. Wise to keep in mind, that is, that just here, in the shape of the argument, is where you appear most strikingly in your writing. Your decisions at this point in the act of composition count for much more in the total impression than images, similes, metaphors, big vocabularies and most of the other items people have in mind when they rattle on about "style." For those decisions embody and display your habits of thought, your manner of assimilating your ideas with the available evidence and with the imaginable counter-propositions; they *are* the image your reader sees.

And the chance of faking the reader out, moreover, playacting a non-existent self, is, for a beginning writer, negligible. Going against your nature isn't easy when you're dealing with materials or points of view that don't comfortably fit your opinions, or when you're deciding whether to come on strong from the start, or to maintain a neutral stance at the beginning and through the middle and then ride in hard from the flanks in the final reel. The irreducible You invariably breaks through. If you are forceful in life when you mean to persuade someone to see a subject your way, your writing probably will come across as forceful—no way to hide. If you are the kind of person who rarely bothers to imagine other people's feelings or the inner surroundings of ideas held by those you disagree with, or by those whose social circumstances aren't like your own, then this obliviousness will stare straight up at the reader of your page. If you incline to the view that your ideas are necessarily superb because they are yours, this too will shout aloud in your writing. And while your reader or teacher may comment, in polite response to his glimpse of these features of your character, that the style is bad, he will sometimes wish he could tell you, without hurting you: Look, these sentences you've written are the sentences of a snob, a windbag, a braggart, or a bore.

For, to say it once more: style is man naked: your inward weight, height, coloring, timbre of mind, modes of self-deception are published on your page. Never think, then, of style as decor or as clothes or jewelry — costumes, beads vs. fringe, socks vs. no socks, wide ties vs. narrow, "figures of speech" vs. whatnot. Think of it as a force flowing directly from the central being, holding you together, making you what you are. And never think that good writers ever ask themselves, How'm I doing style-wise? The only serious question is, Am I being stupid or intelligent? And the power to keep that question blinking in the forehead at all times is the key human energy behind every good writer's good style.

Of course it's one thing to ask yourself, Am I being intelligent? — and another to answer the question correctly. And still another to know what to do if the answer is No. If men's ways of arguing vary according to their personal nature, and if a man's way of persuading does determine his style, and if the foundation of everything really is personal character, going hunting for troves of helpful advice about style would seem pointless. Right: it is pointless. A list of Methods of guarding against stupidity (i.e., bad style) that looks reasonable to one man usually looks perverse, obvious, superstitious, finicky or trivial to the next. There are, however, some means of helping yourself to stay in touch with your full human resources when you're writing, and knowing a little about them never hurt anybody. Character, after all, includes many selves, some lazier than others, some beautiful, some ugly. A piece of writing should project your best self. Toward that end:

1. Remember that writing is thinking. If, after a spell of writing, you find yourself coming out on this or that issue exactly where you were before you began to write, chances are that there's no motion of thought in your paper — just dullness, static, showing off, possibly too many quotations.

2. Remember that the statement that looked like your conclusion before you began writing probably should emerge, in the course of the work, as your premise or starting point. For again: if writing is thinking, how can I come out — after a spell of thinking — where I was before I began to think?

3. Eyes and ears alert always for the next sentence gestating in the sentence you're composing. Thought has to be allowed to drive itself along on its own firm energy, following its own inner signs. Sometimes the seed is a phrase inside a sentence, something that dictates an interruption, a qualification. Sometimes it's an idiom that can be turned or built on at the start of the next sentence. Sometimes the sentence creates an additive or subtractive situation (*and* or *but* must be the word to come). The sense of intelligent movement and pressure in writing often comes from permitting phrases or tones to couple inside the sentence and create the next sound — and notion — on their own.

4. Eyes alert always for *sequence*, clear links, tight cueing — the sense that every word, every phrase "follows hard upon." Here are three sentences from a book review:

This brief book is a work of art. If you like to have vicarious experience, this moving and lyrical book will turn you on. A very private, very delicate book, occasionally reminiscent of the movie "A Man and a Woman," it is told succinctly with great feeling.

Book-book-book, very-very—how the words thud on each other!—a feeling of being stuck in mud, rocking back and forth, no release . . . The author's name, the title of the work, a neat pronoun usage—any of these could help the writer out of this jam, and sustain the desired sense of forward motion. *Connect. Weave sentences tight.* Otherwise the mind looks sleepy.

5. Eyes alert always for the chance of registering several distinctions simultaneously. Developed intelligence perceives a great number of qualities at once. Slow minds lumber through a whole sentence to deposit—half-exhausted by the great weight they've lugged—one commonplace dinky adjective. Readers love the sensation of speed and strength. Look at the sentences quoted above—the book review. Why not one sentence reading as follows?—*Delicate, private, lyrical, moving, this little book is a work of art.* Why hide the peas in the potatoes?

6. Keep your self-respect, never grovel. Think your way to the probable top person in your audience and then ask yourself this question: If accident suddenly set me down before him as he was reading what I've just written, would I have to blush? The review twice quoted above begins with this sentence:

The dreamboat author of this book has a publishing pedigree a mile long.

The lady who wrote the sentence lives in California; the author she was reviewing lives in the East; the lady's piece made it plain that the author was known to her only through the dust-jacket photograph. Should she not have had sufficient self-respect to be skeptical about dust-jacket photographs? It's possible, to be sure, that she lacks self-respect, in which case we read her character in the sentence. But the odds are that there's a decent amount of skepticism in the lady's best self, and she's failed to keep it up to the mark. Avoid such failures. Examine what you write to make certain that your beamish side, the careless gullibility within you, hasn't taken command. Beamishness always offends.

7. Remember that intelligence is independent of received notions. It moves away from conventional wisdom and seeks a different understanding—more personal than Everyman's, more speculative, more surprising. Common thought regards the hen as the source and the egg as the product. Common thought holds that the White House in Washington, D.C., belongs to nobody in particular. Or to "the taxpayers." Yet the light of intelligence snapped on

when Samuel Butler remarked that a hen is an egg's way of producing another egg. And it's also burning nicely when President Kennedy begins (back in 1961) a talk about the Adams family papers with this personal greeting to a direct descendant of the family in his audience: "I want to say to Mr. Adams that it is a pleasure to live in your family's old house, and we hope that you will come by and see us." The idea is to turn common understandings ever so slightly, in order to freshen — or re-create — them as subjects for thought.

8. Stop frequently to restate, to yourself, your chief assertion, proposition, destination, conclusion, point or whatever. Ask yourself over and over again: *What am I asserting? How does what I'm saying in this paragraph bear on my major assertion of the essay as a whole?* "He who has nothing to assert," said Shaw, "has no style and can have none."

9. Never take up a position without first attempting to discover the worst that can be said about it. See around all your thoughts. No need to represent every idea doubtfully, tentatively, apologetically. Avoid self-laceration. But your manner should testify to your lively awareness that there's something to be said against any thesis, and that fools alone believe in self-evident propositions.

10. Come out somewhere. Force your best self to take a stand. Remember that intelligence sees around and sees around, watches itself and teases itself, but that it also accepts the obligation to hold firm finally — to render judgment, to establish the hierarchy. Your *tone* should say, on toward the end: "Well, the answer I'm coming up with has deficiencies — what has not? — but I've named them fairly for you, reader. And the alternative positions have worse deficiencies and fewer strengths, and while I believe in comparative evaluation and understand the conditioned nature of man, I nevertheless also know that choice is what lifts us above animal levels of life: here, then, is the best choice I can make."

Could other reminders and exhortations, other ways of prodding the best self into action, be cited? Certainly. Dozens. Perhaps hundreds. And one or another of them might become, for you, the perfect slogan, the catch phrase that would invariably stimulate you to press your mind to the fullest when engaged in the act of writing. There was a time, remember, when the bare word THINK on a sign struck somebody as an obeyable directive. And there surely is now, for someone holding this book in his hand, an instruction — whether about word order or the right way to use the dash or how to keep an ear out for repetitions or how to make the turn from the middle to the conclusion — an instruction that exactly fits the mind, gains mysterious moral dimensions, chimes with personal need. Advice about writing is like advice about serving in tennis or driving for distance. There are words to be said about throwing the ball up or about breaking your elbows on the backswing, but the words must coincide with an answerable feeling within the server: he has to be able to take the words into his system, to act with them, to make them his own flesh.

Which is to say: it's sensible to keep an ear and eye out for good talk about writing. You can't tell when or where the coaching word on style that precisely matches your character will be said. Some professionals lie awake, waiting for the whisper, the one sweet signal . . .

One more word: assessing intelligence and character is a messy operation. And being assessed can be a humiliating experience, even when the assessor is friendly and thinks your stuff is swell. A beginning writer should allow for the possibility that the person who tells him he has a bad style couldn't recognize a good one. He should also allow for the reverse possibility. And, most important, he should refuse to let himself be dragged down into thinking about writing in terms of academic grades. If I want a style, I must work for it with my mind, I must think in a more interesting, more complicated, more flexible, more surprising, more unrelenting way. I must be a more intelligent human being.

And that is a higher objective than A− or B+. You can achieve it only by thinking *aside*—thinking aside school, college, even career itself. Hold fast to Nietzsche's counsel: "To improve one's style means to improve one's thoughts and nothing else: he who does not admit this immediately will never be convinced of it." Accept the truth that working for a style is a labor of self-transformation and has a noble dimension (one great thinker called style "the ultimate morality of the mind"). See the good stylist for what he is: an idealist and an exemplar: a character whose radiance confirms our right to prize the mind.

WRITING, IMAGINATION, AND STYLE

By Theodore Solotaroff

A friend of mine who teaches English recently told me this story. Toward the end of an undergraduate survey course, he passed out a list of suggested topics for term papers. At the next meeting of the class, two of the students approached him and said that they had come up with a topic of their own — Romanticism and Rock — which they would like to work on together. Both requests were unusual, but my friend was an unusually receptive teacher and asked them what they had in mind. They stumbled around, trying to explain the relationships they would develop. "Well, like there's Wordsworth and Dylan and like they put it together the same way. . . ." As my friend said, "It was like listening to the dawn of language," but thinking of reading their term papers on one or another of the assigned topics, he told them to go ahead.

On the last day of the course, the teacher collected the assignments. After the others had left, the two students approached him.

"Where's your paper?" he asked.

"Right here," one of them said. From his pocket he brought out a reel of tape, while the other student produced a box of slides.

"What am I supposed to do with these?"

"Well, if you can give us an hour, we'll put it together for you."

So, off they went, my friend bitterly wondering what he had gotten himself into. Several hours later, he finally left the two students, having sat through their performance three times.

"It was amazing," he said. "The relationships they came up with. They'd read a passage from the 'Preface' to the *Lyrical Ballads*, then play some Dylan. Or move from De Quincey to the Doors. And with a very sharp commentary tying it together. At the same time, there were the photographs, blending in with the content of what was being said or sung. You know, '. . . Westminster Bridge' and shots of downtown Chicago at 6 a.m. The poetry and the graphics beautifully coordinated like a good experimental film. I couldn't stop listening to it. I kept learning things."

"What do you make of it?" I asked. "You said they could hardly express themselves when they first told you about the idea."

"Yes, that's just the point," my friend said. "Give them their own medium and they're articulate as hell. And they're not alone, believe me."

I begin with this story because it's been on my mind as I try to think of what I might say to you, knowing that you're not simply myself twenty years ago. It has frequently been said that a generation raised on television rather than on books is more responsive to images than to words, and better able to organize their minds by means of the "mosaic" of audio-visual impressions provided by film than by the "linear" progression of sentences. My friend also told me that students who are relatively blind to the organization of a piece of writing can make the most subtle connections in the structure of a film. Moreover, the characteristic style of much of the published writing that comes out of the "youth culture" tends to be a kind of transcription of the spoken language: simple syntax, a personal tone, a vocabulary that is more or less restricted to the vernacular of the day, as though words can be trusted only insofar as they stay as close as possible to common speech. Literary or learned language is out, the presumption being that it can't "tell it like it is."

As it happens, I'm in sympathy with this point of view and would tend to encourage it in young writers. I think it's good that writing should be regarded as one medium among several, and not necessarily the most vivid, affecting, or resourceful one. I also think it's good to distrust highfalutin and abstract language because it is often a breeding ground of false consciousness. I think that the plain style enables a young writer to stay level with his experience and to avoid the pitfall of pretentiousness, where nothing is quite real, least of all himself. Finally, I think that the indifference of students to formal writing, which is nothing new, should lead the teachers of composition to realize that what is lacking is the motive for the activity: the natural desire to express oneself.

Why is it that most people write more dully than they speak? The main reason, I think, is that from an early age they have been trained to associate writing with correctness, with rules and regulations. From the emphasis on good grammar, penmanship, and the other mechanics of the third grade up through the jargon and stiffness of the Ph.D. thesis stretches a continuity of inhibition and intimidation, of propriety overcoming expressiveness. Those students to whom such propriety makes no sense lapse into apathy and we say they have a "writing problem." In his book, *Thirty-Six Children*, Herbert Kohl describes how this problem virtually disappeared among a class of sixth-graders in Harlem once he managed to let them off the leash of the curriculum and encouraged them to let their imaginations run free among words: stories, legends, etymologies, the idioms of the street. At the same time, he encouraged them to invent and describe, to write on subjects that intrigued or mattered to them. By giving writing a place in their lives, he made them want to do it and, as time went on, to do it well.

I suspect that the two college students my friend told me about were attracted to tape partly because it enabled them to bypass the constraints of the formal term paper and of their writing "set" in general, and to approach their subject in a more free, inspiriting, as well as more dexterous way. To be sure, tape is a better medium than writing for presenting rock music; but the fact remains that most of their presentation was constructed from language: the passages from Romantic prose and poetry, the rock lyrics, and their own comments that provided continuity. This language had not come easily to them when they were initially describing their project and hardly making sense. What magical spell descended, then, to make them fluent and articulate?

The answer does not seem to lie in tape itself, which is simply a means of recording what is already there. The two students, though, would probably say that tape, and film, had "turned them on." By which they would mean that tape and film were also means to energize, concentrate, focus, and extend their consciousness of the relationships between Romanticism and Rock. What these means, or media, mainly turned on was their imaginations, precisely in the sense that we say, "Use your imagination," when we want someone to perceive a relationship that is not immediately apparent to him: say, the causal one of why John is dating Mary, or the associative one of what John and Mary have in common. The vehicle of imagination that they developed through their tape and film is called a "style," in the sense that the French poet, Paul Valéry, speaks of style as "an organization of creativity."

Viewing Your Subject

Imagination enters writing in several ways. The first is in how you view the subject. Imagination enables you to move beyond the vague, pat, superficial responses that come off the top of our minds. On leaving the theater, Harold Clurman, the drama critic, was asked how he felt about the play he had seen. "I don't know yet," he said. "I haven't talked to my pencil." What he meant was that he hadn't opened a line of inquiry into the play by using his own words to restage it in the theater of his imagination: not only the visual and verbal images of what he had just seen and heard but also the central image by which he would begin to characterize and judge the play.

If, for example, I say that *Easy Rider* is a movie about a motorcycle trip across the Southern part of the United States, and go on to describe the sequence of happenings—"After leaving the commune, Peter Fonda and Dennis Hopper are thrown in jail, where they meet Jack Nicholson, who plays a dissatisfied, alcoholic lawyer" and so on—the chances are that my literal account will be thin and obvious, as boring to write as it is to read. If, on the other hand, I start with one of the distinctive features of the film, such as the outfits worn by the two main characters, and go on to inquire why one is dressed like a patriotic, comic book hero and the other like a derelict from a horse opera, I can feel a certain mental excitement that comes from my imagination being activated. A whole range of fresh responses to the film begins to come into view as well as a perspective for focusing and connecting them. Or again, if I had seen a comparable movie about the "youth culture" of the previous decade, such as *Rebel Without a Cause* or *The Wild Ones*, I could set my mind and my essay to work comparing and contrasting and, likely, discovering fresh characteristics and implications of the films. Or if I can't get Captain America's last statement — "We blew it" — out of my mind, then I might well begin to review (in both senses of the term) the movie from that point of interest.

You can usually tell your imagination has been engaged when live and complex questions arise that you don't quite know the answers to yet. Or, to put it another way, the truly interesting is likely to have an element of risk in it, a pushing off in the mind from the safety of the obvious and familiar. By the same token, you can tell that an approach hasn't activated your imagination if it bores you to pursue it.

The point is to energize your mind, to stop writing under the wraps of boredom and timidity. A subject is not a problem to be worked out by performing a certain set of operations which, if done correctly, yields the right result. Nor for that matter is a sentence or a paragraph. If writing were like algebra, this procedure would work well enough, but the truth is that it's more like skiing. One learns the fundamentals in order to stay more or less in control while he tries to extend the scope and effectiveness of his ability. The two activities are complementary after a certain point, rather than consecutive. Otherwise, one would perpetually ski the novice slope, in a dull, correct way. You can use your imagination, then, to transform your approach to the subject from a pat answer to an open question. Like an intermediate trail to a novice skier, it may seem scary at first and you're sure to fall a few times, but your performance will improve and so will your attitude. Perhaps even the excitement of writing will descend upon you. At the very least, you'll stop being bored. The chances are so will your instructor: he'll be more interested in helping you because he has something interesting to work with, a willingness that approaches courage.

Activating Your Prose

The second way imagination enters writing follows, as I've just suggested, from the first. The more spirited, inventive, and inquiring your perspective, the more likely it is that these qualities will come into your prose: the energy of the central idea or feeling or conviction finding its natural expression in fresh examples, turns of phrase, images, and so forth. Just as the literal, pat approach tends to spawn a progeny of wooden, trite words and phrases, so does an imaginative one tend to stimulate one's powers of expression. Here are some examples of opening paragraphs:

My street is called Whyte Road. It is in Riverdale, New York, which is a suburb of New York City. On one side of the street is a row of nice brick houses. The houses on the other side run the gamut from a handsome mansion to a group of the original houses on the block, which are now rundown. Recently, a large apartment house was built at the bottom of the street. Most of the residents have lived there for a long time and get along well because they have mutual interests such as gardening and the maintenance of their property. Also most of them work in offices or other white-collar jobs. The people who have moved into the apartment house are a different breed; many of them belong to minority groups. The "old-timers" do not like having them there and feel that they lower the tone of the neighborhood.

Such a description is flat and mechanical. Lacking a point of view, the writer is mainly putting down what comes to mind, like making a shopping list. As a result, the language is dull, timid, cliché-ridden—the verbal equivalent of the emptiness of vision and feeling. It is the prose of someone who is concerned about doing the assignment and not making any errors.

Whyte Road might also be described in this fashion:

Ever been to Suburbia? Well, if you've seen one, you've seen them all. Like my block in Riverdale, New York. It's so square, it's practically cubic. Everything is buttoned-down and plastic, including the faces, and most of the houses look like they came off the same assembly line. People are more concerned about crab grass and dutch elm disease than they are about defoliating Viet Nam. They're also very uptight about drugs, long hair, and blacks. Recently a few "brothers" have moved into the new apartment house and it's like the Chinese Communists were invading the block.

Though the writing here seems more animated, there is as little imagination behind it as in the first example. The writer isn't seeing Whyte Road in his mind's eye or allowing the reader to see it. His point of view screens out concrete details that would characterize the life of the block and instead presents generalizations that caricature it. Strictly speaking, the passage doesn't create a perspective but rather trots out a ready-made attitude that requires as little effort to maintain as does the vacuity of the first passage. As such, it generates merely a different convention of clichés: the jargon of the "counter-culture."

Here is another example:

On Sunday morning, after church, Mr. James Boyle likes to walk with his family along Whyte Road, the street he lives on in Riverdale. A former bartender who owns two taverns in the Bronx, Mr. Boyle carries himself with the double assurance of a large and a self-made man. His wife follows a dutiful step or two behind with her two daughters; then come his four sons — ages fifteen to nine — normally the terror of Whyte Road but now as docile as choir-boys. Mr. Boyle looks about him as he moves down the "good side" of the block where a row of semi-detached brick houses with white colonial trims stand solidly, as though at attention. Through their polished storm windows they gaze at the world with the same sobriety as Mr. Boyle's eyes behind their gleaming rimless glasses. "Rinaldi's trim needs some touching up," he notes. "And the lawn could do with some looking after." He regards with approval the flagstone walk that George Miller has just finished laying. "Might try it myself," he thinks. "Adds a bit of class." Since moving to Whyte Road from the Bronx five years ago, Mr. Boyle has put $6200 and most of his weekends into repairs and improvements. As he nears the bottom of the block, he braces himself, for the big apartment house that has gone up there offends him as an "eyesore" and threatens him as a place for the "riff-raff" who will bring the problems and corruptions of the city with them and eventually lower his "property value."

This writer has used his imagination to show how Whyte Road looks to a typical resident. As such, its point of view is concrete and vivid, unlike the first example, and open to complexity, unlike the second. Moreover, it doesn't just state that Mr. Boyle is a typical resident; by a series of images and details that relate the man to the block, it illustrates this typicality, enabling the reader to see it for himself, to employ his own imagination. Similarly, the prevailing manners and mores of Whyte Road, its way of life, emerge from the actuality of a particular life being led there rather than as a series of familiar generalizations. In attempting to view Whyte Road in a perspective different from his own, the writer has probably also begun to learn something new, or at least to understand better why, say, Mr. Boyle holds the attitudes he does. Finally, this fresh perspective has led the writer to experiment with a style that assimilates Mr. Boyle's language to his own and that is both idiomatic and suggestive, springing the description to life.

Realizing Yourself

The third way that imagination enters writing is in the way we present ourselves by means of our style. Or, to put it another way, style is a form of self-characterization. This is why it is mistaken to regard style as an enhancement of writing, like the icing on a cake, for an authentic style has an organic relation to the temperament of the writer. When we say that a girl dresses with "real style," we mean that she has put together an ensemble of striking clothes in a way that becomes her. The same outfit on another woman might well look all wrong. Or again, when we marvel at Earl Monroe's playing style, we have in mind his individual way of passing, dribbling, and shooting, which he combines into a fluent whole. It is his particular way of being on a basketball court and expresses an imaginative conception of himself—graceful, quick, flamboyant, deadly.

Writing offers a similar opportunity to characterize yourself, to develop a style that expresses qualities that you possess and value. That is why young writers should try as much as possible to write to their strengths. If you have a good sense of humor, let it come into your prose. If you have a good ear for spoken language, for the idioms and rhythms of a region or group, try to incorporate them into your style. If you pride yourself on being clear and direct, then make your prose as explicit as possible. If you like to play around with images and puns, to catch your point on the wing, as it were, then let this be a feature of your style. In short, try to arrange your writing to give scope to what is good in you. By the same token, don't give yourself airs and graces, or indulge what is weak, lazy, or trivial in yourself.

Until something better comes along, writing is the best way man has developed to talk to himself, to find out what he is capable of understanding. If you have been faked out of this truth by your training, if writing has become a boring, intimidating, or depersonalizing activity, then keep a journal for a while, in which you can express yourself in your own way about what matters to you, what you need to understand. The chances are that writing will begin to matter to you, too; and once that happens, you will also have made the first step toward developing your own style.

EXERCISES

1. What conceptions of style are set forth in "On Style" and in "Writing, Imagination, and Style"? In what ways do DeMott and Solotaroff agree, and in what ways do they disagree, about what style is and what makes a good style?

2. How, according to each of the authors, can you go about developing a good style? How does the approach to

writing in each essay resemble, and how does it differ from, the approach to writing that is expressed or implied in earlier chapters of this book, especially in Chapters One, Two, Eleven, and Twelve?

3. Review the two essays, paying close attention to the style of each. How does the tone further what the writer is saying? Is the style appropriate to the rhetorical situation? How do you account for the differences between DeMott's style and Solotaroff's? How, according to their theories of style, would DeMott and Solotaroff account for the differences? Do you find a noticeable difference in style between the beginning and the ending of DeMott's essay? Between the beginning and the ending of Solotaroff's? If so, how do you account for the change?

4. Is style the man? Is style choice? Is style the man choosing? Consider these and other theories about style, and, for an audience of editors of high-school newspapers and literary magazines, discuss ways of developing and improving style. Illustrate your discussion by analyzing the essays by DeMott and Solotaroff, passages by other professional writers quoted in this book, and passages from your own essays.

Chapter Fourteen

THE RESEARCH PAPER

Although a college graduate can't be expected to know everything about everything, he should know how to find out about almost anything; he should know where to look and how to find what he wants quickly and efficiently. This chapter deals with a special form of expository writing, the research paper, which grows out of the writer's efforts to find information, reclaim it, and adapt it to his purposes. As such, the research paper—sometimes called the reference paper, library paper, term paper, or source paper—is basic to most college courses. To write a satisfactory one calls for resourcefulness in using the library and other facilities of scholarship, the exercise of critical judgment in transforming a collection of data into cogent support of a thesis, and skill in organizing and writing an essay of some length.

Preparing a research paper in your writing course will give you practice in finding material, taking notes on it, evaluating its reliability and its relevance to a thesis, and ordering and presenting it. Advanced study, especially in literature, history, and the social sciences, depends on this sort of work, and in the physical sciences a laboratory experiment is often supplemented by research in records of previous experiments. These same methods, more elaborately developed, are used in writing monographs, theses, and dissertations in graduate school and in preparing many business reports and industrial studies. Your freshman reference paper, then, is an introduction to scholarly activity and practice for research— professional or personal—that you may do later.

THE NATURE OF THE RESEARCH PAPER

A research paper is an ambitious and complicated undertaking; every stage takes time, patience, and judgment. At first your personal contribution may seem negligible. The material comes from sources outside your immediate experience, the style you write in will probably be more impersonal and Formal than you are used to, and your primary objective will be to inform and interpret rather than to express your feelings. But serious work on the project will show how wide a scope for originality you actually have in the range and direction of your research. And though the methods of gathering material have been worked out by thousands of research workers before you and the form of the manuscript standardized, the actual content, organization, and style of your essay are the product of your thought and judgment and imagination.

It would be wrong, then, to regard the research paper as totally unlike other kinds of writing we have discussed. Although following the conventions of proper footnote form is an indispensable obligation in writing a research paper, meeting that obligation does not guarantee that the paper will be worth reading. To produce a really effective paper, you must first find in your subject a problem you want to solve, one that stirs your curiosity. The conviction that a problem exists and that you want to engage it and perhaps solve it can turn what might be a dreary canvassing of sources into a coherent, purposeful investigation — an investigation that interests you and will ultimately interest your reader. Regardless of the topic, your essay is not likely to be satisfactory unless it gives the impression that in writing it you found out something you consider worth knowing.

If you are to produce a good research paper, your intelligence and your intellectual curiosity must dominate your research. Fatigued by hours in the library and confronted by a stack of note cards, you may find yourself losing both your confidence and your enthusiasm (they are related) and you may be tempted to fit together mechanically the bits of information you have collected. A paper composed in this fashion is bound to be unsatisfactory — its proportions bad, its continuity rough and awkward, its thesis unfocused or nonexistent. What your reader is mainly interested in is the solution of the problem you have set out to solve. Only if he sees clearly how you move toward that solution can he judge the pertinence and value of the evidence you give to support it. A good research paper — like any other kind of effective writing — gives the impression not simply that material has been collected but that a mind has been at work analyzing it — turning it this way and that, asking questions of it — interpreting it, and organizing it.

One note of caution about the methodology outlined in the following pages. During the time you spend on the project, you will need to strike a balance between your interest in the subject for its own sake and your interest in the procedures of research. Exclusive absorption in either is costly and unwise. At first you may feel a certain impatience at having to follow a rather rigid pattern in preparing and documenting your essay, particularly if you begin by simply wanting to know more about your subject. Meticulousness in recording bibliographical data and taking notes may seem to be a waste of good hours. But in the long run what you learn about the procedures and standards of scholarship will probably be more valuable to you than the essay itself.

This is not to say that the *writing* of the essay can be treated lightly. It is as unwise to concentrate solely on method as it is to slight it. In the end, converting material gathered from many sources into an essay that has its own integrity presents more challenges and offers more rewards than hunting for the material. If you become absorbed in the minutiae of preparing extensive bibliographies and taking full notes, you may exhaust your interest and enthusiasm as well as your time before you begin to cope with the central task of the whole project—writing a purposeful essay that reflects discriminating use of a variety of sources.

EXERCISES

1. The subjects in the following list are too broad or too general for successful treatment in a reference paper of moderate length. Select two that interest you, and make up for each at least three topics that could be treated adequately in papers of the length assigned for your course. You may see a possibility at the point where one topic impinges on another; for example, George Bernard Shaw and the Salvation Army.

Acid rock	Harpsichords
Anarchism	Hesse's novels
Atomic Energy Commission	Hobbits
Blood banks	I.W.W.
Censorship	Insanity in modern poetry
Chairman Mao's poetry	Lasers
Chinook Jargon	Lewis and Clark
Civil rights	Libel laws
Detective stories	Linguistics
Electoral college	Marine Corps
Eskimos	Herbert Marcuse
Euthanasia	Mass media
Existentialism	Medicare
Folk sayings	Metropolitan Opera Company
Game laws	Modern productions of *Hamlet*
George Bernard Shaw	Music in industry

Nonobjective painting
Pan-African movement
Peace Corps
Peyote cults
Poetry readings
Pollution
Primitive peoples
Prison conditions
Radar

Rural poverty
Salvation Army
Satellites
Simplified spelling
Stereophonic sound
Televised political debates
Utopias
Voting at eighteen
Witchcraft

2. Choose a subject for a research paper, and prepare brief statements on the following:

a. Your reason for choosing the subject.

b. Your present knowledge about the subject and the gaps you will have to fill.

c. The audience you have in mind and the information you assume this audience already has about the topic.

d. The bibliographies, indexes, and other reference works that you will consult.

e. The main points you now think you will make and the methods you will use to develop them.

SOURCES OF REFERENCES

Almost everyone starts work on a research paper with one or two sources in mind—a discussion in a textbook, a magazine article, the name of a writer, the title of a book. Very often, preliminary reading furnishes references to other works, and these make a natural starting point for the working bibliography. But to assemble a fairly comprehensive list of possible sources, you must make informed use of the resources of the library. There are several aids planned specifically to direct you to books and periodicals. No matter what your choice of topic, you will invariably want to consult your library's card catalog, its periodical indexes and special bibliographies, and its other general and special reference works.

The Card Catalog

The library card catalog lists all the books in the library by *author*, by *title*, and by *subject* (sometimes under more than one subject heading). If you know of an author who has written on your subject, find his name in the card catalog. If you know a book title dealing with your topic, find it in the catalog. And look up the subject you are writing about, watching for cross-references made by *see* and *see also* cards. If you are looking for material on athletics, you may find a card headed ATHLETICS, SEE SPORTS; this indicates that in your library the cards relating to athletics are filed under the heading SPORTS. When you look up SPORTS, you may find, in addition to a number of cards with that heading, a card labeled SPORTS, SEE ALSO GAMES, indicating that additional related material will be found under the subject heading GAMES. Early in your search it will be worthwhile to make a list of subject titles synonymous with or related to your main title. For a paper on the first ascent of the Matterhorn you would list ALPS and MOUNTAINEERING, and you might go as far afield as ENGRAVING, NINETEENTH-CENTURY. Edward Whymper, who led the first climb, was a celebrated engraver.

The library subject card below illustrates the information given about a book. In preparing your working bibliography (see p. 406), you would transfer items 2, 3, 4, and 5 to a bibliography card (p. 408). The entry on the bibliography card should follow the form prescribed for the final bibliography (pp. 424–26) so that making the bibliography will be simply a matter of arranging the cards alphabetically and copying the entries, inserting conventional punctuation.

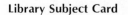

1. Card catalog subject heading
2. Library call number
3. Author
4. Title
5. Facts of publication
6. Relevant facts about the book
7. Subject index
8. Information for librarians

378.1
K41u
① EDUCATION,HIGHER.
③ Kerr, Clark, 1911–
⑤
④ The uses of the university. Cambridge, Mass., Harvard University Press, 1963.

vii, 140 p. 21 cm. (The Godkin lectures at Harvard University, 1963)

⑥ "Based on the 1963 Godkin lectures, delivered at Harvard University on April 23, 24, and 25, 1963."
Bibliographical references included in "Notes" (p. ₍127₎–135)

⑦ 1. Education, Higher—Addresses, essays, lectures. ɪ. Title.
(Series: Godkin lectures, Harvard University, 1963)

LB2325.K43   378   63—20770

⑧ Library of Congress   ₍64n2₎

Library Subject Card

Periodical Indexes

Next to the card catalog, your most useful source of references will probably be *Readers' Guide to Periodical Literature* and other periodical indexes. *Readers' Guide* indexes magazines published since 1900 and gives, under author and subject entries (see illustration below), references to articles in over two hundred current magazines of general interest. It appears twice a month from September through June, monthly in July and August. Cumulative volumes covering one or more years have been issued since the 1940's. The following is an excerpt from the July 1971 issue of the *Guide:*

CANDIDATES, Political
  See also
  Presidential candidates
CANDLES
  Details that make the difference. W. Baldwin. House & Gard 139:10+ My '71
  More power to the candle. il Time 97:72 Je 21 '71
CANOE trips
  Canoe trails of North America. F. M. Paulson. il Field & S 76:138-41 My '71
  Counselors' post-camp Canadian canoe trip brings staff back again next year; Camp Fairfield, Pa. B. T. Vance. il Camp Mag 43:16-17 Je '71
CANON law
  Strait jacket for the mystical body. F. X. Murphy. America 124:611-13 Je 12 '71
CANTWELL, Mary
  Living off the land. il Mlle 73:126-9 Je '71
CANTWELL, Robert
  In the mood for baseball. il Sports Illus 34:54-6+ Je 7 '71
CAPE COD
  Trees of Cape Cod. G. S. Smith. il Am For 77:6-7 Je '71

Readers' Guide uses abbreviations, explained at the beginning of each issue, for the titles of magazines indexed, for the months, and for various facts about the articles. When using *Readers' Guide*, write out all important words on your bibliography card in order to avoid confusion later and to have the data in correct form. In the references the number before the colon refers to the volume and the numbers after the colon refer to the pages of the articles (34:54 − 6+ means volume 34, pages 54 to 56 and continued).

A number of other magazine indexes list articles from specialized periodicals not covered by *Readers' Guide.* Many appear annually, some more frequently than that. The ones marked with a † are the most generally useful.

Agricultural Index, 1916–1964. In 1964 it became *Biological and Agricultural Index.* Subject index to a selected list of periodicals, bulletins, documents.

Annual Magazine Subject Index, 1908– . Subject index to American and English periodicals.

Art Index, 1929– . Author and subject index to fine arts periodicals and museum bulletins.

Bibliographic Index, 1938– . Subject index to bibliographies in books and periodicals.

Biography Index, 1946 – . Subject index to biographical material in books and periodicals.

†*Book Review Digest,* 1905 – . Author, subject, and title index to published book reviews. Gives extracts and exact references to sources.

†*Bulletin of the Public Affairs Information Service,* 1915 – Subject index to books, periodicals, pamphlets, and other materials in economics, government, and other public affairs.

Catholic Periodical Index, 1930 – . Subject index to a selected list of Catholic periodicals.

Dramatic Index, 1909 – 1949. Index to articles and illustrations concerning the American and English theater.

†*Education Index,* 1929 – . Subject index to educational periodicals, books, and pamphlets.

Engineering Index, 1884 – . Subject index to technical periodicals; transactions and journals of engineering and other technical societies; reports of government bureaus, engineering colleges, research laboratories.

Index to Legal Periodicals, 1908 – . Author, subject, and book review index to legal periodicals.

†*Industrial Arts Index,* 1913 – 1957. In 1958 it became two separate indexes: *Applied Science and Technology Index* and *Business Periodicals Index*. Subject index to a selected list of engineering, trade, and business periodicals.

†*International Index to Periodicals,* 1907 – 1965. In 1965 it became the *Social Sciences and Humanities Index.* Author and subject index to periodicals from various countries; devoted chiefly to the humanities and the social sciences.

†*Nineteenth Century Readers' Guide to Periodical Literature,* 1890 – 1899. An index to periodicals, with supplementary indexing, 1900 – 1922.

Poole's Index to Periodical Literature, 1802 – 1881. Supplements cover years through 1906. Subject index to American and English periodicals, many of which are no longer published but are still important; precedes coverage of *Readers' Guide.*

Quarterly Cumulative Index Medicus, 1927 – 1956. Author and subject index to medical literature in many languages. Continued by *Cumulated Index Medicus,* 1960 –

United States Government Publications, Monthly Catalog, 1895 – . A bibliography of publications issued by all branches of the government.

Ulrich's International Periodicals Directory (13th ed.,

1969–70) lists periodicals under subjects they treat, answering the question: What periodicals are there in this field? It also tells where each is indexed so that it becomes an indirect guide to the contents of all magazines.

The New York Times Index now appears semimonthly and runs back to 1913. Although it indexes only *The New York Times,* it can be used as a rough general index to material in other newspapers, since the dates indicate when the news stories were breaking. Through this index you can find many speeches and important documents as well as news stories of significant events.

Special Bibliographies

Besides these periodical indexes there are many annual bibliographies in the learned journals in special fields and bibliographies of one or more volumes that survey a complete field. The key to these special lists is Besterman's *World Bibliography of Bibliographies* (4th ed., 5 vols., 1965), a standard and comprehensive work, or the shorter Ireland's *An Index to Indexes* (1942). The following are standard bibliographies in history and literature:

Articles on American Literature, 1900–1950 (Leary), 1954.

Articles on American Literature, 1950–1967 (Leary et al.), 1970.

A Reference Guide to English Studies (Bond), 1962.

A Concise Bibliography for Students of English (Kennedy and Sands), 4th ed., 1960.

Bibliography of Writings on the English Language from the Beginning of Printing to the End of 1922 (Kennedy), 1927.

The Cambridge Bibliography of English Literature (Bateson), 1940, 4 vols.; supplement, Vol. 5, 1957.

The Concise Cambridge Bibliography of English Literature, 600–1950 (Watson), 2nd ed., 1965.

The New Cambridge Bibliography of English Literature (Watson), 1969, 5 vols.

Reader's Guide to English and American Literature (Wright), 1970.

Selective Bibliography for the Study of English and American Literature (Altick and Wright), 4th ed., 1971.

Literary History of the United States (Spiller et al.), 3rd ed., rev., 1963, 2 vols.

Contemporary British Literature (Millett), 3rd ed., rev., 1943.

Contemporary American Authors (Millett), 1940.

Literature of American History (Larned) and supplement, 1902.

Bibliographies in American History (Beers), rev. ed., 1942.

Harvard Guide to American History (Handlin et al.), 1955.

Guide to Historical Literature (Howe et al.), 1961.

Twentieth Century British Literature (Temple and Tucker), 1968.

These miscellaneous indexes are useful for many research projects:

Vertical File Index, 1932— . An annotated subject and title catalog of pamphlets, booklets, leaflets, and mimeographed materials.

Books in Print, 1948— . Author, title, series index to books currently in print in the United States.

United States Catalog: Books in Print, 1899— . Four editions and their supplements, constituting a comprehensive record of American book publication from 1899 to date.

Cumulative Book Index, 1898— . An author, subject, and title index to books printed in English.

Catalog of the Public Documents of Congress and of All Departments of the Government of the United States for the Period March 4, 1893–Dec. 31, 1940, 1896–1945, 25 vols.

Essay and General Literature Index, 1900— . Author and subject index to essays and articles in collections and miscellaneous works.

Granger's Index to Poetry, 5th ed., 1962. Author, title, and first-line index to poetry in collections published through June 30, 1960.

Short Story Index, 1953. Author, title, and, in many cases, subject index to stories in collections published through 1949; supplements 1950–1954, 1955–1958, 1959–1963, 1964–1968.

Song Index, 1926; supplement 1934. Author and title index to more than 19,000 songs in collections.

Index to Plays, 4th ed., 1963. Author, title, and subject index to plays in collections or separately published.

Play Index, 1949–1952, 1953–1960, 1961–1967. Augments but does not supersede the *Index to Plays.*

Index to Reproductions of American Paintings, 1948.

Index to Reproductions of European Paintings, 1956.

Reference Works

Reference works are a good starting point for compiling a bibliography because their articles almost always refer you to authoritative specialized works. Two comprehensive lists of reference works of all kinds are *Guide to Reference Books*, by Constance M. Winchell (8th ed., 1967), and *Reference Books: How to Select and Use Them*, by Saul Galin and Peter Spielberg (1969). *How and Where to Look It Up: A Guide to Standard Sources of Information*, by Robert W. Murphey (1958), provides a variety of reference sources.

There are numerous general encyclopedias, varying in size from the single-volume *Columbia* to the multivolume *Britannica*, with supplements. Though by no means infallible and always in need of revision (the larger ones revise some articles for each new printing), they are storehouses of information on a vast number of subjects.

Even more important for college work are special reference works—the encyclopedias and general reference books in specific fields. Most of them give brief, carefully selected bibliographies. Some of the best known are:

Architecture: *A History of Architecture on the Comparative Method* (Fletcher), 17th ed., 1961.

Art: *Encyclopedia of World Art*, 1959–1968, 15 vols. *Encyclopedia of the Arts* (Read), 1966. *Lives of the Painters* (Canaday), 1969, 4 vols. *McGraw-Hill Dictionary of Art* (Myers), 1969, 5 vols.

Biography (American): *Dictionary of American Biography*, 1928–1937, 20 vols. and index; supplements 1944, 1958. *Who's Who in America*, biennially since 1899. *Who Was Who in America*, Vol. I, 1897–1942; Vol. II, 1943–1950; Vol. III, 1951–1960 (*Who's Who* subjects who died during those years). *Who Was Who in America*, Historical Volume, 1607–1896, 1963.

Biography (British): *Dictionary of National Biography*, 1885–1901, 63 vols. and first supplement (2 vols.) with other supplements through 1950. *Who's Who*, annually since 1849.

Biography (General): *Current Biography*, monthly since 1940, with annual cumulative volume. *International Who's Who*, 1935– *World Biography*, 5th ed., 1954.

Business: *Encyclopedia of Banking and Finance* (Munn), 6th ed., 1962.

Chemistry: *Encyclopedia of Chemistry* (Clark), 2nd ed., 1966. *Thorpe's Dictionary of Applied Chemistry* (Thorpe and Whitely), 4th ed., 1937–1956, 12 vols.

Education: *Encyclopedia of Educational Research* (Harris), 3rd ed., 1960. *The Encyclopedia of Education* (Deighton), 1971, 9 vols.

Government and Political Science: *Cyclopedia of American Government* (McLaughlin and Hart), 1914, 3 vols. *Political Science: A Bibliographic Guide to the Literature* (Harmon), 1965, supplement 1968. *United States Government Organization Manual*, 1935– , annual.

History (General): *An Encyclopedia of World History* (Langer), 4th ed., 1968. *The Cambridge Ancient History* (Bury et al.), 2nd ed., 1923–1939, 12 vols. of text and 5 vols. of plates. *The Cambridge Medieval History* (Bury et al.), 1911–1936, 8 vols. *The Cambridge Modern History* (Ward et al.), 1902–1926, 13 vols. and atlas. *The New Cambridge Modern History*, 1957– , 14 vols.

History (American): *Dictionary of American History* (Adams), 1940, 5 vols.; supplement, Vol. 6, 1961. *Encyclopedia of American History* (Morris), rev. ed., 1965. *The Oxford Companion to American History* (Johnson), 1966.

Literature (General): *Dictionary of World Literature* (Shipley), rev. ed., 1966. *Columbia Dictionary of Modern European Literature* (Smith), 1947. *A Handbook to Literature* (Thrall, Hibbard, Holman), rev. ed., 1960.

Literature (Classical): *The Oxford Companion to Classical Literature* (Harvey), 2nd ed., 1937. *The Oxford Classical Dictionary* (Hammond and Scullard), 2nd ed., 1970.

Literature (English): *The Cambridge History of English Literature* (Ward and Waller), 1907–1933, 15 vols. *The Concise Cambridge History of English Literature* (Sampson), 3rd ed., 1970. *The Oxford Companion to English Literature* (Harvey), 4th ed., 1967. *A Literary History of England* (Baugh et al.), 2nd ed., 1967, 4 vols.

Literature (American): *The Oxford Companion to American Literature* (Hart), 4th ed., 1965. *The Reader's Encyclopedia of American Literature* (Herzberg), 1962. *Literary History of the United States* (Spiller et al.), 3rd ed., rev., 1963, 2 vols. *Twentieth Century Authors* (Kunitz and Haycraft), 1942. *American Authors* (Kunitz and Haycraft), 1938.

Music: *Grove's Dictionary of Music and Musicians* (Blom), 5th ed., 1954, 9 vols.; supplement, Vol. 10, 1961. *The International Cyclopedia of Music and Musicians* (Thompson, rev. Sabin), 9th ed., 1964. *Harvard Dictionary of Music* (Apel), 2nd ed., rev., 1969. *The Oxford Companion to Music* (Scholes), 10th ed., 1970.

Philosophy: *The Encyclopedia of Philosophy* (Edwards), 1967, 8 vols.

Psychology: *Encyclopedia of Psychology* (Harriman), 1946. *A Dictionary of Psychology* (Drever), rev. ed., 1964.

Quotations: *Familiar Quotations* (Bartlett), 14th ed., 1968. *Dictionary of Quotations* (Evans), 1968. *The Oxford Dictionary of Quotations*, 2nd ed., 1953. *The Home Book of Quotations, Classical and*

Modern (Stevenson), 10th ed., 1967. *The Home Book of Bible Quotations* (Stevenson), 1949. *The Home Book of Shakespeare Quotations* (Stevenson), 1937.

Religion: *New Catholic Encyclopedia*, 1967, 15 vols. and index. *Universal Jewish Encyclopedia*, 1939–1944, 10 vols. *Encyclopedia of Religion and Ethics* (Hastings), 1908–1927, 12 vols. and index. *New Schaff-Herzog Encyclopedia of Religious Knowledge* (Jackson), 1908–1912, 12 vols. and index; reprinted 1949–1950, 13 vols. *Twentieth Century Encyclopedia of Religious Knowledge* (Loetscher), 1955, 2 vols., an extension of *New Schaff-Herzog Encyclopedia of Religious Knowledge. Dictionary of the Bible* (Hastings), rev. ed., 1963.

General Science: *Dictionary of Scientific Terms* (Speel and Jaffe), 1965. *Harper Encyclopedia of Science* (Newman), rev. ed., 1967. *Hutchinson's Technical and Scientific Encyclopedia* (Tweney and Shirshov), 1935, 4 vols. *The New Space Encyclopedia*, 1969. *Van Nostrand's Scientific Encyclopedia*, 4th ed., 1968. *Dictionary of Scientific Biography* (Gillispie), 1970, 2 vols. *McGraw-Hill Encyclopedia of Science and Technology*, 3rd ed., 1971, 15 vols.

Social Sciences: *Encyclopedia of the Social Sciences* (Seligman and Johnson), 1930–1935, 15 vols. *International Encyclopedia of the Social Sciences* (Sills), 1967, 16 vols. and index.

For dictionaries of the language, see pp. 350–54.

Yearbooks and Almanacs

Various publications are valuable for the facts they contain or can direct you to.

World Almanac and Book of Facts, 1868–

Information Please Almanac, 1947–

The American Yearbook, 1910–1919, 1925–1950. Annual record of events in the U.S.

The Americana Annual, 1923–   . Annual supplement to the *Encyclopedia Americana.*

Britannica Book of the Year, 1938–   . Annual supplement to the *Encyclopaedia Britannica.*

Facts on File, 1940–   . Weekly digest of world and domestic news, with index.

The New International Yearbook, 1907–1965. Annual supplement to the *New International Encyclopedia.*

The New York Times Encyclopedic Almanac, 1969–   . New comprehensive annual.

Statistical Abstract of the United States, 1878–   . Summary statistics on the industrial, social, political, and economic organization of the U.S.

Social Work Yearbook, 1929–1960. In 1960 it became *Encyclopedia of Social Work.* Biennial survey of social work and related fields.

Statesman's Year-Book, 1864–   . Descriptive and statistical information about world governments.

Reference Shelf, 1922–   . Reprints of articles, bibliographies, and debates on topics of current interest.

University Debater's Annual, 1915–   . Annual survey of debates in American colleges.

Yearbook of the United Nations, 1956–

Apart from standard sources like these, you will always find some important references indirectly, unexpectedly, by hunch or by chance. Almost every article or book will refer to some other source or give you a clue to follow up. Your instructor and specialists in the field will offer suggestions. If you combine orderly work habits with a certain alertness and ingenuity in following up clues, the sources of material on your topic will begin to spread out before you like a river system, with one stream leading into another.

Since one of the values in undertaking a research paper is to become self-reliant in the use of research methods, you should do as much as possible on your own. The library has trained reference librarians, and your instructor knows his way around the Reference Room; but you should not ask for help in finding out what is known about your subject until you have exhausted your own resources.

 ## THE WORKING BIBLIOGRAPHY

Before you concentrate on gathering material for your topic, you should compile a *working bibliography* of sources you expect to consult. Check reference works of the kind described in the preceding section, and consult the appropriate subject headings in the card catalog and the periodical indexes. To make sure that enough material on your subject is available in the library, compile the working bibliography before you start to take notes. This preliminary survey of materials will save you time and worry when you begin reading and will help you make an intelligent selection of books and articles.

Everyone should have a consistent method for keeping track of references and for taking notes. For casual study, notebooks and odd sheets of paper may do, but for large projects standard filing cards, either 3x5 or 4x6 inches, are most efficient. To begin with, you should prepare a separate bibliography card for each reference. Later you will add note cards on the content of the reference.

The bibliography card records all the facts you need to identify a book or an article, to find it in the library when you want it, and to make the formal bibliography that will appear at the end of the paper. Each card should carry these facts:

For the formal bibliography:

1. *The author's or editor's name*, last name first; *ed.* after editor's name. If no author or editor is given, omit this item and start with 2.

2. *The title* of the article (in quotation marks) or of the book (underlined to represent italics). Put *a, an, the* last, so that the entry begins with the first definitive word of the title: for example, *Long Voyage Home, The.*

3. *The facts of publication:*
   a. Of a book, the city, the name of the publisher, and the date.
   b. Of a magazine, the name of the magazine (underlined), the volume, the date, the pages on which the article appears.
   c. Of a newspaper story, the name of the paper (underlined), the date, and the page. You may also include the edition and the column number.

For your own use:

4. *The library call number* or location of the source—"Per." for Periodical Room, for instance—preferably in the upper left corner, as it is in the card catalog. If you are working in two or more libraries, put an identifying symbol before the call number.

5. *Any other facts* that relate to the use of the reference, such as the pages that treat your subject or the value of the source—preferably at the bottom of the card.

6. *A subject heading*, a phrase for the particular part of your topic that the reference pertains to, at the top center of the card. This label is known as a *slug.*

7. *A code reference* in the upper right corner. This reference may be a number, a letter, or the author's last name. Using it instead of a full citation on each note card taken from this source will save a great deal of needless copying.

The form and arrangement of bibliography cards are illustrated on the next page. Numbers on the cards correspond to the items in the preceding list.

(4) 378.1 (6) Role of the University (7) Kerr
     K41u   President

(1) Kerr, Clark

(2) Uses of the University, The

(3) Cambridge, Mass.: Harvard
    Univ. Press, 1963

(5) pp. 29-41 The university president
    can no longer be an autocrat; his
    role is chiefly as mediator.

Bibliography Card for a Book

(4) Per.   (6) Race Relations   (7) Winter

(1) Winter, Sara K.

(2) "Black Man's Bluff"

(3) Psychology Today, 5 (Sept. 1971),
    39-43, 78-81

(5) Analysis of interracial encounter
    groups at Wesleyan University.

Bibliography Card for a Magazine Article

(4) Per.   (6) Capitol Bombing (7) Chicago
                                       Sun-Times

(2) "'Weather Underground' Takes
    Credit for Explosion"

(3) Chicago Sun-Times, March 3, 1971,
    p. 9, col. 1

(5) "The Weather Underground" says
    they bombed the Capitol Building
    in retaliation for the U.S.'s
    escalation of Vietnam War.

Bibliography Card for a Newspaper

Keep your bibliography cards in alphabetical order according to author or, if no author is given, according to title.

The number of references depends on the nature of the topic. An undergraduate paper should represent adequate coverage of the subject; it should be clear that the writer has located and consulted the most important and influential commentary, especially by modern authorities, and has not merely used the first three books he came across, regardless of their dates or their quality. On the other hand, most undergraduate research projects by their nature impose a limit of some sort: there comes a time when sleuthing must give way to the critical job of reading, note-taking, and evaluating.

TAKING NOTES ON READING

Good notes are crucial in the preparation of a reference paper. Illegible handwriting, meaningless phrases (clear when the note was taken but not when it's cold), and inadequate labeling of the source may send you back to the library when you should be settling down to write. As you become experienced in note-taking and at home with your topic, you will learn to evaluate the importance of a source and to vary the kind, length, and number of your notes accordingly. From some sources you may need only a few facts or statistics; from others you will want not only direct quotations but careful summaries of whole paragraphs, sections, or even chapters; for a few you may simply jot down a sentence or two describing and briefly evaluating the content. In the beginning, of course, you will be taking notes partly on faith, feeling your way note by note toward a thesis. Once you have defined your thesis, it will determine what material should be recorded.

Form of Notes

Notes on 3x5 or 4x6 cards are easy to sort, discard, and rearrange; they can be accumulated indefinitely and kept in good order in an indexed file box. The three essential parts of a note card are: (1) the *material*—the facts and opinions to be recorded; (2) the exact *source*—title and page from which the material is taken; and (3) a *subject label* or slug for the card, showing what it treats.

The sample note card shows a convenient form. In the upper right-hand corner put the author's name and the source—just enough to make reference to the full bibliography card easy and sure. Before writing the note, set down the exact page on which the material was found. Inclusive pages (such as 87−92) should not be used unless the note actually describes or summarizes what those pages say. The slug is best placed in the upper left corner and should identify the subject matter of that particular card, making it possible for you to sort the cards when you get ready to outline and write.

Label

Note with page reference

> Nudity in American Theater — Bentley, "The Naked American" (*New Republic*)
>
> 32 Producers have so far neglected the real dramatic possibilities of nudity on the stage, being interested chiefly in good box office.

Sample Note Card

A single card should contain only one point or a few facts that bear on one point. If unrelated bits of information are included on one card (the temptation is always strong), you will find when you sort the cards that one bit belongs here and another there. One hundred items of information on one hundred cards can be organized and reorganized speedily and efficiently; fifty items on ten cards will cause confusion, exasperation, and error.

It is good practice to use only one side of each card. Cards written on both sides are difficult to handle, and you run the risk of forgetting to turn a card over. If only a few words remain at the end of a statement, they can be written on the back, but the signal OVER should be put on the front as a reminder.

Not all notes need be taken in full sentences. Words, phrases, and topics are enough if you are not quoting directly and if you are sure the note will be meaningful after you have laid it aside for a while. Take notes in ink as you do the reading, but don't bother to recopy them except for some very good reason. They are only means to an end—a good essay.

Suggestions for Note-Taking

It is impossible to give exact rules for taking notes. As you gain experience, your judgment will improve, and you will probably formulate your own special rules as you go along. But it is wise to begin by reading through the article or chapter rapidly to see what it contains for your purpose. Then go over it again, this time taking notes. From your first few sources you will probably take a good many, but after you have accumulated material covering the major points of your topic, a new reference may give only a few additional facts. In taking notes:

1. Distinguish between the author's facts and his opinions. If there is any chance of confusion, label the opinions "So-and-so thinks. . . ." In general, pay most attention to the *facts* presented, unless you are writing on a topic for which the sources are chiefly expressions of critical opinion. You will need facts as the basis of your own interpretations and as evidence to support them in the paper.

2. Distinguish carefully between direct quotation and summary. Anything you are quoting should be taken down exactly as it appears in the original and enclosed in quotation marks. If you omit a word or more in a direct quotation, use an *ellipsis. After an obvious error in the source, write *sic* (thus) in brackets to indicate that the error was in the original.

In the early stages of note-taking, before you have a clear perspective on your subject, you may want to quote rather fully. Many of these quotations will not appear in the final draft, but having a quotation before you as you write can help you work the summary of it into your discussion more smoothly. In the later stages of note-taking, quotations should be copied out only for good reason: material that is crucial for your paper; controversial or difficult material that you want to think about; a striking statement that you want to quote for its pithiness or its authority.

3. Distinguish between what you take from a source and comments of your own. Either put the latter in brackets or circle them and write your initials alongside. Such "notes to myself" often prove very valuable when you begin to write. Indeed, as you take notes, it is a good idea to keep a running log of questions, notions, and leads on a separate pad.

Taking notes on literary works may require some changes in method. As each work is a developing whole and cannot be broken down into "main points" as an article or chapter can, it may be advisable to take running notes (on paper) on your impressions and questions while reading and then go back over these comments to find out what lines of interpretation are worth pursuing in detail. A running commentary on William Stafford's poems in *Traveling Through the Dark*, for example, might reveal to you his preoccupation with small towns and cities as types of the human community; then you could go back and make proper note cards on the poems that deal with this motif.

The Summarizing Note

The summarizing note is made when an argument or explanation in one of your sources seems crucial to your project. Doing a good summary tests your ability to read critically. You need to read the material several times. First, watch for the main ideas and see how each is developed. Move from the general to the specific. Try to determine the overall meaning or purpose, then the main points, and then the subdivisions supporting each main point. The author's transitional expressions give clues to the pattern of his ideas. As in any other note-taking, you must be sure you understand and record the author's ideas, not your own, even though you disagree violently with his point of view. A summary should not be interrupted or distorted by your personal opinions. They will come into play later.

Your success in producing a good summary will depend partly on the care with which you read the original and partly on your skill in cutting unnecessary passages and in condensing. A good summary reproduces as faithfully as possible the ideas and the emphasis of the original—and if incorporated in the final paper must credit the original. Condensation is accomplished by eliminating nonessentials—anecdotes, descriptive details, digressions, illustrations, and all kinds of repetition—and by using appositives, series, and verbals to make the phrasing more compact.

Original	*Summarizing Note*
At the top of agricultural society are the minority of corporation farms and big farm owners. For them, the technological revolution has meant enormous profits and fantastic feats of production. In 1954, some 12 per cent of the operators controlled more than 40 per cent of the land and grossed almost 60 per cent of the farm sales. These were the dramatic beneficiaries of the advance in the fields.—Michael Harrington, *The Other America*	The technological revolution in farming benefited most dramatically a small minority of big operators.
As the nuclear reactor program expands, its wastes will also increase, and the burden of radio-activity in our surroundings will rise, and go on rising. At some point the deleterious effects of this radiation will become unacceptable even to a	Radioactivity produced by wastes from our nuclear reactor program will ultimately saturate our environment.

nation which is able to tolerate
50,000 deaths on its roads each
year. Because the effects of radiation
go on making themselves felt
decades after the first damage is
done, it would be well to anticipate
the eventual saturation of our
surroundings. For the environment
which supports us has only a limited
capacity for radiation, and that
capacity can only be used once.
—Sheldon Novick, *The Careless
Atom*

Many words from the original necessarily reappear in a summary. But if you deliberately use a phrase exactly as it appears in the original, enclose it in quotation marks and cite the page number in parentheses.

EVALUATING MATERIAL

Because preparing a reference paper is largely an exercise in critical judgment, it is essential to evaluate the sources you use. "I found a book in the library that said . . ." is a confession of uncritical work; some sources are better—more comprehensive, more accurate, more penetrating—than others. Your aim should be to find the best books and articles, the most recent and most reliable material on the subject. When you find contradictions or differing estimates in two sources, you should investigate to determine which is more accurate or more probable. At first you will have to rely on the judgment of others. In your reading you may find that the author of one of your sources is generally accepted as the authority in his field but that the scholarship or the fairness of another has been questioned. Judgments like these should be noted and, if possible, substantiated or disproved by further investigation.

For recent books it is often possible to find reviews that will give some indication of their value. The best sources of reviews of serious works are the learned journals—the *American Historical Review* for historical works, for instance, and *American Literature* and similar journals for literature. The *Book Review Digest* will lead you to reviews of less specialized works.

After you have worked on a subject for a while, you can evaluate a good deal of the material yourself, and your considered judgment should influence your further choice of materials. If you are impressed by what a writer has to say about the influence of Mack Sennett films on modern drama, you may decide to examine his book on dramatic theory.

Sources are classed as *primary* (or *original*) and *secondary*. A primary source is a first record of facts or the closest that a person now writing can come to the subject he is discussing; a secondary source is something written by someone else using original sources. In a paper on an author, for instance, the primary sources are the works written by the man you are discussing and the letters, diaries, and so on written by him or by others who knew him; secondary sources are what a critic or historian has written about the author on the basis of these materials. In a science, primary sources are records of observations or experiments; secondary sources are discussions and analyses of such records. In history, primary sources are records and artifacts of all sorts; secondary sources are historians' accounts based on this evidence. Most textbooks and reference works are secondary sources.

Particularly in research papers on works of literature, you should try to come to grips with the major primary sources in your subject before immersing yourself in commentary. A study of the theme of corruption of language in Orwell's *1984* and *Animal Farm* obviously should begin with a reading of these works; without this informing experience you will have no way to evaluate the critics' views when you take up the substantial body of Orwell criticism. Scholarly interpretations are sometimes more authoritative in style than substantial in content. The danger in reading criticism before you have really engaged the subject of that criticism is that you may be seduced by well-written but ill-founded argument.

You will find that it is helpful to make a tentative outline—a *tentative* one—fairly early in the note-taking stage. This should reflect but not necessarily replace your running log of notes and queries. In the first few days of looking for material, you will no doubt have in mind a few points you want to develop or problems you want to solve; but if you let them control your note-taking, you will overlook many interesting approaches to your topic. On the other hand, if you have only a hazy notion of your subject—if you have not begun to ask questions of it—you can hardly take notes intelligently and economically; and because your full notes represent a sizable investment of time and energy, you may later find yourself working desperately to incorporate into your paper an unfocused miscellany of information. Some notes are bound to be wasted; every researcher duplicates information and jots down irrelevancies. But you can reduce the duplications and irrelevancies if you keep a tentative outline beside you as you take notes and if you revise it regularly. After every heavy session of reading, while your notes are still fresh in your mind, spend some time studying, modifying, and developing your tentative outline, trying always to arrive at what will be the heart of your paper, its *thesis sentence.*

In a research paper, with its considerable length and multiplicity of details, the thesis statement — an exact formulation of topic and purpose — is especially important. It is often a difficult sentence to write, requiring a good deal of juggling and testing of ideas. The point is to force yourself to define the purpose of your essay *to yourself.* It may help to conceive of the thesis sentence as the answer to a question: "What is the significance of Orwell's striking emphasis on language in *1984* and *Animal Farm?*" Answer and thesis sentence: "In *1984* and *Animal Farm* George Orwell uses fiction and fable to demonstrate the point he makes explicitly in 'Politics and the English Language' — that in the hands of demagogues, language itself can be corrupted until it becomes an ultimate instrument of tyranny." In point of fact, you may never use exactly this sentence in your essay; but no matter. It will have served its purpose in focusing your ideas and your source materials. Without it, your final selection and organization would be aimless and diffuse, with innumerable supporting details in search of something to support.

As you survey your notes and make your final outline, you will be sorting your facts into those that must be used, those that will probably be used, those of incidental interest that may be used, and those that clearly do not belong. To avoid wasting time in planning and writing, you may want to sort your cards into four groups: *Must, Probably, Maybe,* and *No.*

PLANNING AND WRITING

Writing a research paper does not differ essentially from writing other essays in which the purpose is to explain or persuade, interpret or criticize, but some of the procedures discussed in earlier chapters have special pertinence. For one thing, it is imperative to budget your time and work systematically at every stage of the project. However thorough your research and however lucid your report on your findings, your paper will not be satisfactory if the footnoting is inconsistent and the proofreading careless. And however elegant the footnoting, shoddy basic research will undermine its effect. A good reference paper shows deliberate care in all its aspects — enough evidence of care that the reader feels he can take the accuracy of text, documentation, and mechanics for granted and concentrate on the thesis, the evidence, and the qualities of style.

Planning

The quantity of material and the length of the essay make it advisable to have your outline clear—and on paper—before you begin writing. But consider several possibilities before you commit yourself to one plan, just as a short-story writer often resists telling a story as it occurred to him until he thinks it through from other approaches. Your material will fall into blocks, probably from three to eight. The order of these blocks, which will be your paragraph sequences as you write, should grow logically out of your material, your approach, and your purpose. So that your instructor can examine your plan and offer suggestions, draw up your outline in one of the standard forms (see pp. 215–16 and *Outline form).

Because of its length, some of the typical problems of writing any essay recur in more exaggerated form in the research project. Many writers waste an alarming amount of time making a beginning. The usual advice holds: Pull yourself out of a bogged-down introduction and get on with the rest of the paper. After the whole essay has begun to take shape, go back and compose an introductory passage. This advice assumes that you are in command of a workable thesis. Sometimes a writer's floundering at the outset is symptomatic of a vagueness of purpose that he has not faced up to. If you are in that predicament, the thing to do is to admit the problem and think through the material again, working toward a thesis that you believe in and find manageable.

Even when you are well launched into the writing and feel thoroughly at home with your material, it is wise to review all your notes periodically. Much of your essay will be a digest of sources in your own words, and you need to have a good grasp of the ideas and facts so that you will not rely too heavily on what you wrote on the cards. A great deal of rephrasing of even your best summaries will be necessary if they are to fit comfortably into the essay and harmonize with your own style. Make your direct quotations count, but don't overdo them. A research paper is not a string of quotations knotted together with transitional sentences. What you are expected to do is to give the material a form and thrust of meaning of its own. Direct quotation certainly has its uses, but if you fall into the habit of stringing one quotation after another, you will soon lose control of the shape of the paper. As you write, indicate all direct quotations by quotation marks or, if a passage is more than three lines long, by single spacing and indention (see *Quotation marks).

Because the finished paper gives credit in footnotes to the sources used, you will want to indicate those sources in the first draft. You can put an abbreviated reference to the source in parentheses after a statement (see the draft reproduced on p. 442) or write the reference in the margin. Either method enables you to transfer the data to a footnote when you make your final copy.

As you write, you will almost certainly encounter unexpected problems. What seemed like intersecting avenues of meaning will become blind alleys. Authorities you took to be unshakable will totter and fall. But as you struggle with a desk load of recalcitrant material, you will often surprise yourself by coming up with new connections between ideas, new alignments of facts. The important thing is to cultivate an attitude of openness to such possibilities as you write— and to proceed with the deliberateness of a writer to whom each sentence and paragraph is a matter of rhetorical calculation. Given the nature of the subject, the audience, and your own intentions, what strategies of language, method, organization, and argument will produce the highest degree of clarity and persuasiveness?

Style and Point of View

The conventional style of research papers is relatively formal and impersonal. Usually the writer does not refer to himself extensively—though there is no good rhetorical reason why the first person pronoun should not be used for special emphasis (it is certainly to be preferred to the stuffy use of "the present writer" or the editorial "we"). Writing that strives for accuracy and objectivity in its treatment of a subject does not have to be dull, nor does it require total self-effacement. Just keep in mind that your reader will be more interested in what you have done with your material than in what it has done to you—and strive to write a prose that is concise, specific, readable, and calculated to reach your audience.

What assumptions to make about your reader? This question, like others about rhetorical strategy that may occur to you, should be discussed with your instructor. A safe general rule is to pitch your essay at the brightest members of your class—intelligent, critical readers who know little about your subject but want to know more. Assume that you will be asked to read parts of the essay aloud to them.

Beginning and Ending

Although there is more reason for a research paper to have formal introductory and concluding sections than for a short essay to have them, most professionals studiously avoid the kind of beginning that self-consciously announces what is going to be said and the kind of ending that solemnly sums up point by point what *has* been said. Instead, the best practice involves finding a provocative "angle" in the research material and building an introduction around that—one that succeeds in stirring interest and at the same time defines the nature of the inquiry. An essay on ideas about the political significance of language in George Orwell's novels might, for instance, begin with the image a friend has given of Orwell propped up in bed in his final illness, happily cutting out newspaper articles confirming his fears about the general decline of English through political misuse and propaganda.

As for the conclusion, a skilled writer will generally resist the urge to grandly recapitulate his argument one more time, choosing instead to end the paper with a final, clinching point that grows directly out of the body of the paper. If he offers a summary at all, it will be brief and straightforward, a final demonstration that the essay's argument speaks for itself.

Proofreading

Proofreading is not just a matter of striving to please your instructor—"profreading" one student called it. It is a crucial if unexciting part of a research writer's job. The attention he gives to it is a courtesy to his readers and a basic way of serving his paper's best interests. What would you think of the authority and dependability of an essay on, say, pollution in Lake Ontario that spelled *effluent* three different ways, omitted several footnotes, put Chart I where Chart III should have gone and vice versa, and added three zeros to the 1970 population of Rochester, New York? You might not be especially impressed to find all such errors *avoided* in a paper, to be sure; but the positive virtues of an essay rest in part on such negative virtues, the results of careful proofreading.

 FOOTNOTES AND FINAL BIBLIOGRAPHY

Any paper based on the writings of others should acknowledge the sources used. Common courtesy and honesty require that credit be given where credit is due, and a scrupulously documented source allows the reader to judge for himself the evidence an assertion is based on. It also allows the reader to turn to the sources for further information. College students are expected to draw their materials from various sources, but they are also expected to make a frank acknowledgment of these sources. Fundamentally, the forms of documentation are symbols of the courtesy and consideration shown by scholars to each other.

In formal academic papers it is conventional to give exact references in footnotes. The forms differ slightly, but the purpose of all is the same—to record in some brief and consistent form the author, title, facts of publication, and exact page from which each quotation and each fact or opinion is taken. Your instructor will prescribe the style of documentation he wants you to follow. The style of footnotes and bibliography suggested in this section, suitable for documentation in most college research papers, follows the recommendations of the *MLA Style Sheet*, which has been adopted by many university presses and by most journals in literature and history.

Footnotes are needed for:

1. All direct quotations, except for lines from the Bible, proverbs, and other familiar sayings.

2. All important statements of fact, interpretations, opinions, and conclusions that you have derived from the work of another writer. You need to give the source for all statistics, descriptions of situations, scientific data, and the like that are neither common knowledge nor the product of your own investigation.

Presenting the work of others as one's own is a serious intellectual offense—first of all against one's own neglected capabilities. You must acknowledge your source not only when you reproduce verbatim a paragraph, a sentence, or even a significant phrase, but also when you reword or summarize. Whenever you use in a paper information and ideas you have obtained through research, it is up to you to credit the authors and the works the information and ideas came from. (See also the *Index* article *Plagiarism.) Any question about what to footnote that is not resolved by these guidelines should be raised with your instructor. (To test your knowledge of how a single passage in a book should be incorporated in an essay, see the exercise on p. 434.)

Placing Footnotes

The footnote number is placed slightly above the line after the statement or quotation, following all marks of punctuation except the dash. The notes are numbered from 1 up throughout the paper.

The *MLA Style Sheet*, which deals with the style of papers submitted for publication, calls for notes to be typed double-spaced on separate sheets at the end. If you are asked instead to put your footnotes at the bottom of each page on which they belong, look ahead in your rough draft to see how many notes will be needed on a page, and put a light pencil mark where you should begin the footnote series. Separate the first footnote from the bottom line of text by a triple space; type the notes single-spaced; and double space between notes. Whether the notes are placed at the bottom of the page or on separate sheets at the end, the footnote reference number is slightly raised, as in the text. It is not followed by a period. The first line of each footnote is indented.

Form of Footnotes

The purpose of a citation footnote is to tell the reader the exact source of a statement. Uniformity is a convenience for the reader and is obligatory in scholarly papers and articles intended for publication. This section gives models for undergraduate papers.

Books. The *first* reference to a book gives the author's full name (first name first); the full title copied from the title page and underlined; the place of publication, the publisher, and the date of publication in parentheses; the page or pages. A period is placed at the end of the footnote:

[1]Paul Ehrlich, The Population Bomb (New York: Ballantine, 1969), p. 34.

The *MLA Style Sheet* calls for the use of "short forms" for publishers, as illustrated above and throughout this chapter—but your instructor may want you to use their full titles instead—for example, "Ballantine Books" in the note above.

Variations on the basic footnote form are introduced for the following reasons, illustrated in order below: (1) more than one author, (2) an edited work, (3) a translated work, (4) a compilation by an editor, (5) an item in a collection, (6) a work in more than one volume, (7) an indication of an edition, (8) a work whose author is not known, (9) material quoted at second hand.

[1]Sigmund Freud and William C. Bullitt, Thomas Woodrow Wilson, 20th President of the United States: A Psychological Study (New York: Houghton, 1967), p. 49.

[2]S. Y. Agnon, Twenty-one Stories, ed. Nahun N. Glatzer (New York: Schocken, 1970), p. 8.

[3]Richard Lattimore, trans., The Iliad, by Homer (Chicago: Univ. of Chicago Press, 1962), p. iii.

[4]Ralph Mills, Jr., ed., Selected Letters of Theodore Roethke (Seattle: Univ. of Washington Press, 1968), p. 110.

In editions, translations, and compilations, the author's name is placed first when the text is referred to, the name of the editor, translator, or compiler when it is his work that is under discussion.

[5]George Fraser, "Writing," in The New Outline of Modern Knowledge, ed. Alan Pryce-Jones (New York: Simon, 1956), p. 321.

⁶Immanuel Wallerstein and Paul Starr, eds., The University Crisis Reader (New York: Random, 1971), II, 3–92.

⁷Lewis A. McArthur, Oregon Geographic Names, 3rd ed. (Portland: Binfords, 1952), p. 74.

⁸Soviet Handbook, 1959–1965 (London: Soviet Handbooks, 1965), p. 22.

⁹Emmanuel Lavine, The Third Degree (New York: Vanguard, 1930), p. 138, quoted in Dictionary of American Slang, comp. and ed. Harold Wentworth and Stuart Berg Flexner (New York: Crowell, 1967), p. 378.

Pamphlets and government bulletins are referred to in the same form as books. The items always appear in the same order: author, title, place, publisher, date, page.

For *later* references to the same book, use a short form, enough to identify the work in the bibliography, instead of the now generally neglected *op. cit.* The author's last name is sufficient if only one work by the same man is used:

³Ehrlich, p. 31.

Magazine and Newspaper Articles. In the *first* reference to a magazine article give: (1) the author's name in normal order, (2) the title of the article in quotation marks, (3) the name of the magazine underlined, (4) the series number, (5) the volume number in arabic numbers, (6) the issue number in arabic numbers, (7) the year in parentheses preceded by month or season, (8) page or pages (numbers only, no "p." or "pp."). The simplest periodical form is in order for a journal which is paginated continuously through one entire volume:

⁴Hugh Staples, "The Rose in the Sea–Wind: A Reading of Theodore Roethke's 'North American Sequence,'" American Literature, 36 (1964), 189–203.

For weekly or monthly magazines and for newspapers, you may omit the volume number and give the complete date of issue, preceding the page number or numbers with "p." or "pp."

⁵Mark Harris, "The Flowering of the Hippies," Atlantic, Sept. 1967, pp. 63–72.

When no author is given, the footnote for a magazine article begins with the title of the article. Reference to an untitled article in a magazine or to a newspaper story includes the name of the periodical underlined, the date (either month, day, year or day, month, year), and the page. For a newspaper story the column number and the edition may be given. If there are sections paged separately, the section should also be identified.

6The New York Times, Aug. 21, 1970, Sec. III, p. 2, col. 4.

A *later* reference to a magazine article or newspaper item may be shortened to the author's last name, the name of the magazine, and the page or, if the article is anonymous, to the name of the periodical and the page:

7Harris, Atlantic, p. 65.

Most articles in major encyclopedias are initialed by the authors and keyed to an author list; the name of a contributor should be given in full if possible, then the title of the entry, and the name and copyright date of the encyclopedia:

12E[dward] B[ernstein], "Marx," Encyclopaedia Britannica, 1911.

Unsigned publications of organizations are listed by title:

131971 General Bulletin (Columbus: Ohio State University, 1971), p. 274.

In a footnote, *ibid.* means "in the same place"—that is, in the same book or article as the preceding footnote. It may be used to refer to the work cited in the immediately preceding footnote when both notes fall on the same page.

8William Stafford, Allegiances (New York: Harper, 1970), p. 39.
9Ibid., p. 40.

Neither *ibid.* nor the short form of subsequent reference (3Ehrlich, p. 31) should appear very often in a sound paper. A succession of such references suggests excessive reliance on one source and, perhaps, faulty organization. Ditto marks are not used in footnotes or in a bibliography.

Split Note.   If the author's name is included in the text, the footnote begins with the title. If the author's name and the title are in the text, the title should still be repeated in the footnote. If you give the original source in the text, cite in the footnote the secondary source in which you found it.

Informational Footnote.   In some scholarly publications, you may find an additional fact, a statement of a different opinion, a quotation, or a reference to other sources given in a footnote. In college writing it is usually best to use footnotes only for citation of sources—everything else belongs in the text.

Bible.   Books of the Bible are not underlined. Modern practice is to cite a biblical source in parentheses in the text. If a footnote is used instead, the book is named first, followed by chapter and verse:

[17]Genesis IV:16 (or, increasingly, 4:16).

Common Abbreviations.   The following abbreviations are commonly used in footnotes. Although you are not likely to use them all, you should know what they mean. The *MLA Style Sheet* notes that practice varies in italicizing abbreviations of Latin words. Of the following only *sic* is italicized in *A Manual of Style*, 12th ed. (Chicago: Univ. of Chicago Press, 1969).

art.	article.
ca. or c. (*circa*)	around a given date (ca. 1480).
ch. or chap.; chs. or chaps.	chapter; chapters.
col., cols.	column, columns.
comp.	compiler, compiled by.
ed.	editor, edition (2nd ed.), edited by.
e.g. (*exempli gratia*)	for example.
et al. (*et alii*)	and others (used in *MLA* style when there are more than three authors; but the English words are also widely used: Walter S. Avis and others).
f., ff.	and the following page (386f.), and the following pages (286ff.). Exact references are preferable: pp. 286–87, pp. 286–91 (*MLA* style); or pp. 286–287, pp. 286–291.
ibid. (*ibidem*)	in the same place.
l., ll.	line, lines.
MS, MSS	manuscript, manuscripts.
n., nn.	note (to refer to a footnote in a source: p. 135, n. 2), notes.
n.d.	no date of publication.
n.p.	no place of publication.
NS or N.S.	new series of a periodical.
OS or O.S.	old series of a periodical.
p., pp.	page, pages.
passim	throughout the work.
sic	thus, so (used to indicate that erroneous or doubtful information has been quoted exactly).
trans. or tr.	translator, translation, or translated by.
vol., vols.	volume, volumes (vol. and p. are not used when figures for both are given: Vol. III *or* p. 176; but III, 176).

The following abbreviations are no longer common in general use:

cf. (*confer*) — compare (used to cite other related passages); "see" is often used.

infra — below (referring to something discussed later in the paper); "below" takes no more space.

loc. cit. (*loco citato*) — in the place cited (referring to a passage cited in a recent footnote; not followed by a page number). It is generally simpler to use the short second-reference form.

N.B. (*nota bene*) — note well, notice especially.

op. cit. (*opere citato*) — the work cited (referring to a work cited in a recent footnote): Ehrlich, op. cit., p. 134. Now the author's name alone (Ehrlich, p. 134) or, if more than one book by the same author has been referred to, his name and the title, or shortened title, of the book is more common.

q.v. (*quod vide*) — which see (used for cross-reference); "which see" is common.

supra — above (referring to something discussed earlier in the paper); "above" takes no more space.

If you are writing your research paper from a casebook, source book, or "controlled research" text, footnote your references to sources in the book as if you had found them in the library. Most casebooks provide full bibliographical information and original pagination (indicated in the text itself by numbers in brackets or slashes); document according to this information instead of citing the casebook each time. Your instructor will probably ask you to provide an identifying footnote for the casebook, too.

The Final Bibliography

The bibliography of the sources actually used in the preparation of a reference paper comes at its end. It contains not all the sources consulted but only those that have actually furnished material. (Your instructor may, however, ask you to supply a supplementary list, "Other Works Consulted.") Its purpose is to enable a reader to see at a glance the range of works cited in the footnotes; therefore authors' names that begin entries are inverted for alphabetizing. When no author is given, the first important word of the title is used as the key word for alphabetizing.

The first line of each entry in a bibliography is begun at the left margin, and succeeding lines are indented five spaces. The sample entries that follow, illustrating the bibliography form recommended by the *MLA Style Sheet*, are for works used earlier to illustrate footnote form. Comparison will make clear how the two differ. See also the bibliography for the sample paper, p. 447.

A book

Ehrlich, Paul. The Population Bomb. New York: Bal-
     lantine, 1969.

More than one author

Freud, Sigmund, and William C. Bullitt. Thomas
     Woodrow Wilson, 20th President of the United
     States: A Psychological Study. New York: Hough-
     ton, 1967.

A subtitle may be omitted from a footnote, but it must be included in a bibliography.

An edited work

Agnon, S. Y. Twenty-one Stories. Ed. Nahun N. Gla-
     tzer. New York: Schocken, 1970.

A translated work

Lattimore, Richard, trans. The Iliad, by Homer.
     Chicago: Univ. of Chicago Press, 1962.

If the text rather than the translation is the main concern, the author rather than the translator would come first.

A compilation by an editor

Mills, Ralph, Jr., ed. Selected Letters of Theodore
     Roethke. Seattle: Univ. of Washington Press,
     1968.

An item in a collection

Fraser, George. "Writing," in The New Outline of
     Modern Knowledge, ed. Alan Pryce-Jones. New
     York: Simon, 1956.

A work in more than one volume

Wallerstein, Immanuel, and Paul Starr, eds. The
     University Crisis Reader. 2 vols. New York:
     Random, 1971.

An indication of an edition

McArthur, Lewis A. <u>Oregon</u> <u>Geographic</u> <u>Names</u>. 3rd
    ed. Portland: Binfords, 1952.

A work whose author is unknown

<u>Soviet</u> <u>Handbook,</u> <u>1959–1965</u>. London: Soviet Handbooks,
    1965.

For a work quoted at second hand (see footnote 9, p. 421), the bibliography would give only the secondary source:

<u>Dictionary</u> <u>of</u> <u>American</u> <u>Slang</u>. Comp. and ed. Harold
    Wentworth and Stuart Berg Flexner. New York:
    Crowell, 1967.

EXERCISES

1. Put the following references to source material in consistent footnote form as they would appear in a reference paper. Keep them in the present alphabetical order.

a. To page 225 of this book.

b. To an editorial in the Boston Traveler on December 2, 1940, entitled The Responsibility of the Press.

c. To pages 139 and 140 in the second volume of a book by George Philip Krapp called The English Language in America. The book was published by the Century Company of New York and the date on the title page reads MCMXXV.

d. To pages 228 to 231 inclusive of the book mentioned in *a.*

e. To an unsigned editorial called TV Politics: Too High a Price in volume 69 of Life for September 11, 1970, page 2.

f. To page xvii in the Introduction of a book called Burke's Politics. The book has a subtitle Selected writings and speeches of Edmund Burke on Reform, revolution and war. It was edited by Ross J. S. Hoffman and Paul Levack, and was published in 1949 by Alfred A. Knopf in New York.

g. To an article entitled Report from Greece: Under the Junta, written by two men, Nicholas Gage and Elias Kulukundis, and printed in the American Scholar for Summer 1970, pages 475 to 497. This issue was part of volume 39.

h. To the same pages of the article mentioned in *g.*

i. To a passage by Irving King in the October 1910 issue of the American Journal of Theology, quoted on pages 203 to 204 of the American Myth of Success, a book by Richard Weiss published in 1969 in New York by Basic Books, Inc.

j. To an unsigned article called Isle of Man in the 1941 edition of the Encyclopedia Americana, a thirty-volume work published in New York and Chicago by the Americana Corporation. This article appeared on page 414 of volume XV.

2. Put the items above in proper form and order for a bibliography.

In short bibliographies all the items are run in one list, alphabetically arranged. Very long bibliographies are sometimes grouped by type of material: primary sources, secondary sources; works by an author, works about him; and so on. They should not be grouped according to type of publication, such as books and periodicals, except in a list of the works of a single writer.

Typically the completed paper comprises the following units (those in brackets are optional):

Title page: Give the title of the paper, the writer's name, the date submitted, and any other required information, such as course and section number.

[*Preface:* In a preface a writer talks about his work. Because they lend themselves to pretentious forms of special pleading, prefaces are generally best avoided. You will not need one unless you wish to thank someone for special help, call attention to unusual material, or note some point that you were unable to develop. The preface stands on a page by itself.]

Outline and table of contents: Make the type of outline assigned. Be sure that it conforms to the order of material in the finished paper. Check its form by referring to the modals on p. 216 and to *Outline form. The outline can serve as a table of contents if you give at the right of each main topic the page on which it begins.

Text of the paper: This is the final copy of the paper, complete with footnotes and diagrams or any other illustrative material used. Put the title at the top of the first page, and follow the manuscript form required by your instructor. Before making this final copy, go through pp. 420–24 of this chapter and the sample paper on pp. 433–45 to make sure your footnotes follow the suggested form.

Bibliography: On a separate page, list in the form suggested on pp. 425–26 the books and articles you actually used in writing your paper.

[*Appendix:* Occasionally a paper needs a table of statistics too long to work into the body of the essay, or it may require a long quotation, such as part of a treaty or other document that much of the paper is based on. Such material can be placed in an appendix, but in student research papers it generally should be abridged and included in the text.]

The sample research paper on the right-hand pages beginning with p. 433 follows the guidelines for research and writing set forth in this chapter and the style of documentation described on pp. 418–26. On the left-hand pages are comments and further exercises.

Comment

The outline below is a preliminary version of the outline on the next page. Study it and prepare to answer the questions in the exercise.

```
        Out in the Sticks (rough outline)

    Our expression "out in the sticks" probably comes
from an Indian word having to do with forest spirits.
    I. Introduction
   II. Words and sayings often change their meaning
  III. The expression's widespread use
       A. 19th century
   IV. Specific professional meanings
       A. Theater
       B. Baseball
       C. Loggers
       D. Hoboes
    V. Confusion with "Styx"
   VI. Meaning of stick
       A. In Chinook Jargon
       B. Western loggers' meaning
  VII. Indians told about "stick Indians" who lived in
       the sticks
       A. Henry Gibbs' report
 VIII. Essay by C. B. Bagley makes it clear that Indi-
       ans believed "stick Indians" were spirits
   IX. Indian words for spirit
       A. goblin
       B. Shitike Creek in Oregon
    X. Warm Springs Indians' belief in "stiyakha"
   XI. Conclusion
```

Exercise

Compare the preceding outline and the one below, and analyze the differences.

a. What changes were made to regularize the form? Why is the revised thesis sentence more satisfactory? Why has the order of topics been changed? Which sections of the rough outline overlap?

b. Convert the following sentence outline to a topic outline.

EXPLORING THE LAND OF THE STICKS

The familiar expression "out in the sticks" evolved from explorers' and loggers' use of the Chinook Jargon word for <u>forest</u> and may have originated in an Indian word, <u>stiyakha</u>, meaning "a forest spirit," known to white men as a "stick Indian."

I. Many words and expressions become detached from their origins, and change their meanings.

II. The expression has been widely current since the nineteenth century and has come to have special professional meanings, generally unfavorable.

   A. Uses in the nineteenth century are on record.

   B. Baseball players speak of farm clubs "in the sticks," and actors use the expression to denote uncultured regions.

   C. Hoboes speak of their jungles as "sticks."

III. Speculation that the word is a corruption of "Styx" is unfounded.

IV. Western loggers borrowed the Chinook Jargon word <u>stick</u>, meaning everything relating to wood, to describe "woods."

V. Indians told about a wild race of "stick Indians" living in the forest.

   A. Henry Gibbs understood that these were simply less civilized Indians.

   B. Reports by C. B. Bagley and others suggest on the contrary that they were spirits.

VI. The expression may derive from an Indian word for
    "spirit" sounding like <u>stick</u>, rather than from
    the Jargon word itself.
    A. The Jargon and dialect word for "goblin,"
       <u>tsiatko</u>, sounds like <u>stick</u>.
    B. Shitike Creek in Oregon is another possible
       form of the word.
    C. Warm Springs Indians tell of "stick Indians,"
       mountain spirits who lived around Shitike
       Creek and were called <u>stiyakha</u>, or spirits.
VII. If this origin were confirmed, the connotations
     of "out in the sticks" might change from
     unfavorable to favorable.

Comment

In a manuscript prepared for a printer, footnotes should be placed on a separate page, following the bibliography, and this form may be used for course papers. The more convenient place for footnotes, however, is at the bottom of the page, where the eye can pick them up easily and relate them to the material in the text.

A line across or partially across the page may be used to separate the footnotes from the text. An extra space, however, is usually considered adequate (see opposite page).

Variant forms for a footnote to a book differ mainly in content. Sometimes the publisher is omitted and only the place and year appear in parentheses; sometimes these are omitted as well.

Note 1: In the citation of a book by two authors, both names are given.

Exercise

Write a rough draft of the first four paragraphs of your essay. Submit it with a trial sentence outline of the paper to your instructor.

EXPLORING THE LAND OF THE STICKS

One of the rewards of acquiring more than a
speaking acquaintance with the English language lies
in the discovery of words and sayings whose popular
usage has wandered far from their original
sources. Thus, many of our words—bloomers, macadam,
guillotine—are unsuspected memorials to people whose
names somehow or other got attached to new items and
eventually became, in uncapitalized form, common
currency. The process by which the origins of new
words are forgotten and the words become literally
nonsense can be surprisingly rapid. For example,
everyone has heard and probably used the word
boondocks, meaning "the sticks," the "backwoods," and
so on—but who remembers now that this odd-looking
word came into English in the Second World War, when
American soldiers picked up the Philippine Tagalog
word bunduk, which means "mountains"?[1]

And what about "the sticks" itself? We use the
expression to refer to back country, hillbilly
territory, or, as Webster's Third New International
Dictionary puts it, "wooded lands, rural districts,
sections of a country remote from or held to be little
touched by centers of civilization." The dictionary
definition is connotatively neutral; but in fact,
although we Americans tend to be sentimental about
"country . . . little touched by centers of
civilization," we generally use "out in the sticks"
(like "boondocks") somewhat contemptuously. Does the
current usage bear any relation to its origins?

The phrase apparently entered American popular
speech in the nineteenth century,[2] and it seems to
carry with it a generally Western flavor, although it

[1]William Morris and Mary Morris, A Dictionary of
Word and Phrase Origins (New York: Harper, 1962), I,
43.

[2]C. Merton Babcock, "The Social Significance of
the Language of the American Frontier," American
Speech, 24 (1949), 256.

Comment

Note 4: When two sources supply information for the same sentence, they are cited in one footnote and separated by a semi-colon.

Note 5: Besides this short form for immediate subsequent citation of work after an initial full citation, "Ibid., p. 520" is also correct as a reference to the note immediately preceding; but it is not recommended unless the preceding note is on the same page, and it may be confusing after a double citation.

Exercise

Read the following passage on academic hiring and determine which incorporations of the passage in a text are satisfactory and which are unsatisfactory. A superior number means that the writer intends to footnote.

Original passage

When we examine the specific procedures of hiring in the American university, they turn out to be almost unbelievably elaborate. The average salary of an assistant professor is approximately that of a bakery truck driver, and his occupancy of a job is likely to be less permanent. Yet it may require a large part of the time of twenty highly-skilled men for a full year to hire him. — Theodore Caplow and Reece J. McGee, *The Academic Marketplace*

Uses made of the passage

a.   Hiring university teachers is so elaborate nowadays that twenty professors will spend a good deal of their time for a whole year hiring one assistant professor.[7]

b.   Most assistant professors get about the same salary as bakery truck drivers, but the driver is likely to hold his job longer.

c.   When we look at the specific procedures of hiring in U.S. colleges, they turn out to be incredibly complex. The pay of an assistant professor is approximately the same as that of a bakery truck driver, and his tenure in the job will probably be less permanent. Yet it might take much of the time of twenty highly trained men for a whole year to appoint him.[6]

d.   Hiring teachers, even at the lower ranks, is a complicated process.

e.   Hiring methods in our universities are "almost unbelievably elaborate." Though an assistant professor makes about the same salary as a bakery truck driver, and though the driver will probably hold his job longer, "yet it may require a large part of the time of twenty highly-skilled men for a full year to hire" the teacher.[8]

(continued on p. 436)

has come to have a Southern usage too.[3]   In addition
to its general application, the phrase has been
appropriated by a number of professions in which a
sharp distinction is drawn between "bigtime" status
and lower levels of fame and glory.   Baseball players,
for example, shudder at the prospect of a career on a
farm club somewhere "in the sticks," and actors
traditionally would do almost anything rather than go
on an extended tour "back in stick country"—that is,
out of New York City![4]   In a rather different kind of
profession, hoboes sometimes refer to their camps or
"jungles" as "the sticks."[5]

But if the expression has a clear currency in
American speech and writing, _how_ did it come to make
its small enrichment of our vocabulary?   And would its
original users recognize the way we use it today?   The
answers are strange ones, proving again that the
meaning of a familiar idiom sometimes rests on
unexpected and romantic foundations.

The educated guess might be made that _sticks_ is
only a corruption of _Styx_, the mythological river of
Hades.   But if by stretching things a little the
connotations of the two words seem to match up (our
unsuccessful baseball player might feel that he is
being sent down to a kind of Hades, perhaps), in more
particular terms "the sticks" has apparently never
denoted "river" or "river-country," or anything
especially suggestive of the Underworld; and in fact
no modern dictionary offers this explanation of the
expression's etymology.

In their _Dictionary of Word and Phrase Origins_,

[3]_A Dictionary of Americanisms on Historical
Principles_, ed. Mitford M. Mathews (Chicago: Univ. of
Chicago Press, 1951), II, 1649.

[4]Lester V. Berrey and Melvin Van den Bark, _The
American Thesaurus of Slang_ (New York: Crowell, 1942),
p. 576; _Dictionary of American Slang_, comp. and ed.
Harold Wentworth and Stuart Berg Flexner (New York:
Crowell, 1967), p. 519.

[5]_Dictionary of American Slang_, p. 520.

Comment

Note 7: An example of an "informational footnote." In college research papers the general recommendation is to incorporate such detail in the text if it is sufficiently pertinent and otherwise to omit it.

Is the transition clear at the beginning of the first new paragraph on the facing page?

Note 8: When a work has more than three authors, use the name of the first followed by "et al." or, in some current styles, by "and others."

(continued from p. 434)

f. The average salary of an assistant professor is approximately that of a bakery truck driver.

g. The hiring methods in American colleges are almost unbelievably elaborate.

h. The hiring methods in American colleges are "almost unbelievably elaborate."

i. The average salary of an assistant professor is approximately that of a bakery truck driver.[11]

j. "Hiring teachers, even at the lower ranks, is a complicated process," according to Caplow and McGee.

k. The salaries of assistant professors and bakery truck drivers are about the same: they are about equally underpaid, that is.[9]

1. According to Caplow and McGee, "The average salary of an assistant professor is that of a bakery truck driver, and yet it may require a large part of the time of twenty men for a full year to hire him."[17]

m. The main point of Caplow and McGee's discussion of hiring in *The Academic Marketplace* is that hiring procedures in the colleges should be more like those used in the business world.[6]

William and Mary Morris offer some clues. "The phrase
was originally used . . . by loggers to designate
timberlands. Gradually it has come to mean any rural
district, especially, but not necessarily, a backwoods
area."[6] Now it is a fact that Western loggers still
sometimes refer jovially to the huge evergreens they
cut as "sticks"[7] (perhaps this is what Theodore
Roosevelt had in mind when he proposed to "speak
softly and carry a big stick"), so, logically, "out in
the sticks" would be where the big trees grow, out in
the tall timber. But the true origins of the saying
are not so simple: Why did Western loggers start
calling their trees "sticks" in the first place?

Our expression is current in Canada, too, and A
Dictionary of Canadianisms points out that in the
Chinook Jargon (the famous lingua franca through which
Western Indians communicated with each other inter-
tribally and with the first white explorers and
settlers) the word stick, according to the simplifying
diction of the Jargon, denoted literally everything
made of wood--from spears to ships' masts, from twigs
to whole forests of pine and fir.[8] A standard
dictionary of the Jargon notes that "The word 'stick'
is used to denote 'tree' or wood of any kind; anything
made of wood"[9]--thus, tree bark was known as stick-
skin, a wooden eating bowl was a stickpan, and a
forest was simply sticks. So it seems logical that
early settlers, loggers, and traders would turn this
all-purpose Jargon word into our metaphorical
expression. At this point, however, our search takes
a very odd turn. We must ask why the Indians

[6]Morris and Morris, p. 338.

[7]In his Woods Words: A Comprehensive Dictionary
of Loggers' Terms (Portland: Binfords, 1952), p. 182,
Walter F. McCormick notes that loggers also use the
word to specify tall spars used as booms.

[8]A Dictionary of Canadianisms, ed. Walter S. Avis
et al. (Toronto: W. J. Gage, 1967), p. 752.

[9]W. S. Phillips, The Chinook Book (Seattle:
privately printed, 1913), p. 91.

Comment

Note 11: The date of Gibbs' essay is included in the text in parentheses to make it immediately clear that it is an early first-hand account. Because the text passage and the footnote passage appear on the same page in the original, one footnote suffices. Ellipses are used in the second passage to eliminate extraneous phrasing. A quotation of three or more lines should be indented and single-spaced; it should not be enclosed in quotation marks unless the quotation marks appear in the original source. Single quotation marks appear in these passages to correspond with Gibbs' usage. (Because the *MLA Style Sheet* is concerned with papers prepared for publication, it does not permit single spacing.)

The citation of an unusual source (a phonograph record, mimeographed pamphlet, personal letter, etc.) that does not fit any of the conventional forms should resemble as closely as possible the style used for other footnotes. For example:

[19]W. S. Merwin, letter to the editor, June 24, 1969.

themselves (whose own words from many dialects make up
the great bulk of the Jargon) used this particular
word.

Many early Western explorers (before the rise of
the logging industry and the development of trade
generally) report that Indians told them about other,
wilder natives who lived back in the forest and were
called "stick Indians." In Canada, for example,
Indians on the Pacific Coast reported having dealings
with "the interior, or 'stick' Indian, as he was
known, because he came from the land of forests, or
'sticks.'"[10] In his "Account of Indian Mythology in
Oregon and Washington Territory" (1865), the explorer
and anthropologist George Gibbs observes that

> the foreign medicine men are apt among the
> Indians, as among some other peoples, to enjoy a
> greater reputation than their own, those of the
> wilder tribes, the 'stick Indians' in particular,
> being supposed to have the most potent spirits at
> their command.

In a footnote Gibbs explains that

> a race of tall Indians, called 'wild' or 'stick'
> Indians, was said to wander through the forest.
> . . . Their homes were hollowed out like the
> sleeping places of animals. . . . It is because
> of this lack of any houses or villages that they
> were characterized as 'wild.' A young Quinault—
> Chehalis told me that they were called 'Stick
> Indians' simply because they lived in the
> woods.[11]

Now the more one reads about these "tall," "wild"
Indians who lived in the deep forest and who were
somehow never directly encountered by white explorers,
the more one suspects that to the Indian informants
they were something more than human, not mere figments

[10] _A Dictionary of Canadianisms_, p. 752.

[11] "Account of Indian Mythology in Oregon and
Washington Territory," ed. Ella E. Clark, _Oregon
Historical Quarterly_, 57 (1956), 133-34.

Comment

As is shown in the sample note cards, the page number is written first. On Card 1, a lengthy part of a paragraph was taken down in a quotation because the author's exact words promised to be useful in the final text. In general, when quoting use the author's exact words, and enclose them in quotation marks on your note cards, being careful to note ellipses; in summarizing, do not use his words but paraphrase, as in the three lines at the top of Card 2. Note that the last two items on Card 2 were not used in the final text. Should they have been?

On Card 2 several notes have been taken on the same card because they will obviously be used at the same point in the paper.

Page notes

> Stick Indians   Bagley, *Indian Myths of the Northwest*
>
> 118 "When a boy, the Yakima Indians told me of the 'Eliquas Tein' (Stick Indians), a wild race of people who inhabited the high craggy peaks along both sides of the summit of the Cascade Mountains around the headwaters of the Chelan and Skagit Rivers. They were held in superstitious awe by many who believed that they were the spirits of departed warriors."

Card 1

Page notes

> Stick Indians   Bagley, *Indian Myths of the Northwest*
>
> 119-- Notes that because S.I.'s were seen only around precipices and peaks, Indians thought they were winged.
>
> Some Indian hunters claim to have talked to the spirit chief, who told them to kill all the game they needed, for his people had plenty.
>
> -- Legend of the young squaw who was kidnapped by a Stick Indian.

Card 2

of the imagination or jokes played upon gullible
whites but supernatural beings, perhaps too important,
too sacred for ordinary Indians to identify exactly to
unbelieving or evangelizing white foreigners.
Confirmation of this hunch is found in C. B. Bagley's
Indian Myths of the Northwest, a collection of
stories and tales which includes the following from
the state of Washington:

> When a boy, the Yakima Indians told me of the
> 'Eliquas Tein' (Stick Indians), a wild race of
> people who inhabited the high craggy peaks along
> both sides of the summit of the Cascade Mountains
> around the headwaters of the Chelan and Skagit
> Rivers. They were held in superstitious awe by
> many who believed that they were the spirits of
> departed warriors.[12]

Bagley goes on to note that, because these
creatures were usually glimpsed just as they
disappeared over a crag or leaped into a mountain
abyss, the Indians believed that they possessed
wings.[13]

So, it seems clear, the original denizens of "the
sticks" were not uncultured hillbillies, not white
loggers, but a race of elusive nature spirits,
haunting lonely areas of the West where the Indians
themselves were not inclined to travel. Is it
possible that our expression actually derives from an
Indian word for spirit or supernatural being then,
perhaps in a particular dialect rather than the
Jargon, and that it does not come from the Indian—
English Jargon word for wood, as is generally
accepted?

In the Chinook Jargon, a strong evil spirit was a
skookum, and a great spirit was a tahmuhnawis. More

---

[12]Indian Myths of the Northwest (Seattle: Lowman,
1930), p. 118.

[13]On p. 3 of the magazine section of the
Portland Oregonian for April 28, 1940, Robert L.
Sicade describes similar beliefs: "The Indians Have
Bogey—Men Too: Old Legends Tell of the Tsiatko Who
Roamed the Woods at Night."

Comment

Note 14: The three page references to Thomas' book in this note are to entries for the three Indian words given; since they appear in sequence, they need only one footnote. The Indian Jargon words here and throughout the essay are underlined to indicate that, as foreign words, they should be italicized.

Note 16: Occasionally, to give special emphasis to some portion of a quoted passage, you may want to underline, as here. Be sure to acknowledge that the underlining is your interpolation and does not represent italics in the source.

A rough draft should be triple-spaced or written with wide margins to leave room for revisions. In the rough draft below, a brief citation in parentheses records temporarily the source of material used. Footnotes put at the bottom of the page may be overlooked if the draft and final copy do not correspond page for page.

So, ~~it appears to be a safe speculation that the first~~ *it seems clear, the original denizens of*
~~Stick dwellers~~ were not ~~backwoodsmen but Indian~~ nature *"the sticks" uncultured hillbillies, not white loggers, but a race of*
spirits ˏhaunting lonely areas of the West ˏ ~~Whether~~ *where the Indians themselves were not elusive inclined to travel.*

~~they were tall or short, malevolent or good-hearted~~

~~seems to vary with the informant; the important thing~~

~~is that, disguise their belief as they might (Gibbs~~

~~was probably misinformed by his informant), the~~

~~Indians did believe in their existence.~~ *Is it* ~~It appears to~~

~~be~~ possible, ~~then,~~ that our expression actually ~~was~~
~~developed~~ from ˏa ~~dialect word meaning spirit, rather~~ *derives an Indian word for spirit or super-natural being then, perhaps in a particular dialect*
~~than from the Jargon word for wood.~~ *rather than the Jargon, and that it does not come from the Indian-English Jargon word for wood, as is generally accepted?*

In the Chinook Jargon, a strong evil spirit was a

skookum, and ~~Indians called~~ a great spirit ˏ *was*
More suggestively
tahmuhnawis. ~~However,~~ a goblin was a tsiatko in many

individual dialects as well as in the Jargon, and this
word ~~father sounds like~~ˏ *might be twisted into something sounding like* "stick." (Thomas, pp. 102, 104, 106)

suggestively, a goblin was a <u>tsiatko</u> in many
individual dialects as well as in the Jargon, and this
word might be twisted into something sounding like
"stick."[14] In central Oregon on the Warm Springs
Indian Reservation, there is a large tributary of the
Deschutes River known as Shitike Creek,[15] which,
again, could easily be corrupted into our word: the
name is thought to be a Wasco term, but its meaning is
unrecorded. And a recently-published Indian myth from
this area seems to give strong support if not
confirmation to our etymological hunch. It is worth
quoting in full:

> When an Indian is traveling up in the mountains
> in a lonely place and hears a certain bird
> singing, he knows it is probably a 'stick'
> Indian. The stick Indians are spirits who live
> in high gloomy places, like Grizzly Flats (in the
> Cascades south of Mt. Jefferson) and upper
> <u>Shitike</u> Creek (southwest of Warm Springs Agency),
> and their favorite trick is to sing like a bird
> in the evening when birds don't sing. If you
> follow the song, the stick Indians will lead you
> deeper and deeper into the woods--and you just
> won't come out, maybe you will lose your mind in
> there. Some Indians when they're out huckle-
> berry-picking or hunting scatter matches all
> around their camp at night--they say the stick
> Indians like matches best of all, living in the
> dark.[16]

The word "stick," according to the Indian informant,
is a white man's corruption of a Wasco-Warm Springs
word, <u>stiyakha</u>, meaning "a kind of mountain spirit."

It should be acknowledged that no other instance
of this Indian word has yet found its way into print;
and it is barely possible, of course, that <u>stiyakha</u>
might represent a late corruption of the Jargon word
<u>stick</u> in the Wasco dialect! But at least we have

[14]Edward Harper Thomas, <u>Chinook: A History and
Dictionary</u> (Portland: J. K. Gill, 1935), pp. 102, 104,
106.

[15]Lewis A. McArthur, <u>Oregon Geographic Names</u>
(Portland: Binfords, 1944), p. 468.

[16]Jarold Ramsey, "Three Wasco-Warm Springs
Texts," <u>Western Folklore</u>, 29 (Winter 1970), 97.
Italics added.

Comment

Last paragraph: Should the author acknowledge the limits of his theory here at the end as he does? Should he be more emphatic in his claim to have discovered the true etymology of the saying? Would the essay be improved substantially if the crucial material about the *stiyakha* was introduced at the beginning of the paper, rather than built up to and disclosed near the end?

Exercises

1. The writing of précis, formal condensed paraphrases of someone else's writing, is excellent practice for writing summary notes. Moreover, it is instructive for the challenge it offers to the writer's vocabulary and command of sentence structure. Like the practical summaries you will make for your paper, the précis calls for a scrupulous rewriting of the original, aimed at condensing the original while retaining its information and point of view. Rules for the formal précis prohibit quoting from the original and require that, through the use of appositives, verbals, and series and the elimination of nonessential details, the final version should be from one third to one fifth as long as the original passage. To accomplish all this, keep the emphasis and point of view of the original, and still maintain readability is a large order — but it can be done, and it gets easier with practice. Write précis of two of the following:

a. "The Rhetorical Situation," pp. 19–22.

b. The first two paragraphs of the Declaration of Independence.

c. The sample paper given on these pages.

d. George Orwell's essay, "Politics and the English Language."

e. An article you plan to use in your paper, or a chapter from a book you mean to refer to.

2. Write a brief report on one of the following topics:

a. Different methods by which you could have developed your paper, and why you chose the one you did.

b. The sources you found most useful, and why.

c. Some problems you encountered in organizing your paper, and how you solved them.

d. Some by-products of your research — what you have learned about finding material, about the subject itself, or about areas for further investigation.

3. Write a summary or précis of your paper, giving the essential ideas and emphasis of the original.

traced our familiar saying back to the real "forest
primeval" where it began its journey into the American
vocabulary, and we have uncovered the possibility that
the first inhabitants of "stick country, stickdom, the
sticks, the stix"[17] were supernatural beings who gave
their magical name to the wild woods where they lived
and thence, through who knows what process, to the
language at large.

The irony is that if this etymology were
confirmed, instead of using "out in the sticks" with
an unfavorable twist, we might use it with positive,
even reverent connotations in mind. The growing
number of Americans who long nostalgically for
untouched wilderness frontiers and for the supposed
simplicity of Indian life would find themselves
expressing an urge to retreat to "_Stiyakha_
Country." But as the popular usage now stands, cut
off from its romantic origins, most of us don't crave
to be _that_ deep in the sticks.

[17]Berrey and Van den Bark, p. 576.

Comment

The sample bibliography cards given below are for entries 1 and 2 in the bibliography on the facing page.

Location   Slug   Code

Author

Title

Publication data

Comment

> Per.   "Sticks" - First Uses   Babcock
>
> Babcock, C. Merton
>
> "The Social Significance of the language of the American Frontier"
>
> American Speech
> 24 (1949), 256
>
> "in the sticks" - 19th century usage

Call number   Slug   Code

Author

Title

Publication data

Comment

> L970.62   Stick Indians   Bagley
> B146   as Spirits
>
> Bagley, C.B.
> Indian Myths of the Northwest
> Seattle : Lowman and Hanford, 1930
> Yakimas believed in Stick Indians as mountain Spirits --
> pp. 118-19

Exercise

Evaluate the sample paper as a piece of writing. Pay particular attention to the organization, to the development of the thesis, and to the quality of the prose. What would you have done differently?

Bibliography

Babcock, C. Merton. "The Social Significance of the
    Language of the American Frontier." American
    Speech, 24 (1949), 256.

Bagley, C. B. Indian Myths of the Northwest. Seattle:
    Lowman, 1930.

Berrey, Lester V., and Melvin Van den Bark. The
    American Thesaurus of Slang. New York: Crowell,
    1942.

Dictionary of American Slang. Comp. and ed. Harold
    Wentworth and Stuart Berg Flexner. New York:
    Crowell, 1967.

A Dictionary of Americanisms on Historical
    Principles. Ed. Mitford M. Mathews. 2 vols.
    Chicago: Univ. of Chicago Press, 1951.

A Dictionary of Canadianisms. Ed. Walter S. Avis et
    al. Toronto: W. J. Gage, 1967.

Gibbs, George. "Account of Indian Mythology in Oregon
    and Washington Territory," ed. Ella E.
    Clark. Oregon Historical Quarterly, 57 (1956),
    128-56.

McArthur, Lewis A. Oregon Geographic Names.
    Portland: Binfords, 1944.

McCormick, Walter F. Woods Words: A Comprehensive
    Dictionary of Loggers' Terms. Portland:
    Binfords, 1952.

Morris, William, and Mary Morris. A Dictionary of
    Word and Phrase Origins. 2 vols. New York:
    Harper, 1962.

Phillips, W. S. The Chinook Books. Seattle: privately
    printed, 1913.

Ramsey, Jarold. "Three Wasco-Warm Springs Texts."
    Western Folklore, 29 (Winter 1970), 95-97.

Sicade, Robert. "The Indians Have Bogey-Men Too: Old
    Legends Tell of the Tsiatko Who Roamed the Woods
    at Night." Portland Oregonian, April 28, 1940,
    Magazine section, p. 3.

Thomas, Edward Harper. Chinook: A History and
    Dictionary. Portland: J. K. Gill, 1935.

Postscript

SO YOU HAVE TO WRITE A CRITICAL ESSAY: SOME TIPS AND CHEERS

By Benjamin DeMott

What Am I Really Trying to Do?

The name of the game is precision, as exact a description of the literary object as you see it as can be achieved. Most poems or stories that are interesting have a local and peculiar air about them. They are "special," they occupy space in their own way, they rouse unique feelings, have a voice-print of their own. The same love song sung by Simon and Garfunkel, Buffy St. Marie and Donovan isn't the "same love song"; there are differences among the performers that can be described in words. As a critical essayist you're in the business of describing differences among performers, making your reader feel the timbre of the work you've been studying, rendering an exact impression of what it feels like to read it. The job is demanding. Choosing your words carefully is essential. So too is working for apt, revelatory metaphors. (When relying on metaphor, shop your mind like a tough consumer: don't settle for the first figure offered.) Many people believe that scientists alone struggle for exactitude. Not true. Exactitude of description haunts the mind of every good critic and it's the basis of every good critical performance.

What Exactly Does Exactitude Look Like?

Quick examples are best drawn from commentary on poems—in particular, on the sound or rhythm of individual passages, phrases, lines. The English critic Christopher Ricks singles out two bits of critical commentary as classic. The first is a remark by F. R. Leavis about the following lines from Keats's *To Autumn:*

> And sometimes like a gleaner thou dost keep
> Steady thy laden head across a brook . . .

Leavis was exact about the effect of the line division and the rhythm. He remarked that, "As we pass across the line-division from 'keep' to 'steady' we are made to enact, analogically, the upright steadying carriage of the gleaner as she steps from one stone to the next." The other classic brief commentary, by Donald Davie, is about a line-ending in Milton's *Paradise Lost* (Book III, ll. 37 – 40):

> Then feed on thoughts, that voluntarie move
> Harmonious numbers; as the wakeful Bird
> Sings darkling, and in shadiest Covert hid
> Tunes her nocturnal Note.

Davie writes that:

The language is deployed, just as the episodes are in a story, so as always to provoke the question 'And then?' — to provoke this question and to answer it in unexpected ways. If any arrangement of language is a sequence of verbal events, here syntax is employed so as to make the most of each word's eventfulness, so as to make each key-word, like each new episode in a well-told story, at once surprising and just. The eventfulness of language comes out for instance in 'Then feed on thoughts, that voluntarie move,' where at the line-ending 'move' seems intransitive, and as such wholly satisfying; until the swing on to the next line, 'Harmonious numbers,' reveals it (a little surprise, but a wholly fair one) as transitive. This flicker of hesitation about whether the thoughts move only themselves, or something else, makes us see that the numbers aren't really 'something else' but are the very thoughts themselves, seen under a new aspect; the placing of 'move,' which produces the momentary uncertainty about its grammar, ties together 'thoughts' and 'numbers' in a relation far closer than cause and effect.

How Can I Find a Pattern?

A good workable pattern for a critical essay is as follows: Open by telling your reader what the text has in common with other works in the same category, advance to a description of the qualities that lend it uniqueness, close by choosing from among the latter qualities one that rouses in you the strongest positive or negative response, and use that as the foundation of your final assessment. Other patterns exist, to be sure. What's important is that you select a simple unfussy pattern, one that permits your reader to feel confident at every moment that he understands where he is and where you are: complication and subtlety should enter, but they should enter through the accuracy and fullness of your description of particular effects, not by way of a tricky structure. Aim at sharpness of execution rather than at novelty of plan or strategy, and you'll seldom go wrong.

My Ideas Keep Changing As I Write: Is That Bad?

No, it's good. Writing an essay is like traveling to a place new to you. You begin with some preconceptions, these are modified en route, and often as you bear down on your conclusion (the destination), you're surprised to find that it's not at all what you'd assumed or predicted it would be. The process just described creates an irritating problem for the writer: how to make the parts of his piece work together. After a draft of an essay is begun in one frame of mind, how can it end in another? And while it's sometimes true that consistency is the hobgoblin of little minds, it's not true that inconsistency is a virtue in a critical essay. Differences do need to be reconciled. Contradictions can be left standing only at the price of rousing skepticism about the ultimate conclusion. A persuasive critical essay has the air of having thought its way through to a conclusion — but that air is secured only when the essayist seems to know his direction from the start, what possibilities will be weighed and at length found wanting, which arguments will be assessed as crucial, and exactly how the whole case will come out. It's most unusual for a first draft of an essay to communicate this much from beginning to end. First drafts are records of an "emergent opinion," of erratic steps toward the discovery of a defensible position. Once the writer has made his way to the end of a first draft, he can look back over the terrain and see his missteps, his misjudgments, and the like. He can perceive as errors of response or of reasoning items that initially had seemed immensely promising. And he can go on to write a finished essay that may even focus in part on those errors — showing why someone might make them, commenting on their deluding plausibility — as it makes its firm confident progression to the conclusions that can't be teased or mocked.

Grasping the Whole Idea

Many assigned critical essays invite students to concentrate on the ways in which individual words and phrases develop special meaning and force in the context of a given poem, play or novel. Or the student is asked to show how a particular stanza serves as a crisis point in a poem, drawing together themes introduced separately before, or clarifying an ambiguous tone. Approaches of this sort often pay off in concrete understanding of the verbal organization of the work under study; they reveal details of complex interrelationships that might otherwise have gone unnoticed. But they can also be bad news for paper-writers, especially to those who become so absorbed in tracking out the details, the links among images, etc., that they can't keep in mind the nature of the whole poetic experience they're trying to illuminate.

A good injunction to yourself is this: Remember The Whole Idea. Or, putting it differently, keep as full a sense as you can of the poem in its entirety alive in your mind, even as you work from detail to detail. Facts of verbal structure are interesting and significant only insofar as they reveal more precisely what a poem is fundamentally all about, where its primary energies and concerns are located. Show your reader that you're in touch with the poem as a whole object, that you aren't dealing with it as a puzzle to be inched through piece by piece. The job is to render the experience of reading the work as that experience occurs within you — and this means doing justice to the whole impact of the thing, not merely to verbal patterns lifted out of their context like birds' eggs in a bio lab.

How Can I Keep "the Whole" in Mind? How Will I Remember the Book After I've Read It?

Nervousness on this score is completely understandable. Usually when we read we're not in the position of having to worry about writing an essay on the book. We sit back, relax, "enjoy ourselves." Change the scene, put an assignment into the equation, and pressure mounts. We worry about whether we'll be able to remember what happens in the book — who marries whom, who stole the money, who whipped the child, and so on. We worry about whether this or that passage may be the "key passage" — the place where the writer tips his hand, shows the reader his full meaning. We worry about whether we'll be able (afterward) to find the scene that was the obvious crisis of the story or to remember how events led up to the crisis. We worry that we'll not be able to recall even the net impression the book made on us as we were reading. We worry so much that we sometimes think best to go out and buy a plot summary of the very book we've just "finished."

The source of all this anxiety is our (correct) awareness that our memories aren't perfect, and that the narrative circumstances and arrangements of a work of imaginative literature are hard to keep in mind after but one reading. Still, we're often a lot more anxious than we should be. As was just said, it's the whole effect of the work — our unified impression of the experience in the large—that constitutes the subject of a good critical essay. And actually it's astonishing how long that impression remains vivid in the mind of any reasonably alert reader. You may feel, at the moment you finish the book, that recovering its details, even offering a general synopsis of events, would be beyond you. But if you put the book aside for a while, and then turn the pages more or less at random, the chances are strong that the patterns and sequences will come swiftly back to mind: not only will you be on top of the story, but you'll discover that you can remember what you felt and thought as you read this or that page the first time through. Holding the details of an entire book in mind at once is difficult, to be sure, but keeping in touch with your whole impression of a book is really quite easy. And riffling the pages, reading a paragraph or so here and there, usually suffices to restore a sense of thorough familiarity with the events and people.

Quoting

Three important rules about quoting are too frequently forgotten. One is that the passages chosen should be rich enough for you to return to and discuss from several perspectives. (The principle is that of economy.) Another rule is that the passages quoted should be shrewdly clipped from their context: no more wordage than you need in order to illustrate your point, but no less than is necessary to allow your reader to find his bearings quickly. A third rule is that quoting is serious business. Passages should be copied word for word, comma for comma, and your remarks about them should be keyed to their tone and meaning. It's in the act of quoting and commenting and quoting again that the critic sets his mind, feelings and understanding in clearest relation to those of the author. When you copy out a piece of the text, and place your own writing in adjacency to it, and let your observations flow, you are in effect laying yourself on the line, creating a moment of truth. The reader of your paper becomes an eavesdropper; he compares the quality of your response to the quality of the writing that elicited the response. Accordingly, when you arrive at the point in your essay at which you're going to stand forth as a witness—a man declaring that this and this alone is what he sees—your mind should be working at its most intense pitch.

Two Items to Check When Revising

When you're finished with a first draft, read your words with an eye to deciding whether your way of talking fits the poem or story at hand. Are you flip when the story itself is sober? Are you solemn when the poem is tongue-in-cheek? Obviously you don't always have to accept another writer's tone. By refusing to accept it you can counterpunch at pretentiousness or over-solemnity — if you think these are present in the work itself. But whenever your manner and voice aren't adjusted to the manner of the work you're confronting, you should have a good reason for your intransigence, and that reason must be made plain to your reader.

Further: remember your audience, and beware of telling it things it already knows. You can reasonably assume, if you are writing about *Hamlet* for your English teacher, that he or she knows the nature of the familial relationships in that play: it's not necessary to identify Gertrude as Hamlet's mother. If you are writing about a novel that it's possible your teacher or fellow students haven't read, you should go to some pains to be (briefly) explicit about the character links, taking less for granted. The rule is that straight information should be supplied in accordance with the nature of the situation: an explanation that in one instance would appear to be pedantry might in another instance be courtesy or even absolute necessity. Decide how much your reader can be assumed to know about the book you're addressing, and let that decision determine your practice.

Should I Read with a Pencil in My Hand?

It depends. If your reason for doing so is anxiety of the kind just mentioned — worry about forgetting what happens — you are probably making needless trouble for yourself. If your reason for doing so is that you've always been a great underliner, marking your books or writing marginal notes even when you weren't going to write an essay about them, there's no sense changing your habits now. The important point is this: you don't want to approach the text in a wary, guarded, armed spirit, but rather in a natural, responsive way. A "critical reading" doesn't necessarily mean a negative or skeptical reading. Neither does it mean "a reading by a person who was constantly harassing himself, as he turned the pages, with anxiety about finding a subject or theme for an essay." The best kind of critical writing flows from comfortable engagements between writer and reader — a relationship in which the reader confronts the book in his usual way, open and hopeful, looking for pleasure and instruction, initially disposed to friendship. Virginia Woolf gives fine guidance in *The Second Common Reader:*

Do not dictate to your author; try to become him. Be his fellow-worker and accomplice. If you hang back, and reserve and criticize at first, you are preventing yourself from getting the fullest possible value from what you read. But if you open your mind as widely as possible, then signs and hints of almost imperceptible fineness, from the twist and turn of the first sentences, will bring you into the presence of a human being unlike any other. Steep yourself in this, acquaint yourself with this, and soon you will find that your author is giving you, or attempting to give you, something far more definite.

How to Get Started If You're Stuck

Follow Virginia Woolf's hint. Think about the author of the assigned book or poem *in relation to you*. Decide in your mind what kind of person he is, and whether or not you would be comfortable with him, and why. The text you're writing about is, after all, a human act, a statement made by a person, and therefore something you yourself can respond to in a personal way. There are limits to how much "personalizing" you can do, of course: a critical essay is no place for telling the story of your life. But thinking about the author personally often helps to start a flow of ideas, loosens you up, makes it easier to articulate your views about the experience of reading the book. It's a rare work that isn't self-revealing, and time and again the attempt to "piece out" the revealed self of the author shows the critic a subject well worth digging into.

What About Me? Who Should I Try to Be When I Write?

Be your best self. That is, be a person who knows that books are part of the whole life of men, that they don't just refer to themselves but to general experience, that they are sometimes signposts, sometimes symptoms, sometimes models. Be a person who habitually looks hard for meaning and implication in events, who tries to break out from cramped circles of knowledge and reference to wide ones, who knows what it's like to speculate and regularly practices this activity. Above all, be a person with all his aptitudes for animation, delight and discovery tuned and poised, eager for use: you are on a journey, to repeat, an intellectual journey through and around the resources of your mind, and many a traveler who's headed out this way before you has had marvelous times en route.

To make good use of this *Index*, first read Chapter One of the *Guide* so that you understand the principles of usage presented there, including the division of Standard English into Formal, General, and Informal. Then read a few consecutive pages of *Index* articles to see how those principles are applied. With this preparation, you will find it helpful to refer to the *Index* as you write and revise.

The *Index* articles, arranged alphabetically, fall roughly into four categories:

Articles on particular words and constructions, such as *continual(ly), continuous(ly); *get, got; *like, as; *plenty; *shall, will; *who, whom. Information about the standing of the locutions in current usage is often supported by quotations from books and periodicals. The examples should not be taken as recommendations. Read the articles to see what the attitudes of readers are, and then decide whether the usage fits your style and the particular rhetorical situation. The entry words are not capitalized.

Articles for correction and revision of papers, indicated by longhand abbreviations. These articles are listed on the end papers at the back of this book. Some of the topics are also treated in the *Guide*. The entries are capitalized.

Articles on English grammar, offering definitions and discussions of such matters as *case, *plurals of nouns, *principal parts of verbs. The approach to grammar is eclectic: some of the articles make use of traditional, structural, and transformational methods of analysis. Entries are capitalized.

Articles about language and language study, such as *American and British usage, *Analogy in language, *Foreign words in English, *Linguistics. Entries are capitalized.

As in the *Guide*, an asterisk preceding a word or phrase indicates an entry in the *Index*.

The pronunciation key is in the article *Pronunciation.

Many articles include references to books and journals where you can find further discussion. The titles of the following journals are abbreviated:

American Speech	AS
College Composition and Communication	CCC
College English	CE
English Journal	EJ

For books that are referred to only occasionally, complete bibliographical information is provided. Books that appear frequently as references are cited by author's name only or, if the author is represented by two or more books, by author and title, usually abbreviated. The frequently cited works are listed here, with short forms for titles noted:

Baugh, Albert C. *A History of the English Language.* 2nd ed. New York: Appleton, 1957.
Bloomfield, Leonard. *Language.* New York: Holt, 1933.
Bolinger, Dwight. *Aspects of Language.* New York: Harcourt, 1968.

Bryant, Margaret M. *Current American Usage*. New York: Funk, 1962.

Christensen, Francis. *Notes Toward a New Rhetoric*. New York: Harper, 1967.

Curme, George Oliver. *Parts of Speech and Accidence*. Boston: Heath, 1935. [*Parts of Speech*]
————. *Syntax*. Boston: Heath, 1931.

Evans, Bergen, and Cornelia Evans. *A Dictionary of Contemporary American Usage*. New York: Random, 1957.

Fowler, H. W. *A Dictionary of Modern English Usage*. 2nd ed. Rev. by Sir Ernest Gowers. New York: Oxford Univ. Press, 1965.

Francis, W. Nelson. *The Structure of American English*. New York: Ronald, 1958.

Fries, Charles Carpenter. *American English Grammar*. New York: Appleton, 1940. [*AEG*]
————. *The Structure of English*. New York: Harcourt, 1952. [*Structure*]

Hall, J. Lesslie. *English Usage*. Chicago: Scott, 1917.

Jacobs, Roderick A., and Peter S. Rosenbaum. *English Transformational Grammar*. Waltham, Mass.: Blaisdell, 1968.

Jespersen, Otto. *Essentials of English Grammar*. University, Ala.: Univ. of Alabama Press, 1964. [*EEG*]
————. *Language: Its Nature, Development and Origin*. New York: Norton, 1964. [*Language*]
————. *A Modern English Grammar on Historical Principles*. 7 vols. New York: Barnes & Noble, 1954. [*MEG*]

Joos, Martin. *The English Verb*. Madison: Univ. of Wisconsin Press, 1964.

Long, Ralph M. *The Sentence and Its Parts*. Chicago: Univ. of Chicago Press, 1961.

Marckwardt, Albert H., and Fred G. Walcott. *Facts About Current English Usage*. New York: Appleton, 1938.

Mencken, H. L. *The American Language*. Abridged 4th ed. Ed. Raven I. McDavid, Jr. New York: Knopf, 1963.

Pooley, Robert C. *Teaching English Usage*. New York: Appleton, 1946.

Pyles, Thomas. *The Origins and Development of the English Language*. 2nd ed. New York: Harcourt, 1971.

Roberts, Paul. *Understanding Grammar*. New York: Harper, 1954.

Robertson, Stuart. *The Development of Modern English*. 2nd ed. Rev. by Frederic G. Cassidy. Englewood Cliffs, N.J.: Prentice, 1954.

Sledd, James. *A Short Introduction to English Grammar*. Chicago: Scott, 1959.

Summey, George, Jr. *American Punctuation*. New York: Ronald, 1949.

Whitehall, Harold. *Structural Essentials of English*. New York: Harcourt, 1956.

Williams, Joseph M. *The New English*. New York: Free Press, 1970.

Two stylebooks are frequently referred to:

A Manual of Style. 12th ed. Chicago: Univ. of Chicago Press, 1969. [*Chicago Manual*]

United States Government Printing Office Style Manual. Rev. ed. Washington, D.C.: Government Printing Office, 1967. [*U.S. Style Manual*]

a-

The prefix a- (from Greek meaning "not") forms many words in the Formal and scientific vocabularies (*amoral, asexual, asymmetrical, atypical, achromatic*). An Old English prepositional prefix a-, found in *abed, aloud, asleep, alert, afraid*, and other words, survives in such regional phrases as *going a-fishing, a-hunting.*

a, an

The choice between *a* and *an* depends on the initial sound, not on the initial letter, of the word that follows. *A* is used before all words beginning with a consonant sound: a business, a European trip, a D, a usage. *An* is used before all words beginning with a vowel sound, including words spelled with initial silent *h:* an apple, an F, an hour apart, an honor.

In words beginning with *h* but not accented on the first syllable, as in *histo'rian, hyster'ical, h* was formerly not pronounced, so *an* was used. Although the *h* is now often pronounced, some people continue to say and write *an histor'ical event* (but *a his'tory*). In contemporary usage *a* is the more common in such locutions, but usage is divided: "an habitual set of choices" (Josephine Miles, *CCC*, Oct. 1963).

Repeating *a* or *an* before each noun of a series tends to keep the various words distinct and make the expression emphatic: a pen, a sheet of paper, and an envelope.

See *awhile, a while; *half; *kind of a, sort of a.

Abbreviations

Ab

Revision: Write in full the word or words inappropriately abbreviated. (Or use the correct form of the abbreviation marked.)

1. *Appropriateness.* Abbreviations are usually appropriate in manuals, reference books, business and legal documents, scholarly footnotes, and other works in which saving space is important. They are also suitable in Informal writing—notes for one's own use, letters to friends. In General writing abbreviations are usually restricted to those fully established in Standard usage (see §2) or those regularly used in discussions of a particular subject. In most Formal writing abbreviations are held to an absolute minimum.

2. *Standard abbreviations. Dr., Mr., Mrs., Messrs.* are always abbreviated when used with names. A number of abbreviations, such as *St.* (see **saint*), **a.m.* and *p.m.*, and abbreviations for government agencies like *CIA* and *SEC*, are Standard. In Formal writing, titles like Reverend, Professor, President, and Senator are not abbreviated, but in most other contexts they are abbreviated when initials or given names are used: Professor Hylander or Prof. G. W. Hylander (but not Prof. Hylander).

Scholarly writing still uses some abbreviations of Latin words:

cf. (*confer*)	compare (for which *see* may be used)
e.g. (*exempli gratia*)	for example
ibid (*ibidem*)	the same (used in footnotes)
i.e. (*id est*)	that is

Such abbreviations are no longer customarily italicized, since they are regarded as English words. Less commonly used abbreviations from Latin are often italicized: **c.* or *ca.* (*circa*, "about," used with uncertain dates), *seq.* (*sequentes* or *sequentia*, "following").

Dictionaries give frequently used abbreviations in the main alphabetical list of words or in a special list. (See *Guide*, p. 423, for abbreviations used in footnotes of reference papers.)

3. *Period with abbreviations.* Where standard practice requires the period, its omission is a careless slip. Only one period is used after an abbreviation at the end of a sentence.

Periods are increasingly omitted from the abbreviations of names of government agencies (*NASA, FBI, VA*) and of other terms if the abbreviation is generally used instead of the name (*AFL-CIO, CBS, ID, IQ*), and with abbreviations like *mph, hp, kwh, rpm* in scientific contexts or when used with figures (780 rpm).

Abbreviations that are pronounced as words (*WASP, UNESCO*) are called *acronyms*. Dozens of acronyms entered the language during World War II (*Nazi, Gestapo, radar, sonar, Wac, Wave*), and thousands have been created since that time (*NATO, CORE, WHO, laser*).

For information on abbreviation of dates, see **Months*. Compare **Contractions, *Origin of words* § 3d.

ability to

The idiom with *ability* is *to* and an infinitive (ability *to do*, not *of doing*): He has the ability to design beautiful buildings. The idea is often better expressed by an adjective or verb: He is able to [He can] design beautiful buildings; He designs beautiful buildings.

-able, -ible

These two suffixes, exactly alike in meaning and pronunciation, cause trouble in spelling. Since pronunciation is no help, the only solution is to learn the spelling of each word or check it in a dictionary. The suffix *-able* is by far the more common form and should be used in coining words (like *copable* or *have-at-able*). Several words are found with either *-able* or *-ible*. The more common form is put first:

ascendable	ascendible	discernible	discernable
collapsible	collapsable	indispensable	indispensible
collectible	collectable	preventable ·	preventible

able to

Able to is rarely followed by a passive infinitive (like *to be done* or *to be ended*) because the construction sounds awkward: This was not able to be done because of lack of time. Revised: This could not be done because of lack of time. Or: They were not able to do this because of lack of time. Though *able to* can sometimes be replaced by *can* or *could*, it must be used to express some time relationships: *will be able, might be able.*

about

Like most English preposition-adverbs, *about* has a variety of uses, a few of which may be troublesome.

1. *about – around.* In describing physical position these are nearly interchangeable, though *around* is the more common (about the barn – around the barn). In the sense of "nearly" or "approximately," *about* is more common (about 70°) but both are Standard American usage.

2. *about – almost.* In the sense of "almost" (about finished), *about* is Standard but mainly Informal.

3. *at about.* Strictly speaking, something would be either *at* or *about*, but except in Formal English the two words are frequently used together (At about four o'clock we crossed the line). Reference: Bryant, pp. 31 – 32.

4. *About* followed by an infinitive is a convenient General idiom for "on the point of," with the added advantage of allowing a future or anticipated act to be put into past time: He was about to make a third try. The negative *not about to (for "not going to") is more Informal: ". . . I am not about to throw out the electoral process mindlessly . . ." (Edgar Lockwood, *Ramparts*, Oct. 1970).

above

Above is primarily a preposition (above the clouds) and an adverb (dark above and light below). Its adverbial use in such phrases as "the evidence cited above" is common in contemporary prose; but many writers prefer "the evidence already cited" or some such expression. The use of *above* as an adjective (the above prices) or as a noun (the above is confirmed) is also avoided by some careful writers, though not by others: ". . . for a comment on the above use of the word 'claims' . . ." (Theodore Bernstein, *Watch Your Language*). Reference: Bryant, pp. 3 – 4.

Abridged clauses
    See *Clauses § 3b.

Absolute phrases

   1. *Classification.* Absolute phrases like "The narrows passed" in "The narrows passed, we went along at a fairly good speed" are traditionally said to modify the sentence as a whole. They are absolute not because they are independent but because they lack connectives that define their relationship to other sentence elements. When absolute phrases follow the main clause, they are a convenient way of adding details:

It was about four of a winter afternoon, the sky about thirty feet up, the flats looking like a testing ground for biological warfare, the horizon smoking away. — Theodore Solotaroff, *The Red Hot Vacuum*

Here everything except the main clause, "It was about four of a winter afternoon," is in what are traditionally known as absolute phrases.
   Absolute phrases are explained in transformational grammar as the product of an underlying sentence with a *be* verb deleted:

The narrows [were] passed, we went along. . . .
It was about four of a winter afternoon, the sky [was] about thirty feet up. . . .
The battle [was] lost, the army surrendered en masse.

A transformational grammar would also point out that these are little different from what is traditionally called an introductory participial phrase: *Wearing a heavy fur coat*, she sat through the performance in absolute agony. The difference is the result of a very general process in English. When the subject of the main clause is identical to the subject of an embedded sentence, the subject of that embedded sentence is often deleted: [*She* was] wearing a heavy fur coat, *she* sat through the performance. . . . The so-called absolute differs from the participial phrase only in that the absolute does not share a subject with the main clause, and so its subject is not automatically deleted. Note that in both cases, however, a form of *be* could be reconstructed.

   2. *Use of absolute phrases.* When they are short, absolute phrases are direct and economical: *Camp made*, the boys settled down to relax. But when they are long, especially if they include an auxiliary (*being, having, having been*), they may seem clumsy. Often the relationship implied in an absolute phrase can be more exactly stated by a subordinate clause: The dry falls were formed by the erosive glacial waters, *the ice cap having changed the course of the Columbia.* Clause: . . . after the ice cap had changed the course of the Columbia.
   Some absolute phrases have been used so frequently that they have become fixed formulas or idioms in everyday speech and writing: all things considered, other things being equal, this being the case, God willing.

See *Dangling modifiers, *Idiom, *Participles § 3. References: Christensen, pp. 82 – 94; Jespersen, *MEG*, V, 6; Dorothy Petitt, *CCC*, Feb. 1969, pp. 29 – 34; Arthur Schwartz, *Language*, Dec. 1968, pp. 747 – 83.

Absolutes, comparison of
See *Comparison of adjectives and adverbs § 4.

Abstract and concrete words

Abst

Revision: Replace the abstract word or words with a concrete word or words.

Nouns that name things without mass — relationships, emotions, ideas — are abstract: *love, civilization, danger, square root*. They contrast with concrete nouns, which name persons and things that can be seen and touched: *roommate, computer, mercury, galoshes*. Though abstract terms are necessary in discussing ideas, too much reliance on an abstract vocabulary can mean loss of contact with the world of human experience. The concrete words in the second of the next two sentences give meaning to the abstract language in the first:

The survey's assumption that the bodily symptoms in question are indicators of psychological distress leads to the conclusion that the working class tends to somatize its emotional troubles, whereas the middle class experiences them more directly. In other words, clammy hands and upset stomach are apt to be the poor man's substitute for angst. — Charles J. Rolo, *Atlantic*, Jan. 1961

See *Nominalization; *Nouns § 3b; and *Guide*, pp. 42 – 43, 343 – 44, 363 – 64. Compare *Imagery.

Academic writing
Partly because many works by scholars and research workers are written more impersonally than they need be, *academic* is often used to describe writing that is unpleasantly abstract, distant, and dry, and to describe the style of many books supposedly for general reading that do not show sufficient adaptation to the expected readers. But such partial failures in communication should not hide the importance of academic writing. Very often the men engaged in discovering new facts, in originating interpretations of facts, are not particularly interested in popularizing and leave that task to others. This passage, itself in the Formal style of academic writing, discusses the language of specialists:

The truth is that the language of science and scholarship and that of ordinary literature are different engines of communication, though they have something in common. It is essential for academics to write as far as possible in normal language, and desirable for them to write well. It is essential for them to explain what they are doing to non-specialists and this task, if it is to be carried out adequately, requires them to write well. But they will not themselves judge the value of academic writing by literary standards. When a mathematician or nuclear physicist speaks of beauty and elegance — and he speaks of both as often as the composer or chessplayer, and may strive for both as hard as the poet — he has not in mind the proper ordering of words, but of ideas. And for him as for Spinoza, their beauty may be so great that it altogether dwarfs the lesser beauties of the word. But those of us who do not share his aesthetics, and perhaps cannot understand them, are ill at ease. — *Times Literary Supplement*, Aug. 17, 1956

Accent marks

Accent (or diacritical) marks over, under, or through letters indicate that the letters are not pronounced as they would be if unmarked. English uses few accent marks except those still retained on words taken from foreign languages:

Acute (´): attaché, resumé
Grave (`): cortège, derrière
Circumflex (ˆ): crêpe, rôle
Dieresis (¨): doppelgänger, naïve
Tilde (˜): cañon, piñon

In General writing, accent marks are usually dropped; newspapers rarely use them. An accent mark is sometimes used in English words to show that a syllable is pronounced, expecially in verse (*blessèd*). See *Foreign words in English.

accept, except

See *except, accept.

Accusative case

In English six distinctive pronoun forms are often called accusative (or objective) forms and usually occur in the object function: *me, her, his, us, them, whom.* See *Case; *Gerunds § 2; *Infinitives § 5; *It's me; *Objects; *who, whom.

Acronyms

See *Abbreviations § 3.

Active voice

See *Voice. Compare *Passive verbs.

actually

Actually, like *basically* an overused word of spoken emphasis, is usually unnecessary in writing even when used literally: "My nomination for the 'most neglected book' is actually a trilogy . . . " (Carlos Baker, *American Scholar*, Spring 1970).

ad

> *Ad*, the clipped form of *advertisement*, is spelled with one *d* and no period. Like other clipped words it belongs to General and Informal speech and writing.

Addresses

> When the various parts of a person's address are written on the same line, they are separated by commas: Miss Louise Finney, 48 Adirondack View, Middlebury, Vermont, is a native of Carroll County, Virginia, and a graduate of Smith College.

ad hoc, ad hominem

> Most Latin phrases beginning with the preposition *ad* are italicized in English, especially Formal English. Because of their frequent use in General English, *ad hoc* and *ad hominem* are the most common exceptions. The first describes committees established for a special purpose, as opposed to standing committees; the second describes arguments attacking a man's character instead of his facts or his logic. See *Guide*, p. 172.

Adjective clauses

> See *Clauses § 2b, *Relative clauses, *Restrictive and nonrestrictive.

Adjectives

Adj

Revision: Reconsider your choice of the adjective marked.

> Problems with adjectives are more likely to be rhetorical and stylistic than grammatical. For discussion, see §§ 4b and 6.

> **1.** *Forms.* Many adjectives are compared by adding *-er* or *-est* to the positive (or base) form or by preceding the positive form with *more* or *most: warm, warmer* or *more warm, warmest* or *most warm; talkative, more talkative, most talkative.* See *Comparison of adjectives and adverbs. See also *unique.

> While many adjectives have come down from an early period of the language (*high, handsome, civil*) without a distinctive adjective form, many others have been made and are still being made by adding a derivational ending or suffix to a noun or verb. Some suffixes that are still active are *-able* and *-ible* (*translatable, edible*), *-al* (*critical, hypothetical*), *-ed* (*sugared, four-footed*), *-ful* (*playful, soulful*), *-ish* (*darkish, womanish*), *-less* (*harmless, fearless*), *-ous* (*callous, ferrous*), *-y* (*cranky, dreamy, corny*).

> **2.** *Position.* We recognize adjectives in sentences chiefly by their position in relation to the nouns they modify, especially by the fact that they can stand between an article (*a/an, the*) or word like *our, this, some* and a noun: an *old* parka, our *youngest* son, this *characteristic* gesture, some *favorable* opportunity.

According to its position in a sentence, an adjective is either *attributive* or *predicate*. Attributive adjectives are placed next to their nouns, usually preceding, as in *tiny* brook, *horseless* carriages. Predicate adjectives, also called *predicatives*, come after some form of the verb *be* or some other linking verb, stated or implied (*taste, feel, turn*): The day is *warm;* That pie smells *good.* They precede the verb only in inverted sentence order: *Silent* was the night. See *Linking verbs, *Predicate adjectives.

3. *Types.* Adjectives may be divided into two types, according to their meaning and the character of their modification.

a — Descriptive adjectives, the most common type, are said to modify the noun by naming a quality or condition of the object named: a *gray* shutter, *vivid* colors, *difficult* words. They are ordinarily compared and may themselves be modified by *qualifiers, words like *almost, very, quite.* Participles (*laughing, wrecked*) function like descriptive adjectives but usually are not compared or modified by qualifiers. Because this class of words has no definable limits and new members are constantly being added, it is called an *open class.*

b — Proper adjectives, derived from proper nouns, originally are limiting — *French* possessions, the *Puritan* colonies — but also become descriptive — *French* culture, *Puritan* manners. Sometimes they mingle both functions, as *Elizabethan* in the *Elizabethan* drama both limits drama to a period and brings to mind qualities of a group of plays.

Often a proper adjective is used so frequently in a merely descriptive sense that it loses its relation to the proper noun and becomes a simple descriptive adjective, written without a capital: *bacchanalian, pasteurized, diesel, india* ink, *paris* green. Like descriptive adjectives, they are an open class and may even be compared: He is Frencher than the French.

4. *Adjectival function.* The function of an adjective is to modify a subject, object, or indirect object — that is, to restrict or limit it. Since phrases, clauses, and words that are usually other parts of speech also perform this function, we can speak of the function as *adjectival.*

a — Phrases and clauses used in adjectival function:

The man with his hat on is Harry.
I like the one *on the end* best.
Everyone *who approves* will raise his right hand.
That was the summer *we went to Bermuda.*
He asked the first man *he met.*
They saw a bird *with a long bill* [= a *long-billed* bird, a descriptive adjective].

b — Other parts of speech in adjectival function. One of the outstanding traits of English is the use of nouns in the adjectival function: a *glass* jar, the *Churchill* government, *adjective* modifier, *high-school mathematics* test. Grammarians have occasionally argued that such words are "really" adjectives because they modify nouns. Formally such words are nouns. They all may be inflected for plural and genitive. In context, because they occur in the same position formal adjectives occur in, we may call them adjectiv*als*. Thus in isolation they are nouns; in context they may be either adjectivals, adverbials (as in "He went *home*"), or nominals (as in "My *home* is your *home*").

Rhetorically, piling up nouns in front of nouns results in a rather awkward and heavy style: The progress report committee chairman fund is low = The chairman of the committee on the progress report doesn't have enough money. While a string of prepositional phrases is not very graceful, a string of nouns is less so.

Traditionally, such *determiners as *this, that, his, other, former, two, second, both*, etc., have been called limiting adjectives. Again, it may be clearer to classify them as determiners that usually perform adjectival functions. Unlike regular adjectives, they cannot be compared, they ordinarily do not occur as predicates, they are lexically empty, and they belong to a closed class — new ones are not added.

Participles are verbals which function like adjectives: a *coming* man, a *deserved* tribute.

5. *Adjectives as subjects and objects.* Preceded by an article, words that are ordinarily adjectives occur in the functions of nouns: the *just*, the *rich*, the *unemployed*, an all-time *high*, a new *low*. As a rule such words do not have genitive or plural forms.

References: Curme, *Parts of Speech*, Chs. 3 and 11, *Syntax*, Chs. 5, 13, 14, 25; Francis, pp. 268 – 81; Roberts, Chs. 4 and 14; Sledd, pp. 79 – 80, 92 – 93.

6. *Style.* Adjectives should make a writer's statements more precise or more telling. As Herbert Read puts it, "Appropriate epithets may be either exact or happy." We can judge how effective adjectives are only in context, but there are general criteria for their appropriateness. Some adjectives are redundant: in *briny ocean*, *briny* adds nothing because all oceans are briny; *stark* adds nothing to *tragedy* or *madness* because most tragedies and madnesses are stark; all emergencies are sudden, so *sudden emergency* is redundant. Very general adjectives are equally useless: *good, bad, beautiful, wonderful, terrific, fantastic, incredible, awful,* and so on communicate an attitude toward something, rarely any of its characteristics. The reader wants to know the particular sort of *good* — generous? affable? efficient? Many adjectives that are exact enough have been used too often with certain nouns (*fond* farewell, *beady* black eyes) and are merely trite. Though most of us use inexact adjectives in conversation, in writing we should think twice before using any combination of adjective and noun that comes automatically to mind. See *Trite.

A writer may try too hard to paint a picture. A few of the adjectives in the following passage from a student's essay are satisfactory, but most should be deleted:

In a hotel dining room there is not the clamorous, raucous bedlam of its immediate surroundings, but a refined, subdued atmosphere, pervaded by distinct, faintly audible sounds. The orchestra, with a barely perceptible diminuendo, concludes the melodic, slow-tempo arrangement, climaxed by the beautiful strains of the "Merry Widow" waltz — rising, falling, fading with plaintive supplication.

Used sensibly and sensitively, adjectives can make a valuable contribution to both meaning and style. In most factual writing the first requirement of adjectives is exactness; they must answer the needs of the material. And in writing that makes a definite attempt to capture the feelings and sensations of the reader, the adjectives must also deserve the epithet "happy"; that is, they must seem to fit, as in this account of an actual experience:

He had a quick impression of hard-faced men with gray eyes burning some transparent fuel for flame, and said, "I won't go back. If you don't arrest me, I'm going on to the Pentagon," and knew he meant it, some absolute certainty had come to him, and then two of them leaped at him at once in the cold clammy murderous fury of all cops at the existential moment of making their bust . . . and a surprising force came to his voice, and he roared to his own distant pleasure in new achievement and new authority — "Take your hands off me, can't you see? I'm not resisting arrest. . . ." — Norman Mailer, *Harper's*, March 1968

Carl Sandburg has been credited with advising a writer, "Think twice before you use an adjective." This is probably sound advice for anyone who automatically attaches an adjective to every noun. And according to E. B. White, "The adjective hasn't been built that can pull a weak or inaccurate noun out of a tight place." But it is also important for a writer to fix his eye on his subject and write about it as he really sees it. Without stuffing in adjectives, he should make it possible for the reader to re-create the picture or idea for himself. The adjectives then should be at least exact, and some may be happy.

Compare *Adverbs § 4.

Adverbial clauses

See *Clauses § 2c.

Adverbs

Adv

Revision: Revise the form of the adverb marked (§ 1), or reconsider its choice (§ 4).

Traditionally the adverb as a grammatical category has been a ragbag, including a variety of words that modify verbs, adjectives, other adverbs, and whole clauses and sentences. (Some words in the category, like *almost, very, quite, yes, no,* obviously differ in certain respects from more typical adverbs — they cannot be compared — and could be set off as different parts of speech; but because some of their functions resemble those of adverbs, they can also be regarded as adverbial and assigned to appropriate subgroups.) Grammarians are experimenting with various new classifications, but since none as yet has been accepted widely, this article follows the traditional grouping. See *Parts of speech, *Particles.

1. *Forms.* Most adverbs are formed by adding *-ly* to adjectives or participles: *badly, deservedly, laughingly, surely.* Some adverbs have developed from Old English forms without a special adverbial sign: *now, then, here, there.*

There are a number of adverbs with the same forms as adjectives, most of them in use for hundreds of years. They include:

bad	doubtless	hard	much	slow
better	early	high	near	smooth
bright	even	late	new	straight
cheap	fair	loose	right	tight
close	fast	loud	rough	well
deep	first	low	sharp	wrong

Most of these unchanged adverbs are matched by forms in *-ly*, with which they may or may not be interchangeable. We can say either "He sang loud" or "He sang loudly," but only "That shot came too close" (not "too closely"). The *-ly* words are likely to be preferred in Formal English and the shorter and often more vigorous words in speech and Informal writing. The choice, when a choice is open, is chiefly a matter of style.

In Nonstandard usage even more adverbs without *-ly* occur, such as *common, considerable, different, regular.* For "bobtail" adverbs of this sort, the safest policy is to use the *-ly* ending unless its omission is recognized as Standard in a good dictionary.

Adding *-ly* to a word already in General use as an adverb (*kindlily* for *kindly*) is a blunder, and adding it to an Informal qualifier (*really* for *real*) does not make the word appropriate in General and Formal writing. (See *real, really.*) The *-ly* form should also be avoided after a *linking verb, where a predicate adjective is called for: The breeze smelled sweet (not sweetly).

Most adverbs are compared, either by adding *-er* and *-est* or by preceding them with *more* and *most.* See *Comparison of adjectives and adverbs.

Linguists occasionally debate whether a word like *home* in "He went home" or *days* in "He works days" is an adverb or a noun. The simplest solution is to define such words formally as nouns but functionally as adverbials. In most contexts and by most tests, *home* and *day* would be nouns: they occur in all noun contexts and with all noun inflections. But since they may also occur in positions normally occupied by adverbs, we can say that in such sentences they are nouns in adverbial functions or, alternatively, adverbials. The *-al* ending indicates that we are defining them in context by their syntactic function, not by their formal characteristics such as potential inflection.

2. *Functions.* Adverbs are typically used in two functions:
a—Modifying single words, phrases, and entire clauses: He came early (*early* modifies *came*); They were practically in the street

(*practically* modifies *in the street*); Fortunately, no one was home (*Fortunately* modifies all of *no one was home*). In direct and indirect questions, *when, where, why*, and *how* perform adverbial functions even though they are not in the adverbial position at the end of a statement:

When did he leave? (Compare: He left yesterday.)
Do you know why he left? (Compare: He left because he was tired.)

As in all information questions, the item being questioned — in this case a time, place, reason, or degree question-word — is shifted to the beginning of its clause.

b — Connecting separate sentences or the main clauses of a compound sentence (see *Conjunctive adverbs):

We found the dormitories empty, the classrooms silent and deserted. *Consequently* we returned to the city.

They agreed to call the matter closed; *however*, they were by no means convinced.

Phrases and clauses may also have the function of adverbs (see *Phrases) and thus be classed as adverbials: He came *in the morning; After the exam* he quit; *When it was time to go*, she didn't know what to do.

3. *Position.* Different subclasses of adverbs occupy different positions in sentences, and often a single subclass can occupy more positions than one. Among the one-word adverbs, for example, qualifiers precede the words they modify, different negatives (like *never* and *not*) occupy different positions with respect to the verb, and adverbs of manner (like *worse, keenly, openly*) may often stand initially, medially, or finally:

The air was *extremely* clear.
Tom had *never* liked pizza. Tom *never* had liked pizza.
Patiently she replied. She replied *patiently*. She *patiently* replied.

Adverbs and adverb clauses whose positions are variable should be so placed (first of all) that their meanings are clear: not "She answered the questions that the students asked patiently" but "She patiently answered the questions that the students asked," if it was the answers and not the questions that were patient. Other considerations are rhythm and emphasis. The second of the following sentences moves more slowly than the first and puts a stronger emphasis on the *when* clause:

When the tide turned, all the boats headed for the channel.
All the boats, when the tide turned, headed for the channel.

Similar differences are likely to result whenever an adverb is shifted to separate closely related sentence elements.

4. *Style.* The use of adverbs, like the use of adjectives, should be at least precise and if possible happy. Adverbs are used unhappily when they are used unnecessarily and redundantly (Shrill horns scream *threateningly;* automobiles career *wildly;* giant buses lumber *dominantly* along), when they qualify excessively (The *seemingly* difficult problem of race relations . . .), and when they set up a flutter of unstressed syllables (as in the first part of this sentence). Sometimes writers use an adverb to shore up an imprecise adjective or verb when an exact adjective or verb would have been neater and at least as expressive:

Scholarships should be kept *for those who are academically industrious* [for the studious].

When no one was looking, I took the goggles and *swiftly made my way* [hurried] out of the store.

Many of the adverbs regularly used in conversation are better omitted in writing: *continue* [*on*], *refer* [*back*].

References: Curme, *Parts of Speech*, Ch. 5; Stanley Greenbaum, *Studies in English Adverbial Usage* (Coral Gables: Univ. of Miami Press, 1970).

advise

Besides meaning "to give advice," *to advise* is used to mean "to inform, to give information." In this sense the verb is in General use when the information is rather formally given: Reporters were advised by an administration spokesman that. . . . In less formal situations simple *tell* is more appropriate: Peter tells us he won't be back next year.

affect, effect

Affect is usually a verb, meaning "influence" (This will affect the lives of thousands) or "put on" (He affected a stern manner). The noun *affect* is a technical term in psychology. *Effect* is usually a noun, meaning "result": The effects will be felt by thousands. *Effect* is also a Formal verb, meaning "bring about": The change was effected peaceably.

aggravate

In General and Informal usage *aggravate* ordinarily means to "annoy" or "irritate": "Lindsay further aggravated some policemen by creating the Civilian Review Board . . ." (Richard Reeve, *New York Times Magazine*, Jan. 1, 1967). Formal writing still limits *aggravate* to the sense "intensify or increase something unpleasant," as to aggravate suffering or a wound or a crime: ". . . internal race friction . . . is aggravated by continuing efforts of some employers to use traditional antipathies as a union-busting device" (Wilson Record, *American Sociological Review*, Feb. 1967). The same distinction is made with the noun *aggravation*.

Agreement

Agr

Revision: Make the verb or pronoun marked agree in form with the word to which it is related — its subject if it is a verb, its antecedent if it is a pronoun.

Sentence elements or parts of speech "agree" when one of them determines certain corresponding forms of the other to express a relationship of *gender, *person, or *number.

1. *Subject* and *verb* agree in number (The *man is* old; The *men are* old) and person (*I go* tomorrow; *He goes* tomorrow). Most mistakes in agreement take place when a writer fails to identify the subject correctly; he makes the verb agree with a word other than the subject. The mistake is most likely to occur when a long phrase or clause containing plural nouns intervenes between subject and verb: An analysis of the extent to which audio-visual aids are used in schools make me conclude that books are no longer the chief means of education. (The subject *analysis* calls for the singular verb *makes.*)

With *collective nouns the problem is chiefly one of consistency between the related pronoun and the verb: With *its* [not *their*] big game only a week away, the team *was* very much on edge.

See *Subject and verb, *Collective nouns.

2. A *pronoun* agrees with its *antecedent* in number (The *boy* had lost *his* way; The *hikers* had lost *their* way), in gender (The *girl* found *her* keys; Every *question* has *its* answer), and in person (*I* felt it near *me; He* had *his; You* will need *yours; We* will take *our* own). In correcting an error in pronoun agreement, you may have a choice of revisions: The value that *a person* can receive from understanding these give-and-take methods will stand *them* in good stead for the rest of *their* lives. The sentence could be improved by making the reference consistently singular: . . . will stand *him* in good stead for the rest of *his* life. But the notion seems plural — a statement of general application — so a better revision might be to change *a person* to *people.* It is not always the pronoun that needs changing. See *Reference of pronouns, *each, *every and its compounds.

3. A *demonstrative adjective* usually agrees in number with the noun it modifies (*That coat* is expensive; *These shoes* cost more than my old pair did). See *Demonstrative adjectives; *this; *kind, sort.

The chief cause of lack of agreement is that since formal agreement in English is not vital for intelligibility, we tend to ignore the form of what we started with. This is especially true if the subject is a collective noun or pronoun or if several words, some of them plural, come between a singular subject and its verb, so that we are tempted to use a plural verb. There may also be a conflict between agreement by form and agreement by meaning. In Formal English agreement by form is quite strictly followed, but in General and Informal English agreement by meaning has become acceptable in many locutions. See, for example, *any § 3; *either; *one of those who; *who, whom.

agree to, agree with

One agrees *to* a plan and agrees *with* a person. One thing agrees *with* another. Other idioms are: I agree *in* principle; we agreed *on* a plan of attack; he agreed *to* fly or *on* flying or *that he would* fly.

ain't

Though *ain't* is used in speech every day by millions of Americans as a contraction for *am not, is not, are not, has not*, and *have not*, it is never used in Formal writing or in ordinary expository prose. Where *ain't* does appear in General writing, it is often in set colloquial phrases like "That ain't hay" or "There ain't no such animal" and almost always as a deliberate affectation of untutored spontaneity:

It will never reach the audience Welles might have and should have reached, because there just ain't no way. — Pauline Kael, *New Republic*, June 24, 1967

Those tiresome people with their tiresome quotes from Socrates about the fact that youth is going to the dogs are just trying to reassure themselves that it's all just a little bit more of the same. It ain't. — John M. Culkin, *New York Times*, June 2, 1967

See *Divided usage. References: Bryant, pp. 16–17; Marckwardt and Walcott, pp. 48, 95–96.

a la

A la is regarded as an English preposition, meaning "in the manner of": a la Whistler, a la *The New Yorker*. In Formal writing and in some advertising (as of cosmetics and fashionable clothes), the accent mark is usually kept (*à la*). The other French forms, *à l'* and *au*, occur only in borrowed phrases: *au gratin*.

albeit

Albeit has been revived and is used in the sense of "although": They formed an alliance, albeit an uneasy one. *Though* or *but* is more appropriate in most contexts.

all

Watch the following words and phrases:

all ready (adjective phrase): At last they were all ready to begin.
already (adverb of time): They had already begun.
all right (adjective phrase): The seats seemed all right to me.
all together (adjective phrase): We found them all together in an old trunk.
altogether (adverb, equivalent to *wholly*): That's another matter altogether.

See *all the farther.

Alliteration

Alliteration is repetition of the same sound, usually at the beginnings of several words in a series or at the beginnings of stressed syllables within several words. Besides possibly appealing to the reader's or listener's ear, alliteration serves to bind the phrase, or sometimes a whole series of phrases, into a unit:

. . . the crowded, cloistered colleges of Oxford. — Paul Elmer More

. . . carried by wind and water and soil and seed to the far corners of the globe. . . . — John F. Kennedy

Alliteration is one of the figures of sound that contribute to the musical effect of poetry.

> Here I am, an old man in a dry month,
> Being read to by a boy, waiting for rain.

> T. S. Eliot

> The lunar silences, the silent tide
> Lapping the still canals . . .

> Dylan Thomas

In ordinary expository prose, conspicuous alliteration is usually out of place because it tends to attract attention to the expression at the expense of the idea. It is more appropriate in Formal prose, especially in prose with an oratorical or poetic background. In writing of any kind, unconscious alliteration is usually distracting and may be disastrous.

all of

In General and Informal usage *all* is followed by *of* in many constructions where the *of* is less likely in Formal writing: All of the milk was spilled; They passed all of the candidates; You can't fool all of the people all of the time. With personal pronouns and the relatives *who* and *which*, *all* may follow the pronoun (we all), or *all of* may precede it (all of us). Locutions like *all we* are no longer current (All we like sheep have gone astray); but *all you* is Standard. *All of which* and *all of whom*, as subjects of relative clauses (four attempts, all of which failed), are especially common and are more Formal than their alternatives, *which all*, and *who all* (four attempts, which all failed).

all the farther

Although in some regions *all the farther* is often heard in Informal and General speech (This is all the farther I'm going), Standard written English commonly uses an *as . . . as* construction: This is as far as I am going. References: Bryant, pp. 19–20; Russell Thomas, *CE*, Jan. 1959, pp. 190–91.

Allusion

See *Echo phrases; Guide*, pp. 373–74.

-ally

English has a number of adjectives with the (Latin) endings -al and -ical: fatal, final, medical, historical, political. As usual, the adverbs are made by adding -ly to these words. Although resultant -ically is often pronounced as just two syllables, all three appear in the written forms.

accidental	accidentally	mental	mentally
fundamental	fundamentally	political	politically
incidental	incidentally	practical	practically

Several adjectives ending in -ic seem to be replacing their synonyms in -ical in some uses: alphabetic, biographic, geographic, grammatic, and philosophic, following the example of academic, frantic, emphatic, pathetic, and poetic. Many of these words, however, retain the -al in the adverb form: academically, heroically, specifically, and so on.

almost

See *most, almost.

also

Also as an adverb ordinarily stands within a sentence, not at its beginning (They also serve who only stand and wait), but inversion may shift an also to initial position: Also defeated was the party's candidate for mayor. As a loose conjunction meaning "and," also is usually a weak sentence opener:

He subscribed to eight magazines. Also he belonged to the Book-of-the-Month Club.

See *Conjunctive adverbs.

alternative

Alternative comes from the Latin alter, "the second of two." Some Formal writers, in deference to the word's origin, confine its meaning to "one of two possibilities," but it is regularly used to mean one of several possibilities and is so defined in dictionaries.

although, though

Although and though connect with the main clause an adverbial clause of concession—that is, a statement that qualifies the main statement but does not contradict it.

Although [Though] the rain kept up for almost three weeks, we managed to have a good time.

We managed to have a good time, though [although] the rain kept up for almost three weeks.

Here there is no distinction in meaning; the choice between the two may be based on sentence rhythm. *Although* is slightly more Formal and hence occurs less frequently. (Reference: Bryant, pp. 216–18.) Only *though* is used as a conjunctive adverb: He did it, though.

Often one of two clauses connected by *but* can be thrown into an *although* clause for a slight change of emphasis:

We had rehearsed the act time and time again, but we all missed our cues the first night.

Although we had rehearsed the act time and time again, we all missed our cues the first night.

The simplified spellings *altho* and *tho* are much less in favor now than they were a generation ago. In most General contexts they would look eccentric. See *but. Reference: Curme, *Syntax*, pp. 332–40.

a.m. and p.m.

These abbreviations (for *ante meridiem*, "before noon," and *post meridiem*, "after noon") are most useful in tables and lists of times but are also used in General writing for specific hours, usually with figures: from 2 to 4 p.m. (Not: I'll see you this p.m.)

Though *m.* is the abbreviation for noon (12 m.), *12 noon* is more common; midnight is *12 p.m.*

Ambiguity

Amb

Revision: Make the meaning you intend unmistakable.

Although inexact writing is common enough, a truly ambiguous statement, with two or more meanings that are equally plausible, is relatively rare. The context usually shows which of the possible meanings is to be taken. The most common sources of actual ambiguity are:

1. *Inexact reference of pronoun*, especially in *indirect discourse: He told his father he had been talking too much. Such a sentence usually needs rewriting, perhaps as: He admitted to his father that he had been talking too much. Or as: He criticized his father for talking too much. Recasting in direct speech would be another solution. See *Reference of pronouns.

2. *Modifiers.*
a – Squinting modifiers that may refer to either of two words or constructions: The governor penalized those office holders who had opposed him *for good reason*. This could be clarified as: The governor had good reason for penalizing those who had opposed him. Or

as: The governor penalized those who had had good reason to oppose him. The sentence "Some people *I know* would go there anyway" would be clearer if it began, "Some people whom I know," or if it read, "Some people would go there anyway, I know."
b—Temporarily misleading modifiers, as in headlines: Police Repair Man Killed by Car. Writers should not pose such puzzles for their readers. See *Hyphen.

3. *Incomplete idioms*, especially in comparisons: "I like Alice as well as Will" might mean "I like Alice as well as Will does," "I like Alice as well as I do Will," or "I like both Alice and Will."

4. *Changing meanings.* Many words in English are undergoing changes in meaning. Sometimes the transition can be completed without risk of ambiguous communication because the context makes the intention clear. Before *car* came to apply primarily to an automobile, such restricting labels as *motor, railroad,* or *street* prevented misunderstanding. But when such safeguards are not present, serious ambiguity may occur. Examples: *censor, censure; *disinterested, uninterested; *imply, infer; *incredible, incredulous; *rhetoric; *transpire.

5. *Intentional ambiguity.* Incomplete or ambiguous statements are sometimes intentional, like the sign in an airport limousine, "Tipping for this service not required," which drew tips from most passengers. And multiple meanings may be used deliberately for literary ends. Good writers constantly invite their readers to draw inferences, to understand more than is said. Manipulation of inferences, if it is one source of ambiguity, is also a source of powerful effects in writing.

See *Comma § 7 for information on using a comma to avoid ambiguity. References: W. Nelson Francis, *AS*, May 1956, pp. 102–06; Norman C. Stageberg, *EJ*, Nov. 1958, pp. 479–86; William Empson, *Seven Types of Ambiguity*, 3rd ed. (New York: New Directions, 1957).

American

Because there is no word to describe the United States (as *Italian*, for example, describes Italy), *American* is ordinarily used. It is obviously inexact, since Canadians and Mexicans and Brazilians and others are as American as we are; and many Latins refer to themselves as Americans. But it is no more inexact than many other words, and the usage is Standard. Use *American* as the adjective and the name of an inhabitant. References: H. L. Mencken, *AS*, Dec. 1947, pp. 241–56; R. S. Boggs, *AS*, Dec. 1949, pp. 312–13; Allen Walker Read, *AS*, Dec. 1950, pp. 280–89.

American and British usage

In the written language some spelling differences stand out. The British still prefer *-re* to *-er* in spelling words like *center* and *theater*, though they use both forms; they still keep *-our* in a number of words (see *-or, -our), though they are gradually simplifying; they use x in a few words like *inflexion;* they double more consonants, as in *traveller, waggon;* and various individual words differ, such as *tyre* (automobile *tire*). But these distinctions affect only a small number of words, and for most of them usage is divided in both countries. Though they are just pervasive enough to show that a book is of British or American origin, they do not interfere with reading.

The grammar of the popular levels of British and American English differs somewhat—contrast the speech of ordinary people in novels and movies of the two countries—though less than vocabulary. *Collective nouns are more likely to be plural in British usage (the government intend); British writers differ in small matters like the position of *only*, the proper preposition with *different*, the use of *shall*, and various idioms.

A fairly long catalog of such minor differences between these two branches of English could be drawn up, but their importance should not be exaggerated or allowed to obscure the fundamental fact that the resemblances far outnumber the differences and that the speech of the two countries represents two different strands of the same language. A number of entries in this *Index* note differences between British and American usage.

Americanism

Americanism, as a usage term, means a word or construction originating in the United States (*hydrant, zipper, realtor*) or first borrowed here, as from an Indian language (*hominy, caucus, mugwump*) or from Spanish (*canyon, rodeo, lariat*). It also refers to a sense of a word added in the United States (*campus, carpetbagger, creek*). A *Dictionary of Americanisms*, edited by Mitford M. Mathews (Chicago: Univ. of Chicago Press, 1951), lists vocabulary of this sort.

Americanism may be extended to include words continued in the United States after becoming obsolete in England (*loan* as a verb, *gotten*) or any item of usage characteristic of the United States and not of other areas of the English-speaking world. The label *American* or *chiefly U.S.* in dictionaries records such facts of usage. Americanisms in this extended sense are included in the Craigie-Hulbert *Dictionary of American English* (Chicago: Univ. of Chicago Press, 1938–1944).

among, between

See *between, among.

amount, number

Number is used only of countable things: a number of mistakes, a number of apples. *Amount* is normally used with *mass nouns (a small amount of money, a certain amount of humor) but is sometimes used to mean "number" (a very limited amount of changes). Distinguishing between the two words often improves clarity and is therefore recommended. Compare *fewer, less.

Ampersand

Ampersand is the name for the & sign (originally a linking of the letters of Latin *et*), called also *short and*. Its primary use, obviously, is to save space; therefore it belongs only where abbreviations are appropriate. In addressing firms, use the form they habitually use ("and Company" or "& Company"), and in quoting follow your original carefully. In all other General contexts, *and* should be written out.

Analogy

Analogy is a variety of comparison that points out resemblances, real or imagined, between two things that are not normally thought of as alike. The coming of spring has been analogized to human birth (and rebirth), hippies to early Christians, advertising to poetry. Historical analogies bring out resemblances between two periods or institutions: Augustan Rome and eighteenth-century England, the United Nations and the League of Nations. Analogies may be used solely for clarification; presenting the unfamiliar in terms of the familiar is one of the commonest techniques for explanation. It becomes the basis for argument when the writer tries to persuade his audience that because two things resemble each other in some respects, they must resemble each other in another, vital respect (or because a solution worked in one set of circumstances, it will work in another). The strength of an analogy depends on whether the resemblances adduced are trivial or fundamental.

For the uses and abuses of analogy in explanation and argument, see *Guide*, pp. 88 – 90, 142, and 152 – 53.

Analogy in language

In linguistics *analogy* is the name for the natural tendency in users of a language to make their speech more regular by forming new words on the pattern of existing ones, bringing old words closer together in form, or bringing less common constructions in line with more familiar patterns. It results from the fact that, in general, the patterns of a language form a consistent though complex system (most English noun plurals end in *-s*, past tenses in *-ed*, and so on). It is easiest to observe analogy in the attempts of children to master their language. Before they learn the irregular conventional forms used by grownups, they regularize on the basis of the patterns they are familiar with, saying *mans*, perhaps, for *men* or *singed* for *sung*.

Analogy has removed many irregularities in the main body of language. Out of various plural forms used in Old English, *-s* has won in all but a few words, and analogy is still bringing more words to that form, like **formula, formulas*. Occasionally words are changed in spelling by analogy, as the *-b* was rather recently added to *crumb* and *thumb* from analogy with *comb* and *dumb* — showing that analogy does not always bring improvements in the direction of simplicity. Other words are in the process of changing: *cole slaw* is often replaced by *cold slaw*, and *alright* is slowly making its way from analogy with *already*. New words are formed on analogy with old ones, like *astronaut, telecast*.

The extension of *was* to the plural—a common form in Nonstandard English, based on the analogy of most English verbs in the past tense (I did—we did; he went—they went)—illustrates not only the force of analogy but the fact that the result, however logical and consistent, is not necessarily acceptable. To be accepted in Standard English the analogical form must be frequently used by educated writers and speakers—and "we was" is not. See *Change in language, *due to, and various other examples of analogy treated in particular *Index* articles. References: Bolinger, pp. 114–17; Bloomfield, Ch. 23; Henry M. Hoenigswald, *Language Change and Linguistic Reconstruction* (Chicago: Univ. of Chicago Press, 1960); E. H. Sturtevant, *Linguistic Change* (Chicago: Univ. of Chicago Press, Phoenix Books, 1961), Chs. 2 and 6.

and

1. *Appropriate uses. And,* the most frequently used connective, joins two or more elements of equal grammatical rank:

Adjectives: a *pink* and *white* apron; a *blue, green,* and *white* flag

Adverbs: He drove *very fast* and *rather carelessly.*

Nouns: trees and *shrubs; trees, shrubs,* and *plants*

Verbs: I *found* the book and *opened* it at the exact place.

Phrases: in one ear and *out the other*

Dependent clauses: While the boys were swimming and [*while*] *the older folks were resting,* I was reading.

Independent clauses: The first generation makes the money and *the second spends it.*

2. *Inappropriate uses.* In careless writing, elements of unequal grammatical value are sometimes connected by an unnecessary *and:*

Main verbs and participles: Three or four men *sat* on the edge of the lake with their backs to the road, [and] apparently *watching* the ducks.

Independent and dependent clauses: A contract has been let to install new copper work on the Post Office [and] *which will require 4500 pounds of lead-coated copper.* See *which § 4.

And sometimes appears where no connective is needed or where some other connective would show more clearly the logical relation: The freshmen have a number of required courses and [but] the upperclassmen almost none. See *Guide,* pp. 316–17.

3. *At beginning of sentences.* In current writing of all varieties, *and* may stand at the beginning of a sentence. Used with restraint, it can contribute to movement and emphasis. Overused, it can be damaging to both, as well as boring for the reader.

4. *Omission and repetition.* In some compact writing *and* is omitted between series of items. Judiciously used, this omission makes for economy, but overused it contributes to a "telegraphic" style usually inappropriate for General writing. Repetition of *and* in a series may be an effective means of giving emphasis to the individual items: "I do not mean to imply that the South is simple and homogeneous and monolithic" (Robert Penn Warren, *Southern Review*, Summer 1965). These *Index* articles involve *and:* *Compound predicate, *Compound sentence, *Compound subject, *Coordinating conjunctions, *Coordination, *Series, *which.

and etc.

See *etc.

and/or

Though *and/or* is primarily a legal and business locution, it may be useful when three alternatives exist (*both* items mentioned or *either one* of the two): *fruit and/or vegetables* means "fruit" or "vegetables" or "fruit and vegetables." Its use in General writing is objected to by many readers both because *and/or* looks odd and because *and* or *or* alone is very often sufficient.

angle

Angle meaning "point of view" or "aspect" (from an economic angle) is General but often carries a strong suggestion of *jargon. In the sense of "scheme" or "plan" (What's his angle?), *angle* is *slang.

Anglo-Saxon

See *English language.

Antecedent

An antecedent is the word, clause, or sentence that a pronoun or *pronominal adjective refers to. It usually stands before the pronoun, but not always: We did not hear their call again, and when we found the Thompsons, they were almost exhausted. (*The Thompsons* is the antecedent of the pronominal adjective *their* and the pronoun *they*.) For relations between antecedents and their pronouns see *Agreement, *Reference of pronouns.

Anticipatory subject

See *it; *there is, there are.

Anticlimax

An anticlimax ends a series with an element much weaker than what precedes it. It may be intentional, as a form either of serious irony or of humor (as in Pope's "Men, monkeys, lap-dogs, parrots, perish all"), or unintentional, a lapse of judgment on the writer's part (She had a warm and sympathetic personality, a quick and perceptive intelligence, beautiful features, and real skill at Scrabble).

Antithesis

The stylistic device of using neighboring statements that contrast sharply in meaning is called antithesis. Often the statements are presented in parallel form: He is shamed for being backward; he is scolded for being forward. See *Guide*, pp. 324–25.

Antonomasia

Antonomasia is the technical term for some common figurative uses of names. One is the substitution of a title—the Boss, the Champ, the Major—or an epithet, like the Nose for Jimmy Durante. Another is the use of one person's name for another person with similar characteristics: a Judas, a Jonah, a Pollyanna.

Antonyms

An antonym is a word that means approximately the opposite of another word: *hot, stingy, boring* are antonyms of *cold, generous, entertaining*. Most books of synonyms also give antonyms, as do the synonym entries in dictionaries. Reference: Bolinger, pp. 234–38.

any

1. *Any*, deriving from the same source as *one, a, an*, is used primarily as an adjective (any member of the family; Any dog is a good dog) but also as a pronoun (Any will do).

In comparisons of things of the same class, idiom calls for *any other*: This book is better than any other on the subject. But *any* alone is used when different classes are compared: I like a movie better than any book.

2. *Compounds with* any. *Anybody, anyhow, anything*, and *anywhere* are always written as single words. *Any rate* is always two words: at any rate. *Anyone* is written as one word when the stress is on the *any* (Anyone /en' ē wun/ would know that) and as two when the stress is on the *one* (I'd like any one /en ē wun'/ of them).

Anyway is one word when the *any* is stressed (I can't do it anyway /en' ē wā/), and two when the stress is about equal (Any way /en' ē wā'/ I try, it comes out wrong). If the word *whatever* can be substituted for the *any* (Whatever way I try, it comes out wrong), *any way* should be written as two words.

3. *Pronouns referring to* anybody, anyone. *Anybody* and *anyone* are singular in form and take singular verbs (Anybody [Anyone] feels bad at times). They are referred to by *he, his, him* (Anybody knows what *he* deserves) or, since they are often felt to be collective, by a plural pronoun with the meaning "he or she," "his or her," "him or her": ". . . it is not usually possible to achieve intimacy with anybody in the back seat of a car; you have to live with them in every sense of the phrase . . ." (Edgar Z. Friedenberg, *New York Review of Books*, May 6, 1965). Formal usage insists on a singular pronoun. See *Divided usage. Compare *every and its compounds. Reference: Fries, *AEG*, p. 50.

4. *Other forms.* *Anyways* is regional for the generally used *anyway,* and *anywheres* is Nonstandard for *anywhere.* Though objected to by many, *any more* now frequently appears in print as one word:

Hardly a day passes anymore without disclosure of yet another organization that is being secretly financed by the silent service.—Russell Baker, *New York Times,* Feb. 19, 1967

They want to protect all those traditional events whether or not they mean something anymore. . . .—Herbert Warren Wind, *New Yorker,* Oct. 2, 1971

Any more (or *anymore*) in a strictly affirmative context (Any more I do that) is a regional idiom.

Anyplace (now usually written as one word) has become a General synonym for "anywhere": "Life can be as good and rich there as anyplace else" (Granville Hicks, *Saturday Review,* Dec. 24, 1960).

Aphorisms
See *Epigrams and aphorisms.

Apostrophe

Apos

Revision: Insert an apostrophe where it belongs in the word marked; or take out an apostrophe that is incorrectly used.

Although the apostrophe is an anachronism, you need to know and follow the conventions governing its use.

1. *In genitives.* The most common use of the apostrophe is in spelling the *genitive (possessive) case of nouns and of the indefinite pronouns (*anyone, nobody, someone . . .*): Dorothy's first picture; The companies' original charters; Everybody's business is nobody's business; The boys' dogs. It should be used in singular genitives of time and value even though they carry no idea of possession: a day's hike, this month's quota, a dollar's worth. The genitive is also preferred in plural genitives of this kind, though usage is divided. For discussion of special examples of possessive form, see *Genitive.

2. *In contractions.* The apostrophe is used to show the omission of one or more letters in contractions: *can't, I'm, I'll, it's* [*it is*].

3. *In plurals.* An apostrophe is ordinarily used in plurals of figures, letters of the alphabet, and words being discussed as words: the 1920's, three e's, the first of the two *that*'s. But usage is divided, and the plurals of figures in particular are often made with no apostrophe: ". . . the intractable social problems of the 1960s . . ." (*Newsweek,* June 30, 1969).

4. *In representing speech.* An apostrophe may be used to show that certain sounds represented in the usual spelling were not spoken: "He turned to someone else on the landing outside and said, 'Paddy, 'ere, 'e doesn't want 'is duff,' and went to walk on'' (Brendan Behan, *Borstal Boy*). This is a legitimate use, but too many apostrophes spot the page and confuse the reader. It is better to suggest occasional pronunciations of this sort than to try to represent all of them.

5. *Personal pronouns.* Apostrophes are not used in the genitive of the personal pronouns: *his, hers, its, ours, theirs, yours.*

6. *Spelling.* Apostrophes should not be introduced into words that do not have them. *Till* is not *'till* or *'til.*

Apostrophe

Apostrophe as a rhetorical term means literally "a turning away." In its narrowest sense it occurs when a speaker or writer turns away from his audience to address a particular person or thing. More broadly, *apostrophe* is applied to any formal utterance addressed to someone or something, usually not present, as in Wordsworth's "Milton! thou shouldst be living at this hour."

appendix

The English plural *appendixes* is now more common than the Latin *appendices* in General usage. Formal usage is divided.

Apposition, appositives

Beside a noun or noun-equivalent in a sentence, we may place another nominal expression called an appositive: My aunts, Mary and Agnes, moved to Boulder in 1969. The noun *headword, or head, and its appositive refer to the same person or thing. Sometimes no punctuation is needed between them—"My son Jim was so successful that we called him Jim the fisherman"—but typically the appositive is set off by commas.

An appositive agrees in case with its head; the case of the head is determined by its relation to the rest of the sentence: The winners [subject], Al and I, will lend bus fare to the losers [object], you and him.

Appositional definitions or explanatory tags can be insulting to readers. For example, in referring to the President of the United States, either the President's name or "the President" is sufficient identification.

References: Curme, *Syntax*, pp. 88–92; Jespersen, *EEG*, pp. 93–95.

apt

See *liable, likely, apt.

Arabic numerals

See *Numbers § 3.

Archaic words

When words drop out of all spoken and written use, they are said to be obsolete. When they are old-fashioned but still used at least occasionally, if only in special circumstances, they are called archaic. Archaic words should be used only for very good stylistic reasons. In most General writing they are incongruous. See *Guide*, p. 40.

arise

See *rise, arise, get up.

around

See *round, around.

Articles

Traditionally *a* and *an* are known as indefinite articles, *the* as the definite article. The absence of an article signals indefiniteness for mass nouns and plural count nouns (see *Nouns):

The money you earned is yours. Money is the root of all evil.
The boys arrived late. Boys will be boys.

Traditional grammars call articles adjectives; structural grammars call them function words; transformational grammars group them under determiners. See *a, an; *the; *Parts of speech. Reference: David Perlmutter, "On the Article in English," in *Recent Advances in Linguistics*, ed. M. Bierwisch and K. Heidolf (The Hague: Mouton, 1970).

as

Among the meanings of *as* are "while" (As we walked along, he told us stories) and "because" (His speed is amazing, particularly as he weighs 260 pounds). *While* is preferable to *as* if the emphasis is on the time of the action (While we were walking along, he told us stories). And though *as* is used to mean "because" (or "since") in all varieties of English, many readers dislike the usage, which can easily be ambiguous: As we have continued responding to erratic change in Asia, our position has inevitably become more complex. (Does *as* mean "because" or "while"?)

For the growing tendency to use *as* where *like* would be expected, see *like, as.

as . . . as

1. As I *or* as me. In a sentence like "He dislikes her as much as I/me," meaning determines whether the nominative *I* or the accusative *me* is used. The nominative implies the sense "as much as I dislike her"; the accusative, "as much as he dislikes me."

In a sentence like "They sent for someone as big as I/me," the choice of *I* or *me* does not affect the meaning. Both the nominative and the accusative are good English.

For a third type of sentence—"He is as big as I/me"—in which there is no preceding noun or pronoun in the accusative position, usage has always been divided. The nominative *I* is preferred in Formal contexts and is insisted upon by many teachers and editors. References: Hall, pp. 153 – 57; Jespersen, *MEG*, VII, 231 – 33.

2. *Omitted* as. Writers frequently omit the second *as* in a comparison of equality (as big as) when it is joined by *or* or *if not* to a comparison of inequality (bigger than): It was as large or larger than last year's crowd. But many readers and writers regard the omission as inelegant and prefer the complete form: It was as large as, or larger than, last year's crowd. Sometimes the second comparison can be moved to the end of the sentence: It was as large as last year's crowd, if not larger. References: Bryant, p. 57; Jespersen, *MEG*, VII, 385 – 86; Marckwardt and Walcott, p. 113.

3. As . . . as *and* so . . . as. *As* . . . *as* is much more common than *so* . . . *as* in simple comparisons of degree (as big as that, as late as you like). Unlike *so* . . . *as*, it is suitable for both affirmative and negative statements. Many handbooks of grammar have urged that *as* . . . *as* be used only in affirmative statements (She's as clever as any of them) and *so* . . . *as* in negative statements (She's not so clever as she thinks); but the distinction has never become established in practice. References: Bryant, pp. 26 – 27; Curme, *Syntax*, pp. 294 – 95; Marckwardt and Walcott, pp. 27, 111.

as if, as though

In Formal English the *subjunctive is commonly used after *as if* and *as though:* He acted as if [or as though] he were losing his temper. In General English the past tense is usual: He acted as if [or as though] he was losing his temper; and in some contexts the present is used: It looks as though we are condemned to a lifetime of apprehension. Often in Informal English and sometimes in General, *like* is used instead of *as if:* He acted like he was losing his temper. The subjunctive is never used with *like*. See *like, as.

as it were

This set expression now seems old-fashioned and is better avoided.

as, like

See *like, as.

Assonance

Assonance is the repetition of vowel sounds in words having different consonant sounds (*brave—vain, lone—show*). It is an effective sound element in verse and is also common in prose, especially in heightened style: "that ideal country, of green, deep lanes and high green banks" (Osbert Sitwell).

Asterisk

Except in reference works and advertising, the asterisk or star is not used so much now as formerly, because it is a conspicuous mark and attracts too much attention.

1.　In works that have very few footnotes an asterisk may be used as a reference mark, placed after the statement calling for a note and again at the beginning of the note; but numbers are more common.

2.　Asterisks sometimes indicate a rather long omission in a quotation—a stanza or more from a poem, or a paragraph or more from prose—though spaced periods are now more common. See *Ellipsis.

3.　In fiction a series of asterisks has been used to suggest that action is omitted or to indicate passage of time between movements of a story, but here again a line of spaced periods or extra space is more common. See *Ellipsis.

4.　Asterisks are often given specific functions in a particular field or a specific book. In works on linguistics, the asterisk is used before hypothetical, or reconstructed, forms: Indo-European *pater "father." Or it is used to indicate an ungrammatical form: *A money is the root of all evil. In this book an asterisk means that there is a separate *Index* entry on the item marked.

as though
See *as if, as though.

as to
As to is often a clumsy substitute for a single preposition, usually *of* or *about:* Practice is the best teacher as to [in, for, of] the use of organ stops. But it is preferable to more cumbersome expressions like *as regards, in regard to, as concerns, with respect to.*

as well as
When an *as well as* phrase comes between subject and verb, some writers treat it as part of the subject and let it influence the number of the verb. According to traditional grammarians, however, the phrase is parenthetical and has no bearing on the verb: "This volume, as well as others, consists of a collection of basic articles" (Robert R. Wilson, *ISIS*, Fall 1967).

at about
See *about § 3.

athletics
When the *collective noun *athletics* refers to sports and games, it usually takes a plural verb and pronoun: Our athletics *include* football, basketball, and baseball. When *athletics* refers to a skill or activity, it usually takes a singular verb and pronoun: Athletics *is* recommended for every student.

Attributive
An adjective that stands next to its noun is attributive (a *blue* shirt; a shirt, *blue* and *clean*), as contrasted with a predicate adjective that is related to its noun by a *linking verb (The shirt is *blue*). A noun modi-

fying another noun (*horse* race, *football* field) is used *attributively.*
See *Adjectives § 2.

author

Author is a handy verb for referring to publication by a group: The
report was authored by the President's Commission on Campus Unrest. But taken one at a time, men are ordinarily said to *write* their
messages.

Auxiliary verbs

A verb used with another verb to form a phrasal tense or voice is
called an auxiliary verb or helping verb: I *am* going; He *will* go; They
were lost; He *should* watch out. *Be, do, have* are the commonest
auxiliaries; *can, may, shall, will, must, ought, should, would, might*
are primarily used as auxiliaries; *get, let, need,* and *used* sometimes.
See *Index* articles for these verbs, *Verbs, and *Modal auxiliaries.
Compare *Parts of speech.

awful

In Formal English *awful* means "inspiring with awe." In Informal English it is a convenient utility word of disapproval — "ugly, shocking,
ludicrous" (awful manners). As a result of this contamination the
word is seldom used in General writing. *Awfully* is common in
speech to intensify meaning, but in writing it is usually an example of
*schoolgirl style.

awhile, a while

Awhile is an adverb (They talked awhile). Strictly, a prepositional
phrase in which *while* is a noun should be in three words (for a
while, in a while), but *awhile* is increasingly common: ". . . it had
been found that many nonimmigrants, after they had been here for
awhile, decided that they would like to stay . . ." (Marion I. Ben-
nett, *Annals,* Sept. 1966).

Awkward

Awk (K)

*Revision: Rewrite the passage marked to make the phrasing smoother and
more effective.*

Awkward is a general word of disapproval sometimes used in correcting essays. It may refer to unnecessary repetition of a sound or
word, unsuccessful departure from normal word order, an overloaded sentence, or any phrasing that attracts unfavorable attention or
handicaps a reader. Several kinds of awkwardness occur in this passage:

Primarily an agricultural country, New Zealand's dairy products are of a
quality unknown to pollution-threatened, chemical-saturated America. As

high as anywhere in the world are New Zealand's sanitation standards, and rigid animal inspection procedures are, even in the sparsely populated areas, rigidly enforced. These facts, combined with cattle and sheep which graze all year round on natural grass pasture lands, produce products with a uniquely wonderful fresh-tasting flavor.

The way to correct a phrase or sentence marked *awkward* is to rewrite. *Index* articles that deal with and illustrate specific weaknesses that may be labeled *awkward* include *Coordination, *Nominalization, *Passive verbs, *Reference of pronouns, *Repetition, *Shifted constructions, *Subordination, *Wordiness, and *Word order.

Back formations
See *Origin of words § 3e.

bad, badly
Bad is ordinarily used as the adjective (a bad apple) and *badly* as the adverb (He speaks badly). Because the position after a linking verb is usually filled by a *predicate adjective, we would expect "I feel bad about it," as well as "He looks bad" and "It tastes bad." But after *feel, badly* is widely used to modify the subject, particularly in speech. In written usage, *bad* is preferred.

The use of *bad* as an adverb (I played bad all day) is Informal.

Badly meaning "very much" (He wanted it badly) is Standard, and *badly off* is General as a group adjective: "But we are not Satan. Fallen though we are, we are not that badly off" (John Morris, *American Scholar*, Winter 1963).

References: Bryant, pp. 35–36; Lillian M. Feinsilver, *AS*, Oct. 1949, pp. 161–70.

Bad grammar
Bad grammar is used as a term of reproach and is applied to all sorts of locutions from "I ain't got none" to imaginary confusions in the use of *shall* and *will*. It is too vague and emotional a term to be useful. See *grammatical, ungrammatical.

Balanced sentences
When parallel structures in a sentence are noticeably alike in length and movement, the sentence is said to be balanced: "But we must go on or we will go under" (Douglas MacArthur, *Centennial Review*, 1961). Though associated with ornate style, balanced sentences can be effective for emphatic statements and for comparisons and contrasts. See *Guide*, pp. 324–25.

Base rules
Base rules or, as they are variously known, constituent-structure rules, phrase-structure rules, or rewrite rules, generate the *deep structure

of sentences. They are of the form S→NP + VP; that is, a sentence is made up of a noun phrase and a verb phrase. The noun phrase, in turn, is made up of an article and a noun: NP→A + N.These rules are very much oversimplified. For a fuller though still oversimplified description, see *Guide*, pp. 268–76.

Basic English

Basic English is a simplified form of English devised by C. K. Ogden and intended to facilitate international communication. It has a vocabulary of only 850 words. Reference: C. K. Ogden, *Basic English: International Second Language*, ed. E. C. Graham, rev. ed. (New York: Harcourt, 1968).

be

1. *Forms.* The forms of *be* are more numerous and more varied than those of any other English verb:

Present: I am, you are, he is; we, you, they are
Past: I was, you were, he was; we, you, they were
Infinitive: be
Present participle: being
Past participle: been

Sometimes *be* (in all persons) is used as a present subjunctive and *were* (both singular and plural) as a past subjunctive.

Some old forms survive in stock phrases (the powers that be) and in the Nonstandard "You ain't [sometimes "be'n't"] going, be you?" Nonstandard also uses *was* in the plural (Was the Adamses there?), leveling the past tense to one form (*was*), like the past of other English verbs.

2. *As a linking verb. Be* is the most common *linking verb, joining a subject and a predicate noun (Jerome was the secretary) or predicate adjective (She is sick).

With the *finite parts of *be*, a pronoun in the predicate is in the nominative form in Formal written English: It was *he*. Informal: It was *him*. "It's I" is Formal for the General "It's me." See *It's me.

When the infinitive has a subject and complement, both are in the accusative form: I wanted *him* to be *me*. When the infinitive has no subject, Formal usage has a nominative as the complement (I wanted to be *he*), but General usage more often has an accusative (I wanted to be *him*).

3. *As auxiliary verb.* Forms of *be* are used with the present participles of other verbs to make the progressive tense form: I *am* asking; he *was* asking; you *will be* asking. Forms of *be* with past participles form the passive voice: I *am* asked; you *will* be asked; he *was* asked. In General usage, particularly in speech, a single form of *be* may do the work of both a linking verb and an auxiliary, as in "They were ready and getting into the car." Formal style repeats the *were:* . . . and were getting into the car. Similarly, in General English a form of *be* may be omitted in the second of two clauses with subjects of different number: One was killed and six wounded. Formal style would have "were wounded."

4. *As verb of complete predication. Be* is sometimes considered a verb of complete predication when indicating states or positions: He *was* at home anywhere; The fire *was* just across the street. In its unmistakable use as a verb of complete predication to mean "exist," "live" (Hamlet's "To be, or not to be"; Can such things be?), *be* is now rather rare.

See *ain't, *Subject and verb, *Subjunctive.

because

Because introduces an adverbial clause giving the reason for the statement in the main clause: *Because* we were getting hungry, we began to look for a convenient restaurant. *Since* and *as* can be used in such clauses, but they are less definite, more casual.

Because also finds some use in Informal contexts where a more formal style would insist on **for*—that is, where *because* introduces the premise for a conclusion, not the cause of an effect:

Informal: Komarov clearly had some control over his ship, because he was able to orient it well enough to accomplish re-entry.

More formal: Komarov clearly had some control over his ship, for he was able to orient it well enough to accomplish re-entry. — *Newsweek*, May 8, 1967

See *reason is because, *for, *as. For *because of*, see *due to.

Begging the question

Begging the question is the logical fallacy of assuming a conclusion that needs to be proved. The debater who asks, "Should this antiquated electoral system be abolished?" begs the question of the system's obsolescence. See *Guide*, pp. 171–72.

Beginning of an essay

Beg

Revision: Revise the opening of your essay to make it lead more directly and smoothly into your subject and to arouse your reader's interest.

The best advice for beginning a short paper is "Get on with it." An elaborate windup is inappropriate—indeed, silly—when the pitch is to be no more than a straight throw in a backyard game of catch. And an opening that indulges in philosophizing ("Since the days of Plato's Academy, violence and learning have been alien entities") or announces a grand strategy ("In the paragraphs that follow, I shall attempt, first by analyzing and then by synthesizing, . . .") is equally inappropriate in a two- or three-page paper on a campus controversy.

Ordinarily, the first step is to let your reader know what you are writing about—not by telling him what you are going to discuss but by discussing it: "By any rational political or intellectual standard, Republican economic policy has dismally failed" (Robert Lekachman, *Harper's*, Aug. 1970). This does not rule out a personal approach to the topic; there may be good reason for you to tell why you have chosen it or how you are qualified to discuss it. It does rule out beginnings that fail to begin.

In addition to getting the essay under way, the opening paragraph or two should interest a reader enough to persuade him to continue. But straining for humor or excitement or cuteness or sentiment is no way to go about it. For one thing, such attempts often distract or mislead. For another, as imitations of the techniques used by some professional journalists, they are very likely to fail in their purpose: the humor doesn't amuse; the excitement doesn't stir; and so on. Instead of trying out gimmicks, move into your topic, and treat it with the interest *you* feel. If it doesn't interest you, your chances of making it interest your readers are slim. If it does interest you, and if you write about it as honestly and directly as you know how, your readers will keep reading.

For long papers—from five to ten pages, say—somewhat more elaborate beginnings are justified and perhaps necessary. But getting on with the discussion remains fundamental. If you sketch the historical background of a problem or indicate its significance, make sure that this material functions when you go about solving the problem. See *Guide*, pp. 205–07, 416–18.

beside, besides

Beside is used chiefly as a preposition meaning "by the side of," as in "beside the road," "beside her"; it is used figuratively in a few rather Formal idioms like "beside the point," "beside himself with rage." *Besides* is used as an adverb meaning "in addition" (We tried two other ways besides) and as a preposition meaning "in addition to" (Besides ourselves, no one was interested). Sometimes *beside* is used synonymously with prepositional *besides:* "Other comic talents beside mutism stood our hero in good stead . . ." (A. H. Weiler, *New York Times Book Review*, April 30, 1961). More rarely, *beside* is used as an adverb: the foreman and six others beside.

Besides is also used as a conjunctive adverb: He didn't think that he ought to get into the quarrel; besides, he had come to enjoy himself.

between, among

Among implies more than two objects: They distributed the provisions among the survivors. *Between* is most strictly used of only two: They divided the prize between Kincaid and Thomas. But attempts have failed to limit *between* to use with only two items. When the relationship is between individual items, *between* is the word to use no matter how many items there are:

. . . there are often two or more possible arrangements between which a choice must be consciously made.—H. W. Fowler, *Modern English Usage*

This is so . . . of some part of the debate between Einstein, Bohr, Wolfgang Pauli, and Max Born. . . .—George Steiner, *Atlantic*, Aug. 1971

When a group is treated as a collective unit, only *among* is used: Divide the books among the poor. References: Bryant, pp. 38–40; Pooley, pp. 135–37.

between you and me

Although *you and I* as the object of a preposition or a verb is frequently heard and has a long history in written English, anyone who uses it now is apt to be thought only half-educated. *Between you and me* is always correct. *Between you and I* should be avoided. See *Hypercorrectness.

bi-

There is much confusion about time words beginning with *bi-*. *Bimonthly* and *biweekly*, for example, may mean either "every two . . ." or "twice a. . . ." And *biennial* means "every two years" whereas *biannual* means "twice a year." In places where the context does not distinguish exactly the time meant, it is safest to avoid the prefixes and use phrases like "every two months," "twice a day," "twice a year."

Bible, bible

When referring to the Christian Scriptures, the word is capitalized but not italicized: You will find all that in the Bible. In the sense of an authoritative book, the word is not capitalized: Gray's *Manual* is the botanist's bible.

The usual forms of particular references to parts of the Bible are: the Old Testament, the New Testament, the Ten Commandments, Exodus 20 (or Exodus XX), Exodus 20:3–17, I Corinthians 4:6. The adjective *biblical* ordinarily is not capitalized.

Bibliography

See *Guide*, pp. 406–09, 424–26.

Big words

Big W

Revision: Use a simpler, more natural word instead of the Formal or heavy one marked.

A word is "big" if it is too heavy or pretentious for the subject. Big words may not be long or obscure—*deem*, *doff*, and *dwell* are examples—but they are big in that they are inappropriate for their place. You can catch the big words in your essays by reading aloud what you have written. If you have written it very differently from the way you would tell the same thing in your best style to a friend, reconsider your words carefully, and see if you can't use simpler ones that are just as precise and effective but more natural to you. See *Guide*, pp. 360–61.

black

Of those who find the term *Negro* offensive, many prefer *black*, usually not capitalized (blacks, black women, black culture, black studies, but Black Power). Others prefer *Afro-American*. The older term *colored people* survives in the full name of the NAACP, the National Association for the Advancement of Colored People. References: G. A. Maddox and R. S. Ross, *Childhood Education*, Jan. 1969, pp. 260–64; *Newsweek*, June 30, 1969, p. 20.

Blends

See *Origin of words § 3c.

blond, blonde

Usage is not settled. Perhaps the best solution is to use *blond* as the adjective and as a noun for a male or a neutral object, *blonde* as a noun for a woman.

born, borne

In most senses the past participle of *bear* is spelled with a final *-e:* The tax burden was borne by the middle class; The conclusion was borne out by the evidence; The ewes had borne many more lambs. But the spelling *born* is used in the senses "brought into being," "determined by birth," in the passive voice: A child was born; Corruption is born of public apathy; He was born to be hanged. Thus "She has borne three children," but "Three children were born to her." Both *borne* and *born* are used as modifiers: an airborne soldier, a born soldier.

both

Both is a favorite way of emphasizing two-ness: The twins were both there; Both Harry and his brother went. Though neither is necessary, each of these *both*'s gives a legitimate emphasis. In "They were both alike," on the other hand, *both* awkwardly duplicates the meaning of *alike*. "The both of them" is a fairly common spoken idiom, usually avoided in writing.

both . . . and

See *Correlative conjunctions.

Bound modifiers

See *Restrictive and nonrestrictive.

bourgeois, bourgeoisie

Bourgeois is used both as an adjective (bourgeois standards) and as a noun (the new bourgeois). *Bourgeoisie* is a noun only (young women of the bourgeoisie).

Brackets

Brackets are rarely used in General writing, but in much academic and professional writing they have specific uses. If your typewriter does not have them, you can make them with diagonals and underscores (/‾ ‾/) or put them in by hand.

The main function of brackets is to enclose editorial interpolations within quoted material. Here they are used in clarifying references: "The story answers precisely . . . to that told in the third paragraph of Curll's *Key:* 'But when he [Thomas Swift] had not yet gone half way, his Companion [Jonathan Swift] borrowed the Manuscript to peruse'" (Robert Martin Adams, *Modern Philology*, Feb. 1967).

In quoting material, *sic* in brackets is sometimes used to indicate that an error in the original is being reproduced exactly: New Haven, Connecicut [*sic*]. . . . Brackets may also be used to insert a correction: When he was thirty-eight [actually he was forty-three], he published his first novel. And brackets function as parentheses within parentheses, particularly in legal documents and scholarly footnotes.

In this *Index* brackets are used in examples of faulty writing to enclose words that might better be left out (In [the course of] the next year I read such books as . . .) and to suggest improved expression (The contraption made a noise similar to [like] a concrete mixer).

bring, take

Bring implies motion toward the speaker (Bring it with you when you come); *take* implies motion away from him (Take it with you when you go). In situations in which the speaker is not involved, either form is used: Potatoes were brought [or taken] from Ireland to France.

bring up

Bring up (like *raise*) is General usage (That's the way I was brought up) for the more Formal *rear* or *nurture*. It also means "to introduce" a subject: Having brought it up, he couldn't stop talking about it. See *raise, rear.

British usage

See *American and British usage.

Broad reference

A pronoun referring to a preceding idea rather than to a particular antecedent is said to have a broad reference. See *Reference of pronouns § 1.

bunch

In Formal English, *bunch* is limited to objects that grow together like grapes or can be fastened together like carrots and to other objects only in certain established contexts (a bunch of cattle). Used of people, *bunch* is moving into the General vocabulary: ". . . another monumental American myth—that Washington is run by a bunch of cynical, untrustworthy fools" (Nona B. Brown, *New York Times Book Review*, Dec. 2, 1962).

burst, bust

Burst is the unchanged past tense and past participle of the verb *burst*. *Bust* (with *bust* or *busted* as past tense and participle) is a Nonstandard variant of *burst* in its literal meanings: dams and balloons burst (not bust).

But in contexts where the meaning is figurative, *bust* (frequently with the adverbs *up* and *out*) is now common, though still somewhat Informal (The President's consensus was busted wide open). And of broncos and trusts and noncommissioned officers, *bust* is General; *burst* cannot be substituted in these senses.

In recent years the use of *bust* for a police raid and *busted* for arrested has become increasingly popular.

business world

See *world.

but

But is the natural *coordinating conjunction to connect two contrasted statements of equal grammatical rank. It is lighter than *however, less Formal than *yet, and, unlike *although, does not subordinate the clause that follows it.

1. *Connecting equals.* The locutions connected by *but* should be of equal grammatical rank:

Adjectives: not blue but green

Adverbs: He worked fast but accurately.

Phrases: He finally arrived, not in the forenoon but in the early evening.

Clauses: The first day we rested, but the second we got down to work.

Sentences: Enigma of the semitropics, the Rio Grande defied the best engineering minds of two countries for a century. But $10,000,000 in flood-control work harnessed the treacherous stream.

See *which § 4 for comments on *but which.*

2. *Connecting statements in opposition.* The statements connected by *but* should be in actual opposition: "He knows vaguely that the nation is not much good any more; he has read that the crust of the earth is shrinking alarmingly and that the universe is growing steadily colder; but he does not believe that any of the three is in half as bad shape as he is" (James Thurber, *My Life and Hard Times*).

But should not be used between clauses that are not really opposed: Our view was limited to about twenty yards down Tuckerman Ravine; [not but] beyond that everything was in clouds. "Our view was limited to twenty yards" includes the idea of "only," and therefore the two clauses are not opposed. They can stand side by side as partial statements of a complex fact, an effect and its cause.

3. *At beginning of sentences. But,* like **and,* often stands at the beginning of sentences, especially if the sentences are short. The separation emphasizes the contrast with the preceding clause.

4. *Punctuation.* Two clauses connected by *but* should ordinarily be separated by a comma. The contrast in ideas suggests the use of punctuation even when the clauses are relatively short: I couldn't get the whole license number, but it began with A30. No punctuation should follow *but* to separate it from the clause it introduces.

5. *Minor uses.*
a — As subordinating conjunction, after some negative constructions and in some questions:

Who knows but everything will come out right?

Nothing would do but I must spend the night with them.

I never go by a hospital and smell anesthetic, but I know we die. — Harvey Breit, *Esquire*, Dec. 1965

b — As a preposition, equivalent to *except* (no comma preceding):

We didn't get anything but a couple of shad.
A New Englander talks about everyone's income but his own.

c — As a rather Formal adverb, equivalent to *only:* If he but stops to think, he can interpret his own reactions.
d — As a relative pronoun (who . . . not) in Formal constructions like "There was no one in town but knew [who did not know] the whole story."

See also *Correlative conjunctions. References: Fowler, "but"; Curme, *Parts of Speech*, index references.

but that, but what
Although Formal style avoids *but that* as a subordinating conjunction (I do not doubt [but] that he will come), it is common in General and Informal. *But what* occurs less often in print: "Scarcely a season goes by but what some new espionage scandal erupts . . ." (Richard B. Stolley, *Life*, Nov. 22, 1968). Reference: Bryant, pp. 46 – 47.

but which
See *which § 4.

c.
Both c. and ca. are abbreviations for the Latin *circa*, "about," and are used to indicate that a date is approximate or uncertain. "Geoffrey

Chaucer (c. 1340–1400)" means that Chaucer was born around 1340. The same uncertainty may be signaled by a question mark after the date. *C.* and *ca.* are often italicized.

calculate, reckon

Calculate and *reckon* are regional usages for the *think, suppose, expect* of General English. See *guess.

can, may (could, might)

1. Both *can* and *may* are used to express possibility. *Can* is reserved for simple ability ("I can swim" meaning "I am able to swim") and for feasibility ("I can swim today" meaning "There is nothing to prevent me from swimming today"). *May* is also used to express feasibility, particularly in Formal writing:

No absolute date for the wall may be given. . . . —Kyle Meredith Phillips, Jr., *American Journal of Archaeology*, April 1967

The Introduction only hints at the many paths the reader may follow. . . . —Anna Benjamin, *Classical Philology*, April 1967

Stylistically, habitual use of *may* in this sense can create an excessively tentative tone.

2. In requesting permission, *may* has a cool politeness appropriate to Formal occasions: May I add one further point? Informally, *can* requests permission.

In granting or denying permission, *may* is also Formal: ". . . the Board adhered to the view that an employer . . . may not lawfully refuse recognition . . ." (Howard Lesnick, *Michigan Law Review*, March 1967). But except in institutional contexts, where the notion of authority is central, the more democratic *can* is apt to be chosen: ". . . after forbidding the Colonel to speak of love to her, she . . . tells him he can" (Henry Hewes, *Saturday Review*, July 18, 1964).

3. Might *and* could. *Might*, originally the past of *may*, and *could*, the past of *can*, are now used chiefly to convey a shade of doubt, or a smaller degree of possibility than *can* and *may:* He could be here by Sunday; I might have left it in my room.

See *Divided usage. References: Bryant, pp. 48–49; Gladys D. Haase, *CE*, Jan. 1950, pp. 215–16; Long, pp. 138–42.

cannot, can not

Usage is divided; *cannot* is more common.

cannot help but, cannot seem to

Cannot (or *can't*) *help but* and *cannot* (or *can't*) *seem to* are established General idioms:

. . . the reader cannot help but question whether they, indeed, were so universally excellent. —Peter Wall, *Annals*, Sept. 1966

What they can't seem to tolerate is unemployment, the feeling of being useless. . . . — Alfred Kazin, *Saturday Review*, Oct. 13, 1962

But *cannot help but* is avoided by many conservative stylists (who may
prefer *cannot but*, or *cannot help* followed by a gerund: cannot help
saying); and Formal usage would have *seems unable to* rather than
cannot seem to. See *seem. References: Bryant, pp. 49–50; Russell
Thomas, *CE*, Oct. 1948, pp. 38–39.

Capital letters

Cap

*Revision: Capitalize the word marked, for one of the reasons given in this
article.*

    Certain uses of capitals, as at the beginning of sentences or for
proper names, are conventions followed by everyone; certain others
show divided usage or are matters of taste. Formal English tends to
use more capitals than General English, and newspaper usage tends
to cut them to a minimum. The best policy is to follow convention
where it is well established and in other situations not to capitalize
without a specific reason.

    This article summarizes the principal uses of capitals in current
writing. Further discussion and examples will be found in the articles
marked by asterisks.

1. *Sentence capitals.* The first word of a sentence is capitalized.

    Complete sentences that stand in *parentheses are always capi-
talized if they stand between other sentences, but if they stand within
sentences they usually are not. Similarly, a sentence following a
dash, or between dashes, within a sentence is usually not capitalized.

    A complete sentence standing after a *colon is ordinarily capital-
ized only if the writer wants to emphasize it or keep it distinct:

With stage drama the problem is reversed: scripts abound while performances available to students are only occasional and fortuitous. — Richard
Gallin, *College English*, March 1969

He promised this: The company will make good all the losses. — *New York
Times Style Book* (1962)

    In dialog the first word of any quoted utterance is capitalized but
not the second part of an interrupted quoted sentence: "Well," he
said, "it's nice to see you again." Except in dialog, quoted parts of
sentences are not capitalized:

It was, he said, "a restrained and diplomatic use of power." — *Time*, Oct. 12,
1970

2. *Proper names.* Proper names and abbreviations of proper names
are capitalized: names of people and places, months, days of the

week, historical events (the Civil War, the Council of Trent, the New Deal), documents (the Treaty of Paris), companies and organizations, trade names, religious denominations, holidays, races and ethnic groups (but see *black), languages, ships, named trains and planes, and nicknames. See *Course names.

The names of the seasons (summer, fall, midwinter) are not capitalized except for stylistic reasons.

The points of the compass (north, southwest) are not capitalized when they indicate direction but are usually capitalized when they denote a region in the United States: He started west in 1849; He was much more popular in the West than in the East.

Army, Navy, and so on are capitalized in full titles: the United States Army, the British Navy; and in this country "Army" and "Navy" are customary for the athletic teams of the Military Academy and the Naval Academy. In other cases usage is divided: the American army (or Army), their navy (or Navy). Also: He went to college; He went to Beloit College; He didn't do his graduate work there, but he went to the College [or: the college].

Proper nouns that have become common nouns (*tweed, sandwich, bohemian, diesel engine, plaster of paris, silhouette, guillotine*) are not capitalized, nor are many proper adjectives in senses that no longer suggest their origin: Paris fashions (fashions created in Paris) but paris green. Other such adjectives are usually capitalized: French cuffs, Bessemer process, Bordeaux mixture.

3. *Lines of verse.* Quotations from poetry should follow the poet's capitalization.

4. *Titles of books, articles, etc.* The usual convention is to capitalize the first word and last word (and the first word after a colon), all nouns, pronouns, verbs, adjectives, and adverbs, and all prepositions that contain more than four (sometimes more than five) letters: *With Malice Toward Some; Socialist Humanism: An International Symposium; Now Don't Try to Reason with Me; Pity Is Not Enough;* "Theories of Style and Their Implications for the Teaching of Composition."

5. I, O. The pronoun *I* is always capitalized. The exclamation *O* is capitalized, but *oh* is not unless it begins a sentence or is especially emphatic. See *O, oh.

6. *Titles, positions, relatives.* Titles are regularly capitalized before proper names: President Taft, Ambassador Galbraith, Senator Lodge, Sergeant York. When the title alone is used to refer to an individual (the Colonel was there), usage is divided, though "the President" for the President of the United States is still customary.

When they are used as proper nouns, names for members of one's family are generally capitalized: We had to get Father's consent. They are not capitalized when used as common nouns: My sister and two brothers are older than I.

7. *Deity. God, Jesus,* and nouns such as *Saviour* are capitalized; practice is divided on pronouns referring to them:

After all, it is God — and not the Girl — who is God. . . . The identity he confers frees men from all pseudo-identities. . . . — Harvey Cox, *Christianity and Crisis*, Aug. 7, 1961

We all know . . . what a smart thing it was for Jesus to say, "Lead us not into temptation," because He knew well that once we got there we were all so very weak. — Joan Baez, foreword to *Long Time Coming and a Long Time Gone*

Pronouns referring to other than Judeo-Christian deities (Zeus, Jove, Venus) are not capitalized.

8. *Street, river, park, etc.* Usage is divided over capitalizing such words as *street, river, park, hotel, church* when they follow a proper name: Fifth Avenue (or avenue), Missouri River (or river). Formal and General styles (books, most magazines, addresses in and on letters) have capitals; Informal usage and some newspapers do not. When abbreviations are used, they are capitalized: 2319 E. 100th St.

9. *Abstract nouns.* Abstract nouns are likely to be capitalized, more often in Formal writing than in General, when the concept they refer to is personified or when they refer to ideals or institutions: The State has nothing to do with the Church, nor the Church with the State.

10. *Stylistic capitals.* Some writers use capitals as a form of *emphasis, to lead the reader to stress certain words or give them more attention: "And a woman is only a woman, but a good Cigar is a Smoke" (Rudyard Kipling, "The Betrothed"). Such unconventional use of capitals is usually better avoided, though sometimes the device works: "They will learn, like the boy who cried wolf, that people who mock the Last Laugh are incinerated by it when it finally sounds" (*New Yorker*, Sept. 21, 1963).

For additional information on capitals, see *Foreign words in English § 2b, *Proper adjectives. See also *Chicago Manual, U.S. Style Manual*, and *Webster's Third New International Dictionary*.

Careless mistakes

X

Revision: Correct the obvious and apparently careless mistake marked.

Conferences with students indicate that carelessness, not ignorance, is responsible for well over half the mistakes they make in diction, sentence structure, spelling, and punctuation. Careless lapses are inevitable in hurried work. But a course essay is not expected to be hurried work. Most *comma faults and *fragments, mistakes in the forms of verbs and pronouns (*broke* for *broken, it's* for *its*), and scores of other slips result from haste or lack of attention in the final stages of preparing a paper.

Train yourself to proofread carefully. Check your manscript for such elementary mistakes as these: omitting letters (the *n* of *an*, the

-ed of *used to*, a final *y*); omitting end punctuation, including the closing quotation marks after a quoted passage; running together small words (*a/lot, in a/while*); interchanging words that are closely related in sound or spelling (*to, too; than, then; affect, effect; whether, weather; quite, quiet; principal, principle*). Check for the unnecessary repetition of a preposition or a conjunction (It is only natural *that* with the sudden change in the Administration *that* people are worrying about what new policies might be instituted).

If you are uncertain about the spelling of a word, consult your dictionary. If you are unsure about what grammatical form is correct, consult this *Index*. The exercises in the *Guide*, especially those on pp. 284–93, will give you practice in identifying and correcting common blunders in sentence structure. See *Proofreading.

Caret

This inverted *v*, made with its point just on a line of manuscript or just below it, shows that something written between the lines or in the margin should be inserted at that point:

```
                                             because
There was no reason for them not to get good grades,ʌ
all they did was study.
```

This is an acceptable way to revise papers as long as the revisions are completely clear and not very numerous.

A caret used by an instructor as a correction mark indicates an omission.

Case

The case of a noun or pronoun indicates its relationship to other elements in the sentence. In languages like Latin and German, whose nouns and pronouns (and adjectives too) are elaborately declined, the case endings of the nominative, genitive, dative, and accusative (and ablative in Latin) are important clues to the function and meaning of the words. In English, the few forms that survive are much less useful as clues. Our adjectives have no case endings; regular nouns have only two fòrms, the common form (*soldier*) and the form ending in *-s* for genitive and plural, distinguished from each other only in writing (*soldier's—soldiers*); and the personal pronouns and *who* keep at most three forms, a nominative, genitive, and accusative: *I, my, me*. *You* has only two: *you, your*.

We signal the relation of nouns and pronouns to other sentence elements through word order (an object following its verb or preposition, for example) and by means of prepositions (to Fred) rather than inflectional endings. The few problems that we have come chiefly from the surviving accusative form of pronouns (*It's me; *who, whom).

This *Index* has articles on four cases to call attention to the few functions in which the case forms are significant and to note problems in usage that are due to case forms:

Nominative (or subjective): the subject of a verb, complement of a linking verb

Genitive (or possessive): indicating not only possession but various adjectival and adverbial relations

Dative: principally notions of interest or location or "indirect objects"

Accusative (or objective): the object of a verb or preposition

Fuller accounts of the grammatical points involved will be found in *Subject and verb, *Objects, *Infinitives § 5, *Linking verbs, *Gerunds § 2, *Nouns, *Pronouns, *Word order. For more complex treatments of problems of English cases, see Jespersen, *EEG*, Ch. 14 (the two-case system); Curme, *Parts of Speech*, pp. 127–36 (the four-case system).

case

Various locutions with *case* are targets for stylistic criticism. "In case" for *if* (In case you're driving east, I'd like a ride) is a General idiom that is avoided in Formal writing. "In any case" appears in Formal usage but is objected to by some as vague and ambiguous. And the group preposition "in the case of" is frequently *deadwood: This goes for all artists, though in [the case of] the first two groups the issue may be obscured.

catholic

Written with a small letter, *catholic* is a rather Formal synonym for "universal or broad in sympathies or interests." In General usage, *Catholic* written with a capital is taken as equivalent to *Roman Catholic*, both as a noun (She is a Catholic) and as an adjective (Catholic labor unions).

Cause

The use of cause-effect analysis in developing a paper is discussed in the *Guide*, pp. 93–95, the problem of testing a causal hypothesis on pp. 150–52. Following (with very simple examples) are the five methods or canons formulated by John Stuart Mill for testing causal relationships:

1. *The method of agreement.* If two or more instances of the phenomenon under investigation have only one circumstance in common, the circumstance in which alone all the instances agree is the cause (or effect) of the given phenomenon. (If several people have an attack of food poisoning after eating lunch in the same cafeteria, and if it is learned that the one item their meals had in common is smoked fish, it is probable—but not certain—that the smoked fish caused the food poisoning.)

2. *The method of difference.* If an instance in which the phenomenon under investigation occurs, and an instance in which it does not occur, have every circumstance in common save one, that one occurring only in the former; the circumstance in which alone the two instances differ, is the effect, or the cause, or an indispensable part of the cause, of the phenomenon. (If two people had exactly the same menu except that one added smoked fish, and if he became sick while his companion did not, the fish was probably — but not certainly — the cause of his illness.)

3. *The joint method of agreement and difference.* If two or more instances in which the phenomenon occurs have only one circumstance in common, while two or more instances in which it does not occur have nothing in common save the absence of that circumstance, the circumstance in which alone the two sets of instances differ is the effect, or the cause, or an indispensable part of the cause of the phenomenon. (This method combines the first two; it suggests the process of testing over an extended period of time used by doctors to isolate, through elimination of various possibilities, the cause of an allergy.)

4. *The method of residues.* Subduct from any phenomenon such part as is known by previous inductions to be the effect of certain antecedents, and the residue of the phenomenon is the effect of the remaining antecedents. (If only four people could have committed a crime and three can be proved not to have done it, then the fourth is presumed guilty.)

5. *The method of concomitant variation.* Whatever phenomenon varies in any manner whenever another phenomenon varies in some particular manner is either a cause or an effect of that phenomenon, or is connected with it through some fact of causation. (If a field which is heavily fertilized yields a better crop than one which has received half as much fertilizer and a much better crop than one which has received none at all, the farmer concludes that there is probably a connection between the amount of fertilizer he uses and the yield of the crop.)

For discussion and criticism of Mill's canons, see Irving M. Copi, *Introduction to Logic*, 3rd ed. (New York: Macmillan, 1968); Philip Wheelwright, *Valid Thinking* (New York: Odyssey, 1962).

Cedilla

The cedilla is the mark placed under the letter *c* (ç) to show that before *a* or *o* it is pronounced /s/ rather than /k/. In English spelling the cedilla persists in such borrowings from French as *façade, Français, Provençal, garçon, aperçu, soupçon*. In General writing the cedilla is often dropped from common nouns, especially from *facade*.

-ce, -ge

A word ending in -ce or -ge keeps the final *e* before suffixes beginning with *a, o,* or *u* to indicate the pronunciation: *courageous, noticeable, peaceable, vengeance* (but *mortgagor*). Before a suffix beginning with *e* or *i* the final *e* is dropped: *diced, noticing, encouraging.*

censor, censure

When we *censure*, we condemn or blame or disapprove. When we *censor*, we delete or suppress. But the adjective *censorious* refers to *censuring*.

center around

Although some find it illogical, *center around* (The story centers around the theft of a necklace) is the Standard idiom:

. . . we could sometimes look out on shooting and fights that seemed to center around this saloon. — Edmund Wilson, *New Yorker*, May 6, 1967

. . . accompanied by a propaganda war centered around her rightness and fitness for the throne. — Kerby Neil, *Modern Philology*, Nov. 1966

In Formal styles precisionists may substitute *on* or *upon* for *around* or use *revolve* instead of *center*.

Centuries

The first century A.D. ran from the beginning of the year 1 to the end of the year 100, the nineteenth century from January 1, 1801, through December 31, 1900. Thus to name the century correctly, add one to the number of its hundred except in the last year, when the number of the hundred is the number of the century, too. You live in the twentieth century.

Popularly the distinction is not closely kept, since people feel that the century changes when the figure for the hundreds changes: there were celebrations for the beginning of the twentieth century on January 1 of both 1900 and 1901, and there was debate over whether the second half of our century began with 1950 or 1951.

For clarity, the hundreds can be named, even in Formal writing: Dr. Johnson lived in the seventeen hundreds. Similar practice — with and without the century — is Standard in naming decades: the nineteen twenties, the thirties.

cf.

See *Abbreviations § 2.

Change in language

The inevitability of change in language is attested by the records of all languages whose histories have been traced. Sometimes changes appear to be relatively sudden and far-reaching, as after an invasion, but ordinarily they are slow — the accumulation of slightly different pronunciations and gradual shifts in grammatical forms and constructions. Vocabulary varies much more rapidly and less consistently than the basic structure of a language.

Every writer should be aware of the natural process of change in language and should cultivate the habit of watching for change in speech and writing. He needs also to decide whether he is going to oppose change, to welcome it, or to try to discriminate, adopting in his own work those new words and forms that seem to be more convenient and more expressive than older ones. A good general principle is to follow cautiously the direction in which English has already been moving.

Several articles treat points of change in current English: *Analogy in language, *Origin of words, and specific articles like *-ally; *due to; *like, as; *shall, will. The *Oxford English Dictionary* gives the history of individual words from their first appearance in the language, recording their changes in form and meaning. References: Histories of the language, like those by Baugh, Pyles, and Robertson, tell the story in detail. The general and orderly process of change is described in Jespersen, *Language*, Book IV, and in E. H. Sturtevant, *Linguistic Change* (Chicago: Univ. of Chicago Press, Phoenix Books, 1961). See also Bloomfield, Ch. 20 ff.

check, cheque

Check is the American spelling for the order on a bank, but the British spelling *cheque* is sometimes used, as in American Express Travelers Cheque.

Chiasmus

Chiasmus is a figure of speech in which two words or constructions are reversed in consecutive parallel locutions: "The sabbath was made for man and not man for the sabbath" (Mark 2:27).

Chinese

Chinese (a Chinese, three Chinese, the Chinese) is preferred by people of Chinese descent because of the occasionally belittling connotation of *Chinaman, Chinamen*. In Formal compounds *Sino-* is used as an adjective: the Sino-Japanese War.

Circumflex

A circumflex—the accent mark ^ over a vowel—is used in French spelling to indicate that a following *s* in Old French has been dropped (*île—isle*), to distinguish homonyms (*dû*—English *due*—from *du*—English *of the*), and to mark long vowel sounds (*âne, rôle*).

Circumlocution

See *Wordiness.

claim

Used in the sense of "say" or "declare," *claim* suggests to many readers that the assertion should be regarded skeptically or scornfully: He claims to be opposed to thought control. Therefore, using it as a mere variant of *say* (He claimed he was a graduate student in chemistry) can be misleading and confusing.

Clauses

1. *Definition.* Each combination of a complete subject with a complete predicate is traditionally called a clause. A simple sentence consists of a single independent subject-predicate combination. In compound and complex sentences the clauses are related one to another by means of conjunctions or implied connections. Compound sentences have two or more coordinate clauses — independent (or main) clauses of grammatically equal value connected usually by *and* or another *coordinating conjunction. Complex sentences have at least one independent clause, grammatically capable of standing alone, and one or more dependent (subordinate or included) clauses, joined typically to an independent clause or some part of an independent clause by *as, because, since, when,* or some other *subordinating conjunction, or by a *relative pronoun, such as *that, who, which.*

[*Complex sentence, dependent clause:*] When Castro came to power, [*Independent clause:*] Cuba was already well-endowed with mass media facilities. [*Compound sentence, first coordinate clause:*] There has been some expansion under the Revolutionary Government, particularly in the electronic media, [*Second coordinate clause:*] but basically the physical plant in use is the one inherited from the Batista regime. — Richard R. Fagen, *Journal of International Affairs,* Vol. XX, No. 2, 1966

2. *Functions of dependent clauses.* Dependent clauses are classified according to the grammatical functions they serve in sentences:
a — Noun or nominal clauses stand in noun positions — for example, as subjects and objects of verbs or as objects of pronouns:

Subject of *was: That herons fed at night* was news to him.
Object of *knew:* No one knew *who was to blame.*
Object of *to:* The prize went to *whoever had the most right answers.*

b — Adjectival clauses modify nouns and pronouns:

The man *whom they met* [or: The man *they met*] did not return.

The cement road turned into a macadam road, *which in time turned into a clayey unsurfaced road.*

c — Adverbial clauses function as single-word adverbs do:

When they finally got straightened out, it was too late.
They were discouraged *because they had tried very hard.*

3. *Reduced clauses.* Though the typical clause as traditionally defined has an expressed subject and a predicate with a full finite verb, many constructions lack one or the other of these elements and yet function in sentences much as typical clauses do. These can be explained in transformational grammars by a deletion transformation that usually deletes either a repeated verb or a form of *be* and a repeated subject:
a — Elliptical clauses, in which a full verb can be reconstructed because it occurs earlier in the sentence:

I don't *believe it* any more than you [*believe it*].
They can *speak Russian* and so can Bill [*speak Russian*].

b — Abridged clauses in which a subject and form of *be* are deleted:

While [*I was*] waiting, *I* read the newspaper.
When [*he was*] sixteen, *he* went to work.
Though [*he was*] a rapid reader, *he* disliked books.
After [*I had been*] standing in line for an hour, *I* left.
Though [*she was*] tired, *she* continued to work.

When the deleted subject is not the same as the subject of the main clause, the result is often a *dangling modifier.
 Because reduced clauses exist and because in a finished sentence the elements of many underlying clauses have often been deleted and combined, use of the term *clause* itself varies considerably among grammarians. Constructions that are clauses in *deep structures may emerge in *surface structures as single words:

  Students [students are *intelligent*] get good grades.
⇒ Students [who are *intelligent*] get good grades.
⇒ [*Intelligent*] students get good grades.

 See *Complex sentence, *Compound sentence, *Elliptical constructions, *Restrictive and nonrestrictive. References: Curme, *Syntax*, Ch. 10; Jerrold J. Katz, *The Philosophy of Language* (New York: Harper, 1966), pp. 119–51; Ralph B. Long, *AS*, Feb. 1957, pp. 12–30; Roberts, pp. 343–45.

Cliché
A cliché is a worn-out word or phrase. See *Trite.

Clipped words
See *Origin of words § 3d.

Cognate
Cognate means "related, of the same family." It is applied to languages that are from the same stock, as Spanish and French are both descended from Latin. In speaking of cognate languages, *cognate* is also applied to groups of words derived from some one word in an ancestral language: German *Wasser*, English *water*.

Coherence

Coh

Revision: *Make the relation between the parts of this sentence or between these sentences or paragraphs exact and clear.*

Coherence — the traditional name for relationship, connection, consecutiveness — is a difficult but essential virtue in writing. It is essential because the reader's mind differs from yours; he must be guided from one idea, from one sentence, to another. It is difficult because to make a coherent presentation you have to triumph over natural human casualness and arrange your ideas so that they can be grasped by others.

Though careful planning in the prewriting stage will help to make clear the relationship of consecutive ideas, for the most part coherence must be tested after writing. You should try to go over your copy impersonally to see if what you have written hangs together not only for you but for those who will read it. Ask yourself, "Is the relation between these statements clear? Can a reader move from this sentence or from this paragraph to the next without losing the thread?"

A natural arrangement of material is not enough; you often need to signal the relationship between sentences and paragraphs. These signs, various suggestions for establishing coherence, and examples of successful and unsuccessful attempts at coherence are discussed in *Conjunctions; *Prepositions; *Reference of pronouns; *Transition; and *Guide*, pp. 201–04 and 247–62. Reference: E. K. Lybbert and D. W. Cummings, *CCC*, Feb. 1969, pp. 35–38.

Collective nouns

Coll

Revision: Change, according to the conventions outlined in this article, the verb and/or the pronoun to agree with the collective noun marked.

1. A collective noun is one whose singular form names a group of objects or persons or acts. Some common collective nouns are:

army	contents	gang	*number
*athletics	*couple	group	offspring
audience	crowd	herd	*politics
class	dozen	jury	*public
*committee	faculty	*majority	remainder
company	family	mankind	team

When the group as a whole is intended, the collective noun takes a singular verb and singular pronoun; when the individual units of the group are intended, the noun takes a plural verb and plural pronoun:

The *crowd* that *has* been noisily engaged in finding *its* seats *settles* down and the incessant murmur of voices slowly quiets.

The first *couple* on the floor *was* Tom and Janet.

One day when we were near where the old *couple were* living, we dropped in to see *them*.

The inner *circle* of Kennedy aides, too, *have* gone *their* separate ways. . . . —*Newsweek*, Feb. 1, 1971

The rule is simple enough. Its application is more complicated because (1) some collectives have regular plural forms (*army* – *armies*), others (*athletics, offspring*) do not; (2) even in the same sentence the sense may shift from singular to plural (see § 2 below); (3) words which are not ordinarily collectives may be so used (the baseball *nine* were . . .); (4) some collectives more commonly take singular verbs (*herd, mankind*), others plural verbs (*people*).

British and American practices differ somewhat; for example, *government* and *party* referring to political groups are plural in England, singular here.

2. In speaking we often make casual shifts in number. In writing, especially Formal writing, a collective should not be treated as both singular and plural in the same context:

The *company was* organized and immediately sent out *its* [not *their*] representatives.

Mess is over and the *guard have* a busy morning ahead of *them* [not *it*]. Or: . . . the *guard has* . . . ahead of *it* [not *them*].

In using a collective noun, there is often a temptation to try to keep it singular when the meaning really calls for a plural construction. Then the writer may slip unconsciously from singular to plural:

The entire *town troops* into the church, *seats itself* on the uncomfortable wooden benches, and *remains* there for a good two hours, while an aged curé preaches to *them* [consistency demands *it*] of *their* [*its*] wicked lives and awful sins.

In making constructions consistent, you will often find, as in the example just given, that it is the first member, the collective subject, that needs to be changed, rather than its pronouns. Beginning with "All the people of the town troop to the church, seat themselves . . ." would avoid the problem.

Also operating is our tendency not to sustain constructions across intervening words. A verb that follows a collective noun closely is likely to be singular, but an intervening plural modifier may make it plural: The inner circle *of aides* have. . . . More common is the shift from a singular verb, close to the noun, to a plural pronoun, some distance from it: The *team was* called together for last-minute instructions and then sent to *their* positions in the field. Here, too, a change in the subject is easiest: The players were called. . . .

3. The plural of a collective noun signifies different groups: The audiences of New York and Chicago differed in their reception of the play.

4. In measurements and amounts a plural noun is often followed by a singular verb: About eighty pounds of carbon disulfide *is* [or *are*] added.

See *Subject and verb § 3a, *Reference of pronouns § 2, *every and its compounds § 1. References: Bryant, pp. 6–7; Curme, *Syntax*, pp. 50–51, 539–40; Fries, *AEG*, pp. 48–50, 54, 57–59; Jespersen, *EEG*, pp. 210–12; Pooley, pp. 85–88.

Colloquial English

Usage that is characteristic of speech is colloquial. In modern writing the division between what is spoken and what is written is not nearly so sharp as it once was, though some spoken usages may be inappropriate in writing just as some features of written English are inappropriate in speech. See *Spoken and written English, *Vernacular, and *Guide*, pp. 5–14.

Colon

Colon

Revision: Use a colon here.

The colon is a mark of anticipation, indicating that what follows the mark will supplement what preceded it.

1. *Introductory uses.* A colon is used before a series of words, phrases, or clauses when there is no introductory word or phrase or when they are formally introduced by a set phrase like *as follows* or *including the following*. It should not be used after less Formal introductory words (*like, such as*) that tie the series closely to the rest of the sentence.

Seen from another perspective it is a heterogeneous collection of documents: poems, fragments of poems, letters, notebooks, undergraduate papers, lecture notes, incomplete commentaries, sermons, and so on. — J. Hillis Miller, *Journal of English Literary History*, Dec. 1955

Classifying the poetry written from 1500 to 1900 in accordance with this distinction, we discover a sequence which runs as follows: predicative, then balanced; predicative, then balanced. — Josephine Miles, *PMLA*, Sept. 1955

. . . Hesse is bold and realistic, anticipating existential thinkers such as Camus and Sartre. — Joseph Mileck, *Modern Philology*, Feb. 1967

The colon is also used to introduce quotations in factual writing, especially if they are complete grammatical units and run to more than one sentence. Again, the colon is more common in Formal than in General and Informal, and its suitability depends in part on the way the quotation is introduced. If it is closely built into the sentence, a comma is usual; if the introduction is more formal, a colon: "For example, the report cannot say, 'It was a wonderful car,' but must say something like this: 'It has been driven 50,000 miles and has never required any repairs' " (S. I. Hayakawa, *Language in Thought and Action*).

2. *Between clauses.* A colon is sometimes used between the clauses of a compound sentence, particularly in Formal writing, when the second clause is an illustration, a restatement, or an amplification of the first:

In all our ordinary experience the metaphor is non-literal: nobody but a savage or a lunatic can take metaphor literally. — Northrop Frye, *Journal of English Literary History*, June 1956

The form of the stanza is set: even in these very early drafts Yeats never rhymes line 1 with line 3. . . . — Curtis Bradford, *Yeats at Work*

The supposition that words are used principally to convey thoughts is one of the most elementary of possible errors: they are used mainly to proclaim emotional effects on the hearers or attitudes that will lead to practical results. — H. R. Huse, *The Illiteracy of the Literate*

Particularly in less Formal writing, a semicolon or a period is common in this position. It is the one use in which the colon and the semicolon are sometimes interchangeable; a semicolon should never be used to introduce a series or a quotation.

3. *Conventional uses.* The colon has a number of conventional uses.
a — After the salutation of business or other Formal letters: Dear Sir:
b — Between hours and minutes expressed in figures: 11:42 a.m.; 3:28 p.m.
c — In formal bibliographies and formal citations of books:

Between volume and page: *The Mt. Adams Review*, 160:129 – 40 (A comma is now more common.)

Between title and subtitle: *The Great Tradition: An Interpretation of American Literature Since the Civil War*

Between place of publication and publisher: Glenview, Ill.: Scott, Foresman

Between Bible chapter and verse: Genesis 9:3 – 5

d — In ratios and proportions when the numbers are written as numerals: concrete mixed 5:3:1. Two colons are used instead of an equals sign in a full proportion: 1:2::3:6.

4. *Stylistic use.* Sometimes, for stylistic effect, a writer will use colons where other writers would use commas, dashes, semicolons, or periods:

And whether this shall descend upon us over the steep north crown I shall not know, but doubt: and after how many false deliverances there can be no hopeful imagining: but that it shall come at length there can be no question: for this I know in my own soul through that regard of love we bear one another: for there it was proved me in the meeting of the extremes of the race. — James Agee, *Let Us Now Praise Famous Men*

Similar uses are found in verse, where the syntactical relationships may be unconventional.

5. *Capitals following.* After a colon either a capital or a small letter may be used, but a small letter is much more common. The capital is most often used when the matter following the colon is a new paragraph or an elaborate enumeration. A new sentence may be capitalized in a rather Formal presentation:

The ways in which the kings settled social disputes were very different, in spirit as well as in technic: The kings of France . . . protected the social privileges of the nobility . . . ; the kings of Prussia . . . tried to restrict exploitation of the masses . . . . —Carl Landauer in *The American Way*

But in most cases a new sentence introduced by a colon is begun with a small letter:

If someone is rude enough to ask who the serious writers are, the answer is easy: they are those whom one could never suspect of writing with the reader in mind!—Wayne C. Booth, *The Rhetoric of Fiction*

The will of the majority is otherwise: the black man believes, 3 to 1, that he can win short of war. —*Newsweek*, June 30, 1969

For other uses of the colon, see the *Chicago Manual* and the *U.S. Style Manual*.

Comma

Comma

Revision: Insert or remove a comma at the place marked, in accordance with one of the sections in this article.

About half the punctuation marks in normal writing are commas, and the most common question in punctuating is "Should there be a comma here?" The general advice of this book is to use commas wherever they are considered obligatory and to use them optionally where they contribute to understanding. When choice is possible, the final decision depends on fitness with other traits of style: the complex syntax and deliberate pace of much Formal writing call for more commas than the simpler, brisker sentences of General.

C_1 **1.** *To separate coordinate clauses.*
a—A comma before the conjunction is particularly common when the independent clauses are rather long and when it is desirable to emphasize their distinctness, as when they have different subjects:

To have survived all this, to be on high display in the very center of gone-with-the-wind country is a just cause for a little waggish arrogance, and when Ali stops for a moment as he passes three large, T-shirted, white Atlantans and laughingly challenges the largest of them . . . to a little tune-up fight . . . , the glee at the deferential refusal bubbles all over downtown Atlanta. —Jack Richardson, *Harper's*, Jan. 1971

A comma is often not used when the coordinate clauses are fairly short and closely related in meaning, especially in easy narrative:

Uses of the comma

The following list of uses of the comma outlines the treatment in this article. The numbers and letters refer to sections and subsections.

1. *To separate coordinate clauses*
   a — Between long clauses
   b — Between clauses connected by *but*
   c — Between clauses connected by *for*

2. *With preceding and following elements*
   a — After a dependent clause or long phrase preceding the main clause
   b — Before a dependent clause or long phrase following the main clause and not essential to its meaning

3. *To set off nonrestrictive modifiers*

4. *To enclose interrupting elements*
   a — Around interrupting elements
   b — Around conjunctive adverbs

5. *In lists and series*
   a — Between units in lists and series
   b — Between coordinate adjectives

6. *For emphasis and contrast*

7. *For clarity*

8. *With main sentence elements*
   a — Subject and verb
   b — Verb and object
   c — Compound predicates

9. *In conventional uses*
   a — In dates
   b — In addresses
   c — After salutations in informal letters
   d — After names in direct address
   e — In figures
   f — With degrees and titles
   g — With weak exclamations
   h — To show omission

10. *With other marks of punctuation*
    a — With parentheses
    b — With dash (*Dash § 6)
    c — With quotation marks (*Quotation marks § 4, b and c)

"The mother had killed a bull gaur in a shallow ravine and I watched the family throughout the night . . ." (George B. Schaller, *Life*, June 25, 1965).

b — A comma is generally used between two coordinate clauses joined by *but*, to emphasize the contrast: "His achievements in office have been difficult to assess, but they have been formidable"(John David Hamilton, *Atlantic*, Jan. 1971).

c — A comma is generally used between clauses connected by the conjunction *for*, to avoid confusion with the preposition *for:* They were obviously mistaken, for intercollegiate sports are always competitive.

For commas between clauses that could stand as separate sentences, see *Comma fault; *Contact clauses; and *Guide*, pp. 280 – 90.

C₂ **2.** *With preceding and following elements.*

a — A comma is used after an introductory dependent clause or an introductory phrase if the clause or phrase is long or if it is not closely related to what follows:

If a time comes when we are no longer free to laugh at our own generation, the situation will be far worse than that caused by intergenerational gaps.

Although willing to use his athletic ability, he refused to let the demands of the football schedule interfere with his academic work.

When the preceding clause or phrase is short or closely related to the thrust of the main clause — especially when the two clauses have the same subject — there is often no comma following it in General writing:

For this reason [ ] it was particularly necessary to share the experiences of as many as possible. (Short phrase)

When we had completed the long hike to the summit [ ] we passed around the wineskins. (Subjects the same)

Every time appropriations are before the House [ ] he continually checks the Democrats' expenditures. (Close relationship)

b — A comma usually stands before a dependent clause or long phrase that follows the main clause if the subordinate element is not essential to the meaning of the main clause:

The foregoing was written before the upheavals of last May, when the fatality of Cambodia and the tragedies of Kent State and Jackson State further unhinged American campuses. — Fritz Stern, *American Scholar*, Winter 1970 – 71

They had tried four times to start the engine, with the breeze freshening and the tide beginning to turn.

C₃ **3.** *To set off nonrestrictive modifiers.* Word groups that do not restrict the meaning of the noun or verb or clause they modify are set off by commas. The italicized word groups in the following sentences are nonrestrictive:

From where I was standing, *almost directly above the trunk*, I could see many of the articles that had been lost.

Pigeons breed in the spring and the hen lays two eggs, *one of which usually hatches into a hen and the other into a cock.*

A modifier that restricts the reference of the word it modifies (as "that had been lost" restricts "articles" in the first of the illustrative sentences above) is essential to correct understanding and is therefore not set off by commas. Out of context, many modifiers could be either restrictive or nonrestrictive. The word groups in italics in the following sentences might or might not be set off, depending on the writer's meaning:

A winding road *which seemed to lead nowhere in particular* passed through the village.

The man *who was carrying a gun* walked across the campus and into the administration building.

See *Restrictive and nonrestrictive; *Guide*, p. 300.

C₄ **4.** *To enclose interrupting and parenthetical elements.*
a—A word, phrase, or clause that interrupts the main structure of the sentence should be enclosed in commas:

Next summer, no matter what happens, I intend to go to Africa.
The prank, I assume, seemed amusing at the time.
My uncle, as was his habit, stopped for a drink on his way home from work.

Forgetting to complete the enclosure with a second comma can result in a confused sentence: "If factory workers and farmers became more efficient, Soviet citizens were told this week [ ] they would get more domestic goods, food, housing, hospitals and schools" (*Newport Daily News*, Dec. 26, 1970).

Usage is divided over setting off short parenthetical expressions like *of course.* Enclosing them in commas is more characteristic of Formal than of General writing. There is often a difference in emphasis as well as tone according to whether or not commas are used:

And of course there are those who talk about the hair of the dog. . . .
—*Providence Sunday Journal*, Dec. 27, 1970

The question, of course, is not whether the family will "survive." . . .
—*Time*, Dec. 28, 1970

b—When a *conjunctive adverb stands after the first phrase of its clause, it is usually enclosed in commas: It was this ridiculous proposal, however, that won majority approval. At the beginning of a sentence such adverbs may or may not be set off: Therefore [ ] I have decided to withdraw my application.

But and other coordinating conjunctions are a part of the clauses in which they appear and should not be set off: But a solution must be found.

C₅   **5.** *In lists and series.*

a—The comma is the natural mark to use between the units in lists and series: "He has read everything he could lay his hands on, manuscript and printed, that was written during the period: plays, sermons, ballads, broadsides, letters, diaries, and, above all, court records" (Edmund S. Morgan, *New York Review of Books*, May 9, 1968).

Usage is divided over the use of a comma before the conjunction in a series: "letters, diaries, and records" or "letters, diaries and records." Use of the comma is a safeguard against ambiguity: "He had small shoulders, a thick chest holding a strong heart [ ] and heavy thighs . . ." (Richard Mandell, *Sports Illustrated*, April 12, 1971). See *Series.

b—The comma is used between adjectives modifying the same noun. In the sentence "Though it was a hot, sticky, miserable day, Mrs. Marston looked cool in her fresh gingham dress," there are commas between *hot* and *sticky* and between *sticky* and *miserable* because each stands in the same relation to the noun *day*. There is no comma between *fresh* and *gingham* because *fresh* modifies *gingham dress*, not just *dress*.

By separating, a comma provides emphasis. Compare these two versions:

His long, greasy hair hung down to the shoulders of his worn, faded jacket.
His long greasy hair hung down to the shoulders of his worn faded jacket.

In the first, *greasy* and *faded* stand out as separate modifiers of their nouns.

C₆   **6.** *For emphasis and contrast.* When two words or phrases are connected by *and*, they are not usually punctuated; but because a comma tends to keep distinct the elements it separates and to emphasize slightly the element that follows it, writers may use commas for these purposes alone: My brother was delighted with the prestige of his new position, and with the increase in pay.

C₇   **7.** *For clarity.* Often a comma will guide a reader in interpreting a sentence and make it unnecessary for him to go back over it for meaning. A comma between clauses joined by *for* makes it clear that the word is functioning as a conjunction rather than as a preposition. Similarly, a comma can prevent the subject of one verb from being mistaken even momentarily for the object of another:

When the boll weevil struck, the credit system collapsed and ruined both landowners and tenants. Not: When the boll weevil struck the credit system. . . .

Soon after the inspector left, the room was crowded with curious onlookers. Not: Soon after the inspector left the room. . . .

A comma can also make immediately clear whether a modifier goes with what precedes or with what follows: A great crowd of shoppers milled around inside, and outside hundreds more were storming the doors. Not: . . . milled around inside and outside. . . .

And a comma helps when the same word is used twice in a row: What he does, does not concern me.

C_8 **8.** _With main sentence elements._

a — Subject and verb. Although a comma is sometimes placed between a very long subject and its verb in old-fashioned Formal usage, subjects are not separated from their verbs in General or current Formal writing.

b — Verb and object. There is some temptation to put a comma after a verb that in speech would be followed by a slight pause; but conventional punctuation does not follow speech at all precisely, and a verb should not be separated from its object.

c — Compound predicates. Ordinarily no comma is needed or should be used between the verbs of a compound predicate. An exception should be made only when the sentence is long and involved, as in some Formal prose, and a comma between the widely separated verbs makes reading easier, or when you feel the need for special emphasis or contrast: "He must believe, too, that mobilization of science and knowledge in peace should not be confined to cosmic forces, but must be extended to his other needs . . ." (Norman Cousins, _Saturday Review,_ Aug. 18, 1945).

C_9 **9.** _In conventional uses._

a — In dates, to separate the day of the month from the year: May 26, 1971. When the day of the month is not given, a comma may or may not be used: In September 1846 or In September, 1846. If a comma precedes the year, punctuation should also follow: In September, 1846, the government fell.

b — In addresses, to separate smaller from larger units: Washington, D.C.; Chicago, Illinois; Hamilton, Madison County, New York; Berne, Switzerland.

c — After salutations in informal letters: Dear John,

d — After names in direct address: Jim, try that one again.

e — In figures, to separate thousands, millions, etc.: 4,672,342. In some styles no comma is used in figures with four digits: 2750.

f — To separate degrees and following titles from names: George Emmett, M.A.; Charles Evans Hughes, Jr.; Elihu Root, Esq.

g — After a weak exclamation like _well, why, oh:_ Oh, what's the use?

h — Sometimes to show the omission of a word that is required to fill out a construction: He took the right-hand turn; I, the left.

C_{10} **10.** _With other marks of punctuation._

a — When a parenthesis comes within a phrase or clause that is followed by a comma, the comma belongs after the parenthesis.

b — Use a comma or a dash, not both. See *Dash § 6.

c — For the use of commas with quotation marks, see *Quotation marks § 4, b and c.

References: Summey, index entries under _Comma;_ Whitehall, pp. 126 – 29.

Comma fault

CF

Revision: Revise the sentence marked by changing the comma to a semi-colon or a period, or by inserting an appropriate conjunction, or by rephrasing to make a more satisfactory sentence.

A comma fault (comma blunder, comma splice, *fused sentence) occurs when two or more independent clauses are punctuated as a single sentence — that is, with a comma between them. Occasionally sentences of this sort may be effective (see *Contact clauses), but the term *comma fault* marks those that are unjustified by their form or the semantic relation between the clauses or both.

There are various remedies for a comma fault:

1. The most obvious is to put a semicolon or a period in place of the comma, but inserting a period sometimes makes two weak sentences instead of one.

2. If the statements really belong together in one sentence, they may be joined by a conjunction that shows the relationship. When the choice is a coordinating conjunction, ordinarily the comma is retained (see *Comma § 1a); when the choice is a conjunctive adverb, it is replaced by a semicolon (see *Semicolon § 1b).

3. Often the sentence needs to be rewritten, perhaps subordinating one of the clauses, perhaps making a single independent clause. The aim is to produce a satisfactory sentence, not just to remove the comma fault.

The following examples show some common types:

I think Americans should read this book, they would get a more accurate picture of problems in the Middle East.
Revised: I think Americans should read this book for [or: because it would give them] a more accurate picture of problems in the Middle East.

The captain was endowed with great vitality, he had what amounted to a genius for survival.
Revised: The captain was endowed with great vitality; [or colon or period and a new sentence, depending on the emphasis desired] he had what amounted to a genius for survival.

One part receives the stimulus from outside and transmits the impulse to the cell, this is known as the dendrite.
Revised: One part, known as the dendrite, receives the stimulus from outside and transmits the impulse to the cell.

I wanted to see the movie, however, I decided I could not spare the time.
Revised: I wanted to see the movie; however, [or: . . . movie, but] I decided I could not spare the time.

If you can make a sure distinction between an independent clause and a dependent clause, you should find it easy to spot any comma faults in your sentences. Look first to see how many independent subject-verb combinations you have in each group of words punctuated as a single sentence. If there are two independent clauses, see if you have a connective between them. If there is no connective but only a comma, you have probably produced a comma fault. For exceptions, see *Contact clauses. See also *Guide*, pp. 288–90.

Commands and requests

Direct commands (also called imperatives) are expressed by the simple (infinitive) form of the verb:

Hurry up!
Shut the door, please.
Fill out the coupon and *mail* it today.

In speech the force of the command or request is shown by the stress and tone of voice, which are hard to represent on paper. Emphatic commands are punctuated with an exclamation mark, less emphatic ones with a period. The form with *do* is often emphatic (*Do come!*). Negative commands are expressed with *not* and the *do* form of the verb: Don't go yet.

Softened or more polite commands and requests depend on phrasing and usually involve auxiliaries or adverbs of courtesy. Often they are in the pattern of a question, written with either a period or a question mark, depending on the intonation intended.

Try to get them in on time.
You will write at least six pages.
Please think no more of it.
Would you be willing to take part in this program?
Would [or Will] you please close the window.
Let's go around and see what we can do with him.
Suppose we say nothing more about it.

In indirect discourse a command becomes an infinitive with *to* or a clause with *should:*

He told us to write a 5000-word paper. Or: He said that we should write a 5000-word paper. Direct form: Write a 5000-word paper.

He wired me to come at once. Direct: Come at once.

References: Curme, *Syntax*, pp. 419, 430–36; Long, pp. 76–79.

committee

Committee is a *collective noun, usually construed as singular but sometimes as plural when the writer is thinking of the several individuals who compose it. In the latter situation "the members of the committee" is more usual.

Common case form

See *Accusative case, *Case.

compare, contrast

Compare is used: (1) to point out likenesses (used with *to*); (2) to find likenesses or differences (used with *with*). *Contrast* always points out differences.

He compared my stories *to* Maupassant's [said they were like his].

He compared my stories *with* Maupassant's [pointed out like and unlike traits].

When the things compared are of different classes, *to* is used: He compared my stories to a sack of beans. In the common construction with the past participle, either *to* or *with* is used: Compared with [or to] Maupassant's, mine are feeble. *In comparison* is followed by *with:* In comparison with Maupassant's mine are feeble. *Contrast* ordinarily takes *with:* He contrasted my work with [sometimes to] Maupassant's. *In contrast*, however, usually takes *to:* In contrast to Maupassant's, my stories are feeble.

Comparison and contrast

For comparison and contrast as a method of developing paragraphs, parts of essays, or entire essays, see *Guide*, pp. 80–90.

Comparison of adjectives and adverbs

Comp

Revision: Change the form or construction of the adjective or adverb marked, in accordance with the section below that applies.

To express degrees of what is named, the forms of adjectives and adverbs are changed by adding -er or -est to the root (*long, longer, longest*), or the base form is preceded by *more* or *most* (*more beautiful, most beautiful*). The forms are simple enough, but a number of problems arise in using them.

1. *Choice of forms.* English adjectives and adverbs are compared in two ways:

a—By adding -er, -est.

	Positive	Comparative	Superlative
Adjective	early	earlier	earliest
	hoarse	hoarser	hoarsest
	unhappy	unhappier	unhappiest
Adverb	fast	faster	fastest
	soon	sooner	soonest

b – By using *more, most.*

	Positive	*Comparative*	*Superlative*
Adjective	exquisite	more exquisite	most exquisite
	afraid	more afraid	most afraid
	pleasing	more pleasing	most pleasing
Adverb	comfortable	more comfortable	most comfortable
	hotly	more hotly	most hotly

Three-syllable modifiers are ordinarily compared with *more* and *most,* one-syllable words with *-er* and *-est.* Most two-syllable modifiers are compared with *more* and *most,* but many can take either form: *able – abler, more able – ablest, most able; empty – emptier, more empty – emptiest, most empty.*

For two-syllable words, *more* and *most* are the safer choices when in doubt. Many words that ordinarily took *-er* and *-est* a generation ago are now regularly compared with *more* and *most.* For example, *commoner* and *commonest* are becoming rare. It was once possible to use both methods of comparison in one locution, as in Shakespeare's "most unkindest cut of all," but double comparatives and double superlatives are no longer Standard English.

Some problems of usage that arise with irregular forms of comparison are discussed in *elder, eldest; *farther, further; *former, first – latter, last;* and *last, latest.* References: Curme, *Parts of Speech,* Chs. 11 and 13; Fries, *AEG,* pp. 96 – 101.

2. *Uses of the comparative.* The comparative expresses a greater degree (It is *warmer* now) or makes specific comparison between two units (He was *kinder* [*more kind*] than his wife). The two terms of a comparison should be actually comparable:

Comparable: His salary was lower than a shoe clerk's. Or: . . . than that of a shoe clerk. Not: . . . than a shoe clerk.

Comparable: His face was round and healthy looking, like a recent college graduate's. Not: . . . like a recent college graduate.

Logic calls for *other* with *any* in comparisons between a thing and the group to which it belongs: She is a better dancer than any of the other girls. The comparative is frequently used absolutely, with no actual comparison involved (higher education, the lower depths, older people). In much advertising copy the task of supplying a comparison is left to the reader (*cooler, fresher, stronger, faster, more economical*). See *as . . . as. Reference: Esther K. Sheldon, *AS,* Oct. 1945, pp. 161 – 67.

3. *Uses of the superlative.* In Formal and most General writing, the superlative is used to indicate the greatest degree of a quality among three or more people or things (He was the *jolliest* of the whole group; This is the *brightest* tie in the showcase). Informally, the superlative of two objects is common (Russia and China compete to see which can be most critical of our policies). Use of the superlative as a form of emphasis is also Informal (She has the loveliest flowers; We saw the best show). The form with *most* is now largely restricted to Formal social correspondence (You are most kind; She is most clever) in which no specific comparison is intended.

Superlatives are not completed by *other:* The Egyptians had obtained the highest degree of cultivation in medicine that had up to that time been obtained by any [not: other] nation.

References: Bryant, pp. 201–02; Curme, *Syntax*, p. 504; Fries, *AEG*, pp. 99–101; Hall, pp. 279–80; Jespersen, *MEG*, II, 203–04.

4. *Comparison of absolutes.* Purists raise objections to the comparison of *black, dead, excellent, fatal, final, impossible, perfect, *unique* on the grounds that there can be no degrees of *deadness* or *blackness* or *impossibility.* But in common use these words are frequently compared: a more equal society, a more complete victory, a more impossible situation; and the Constitution has "to form a more perfect union." Many absolutes are used figuratively with meanings that naturally admit comparison: This is the *deadest* town I was ever in. See *Divided usage. Reference: Bryant, pp. 58–59.

Complement

Complement often refers to the noun or adjective completing the meaning of a linking verb and modifying the subject: He was *busy;* He became *the real head* of the concern. In some grammars *complement* is used to include direct and indirect objects. See *Linking verbs, *Predicate adjectives.

Complex sentence

A complex sentence has one independent, or main, clause and one or more dependent clauses, ordinarily introduced by relative pronouns or subordinating conjunctions: She married the man *who* picked her up *when* she fell. See *Clauses and *Guide*, pp. 278–79.

Compound-complex sentence

See *Compound sentence § 4.

Compound predicate

Two or more verbs with the same subject, together with their modifiers, form a compound predicate: Ruth *wrote* and *mailed* three letters.

Compound predicates help make writing economical. Note how far removed this sentence is from the one-small-idea-to-a-sentence type:

The case is made more interesting if the great daily has, among other things, distorted political news, reported its political opponents with miserable unfairness and glaring prejudice, tried to goad the government into declaring war on Cuba, lowered the mental level of life in the community, debased the language, filled its pages with vast ads for pork butts, storm windows, undergarments, dollar sales, antiperspirants, failed to inform the public on matters of great importance, fought medical care for the aged, and so forth. — Saul Bellow, *Atlantic*, March 1963

For further discussion see *Subject and verb.

Compound sentence

A compound sentence coordinates two or more independent clauses, each with its complete subject and predicate. See *Clauses and Guide, pp. 277–78.

1. *With coordinating conjunction.* Usually the clauses of a compound sentence are connected by one of the coordinating conjunctions: "It doesn't take much special talent to master a simplified programing code, and the ability to consider a problem in logical sequence is not confined to mathematicians" (Gene Bylinsky, *Fortune*, March 1967).

2. *Without connective.* A compound sentence may have a comma instead of a connective between the clauses (see *Contact clauses). But such sentences are usually punctuated with a semicolon: "They are generous-minded; they hate shams and enjoy being indignant about them; they are valuable social reformers; they have no notion of confining books to a library shelf" (E. M. Forster, *Aspects of the Novel*). Since each of these clauses could also be written as a separate sentence, it is apparent that the traditional definition of *sentence* is somewhat arbitrary.

3. *With conjunctive adverb.* The clauses of a compound sentence may be connected by a conjunctive adverb (*however, moreover, whereas, consequently, therefore* . . .): The FBI had proved themselves expert in publicizing their solution of crimes; consequently some local police gave them only grudging support.

4. *Compound-complex.* When one or more of the coordinate clauses of a sentence are modified by dependent clauses, the sentence is called compound–complex:

Yet while there is still much to be done in completing the battle against poverty, the central problems of our time are no longer problems of want and privation, and the central sources of discontent are no longer, as they were in the 1930's, economic in character. — Arthur Schlesinger, Jr., *Reporter*, May 1956

This sentence has two independent clauses (making it compound): "the central problems . . . and the central sources . . ."; and two dependent clauses (making it compound–complex): "while there is . . ." and "as they were. . . ."

Compound subject

Two or more elements standing as the subject of one verb are called a compound subject: "Capitalists, militarists, and ecclesiastics cooperate in education . . ." (Bertrand Russell, *What I Believe*). The verb following a compound subject is usually plural: Christianity and humanity have gone hand in hand throughout history.

Some special cases are described under *Subject and verb § 3. See also *Guide*, p. 280.

Compound words

Compound words in written English are combinations of two or more words which are written as one word or hyphened: *doorknob, notwithstanding, quarter-hour, father-in-law, drugstore*. But the conventions of writing ignore a large number of compounds which, though written as separate words, express more than the sum of the parts: *the White House, high school, post office*. In speech these are usually distinguished by the stronger stress on the first words: compare *a white house* and *the White House*.

Questions about the use of the hyphen in compound words are discussed in *Hyphen, and questions about their plurals in *Plurals of nouns § 5. See also *Group words, and check your dictionary.

comprise

Traditionally, *comprise* means "consist of" or "include": The whole comprises its parts. In current usage the nearly opposite senses of "constitute," "compose," and "make up" are very common:

Of the forty-nine letters and two contracts that comprise this volume. . . .— Grace M. Sproull, *Modern Philology*, Feb. 1967

The four states that at one time comprised French Equatorial Africa. . . .— Harold G. Marcus, *American Historical Review*, Jan. 1967

But some stylists and teachers consider these latter senses unacceptable. Since *comprise* is a relatively Formal word, the more General *make up* is often a better choice.

Conclusion of an essay

Concl

Revision: Revise the end of your paper to round out the discussion more effectively.

When you reach the end of your discussion, wrap it up. Don't simply stop, so that the reader wonders if the last page is missing. And don't keep rambling on until your reader is missing.

If your paper is a long one, you may need to review the ground that has been covered, preferably in fresh phrasing. If the material is complex, you may need to pull together the points that have been made and show how they add up and what they add up to. But short papers, like long ones, must add up to something.

When the reader of an essay finishes the last sentence and thinks "So what?" the writer has written an essay that has no point, or—more likely—he has failed to make clear what that point is. A conclusion cannot save a pointless essay by announcing a point: "I guess what I've been trying to say is that there are worse places to live in than Chicago." (A point like this one should have been emerging step by step throughout the essay.) But by clarifying a fundamental causal relationship, by restating the essential argument, by bringing out an implication, the final paragraph or two can greatly strengthen an essay.

The final sentences should avoid tag ends and anticlimax, build to a firm conclusion instead of trailing away to a dying fall. They should wrap up the essay in such a way that the reader not only recognizes its completeness but feels satisfied that the last words were the right ones. See *Guide*, pp. 207–08, 417–18.

Concrete words

See *Abstract and concrete words.

Conditions

A conditional clause states a condition or action necessary for the truth or occurrence of what is stated in the independent clause that the conditional clause modifies. *If* is by far the most common conjunction for conditional clauses, with its negatives *if not* and *unless* (=*if not*), and *whether* (=*if* . . . *if, if* . . . *or if*). Somewhat more Formal words and phrases introducing conditions are *in case, provided, provided that, on condition that, in the event that.*

1. *Simple conditions.* Simple (or practical) conditions are statements of actual or reasonable conditions under which the main statement will hold. The indicative (ordinary) verb forms are used:

If the red light is on, you know a train is in that block of track.
He will be there *unless something happens to his car.*
Whether he comes or not, I shall go just the same.

An older type of condition survives in some proverbs: Spare the rod and spoil the child. (*If you spare the rod,* you will spoil the child.)

In speech, we often express condition by a compound sentence: You just try that and you'll be sorry.

2. *Less vivid conditions.* Less vivid (theoretical or hypothetical but still possible) conditions are usually made with *should* . . . *would* or with the past tense: *If he should offer another $100,* I would take it. Or: *If he raised his offer,* I would take it.

3. *Contrary to fact conditions.* Conditions that cannot be met or that are untrue—contrary to fact—are indicated by the past tense of the verb used in a present or future sense (If he *was* here [now], we would have seen him). In some Formal English, especially in writing, the plural form of the past tense is not uncommon in the third-person singular, usually called a subjunctive (If he were here . . .); and "If I were you" is a firmly established petrified construction. Formal English also sometimes uses a rather archaic inversion (*Were* he here. . .).

See also *if, whether; *Subjunctives. References: Curme, *Syntax,* pp. 317–32, 421–29; Fries, *AEG,* pp. 104–07; Jespersen, *EEG,* Ch. 24.

Conjugation

The conjugation of a verb is the set of inflected and phrasal forms in which it may occur to show person, number, voice, and tense. See *Principal parts of verbs, *Tenses of verbs, *Verbs.

Conjunctions

Conj

Revision: Make the conjunction marked more accurate (§ 1) or more appropriate to the style of the passage (§ 2).

Conjunction is the traditional term for a limited group of words without distinctive formal traits, which join words, phrases, clauses, or sentences. In this *Index* conjunctions are further defined and discussed according to their conventional classification:

*Coordinating (*and, but, for,* etc.)
*Correlative (*either . . . or, not only . . . but,* etc.)
*Conjunctive adverbs (*however, therefore, consequently,* etc.)
*Subordinating (*as, because, since, so that, when,* etc.)

There are also articles on many of the particular conjunctions. Since most conjunctions are used in other capacities as well, especially as prepositions and adverbs (*as, for, so* . . .), the exact application of the term is not always possible, nor is the distinction between coordinating and subordinating conjunctions always apparent. Though *relative pronouns (*who, which, that* . . .) also have a connective function, they are not classed as conjunctions.

1. *Accurate conjunctions.* An exact use of conjunctions in fitting clauses together is a sign of mature, practiced writing. In everyday speech we get along with a relatively small number—*and, as, but, so, when,* and a few others—because we can emphasize shades of meaning and exact relationships by pauses, tones, gestures. In writing, careful choice of connectives goes a long way toward making up for the absence of these means of holding ideas together.

Conjunctions are often used carelessly: *but* may be tossed in when there is no contrast between statements (see *but § 2). *As* means "because," but it is a weak *because* (see *as); *while* may mean "although" or "whereas," but the core of its meaning relates to *time. Sometimes, if a writer's thinking has been truly consecutive, the most satisfactory linkage will be implicit: a *therefore* or an *accordingly* will be unnecessary and unwelcome. See the articles on the particular conjunctions; *Transition; *Guide,* pp. 255–57, 317.

2. *Weight.* Conjunctions should be appropriate to other traits of style. In General contexts, such conjunctive adverbs as *furthermore, moreover, consequently,* and *nevertheless* may be unnecessarily heavy. Often simple *but* is a better choice than *however:* The trail presents few problems until you reach the canyon; from there on, however, it is no route for Sunday strollers. Better: . . . canyon, but from there on. . . . See *Conjunctive adverbs § 2.

3. *Repetition of conjunctions.* Repeating a conjunction at the beginning of each element of a series makes each element distinct, avoids possible confusion, and achieves the advantages of strong rhythm and clear-cut parallelism:

I took an old shutter and fixed a sort of porch roof on it, and nailed it to a locust tree nearby, and set the nest with the eggs carefully on it.—Wendell Berry, *The Long-Legged House*

Barry Lydon, too, has stolen and cheated and lied.—Jean Sudrann, *Victorian Studies*, June 1967

In contrast, omitting *and* before the last member of a short series is crisply emphatic:

The most important of these, the most characteristic, the most misleading, is called *Some Glances at Current Linguistics*, and it's largely a polemic against Chomsky.—William H. Gass, *New Republic*, May 11, 1968

It may also suggest that the series is only a sample, not a complete enumeration:

. . . many were the Northerners who, during and after the Civil War, went South to train, to educate, to rehabilitate Negro refugees and freedmen.—William H. Pease, *Journal of Southern History*, Feb. 1967

See *Series.

4. *Coordination versus subordination.* For discussion of this phase of the use of conjunctions, see *Coordination, *Subordination, and *Guide*, pp. 313–17.

References: Curme, *Parts of Speech*, Ch. 7, and *Syntax*, pp. 161–73, 181–95.

Conjunctive adverbs

1. A number of words that are primarily adverbs are used also as connectives. They are called conjunctive adverbs (or transitional adverbs or adverbial connectors or sentence connectors or sentence adverbials). Their adverbial meaning remains rather prominent, so that their connective force is relatively weak. They are used after a semicolon between coordinate clauses and also after end punctuation to introduce separate sentences. The most common are:

accordingly	furthermore	*namely
*also (see *too)	hence	nevertheless
anyhow	*however	otherwise
anyway (colloquial)	indeed	*still
*besides	likewise	*then
consequently	moreover	therefore

Adverb: No campaign, *however* violent, could make him vote.
Conjunction: The results were poor; *however,* we were not surprised.

2. *Weight and use.* Because most of the conjunctive adverbs are relatively heavy connectives, they are most appropriate in Formal writing and in sentences of some length and complexity; they are less appropriate in most General writing. They are now more likely to serve as transitional devices between sentences than to connect clauses within a sentence. The stilted use of conjunctive adverbs is a major barrier to simple, straightforward writing.

Note these appropriate and inappropriate uses:

The armored saurians, the dodo, and a few other extinct creatures are supposed to have become unviable through their exaggerated specialties; usually, *however,* such excesses are not reached. [Appropriate with the Formal sentence structure] — Susanne K. Langer, *Philosophical Sketches*

In the morning I still felt sick; *nevertheless* when the bugle sounded, I got up. [Inappropriately heavy. Could substitute *but.* Better to rewrite as complex sentence: Though I still felt sick the next morning, I got up when the bugle sounded.]

3. *Position.* Conjunctive adverbs are often placed inside their clauses instead of at the beginning. This helps take the initial stress from them and gives it to more important words. When they are so placed, they are usually set off by commas as in the first example in § 2.

4. *Punctuation.* A clause introduced by a conjunctive adverb is preceded by a semicolon.

Connectives

See *Conjunctions, *Conjunctive adverbs, *Parts of speech, *Relative pronouns.

Connotation

See *Guide*, pp. 357–59.

Construction

A construction is a group of words which stand in some grammatical relationship to each other, as that of modifier and headword (black cat), preposition and object (to the roof), or subject and predicate (They walked slowly). Any grammatical pattern may be spoken of as a construction, as in *shifted constructions.

contact

The verb *contact*, meaning "get in touch with, communicate with" (Will you contact Mr. Hubble?), is more acceptable in nonbusiness contexts today than it was a generation ago, though it remains rare in Formal usage. Its General use may be explained by its inclusiveness, embracing as it does the notions of "call," "write," "visit," and even communications conducted through intermediaries: "He contacted a leading American corporation, but the corporation heads were skeptical" (Grace M. Spruch, *Saturday Review*, Dec. 4, 1965). See *Divided usage. Reference: Bryant, pp. 60–61.

Contact clauses

Two or more clauses of a sentence, written together without a connective, are called contact clauses. A contact clause may be a restrictive dependent clause, as in "He found the key *you lost yesterday*." It may also be one of two or more independent clauses that are neither joined by conjunctions nor linked by semicolons but instead are separated by commas.

The ranging of clauses one after the other (known as parataxis) is found in classical literature; Julius Caesar's "I came, I saw, I conquered" is the most familiar example. In current prose the practice serves a variety of purposes. Writers sometimes use contact clauses to speed the movement and reduce formality:

The intellect gets busy, means and methods are studied, purposes are assessed. —Gerald Warner Brace, *The Stuff of Fiction*

Or they use them to emphasize relationships:

Both colloquial styles—consultative and casual—routinely deal in a public sort of information, though differently: casual style takes it for granted and at most alludes to it, consultative style states it as fast as it is needed. —Martin Joos, *The Five Clocks*

The clauses are usually short and direct, but they may be joined in a lengthy series:

The good times seem a little sweeter, the bad times fade into the background; there was no loneliness, my decrepit cars never broke down, I was always able to pay my phone bills, I was never frightened to death covering Klan meetings. —David Halberstam, *Harper's*, Jan. 1971

The choice of commas alone instead of coordinating conjunctions (with or without commas), subordinating conjunctions, or semicolons is a matter of style. In the first example above, many writers would substitute semicolons for the commas. In the second, some would precede "consultative style" with "but" or "while." In the third, some would put a semicolon after "sweeter," a period after "background," and an "and" before "I was never frightened. . . ." In every case, the effect would be changed. Semicolons, for example, slow the pace and add a touch of formality.

Objection to the use of commas between contact clauses like these has a basis in one of the perennial problems of writing, the *comma fault. See *Guide*, pp. 288–90. References: Curme, *Syntax*, pp. 170–73; Jespersen, *EEG*, pp. 360–61.

Context

In writing, the context is the discourse that surrounds and limits a word or passage that is being separately discussed.

1. The context is tremendously important in revealing the particular meanings of words. What, for instance, does the word *check* mean? By itself, no one can tell which of the forty or so dictionary senses of the word is meant. Yet in actual use, in definite contexts, it gives no trouble:

They were able to *check* the fire at the highway.
The treasurer's books *check* with the vouchers.
He drew a *check* for the entire amount.
The tablecloth had a red and white *check*.
He moved his bishop and shouted *"Check!"*
With difficulty he held his temper in *check*.
He had the *check* list on the desk in front of him.

And so on. Though *check* has more senses than most English words, a very large proportion of our words have more than one sense, so their particular meaning must be gathered from the context—and ordinarily it can be. Context is important in indicating not only the particular denotative sense of a word, as illustrated with *check*, but also the connotative value of the word, as suggested in statements like "By itself the word might seem insulting, but in its context it couldn't possibly give offense."

2. Statements of ideas depend for full understanding upon the context in which they stand, and in quoting or alluding to a writer's thought we should be careful to take the context into account. Cardinal Newman's definition of a gentleman as a man who never inflicts pain is often referred to as though it represented Newman's ideal, but the context (*The Idea of a University*, Discourse viii) reveals that the gentleman without religious conviction falls far short of the ideal. An honest writer takes care that allusions and quotations are true to the context in which they occur, that they really represent the ideas of their authors.

3. The rhetorical context includes the writer, his subject, his purpose, and his audience. See *Guide*, pp. 19–25 and 123–27.

continual(ly), continuous(ly)

In the sense "uninterrupted," with reference to space, *continuous(ly)* is the word: The mountains stretch continuously from Montana to Mexico. In the same sense with reference to time, conservative stylists prefer *continuous(ly)*, but *continual(ly)* is also used: For weeks we observed an almost continuous eruption of the volcano. In the sense "recurring rapidly and often," the situation is reversed — conservative stylists insist on *continual(ly)*, but *continuous(ly)* is also Standard: The governor broke his promises, not just repeatedly but continually.

Contractions

This term is applied to the written forms of words in which an effort is made to indicate the colloquial pronunciation, usually by substituting an apostrophe for one or more letters of the standard spelling. As a trait of spoken English, contractions abound in Informal usage but are notably rare in Formal. In General usage a writer will favor or avoid them just as he makes other rhetorical choices, considering the rhythm of the particular sentence, how much distance he wants between himself and his readers, and whether the subject and the occasion call for a relaxed or a restrained style. Contractions are necessary, of course, in actual representations of speech, as in dialog.

Though letters may be omitted from more than one place in a contraction (as in *shan't*), current usage employs only one apostrophe.

See *have § 3.

contrast, compare

See *compare, contrast.

Conversion

When a word most commonly used in one part-of-speech function is used in another part-of-speech function, it is said to have undergone conversion or functional shift: a *must* book; a *commercial* (adjective used in the function of a noun, meaning the advertising part of a television program); in the *know*; I wouldn't *fault* him. The principle of functional shift is well established, but a writer should be cautious in experimenting with new conversions. The student who wrote the following sentence was experimenting — unsuccessfully: She stooped as if to *negative* her height.

convince, persuade

For a long time some uses of *convince* and *persuade* have overlapped: He persuaded (convinced) me of the necessity for action; He convinced (persuaded) me that I should act. Recently *convince* has become increasingly common in still a third context, where *persuade* is traditional: He convinced me to act. The usage is avoided in Formal writing and deplored by some conservative stylists.

Coordinate clauses

See *Clauses, *Compound sentence.

Coordinating conjunctions

The coordinating conjunctions are: *and, *but, *for, nor, *or, *so, and *yet. They are used between words, phrases, clauses, or sentences to connect two or more elements that are of equal grammatical rank:

Words: books and papers; books, pamphlets, or magazines

Phrases: in one ear and out the other

Clauses: I spoke of the ironies of our current situation in which a broad range of political dissent is tolerated from teachers, but in which no similar latitude is granted them in expressing opinions about changing standards in respect to sex and drugs. — Leslie Fiedler, *New York Review of Books*, July 13, 1967

Independent clauses: At present the common cause between eccentric and hippie is proper hatred of the way things are, and the common inclination is for personal justice. — Jerome Lettvin, *Natural History*, Oct. 1967

For different effects of repeating or omitting conjunctions in a series, see *Conjunctions § 3 and *Series. For coordination versus subordination, see *Guide*, pp. 313–17; *Coordination; and *Subordination. For various uses of coordinating conjunctions, see *Conjunctions, *Clauses § 1, and articles on individual conjunctions. See also *Conjunctive adverbs, *Correlative conjunctions.

Coordination

Coord

Revision: Correct the faulty coordination.

Two or more grammatically equivalent words, phrases, or clauses joined by a *coordinating conjunction are said to be coordinate. Many *shifted constructions result from the writer's failure to put grammatically equivalent elements into matching structures. As used here, the term *faulty coordination* refers not to all such weaknesses but only to those relating to independent clauses. Faulty coordination is not a lapse in grammar or usage; it is a failure to make clear the logical relationships of the material. Often, therefore, it can be discussed satisfactorily only in the context in which it appears. A combination of independent clauses that is perfectly appropiate in one context may be puzzling or ineffective in another. Faulty coordination means that in the particular context the material calls for a relationship or emphasis different from the one reflected in the writer's use or arrangement of independent clauses.

1. Some examples of faulty coordination result from joining two statements that are patently unequal: The condition of the house is deplorable, and the dining nook seats six comfortably. Revision should take the two statements out of the coordinate relationship by putting them in separate — and separated — sentences.

2. Sometimes faulty coordination can be corrected by turning one of the independent clauses into a dependent clause. "He went to France for the summer, and his novel was published" suggests that there is an obvious causal relationship between his going to France and the publication of his novel. In some contexts, this might make sense. But if the only relationship that can be established is a temporal one—two events happening at about the same time but not otherwise related—the sentence needs to be revised: "When he was spending the summer in France, his novel was published" or "At the time his novel was published, he was spending the summer in France," or in some other way.

3. In the example above, coordination might be confusing or misleading. Sometimes it is simply ineffective:

When I reached the intersection, I found a group of people gathered around the body of a man. The left front tire had had a blowout, and the car had gone out of control and rolled over, and the driver was obviously dead.

The independent clause "the driver was obviously dead" needs to be taken out of the coordinate relationship it is in; to gain its proper effect, it should be made a separate sentence. Left in the series, it implies that the death of the man had no more importance than the blowout and the crash.

For further discussion, see *Guide*, pp. 313–17, and *Subordination. Reference: James Sledd, *CCC*, Dec. 1956, pp. 181–87.

Copula
See *Linking verbs.

Corrections in copy
See *Proofreading.

Correlative conjunctions
Some coordinating conjunctions are used in pairs: *both . . . and, either . . . or, neither . . . nor, not only . . . but [also], whether . . . or.* Of these correlatives, *neither . . . nor* and *not only . . . but [also]* are slightly Formal, showing a more conscious planning than is common in Informal or General English: "Neither the gold drain nor the beautification of America deters them from going abroad" (Thomas L. Hughes, *Foreign Affairs*, Jan. 1967).

Since these correlatives are coordinating conjunctions, they mark parallel constructions, joining expressions of the same grammatical rank:

Nouns: He said that both *the novel* and *the play* were badly written.

Adjectives: He must have been either *drunk* or *crazy*.

Prepositional phrases: They can be had not only *in the usual sizes* but also *in the outsizes.*

Verb phrases: The wind scoop not only *caught the cool breezes* but also *picked up the captain's conversation.*

Clauses: Whether *the sale was for cash* or *a generous mortgage was ar-ranged,* it seemed too much to pay.

See *Shifted constructions. Reference: Lillian Mermin, *AS*, Oct. 1943, pp. 171–91, and Feb. 1944, pp. 66–68.

could, might

See *can, may.

Count nouns

See *Mass nouns, *Nouns § 3c.

Counter words

Trite words that appear more frequently in vogue usage than with exact meanings have been called counter words. They are usually words of general approval or disapproval or else rather abstract words that are popularly overused. Counter words and slang are alike in that both are current and popular, but counter words are ordinary English words and lack the element of surprise that good slang has. In Elizabethan times *fair* was such a word; in modern speech *great, lovely, nice, pretty, poor,* and *case, factor, field* are samples.

Counter words flourish in casual conversation. Some of them do no harm in Informal writing, but in serious prose they should give way to more precise terms. See *Vogue words.

couple

The primary meaning of the *collective noun *couple* is two persons or things associated in some way, typically as in "a married couple." In General and Informal usage it is equivalent to the numeral *two:* a couple of pencils; or equivalent to *a few:* a couple of minutes. The *of* is frequently omitted in speech and Informal writing and sometimes in General: "Yet some of his classmates do not sleep through the night, and live happily on a couple hours sleep" (Gay Gaer Luce and Julius Segal, *Insomnia*).

Course names

In general discussions, only the names of college subjects that are proper adjectives (the languages) are capitalized. In writing a list of courses including one or more of these proper adjectives, it is possible to capitalize them all for consistency (and courtesy), though the distinction is usually kept, as in the first example:

My program is biology, chemistry, European history, English composition, and French.

My program is Biology, Chemistry, European History, English Composition, and French.

In referring to the various departments of an institution, all names are usually capitalized, as they also are when preceding the number of a course: the Department of History, History 347.

Cumulative sentences

See *Guide*, pp. 328–33.

cupfuls, cupsful

See *-ful, full.

curriculum

Curriculum has the Latin plural *curricula* and the English *curriculums.* The adjective is *curricular,* and the compound adjective with *extra* is ordinarily written as one word: *extracurricular. Curriculum* is also used as a modifier: ". . . the guidance of college students, curriculum and instructional problems at the college level" (*Current Issues in Higher Education*, 1955).

Dangling modifiers

DM

Revision: Revise the sentence so that the expression marked is clearly related to the word it is intended to modify.

A phrase is said to dangle (or to be misrelated) if its position makes it seem to relate to a word that can only make nonsense of the meaning or if, in a context that demands an explicit relationship, it has no clear relation to any word in the sentence.

In the sentence "Looking farther to the left, we saw the spire of a church," *looking* clearly modifies *we;* if we reconstructed the subject of the verb *look,* it would be *we:* [*We* were] looking farther to the left, *we* saw the spire of a church. In the sentence "Defined in psychological terms, a fanatic is a man who consciously overcompensates a secret doubt" (Aldous Huxley, *Proper Studies*), *defined* clearly modifies *fanatic* for the same reason. We know that the subject of *defined* must be *fanatic:* [*A fanatic* is] defined in psychological terms, *a fanatic* is a man who consciously overcompensates a secret doubt. In both these cases a form of *be* seems to be implicitly reconstructable.

When the phrase does not refer to the subject—that is, when it has a different subject from the subject of the main clause—then the modifier dangles. In the sentence "To get the most out of a sport, the equipment must be in perfect condition," the reconstructed subject of the introductory phrase would be something like "[For *someone*] to get the most out of a sport, *the equipment* must be in perfect condition." But since *someone* is different from *equipment, someone* should not be dropped. If the sentence "At eleven, my family moved to Denver" is reconstructed, it reads "[When *I* was] eleven, *my family* moved to Denver." *I* does not equal *family,* so *I* should not be deleted. In the following examples, try to reconstruct the subject of the introductory phrase:

Driving toward the city, many signs read "Visit Our Snake Farm."

Upon telling my story to my adviser, he stopped and thought.

Born in England in 1853, John MacDowell's seafaring activities began after he had migrated to this country. (This type of dangling modifier, in which the phrase refers to a noun — *MacDowell* — represented only by its genitive form modifying the subject, sometimes appears in edited prose.)

Dangling modifiers are to be avoided chiefly because educated readers do not expect to find them. As a rule there is no real question of the intended meaning of the sentence, and in context the dangling phrases are not apt to be conspicuously awkward or so nonsensical as they seem in isolation. But they are distracting in any writing that is meant to be read attentively. By forcing the reader to search for (or make a guess at) the related noun, they can make a piece of writing needlessly difficult.

Such dangling constructions should not be confused with *absolute phrases, in which the phrase has a subject. Compare an absolute phrase, a correct modifier, and a dangling modifier:

Absolute phrase: The car paid for with my last dollar, I was at last out of debt.

Correct modifier: Paid for with my last dollar, the car became my first piece of personal property.

Dangling modifier: Paid for with my last dollar, I drove the car away elated.

See *Gerunds; *Participles; *Guide*, pp. 290–92. See also *Clauses. References: Bryant, pp. 64–65; Curme, *Syntax*, pp. 158–60; Jespersen, *MEG*, V, 407–10; Roberts, pp. 351–52, 358–59, 366–67.

Dash

The dash — typed as two hyphens not spaced away from the words they separate — can be used singly to link a following word or word group to the main structure of a sentence or in pairs to enclose a word or word group that interrupts the main structure. Enclosing dashes indicate greater separation from the core context than enclosing commas, less separation — or less formality — than parentheses.

If used sparingly, the dash suggests a definite tone, often a note of surprise or an emotional emphasis equivalent to a mild exclamation. If used regularly in place of commas, colons, and semicolons, it loses all its distinctiveness and becomes merely a sloppy substitute for conventional punctuation (see *Schoolgirl style). At its best the dash is an abrupt, emphatic mark.

1. *Before a "kicker."* The single dash is often used to throw emphasis on what follows, which may be dramatic, ironic, humorous:

The old nations still live in the hearts of men, and love of the European nation is not yet born — if it ever will be. — Raymond Aron, *Daedalus*, Winter 1964

We do not question the right of an author to spell, capitalize, and punctuate as he wishes — provided he follows consistently a recognizable system. — John Benbow, *Manuscript and Proof*

2. *Before a summary or illustration.* The dash is used singly or in pairs with word groups that summarize what has just been said or provide details or examples:

It takes a cataclysm — an invasion, a plague, or some other communal disaster — to open their eyes to the transitoriness of the "eternal order." — Eric Hoffer, *The True Believer*

He was strongly in favor of peace — that is to say, he liked his wars to be fought at a distance and, if possible, in the name of God. — George Dangerfield, *The Death of Liberal England*

3. *Between independent clauses.* A dash is sometimes used to link independent clauses when the second expands, develops, completes, or makes a surprising addition to the first. In this function, it is less Formal than a colon:

And yet they had a thing in common, this oddest of odd couples — they both cared about the social graces. . . . — George Frazier, *Esquire*, Dec. 1966

In one respect, Welles was unique among the Cabinet members — he did not think himself a better man than the President. — Margaret Leech, *Reveille in Washington*

4. *Enclosing interrupting elements.* Dashes are used to set off words and word groups that break with the main structure of the sentence:

Fitzgerald's people believed in their world — it really mattered who won the Princeton-Harvard game, it really meant something to appear at the theatre or the opera — and because they believed in their world they owned it. — Frank Conroy, *Esquire*, Oct. 1968

5. *As a trait of style.* Writers of heavy, complicated sentences are sometimes forced into using the dash because they have used all the other marks. Other writers use it by choice. At times dashes can be appropriate and effective, but in most straightforward exposition commas, colons, or semicolons are preferable. Dashes easily become conspicuous, and when there are too many of them, their special quality is lost.

6. *With other marks.* The old practice of combining the dash with a colon (Dear Sir: —) has practically disappeared; and instead of the old comma-dash combination, we ordinarily find either a comma or, if emphasis is wanted, a dash alone.

7. *Conventional uses.*
a — To precede a credit line, as at the end of the quoted passages in this book.

b — After introductory words that are implicitly repeated before each of the lines that follow:

We recommend —
    That a constitution be drawn up.
    That it be presented to the student council.

c — To separate run-in questions and answers, as in testimony: Q. Did you see him? — A. No.

8. *Other dashes.* In addition to the ordinary dash, which they call the em dash, printers use the 2-em (or long or double) dash and the en dash. The 2-em dash appears in names (Mr. S——) and as an end stop in dialog to indicate interrupted speech. Printers use the en dash, which is slightly longer than a hyphen, between inclusive figures (1837–1901) and in place of a hyphen when one of the elements in a compound expression is itself made up of two words: the New York–Hollywood axis.

    Reference: Summey, pp. 101–04; Whitehall, pp. 123,129.

data

Formal usage follows the Latin, treating *datum* as singular and *data* as plural. In General usage *datum* is rare, and *data* is treated as a *collective noun, taking a singular verb to emphasize the whole (". . . data so far available makes it seem doubtful . . ." — John Mecklin, *Fortune*, Feb. 1967) and a plural verb to emphasize the parts ("Data cascade out at the reader line after line . . ." — Theodore Levitt, *Boston Sunday Herald Traveler*, Sept. 20, 1970). Reference: Bryant, pp. 66–67.

date

Date as a noun is now General for "appointment, engagement" (I had a date for the evening) and for "a person with whom one has an engagement" (After all, she was his date); as a verb, for "to have or make an appointment with." *Blind date* is a useful and economical expression, saying in two syllables something that would take several words in Formal English. Reference: Bryant, pp. 67–68.

Dates

The typical American form for writing dates is "August 19, 1970." The form "19 August 1970" prevails in British and in American military usage. If the full date is given within a sentence, the year is usually set off by commas; when only month and year are given (In August 1970 he died), no commas are necessary, though they are often used in Formal styles.

    The year is not written out in words except in Formal social announcements, invitations, wills, and some other ceremonial situations and at the beginning of a sentence — and most writers manage to avoid beginning sentences with the year. Expressions like "January in the year 1885" are wasteful; "January 1885" is enough. In business writing and references, months having more than four (or five)

Dates   **539**

letters are often abbreviated: Jan. 3, 1980. In General writing the day of the month is either spelled out (January third) or given by the number and the appropriate ordinal ending (January 3rd). In business writing *-st, -nd, -rd, -th* are omitted: We got your order June 3. When the day of the week is also given, full comma treatment is used: . . . at the seminar on Wednesday, December 9, 1970, in the Physics Building.

In writing dates in figures only, American practice is month-day-year: 9/17/75; European practice is day-month-year, sometimes with the month in roman numerals: 17-IX-75.

Dative case

English does not inflect its nouns or pronouns for the dative case. One relationship corresponding to the dative case in other languages is expressed in English by the indirect object: He gave *the teacher* an apple (an apple *to the teacher*). See *Case, *Objects § 2.

Deadwood

Dead

Revision: Remove the unnecessary word or words, revising the sentence if necessary.

Deadwood is a convenient label for a type of wordiness in which a word or phrase adds nothing at all to the meaning or effectiveness of the statement:

He was a handsome [looking] man.

He was quite conscious [of the fact that] he had failed.

The architecture [of the buildings] and the landscaping [of the grounds] speak of town pride.

[It so happened that] we were the same age.

He kept things moving at breakneck speed throughout [the entirety of] his performance.

The most common deadwood consists of unnecessary phrases like "green *in color*," "seven *in number*," "rectangular *in shape*" and clichés like "in the business world" and "in the field of economics," which we often use without thinking. But good writing requires thought, and when a first draft is being revised, every phrase should be looked at closely. Does "green in color" mean anything more than "green"? Doesn't "in economics" say everything that "in the field of economics" says? Sometimes a phrase that contributes nothing to the meaning of a sentence nevertheless fits its rhythm or has some other stylistic justification. Perhaps adding "in my life" to "for the first time" provides a desired emphasis even though it is tautologous.

But, in general, eliminating deadwood is a step toward a compact, direct, honest prose style. See *Wordiness; *Guide*, pp. 345–46. See also *case, *factor, *field, *world.

Declension

Declension means the list or listing of the forms of nouns and pronouns (and in many languages the forms of adjectives and participles also) to show number (singular, dual, plural), gender (masculine, feminine, neuter), and case (nominative, genitive, accusative, and others in different languages). The English noun has two regular forms: the form ending in *s*, which serves as genitive and plural, though these are written differently (*sister's, sisters', sisters*), and the form without an ending, which is used for all other relationships. Personal pronouns in English have from two forms (*it, its*) to four (*I, my, mine, me*). English adverbs are compared but not declined, and our participles are invariable.

Deduction

Deduction as a mode of inference is discussed and illustrated in the *Guide*, pp. 156–71. The method of organization sometimes called deductive is described in the *Guide*, pp. 189–90, and 238–41.

Deep structure

The deep structure of a sentence is that abstract structure generated by *base rules before any transformations have changed it (see *Guide*, pp. 269–71). It specifies the individual grammatical elements in a sentence: nouns, verbs, prepositions, modal auxiliaries, articles, adjectives, etc.; it specifies their grammatical relationships: subject–verb, verb–object, modifier–head, preposition–object, etc.; and it groups elements into hierarchical structures: The man may give a penny to the boy = [[the man [[may give] [[a penny] [to [the boy]]]

The deep structure of a sentence may resemble the *surface structure very slightly if at all. "Tom's eagerness to please is easy to see" has as its deep structure something like: [someone sees [[Tom is eager [Tom pleases]] is easy]] *Transformations have nominalized *eager* into *eagerness*, deleted the indefinite subject of *see* and the repeated subject (*Tom*) of *please*. Another series of transformations has shifted other elements about so that *to see* occurs after *easy*, and *eagerness* occurs as subject of *is*.

In some cases, the same deep structure can have more than one surface structure. The deep structure above could be realized in at least these three ways:

It is easy to see Tom's eagerness to please.
To see Tom's eagerness to please is easy.
Tom's eagerness to please is easy to see.

Conversely, two different deep structures can have the same surface structure: "The chicken is ready to eat" can have as its deep structure either

[the chicken is ready [the chicken eats something]]
or
[the chicken is ready [someone eats the chicken]]

In recent years some transformationalists have postulated basic underlying structures far more abstract than those described here — structures that might more easily be identified as representative of underlying cognitive or semantic structure than of underlying grammatical structure.

Reference: Paul Postal, "Underlying and Superficial Linguistic Structure," in *Language and Learning*, ed. Janet Emig, James T. Fleming, and Helen M. Popp (New York: Harcourt, 1965), pp. 153–75.

definitely

Definitely has been overused as a *counter word to give emphasis or in the sense of "certainly, quite" (I will not do it, definitely; He was definitely worse than usual; She definitely disapproves of those methods; But definitely!) instead of in its more limited sense of "clear-cut, in a definite manner."

Definition

A lexical or dictionary definition tells how a word is generally used. A real or logical definition describes the essential nature of a class of things — what a thing *is*. Both types of definition are discussed in the *Guide*, pp. 107–16. For further discussion of dictionary definitions, see *Guide*, pp. 350–53.

Degree

See *Comparison of adjectives and adverbs.

Degrees

Ordinarily a person's academic degrees are not given with his name except in college publications, reference works, and articles and letters where the degrees indicate competence in a particular field, as in a doctor's comment on a medical matter. When used, the names of the degrees are abbreviated, and the abbreviations are separated from the person's name by a comma; in alumni publications they are often followed by the year in which the degrees were granted:

Harvey J. Preble, A.B.   Harvey J. Preble, A.B. '08
James T. Thomson, M.A.   James T. Thomson, A.B. '51, M.A. '54
Royce Walton, B. Arch., discussed Wright's mile-high building.

As a rule, except in reference lists, only the highest degree in an academic professional field need be mentioned.

If the institution granting the degree is named, the following forms are usual:

George H. Cook, A.B. (Grinnell), A.M. (Indiana), Ph.D. (Chicago)
D. C. Browning, B.A. (Oxon. [= Oxford])
J. H. Plumb, Ph.D. (Cantab. [= Cambridge])

Two kinds of degrees are granted by American colleges and universities. *Earned* degrees (degrees "in course") are given at the completion of a required course of study. Among those most commonly granted are:

A.B. (or B.A.) – Bachelor of Arts
B.S. – Bachelor of Science
B.E. – Bachelor of Engineering
B.D. – Bachelor of Divinity
B. Mus. – Bachelor of Music
B. Arch. – Bachelor of Architecture
Ph.B. – Bachelor of Philosophy
LL.B. – Bachelor of Laws
A.M. (or M.A.) – Master of Arts
M.A.T. – Master of Arts in Teaching
M.S. – Master of Science

M.E. – Master of Engineering
M.Ed. (or Ed.M.) – Master of Education
M.B.A. – Master of Business Administration
M.F.A. – Master of Fine Arts
Ed.D. – Doctor of Education
J.D. – Doctor of Jurisprudence
Ph.D. – Doctor of Philosophy
S.T.D. – Doctor of Sacred Theology
M.D. – Doctor of Medicine
D.D.S. – Doctor of Dental Surgery

Honorary degrees (degrees "*honoris causa*") are granted by institutions as a token of respect. The most common are:

LL.D. – Doctor of Laws
D.D. – Doctor of Divinity
Lit(t).D. – Doctor of Literature *or* Letters

Sc.D. – Doctor of Science
D.C.L. – Doctor of Civil Law
L.H.D. – Doctor of Humanities
Eng.D. – Doctor of Engineering

Demonstrative adjectives and pronouns

The *determiners *this, that, these, those* have traditionally been called demonstrative adjectives or demonstrative pronouns, according to their use in a sentence:

Adjectives: This car is fast. *Those* people never think of anyone else.
Pronouns: These cost more than *those. That's* a good idea.

See *Agreement; *that; *this; *kind, sort.

Dependent clauses

See *Relative clauses, *Clauses.

Derivation of words

See *Origin of words.

Details

Det

Revision: Develop this topic more fully by giving pertinent details.

Adequate development of a topic in writing usually comes from the use of details — images, facts, evidence, examples, bits of observation, and so on. Details not only help make your ideas understandable but do a lot to make any paper interesting and convincing. In description and narration, details should be so arranged that the reader is led to shape for himself a clear impression of what you have observed or experienced. In explanation and persuasion, details are essential to support your generalizations. See *Guide*, pp. 42–43, 54–55, 71–75, 387–89.

Determiners

Determiner is a general term for the several types of words that precede nouns in English. Chosen usually to fit the semantic context, determiners may be subclassified as articles (*a/an, the*), prearticles (*none, all, half, most, much,* etc.), and postarticles (*two, three; first, second; first, last; former, latter;* etc.). Transformationalists include among the articles a zero form, *φ*, of the indefinite *a/an,* which occurs before indefinite mass nouns and indefinite plural count nouns: *φ* money is necessary to live; *φ* children can be difficult. Thus *many* in *many boys* is a prearticle because the phrase would be transformationally represented as *many φ boys;* the *many* comes before the *φ* article. When the article is definite *the* or a demonstrative article — *this, that, these, those* — an *of* must come between the prearticle and the article: many of the boys, several of those people, much of that food.

The prearticles can serve as transitional devices between sentences when the noun has been deleted:

Several boys walked in the door. A few were wearing black leather jackets.

Demonstrative articles and the postarticles can serve the same function.

These were the last ones. *The first* were more interesting.

Genitive or possessive forms can also serve determiner functions:

George's book was very interesting→George's was very interesting.
My father is a teacher→Mine is a teacher.

In each case the genitive form occurs where the definite article *the* would occur. Since they occur in identical positions in the noun phrase, the definite article and genitives belong to the same class of words.

References: Arthur Norman, "An Outline of the Subclasses of the English Nominal," in *Readings in Applied English Linguistics*, ed. Harold B. Allen, 2nd ed. (New York: Appleton, 1964), pp. 156–63; Owen Thomas, *Transformational Grammar and the Teacher of English* (New York: Holt, 1965), pp. 79–87.

Diacritic marks

See *Accent marks.

Dialects

A dialect is the speech (sounds, forms, meanings) characteristic of a fairly definite region or group. It is speech that does not attract attention to itself among the inhabitants of a region (regional dialect) or among members of a group (group or class dialect) but that would be recognizably different to an outsider. In linguistics a dialect is any development from a parent language: French and Italian are dialects of Vulgar Latin.

*Localism is used in this book for a regional dialectal usage. Conspicuous dialectal words are usually out of place in General and Formal writing except to give a local flavor. They are more effective in speech, in fiction, and in Informal writing. American dialects are discussed in the *Guide*, pp. 5–7. See *English language § 3.

Diction

D

Revision: Replace the word marked with one that is more exact, more appropriate, or more effective.

Diction means primarily the choice of words in speaking or writing. Good diction conveys the meaning and attitudes of the writer or speaker; faulty diction either fails to convey the meaning fully or accurately or in some other way disappoints the expectations of the reader. Weaknesses in diction are discussed in many *Index* articles, including *Abstract and concrete words, *Big words, *Counter words, *Deadwood, *Nominalization, *Vogue words, and *Wordiness; specific words have articles of their own (*claim, *contact, *drunk, *finalize, *hope, *however, *massive, *relate, *viable). See also *Usage; *Words; and *Guide*, Ch. Twelve.

Dictionaries

See *Guide*, pp. 350–54.

Dieresis

Two dots placed over the second of two consecutive vowels to show they are to be pronounced separately are referred to as a dieresis: Aïda, Laocoön, microörganisms. But a hyphen is more usual to keep prefix and root word separate (*re-enlist*), and the tendency is to use neither dieresis nor hyphen in many words (*cooperation, zoology*). Do not confuse the dieresis with *umlaut in German words, which when placed over *a, u,* or *e* makes separate alphabetical entities.

different

Formal usage insists on *different from:* The rich are different from you and me. General usage is divided between *different from* and *different than:* "The young TV generation has a completely different sensory life than the adult generation which grew up on hot radio and hot print" (*Newsweek*, March 7, 1967). *Different than* is particularly common in General writing when the object is a clause: ". . . the story would be different for an investigator who accepts the verdict of the court than for one who doesn't" (Meyer Shapiro, *New York Review of Books*, Feb. 23, 1967). Formal favors the longer expression: . . . verdict of the court from what it would be for one who doesn't.

Formal: "The role of 'laws' in history is fundamentally different from their role in natural science . . ." (Kenneth T. Young, *Foreign Affairs*, Oct. 1966). Less Formal: . . . different than in natural science.

Different to is a British idiom, rare in American usage. References: Gladys D. Haase, *CE*, March 1949, pp. 345–47; Bryant, pp. 69–70; Evans and Evans, "different from."

Digraph

Two letters that together spell a single sound are known as a digraph. English spelling has many digraphs: *ea* as in *head* or *heat*, *ee* as in *seed*, *ei* as in *either* or *neighbor*, *oa* as in *coat*, *oo* as in *book* or *food*, *ph* as in *physics*, *sh* as in *shall*, *th* as in *then* or *thin*.

Diphthong

A diphthong is a vowel-like sound made by moving the tongue, jaw, and lips from the position for one vowel to that of another while vibrating the vocal cords. (The term has also been used as equivalent to *digraph.) The standard method of transcribing these glide sounds is to use two vowel symbols, which are to be interpreted as indicating where the diphthong begins and where it ends. The common distinctive diphthongs of American English are: /ī/, /ä to i/; /oi/, /ô to i/; /ou/, /ä to ü/; and /ū/, /i [y] to ü/.

Most English vowels have some diphthongal quality. For further details about American diphthongs, see John S. Kenyon, *American Pronunciation*, 10th ed. (Ann Arbor, Mich.: Wahr, 1958), §§ 327–76, and the discussions of pronunciation in good modern dictionaries.

Direct address

Direct address is the term applied when the audience being spoken to is named:

My friends, I wish you would forget this night.
What do you think, *Doctor*, about his going home now?
Rain, rain, go away.

Words in direct address are usually separated from the rest of the sentence by a comma or, if in medial position, by two commas.

Direct objects

See *Objects § 1.

disinterested, uninterested

From its first recorded uses in the seventeenth century, *disinterested* has had two senses: (1) "indifferent, uninterested"; (2) "impartial, not influenced by personal interest." But the first meaning gradually disappeared from educated writing, and its revival in this century has met strong opposition—in part, at least, because assigning the two different meanings to two different words set up a distinction that prevented ambiguity. Even though *disinterested* in the sense "uninterested" is established in General usage, a writer who uses it should know that he risks being thought semiliterate:

The House Agriculture Committee . . . is, to state it gently, disinterested in the poor. —Elizabeth B. Drew, *Atlantic*, Dec. 1968

There may be some drab, lethargic, disinterested Greeks, but most of the ones I've met have been bouncy, colorful, wildly ebullient enthusiasts. . . . —Richard Joseph, *Esquire*, June 1964

I began to hate someone once who habitually said "disinterested" when he should have said "uninterested." —Alexander Cockburn, *New Statesman*, Jan. 5, 1968

dissent

Though Formal usage strongly prefers the preposition *from* after the verb *dissent* (the right to dissent from majority opinion), in General usage *against* is common (the right to dissent against administration policies). In the late 1960's, *dissent*, both the noun and the verb, and *dissenters* took on connotations of violence not previously associated with these words, and critics of dissent sought to deny the words their traditional association with difference of opinion.

Ditto marks

Ditto marks are sometimes used in lists and tabulations to indicate the repetition of words, figures, or symbols appearing directly above:

```
m, as in man, men, mine, hum, hammer
n, "  " no, man, manner
```

Ditto marks are not used in consecutive writing or in footnotes or bibliographies.

Divided usage

Usage is said to be *divided* when two or more forms exist in the language, both of them in reputable use in the same dialect or variety. *Divided usage* is not applied to *localisms, like *poke* for *sack* or *bag*, or to differences like *ain't* and *isn't*, which belong to separate varieties of the language. It applies to spellings, pronunciations, or grammatical forms in which those of similar education follow different practices.

There are many more of these divided usages within Standard English than most people are aware of. In addition to hundreds of instances of divided usage in pronunciation, most dictionaries record forms like these:

In spelling: buses, busses; millionaire, millionnaire; catalog, catalogue

In verb forms: past tense of *sing: sang* or *sung;* past tense of *ring: rang* or *rung;* past participle of *show: shown* or *showed;* past participle of *prove: proved* or *proven*

It is hard for some careful users of the language to realize that others who speak or write somewhat differently from themselves are still following Standard practice. Before calling a person to account, either seriously or playfully, for a usage, we should make sure that his is not a variant that is as reputable as the one we prefer. The point about divided usages is that both are acceptable. A person who has learned to say "It's I" does not need to change to "*It's me," and one who says "It's me" need not change to "It's I." When there is a choice between variants of equal standing, choose the one that you use naturally, that is appropriate to your style, or, if you are taking pains to be tactful, the one that is customary among the audience you want to reach.

The entries in this *Index* include a number of divided usages. When one or the other of two acceptable usages is likely to disturb many readers or listeners and arouse emotional attitudes, evidence is usually presented: there is security in knowing what is dangerous ground. For examples, see: *can, may; *different; *disinterested, uninterested; *due to; *-ed; *enthuse; *farther, further; *like, as; *Principal parts of verbs; *reason is because; *slow, slowly.

Division of words

Div

Revision: Break the word at the end of this line between syllables.

To keep the right-hand margin of a manuscript fairly even, you must divide some words at the end of a line with a hyphen. When you are not sure how to divide a word, consult a dictionary. Both the divided parts should be pronounceable: the break should come between conventionally recognized syllables. Words of one syllable, like *matched, said, thought,* should not be divided at all. The following words are divided to show typical syllables: *mar gin, ca ter, hy phen, chil dren, long ing, hi lar i ous, cat ty, ac com plished, ad min is trate.*

Double consonant letters are usually separable (*ef fi cient, com mit tee, daz zling, bat ted;* but they are kept together if there is no syllable break (*im pelled*) or if both belong to a root to which a suffix has been added (*stiff ly,* not *stif fly; yell ing,* not *yel ling*).

A single letter is never allowed to stand by itself: do not divide words like *enough* (which would leave a lone e at the end of a line) or *many* (which would put a lone y at the beginning of a line). Words spelled with a hyphen (*half-brother, well-disposed*) should be divided only at the point of the hyphen to avoid the awkwardness of two hyphens in the same word.

Fuller directions will be found in the stylebooks of publishing houses, like the *Chicago Manual.* Reference: Hans Kurath, *Phonology and Prosody of Modern English* (Ann Arbor: Univ. of Michigan Press, 1964).

do

Do is one of the most important auxiliary verbs in English. Its conjugation follows the regular strong verb pattern (the past tense and past participle are formed by a change in vowel) except for the pronunciation of the third person singular *does* /duz/ and of the contracted *don't* /dōnt/.

1. Do *in verb phrases.*
a — *Do* is used to form what are called emphatic verb phrases with all verbs except the modal auxiliaries (*can, may, shall* . . .) and usually *be*:

Present	*Past*
I, you do wish	I, you, he, she did wish
he, she does wish	we, you, they did wish
we, you, they do wish	

b — *Do* is used with *not* (in speech contracted to **don't, doesn't, didn't*) to negate all English verbs except the modal auxiliaries and *be*: He did not feel well enough to go out. I don't expect to go.
c — *Do* is used to form questions: Do you think I was right? Did you like the show?

2. Do *as a substitute. Do* is used to avoid repetition of a simple verb that has just been used: I like him better than you do [than you like him].

3. Do *in idioms. Do* has many idiomatic meanings and is part of many idiomatic phrases: *do for, do away with, do in, do over, do up.* When in doubt about an idiomatic use, consult a dictionary.
References: Fries, *AEG*, pp. 146 – 49; *Structure*, pp. 96 – 97, 149 – 51.

doctoral, doctor's, doctorate

Doctoral is an adjective, *doctorate* a noun: a man who has earned his doctorate has earned his doctor's degree (his Ph.D.) in a doctoral program.

don't

Don't is the contraction of *do not,* universally used in conversation and often in writing when *do not* would seem too emphatic or when the rhythm seems more comfortable with the shorter form. Until about 1900 *don't* was the usual third person singular (he don't, it don't, that don't) in Informal speech, and though the usage is now regarded as Nonstandard, it still often finds its way into familiar speech and even into casual writing: He don't look as well as he used to.
References: E. Bagby Atwood, *A Survey of Verb Forms in the Eastern United States* (Ann Arbor: Univ. of Michigan Press, 1953), p. 28;

Bryant, pp. 73–74; Karl W. Dykema, *EJ*, Sept. 1947, pp. 370–76; Fries, *AEG*, pp. 52–53; Marckwardt and Walcott, pp. 45, 46, 49.

Double negative

1. *In Standard English.* Two negative words in the same construction are not used in Standard English to express a single negation: not "He couldn*'t* find it *no*where," but "He couldn*'t* find it *any*where" or "He *could* find it *no*where." But two negatives may be used in General English to make an emphatic affirmative: "Its re-emergences into view, out of covering buildings, never are not dramatic" (Elizabeth Bowen, *A Time in Rome*). And in a few constructions one negative statement modifies another negative statement to give a qualified meaning or a meaning with some special emphasis: I wouldn't be surprised if he never spoke to us again; He isn't sure he won't be able to afford it; Don't think he isn't clever. The negated negative, or *litotes*, used in some Formal styles (a not unattractive young woman) is discussed in *Negatives.

2. *Hardly, scarcely.* A concealed double negative sometimes occurs with *hardly* or *scarcely*. Since *hardly* means "not probably" and *scarcely* means the same a little more emphatically, a sentence like "The campus paper contains hardly nothing" should read ". . . contains hardly anything," and "For a while we couldn't scarcely see a thing" should read ". . . could scarcely. . . ." Reference: Bryant, pp. 106–07.

3. *In Nonstandard English.* Two or more negatives are very often used in Nonstandard English to express a simple negation: I don't have nothing to lose. Such a double negative is not a backsliding from the current idiom of Standard English; the form survives from an older period. In early English two negatives were used in all varieties of language. Chaucer wrote:

> In al this world *ne* was there *noon* him lyk
> A bettre preest, I trow that *nowher noon* is.

The objection to a double negative is not that "two negatives always make an affirmative," for they do not. The objection is simply that the double negative is not now in fashion among educated people. References: Bryant, pp. 75–76; Fries, *AEG*, p. 35; Jespersen, *MEG*, V, 449–56.

Double prepositions

See *Prepositions § 2b.

doubt

The word used to introduce a clause after a statement with the verb *doubt* (or: It is doubtful) depends on whether the statement is negative or positive.

1. *Negative* (when there is no real doubt), *doubt that*: I do not doubt that he meant well. (For *doubt but*, see *but that, but what.)

2. *Positive* (when doubt exists), *that, whether,* less often *if:*

But there is reason to doubt that this is so. — Wayne F. LaFave, *Supreme Court Review,* 1967

A couple of days ago, Walter Heller . . . said that he doubted whether that level could be reached. . . . — Richard H. Rovere, *New Yorker,* Feb. 2, 1963

. . . I doubt if this was ever a really important reason for his leaving London. . . . — George Woodcock, *Esquire,* Sept. 1966.

drunk

It seems to take courage to use this General word. We either go Formal — *intoxicated;* or grasp at respectability through euphemisms — *under the influence of liquor, indulged to excess;* or make a weak attempt at humor with one of the dozens of slang expressions like *looped, bombed, stoned.* But *drunk* is the word.

due to

No one complains when *due* (followed by *to*) is used as an adjective firmly modifying a noun: "The failure was due to a conceptual oversight . . ." (William Jaffé, *Journal of Political Economy,* Feb. 1967). And *due to* is used in all varieties of writing in the sense "because of" to introduce prepositional phrases functioning as adverbs:

Cooperative self-regulatory efforts among newspapers in a locality have become rare, partly due to the tradition of independence in the field. — *Harvard Law Review,* March 1967

Due to rising prices, the wage earner's purchasing power is shrinking. . . . — Kenneth Crawford, *Newsweek,* Aug. 29, 1967

This use of *due to* in adverbial prepositional phrases has been strongly criticized, however, on the grounds that *due to* is adjectival only. (The objection ignores the fact that the change of a word from one part of speech to another is commonplace in English.) And though the distinguished lexicographer John S. Kenyon presented evidence in 1930 that this use of *due to* had become Standard, the prejudice (which he shared) remains widespread.

Reference: John S. Kenyon, *AS,* Oct. 1930, pp. 61–70; Bryant, p. 81.

each

1. Though the pronoun *each* is singular (To each his own), we use it to individualize members of a group. As a result, it inevitably attracts plural forms. In Informal and increasingly in General usage, *each* is treated as a collective when the plural idea is uppermost (compare *every):

Each of the stages in child development produce typical conflicts. . . . — Selma Fraiberg, *New York Review of Books,* Oct. 28, 1965

Each of these people undoubtedly modified Latin in accordance with their own speech habits. — Albert C. Baugh, *A History of the English Language*

But in Formal usage *each* is ordinarily singular:

Each of them was asserting its own individuality. . . . — John Higham, *American Historical Review*, Oct. 1966

Each of the [5-year plans] will show the more significant indicators . . . for its own proper period. . . . — Thad P. Alton, *Journal of International Affairs*, Vol. XX, No. 1, 1966

2. As an adjective, *each* does not affect the number of the verb or related pronoun. When the subject modified by *each* is plural, the verb and related pronoun are also plural:

The editions that have appeared since World War I each have their weak and strong points. — James G. McManaway, *PMLA*, Dec. 1964

Two entrants will each win $500 and publication of their stories. . . . — *Mademoiselle*, Dec. 1965

References: Bryant, pp. 8–9; Russell Thomas, *CE*, Oct. 1939, pp. 38–45.

each other, one another

Although some textbooks have insisted that *each other* refers to two only and *one another* to more than two, writers have ignored the distinction: "Humphrey and Kennedy are so comfortable in each other's company that they can kid one another" (Samuel Shaffer, *New York Times Magazine*, Aug. 25, 1963). See *Pronouns § 1. References: Bryant, pp. 82–83; Russell Thomas, *CE*, May 1957, pp. 422–24.

Echo phrases

Sometimes it is convenient to form a phrase on the pattern of a well-known one or to echo one less known but apt. This is a type of allusion. The echoing may be either serious or light:

Vanity of vanities, crieth the trend-watcher. Comfort me with aumbries, stay me with chasubles, for I am sick of sexology. Give me this day our diatribe against the Fabians, our reminiscence of P. G. Wodehouse, our exposé of the lusts of Queen Victoria, the pride, pomp, and circumstances of lovable Dwight Macdonald, whom age cannot wither nor custom stale. — D. A. N. Jones, *New York Review of Books*, Dec. 29, 1966

. . . but democracy means simply the bludgeoning of the people by the people for the people. — Oscar Wilde, *The Soul of Man Under Socialism*

In revising your essays, be on the lookout for unconscious echo phrases, which, like unconscious puns, can have disastrous effects. See *Guide*, pp. 372–74.

-ed

The spelling of the ending commonly written as *-ed* presents some problems.

1. *Consonant clusters.* In spoken English consonant clusters are often simplified across word boundaries, and in the process *-ed* may disappear, as in *released time* /rì lēs' tīm'/ and *relieved to hear* /ri lēv' tə hir'/. Grammatical analogy sometimes favors the forms without *-ed: barb wire*, for example, seems to fit the common pattern of noun + noun, with the noun *barb* in modifying function. In many expressions forms without *-ed* are now Standard: *frame house, ice cream, grade school, high-heel shoes.* Other forms without *-ed* are still debatable at best: *mash potatoes, whip cream, middle-age man.* Since such spellings are very likely to arouse criticism, using the conventional forms with *-ed* is advisable.

2. *-ed or -t.* In the past tenses and past participles of verbs in which *-ed* is (or may be) pronounced as /t/, a simpler spelling with *-t* may match the sound; and a few spellings of this kind have been rather generally adopted: *crept, dreamt, leapt, slept.* But though *asked, jumped,* and *missed* are regularly pronounced with final /t/, the *-ed* ending is the only accepted spelling.

3. *-ed or 'd.* When the ending commonly spelled *-ed* is added to words formed from initials, abbreviations, or proper names, or to nouns ending in vowel letters that would combine oddly with the *-ed* spelling, *'d* is generally used instead: *GI'd, tko'd, shanghai'd.*

References: Curme, *Parts of Speech*, pp. 260–69; W. Nelson Francis, *Word Study*, Oct. 1954, pp. 6–7; Ralph H. Lane, *Word Study*, Feb. 1955, pp. 1–3.

Editorial we

See *we.

-ee

Nouns formed from verbs by the ending *-ee* usually denote the one who receives or is affected by an act or grant of power: *payee* (one who is paid, vs. *payer*, one who pays), *draftee, employee, mortgagee, trainee.* In a few words, however, *-ee* has the *-er* sense of agent or doer: *conferee, devotee, escapee, standee.*

effect, affect

See *affect, effect.

e.g.

See *Abbreviations § 2.

either

The pronoun *either* normally takes a singular verb: ". . . Welsh and Irish are closer to each other than either is to English" (William W. Heist, *Speculum*, April 1968). And while the plural verb is not uncommon after a prepositional phrase with a plural object ("I personally do not find that either of these critics make my flesh creep" — John Wain, *New Republic*, Jan. 28, 1960), a singular verb with *either* is always the safer choice. References: Fries, *AEG*, pp. 50, 56, 59; Jespersen, *MEG*, II, 172.

either . . . or, neither . . . nor

When both elements of a compound subject connected by the *correlative conjunction *either . . . or* or *neither . . . nor* are plural, the verb is naturally plural; and when both elements are singular, the verb is usually singular. When one of the subjects is plural and the other singular, the familiar rule is that the verb should agree with the nearer subject. Actual usage varies:

Neither the cases nor sound policy support such a result. — *Harvard Law Review*, April 1967

I do not believe that either the European nations or the United States have a serious choice. — Daniel Lerner, *Virginia Quarterly Review*, Autumn 1964

Neither Carré nor his characters has any religious belief. . . . — Steven Marcus, *New York Review of Books*, Aug. 5, 1965

elder, eldest

These forms of *old* survive in references to the order of birth of members of a family — "the elder brother," "our eldest daughter" — and in some honorific senses like "the elder statesmen."

Ellipsis

A punctuation mark of three spaced periods in a quotation, indicating the omission of one or more words, is called an ellipsis: "Fourscore and seven years ago our fathers brought forth . . . a new nation . . . dedicated to the proposition that all men are created equal." When the last words in a sentence are omitted, the end punctuation precedes the ellipsis, just as it does when the omission follows the sentence.

The omission of a line or more of poetry is generally indicated by a full line of spaced periods. Traditional practice also uses a line of periods to indicate the omission of a paragraph or more of prose, but more liberal style simply places an ellipsis at the end of the paragraph preceding the omission.

No ellipsis should be used when a quotation is just a phrase: It is worth asking whether we continue to be "dedicated to the proposition." (Not: ". . . dedicated to the proposition. . . .")

In narrative an ellipsis is sometimes used to mark hesitation in action, suggesting passage of time; in dialog, to mark hesitation in speech. It is also used as an end stop to mark a statement that is left unfinished or allowed to die away: "The town was poor then. And like so many who grew up in the Depression, we never expected we would have real jobs. There was no place for us in the world. It was depressing . . ." (John Thompson, *Harper's*, May 1969).

References: *Chicago Manual; MLA Style Sheet; U.S. Style Manual.*

Elliptical constructions

An elliptical construction is one which omits a word or two that can somehow be supplied, usually from a neighboring construction: I work much harder than you [work]. Grammarians differ in the extent to which they use ellipsis as a means of explanation. In the sentence "We had the same experience you did," some grammarians would say that the relative pronoun *that* has been omitted after *experience*, some that it is present in zero position, still others that no relative occurs, even implicitly. Constructions like "The more, the merrier" and "First come, first served" are commonly taken as established idioms, not elliptical.

The choice between the longer and shorter forms is a matter of style. Formal English tends to be explicit and uses relatively few ellipses. General English and Informal use the shorter constructions freely. See *Guide*, pp. 344–45, and compare *Clauses § 3a. References: Otto Jespersen, *Philosophy of Grammar* (New York: Norton, 1965), p. 306 and index references; Arthur G. Kennedy, *Current English* (Boston: Ginn, 1935), pp. 508–12; Long, index references.

else

The intensive *else*, as in "He was running on nothing else but courage and adrenalin," is likely to be *deadwood in writing and should be deleted. In phrases with pronouns like *anyone, nobody,* and *someone, else* and not the preceding pronoun takes the sign of the possessive: The package was left at somebody else's house.

Emphasis

Emph

Revision: Strengthen the emphasis of this passage.

Rightly used, emphasis makes clear the relative importance of the points you are making, so that your reader recognizes the most important as most important, the less important as less important, the incidental as incidental. A lack of emphasis means a failure in guidance; misplaced emphasis means serious confusion.

1. *Proportion.* Ordinarily, mass is evidence of significance: we allot space on the basis of importance. When a paper is finished in a hurry, the major point may be left undeveloped and therefore fail in emphasis. Sometimes a good deal of groundwork must be laid before the central issue in an essay can be presented, but one of the tasks of revision is to see that minor points are not given so much space that the reader is misled as to where the emphasis belongs. See *Guide*, pp. 212–13.

2. *Position.* Generally speaking, the most emphatic position in a sentence, a paragraph, or a full essay is the end (hence the danger of leaving the last point undeveloped). The second most important is the beginning. Through other means, emphasis can be shifted — from the end of a sentence to the beginning, for example, or to somewhere in between — but the positions of natural emphasis should not be wasted. See *Guide*, pp. 207 – 08, 339 – 40.

3. *Separation.* A comma or a dash can be used to set off part of a sentence and thereby emphasize it, lightly or heavily. Making a separate sentence or a new paragraph achieves the same purpose. See *Guide*, pp. 338 – 39.

4. *Repetition.* Repeating significant words drives them home, and repeating ideas in different words, perhaps in figurative expressions, is a useful way to emphasize if it is not overdone. Repeating a structural pattern, especially in a series that builds to a climax, is an excellent device for emphasizing. See *Guide*, pp. 341 – 42.

5. *Economy.* Wordiness is a serious obstacle to emphasis. In the cutting and condensing that is a regular part of revision, special attention should be given to the expression of the ideas that deserve major emphasis. It should be stripped of any verbiage that blurs its clarity and blunts its impact. Emphatic statement need not be harsh, but it must be direct and uncluttered. See *Guide*, pp. 343 – 46.

6. *Mechanical devices.* Included in this category are not only such orthographic devices as underlining, using capital letters, and punctuating with exclamation marks but also announcing that what is said is significant and saying it with words that claim importance for it. These methods are usually too obvious and mechanical to accomplish their purpose. Underlinings, capitals, and exclamation marks are likely to bore the reader or amuse him. Telling him that he should be interested ("It is interesting to note") or impressed ("Here is the really important point that we should all recognize") is likely to irritate him. Pretentious or portentous word choice has the same effect, and the qualifiers used in speech — *very, terribly, extremely, incredibly* — are almost uniformly ineffective in writing. On paper, "a very shocking incident" turns out to be less, not more, impressive than "a shocking incident."

Mechanical devices, then, are poor means for achieving emphasis. They demand the reader's attention instead of earning it.

See *Repetition, *Wordiness.

End stop

An end stop is a mark of punctuation — usually a period, exclamation mark, or question mark — used at the end of a sentence. In writing conversation, the double or two-em dash (see *Dash § 8) is used as an end stop when a speech is interrupted. An *ellipsis may be used as an end stop for a sentence that is intentionally left unfinished.

When two end stops would fall together at the end of a sentence, only one mark, the more emphatic or more necessary for meaning, is used. Here a question comes at the end of a sentence that would normally close with a period; only the question mark is used:

When we say, for example, that Miss A. *plays* well, only an irredeemable outsider would reply, "Plays what?" — C. Alphonso Smith, *Studies in English Syntax*

See *Guide*, p. 298, and articles on the individual marks.

English language

The language we speak is a product of history — subject still to constant change yet reflecting its past in pronunciation, in vocabulary, in anomalous forms that are the fossils of linguistic history, and in productive rules for word and sentence formation. Some knowledge of the history of English can help a writer understand the richness and the complexity of the medium he uses.

To the linguistic historian there is no real beginning for any language. The earliest records of English date from the seventh century A.D., two centuries after invading Germanic tribesmen from northwestern Europe — Angles, Saxons, Jutes, and Frisians — had made their homes in the British Isles, bringing with them the differing but mutually intelligible dialects which are the direct ancestors of the English language. But through those dialects, English is connected to a prehistoric past — to a reconstructed language called Germanic, parent of the Low and High German languages, the Scandinavian languages, and English. Through Germanic, English is connected to a still more ancient reconstructed language, Indo-European, the parent of several language groups besides Germanic: Indo-Iranian, Armenian, Celtic, Albanian, Balto-Slavic, Italic, Hellenic, and the ancient tongues of Hittite and Tocharian. Thus English is ultimately related to most of the ancient and modern languages of Europe and to many of the most important languages of the Near East and the Indian subcontinent.

The history of English is customarily divided into four periods: Old English (OE), c. 450–1100; Middle English (ME), c. 1100–1450; Early Modern English (EMnE), c. 1450–1700; Modern English (MnE), c. 1700–   . To speak of discrete periods does no harm as long as we recognize that language change is continuous and gradual and that the periods refer to accumulated changes, making the language of Tennyson, for example, noticeably different from the language of Chaucer.

The central theme of the history of English is expansion. From very modest beginnings as the tongue of a handful of Germanic adventurers and colonists on a chilly island at the fringes of the civilized world, English has risen to the stature of a world language: first language to hundreds of millions in Europe, North America, Africa, Asia, Australia; perhaps the most popular second language in the world.

1. *Vocabulary.* Of all aspects of language, vocabulary is the surest index to cultural change, since new environments, new inventions, new ideas all require new words for talking about them. English speakers have met their needs for new words by borrowing from foreign languages and by relying on native processes of word formation.

Latin, Scandinavian, and French have contributed most to the common vocabulary of English. Latin makes its mark early—first before the English-to-be had left their continental homes, next when Roman missionaries converted the English to Christianity in the Old English period. Many of the early loans are unmistakably popular: from the pre-English period—*wine, flask, kettle, kitchen, cup, dish, cheese, pepper, copper,* reflecting trade contacts; *camp, wall, pit, street,* reflecting military ones; from the OE period: *cap, sock, mat, beet, lentil, pear, radish,* to cite a mere handful of the words which entered everyday English.

Scandinavian influences strike still more deeply into the core of English vocabulary. Danish and Norwegian armies invaded England in the ninth century; in the tenth, colonists followed to establish permanent settlements in the north and east; by the eleventh, Danish kings ruled England. Because Englishmen and Norsemen lived side by side, and because the languages were similar—perhaps similar enough to make limited communication possible—many Scandinavian words entered English. Although the degree of similarity makes it difficult to tell in all cases whether a word is English or Scandinavian in origin, many loans can be identified. English words beginning with /sk/ are often Scandinavian: *sky, skin, scream, skirt* (the English cognate is *shirt,* showing an English sound change of /sk/ to /sh/); as are many beginning with /g/ and /k/: *gear, geld, gill, give* (where the English cognate would have /y/); *kick, kilt, kindle* (where the English cognate would have /ch/).

French influence, resulting from the Norman Conquest and occupation, is still more pervasive. For almost three hundred years, French replaced English as the tongue of law, learning, politics, and influence. One scholar has calculated that during the Middle English period alone over ten thousand French words were borrowed and 75 percent of them survive. French words dominate our vocabulary for government (*government* itself, *empire, sovereign, parliament, statute, tax, governor, mayor*), law (*bar, plea, suit, attorney, jury, fine, prison*), war (*army, siege, soldier, spy*), social life (*fashion, attire, chemise, lace, dinner, supper, venison, beef, salad*), the arts (*painting, sculpture, music*). It is difficult to find an English paragraph, on any subject, that does not contain French imports.

From the fourteenth century, Englishmen have been invaders more often than invaded, explorers and discoverers more often than passive receptors of foreign influence. Loan words from the modern period reflect an ever-widening circle of contacts. Terms from Low German (particularly Dutch and Flemish) result from late medieval trade across the channel; Italian and Spanish terms show English movements into the Mediterranean. Excursions to more distant lands provided English with loans from Turkish, Arabic, Persian, Indian, Dravidian, Chinese, Japanese, Malayo-Polynesian, Australian, African, and Amerindian languages. Some words from exotic sources have entered the general English vocabulary (*apricot, caravan, coffee, taboo, tulip*); others belong to the common vocabulary of only one national variety of English (e.g., Amerindian loans in American English); still others retain their exotic flavor and are used only in reference to foreign locales (*gaucho, amboyna, parang, punkah*).

Many words have made their way into English through books. Latin and Greek have contributed most to learned vocabulary. The Christian missionaries to the earliest English brought terms related to learning and to church activities: *school, gloss, grammatic(al), master, verse* alongside *abbot, alms, cleric, hymn, priest*. OE borrowings of animal terms show that the world of books is opening: *dragon* (OE *draca*), *elephant* (OE *elpend*), *basilisk, camel, phoenix*. The language of English learning is predominantly Latin through the EMnE period, joined then by Greek as a complementary source. The scholarly, scientific and technical vocabulary of the twentieth century reflects the persistent influence of the classical tongues: *aerospace, allobar, antibiotic, astrophysics, astronaut, biochemistry, chronograph, ecology, electron, isotope, positron, spectroscope, telemetry*.

Of the native processes for forming new words, two have been most productive: compounding and word composition (see *Origin of words). English vocabulary is rich in its collection of noun, adjective, verb, and adverb compound terms. OE *scops* (bards, poets) relied heavily on compounds to meet the demands of alliterative verse; OE prose writers used compounds almost as frequently, often preferring native formations to borrowed terms: e.g., *ānhorn, allmihtig, gōdspell* (literally, "good tidings"), instead of *unicorn* (L. *unicornus*), *omnipotent* (L. *omnipotens*), or L. *ēvangelium*. Some earlier compounds have been acted upon by phonetic changes which obscure their origin: e.g., *hussy* (from OE *hūs* "house" and *wīf* "wife"), *lord* (OE *hlāf* "loaf" and *weard* "ward," "guardian"), *nostril* (OE *nasu* "nose" and *þyrel* "hole"). But compounding has continued as a productive process throughout the history of English; examples abound in modern colloquial English: *highbrow, egghead, hotbed, deadbeat, lowbrow;* in the vocabularies of occupations, sports, and hobbies; and in technical vocabularies—*countdown, earthshine, moonshot, spacewalk*.

History has worked changes in English word composition, but has never restricted its productivity. Over the centuries, some native affixes have disappeared altogether; some survive only as fossils (e.g., *for-* in *forbear*); still others have become restricted in use (e.g., *-dom, -hood, -th* as in *width*). But to its dwindling stock of native affixes, English has added others, principally from Latin, Greek, and French. How completely English has assimilated foreign elements may be seen in the freedom with which it combines foreign and native word elements: to native bases are added foreign affixes—*goddess, endearment, mileage, hindrance, murderous, heathenism, womanize;* to foreign bases, native affixes—*graceful, faintness, courtship, unconscious, forbearance, martyrdom;* foreign elements from two sources are mixed—*postal, socialist, jurist, communism*. With its borrowings and its still flourishing native supply, English possesses a rich and precise system of formatives.

In spite of its cosmopolitan quality, the English lexicon remains fixed to its origins. Perhaps a quarter of the present English vocabulary goes back to the words of Old English, and many of these are the most frequently used of all. The modern descendants of OE words are changed almost always in pronunciation and nearly as often in meaning, as are borrowed words which have long been in common use. As objects change in shape or in the uses to which they are put, the meanings of the terms naming them change: *ship, car, weapon,* are obvious examples; *atom* has a long history in English, but scientists change its definition each time they discover more about its structure. Words naming specific things can be generalized in application (*thing* was once a legal term); general terms can become specific (our word *deer* once meant "wild animal"); words can slide up and down an evaluational scale with the fortunes of the referents (*lust* once meant "pleasure," harmless as well as otherwise; a *marshall* was once a horse-servant, a *steward*, a pig-keeper). Writers must be on their guard for fluctuations in denotation and nuance but quick to seize potentialities in their rich lexical heritage. English offers an everyday vocabulary rich in its synonyms, an exotic vocabulary redolent of distant countries, a learned vocabulary precise in denotation and partially preserved by its literary character from rapid semantic change. The effective writer learns to exploit the nuances of synonymous terms, to respond to the demands of occasion on vocabulary level, and to recognize that the English lexicon is not a closed book.

2. *Grammar.* Although a modern student needs assistance in learning to read Old English, he will recognize more similarities than differences in the grammatical systems of Old and Modern English. The inflectional system of OE has been extensively simplified by historical changes, but in syntax the two stages show fundamental likenesses.

Space permits only hints of the inflectional complexity of OE. The OE noun, for example, had distinctive forms for singular and plural and for four cases (nominative, genitive, dative, accusative) and exhibited grammatical gender (nouns fell into one of several declensions, mainly according to gender). Articles, demonstratives, adjectives agreed with nouns in gender, number, and case. Thus, where MnE has only the form *the*, OE had a separate inflection for masculine, neuter, and feminine forms, for singular and plural, and for five cases (dative and instrumental case are merged in the noun, preserved in articles). Where MnE has an invariant form of the adjective, OE possessed a full array of endings for number, gender, and case.

From the complex of forms in OE comes the sparse inflectional machinery of MnE: *the* and *that* are remnants from an OE demonstrative article; *this, these,* and *those* come from a second demonstrative; *a, an* come from the OE word *ān* (one), separately inflected in OE. Adjective inflections disappeared entirely by the end of the ME period. The noun endings that remain in MnE trace back to OE origins: the *-s* of plural to *-as* in the masculine declension (*cyningas* "kings"); the *-s* of genitive to the OE genitive of the same declension (*cyning-es*). From other noun declensions, MnE retains only fossils: the *-en* of *oxen*; the *-ren* of *children* (a double plural); the vowel gradation of *man, men; goose, geese.* Verb inflections underwent similar processes of decay, particularly of personal endings, and in the conversion of strong (irregular) verbs to the weak pattern. The conversion of irregular verbs has been slowed in the Modern period, but competing forms are easily found in EMnE: *oke* and *ached, stope* and *stepped, rewe* and *rowed, clew* and *clawed. Clomb* (for *climbed*) occurs in Chaucer, Spenser, and Dryden—and now in uneducated dialects of Britain and the United States, in which the historical process of remodeling is not checked by the conservative efforts of teachers seeking to preserve the fossilized forms against the drift of history.

Why the English inflectional system should undergo such extensive simplification is not known, but whatever the ultimate causes, the results are clear—MnE relies more on word order and on grammatical function words than did OE, although the contrast is easily exaggerated. Because OE possessed contrastive inflections for nouns serving major sentence functions like subject, direct and indirect object, OE word order could be somewhat freer than that of MnE. For example, objects as well as subject could precede the verb: *hē him hirngas geaf* (he him rings gave). But in independent clauses the usual OE word order was subject-verb-object as in MnE. Thus OE rules for word order tended to make inflections redundant and to smooth the way for their loss. Similarly, the MnE reliance on prepositions is anticipated in OE, which used prepositions with inflected noun phrases to enforce the meaning: e.g., *Adam ðe wæs of eorþan geworht* (Adam who was made of earth); *ond þus glædlīce tō ūs sprecende eart* (and thus gladly are speaking to us).

Some syntactic changes have occurred. The MnE use of *do* in interrogatives (Do you dance?) and emphatics (You DO dance) is an EMnE addition to the auxiliary system of English (cf. Chaucer's question form, "Lady myn, Criseyde, lyve ye yet?"). The auxiliary *be* in progressive forms first appeared in OE, and only slowly made its way into the English auxiliary system. Forms like "He is laughing" were not common until the sixteenth century; passive progressive (The house is being painted) does not develop until the end of the eighteenth. The full participation of progressive forms in the auxiliary system will be reached when a sentence like "The runner could have been being trained during that time" no longer strikes us with its rarity. But significant innovations are rare in the history of the English grammatical system. To look at deep rather than superficial features of English grammar is to convince oneself of how slowly they alter, no matter what happens to vocabulary and pronunciation, or to surface inflections. Purists sometimes maintain that changes in usage will render the language chaotic and unintelligible. As a consequence, writers are urged to cling to the *whom* in "Whom did you see?" Historical perspective helps us to see that English preserves its basic form, its semantically significant categories and relations, through many superficial changes.

3. *Standardization and the spread of English.* In modern times, English has undergone two developments which may at first glance seem contradictory. On the one hand, large groups of English speakers have migrated from mother England in apparent imitation of their continental Germanic ancestors, whose migrations resulted in the split of Germanic into separate languages — High German, Dutch, Danish, Swedish, English, etc. In North America, Australia, New Zealand, India, and Africa, new national varieties of English have arisen, but none has diverged far enough from its parent or its siblings to be considered a separate tongue. The failure of history to repeat itself may be attributed to the second major development in Modern English — standardization. In England after the ME period, a relatively uniform and powerfully dominant form of English spread to all parts of the island kingdom; in other English-speaking nations, similar tendencies toward standardization have kept the separate national varieties basically alike.

Dialect differences have always existed in English. The major varieties of OE — Kentish, West Saxon, Anglian (sometimes divided into Mercian and Northumbrian) — derive from differences between the dialects brought by Angles, Saxons, and Jutes, and lead in turn to the major varieties of ME — Kentish, Southern, East and West Midland, and Northern. Although West Saxon approached the status of a written standard late in the OE period (most surviving manuscripts are written in that dialect) its ascendancy was cut short by the Norman Conquest. For much of the ME period, French replaced English in official documents, in parliament, in law courts, in schools, and in literature intended for the upper classes — a condition fostering localism in the use of English. Although English emerged from its subservience in the thirteenth century and became common in official use in the fourteenth, the three major English poets of the fourteenth century — Chaucer, Langland, and the Pearl Poet — all wrote their separate native dialects.

Sixteenth-century poets, however, used a uniform written standard based on a late ME form of London English. Thus what is later known as Standard English begins as a regional dialect — the dialect of England's capital, naturally prestigious because it is the dialect of powerful and influential men. Early in the fifteenth century the standard spreads into official documents written outside London, later in the century into private documents such as letters and journals. Its influence is noticeable on late fifteenth-century writers like William Caxton, himself a southern man, who sought to purge his productions of offensive localisms. Caxton was a printer as well as a writer — the first to bring a press to England (1476). Printers felt a particular need for uniformity, especially in spelling and choice of word forms, and helped spread written standard by putting it before the eyes of an ever-growing number of readers. Renaissance scholars and schoolmasters pushed standardization almost as actively, seeking to demonstrate that English was as proper a medium of learning as the classical tongues, pressing their claims by working for spelling reform and by providing English with grammars and dictionaries. What the Renaissance left untidy, eighteenth-century schoolmen sought to regularize and fix. Prescriptive grammarians labored to settle cases of disputed usage: to unravel the uses of *between* and *among*, to decide what case properly follows *than* and *as*, to explicate the differences between *shall* and *will*. Uniformity and correctness were cardinal linguistic virtues.

The benefits of standardization are many: learning to read is made easier as the number of variant spellings and forms is reduced; communication is facilitated; the growth of a national literature is undoubtedly encouraged when writers and audience share a common tongue. But there are disadvantages and dangers when standards are asserted so stringently that no room is left for variations introduced by the natural processes of linguistic change; greater dangers when, as has happened in the history of English, the standard dialect becomes a class dialect invested with the status of its speakers. The process begins early in England with the feeling that one kind of pronunciation must be correct. Sir Thomas Elyot urges sixteenth-century nurses, if they cannot teach a nobleman's son pure and elegant Latin, at least to teach "none englisshe but that which is cleane, polite, perfectly and articulately pronounced, omittinge no lettre or sillable." Such pronunciation is soon equated with the speech of "the better sort": educated and influential people who hover about the seats of power. After the eighteenth century—a great age of snobbism, when aristocrats looked down their noses at the lower classes and lower classes did all they could to imitate their betters—spoken Standard English is firmly a class standard, carefully maintained by gentlemen as an outward sign of status. Those who could not adapt betrayed their origins merely by opening their mouths.

Although most traces of provincial dialects disappear from English writing after the fifteenth century, the dialects themselves continued to be spoken. Earlier dialect differences are, of course, the bases of modern British dialects, and also of differences between British English, American English, Australian English, etc. The retention of postvocalic /r/ in most dialects of American English, for example, reveals that many immigrants to the American colonies left northern British homes and did not speak the British prestige form. The loss of /r/ in America's South and in New England shows that settlers to those regions migrated from the south of England and retained closer ties to the mother country.

But American English has never diverged far from the parent language, partly because of cultural contacts, partly because standardizing processes in American English have retarded linguistic change. British and American usage remained close during the colonial period—the differences consisting mainly of vocabulary items. Growing nationalism after the Revolution led Americans to predict, and eagerly expect, a new American language: ". . . as different from the future language of England, as the modern Dutch, Danish and Swedish are from the German, or from one another" (Noah Webster, 1789). But concern for preserving national unity suggested that American dialects must not be allowed to develop unchecked lest they become so different from one another as to make comunication difficult: "a national language is a band of national union," wrote Webster, and as textbook writer for the new nation he pushed a standard of general (that is, national) custom:

. . . general custom must be the rule of speaking, and every derivation from this must be wrong. The dialect of one state is as ridiculous as that of another; each is authorized by local custom; and neither is supported by any superior excellence.

In Webster's time, America was a nation of the middle class, or of aspirants to that class, with a healthy respect for the primary skills of formal education. The call of prescriptivists for one language linking all fell on receptive ears.

But American prescriptivism has tended to concentrate on the written word. Webster's "general custom" is easily translated into marks on a printed page, and general custom in pronunciation must inevitably be abstract as long as differences in speech exist. America has never had a Received Standard of pronunciation, based—as England's was until very recently—on the speech of a single locale or class. And American prescriptivism has paid more attention to grammar than to pronunciation. Southern, Northern, and Western speakers may sound different but still speak Standard American English; the same is not true of Southerner, Northerner, or Westerner who utters "He don't never do that."

Class dialects do exist in the United States. When we use the terms Standard and Nonstandard English, we refer to the social status of the speakers of each, not to good or bad qualities inherent in the dialects themselves. And while it is true that Standard English in the United States has been more flexible than British Received Standard—more tolerant of regional variation and of importations from Nonstandard—dialect conflict has emerged in our century. The historical flexibility of Standard American English has been based on social flexibility—ease of movement upward in social class, ease of assimilation by minority groups. Immigrants to the United States have wanted to assimilate to American culture and language; the ignorant and the poor have aspired to education and middle economic status—and American institutions have historically been receptive to the wishes of both groups. In twentieth-century America, however, the pressures of urbanization and of rapid technological development have changed attitudes. Massive migration to Northern cities, particularly from the South and South-Midlands, has brought Northern and Southern speakers into close contact. Because many of the migrants have been poor and ill-educated, their speech—regional in its origins—has been taken as indicative of their class. Thus in many Northern cities, Southern speech is equated with Nonstandard speech. In addition, assimilation and upward mobility do not seem as available to the new urban dwellers. Technological societies demand sophisticated skills; fewer workers can produce more, increasing competition for jobs and the hostility of groups contending for them; racial conflicts intensify the hostility as more and more blacks move into cities and spread to previously all-white neighborhoods. Thus the new migrant—particularly if he is black—does not find the city welcoming him with open arms. Hostility toward him, toward his class or race, attaches easily to his language; in return, the migrant may see in Webster's "general custom" only the values of an oppressive class.

Dialects are not merely collections of sounds, forms, words. They are powerful social and psychological symbols—expressive of who one is, what groups he belongs to, what values he shares with others. Standardized languages have vital functions to perform in breaking down intense regionalism and in facilitating international communication: Englishmen, Americans, Canadians, Australians, New Zealanders can talk to one another; they can also talk to English speakers in India, Pakistan, Ceylon, Malaysia, Nepal, the Philippines, Nigeria, Rhodesia, Sierra Leone, Ghana, Kenya, the British West Indies, to name only a few of the nations where English holds some official status. Standardization has helped make English available as a communicative medium for educated people in Africa, Asia, and the Western world, as a potential link between peoples of diverse cultures. The link, however, can be easily broken by an over-zealous commitment to inflexible standards that take no account of the personal, social, and cultural validity of dialect difference. West Indian poets and novelists insist that their own English is the proper medium for their works; African writers do the same; some black authors in the United States insist that they write in Black English—a dialect symbolizing the values and attitudes of black men in coexistence with or rebellion against white society. If Standard American English is defined too narrowly and without reference to the usage of social minorities—if it is identified too closely with the usage of the white middle class, as Received Standard was earlier with the British upper class—we invite the division of America predicted by black militants, by sociologists, and by Presidential commissions.

References: Histories: Baugh; Pyles; Robertson; John C. McLaughlin, *Aspects of the History of English* (New York: Holt, 1970). American English: Mencken; G. P. Krapp, *The English Language in America*, 2 vols. (New York: Ungar, 1960); A. L. Marckwardt, *American English* (New York: Oxford Univ. Press, 1958); Thomas Pyles, *Words and Ways of American English* (New York: Random, 1952). English words: George H. McKnight, *English Words and Their Background* (New York: Appleton, 1923); Mary S. Serjeantson, *A History of Foreign Words in English* (London: Routledge, 1935); J. A. Sheard, *The Words We Use* (New York: Praeger, 1954). Dialects: G. L. Brook, *English Dialects* (New York: Oxford Univ. Press, 1963); Raven I. McDavid, Jr., "The Dialects of American English," in Francis; Carroll E. Reed, *Dialects of American English* (Cleveland: World, 1967); Harold B. Allen and Gary N. Underwood, eds., *Readings in Ameri-*

can *Dialectology* (New York: Appleton, 1971). A survey of British dialects is in process of publication by Leeds University under the editorship of Harold Orton and Wilfred J. Halliday. Many publications have resulted from the survey of American dialects called *The Linguistic Atlas of the United States and Canada.* Bibliographical references may be found in the books by Reed and by Allen and Underwood.

Jay Robinson

en-, in-

In- is either a native English prefix or a prefix of Latin origin; *en-* is the same Latin prefix modified in French. (*Em-* and *im-* are variant forms.) For several common words (*endorse, indorse; inquire, enquire;* etc.) usage is divided, though usually one form is more prevalent. Fowler and other British sources are not dependable guides to American usage on this matter because Americans tend to use *in-* more than the British. When in doubt, consult a recent American dictionary. If dictionaries disagree, the choice is a matter of taste or style.

enormity, enormousness

Because *enormity* looks like a more compact way of expressing the idea of "enormousness," it is often used in that sense. But this use is deplored by those who restrict *enormity* to the meaning "enormously evil" or "great wickedness," as in "the enormity of the crime."

enthuse

Enthuse is a back formation (see *Origin of words § 3e) from *enthusiasm.* Although widely used in General and Informal writing, it is still not established in Formal usage, and many readers object to it. The only other locution we have for the idea is the clumsy *be enthusiastic over* or *about.*

Epigrams and aphorisms

An epigram is a short, pithy statement, in verse or prose, usually with a touch of wit. In prose this means a detached or detachable and quotable sentence. In consecutive prose, epigrams sometimes become too prominent, attract too much attention to themselves, or give the impression of straining for effect. But they can focus attention and phrase an idea so that it will be remembered:

Conscience is the inner voice that warns us that someone may be looking. — H. L. Mencken, *The Vintage Mencken*

Using a blowtorch on the middle of the candle is less aesthetic than burning it at both ends, but more people see the flames. — Richard Fariña, *Long Time Coming and a Long Time Gone*

Closely related to epigrams are aphorisms — pithy statements that are more likely to be abstract and are not necessarily witty. The essays of Francis Bacon are packed with aphorisms:

To spend too much time in studies is sloth; to use them too much for orna-
ment, is affectation; to make judgment wholly by their rules is the humour of
a scholar. . . . Read not to contradict and confute; nor to believe and take
for granted; nor to find talk and discourse; but to weigh and consider. . . .
Reading maketh a full man; conference a ready man; and writing an exact
man. — Francis Bacon, "Of Studies"

A special type of epigram is the paradox, which makes a statement that as it stands contradicts fact or common sense or itself and
yet suggests a truth or at least a half-truth: All generalizations are
false, including this one.

equally as

Although *equally as* is an established idiom (Color is equally as important as design), one of the words is always redundant. A careful
writer will use *equally* or *as*, not both. Reference: Bryant, p. 85.

-er, -or

Names of persons or things performing an act (nouns of agent) and
some other nouns are commonly formed in English by adding *-er* to a
verb (*doer, killer, painter, thinker*); but many nouns of agent — chiefly
nouns taken from Latin or French — end in *-or (assessor, prevaricator)*.
Since the two endings are pronounced the same /ər/, it is hard to tell
whether *-er* or *-or* should be written. A dictionary will settle most
questions. When either *-er* or *-or* is correct (*adviser* or *advisor*), the
choice is a matter of taste or style. A few nouns of agent end in *-ar:
beggar, burglar, liar.*

-er, -re

Many words formerly ending in *-re* are now ordinarily spelled *-er* in
American usage. This group includes *caliber, center, fiber, luster,
maneuver, meager, meter, scepter, sepulcher, somber, specter,* and
theater. Far more *-re* endings are found in British writing.

French words ending in *-re* that have not been completely anglicized retain that ending: *cadre, genre, macabre, timbre.*

Acre, lucre, and *mediocre* keep *-re* to mark the /k/ sound of c
(contrast *seducer*).

-ese

The suffix *-ese* is used to make new nouns, such as *Brooklynese,
journalese, educationese, Pentagonese,* which have the disparaging
sense of "lingo, jargon, or dialect": His mastery of sociologese left us
impressed if uninformed.

Establishment

Establishment (sometimes not capitalized) is a *vogue word for the
powers-that-be: "In the intellectuals' lexicon 'the Establishment' now
seems to include federal, state, and local government, business cor-
porations, foundations, and other philanthropic organizations, Big
Labor, Big Science, and the administrations of universities" (Max

Ways, *Fortune*, April 1967). While sometimes simply descriptive, it is more often a term of abuse, expressing discontent with the ins and sympathy with the outs.

In *The New Yorker*, Oct. 19, 1968, Henry Fairlie tells of launching the term in its present sense in the British *Spectator* of Sept. 23, 1955. At that time Fairlie wrote: "By the 'Establishment,' I do not mean only the centres of official power—though they are certainly part of it—but rather the whole matrix of official and social relations within which power is exercised." *Establishment* has remained anything but precise: "Except as a spread-eagle put-down it has no discernible meaning, and if accepted as a put-down, the problem then becomes to discover who, if anyone, is not in the Establishment" (Irving Howe, *Decline of the New*).

etc.

Though sometimes a convenient way to end an incomplete list, *etc.*, the abbreviation for the Latin phrase *et cetera* ("and the rest"), belongs primarily to business and reference usage: This case is suitable for large photographs, maps, blueprints, etc. In most writing the English *and so forth* or *and so on* is preferable when the reference is to things, and English *and others* is preferable with lists of people. The incompleteness of a list can also be marked by an introductory phrase like *such as* after the category the list exemplifies: This case is suitable for *large papers such as* photographs, maps, and blueprints.

Etymology

See *Origin of words.

Euphemisms

A euphemism is a softened word used in place of one that names more explicitly something unpleasant or something regarded as not quite nice: *perspire* for *sweat, passed on* for *died, senior citizens* for *old people, lavatory* or *powder room* or *bathroom* or *john* for *toilet*. Political, military, and promotional vocabularies offer countless examples. Occasionally euphemisms are warranted, to avoid causing pain or embarrassment, but ordinarily honesty is better—and makes for better writing—than evasion. For further discussion see *Guide*, pp. 365 – 66.

Euphony

Euphony means "a pleasing sound," particularly a pleasing sound produced by words. See *Alliteration, *Assonance, *Consonance.

every and its compounds

1. *Every, everybody, everyone* were originally singular and are still so to the extent that they nearly always take a singular verb: Every man on the team did well; Everybody loathes the mayor; Everyone takes the freeway. Usage is divided, however, for related pronouns that come later in the sentence. The singular is perhaps more common, especially in Formal writing, but the plural appears in all varieties: "Everybody who has praised the inaugural address cannot possibly be as enthusiastic as they sound, unless they are merely reacting to its music" (James Reston, *New York Times*, Jan. 22, 1961). This construction is reasonable, since the reference is to a number of people. Instead of substituting a *he* for each *they*, Formal written usage might replace *Everybody* with an explicit plural: All those who have praised. . . .

There is also a tendency to use a plural pronoun for clarity when the *every* phrase is the object of a verb with a singular subject: "The traditional leader then comes forward and thanks everyone for their attendance and invites them to lunch" (John A. Woodward, *Ethnology*, Jan. 1968). Treating the *every* words as collectives can sometimes prevent confusion and also avoid the awkward *he-or-she* problem. References: Fries, *AEG*, p. 50; Bryant, pp. 8 – 10.

2. *Everybody* is always written as one word; *everyone* is usually written as one word, but when the *one* is stressed, it is written as two:

Everyone knew what the end would be.
Every one of us knew what the end would be.

3. *Every so often*, meaning "occasionally," should not be confused with *ever so often*, meaning "very frequently":

Every so often we have to get away from the city.
Campus pressures ever so often produce symptoms of nervous exhaustion.

4. *Every place* (or *everyplace*), meaning "everywhere," is avoided in Formal usage.

Examples
See *Details; *Guide*, pp. 76 – 79, 148 – 50.

except, accept
Except, verb, means "leave out, exclude": He excepted those who had made an honest effort. It is decidedly Formal. *Excused* would be more appropriate in General writing.

Accept means "receive" or "answer affirmatively" and is slightly Formal: I accept with pleasure; He accepted the position (as contrasted with "He took the job").

Exclamation mark
An exclamation mark (or point) is used after an emphatic interjection, after a phrase, clause, or sentence that is genuinely exclamatory, and after forceful commands. Clear-cut exclamations are no problem:

Oh! Ouch! No, no, no!
Damn those mosquitoes!
It was the chance of a lifetime!

But many interjections are mild and deserve no more than a comma or a period:

Well, well, so you're in college now.
Wow.

Often sentences cast in exclamatory patterns are really statements (What a memorable experience that was), and the type of punctuation is optional.

In deciding whether or not to use an exclamation mark, you should first ask yourself whether you intend an exclamation. Are you in fact expressing strong feeling or saying something that you want to give special emphasis to? Walt Kelly has said, "Using the exclamation point is like wearing padded shoulders." But when used sparingly, to signal genuine emotion, the mark can serve the writer as the raised voice or dramatic gesture serves the speaker:

The Sun Also Rises is a major work, brilliantly constructed and colored—though last year I was taken aback to hear some students complain that Jake Barnes indulges himself in too much self-pity. How imperious the young can be when judging the victims of disasters they don't even trouble to learn about!—Irving Howe, Harper's, May 1969

Exclamations

What distinguishes an exclamation from other kinds of utterance is its purpose: emphatic expression. In form, an exclamation may be a declarative sentence (She's late again!), a question (Can she be late again!), a command or request (Be ready when I call! Please be on time!), a verbless sentence (How terrible for you!), or an interjection (Ouch!). See *Exclamation mark.

expect

In General and Formal writing, expect is ordinarily limited to the senses "anticipate" (He expects it to be a great success) and "require as reasonable" (Winsock, Inc., expects its employees to arrive on time). The sense "to suppose, presume, believe" in reference to past and present events (I expect there were times when Lincoln was heartily fed up) is common in British writing but likely to be limited to Informal contexts in the United States.

expertise

Formal usage prefers to restrict the sense of expertise to "the specialized knowledge of an expert," as distinct from "practical skills": "Aside from Yugoslavia's Marshal Tito, it takes real expertise to recall the names of European resistance leaders" (Bernard B. Fall, Foreign Affairs, Oct. 1966). But expertise has escaped the limitations of its French origin, and a broadened meaning, "the highly developed skills of a craftsman or performer, is common in General usage: ". . . one pupil was embroidering with extraordinary expertise" (New Yorker, Feb. 28, 1961).

Expository writing, exposition

Most of the writing required in college courses is explanatory—writing that is intended primarily to inform and enlighten the reader. *Exposition* (or *expository writing*) is a term commonly used for writing of this kind. Sometimes the term is extended to include argumentative writing; *exposition* then refers to all factual prose, in contrast to fiction.

fact

Fact and phrases in which it appears are often *deadwood. Many times *fact* can simply be omitted: The study demonstrates [the fact] that workers can become affluent. Sometimes phrases with *fact* can be replaced by single words: In spite of the fact = *although;* due to the fact that = *because.* In the redundant *true fact, fact* alone should be retained.

factor

Windy phrases with *factor* should be deleted:

Determination and imagination [were the factors that] brought the program its popularity.

Membership on the committee [was a factor that] influenced his decision.

The censorship code was strained in the Thirties by [two factors:] increased competition and the advent of the talkies.

Factor itself can often be replaced by a more precise, expressive word: A major factor [stimulus? influence? resource?] in creating the system was the artisan class.

Fallacies

The chief formal and material fallacies (errors in reasoning or in facts) are discussed in the *Guide*, pp. 149–73.

famed

Though *famed* for "famous, well-known" is established in all varieties of usage, some prejudice against it persists.

farther, further

Some careful writers make a distinction between *farther*, referring to physical distance (Farther north there was heavy snow), and *further*, referring to more abstract relations of degree or extent (Nothing could be further removed from experience). But the distinction is not consistently maintained, even in Formal English:

He . . . established an imperial foothold at the further shore, and Charles won his greatest victory. — Lynn White, Jr., *American Historical Review*, Jan. 1967

Thematic analysis has revealed the implied author's inconsistencies, but it can take us no farther. — Bernard Paris, *Victorian Studies*, June 1967

Reference: Bryant, p. 87.

fellow

Fellow is General and Informal when used to mean "person, man, or boy" but Formal in the sense "associate." It is most commonly used in writing in the function of an adjective: his fellow sufferers, a fellow feeling ("a similar feeling" or "sympathy").

female

In current usage the noun *female* seems most appropriate in somewhat Formal or technical contexts in which the designation of sex is significant: "Each female is assigned a number of social security quarters at the beginning of the simulation" (James H. Schulz, *Yale Economic Essays*, Spring 1967). As an adjective *female* has more General usefulness but does not entirely escape its pejorative or technical connotations.

Woman (or *girl*) often replaces *female* not only as a noun but as a modifier: woman doctor, woman legislator, all-girl orchestra, woman suffrage (but women's lib).

fewer, less

The rule is that *fewer* refers to number among things that are counted (fewer particles) and *less* to amount or quantity among things that are measured (less energy). Formal usage ordinarily observes the distinction; and though less is applied to countables fairly often in General writing ("I suggested they sell two less tickets to the public. . . ." — Dwight Macdonald, *Esquire*, Dec. 1964), it grates on some readers' ears. Reference: Bryant, pp. 129–30.

fiancé, fiancée

Fiancé and *fiancée* are masculine and feminine respectively. In much General writing the accent is dropped.

field

"The field of" is *deadwood. The phrase can almost always be omitted: He has long been interested in [the field of] psychiatry.

Figures

See *Numbers.

Figures of speech

Fig

Revision: This figure of speech is inappropriate, inconsistent, or threadbare. Revise the passage.

When we talk about music in terms of color or about moral problems in terms of a game, we are using figures of speech. Appropriate, fresh figures render meaning more vividly than literal expression does. But careless, tasteless figures detract. They may be threadbare (a ribbon of concrete, Old Man Winter). They may be strained and unnatural (Over yonder hill Apollo thrust the blade of his golden sword, severing the filmy mist that blanketed the paths of old Onondaga). They may be inconsistent or "mixed" (But then the molehill of annoyance became a mountain of hate and chased love out of the home).

The most common figures make comparisons or establish relationships. A *simile* asserts likeness, using *like* or *as* (The mist was like a blanket). A *metaphor* sometimes asserts identity (The mist was a blanket), sometimes makes the transfer of meaning in other ways (Her anger flared). An *analogy* shows or implies several points of similarity between things that are unlike—between education and mass production, for example. *Synecdoche* substitutes the part for the whole (many mouths to feed) or the whole for a part (The university adopts a policy). *Metonymy* uses one word for another that it suggests: *java*, a source of coffee, for *coffee*.

Overstatement or *hyperbole* is exaggeration used to dramatize or make laughable. *Understatement* or *litotes* achieves the same end by the opposite method (Enthusiasm for the draft was not overwhelming).

The use of figures of speech is discussed in the *Guide*, pp. 367–74. See also *Alliteration, *Analogy, *Assonance, *Chiasmus, *Hyperbole, *Imagery, *Imitative words, *Mixed metaphors, *Negatives, *Oxymoron, *Personification, *Puns.

finalize

Finalize has been in widespread use for more than a generation. Its near-synonyms, *finish, conclude*, and *complete*, lack the connotation "to make official" that gives *finalize* its usefulness in some contexts:

Before they finalize new guidelines they will consult listeners in East Europe to make sure the proposed changes are having the right effect. — Mary Hornaday, *Christian Science Monitor*, March 24, 1965

Dement, who emphasized that the project is not yet finalized, said the CTA is trying to get a federal grant to finance a trial run. . . . —Earl Moses, *Chicago Sun-Times*, Jan. 5, 1968

But no writer can afford to be ignorant of the great prejudice against *finalize*. It was included in Maury Maverick's original list of *gobbledygook in 1942, and it is still extremely rare in Formal writing.

fine

Fine is widely used as a *counter word of general approval, slightly more vigorous than *nice*, but it is of little value in writing and is better omitted. *Fine* may, of course, be used in any of its more restricted senses. Reference: Bryant, pp. 87–88.

Fine writing

Fine writing is generally a term of dispraise, applied to writing that is too pretentious for the material or purpose. Fine writing betrays itself chiefly in the use of *big words and in strained, artificial *figures of speech. If you write more to impress an audience than to express an idea, you are likely to produce fine writing. See *Guide*, pp. 360–61.

Finite verbs

A finite verb is one that is limited (Latin *finis*, "end, limit") in number (singular or plural) and in person (first, second, or third). In English the first word in every finite verb form is a verb in the present or past tense: *drives, drove, can* drive, *has* driven, *are* driving, *may* have driven. Finite verb forms are contrasted with the nonfinite forms—the infinitives (*to drive, drive*), the participles (*driving, driven*), and the verbal nouns or gerunds (*driving*)—which are not limited in person or number. Verbal phrases take their classification from their first words: *may have been driving* is finite because its first word, *may*, is present tense and not past (*might*), but the words that follow *may* (the infinitive *have* and the participles *been* and *driving*) are not finite themselves. Only finite forms can be the verbs of sentences and unreduced clauses.

fix

In Formal usage *fix* means "fasten in place"; in General usage it means "repair" or "put in shape": "My mother's glasses did need fixing, of course" (Shana Alexander, *Life*, May 27, 1966). As a noun meaning "predicament," *fix* has passed from Informal to General: ". . . in some respects economic theory is in the same fix as biology was years ago" (Henry M. Boettinger, *Harvard Business Review*, July–Aug. 1967).

flair, flare

The two forms ordinarily have different meanings: *flair*, "natural talent, knack, aptitude"; *flare*, "sudden burst of flame or light." The distinction is lost when *flare* is used—as it sometimes is—to mean "natural talent."

flaunt, flout

Flaunt, to "wave, display boastfully," is frequently used with the sense "treat with contempt, scorn," the meaning traditionally assigned to *flout*. Readers aware of the traditional distinction deplore the confusion.

flounder, founder

Flounder means "stumble about, wallow." *Founder* is applied literally to horses ("go lame") and to ships ("sink"); in an extended sense it means "fail." Many readers disapprove the frequent use of *flounder* in this sense.

Folk etymology

When people are puzzled by an unfamiliar word or phrase, they sometimes try to make it more regular or more meaningful by reshaping it
from familiar elements: from *aeroplane* they made *airplane*; from
Spanish *cucuracha*, English *cockroach*; from *saler*, "a salt-holder,"
first the redundant *salt-saler* and then *salt-cellar*, which has no more to
do with a cellar than the *sir-* in *sirloin* has to do with a knight (the *sir-*
in the steak is *sur*, "above"). Folk etymology continues to operate, as
in *chaise lounge* from French *chaise longue*.

folk, folks

In Formal writing, *folks* is uncommon. *Folk* is used in the senses "the
common people (usually of a certain region)" and "people (of a
specified type)." In General writing, *folks* for "people," often with
the connotation "ordinary, everyday," and for "relatives, parents" is
carried over from Informal.

Footnotes

See *Guide*, pp. 415 – 24.

for

Since *for* always comes between the clauses it joins, it is classified as
a coordinating conjunction, but coordinating *for* may mean the same
as subordinating *because: He was exhausted, for he had gone two
nights without sleep. A comma is usually needed between clauses
joined by *for*, to keep *for* from being read as a preposition: The tutors
must love the work, for the pay, which is only $300 a year plus room
and board, cannot be very attractive. [Not: The tutors must love the
work for the pay. . . .] Reference: Henry L. Wilson, *AS*, Dec. 1952,
pp. 257 – 60.

Foreign words in English

1. *Anglicizing foreign words.* English has always borrowed words
and roots freely from other languages and is still borrowing, especially from Greek and French. Words usually cross the threshold of English with their foreign spelling, perhaps with un-English plurals or
other forms, and no established English pronunciation. The process of
anglicizing brings them more or less in line with English usage, but
they may keep some of their foreign quality, like the *i* of *machine*, the
silent *s* in *debris*, the *t* where English is tempted to put a *d* in kindergarten.

Many loan words are in a transition stage, showing two spellings
(*maneuver, manoeuvre; role, rôle*) or pronunciations (most dictionaries list at least two acceptable pronunciations for *melee* and *zwie-
back*). Some words that have been in English a considerable time are
still changing, especially in stress (*debris* can be accented on the first
or second syllable) and in consonant sounds (the first letter of *junta*
can be sounded like the *j* in *jump* or the *h* in *hunt*). In these and other

words a rough compromise is worked out between English practice and the original form.

The speed and degree of anglicizing depends on how frequently the word is used, the circumstances in which it is used, and the people who use it. Formal writers and conservative editors keep the foreign spelling longer than writers and editors of General English. If the words come in through the spoken language, like those of the automobile vocabulary, they usually become English or near-English sooner than if they come in by way of literature: we have *chassis, chauffeur, garage, detour*. Words that come in through and remain in literary, scholarly, or "polite" circles change more slowly, in both spelling and pronunciation: *tête-à-tête, faux pas, nouveau riche, laissez-faire*.

2. *Use of borrowed words.*
a — Italics. Words which have not been completely anglicized are printed in italics in magazines and books and should be underlined in copy. Formal writers tend to use more italics; General, fewer. There are always many words on the borderline which will be found sometimes in italics, sometimes not. Consult a recent dictionary for doubtful words — remembering that it represents conservative usage.
b — Accent and other marks. In books and magazines, words recently taken in from French are usually written with accent marks if they were so written in French. After a time the accents are usually dropped unless they are necessary to indicate pronunciation. *Matinee, melee, role* do not need marks; *blasé* does. Similarly *cañon* is now usually spelled *canyon*, but: *piñon*. A *cedilla shows that a *c* before *a* or *o* is pronounced /s/: *façade, soupçon*. General publications are more likely to drop accents marks (*expose, cliche*) than Formal ones (*exposé, cliché*).

In German all nouns are capitalized, and recent or infrequent borrowings from German are capitalized in English, particularly if they are still printed in italics (*Anschluss, Realpolitik, Weltanschauung*, but *hinterland, kindergarten, blitzkrieg*). The *umlaut can be replaced by an *e* after the vowel: *Mädchen* or *Maedchen*.
c — Plurals. English usually brings borrowed words into its own system of conjugation and declension, though some words change slowly, especially words used mainly in Formal writing. *Beaus* is now as common as *beaux*, and *tableaus* is gaining on *tableaux*. See *Plurals of nouns § 4.

A few French adjectives may keep both masculine and feminine forms: *blond, blonde; debonair, debonaire. Reference: *Chicago Manual*.

3. *Pronunciation.* For pronunciation of borrowed words, consult a dictionary. Because the speech sounds of one language differ from those of another, it is almost impossible for someone not thoroughly familiar with a language to speak it as a native does. If there is an established English pronunciation, it is preferable to the foreign one.

See *English language, *Latin and English, *Origin of words. References: Baugh; Mencken; Pyles; Thomas Pyles, *Words and Ways* of *American English* (New York: Random, 1952); Mary Serjeantson, *A History of Foreign Words in English* (London: Routledge, 1935); Kenyon and Knott, § 122; T. R. Palfrey, *Modern Language Journal*, April 1941, pp. 550–57.

Formal English

Form

Revision: The word or passage marked is too Formal for the subject or for the style of the rest of the essay. Revise, making it more General.

Formal English is the appropriate variety for discussions of ideas, for scientific and scholarly writing, for addresses to audiences of considerable education, for literary works that are intended for a somewhat restricted reading public. Its vocabulary includes many words that are not used in everyday speech, and its constructions are generally filled out, with none of the short cuts characteristic of *General and *Informal English. Formal English is not appropriate for ordinary writing, for accounts of personal experience, casual comment, and other sorts of writing intended for the general reading public. For discussion, see *Guide*, pp. 12–13, 20–23. See also *Academic writing. Other *Index* articles dealing with Formal usage include *Abbreviations, *Agreement, *Collective nouns, *Contractions, *Dates, *Gender, *Reference of pronouns.

Form-class words
See *Parts of speech.

former, first—latter, last
Traditionally, *former* and *latter* refer only to two units: ". . . the former called the latter 'little prig'"; and though, in fact, the use of *latter* with more than two is common enough to be Standard, conservative readers would prefer "the last named" in references like this one: ". . . the list of products . . . could include potassium, bromide, chlorine, caustic, and magnesium. The latter might become a very important lightweight metal . . ." (Glenn T. Seaborg, *Bulletin of the Atomic Scientists*, Jan. 1968).

First and *last* refer to items in a series, usually more than two:

The first president had set up a very informal organization.
His last act was to advise his family on their future.

Latest refers to a series that is still continuing (the latest fashions). *Last* refers either to the final item of a completed series (their last attempt was successful) or to the most recent item of a continuing series (the last election). *Latest* for *last* is archaic: his latest breath. See *last, latest.

Forms of discourse
For the last hundred years or so it has been conventional to divide

writing into four "forms of discourse" — narration, description, exposition, and argument. The chief value of this classification is that it emphasizes purpose as the controlling element in a piece of writing. Studying the forms one by one allows concentration on certain traits of content, organization, and style peculiar to each type. The categories are not, however, sharply distinct — description contributes to all, notably to narration; many essays which are primarily argumentative include long stretches of exposition; and so on.

formula

Although the Latin *formulae* is the preferred plural in Formal usage, *formulas* is more common in General writing. Either is acceptable.

Formulas

Every language has some fixed phrases that have become customary in certain situations: Once upon a time, Ladies and gentlemen, Good morning, How are you? How do you do? Best wishes, Dear Sir, Yours truly. Occasionally fresh substitutes can be found, but more often the attempt merely calls attention to itself. Such phrases, though stereotyped, are too useful to be called *trite, and they are not, as most trite expressions are, substitutes for some simpler locution. They should be used without apology and without embarrassment whenever they are needed. See *Idiom, *Subjunctives § 2a.

Fractions

Fractions are written in figures when they are attached to other figures (72¾) or are in a series that is being written in figures (½, ⅔, 1, 2, 4) or are in tables or reference matter. In consecutive writing they are usually written in words (In the local newspaper three fourths of the space was given to advertising, one eighth to news, and one eighth to miscellaneous matters). Hyphens may be used between the numerator and denominator if neither part itself contains a hyphen, and they should be used to avoid confusion (though *twenty seven eighths* probably means "twenty-seven eighths," it could mean "twenty seven-eighths"). But they are less used than formerly and are not used at all when the numerator has the value of an adjective (as in "He sold one half and kept the other"): seven tenths or seven-tenths.

Decimals are increasingly used in place of fractions in factual writing, since they are more flexible and may be more accurate: .7; .42; 3.14159.

See *Numbers.

Fragment

Frag

Revision: The construction marked is not a satisfactory sentence. Revise by joining it to a neighboring sentence, by making it grammatically complete, or by rewriting the passage.

A sentence fragment is a part of a sentence—usually a phrase or dependent clause—that is carelessly or ineffectively punctuated as a whole sentence. Unlike a minor sentence, which is also grammatically incomplete, a fragment is not rhetorically effective and is considered a careless error. The fragment is usually corrected by joining it to the preceding or the following sentence or by making it grammatically complete. Sometimes rewriting is the best solution.

Below, with suggested revisions, are common types of fragments—a prepositional phrase, a participial phrase, and two kinds of dependent clause, each punctuated as a sentence:

The northern part of the city is mainly residential. On the eastern outskirts are the oil refining plants. And to the south beaches and parks.
Revision: The northern part of the city is mainly residential. On the eastern outskirts are the oil refining plants and to the south beaches and parks.

For the first hour he discussed modern poetry. Praising especially Dylan Thomas and W. H. Auden.
Revision: For the first hour he discussed modern poetry, praising especially Dylan Thomas and W. H. Auden. Or: . . . discussed modern poetry. He gave special praise to Dylan Thomas. . . .

These days we keep hearing about power and freedom and how necessary it is for people to have power if they are to be free. Though when you ask exactly what power and freedom mean, you risk being attacked as an enemy of the people.
Revision: These days we keep hearing . . . if they are to be free. But when you ask. . . .

In an unexpectedly heavy turnout, over 80 percent of the citizens voted. A fact that shows how strongly they felt about the issue.
Revision: In an unexpectedly heavy turnout, . . . the citizens voted—a fact that shows. . . . Or: . . . This fact shows. . . .

See *Guide*, pp. 283–88; *Clauses; *Phrases.

Free modifiers
See *Restrictive and nonrestrictive.

freshman, freshmen
The modifier is *freshman,* not only before nouns with an obviously singular reference (a freshman student) but also before plural and abstract nouns (freshman courses, freshman orientation).

-ful, full
When the adjective *full* is used as a suffix to nouns of measure (*basketful, spoonful*) or of feeling or quality (*peaceful, sorrowful, soulful*), it has only one *l*. In the separate word, both *l*'s are kept (a basket full of apples).

The plural of nouns ending in *-ful* is usually made with *-s*: *spoonfuls, basketfuls.* When *full* is written as a separate word, the preceding noun is made plural: *spoons full, baskets full.*

Function words
See *Parts of speech.

further, farther
See *farther, further.

Fused sentence
A *fused* or *run-on sentence* is the name sometimes given to two grammatically complete sentences written with no mark of punctuation between them: If you ask me why I did it, I can only say that at the time it seemed the right thing to do [ ] that is my only explanation. Failing to signal the start of a new sentence usually results simply from carelessness. Compare *Comma fault.

Future tense
English has no specific verb form to express future time and instead uses a number of different phrases. Some examples are: I *am leaving* next week; He *sails* tomorrow; She *is to speak* on Saturday; He *is about to* resign; When I am elected, I *will make* an investigation; They *will try* to be on time; She *is going to* refuse. See *Tenses of verbs.

gap
Of the great variety of gaps that developed in the 1960's, the credibility gap was only the most notorious. Other major gaps included the missile gap, the intelligence gap, the communication gap, and the generation gap. Gaps could even be personal: one writer deplored Senator Eugene McCarthy's "great passion gap" (*Newsweek*, Sept. 21, 1970). See *Vogue words.

-ge, -ce
See *-ce, -ge.

Gender
Modern English does not have regular and distinctive endings for masculine, feminine, and neuter nouns, for articles and adjectives modifying them, or for many pronouns referring to them—grammatical gender. Instead, we call nouns masculine, feminine, or neuter according to the sex of their referents or to their lack of sex. We refer to the names of inanimate objects with *it*, to the names of males with *he*, females with *she*. We use *who* mainly for human beings, *which* and *what* for inanimate objects. Usually, then, in speaking of gender in English, we are talking about the choice of pronouns and about the meaning of words that govern that choice.

Some English nouns refer to living things of either sex (*parent*), some to one sex (*father*), some to the other (*mother*). Some names for animate beings imply no sex distinction (*friend*), though compounds allow the distinction to be made (*girl friend*). When we ignore the sex of an animal, we use *it* to refer to the noun that names the beast, just as we sometimes use *it* of a child. We have no pronoun meaning "either-he-or-she." Though a fair number of nouns have endings that distinguish gender (*actor, actress; alumnus, alumna; comedian, comedienne*), they remain an unsystematized minority.

*Personification (or animation) is possible as a figure of speech in both Formal and Informal English. In rather old-fashioned Formal styles, the sun may be *he*, the moon *she*. In Informal English, *she* sometimes replaces *it*, especially where affection or intimate concern in involved, as when a driver speaks of his car. See *he or she.

General English

General English is the great central strand of words and constructions in our language, lying between *Informal English and *Formal English. We find it in most of what we read—in newspapers, magazines, and books for general circulation. We hear it in most talks for general audiences, in news broadcasts, in discussions, and in conversation other than the chat of intimates. This main strand of Standard English is what most of us use most of the time. See *Guide*, pp. 13–25.

Genitive

1. *Signs of the genitive.* The genitive (or possessive) function in English is shown in four ways:

a—Apostrophe-*s* or apostrophe alone. Singular nouns that do not end in the sounds /s/ or /z/ and plural nouns that do not end in the letter *s* add apostrophe-*s: boy's, horse's, one's, England's, men's, children's, freshmen's.* After plural nouns ending in *-s*, only an apostrophe is used: workers' incomes, dogs' teeth, coaches' rules.

For singular nouns ending in /s/ or /z/, practice varies, as do the recommendations of the stylebooks that encourage systematic rules for the sake of consistency. The system proposed by the *Chicago Manual* calls for an apostrophe-*s* after all singular nouns except *Jesus, Moses*, classical names ending in *-es* (*Socrates, Xerxes*), and words like *conscience* and *goodness* before *sake*; these exceptions take an apostrophe only.

To indicate joint possession, the apostrophe is often added only to the second of two coordinate nouns: "Martha and George's son" (Diana Trilling, *Esquire*, Dec. 1963). In "Mary's and Tom's bicycles," separate objects are possessed, and an apostrophe-*s* is needed for each noun. References: *U.S. Style Manual*, pp. 70–71; *Chicago Manual*, pp. 129–30; Margaret Nicholson, *A Practical Style Guide for Authors and Editors* (New York: Holt, 1967), pp. 93–97.

b—The *of* genitive. Any genitive formed with an apostrophe or apostrophe-*s* can also be formed with an *of* phrase. The choice between the two will usually depend on considerations of rhythm, idiom, and the syntactical pressures of neighboring phrases and clauses. The *of* genitive is easier to work with when the noun in the genitive is to be modified by clauses or by other genitives. For example, both "the car's tires" and "the tires of the car" are acceptable, but if *car* is to be modified by the clause "that John used to drive," the *of* genitive is more lucid: the tires of the car that John used to drive (rather than: the car that John used to drive's tires). If we want to indicate that the car is John's, the *of* genitive avoids a perplexing succession of apostrophes: the tires of John's car (rather than: John's car's tires).

There is also a possible difference of meaning between the two forms. "Jane's picture" probably means a picture belonging to Jane, but it might mean a picture of Jane. "A picture of Jane" can only mean that Jane is represented in the picture. References: Bryant, pp. 50−51; Hall, pp. 202−07; Pooley, pp. 65−67.

c−Double genitive. Using the *of* genitive and apostrophe-*s* together is an English idiom of long and respectable standing. It is especially common in locutions beginning with *that* or *this* and usually has an informal flavor: that boy of Henry's; friends of my father's; hobbies of Anne's. It is useful in avoiding the ambiguity mentioned above: "Jane's picture" is resolved either as "that picture of Jane" or "that picture of Jane's." Reference: Bryant, pp. 74−75.

d−Genitive of the personal pronouns. The personal and relative pronouns have genitive forms without an apostrophe: *my, your, his, her, its, our, their, whose.* It is as important *not* to put apostrophes in these pronouns (and in the forms used without nouns: *ours, yours, theirs, hers*) as it is to put one in a noun in the genitive. See *Pronouns § 1; *its, it's; *which; *who, whom.

2. *Uses of the genitive.* The most common function of the genitive is to indicate possession: the professor's house, Al's dog, my daughter. It also indicates a number of other relationships:

Description: a man's job, children's toys, suit of wool

Doer of an act (the "subjective genitive"): the wind's force, the force of the wind; John Knowles's second novel; with the dean's permission, with the permission of the dean; (the subjective genitive usual with gerunds) the doctor's coming relieved the strain. See *Gerunds.

Recipient of an act (the "objective genitive"): the policeman's murderer, the murderer of the policeman; the bill's defeat

Adverb: He drops in of an evening.

More details of these and other genitive relations will be found in the large grammars. References: Curme, *Parts of Speech*, pp. 133−36, *Syntax*, pp. 70−88; Fries, *AEG*, pp. 72−88; Jespersen, *MEG*, VI, 281−98; Bryant, pp. 93−94.

Gerunds

1. *Form and use.* A gerund−also called a verbal noun−is the *-ing* form of a verb used as a noun. It can serve in any noun function: as subject of a verb (*Seeing* him pleased her), as object of a verb (He taught *dancing*), as object of a preposition (The odds are against your *winning*), or as a predicate complement (Seeing is *believing*). Like a noun, a gerund may be modified by an adjective (Good *boxing* was rare) or may be used as a modifier (a *fishing* boat, a *living* wage). Yet since it retains some of the characteristics of a verb, it can take a subject and an object and be modified by an adverb: One despairs of the author [subject] ever [adverb] *constructing* a really forceful play [object].

A gerund may be in the present or the perfect tense and in the active or passive voice: *seeing, having seen; being seen, having been seen.*

Though the gerund has the same form as the present participle, it differs in use:

Gerund: Running a hotel appealed to him. (*Running* is the subject.)
Participle: He was busy running a hotel. (*Running* modifies *he.*)

2. *Subject of a gerund.* The subject of a gerund is sometimes in the genitive and sometimes in the accusative or objective (in nouns, the "common") case. Formal writing uses the genitive more than General writing does: "Such a view leads to the metaphor's becoming a brief poem in itself . . ." (Alex Page, *Modern Philology*, Feb. 1969). General uses the accusative more often: "The Vice President's humorous remarks about Hofstra not picking up this ball are somewhat offset . . . by the record" (Clifford Lord, *College Board Review,* Summer 1970).

Since the case of the subjects of gerunds is often a worry, some general points may prove useful:
a—When the subject is a personal noun or pronoun, the genitive is more common than with impersonal subjects: They wanted to discuss *my going* AWOL; We overlooked *Joe's* swearing. When the subject is a personal pronoun and begins the sentence, the genitive is required: *Our* [not *Us*] *worrying* won't solve anything; *His* [not *Him*] *lying* deceived nobody.
b—If the subject is a plural noun, it is likely to be in the accusative case even if it refers to persons: I don't approve of *men drinking* or *women smoking.*
c—If the subject is abstract or the name of an inanimate object, it is most often in the common (accusative or objective) form: It was a case of *imagination getting* out of hand; The city was seized without a *shell being* fired.

3. *Phrases with gerunds.* Gerunds are often used in phrases that function somewhat like subordinate clauses: *In coming to an agreement*, they had compromised on all points; *By learning to read*, he embarrassed his father. The relation of the gerund phrase to the word it modifies should be immediately apparent; the reader should not have to pause to make sure just what the writer intended:

Dangling: In coming to an agreement, a compromise had to be voted. (The compromise did not come to an agreement; the voters did.)

Dangling: After sleeping sixteen hours, my headache was finally gone.
Revision: After sleeping sixteen hours, I was finally rid of my headache.

See *Dangling modifiers.

4. *Without* the. In current style there is a tendency to use gerunds without *the* and with a direct object rather than an *of* phrase. This emphasizes the verbal force of the word and makes for economy:

His chief amusement is telling jokes on the President.
Rather than: . . . the telling of jokes. . . .

In revising the first draft, a writer can check all the spellings.
Rather than: In the revising of the first draft. . . .

5. *Idioms with gerunds.* Some words are characteristically followed by gerunds, others by infinitives. For example:

Gerunds	*Infinitives*
can't help *doing*	compelled *to do*
capable of *painting*	able *to paint*
the habit of *giving*	the tendency *to give*
an idea of *selling*	a wish *to sell*
enjoys *playing*	likes *to play*

With many common words, either is used: the way *of doing* something, the way *to do* something.

Compare *Participles, *Infinitives. Reference: Curme, *Syntax,* Ch. 24.

get, got

Either *got* or *gotten* is acceptable as the past participle of *get* except in the following senses:

Got (not *gotten*) is often added to *has* or *have* to emphasize the notion of "possess" (I haven't got a cent) or of "must" (You have got to lend me a dollar). Though seldom used in Formal writing, the emphatic *got* is not uncommon in General: "A lot of adults are bored by Bach because they haven't got the faintest idea of what music is about" (Marya Mannes, *TV Guide,* March 25, 1966). References: Albert H. Marckwardt, *CE,* Feb. 1955, pp. 309–10; Thomas L. Crowell, *AS,* Dec. 1959, pp. 280–86; Bryant, 95–98.

get up

See *rise, arise, get up.

go

Go, in the sense "become," is used as a *linking verb in a number of idioms. While some (*go broke, go native, go straight*) are at most Informal to General, others (*go blind, go lame*) are fully established in all varieties. *Go and,* as an intensive with no actual motion implied, is common in speech and turns up in some General writing: ". . . he has gone and made a genuine commercial film . . ." (Joseph Morgenstern, *Newsweek,* April 22, 1968). *Going for* in the sense "working to the advantage of" is General: "What they had going for them were an attractive temporary theater . . ., a large, reportedly enthusiastic audience . . ." (Richard Gilman, *Holiday*, June 1966). Neither *go and* nor *going for* in these senses is appropriate in Formal writing.

Gobbledygook

Maury Maverick, a Congressman from Texas, coined the term *gobbledygook* for wordy, pompous, overweight prose that confuses and irritates more than it informs. Although government bureaus have produced their full share of examples, business, the military, the social sciences, and the humanities have shown an equal weakness for inflated *jargon. See *Big words; *Guide*, pp. 363–64.

good, well

Good is usually an adjective in Standard English; *well* is either an adjective or an adverb. "I feel good" and "I feel well" (adjectives) are both usual but have different meanings, *good* implying actual bodily sensation, *well* referring merely to a state, "not ill." In Nonstandard usage, *good* takes the place of *well*: He played good; She sings good. Adverbial *good* is also heard in Informal speech and frequently appears in printed representations of speech: "She's running good now," the mechanic said. And adverbial *good* is sometimes used deliberately for stylistic effect in General writing: ". . . the underlying passion of this book is . . . to promise the vested idiots of the book reviews that he can write as good as anyone who writes a book review" (Norman Mailer, *Esquire*, July 1963).

got, gotten

See *get, got.

graduate

The idiom *to be graduated from* an institution has generally gone out of use except in Formal and somewhat archaic writing and has been replaced by *graduated from*: He graduated from Yale in 1950. Omitting the *from* is Nonstandard: He graduated high school in 1969. Reference: Bryant, pp. 102–03.

Grammar

Grammar has several different senses. Just as the word *history* can mean a field of study, events in the past, or the book that describes those events, so *grammar* can refer to (1) a field of study, (2) a set of abilities in our brains, or (3) the book that describes those abilities.

1. As a field of study, grammar is as old as intellectual inquiry itself. The pre-Socratic philosophers in Greece in the sixth century B.C. had begun speculating on language and words (*grammar* comes from *grammatikos*—one who understands the use of letters) long before the Stoics in 300 B.C. singled grammar out as a field separate from rhetoric and poetics. Since then scholars have continued to study the structure of language, not only because language is the central defining characteristic of man but because it seems possible that the very foundations of our knowledge and thought—perhaps even perception itself—are shaped by the grammatical structures of our language. The study of grammar thus becomes an entry to the study of mind.

2. *Grammar* may also refer to this capacity of mind, the ability every normal human being possesses to speak and understand sentences. Thus we all have a grammar in our heads. Every human being understands an indefinite number of new sentences he has never heard before. He can recognize grammatical and ungrammatical sentences (see *grammatical, ungrammatical § 1). He can recognize sentences which are ambiguous in several different ways. He also understands that some sentences relate to other sentences, as this one does to the next two. That some sentences relate to other sentences is also understood by him. It is also understood by him that some sentences relate to other sentences.

The goal of a linguist, a scholar who studies grammatical structure, is to describe in a written grammar this tacit knowledge, this internalized grammar, that all of us share.

3. Though the formal aspects of language have been studied for over 2500 years, linguists are debating more strenuously than ever before both what questions linguists should concern themselves with and how their answers should be formulated in written grammars. At the risk of gross overgeneralization, it can be said that the history of linguistic study in the last hundred years falls into three schools. We shall limit our consideration to these three, because they are now present in a good many English curricula in this country.

a—Classical/traditional. Although this rather arbitrary label is applied to a great variety of approaches, most of the grammars start with semantic definitions for parts of speech and the inflections that are associated with them: nouns are names of persons, places, and things, etc. Once the parts of speech have been described, the grammar describes functions: subjects, verbs, objects, modifiers, etc. The definitions are illustrated by examples. The reader of the grammar is expected to understand the labeling through the descriptions and examples and then to use his native knowledge of the language to apply the label in any new sentence that might contain the pattern. For example:

A sentence adverb modifies a whole sentence rather than any individual word or construction. It usually stands at the beginning of the sentence, though it may occur elsewhere: *Fortunately*, he left; He is *allegedly* still here; No one cares, *obviously*.

Confronted with the sentence "*Apparently*, she left," you could identify *apparently* as a sentence adverb on the basis of the explanation and examples. Such descriptions—semantically based as they are—require the ability of a native speaker to make them work. References: Curme, *Parts of Speech, Syntax;* Long.

b—Structural-descriptive. When, in the early part of this century, anthropologists began to deal more and more with languages that had no written form and were totally unrelated to the Indo-European languages already well-known, a new approach to the structure of the language emerged in this country. It had antecedents in the work of the nineteenth-century French linguist Ferdinand de Saussure and was later influenced by a group of linguists at Prague; but it took its attitude from the problems encountered by field workers trying to decode unknown languages for which there were no written documents and whose grammars were too different from Indo-European languages to allow the investigator to guess what their structures might be.

These linguists, variously called structuralists or descriptivists, tried to devise a set of purely formal and objective techniques for discovering the structure of a language almost entirely from the physical, acoustical signal, techniques that explicitly avoided any reference to lexical meaning. First they identified groups of sounds that native speakers of the language responded to as psychologically the same. (We, for example, respond to the class of /t/ sounds in *eighth, ten, Bertram,* and *button* as "sames" even though we pronounce them in different parts of the mouth and they are thus objectively different sounds.) The linguists then tried to discover units of meaning, ignoring the specific lexical content of these units. Units were grouped into higher classes on the basis of which units occurred next to which other units. In English, for example, *book, house, car,* and *idea* are classed as nouns not because they are names of persons, places, things, and so on but because they all occur before the plural unit of meaning and before the genitive unit of meaning: book, books, book's; house, houses, house's. Once the parts of speech were classified, higher order syntactic sequences were identified (noun–verb, verb–noun, preposition–noun, adjective–noun, etc.) and then further described functionally (subject–predicate, verb–object, modifier–head, etc.). A rough approximation of this technique can be found in the *Parts of speech article. References: Francis; Sledd.

c – Transformational-generative. Through the 1940's and most of the 1950's, structural grammars were thought to be the new wave in English language education. Then in 1957 Noam Chomsky, a linguist at the Massachusetts Institute of Technology, published *Syntactic Structures* and revolutionized the study of language. Chomsky turned linguists away from formal discovery procedures, which he claimed were largely useless, and toward a model of language that tries to account for all the abilities of a native speaker in a set of rules that, loosely speaking, create sentences along with their grammatical structures. A brief description of a transformational grammar is given in the *Guide*, pp. 268–76.

In recent years transformational grammars have virtually replaced structural grammars in scholarly research into English. There are adherents to schools of linguistics other than transformational – tagmemic grammars, stratificational grammars, dependency grammars, and others. But generally speaking the dominant model for research into English structure is provided by transformational-generative linguists. References: Jacobs and Rosenbaum; Williams.

4. So far, we have ignored what may be the most common meaning of *grammar*, the meaning we associate with the word from junior-high-school days. This is *grammar* in the sense of "good grammar"—not splitting infinitives, choosing *who* or *whom*, *shall* or *will*, avoiding prepositions at the ends of sentences, and so on. This is *grammar* in its normative sense. It concentrates only on those areas where usage varies from one social class to another or from the way English teachers think educated people speak to the way their students speak.

The varieties of English are sketched in the *Guide*, pp. 8–19. How we communicate depends on our social class, our geographical roots, the social situation we happen to be in, and our mode of communication—speaking or writing. What most traditionalists teach as grammar are those features that allegedly distinguish written, fairly formal, supposedly upper-middle-class usage from all other varieties. We make a serious mistake if we assume that this form of usage alone defines "correct" usage.

Thus when you use the word *grammar*, you have to distinguish a variety of senses:

1) Grammar is a field of scholarly inquiry dating back beyond Aristotle.

2) A grammar of a language is in the mind of every speaker of that language. Its "real" nature is entirely inaccessible to direct observation.

3) A grammar of a language is that set of rules which can be written down and which will generate the sentences of that language along with a description of each sentence. The object of this grammar is to "model" or explain grammar in sense (2).

4) Grammar in the sense of "He uses good grammar" is the ability we have acquired that allows us to demonstrate that we can observe certain usages that allegedly characterize "educated" upper-middle-class speakers.

5) A grammar of good usage is the list of the prescriptions found in grammar books—usually fewer than twenty or thirty—that allow someone aspiring to membership in the "educated" community to speak as those already in that community allegedly speak.

The last two senses of *grammar* are, unfortunately, the senses most familiar to American students. The associations that cluster about those senses make it very difficult for linguists to communicate the excitement of discovering something about grammar (sense 2) that he can write down in a grammar (sense 3) that reveals the elegantly complex organization of human linguistic knowledge.

grammatical, ungrammatical

Sentences can be grammatical in two senses:

1. Sentences are grammatical when they meet the structural requirements of the grammar used by an individual speaker. "Can't nobody tell me what to do" is ungrammatical for some speakers, but it is grammatical for others, if the grammar they have incorporated into their nervous systems allows them to construct that sentence for ordinary conversation (see *Grammar § 2). "Nobody can tell me what to do" might, conversely, be ungrammatical for those speakers who habitually put the *modal auxiliary and negative first but grammatical for those who do not. In this sense, *grammatical* simply describes the structure of a sentence that is acceptable for use by a particular speaker in his ordinary discourse. And in this sense nobody, except by mistake or by intention, utters an ungrammatical sentence. For example, the made-up sentence "I know the man who and the woman left" is ungrammatical for all speakers of English.

2. Sentences are also said to be grammatical when they meet the structural requirements of the grammar used by those who set the linguistic standards of usage. In this sense, "Can't nobody tell me what to do" is ungrammatical for everyone, and those who might habitually and unselfconsciously say it are speaking ungrammatical English. But in this case it must be called sociologically ungrammatical—that is, social behavior that is unacceptable to those whose judgments often carry the most weight in our stratified society. In many cases, advice based on this sense of *grammatical* can be quite accurate: most educated people in this country do not say "Can't nobody tell me what to do"; in writing, most make their subjects and verbs agree; most avoid *ain't* in all but relatively informal situations. On the other hand, rules for sociologically grammatical usage also involve a good deal of folklore, as many of the articles in this *Index* make clear.

References: William Labov, *The Study of Nonstandard English*, rev. ed. (Champaign, Ill.: NCTE, 1970); Archibald A. Hill, "Grammaticality," in *Readings in Applied Linguistics*, ed. Harold B. Allen, 2nd ed. (New York: Appleton, 1964); Noam Chomsky, "Some Methodological Remarks on Generative Grammar," ibid., pp. 173–92.

Group words

In English many groups of two or more words (that is, phrases) function like single words. Often the division of the elements into separate words in print is quite arbitrary. *High school* is not the noun *school* modified by the adjective *high* so much as a noun in its own right just as *highway* is; but traditionally the first is spelled as two words, the second as one. Many of our verbs are made up of a verb plus an adverb: *close up, hold off, look into;* many prepositions are phrases: *according to, in opposition to.* Other typical group words are:

Nouns: hay fever, back door, holding company, home run, safety razor, baby blue, school year, sacrifice hit

Verbs: dig in, back water, flare up, follow through, follow up, show up, blow up

Prepositions: in spite of, in consequence of, previous to, due to

In this book we ignore the superficial difference between a part of speech written as a single word and one that is written as a group of words. *Noun* or *verb* or *preposition* refers both to single words and to group words functioning as noun or verb or preposition. References: Curme, *Syntax*, Ch. 30; George P. Krapp, *The Knowledge of English* (New York: Holt, 1927), pp. 313–16, where such phrases are called "function groups."

guess

Formal usage limits *guess* to its senses of "conjecture, estimate, surmise": "The employers can only guess whom the victims will choose to sue" (Henry L. Woodward, *Yale Law Journal*, March 1967). But in General and Informal usage *guess* is common in its looser senses of "think, suppose, believe": ". . . I guess I should feel sorry that I have no simple solution . . ." (Tom Prideaux, *Life*, Jan. 29, 1965).

Habitual action

Habitual action is expressed in English in a variety of ways, of which these are samples:

He comes home every weekend.
He came home every weekend.
He would always come home on weekends.
He used to come home weekends.
He usually came home weekends.

had better, had rather

Had better is the usual idiom in giving advice or an indirect command: You had better take care of that cold; You'd better go. The assimilation of the *d* in *you'd* to the *b* of *better* has given rise to the Informal construction without either *had* or *'d*: "But I better get with it if I'm going to be a TV viewer . . ." (Goodman Ace, *Saturday Review*, Dec. 25, 1965).

Had rather and *would rather* are both used to express preference: He would rather ski than eat; He had rather ski than eat. Use whichever seems more natural. In speech both *had* and *would* contract to *'d*: He'd rather ski than eat. Reference: Bryant, pp. 104–05.

half

Though *a half* is traditionally considered the more elegant of the two idioms, little distinction can be found between *a half* and *half a* in current Formal and General usage:

. . . it makes one wonder about the beneficence of Wantage's rural experiments a half century earlier. — David Spring, *American Historical Review*, Jan. 1967

. . . the task of recording, analyzing, and interpreting an age . . . nearly half a century removed. . . . — Roy F. Nichols, ibid.

A half a (a half an hour) is an Informal redundancy.

The number of the noun accompanying *half* or *half of* in a subject determines the number of the verb: Half of the book is . . . ; Half the men are. . . .

hanged, hung

In Formal English the principal parts of *hang* when referring to the death penalty are *hang, hanged, hanged,* the archaic forms kept alive in legal phrases such as "hanged by the neck until dead." In other senses they are *hang, hung, hung:* people are hanged, pictures are hung.

General and Informal usage often ignores this distinction, using *hang, hung, hung* in all senses: "Of course, McCarthy hung himself at the hearing" (Isidore Silver, *New Republic,* Nov. 20, 1965).

hardly

See *Double negative § 2.

have

1. *Auxiliary. Have* occurs most frequently in the perfect tenses, for which it is now the sole auxiliary in English (in earlier English *be* was also so used). *Have* plus a past participle makes the perfect tense (They have come); *shall have* or *will have* plus a past participle makes the future perfect tense (They will have gone by then); *had* plus a past participle makes the past perfect (They had gone to the beach before we arrived). In this use it is a function word—a signal of tense. See *Tenses of verbs.

2. *Independent meaning.* As a verb of independent meaning *have* means "own, possess" in a literal sense (have a car) or a transferred sense (have the measles). Because *have* occurs so frequently as an "empty" auxiliary word, its meaning as an independent word is often reinforced by *got* (see *get, got).

3. *Contractions. He, she, it has* contract to *he's, she's, it's* (He's not tried to in years; It's rained for a week). Contractions with *has* and *is* are indistinguishable: *He's gone* may be *He has gone* or *He is gone. I, you, we, they have* contract to *I've, you've, we've, they've.* Both *had* and *would* contract to *'d* (They'd already spoken; She'd already be waiting).

Would have, wouldn't have are sometimes written *would of, wouldn't of,* an unacceptable transcription of what is spoken as *would've, wouldn't've.*

4. *Had ought. Had ought* and *hadn't ought* occur frequently in speech. *Hadn't ought* (He hadn't ought to lie like that) is regional and Informal. *Had ought* (He had ought to take better care of himself) is a common Nonstandard idiom, sometimes heard in Informal speech. Reference: E. Bagby Atwood, *A Survey of Verb Forms in the Eastern United States* (Ann Arbor: Univ. of Michigan Press, 1953).

5. *Have to.* *Have to* and *must* are nearly synonymous in the affirmative (I *have to* [or *must*] go now), but in the negative there is a difference (I don't have to go; I mustn't go). *Have to* has the advantage that it can be conjugated in all tenses.

6. *Other idioms.* For *have got,* see *get, got. See also *had better, had rather.

Headword, head

A headword, or head, is a word modified by another word, especially a noun modified by one or more adjectives (his first long *sleep*), a verb modified by one or more adverbs (*walk* carefully), or an adjective or adverb modified by qualifiers (very *old,* more *intelligently*). The term is used differently by different linguists but always to mean the word around which the rest of the construction is built: *men,* old *men,* very old *men,* very old *men* in raincoats, very old *men* in raincoats who had been waiting outside. References: Paul Roberts, *Patterns of English* (New York: Harcourt, 1956), pp. 77–105; Long, p. 490; Sledd, pp. 226–27; Whitehall, pp. 9–18.

healthful, healthy

The distinction between *healthful* "conducive to health" (places and foods are healthful) and *healthy* "having good health" (persons and animals are healthy) is maintained in Formal and some General writing, but by and large *healthy* is now used for both meanings.

help but

See *cannot help but, cannot seem to.

hence

See *Conjunctive adverbs.

he or she

The plural pronoun *they* does not indicate sex, but *he, she,* and *it* are masculine, feminine, and neuter. Conventionally, *he* is used with indefinite pronouns like *anyone* and *everyone* and with noun antecedents that may refer to either men or women: Every student must accept responsibility for his acts. Sometimes antecedents make a masculine pronoun inappropriate and the double pronoun *he or she* or *his or her* convenient: "In enabling a young man or woman to prepare for life in a shorter period of time, we direct his or her attention to other values" (Edward H. Litchfield, *Saturday Review,* Dec. 15, 1962).

In most cases, however, *he or she* is unnecessarily awkward: "Unfortunately, sometimes a reader misses a column of personal interest, simply because it has appeared when he (or she) is out of town . . ." (P. J. Steincrohn, syndicated columnist, Oct. 3, 1970). When *he* will not do, *they* is a frequent choice in General writing: In helping a young man or woman to prepare for life . . . , we direct their attention to other values. Reference: Evans and Evans, "his" and "they."

highbrow

After a period of overuse, *highbrow* and *lowbrow* settled down as useful General words. *Middlebrow*, a more recent coinage, has also made its way: "Both highbrows and lowbrows have ferocious champions, and the middlebrows, as become them, have milder ones" (David Cort, *Columbia Forum*, Spring 1961).

himself, herself

Himself and *herself* are used in two ways:

1. As reflexive pronouns, referring to the subject of the sentence: George has always taken himself too seriously; She looked at herself in the window.

2. As qualifiers, for emphasis: He told me so himself; I looked up, and there was the captain himself.
Compare *myself, *self.

historic, historical

Unlike many pairs of adjectives ending in -*ic* and -*ical, historic* and *historical* ordinarily have quite different meanings. *Historic* usually has the sense "important in history, noteworthy, famous": ". . . a historic act: the toast to the French fleet by which the archbishop . . . urged French Catholics to abandon royalist opposition . . ." (James E. Ward, *American Historical Review*, Oct. 1967). *Historical* is much more neutral, meaning "based on the facts of history," "having occurred in the past," "suitable for study by historians or using their methods": "This autobiography . . . provides a wide range of historical persons and events" (Heinz E. Ellersieck, ibid.).

Homonyms

Words of different meanings that are pronounced alike (*bear–bare, plain–plane*) are called homonyms (or homophones). English has a great many such pairs of words that have developed for various reasons. Some Old English words once different in sound have come to be pronounced alike because of changes in form through the centuries: *bear* (the animal) from *bera; bear* (the verb) from *beran. Plain* and *plane* both go back to Latin *planus,* but the spelling of *plain* was altered in coming through Old French. Many words are from different languages, having acquired similar forms by accident. *Rest* meaning "peace" is from Old English, *rest* meaning "remainder" from French; *bark* of a tree is from Scandinavian, *bark* the vessel a more recent borrowing from French-Italian.

There is little chance of misunderstanding such words because the context will tell which is which—though their similarity is often exploited in puns. Where real ambiguity arises, usage has commonly resolved the problem by dropping one or both words: the noun *quean* meaning "a wench" lost currency because the confusion with *queen* was intolerable. But homophones like *plain – plane, assent – ascent, piece – peace, born – borne* make a good deal of trouble in spelling.

Two or more words that are spelled alike but are of different derivation or meaning or pronunciation are called homographs. The verb *bow* (They had to bow in the emperor's presence) and the noun *bow* for the forward part of a ship are both homographs and homonyms. Reference: Bolinger, pp. 159 – 61.

hope

The phrases *in* [*the*] *hope of* and *in hopes of* are used interchangeably:

The Intruder blindly drops bombs . . . in hopes of disturbing the airlift. — William Hedgepeth, *Look*, April 1, 1969

The commission is planning to study . . . the whole range of foundation activities, in the hope of warding off ill-considered regulatory action. — Irwin Ross, *Fortune*, June 1969

hopefully

From an adverb with the established meaning "in a hopeful way, full of hope" (The dog waited hopefully for a handout), *hopefully* became a vogue word meaning "it is hoped": "Hopefully, they will reveal the thickness of the planet's polar ice cap . . ." (Jonathan Spivak, *Wall Street Journal*, July 13, 1965). Sometimes it means no more than "I hope": Hopefully she'll be down in a minute.

So long as it is kept away from the verb and set off by commas, there is little chance of real ambiguity; but prejudice against the usage remains: ". . . [*hopefully*] correctly means *in a hopeful way*, not, as often misused, *it is hoped*" (*Columbia Journalism Review*, Summer 1965).

Hours

In consecutive writing, especially if it is Formal, hours are written in words: at four o'clock; around five fifteen. In newspapers and in much General writing, figures are used, especially if several times are mentioned and always in designations of time with *a.m.* and *p.m.*: at 4 p.m., just after 9 a.m., around 4:30 p.m., from 10 to 12. See *a.m. and p.m., *Numbers § 1b. See also *Period § 2d.

however

Though particularly appropriate as a connective in the fully developed sentences of Formal style, *however* is also the most common *conjunctive adverb in General writing:

Murder is usually reported, and 86 per cent of all reported murders lead to arrests. Among those arrested, however, only 64 per cent are prosecuted. . . . — Ramsey Clark, *Saturday Review*, Sept. 19, 1970

However is more maneuverable than *but;* it can either introduce the clause it modifies or, as in the example, follow the words the writer wants to emphasize ("Among those arrested"). To introduce a clause in General writing, *but* is often the better choice.

Humor

See *Epigrams and aphorisms, *Malapropisms, *Puns, *Spoonerisms.

hung, hanged

See *hanged, hung.

Hyperbole

This very common figure of speech—obvious and extravagant over-statement—is a staple of humor; but we also use hyperbole regularly in ordinary conversation when we describe our troubles as *incredible,* our embarrassments as *horrible,* an evening as *fabulous.* Such efforts to dramatize and intensify rapidly cease to have any effect, including the hyperbolic. They are particularly tiresome in writing. See *Counter words, *Qualifiers.

Hypercorrectness

Hypercorrect forms are used by speakers and writers who think their language is mistaken and extend the patterns of supposed correctness beyond their established limits. Perhaps the most common is the use of *I* for *me* in a compound object: It is a wonderful moment for my wife and I; They invited Jack and I; between you and I. Other common hypercorrect forms include *whom* for *who* (He is critical of the other members of the committee, whom he feels spend more time making accusations than solving problems), *as* for *like* (She, as any other normal person, wanted to be well thought of), the ending *-ly* where it does not belong (Slice thinly), some verb forms (*lie* for *lay, shall* for *will*), and many pronunciations, especially of place names. Hypercorrect forms are also called hyperurbanisms. References: Jespersen, *Language,* pp. 293–95; Robert J. Menner, *AS,* Oct. 1937, pp. 167–68; Margaret Schlauch, *The Gift of Language* (New York: Dover, 1955), pp. 264–68; Bloomfield, index references under *hyperforms.*

Hyphen

The most common use of the hyphen is to mark the division of a word at the end of a line of manuscript or type (see *Division of words). Other uses are in part a matter of style, with Formal writers tending to use more hyphens than General writers.

Compound words are written as two words (*post office*), as one word (*notebook*), or as a combination of words joined by hyphens (*mother-in-law*). In most cases, questions about compound words can be quickly resolved by a good recent dictionary. The general trend is away from hyphenation, toward one-word spelling. Even when a prefix ends and a root word begins with the same vowel, the current tendency is to write the word solid: *cooperate, reelect, preeminent.*

A number of compound adjective forms are conventionally

hyphened when they precede a noun. The ones most commonly used are given in dictionaries. Most of them are an adverb plus a verbal (*clear-eyed, able-bodied, easy-going*); and other phrases formed on this pattern are hyphened when the adverb does not end in *-ly*: a late-flowering iris, slow-moving goods, a well-marked trail (but: a plainly marked trail).

Usage is divided on hyphening noun phrases used as modifiers, as in "seventeenth century philosophy." Formal writers prefer *seventeenth-century;* General, *seventeenth century.*

Occasionally a pair of modifiers is ambiguous without a hyphen: "a light yellow scarf" may be either a scarf that is light yellow or a light scarf that is yellow. *Light-yellow* is safest for the first meaning, and *light, yellow* for the second. Similarly, "new car-owner" might be distinguished from "new-car owner."

A numeral as part of a modifier (5-cent item, nine-inch boards) is hyphened, and a hyphen is used between a prefix and a proper name: *pre-Sputnik, pro-Nixon.*

A hyphen may be used to carry the force of a modifier over to a later noun ("suspension hyphen"): In both thirteenth- and fourteenth-century texts; the third-, fourth-, and fifth-grade rooms.

The conclusion one comes to after reviewing current habits in the use of the hyphen was well put by John Benbow in *Manuscript and Proof,* stylebook of Oxford University Press of New York: "If you take the hyphen seriously you will surely go mad." The best advice for a writer is to consult a recent dictionary when in doubt about hyphens and to use them as consistently as possible.

References: Regina Hoover, CCC, May 1971, pp. 156–60; *Chicago Manual; U.S. Style Manual;* Summey, Ch. 10; and discussion in recent dictionaries.

The pronoun *I* is still written as a capital simply because in the old manuscripts a small *i* might have been lost or attached to a neighboring word; the capital helped keep it distinct. The notion that *I* should not be the first word in a sentence is groundless. *I* should be used wherever it is needed, though if it opens several consecutive sentences the repetition becomes irksome. Circumlocutions to get around the natural use of *I* are usually awkward and are likely to attract attention to themselves: "My present thinking is that relief projects are unsound" is a clumsy way of saying "I think now [or "I think" or "I have come to think" or "At the moment I think"] that relief projects are unsound."

The best way to avoid conspicuous use of *I* is to keep it out of emphatic positions in the sentence, particularly the beginning. An introductory phrase or clause will throw the stress off the *I:* "After a long struggle I decided to go," instead of "I struggled for hours to make up my mind and finally decided that I would go." See *It's me, *myself, *we.

ibid.

See *Abbreviations § 2; *Guide*, p. 422.

-ible

See *-able, -ible.

Idiom

Id

Revision: The expression marked is not Standard idiom. Revise it, referring to an article in this Index *or to a dictionary if you are not sure of the correct form.*

Idioms are phrases that are established in the language but are not easy to explain grammatically or logically. Some examples are "in good stead," "come in handy," "strike a bargain," "look up an old friend," "many's the time," "make good," "in respect to." We learn these phrases as individual units, and if we are native speakers, most of them cause us no trouble. No native speaker is likely to say "the time is many" or "hit a bargain" or "look down an old friend" (though "track down"—another idiom—might be a sound substitute). Many idioms are completely frozen: you can use thousands of words as subjects and verbs of sentences, but you can't substitute any other adjective in the phrase "in good stead."

We have trouble with idioms we have not learned, and most commonly the error is in the choice of preposition. Because we know *conform to*, we may speak of a policy that is "in conformity to public opinion"; but the idiom is "in conformity with." In using the Formal word *arise*, we might attach the preposition *off* instead of the *from* idiom demands. Because logic is no help, the prepositions must be learned in the phrases that determine their usage. Dictionaries generally show the preposition that is conventionally used with particular words. Sometimes usage is divided. See *agree to, agree with; *different; *Gerunds § 5; *it; *Prepositions § 2a; *Subjunctives § 2a; *Verb—adverb combinations.

i.e.

See *Abbreviations § 2.

if, whether

Writers have a choice between *if* and *whether* before interrogative clauses (direct questions) and clauses expressing doubt or uncertainty. *Whether* is almost always chosen in Formal contexts:

. . . it is appropriate to ask whether these decisions are to be considered a victory for those who champion individual rights. . . .—Wayne F. LaFave, *Supreme Court Review*, 1967

One wonders whether Aconcio's flight . . . may have brought suspicion . . . upon his patron.—Lynn White, Jr., *American Historical Review*, Jan. 1967

Both words are used in General writing, but *if* is more common:

The survey first asked people if TV made them feel more opposed to the war or not. — *Newsweek*, July 10, 1967

. . . he never determined if these were true or not. — John Thompson, *New York Review of Books*, April 28, 1961

Whether is required, however, when the clause begins a sentence (Whether it rains or shines . . .), is the object of a preposition (The question of whether . . .), modifies a noun (The question whether . . .), or follows *be* (The question is whether . . .). See *as if, as though; *like, as.

illiterate

Both *illiterate* and *literate* are used in a wider and narrower sense: "(in)capable of reading and writing"; "(un)acquainted with what is written — hence (un)educated." Usage called Nonstandard in this book is often loosely referred to as illiterate.

ill, sick

See *sick, ill.

illusion, allusion, delusion

Illusion, "a deceptive appearance" (The oasis turned out to be a mirage, an optical illusion), is sometimes confused with *allusion*, "a reference to something" (In *Paradise Lost* Milton makes many biblical allusions). A *delusion* is a self-deception: He suffered from delusions of perfection.

Imagery

An image is a word or group of words that makes an appeal to one of the senses: sight (*shiny, ghostly, mist, slime, green, thick brown hair*), hearing (*creaking, faraway shouts, the pounding of surf*), taste (*salty, dry, a pickled pear*), smell (*jasmine, fresh paint, a blown-out candle*), touch (*smooth, glassy, razor sharp*), and the muscular tension known as the kinesthetic sense (*squirm, jerky, jogging heavily along*). Though a word may appeal to more than one sense (*glassy, ghostly mist*), in a specific context one is usually dominant.

Imagery is especially characteristic of poetry, in which the content or activity of the mind is often rendered concretely, thought manifested in things. But even in expository prose that is primarily intellectual, most writers keep in close touch with the visible and tangible world:

The first attempt of men to live collectively under the rule of reason ended in the bloodletting of the French Revolution. This was a sorry disappointment to liberals, but they accommodated it to their thesis by arguing that rational behavior could not be expected to sprout overnight from soil that had for centuries been eroded and poisoned by injustice and oppression. — Reinhold Niebuhr, *The Search for America*

Studying the images in a writer's work will usually show what has impressed him in his experience, what appeals to him — colors, lines, odors, sounds. Your own writing will be richer and stronger if it includes images drawn from your own experiences. A borrowed image is likely to be a dead one. An image drawn from experience is a live image; and a live image is like a good photograph: it reveals something of the photographer as well as showing what he has photographed. See *Figures of speech; *Guide*, pp. 361–62, 367–72.

Imitative words

By their pronunciations, some words suggest particular sounds: *buzz, bang, clank, swish, splash, whir, pop, clatter.* Such imitative or echoic words are established in the English vocabulary. Occasionally new ones are more or less playfully formed, but ordinarily a writer is wise to use the conventional forms, even when they are not very exact (*humph, uh huh*), rather than make up new ones that may only puzzle a reader.

By the stylistic device known as onomatopoeia, sounds that match the sense of a passage can be used to intensify its meaning. In *The Red Badge of Courage*, Stephen Crane frequently uses imitative words to good effect:

The regiment snorted and blew. . . . The song of the bullets was in the air and shells snarled among the tree-tops. . . . Near where they stood shells were flip-flapping and hooting. . . . Occasional bullets buzzed in the air and spanged into tree trunks. . . .

But conscious striving for words like *flip-flap* and *spang* can produce embarrassing results.

Imperative mood

The form of the verb that is used for direct commands and requests is called an imperative and is said to be in the imperative mood: Bring the tapes when you come; Run! English imperatives have no overt ending and usually no expressed subject. See *Commands and requests.

implement

The catchall verb *implement*, meaning to "give effect" to policies or ideas (It's a great theory, but who's going to implement it?), might often be replaced by *fulfill, execute, put into practice*, and *carry out*, if only for variety. See *Vogue words.

imply, infer

Careful users of English make a distinction between *imply* and *infer:* a writer or speaker *implies* something in his words or manner, suggesting a conclusion without stating it; a reader or listener *infers* something from what he reads or hears, drawing a conclusion from the available information. Indeed, both implying and inferring can be wordless: The dean implied by his half smile that he doubted my story; They inferred from his silence that he disapproved of the new policy.

Having a word for each of these acts contributes to clear communication. But for centuries *infer* has also been used to mean "imply," and today many dictionaries recognize this meaning (as well as the traditional meaning) of *infer* as Standard. Thus when clarity is essential, the safe course is not simply to distinguish between *imply* and *infer* but to provide a context that underlines your meaning: From the President's words, I infer that he. . . .

Incoherence

Writing is incoherent when the relationship between parts (of a sentence, of a paragraph, of a whole paper) is not made clear. The cause may be that there actually is no relationship between the parts, or it may be that the writer has failed to indicate the relationship that he perceives. See *Coherence; *Transition; *Guide*, pp. 247–62, 311–13.

Incomplete sentence

See *Fragment.

incredible, incredulous

A story or situation is incredible ("unbelievable"); a person is incredulous ("unbelieving").

Indefinite article

See *a, an.

Indefinite nouns

See *Parts of speech.

Indefinite pronouns

See *Reference of pronouns, *you.

Indention or indentation

Indenting in manuscript or printed copy is beginning the first line of a paragraph some distance to the right of the left-hand margin—about an inch in longhand copy, about five spaces in typewritten copy. Hanging indention is indention of all lines below the first line, as in many newspaper headlines, outlines, headings, and addresses of letters. If a line of verse is too long to stand on one line, the part brought over to the second line should be indented. For indenting quotations, see *Quotation marks § 1d.

Independent clause

See *Clauses.

Indicative mood

Verb forms that ask questions or state facts are said to be indicative or in the indicative mood. Hence the indicative is the mood of most verbs in English sentences:

They *sat* on the porch even though it *was* late October.
Will you *come* if you *are* invited?

See *Verbs. Compare *Imperative mood, *Subjunctives.

Indirect discourse (indirect quotation)

When someone's words are reported in paraphrase or summary instead of being quoted exactly, they are in indirect discourse:

Direct: He said, "I won't take it if they give it to me."
Indirect: He said he wouldn't take it if they gave it to him.

An indirect question restates a question at second hand:

Direct: "Is everyone all right?" he asked.
Indirect: He asked if everyone was all right.

Personal pronouns and verb tenses in the indirect quotation are made to match the pronouns and tenses in the enclosing statement. See *Commands and requests, *Quotation marks §2b, *Tenses of verbs §5.

Indirect objects

See *Objects §2.

Indo-European languages

See *English language.

Induction

Induction as a mode of inference is discussed and illustrated in the *Guide*, pp. 148–53. The method of organization sometimes called inductive is described in the *Guide*, pp. 190–91, 241–43.

in-, en-

See *en-, in-.

infer, imply

See *imply, infer.

Infinitives

Infinitive is a Latin grammatical term for a verb form expressing the general sense of the verb without restriction as to person, number, or tense. In Old English the infinitive had a distinctive form, but in Modern English the bare form of the verb is used, often with *to* before it.

1. *Tenses*. These are traditionally called the infinitive forms:

Active

Simple	Progressive
Present: (to) ask	(to) be asking
Perfect: (to) have asked	(to) have been asking

Passive

Simple	Progressive
Present: (to) be asked	(to) be being asked
Perfect: (to) have been asked	(to) have been being asked

The present infinitive indicates a time the same as, or future to, that of the main verb: He is here to help; They came to play. The perfect infinitive primarily indicates action previous to the time of the main verb: I am glad to be one of his friends.

2. *The* to *infinitive. To* is the "sign of the infinitive" used in many infinitive constructions. It connects the infinitive to some other part of speech: He is the man to see; He was glad to leave; He tried to stop.

3. *The "bare" infinitive.* After the *modal auxiliary verbs and some full verbs, *to* is never or seldom used: I can see; He must carry it; We might be seeing him; He does care; I helped him study; We let him go; I saw him leave.

In short, clear, unemphatic series of infinitives in parallel constructions, *to* is not repeated: He decided to shower, shave, and dress. When the series is complex or when separate verbs deserve emphasis, *to* is repeated: These were his goals—to escape the city, to avoid routine, and to find contentment.

4. *Other uses.*

Subject: To sit and smoke was his idea of a holiday. To do that again would be a serious mistake.

Object: He prefers to wait until Tuesday. The police attempted to hold back the crowd.

Adjectival modifier: My friend is the man to see. Jane is the person to do that.

Adverbial modifier: Everybody was happy to stay. (Modifies adjective *happy*.) The teacher stopped to find out what had happened. (Indicates purpose.)

5. *Subject of the infinitive.* When *for* + noun precedes the infinitive, the subject of the infinitive is clear: For Tom to say that shocked us. When it does not, the subject is either an indefinite *someone* or a referent expressed elsewhere in the sentence. In the sentence "To ignore the suffering in the world is criminal," the subject is an indefinite *someone* or *anyone*. When there is a potential subject for a verb like *ignore* later in the sentence, then—given certain grammatical deep-structure conditions—it is the subject of the infinitive: To ignore the suffering in the world is criminal of *you*. In a transformational grammar, all infinitives have their source in a complete sentence

structure in the *deep structure. Under certain conditions, such as the indefiniteness or repeated reference described above, the subject is deleted:

[for someone] to ignore the suffering in the world is criminal
[for you] to ignore the suffering in the world is criminal of you

For the pronoun after the infinitive of a *linking verb that has no expressed subject, General English usually has the accusative: I always wanted to be him. Formal would probably have a nominative: I always wanted to be he. But that locution makes the pronoun prominent and might better be rephrased: He was the one I always wanted to be. Compare *Participles, *Gerunds. Reference: Jespersen, *MEG*, VII, 6.

6. *Split infinitive.* See *Split infinitive.

References: Curme, *Syntax*, Ch. 23; Jespersen, *EEG*, Ch. 32; Roberts, pp. 359–67; Peter Rosenbaum, *The Grammar of English Predicate Complement Constructions* (Cambridge, Mass.: MIT Press, 1967).

Inflection

In grammar *inflection* refers to the change of form that some words undergo to indicate certain grammatical relationships, like singular and plural number for nouns or past and present tense for verbs. For English inflections, see *Case and the articles referred to there, *Comparison of adjectives and adverbs, *Plurals of nouns, *Pronouns, *Verbs. Reference: Curme, *Parts of Speech*, Chs. 9–13.

Informal English

Inf

Revision: The word or passage marked is too Informal for the subject or for the style of the rest of the paper. Revise, making it more appropriate.

Informal English, as described in the *Guide*, pp. 13, 24–25, is the variety of the language that we ordinarily use when we talk to close friends or to members of our families. It is appropriate where a casual tone and a conversational atmosphere are appropriate; but it has no place in Formal writing, and its successful use in General papers requires taste and judgment.

in, into, in to

In usually shows location, literal or figurative: He was in the house; He was in a stupor. *Into* usually shows direction: He came into the house; He fell into a stupor. But in General and Informal usage, *in* is common when direction is meant: "Twice a week we get in the car, and drive down the Parkway" (Richard Rose, *St. Louis Post-Dispatch*, Jan. 20, 1963).

The *in* of *in to* is an adverb and the *to* a preposition (They went in to dinner) or sign of the infinitive (They went in to eat).

institutions of higher learning

There is seldom any excuse for using the clumsy and abstract phrase "institutions of higher learning" in the singular, but there is neither a single word nor a group word (like *secondary schools*) for the plural. "Colleges and universities" is often a better choice, and frequently either *colleges* or *universities* is used to refer to both.

Intensive pronouns

See *myself, *Pronouns §1.

Intensives

See *Qualifiers.

Interjections

See *Exclamations, *Parts of speech.

Interrogative pronouns

See *Pronouns §3.

Interrogative sentences

See *Questions.

Interrupted sentence movement

See *Commas §4; *Guide*, pp. 334 – 36.

Intonation

Intonation, a general term for the speech tunes or sentence melodies of a language, is applied by different linguists to somewhat different features of speech sound. In discussions of English, it usually refers to pitch and juncture, but sometimes stress, too, is included. After much intensive research in recent years, the description of English intonation remains controversial.

Intransitive verbs

See *Transitive and intransitive verbs.

Introductions

See *Beginning of an essay.

in-, un-

In- or *un-* (variants *im-*, *il-*) prefixed to many words gives them a negative meaning: *inconsiderate, incapable, uneven, unlovable, unloved*. If you are not sure whether a word takes *in-* or *un-*, consult a dictionary.

Not all words beginning with *in-* are negatives (*inmate, insure, intoxicate*); *invaluable* means having a value so great that it cannot be determined. *Inflammable* has apparently come to be considered so ambiguous as a warning that *flammable* has displaced it on tank trucks. *Un-* is also tricky: see *unbend, unbending* in a dictionary.

Inversion

Inversion means placing the verb, or some part of the verb phrase, before its subject. This is the regular syntactical pattern in questions, with the auxiliary before the subject and the infinitive or participle after it: Is he coming? Will she go? Did they enjoy it? Inversion is also used with expletive *there* and *it* (There was a man at the door) and in a few other situations: What a fool he is; Long may it wave; Here comes the thunder. Otherwise, inversion is rather rare in English. For its stylistic effect in declarative sentences, see *Guide*, pp. 336–37.

invite

The word *invite* is ordinarily a verb. Its use as a noun /in' vīt/ is distinctly Informal: Did you get an invite? Reference: Bryant, p. 116.

Irony

Irony implies something markedly different, sometimes even the opposite, from what is actually said. Light irony is humorous, as in the greeting "Lovely day!" when the weather is wretched. Heavy irony is usually a form of sarcasm or satire.

irregardless

Irregardless is redundant: both the prefix *ir-* and the suffix *-less* are negative. The Standard word is *regardless*.

Irregular verbs

See *Principal parts of verbs.

-ise, -ize

See *-ize, -ise.

it

It is the neuter third-person singular pronoun, used most commonly to refer to inanimates but sometimes to living things. Typically, it replaces preceding neuter noun phrases: Have you seen *the neighbor's new car?*—Yes, isn't *it* a mess? The antecedent may be a clause or a sentence: Some people say *that more money will solve the problem of our schools*, but I don't believe *it*. Sometimes, however, *it* has no antecedent, as in impersonal statements about the weather, time, distance, or events in general, and in numerous idioms:

It's now three hours since *it* began to rain, and *it's* still five miles to camp.
It isn't pleasant in Washington these days.
Damn *it*, we'll have to talk *it* out with the dean.

Though typically neuter, the antecedent of *it* may be an animal or a small child whose sex is unknown or irrelevant. *It* is also used with reference to collective nouns denoting persons (The faculty must decide for itself) and in sentences where individuals are identified (I'm not sure who the violinist was, but it could have been Kreisler).

The more important uses of *it*, stylistically, are those where it fills the position of a subject or object fully expressed later in the sentence. In such sentences "expletive" *it* is called the "formal" or "provisional" or "anticipatory" subject or object:

It is doubtful *that he should be given so much freedom.*

He found *it* painful *living in the same house with his noisy harridan of a mother-in-law.*

It was *Wordsworth* who called his gun a "thundering tube."

The advantages of such constructions are that they offer an alternative to clumsy word order (He found living in the same house with his noisy harridan of a mother-in-law painful) and a means of assigning emphasis: "It was Wordsworth who . . ." emphasizes *Wordsworth*; "Wordsworth called his gun a 'thundering tube'" emphasizes *thundering tube.*

See *there is, there are; *its, it's; *It's me; *Guide*, p. 339. References: Emerson Beauchamp, Jr., *AS*, Oct. 1951, pp. 173–80; Curme, *Syntax*, index references to *it;* Long, pp. 211–12, 342–45; R. W. Zandvoort, *A Handbook of English Grammar*, 3rd ed. (Englewood Cliffs, N.J.: Prentice, 1966), pp. 133–37.

Italics

Ital

Revision: In longhand and typewritten copy, underline words or passages to correspond to the conventions of using italic type.

Words or statements that would be printed in italics are underlined in manuscript. Although newspapers have generally abandoned italic type, most magazines and books use it, and in academic writing — course papers, articles in learned journals, monographs, dissertations, reference books — italics have standardized uses:

1. To indicate the titles of books, plays, motion pictures, and other complete works, and to indicate the titles of periodicals and newspapers. See *Titles of books, articles, etc.

2. To mark words and expressions considered as words rather than for their meaning: There is a shade of difference between *because* and *for* used as conjunctions.

3. To mark unanglicized words from foreign languages: Good clothes were a *sine qua non.* See *Foreign words in English.

4. To indicate words that would be stressed if spoken. This easily abused device is more appropriate in dialog than in exposition.

5. To indicate key words, phrases, or sentences in an argument or explanation. Here also italics must be used sparingly if they are not to lose their force. See *Emphasis, *Schoolgirl style.

References: *Chicago Manual; MLA Style Sheet; U.S. Style Manual.*

its, it's

Its is a possessive pronoun and, like the possessive pronouns *his, her, our, your,* and *their,* has no apostrophe: A car is judged by its performance. *It's* is the contraction for "It is" or "It has": It's a long road; It's been said before. Like other contractions, *it's* is more appropriate in Informal and General styles than in Formal style.

It's me

The argument over "It's me" is a case of theory versus practice. The theory—that after a finite form of the verb *be* the nominative or subjective case should always be used—is consistently contradicted by the usage of good writers and speakers (see *be § 2). We tend to use the nominative form of a pronoun when it is the subject and stands alone directly before the verb, but we are likely to use the accusative in most other positions, especially when it comes after the verb—in "object territory," as Fries calls it. (Compare *who, whom.)

All the large grammars of English regard "It's me" as acceptable colloquial usage. The expression is not likely to occur in Formal writing, but it is fairly common in General:

. . . I don't think I believe in God anymore. It is not only me. . . .—Eve Auchincloss, *New York Review of Books,* Nov. 14, 1963

There was no single phase of his past to which he could go back and say, "This is me. . . ."—Iris Origo, *Atlantic,* Nov. 1963

See *Case. References: Bryant, pp. 120–21; Marckwardt and Walcott, pp. 77–78; Wallace Rice, *AS,* Oct. 1933, pp. 58–63; Robertson, pp. 293–97.

-ize, -ise

The formation of verbs from non-Greek nouns or adjectives by adding the Greek ending *-ize* (often *-ise* in British usage) has been going on since the sixteenth century. Some readers object to recent extensions of the verbs in *-ize,* either because the new verbs duplicate in meaning verbs already in common use (*fantasized, fantasied; formularize, formulate*) or because the proliferation adds to the stock of advertising jargon (*customize, personalize*), much of which is virtually meaningless.

Japanese

Japanese is the customary word both for the modifier (the Japanese economy) and for the noun, either singular or plural (a Japanese, many Japanese). Although once a colloquialism with neutral connotations, *Jap* is now considered highly derogatory.

Jargon

Sir Arthur Quiller-Couch popularized *jargon* as the name for verbal fuzziness of various sorts—wordiness, a high proportion of abstract words, *big words, and words that add nothing to the meaning. *Jargon* and *gobbledygook* are sometimes used interchangeably. See *Guide*, pp. 363–64. Reference: Sir Arthur Quiller-Couch, *On the Art of Writing* (New York: Putnam, Capricorn Books, 1961), pp. 100–26.

Linguists use *jargon* to mean a dialect composed of the mixture of two or more languages, such as the Chinook Jargon of the Pacific Northwest and the Chinese-English jargon, pidgin English. Reference: Jespersen, *Language*, Ch. 12.

job, position

Job is General for the Formal *position:* He got a job at the oil refinery. The word *position* has more dignity, and what it refers to is usually thought of as better paid; but because *position* can sound pompous, many writers use *job* for all levels of employment.

Journalese

See *Newspaper English.

just

Most readers find the qualifier *just* redundant in expressions like *just exactly* and *just perfect.*

kid

The noun *kid* for "child" and the verb *kid* for "tease" are now so widely used in serious contexts that they should be regarded as established in General (but not in Formal) usage:

. . . the real enthusiasms of the young are not handed down from above but are the discoveries, almost the inventions, of the kids themselves.— Walter Allen, *New York Times Book Review*, Jan. 7, 1968

. . . we have been hearing that the motion picture is the art form of the twentieth century, then visited our local movie house only to emerge wondering who is being kidded. — Arthur Knight, *Saturday Review*, Aug. 12, 1967

A problem with *kid* as a noun is that it now may mean not only someone past puberty but someone past adolescence. In many contexts a more specific term is needed.

kind of a, sort of a

Though *kind of a* and *sort of a* are avoided in Formal writing, they are accepted General idioms: "People just didn't trust that kind of an approach" (Charles Mohr, *Esquire*, Aug. 1965). Formal style would have "kind of approach."

kind of, sort of

Kind of and *sort of* are General to Informal as adverbs, equivalent to vague qualifiers like *rather* or *somewhat* in more Formal usage:

She was kind of plump. . . . —Claude Brown, *Commentary*, July 1965

The World Boxing Association . . . is sort of peeved at Cassius Clay. — *Time*, Nov. 12, 1965

. . . everything just sort of limped along. —E. J. Kahn, Jr., *New Yorker*, June 11, 1966

kind, sort

Kind and *sort* are singular pronouns with regular plurals. A problem arises only when singular *kind* or *sort* is followed by *of* and a plural noun. Then there is a strong tendency to treat the plural object of *of*, rather than *kind* or *sort*, as the head of the construction and to use plural demonstratives and verbs: "For men with those kind of overhead expenses . . ." (Lewis H. Lapham, *Harper's*, May 1971); These sort of books are harmless.

The construction is common in speech, and there are numerous examples of its use by esteemed writers (". . . these kind of marks have not been left by any other animal than man . . ." —T. H. Huxley, "The Method of Scientific Investigation"); but strong objection to it continues. For one variety, then: *That kind* of book *is*. . . . For more than one: *Those kinds* of books *are*. . . . References: Bryant, pp. 124–25; Curme, *Syntax*, pp. 544–46; Fries, *AEG*, p. 58; Jespersen, *EEG*, p. 202.

know-how

Although *know-how* occurs in every variety of writing, its connotations remain commercial and technical.

lab

The clipped form of *laboratory* is now appropriate in all but the most Formal usage.

Language study

See *Linguistics, *Usage.

last, latest

Both *last* and *latest* are used as superlatives of *late* (his last book; his latest book). But to avoid ambiguity Formal English uses *last* for the final item in a series and *latest* for the most recent of a series that may or may not be continued: "Mao Tse-tung's latest battle is almost certainly his last" (Mark Gayn, *Foreign Affairs*, Jan. 1967).

last, latter

See *former, first—latter, last.

Latin and English

1. *Latin words.* In general, borrowings from Latin are pronounced as English words — *agenda* /ə jen' də/, *erratum* /i rā' təm/ or /i rä' təm/ — instead of according to the system of pronunciation now taught in Latin classes.

Since Latin is dead as a first language and rare as a second language, new borrowings come in through written rather than spoken use and belong to the Formal dialects, chiefly those of science, law, religion, medicine, and academic work. Several Latin words and abbreviations are used in the footnotes of academic research (see *Guide*, pp. 423 – 24). Prefixes of Latin origin (*ante-, ex-, in-, pre-, re-, sub-*) and other compounding elements, such as *uni-* (*unilateral*), *bi-* (*biweekly*), are active in forming new English words. At present, scientific words are being formed more from Greek than from Latin elements.

2. *Latin forms.* English continues to use the Latin forms for some words that are found principally in the Formal dialects (*alumnus, alumna; bacillus, bacilli*), but many of those commonly used have either English plurals or both (*formula, formulas* or *formulae; focus, focuses* or *foci; stadium, stadiums* or *stadia*). (See *Plurals of nouns § 4, *data.)

3. *Latin and English grammar.* The first English grammars and most later ones were composed by men who were thoroughly familiar with Latin and, in many cases, believed that English should be like Latin. As a result, English, which was a Germanic language in structure, was described in terms of Latin grammar, and rules were devised for making the language fit the picture. Only recently has English grammar been based squarely on a careful examination of the English language itself and freed from some of the categories and rules of Latin grammar. See *Linguistics. Reference: Karl W. Dykema, *CE*, April 1961, pp. 455 – 65.

latter, last

See *former, first — latter, last.

lay, lie

In Standard English *lie (lay, lain)* is intransitive — He let it lie there; She lay down for a nap; The boards had lain there for months. *Lay (laid, laid)* is transitive: You can lay it on the table; They laid the keel; She had laid it away for future reference. In writing, the two verbs are almost always kept distinct; but in much spoken English *lay* does the work of both, and sometimes this usage appears in print: "In 1932, in his luxurious Paris apartment, Ivor Kreuger laid down on his bed . . ." (Eric Goldman, *New York Times Book Review*, Aug. 7, 1960).

The *-ing* forms also give trouble, with *laying* appearing where *lying* is meant: I spent the summer laying around the house.

Leading question

See *Questions § 3.

learn, teach

Nonstandard English often uses *learn* in the sense of *teach:* He learned me how to tie knots. Standard usage makes the distinction: He taught me how to tie knots; I learned how to tie knots from him.

leave, let

See *let, leave.

lend, loan

In referring to material wealth, *lend* and *lends* are preferred to *loan* and *loans* in Formal writing, but the past tense and past participle *loaned* is preferred to *lent* in all varieties:

. . . those who wished to lend had to . . . circumvent the law against usury. — George V. Taylor, *American Historical Review*, Jan. 1967

. . . merchants loaned [industrial machinery] to them. — Ibid.

. . . savings banks . . . have been willing to lend to individuals. . . .— Adolf A. Berle, *The American Economic Republic*

. . . about $4 billion have been loaned for agricultural purposes.— Ibid.

In General contexts, *loan* and *loans* are as common as *lend* and *lends* and are entirely reputable.

In the sense "grant, impart, furnish" or "adapt or accommodate (itself)," *lend* and *lent* are always preferred:

Judge Hoffman lent·the one elegant tone to the trial.— William F. Woo, *St. Louis Post-Dispatch*, Feb. 6, 1966

. . . America always lent itself to personification.— Norman Mailer, *Harper's*, March 1968

less, fewer

See *fewer, less.

let, leave

A common Nonstandard idiom is the use of *leave* for "permit" or "allow," meanings which Standard English assigns to *let*. Both uses are shown in this sentence by a student making a transition between the two varieties: "In high school I was cured of the practice of leaving [Nonstandard] notebooks go, but I fell into the habit of letting [Standard] homework slide."

Only with *alone* and the meaning "refrain from disturbing" are the two verbs interchangeable in Standard English: Leave [or Let] me alone; Americans like to be let [or left] alone. Reference: Bryant, pp. 127–29.

Lexical meaning

In linguistics a distinction is often made between grammatical or structural meaning and lexical meaning. In "Birds were killed," the information that *bird* and *kill* give us is of the sort regularly provided by a dictionary or lexicon—hence, lexical meaning. The information given by the *-s* of *birds* (plural), *were* (past tense, passive voice), and the *-ed* of *killed* (past participle in this position) is of the sort provided by our awareness of the structure or grammar of the language—hence, grammatical or structural meaning. When we fully understand the sentence, we have grasped its total meaning.

liable, likely, apt

Liable is the troublesome member of the trio. In Formal and most General writing, when followed by an infinitive, it is restricted to predictions of undesirable results (The effects are liable to be disastrous). *Liable* plus infinitive to predict desirable results is most likely to be found in Informal and casual General contexts: ". . . in many rivers, walleyes are year-round sport and . . . they're liable to hit any time of the day or night" (Roger Latham, *Field and Stream*, Feb. 1968). *Likely* and *apt* are not restricted in this way.

lie

See *lay, lie.

lighted, lit

Both forms are in good use as the past tense and past participle of *light:* He lighted the fire; He lit the fire. In attributive position, *lighted* is usual: a lighted match.

like, as

1. *As prepositions.* In all varieties of English, *like* is used as a preposition introducing a comparison: The description fits him like a glove; Habit grips a person like an octopus; She took to selling like a duck to water. *As* seems to be increasing as a *hypercorrect form:

The University of Texas, as so many American campuses during the Kennedy years, has exploded with vitality. . . .—Willie Morris, *North Toward Home*

. . . the Basenji is the size of a fox-terrier and cleans itself as a cat.—Natalie Winslow, *Providence Sunday Journal,* Jan. 17, 1971

2. *As conjunctions.* In all varieties of English, *as, as if*, and *as though* are used as conjunctions introducing clauses of comparison: Habit grips a person as an octopus does; He walked as though he was hurt. *Like* as a conjunction is common in speech and appears frequently in Informal and General writing:

"I feel like an evangelist must feel," Nixon added. —*Newsweek*, Oct. 10, 1961

. . . this endless line of people had really loved him, loved Bobby Kennedy like no other political figure in years had been loved. — Norman Mailer, *Harper's*, Nov. 1968

It looks now like it will take us years of John Cage, Godard, Burroughs, *et al.*, to absorb it. — Theodore Solotaroff, *The Red Hot Vacuum*

Many people remain strongly opposed to the use of *like* as a conjunction, perhaps because they associate it with advertising and mass-media comedy, and the usage is avoided in Formal writing. References: Bryant, pp. 133–35; Curme, *Syntax*, pp. 281–82; Fries, *AEG*, pp. 225, 239; Pooley, pp. 153–55; Harold Simpson, *CE*, May 1952, pp. 463–64.

3. *The way. The way* provides an escape from the *like-as* thicket for writers who shy from *like* and find *as* prissy:

The fateful scene between Launcelot and Guinevere is hardly the way I imagined it. — Marya Mannes, *Reporter*, Feb. 2, 1961

Hemingway once told Callaghan, "Dostoevski writes like Harry Greb fights." Unfortunately, Callaghan writes the way Hemingway fights. . . . — *Time*, March 15, 1963

. . . she perched on bandleader Peter Duchin's piano the way flappers used to do back in the 1920's. . . . — *Newsweek*, April 3, 1967

Linguistics

Linguistics is the study of the formal, regular, recurrent patterns in the structures of human languages. A linguist's first goal is to write grammars or parts of grammars that will describe the phonological, syntactic, and semantic structure of sentences in particular languages. A more ambitious goal, one pursued in the eighteenth century and now once again the object of research, is to describe those linguistic features that all human languages share — the universals of language.

There are many schools of linguistics (see *Grammar). While they differ in the particular questions they pose and the methods they use to answer them, all share the desire to be as objective and "scientific" as possible, rejecting conclusions not based on consistent theory and adequate data. For some, this means looking only at those features of language they can directly observe either as marks on a page or as vibrations in the air. They eschew "mentalism," or introspection about their intuitive sense of the structure of a sentence, if it is not supported by observable linguistic features. These "descriptivists" have concentrated on finding objective discovery procedures to "break the code" of known and unknown languages. Others, particularly those writing transformational grammars, believe that the data they must account for includes what they sense about the structure of a sentence, and what they sense may not be found in its objective *surface structure. Descriptivists would consider three sentences such as "The boy is lucky to leave," "The boy is eager to leave," and "The boy is certain to leave" as structurally identical, differing only in the words *lucky, eager,* and *certain.* A transformationalist "senses" a greater difference: *lucky* describes the situation of the boy's leaving; *eager* describes the boy himself; *certain* describes the fact of his leaving. The boy may be both lucky and eager, but he is not certain. These differences exist in a sentence's *deep structure. The goal of a transformationalist is to formalize this deep structure and relate it in equally formal ways to a surface structure. The goal of a descriptivist is to describe only surface structures.

The goal of both these main schools of linguistics, however, is to construct a grammar that will identify the elements constituting a language; to group them into classes and group the classes into higher-order classes; to discover the order in which these classes occur; and to account for the relationship among these classes in the most systematic, general, and economical way possible.

1. *Basic areas.* The three basic areas of linguistic study are phonology, syntax, and semantics.

a—The object of phonological studies is to determine how components of sounds make up units of sound and how those units may and may not be combined into longer sequences in words, phrases, and sentences. The first sound in *pin,* for example, is made up of the features *stop* (the air is completely stopped and then released, as opposed to the first sound in *fin); voicelessness* (the vocal cords are not vibrating, as opposed to the initial sound in *bin); consonantal* (as opposed to the first sound in *win);* and *aspiration* (the little puff of air after the release of the stop, as opposed to no puff of air after the /p/ sound in *spin).* The phonologist then tries to account for the sequences of these combinations and how they affect one another. Some combinations are possible in English and do occur: *tip.* Some are possible but do not occur as words: *tid.* Some, because of the way sequences of English sounds are organized, never occur in ordinary usage: *ftid.* Most sounds, furthermore, are "conditioned" by surrounding sounds. The /t/ sounds in *tip* and *trip* are different because in *trip* we are forced to make the /t/ sound farther back behind the teeth in anticipation of the following /r/. (You can show this by starting to say *trip* and then saying *tip.)* Once these sequences and their effects have been described, the phonologist must then show how sounds change under different stress patterns: *átom, atómic; resígn, resignátion; revólt, revolútion.*

b—The object of syntactic studies is to identify those units of meaning that form words or that combine to form words: *cat* is made up of one unit of meaning, *cats* of two—*cat* and plural *-s. Ungentlemanly* is made up of four: the negative *un-,* the unit *gentle,* the unit *man,* and the unit *-ly,* meaning adverb. When the words are identified, they are classed into *parts of speech and then described in terms of their order, clustering, and relationships.

c—The object of semantics is quite similar to the object of phonological and syntactic studies. The semanticist must first discover—or postulate—the components that make up meaning. In some areas of meaning, such as kinship, this is relatively simple: *father* is composed of the elements *physical object, animate, human, male, adult, with child. Mother* differs only in regard to the feature *male* vs. *female; man* differs only in regard to *with child; person* differs in regard to *male, adult, with child.* Research is only now beginning to discover what features of meaning are necessary to describe semantic content. How, for example, do *pat, press, rub, pet, stroke* as a group differ from *poke, jab, rap,* and *tap?* How do they differ from one another? If we can conceive of words being made up of components of meaning, just as sounds are made up of components of sound, then perhaps the same kinds of questions about combinations and sequence can be answered. Are there combinations of elements which are possible but which have no word attached to them? We call children without parents by a single word: *orphans.* But we have no single noun to name couples without children; we must use a circumlocution—"a childless couple." And we certainly have no words to name parents who had children but lost them as distinguished from couples who have never had children.

The semantic structure of our language determines what sequences of words are acceptable and what sequences are unacceptable. "I poked him with my finger" is acceptable; "I kicked him with my finger" is unacceptable. "I baked a cake," not "I roasted a cake." "I damaged my typewriter," not "I injured my typewriter." The actions are essentially the same in each pair of sentences; the appropriateness of the word combinations depends on their semantic environment.

In recent years some linguists have become so much concerned with semantics that, for them, the distinction between syntax and semantics is breaking down. Their goal is to relate semantic structures to a very abstract sort of phonological manifestation, without worrying whether there is a discrete intermediate field of study called syntax.

Progress in all three of these fields has been enormous in the last decade. But it is progress that must be defined in two ways. We know much more about language than we did in the 1950's when transformational grammars were first formulated, but new questions, posed as a consequence of new theories, have disclosed vast new areas of ignorance. Thus progress must be measured not only by what we know but by what we have discovered we do not know.

2. *Specialized fields.* In addition to describing the grammatical, phonological, and semantic structures of modern languages, linguists are interested in more specialized areas. Dialectology examines the characteristic linguistic patterns that distinguish groups of speakers of the same language. Geographical dialects have been most thoroughly studied; but in recent years social dialects have drawn increasing attention as higher education has encompassed all classes of speakers, forcing teachers to reconsider their attitudes toward the variety of English spoken by those not part of the white, Anglo-Saxon, upper-middle-class community. Historical linguistics attempts to reconstruct the grammars of earlier forms of a current or dead language. Comparative linguistics studies the relationships between languages that are genetically related to a parent language or between languages that differ or resemble each other structurally, without regard to their historical sources. Specialists in child language investigate the development of linguistic competence among infants and young children.

3. *Practical applications.* In lexicography the findings of semanticists and dialectologists are being used in compiling dictionaries. In foreign-language teaching, the findings of comparative and contrastive linguistics have helped pinpoint those differences between a native language and a target language that would make learning the new language particularly difficult. In machine translation the findings of syntactic studies and semantics have been used in attempts, so far largely fruitless, to program machines to translate from one language to another. In literary studies transformational grammars have been used to analyze the syntactic, metaphorical, and prosodic structure of poems and the styles of various prose writers. In composition courses transformational grammars have been used to analyze the characteristics of mature sentence structure to help students write better. In reading, phonological studies have shown how the apparently chaotic system of English spelling is in reality a regular system that, far from preventing a child from learning to read, may actually help him. The findings of phonology have also been used to construct better communications systems. And the scientific attitudes of linguists have forced those concerned with usage to look at language as it really is used rather than as they would like it to be used.

4. *Related fields.* As linguistics has developed theoretically and in its practical applications, a number of related fields have developed. Psycholinguistics studies the correlation between linguistic structures and experimentally describable behavior. Stylistics studies the linguistic characteristics of literary language. One kind of linguistic philosophy studies the nature of meaning in sentences from the point of view of deep and surface structures. Linguistic anthropology uses the semantic structures of individual languages and the verbal interaction of their speakers to discover distinctive patterns of culture. Related to this field is sociolinguistics, the specific study of the verbal interaction between and among social classes.

In short, language is central in a great many different fields and peripheral in still more. One task of the linguist, then, is to provide a theoretical framework in which other scholars can work. A zoologist who knew nothing about the structures of human languages could say little or nothing about the necessary conditions for apes to develop into prehumans. An anthropologist who knew nothing about the variations among human languages could say little about the cultural implications of structures in a particular language. A philosopher who speculated on the meaning of sentences without having some understanding of how sentences mean would contribute little to our understanding of the meaning of "meaning." A literary critic who knew nothing of the structure of language could say little interesting about style. And an English teacher who knew nothing about language would be of little use in helping a student develop a style suited to the different rhetorical demands placed on him by different rhetorical situations.

References: History: R. H. Robins, *A Short History of Linguistics* (Bloomington: Indiana Univ. Press, 1968); John T. Waterman, *Perspectives in Linguistics*, 2nd ed. (Chicago: Univ. of Chicago Press, 1970). Phonology: Archibald A. Hill, *Introduction to Linguistic Structures* (New York: Harcourt, 1958), pp. 13–88; Noam Chomsky and Morris Halle, *The Sound Pattern of English* (New York: Harper, 1968). Syntax: Noam Chomsky, *Aspects of the Theory of Syntax* (Cambridge, Mass.: MIT Press, 1965); Jacobs and Rosenbaum. Semantics: Uriel Weinreich, "Explorations in Semantic Theory," in *Current Trends in Linguistics*, Vol. 3: *Theoretical Foundations*, ed. Thomas A. Sebeok (The Hague: Mouton, 1966), pp. 395–477. Related disciplines: Archibald A. Hill, ed., *Linguistics Today* (New York: Basic Books, 1969).

Linking verbs

When a verb like *be* is so used that it has little *lexical meaning but functions chiefly as a structural bridge between a subject and another noun or a modifier, it is called a copulative or linking verb. It is followed by elements that function as adjectives or nouns (single words, phrases, or clauses) and are traditionally known as predicate adjectives (This bottle was *full*) and predicate nouns or predicate nominatives (The man was a *carpenter*). Some grammarians prefer to call them complements, or subjective complements.

Many verbs besides *be* are used as linking verbs; Curme counts about sixty in current English. For example, instead of having a verb of full meaning like *colden*, English uses the verb *turn* or *get* and the adjective *cold* (which carries the chief part of the meaning) in such a sentence as "The weather turned cold." Many verbs are used both with full meaning of their own (*fell* in "The tree fell into the water") and as linking verbs (*fell* in "She fell silent" or "He fell ill"). Other linking verbs (which could be variously subclassified) appear in the following sentences:

He became a doctor. The butter tastes rancid. She felt sad. He acts old. The ground sounds hollow. He grew moody. He appeared to be recovering. This looks first-rate. His story seemed incredible.

Because many speakers have been taught that verbs are modified by adverbs, and because they are unaware that the same verb can function either as a linking verb or as a transitive, they often correct correctness by substituting an adverb for the correct adjective: "He felt sadly" for "He felt sad." Such *hypercorrectness sometimes appears in writing.

For the most common source of difficulty in using the linking-verb pattern, see *Predicate adjectives. See also *bad, badly; *be §2; *It's me; and *look. References: Curme, *Parts of Speech*, pp. 66–69, *Syntax*, pp. 26–28; A. S. Hornby, *A Guide to Patterns and Usages in English* (London: Oxford Univ. Press, 1954), pp. 62–72; Gustave

Scheurweghs, *Present-Day English Syntax* (London: Longmans, 1959), pp. 19–32.

literally

Literally means "actually, without deviating from the facts," but it is so often used to support metaphors that its literal meaning may be reversed. In statements like "We literally combed the neighborhood to find him," *literally* means "figuratively." Literal-minded readers find this usage absurd.

literate

See *illiterate.

Litotes

See *Negatives.

loan

See *lend, loan.

Loan words

See *Foreign words in English, *Origin of words § 2b.

Localisms

A localism is a word or other expression in regular use only in a certain region, like the "baby cab" used in western Pennsylvania for "baby carriage." Localisms are appropriate to conversation and to Informal writing but are out of place in General and Formal writing except to give a regional flavor. See *Guide*, pp. 5–7, and *Dialects.

locate

Although avoided by some stylists, *locate* is in General use for "settle" (The family located near Nashua) and for "find" (I can't locate the letter now). It is *deadwood in indicating the whereabouts of specific places or people: He is now [located] with the Ford Motor Company in Detroit. But it may be useful when it refers to considered placement: "Thus the small department store is probably wise to locate close to its competition" (Richard H. Holton, in *Competition, Cartels and Their Regulation*, ed. J. P. Miller).

Locution

Locution is a handy term for referring to a word or a unified group of words; that is, it may be applied to a single word or to a phrase or clause considered as a unit. In the preceding sentence, "phrase," "a handy term," and "that is" are locutions.

Logic

Logic

Revision: Reconsider the logical relationship that is expressed or implied.

Logic is a complex and difficult subject covering a broad range of topics, from vagueness and ambiguity in statements to the methods of scientific investigation. But logic is also a necessary part of our daily lives, whether we are making a judgment, deciding on what action to take, or simply trying to understand what goes on around us. It is equally important in our attempts—spoken or written—to communicate with each other. Everyone (whether he's ever heard the term *logic* or not) has at some time or other protested, "That doesn't make sense" or "That doesn't follow from what you just said." Everyone, that is, has some notion of the difference between logical and illogical reasoning.

Unclear or illogical thinking may reflect itself in all aspects of an essay—irrelevant material, faulty organization, sentences that don't hang together, and imprecise choice of words. More narrowly, it shows up in errors in reasoning, in faulty relationships between one idea and another, one statement and another. For a discussion of the kinds of reasoning we use to reach conclusions and for illustrations of the possible sources of error, see *Guide*, pp. 147–73.

References: Three of the many excellent textbooks on logic are Morris R. Cohen and Ernest Nagel, *An Introduction to Logic and Scientific Method* (New York: Harcourt, 1934); Irving M. Copi, *Introduction to Logic*, 3rd ed. (New York: Macmillan, 1968); Philip Wheelwright, *Valid Thinking* (New York: Odyssey, 1962).

Logic and language

Sometimes items of usage are objected to as being "illogical"—for example, "he *don't," "the *reason is because." But the real trouble with "he don't" is simply that it has become Nonstandard. And when the objection to "the reason is because" is elaborated, it is usually that an adverbial clause (*because . . .*) is equated with a noun (*reason*)—terms that are from grammar rather than logic. Logic proper is not involved in either objection.

The meanings of a great many *idioms are not the sum of the meaning of their separate words: get sick, hard to come by, a little water, many is the time, out of order. These show, more clearly than the general patterns and rules of English, that language is a human development, the result of millions of speech situations, not a preplanned system; it is not illogical but simply alogical. The wonder is that it is as systematic as it is.

Probably arguments from logic had an influence in establishing the *double negative as Nonstandard English; in Old and Middle English the more negatives there were, the more forceful the negation. But arguments from logic have had few such successes, and the term *logical* cannot be applied to language in its technical sense but only in its most general popular sense of "more or less systematic."

Long variants

Some writers are tempted to add an extra prefix or suffix to a word that already carries the meaning they intend. They write *irregardless*, though *regardless* already means "without regard to," or *doubtlessly* for *doubtless*. Some like to use sonorous suffixes that add nothing to the meaning, like the *-ation* in *analyzation*, which means no more than *analysis*. Some other long variants that it is wise to avoid are: *certificated* for *certified; confliction* for *conflict; emotionality* when only *emotion* is meant; *hotness* for *heat; intermingle* for *mingle; orientate* for *orient; repay* when simple *pay* is meant, as in "paying dividends"; *ruination* for *ruin; subsidization* for *subsidizing;* and *utilize* when only *use* is meant.

Occasionally a long form acquires a special sense: a *certificated* teacher is one who has a certificate from the state, licensing him to teach. But in general the more compact form is the right choice. See *Big words. Reference: Fowler, "long variants."

look

When used as an intransitive verb meaning "use the eyes, gaze," *look* is modified by an adverb: look longingly, look searchingly. As a linking verb, equivalent to *appear, look* is followed by an adjective which modifies the subject: He looks well [or healthy or tired or bad]. See *Linking verbs.

lot, lots

In the senses "much," "many," "a great deal," the various expressions *a lot, a lot of, lots*, and *lots of* are established in General (though not in Formal) usage:

Everybody smiles a lot, but nobody really can hear. . . .—Jane Howard, *Life*, May 20, 1966

He tells Celine to make herself attractive and buys her a lot of new clothes. — Edmund Wilson, *New Yorker*, May 21, 1966

. . . with lots more titles to choose from. . . .—David Dempsey, *Saturday Review*, Feb. 16, 1963

There is lots of talk. . . .—*Fortune*, March 1967

lousy

Lousy is an Informal *counter word of disapproval, as *lovely* is a counter word of approval.

Lowercase

l c

Revision: Use a lowercase (small) letter instead of a capital.

See *Capital letters. The correction may be indicated by drawing a slant line through the capital, as shown in *Proofreading.

-ly forms

See *-ally, *Adverbs § 1.

m.
See *a.m. and p.m.

Main clauses
See *Clauses.

majority, plurality
Technically, a majority in an election is more than half the total number of votes cast, while a plurality is the largest number of votes cast for any one candidate but not more than half the total. Though the distinction is sometimes neglected, it is worth preserving for clarity.

In Formal usage, *majority* is applied only to groups of at least three things that can be counted. In Informal and General usage it is sometimes used also of the larger part of a single thing or mass: "A majority of the territory would be Vietcong dominated" (Hugh Sidey, *Life*, Oct. 16, 1970). *Most* is usually a preferable alternative.

Malapropisms
A malapropism is a ludicrous confusion of two words that sound alike but differ in meaning. The humor of malapropisms has faded since the eighteenth-century playwright Richard Brinsley Sheridan used them in the speeches of a character, Mrs. Malaprop: "I would by no means wish a daughter of mine to be a progeny of learning. . . . Then, sir, she would have a supercilious knowledge in accounts; — and as she grew up, I would have her instructed in geometry, that she might know something of the contagious countries . . ." (*The Rivals*, act 1, scene 2).

Manuscript form

MS

Revision: Your manuscript is not in the proper form. Revise or rewrite as directed.

Instructors usually establish their own specifications for manuscript form at the beginning of the course. Whatever the details, the goal is a clean, legible copy that can be read easily. Use regulation paper, leave adequate margins, number the pages, make corrections neatly, and observe your instructor's directions for endorsing the paper. See also *Division of words, *Proofreading, *Typewritten copy.

massive
Used with abstract nouns, *massive* became a *vogue word in the 1960's: massive retaliation, massive resistance, massive inequality, massive unemployment. It continues to be overused.

Mass nouns
Mass nouns denote masses that can be divided but not numbered as aggregates of separate units: *dirt, oxygen, wealth*. They are used with

the (not *a* or *an*) or without an article in the singular and ordinarily have no plural. Mass nouns are opposed to count nouns, which can be counted as separate units, are used with both *a(n)* and *the* but not without an article in the singular, and have plurals: *a boy, the stick, horses.* See *Nouns § 3c. References: Jespersen, *EEG*, pp. 206–09; Sledd, p. 225; Williams, pp. 71–73.

may, can
See *can, may.

Meaning

Mng

Revision: The word, phrase, or sentence marked does not make sense in this context. Replace it with one that communicates the meaning you intend.

For a reader to question the meaning of what you have written indicates a rather drastic failure in communication. Ordinarily the problem is not simply the use of one word for another that is reasonably close to it in sound or meaning—*comprehension* for *comprehensibility*, for instance. This would be marked *WW* (wrong word): the reader knows the word is wrong because he knows what the right one is. But *Mng* suggests that he can't make an intelligent guess at what you were trying to say. Rethinking and rewriting are in order. Compare *Ambiguity, *Wrong word.

media, medium(s)
Medium and *media*, the Latin singular and plural forms, were taken directly into English, and Formal usage consistently maintains the distinction in number, while recognizing the alternate plural, *mediums:* "... the moral possibilities of the mediums themselves ..." (Robert J. Reilly, *American Literature*, March 1967). But *media*, like many other Latin plurals, has tended to become singular in American usage and is frequently so used in General writing, with *medias* sometimes as its plural. As the last of the following citations shows, many readers find the usage objectionable:

Never before has any news media brought war . . . so vividly into the living rooms of our people. —James C. Hagerty, *New York Times*, Dec. 25, 1966

We are all the time reading in the medias that this is a nonviolent demonstration. —*Esquire*, Jan. 1964

Nomination for the most common error among men who should know better: "The media is. . . ." —*Columbia Journalism Review*, Spring 1963

Metaphor
See *Figures of speech; *Guide*, pp. 367–73.

Metonymy
> See *Figures of speech.

Middle English
> See *English language.

Midwest, Middle West
> *Midwest* and *Midwestern* are now much more common than *Middle West* and *Middle Western.*

might, could
> See *can, may.

Misrelated modifiers
> See *Dangling modifiers.

Mixed metaphors
> Speakers frequently run two inconsistent metaphors together: The new measure has taken a firm foothold in the eye of the public; If they are to win in November, they need a fresh face on the ticket — one that has not been straddling the Iron Curtain. Writers, who can reconsider their words, have less excuse for such blunders and — since what they allow to stand can be read again and again — more reason for avoiding them. See *Guide*, pp. 369–71.

Mixed usage
> Incongruously mixed language — Formal with Informal, technical with poetic — is often used for comic effect or, in serious discussions, for shock value: "Many of the scenes have a vivid, snotty ambience" (*New Statesman*, July 28, 1961). But such mixtures are not always effective, and if they are unintentional, they are more disconcerting than amusing. Conspicuously Informal words or idioms should usually not stray into Formal writing; Nonstandard locutions and distinctly Formal words and idioms are equally inappropriate in most General writing. See *Guide*, pp. 24–25.

Modal auxiliaries
> *Can, could; may, might; must; ought; shall, should; will, would* are called modal auxiliaries. They differ from other verbs in having no *-s* in the third-person singular, no infinitive, no participles, and therefore no compound or phrasal forms; instead, they themselves always occur as part of verb phrases, complete or elliptical. The generally similar *dare* and *need* are also sometimes treated as modal auxiliaries. See *Elliptical constructions.

Modern English
> See *English language.

Modifiers

Typically, a modifier limits the meaning of its *headword and makes it more exact (an apple vs. a *green* apple). Modification has never been satisfactorily defined, however, and for the present, students of English grammar must be satisfied with examples. In the following illustrations the words in italics modify the words in capitals: A *cold windy* DAY; HE FAILED *miserably;* She was *truly* SUPERB; *Undoubtedly* IT WAS THE CAT WHO STOLE THE BUTTERMILK; *Coming around the corner,* WE met him head on.

See Guide, pp. 271–83; *Absolute phrases; *Adjectives; *Adverbs; *Ambiguity § 2; *Apposition; *Clauses § 2, b and c; *Dangling modifiers; *Gerunds § 1; *Hyphen; *Infinitives § 4; *Nouns § 2; *Participles § 2; *Phrases; *Restrictive and nonrestrictive.

Money

1. Exact sums of money are usually written in figures: 72¢, $4.98, $168.75, $42,810. Though round sums are likely to be written in words (two hundred dollars, a million and a half dollars), figures may be used for them, too, when several sums are mentioned.

2. In consecutive writing, amounts are usually written out when they are used as modifiers: a million-dollar project. Informally, figures are often used: a $2 seat.

3. For amounts in millions and billions, the dollar sign followed by the number followed by the word is most common: $50 billion, $910 million.

4. Sums of money are construed as either singular or plural: More than $9 million *was* invested in paintings; Over $40 million *were* spent on luxury items.

Monosyllables

A monosyllable is a word of one syllable: *asked, bright, feel, fill, longed, word.* Monosyllables should not be divided at the end of lines (see *Division of words).

Months

In reference matter and Informal writing, the names of months with more than four or more than five letters are often abbreviated in dates: Jan. 21, 1972; Dec. 2, 1964; but May (June, July) 12, 1970. In Formal writing the names of months are not abbreviated. When only the month is given, or the month and year, abbreviation is rare in any style: He was born in January 1959; Every June he tries again. See *Numbers § 1a, *Dates.

Mood

The different forms a verb has for different moods show how the speaker regards what he is saying:

Indicative: as a statement of fact or a question concerning fact
Subjunctive: as a wish or an expression of possibility or doubt
Imperative: as a command

See *Commands and requests, *Indicative mood, *Subjunctives, *Verbs.

more, most
See *Comparison of adjectives and adverbs § 1.

most, almost
In speech, *almost* is often reduced to *most:* A drop in prices would appeal to most anybody. *Most,* used thus, is occasionally seen in factual prose (". . . most everywhere there were lame explanations of the unimportance or irrelevance of regular classes"—*Life,* May 29, 1970); but in all Formal and most General writing, if you can substitute *almost* for *most* in a sentence (almost always, almost everywhere), *almost* is the word you need.

MS
MS, usually in caps, is the conventional abbreviation for *manuscript.* Plural: *MSS.* Though usage is divided, both the *Chicago Manual* and the *MLA Style Sheet* recommend that in most contexts the abbreviation be used without a following period.

must
In General English (but not in Formal) *must* has become a noun meaning "necessity" and an adjective modifier meaning "essential":

It has never been a must. . . .—Henry Brandon, *Saturday Review,* July 29, 1967

This book is a must assignment for reporters. . . .—Robert O. Blanchard, *Columbia Journalism Review,* Spring 1967

myself
Myself is a reflexive or an intensive pronoun, referring back to *I:* I shave myself (reflexive); I saw the whole thing myself (intensive). Besides these uses, *myself* and the other *-self* pronouns are now in General use, in some grammatical environments, as ordinary subjects and objects:

The writing was then done by myself, taking perhaps fifteen days.—Hollis Alpert, *Saturday Review,* Oct. 27, 1962

Then the two of us, President Johnson and myself, walked out. . . .—Malcolm Kilduff, *Columbia Journalism Review,* Winter 1964

Such usage is widely criticized. For the *-self* forms, Formal English would substitute the regular nominative or accusative (*me* in the first example above, *I* in the second). See *Pronouns § 1; *self; *himself, herself. References: Josephine M. Burnham, *AS,* Dec. 1950, pp. 264–67; Bryant, pp. 141–43.

namely and other introductory words

The beginning of wisdom with introductory words like *namely, *that is, for example* is to use them as seldom as possible. Very often they can be omitted altogether in compact, General writing: His topic was a particularly unpleasant one — [namely] napalm.

Names

In factual writing use the real names of people and places unless there are cogent reasons for avoiding them. If there are, invent convincing names (not obviously phony or supposedly funny ones), or use pronouns or "a man" or a less conspicuous device.

nauseous, nauseated

Nauseated usually means "sickened, disgusted" (I felt nauseated at the sight); *nauseous* usually means "causing sickness or disgust" (The food looked nauseous). But speakers, and some writers, frequently use "feeling nauseous" and "getting nauseous." The ambiguity involved (sickened/sickening) suggests the wisdom of retaining the distinction between the two words — a distinction on which many writers insist: "The translator . . . has done a good and sensitive job: except that she will say that a character is 'nauseous' when she means 'liable to vomit'" (Kathleen Nott, *Encounter*, Feb. 1963).

need, needs

Both *needs* (with the ending of regular verbs) and *need* (without the ending, like the auxiliaries) are used as the third-person singular of the verb *need*, but in different idioms. *Needs* is the usual form in affirmative statements, either with noun objects (He needs a haircut) or with *to* and an infinitive (He needs to have a haircut). *Need* is sometimes used, with an infinitive but without *to*, in negative statements and in questions: He need not come; Need she come? In rather Formal English *need* may be used even when the negation is merely suggested by a word like *only:* He assumed that he need only identify himself and all charges would be dropped.

Negation

The meaning of a negative in language is not always equivalent to its meaning in mathematics, where -3 is as much less than 0 as $+3$ is more than 0 and $-(-3) = +3$ because the only mathematical alternative to $-$ is $+$. In language a contrary is likely to be stated by another positive (good — evil, short — tall); the negative usually means "less than" or "different from": *not good* is "less than good" but not necessarily "evil," and *not short* is "different from short" but not necessarily "tall." This quality of negation provides the weakened positive that results from a negated negative. In *not uncommon*, we get a reduced reduction: *uncommon* is "less than common"; *not uncommon* is "less than less than common" or "not quite common" — an unemphatic or understated affirmative.

On the other hand, when *not* negates the verb, and one or two additional negatives modify either the verb or some other sentence element (as in "He can't never do no work"), the multiple negatives may actually reinforce the negation. But this cumulative effect is no longer used in Standard English. See *Double negative.

Sometimes the negative form shows unexpected variation from the affirmative: "must go" and "have to go" are nearly synonymous; "mustn't go" and "don't have to go" are not. See also *Negatives. References: Otto Jespersen, *The Philosophy of Grammar* (New York: Norton, 1965), Ch. 24; Edward S. Klima, "Negation in English," in *The Structure of Language*, ed. Jerry A. Fodor and Jerrold J. Katz (Englewood Cliffs, N. J.: Prentice, 1964), pp. 246–323.

Negatives

When you use both negative and positive words in the same sentence, be sure the combination says clearly what you intend: "The vocational counseling office will try to increase their inability to support themselves" would be better phrased either as "to increase their ability" or as "to remedy their inability."

Poor sentences often result from stating negatively what might better be put positively: This mob violence does not reflect the sentiment of an overwhelming majority of the students. Better: This mob violence reflects the sentiments of only a small minority of the students.

Rather formal writers seem to be especially fond of tricky negative constructions, including litotes, a variety of understatement in which an affirmative is expressed by the negative of its contrary: "Although Marquand is not unfond of poor Apley . . ." (Alfred Kazin, *Saturday Review*, Feb. 2, 1963). Litotes can be effective, but it is best used sparingly. Overused, it makes the writer sound coy, evasive, or simply tiresome. See *Double negative.

Negro

See *black.

neither

As a pronoun, *neither* is ordinarily construed as singular and followed by a singular verb. But when the verb is separated from *neither* by a prepositional phrase with a plural object, a plural verb is frequently used in Informal writing and sometimes in General: ". . . Marx and Trotsky, neither of whom were notably gentle or vegetarian . . ." (Dwight Macdonald, *Esquire*, Oct. 1966). In such cases, Formal writing and most General writing continue to use a singular verb.

As an adjective, *neither* modifies a singular noun (neither man), and a pronoun referring to the noun should be singular by grammatical convention, though some General writers treat the modified noun as a collective and follow it with a plural pronoun: ". . . neither sale took place and, even if they had, . . ." (Henry Cecil, *Holiday*, Jan. 1963).

References: Bryant, pp. 8–10; Fries, *AEG*, p. 50.

Newspaper English

Much newspaper writing is marked by journalese and headlinese. The symptoms of journalese are *big words and *triteness. Granting that "our fair city," "ample outlet for her histrionic ability," and scores of such inflated phrases belonging to paleojournalism are now largely restricted to small-town papers, there is still a vast amount of wordy, lazy writing in newspapers.

The special usage of headline writers enters General spoken English both directly from the newspapers and indirectly through local radio and television reporters, who often base their summaries on newspaper stories. Words like BAN (prohibition), EYES (considers), FLAYS (castigates), PACT (agreement), PROBE (investigation), READIES (prepares), SHIFT (change), and SLAP (criticize) are supposedly chosen by headline writers because they are shorter than their synonyms, but there is also a preference for words that give the impression of urgency, danger, or crisis. The inevitable result of this dramatic inflation is boredom.

The same attempt to save space and achieve vigor results in the telegraphic style of the headline, with articles, connectives, and other function words omitted: GANG FLEES COP; TOT SLAYS FIVE. It is not appropriate in ordinary writing.

nice

Nice is a *counter word indicating mild approval, useful in speech but so general in meaning that it is out of place in most writing. In Formal prose *nice* is usually restricted to meanings like "precise," "subtle," or "discriminating": Kirk raises a nice point in his article on Camus.

nobody, no one

The pronouns *nobody* and *no one* take singular verbs, and strictly speaking a pronoun referring back to either of them must be singular: No one lowered his voice. But sometimes meaning demands a plural pronoun:

Nobody spoiled her. They just took her for granted. . . . — Tom Prideaux, *Life*, June 23, 1967

No one sings; they simply listen reverently. — Ray Jenkins, *New York Times Magazine*, April 7, 1968

In Formal writing the last sentence might be recast: No one sings; everyone simply listens reverently.

Nominalization

Nom

Revision: Change the abstract nominalization into a concrete verb.

For most purposes the best writing is direct writing, writing that avoids three words where two will do, writing that represents an action in a verb and the agent of that action as its subject. The difference between indirect and direct writing is the difference between these two sentences:

It seems to be the case that certain individuals in attendance at this institution of higher education are in a state of anger over recent announcements on the part of the dean in regard to a necessity for greater restrictions where demonstrations are concerned.

Some students here are angry because the dean announced that he would not let them demonstrate as freely as they had.

Probably the most common source of indirect writing is the abstract nominalization, a noun that has been transformationally derived from a full subject + verb in the *deep structure of a sentence:

Tom *paid* the money	⇒ Tom's *payment* of the money
Someone *rejects* material things	⇒ Someone's *rejection* of material things
The common man is intelligent	⇒ The common man's *intelligence*
The students are responsible	⇒ The students' *responsibility*

The direct subject-verb-object or subject-*be*-adjective construction is made indirect and usually less vivid and forceful. When this kind of construction occurs often (about once every seven or eight words), your writing can become heavy, abstract, even pretentious, and possibly dishonest.

To improve such a style, first look for nouns made out of verbs and adverbs: A study is being made of the causes for the decline in the birthrate. When you find them (*study, causes, decline, birthrate*), ask whether the crucial action is in the main verb or in one of these abstract nouns. If it is in the noun (*study*), change the noun to a verb (*are studying*); find a subject for it, if necessary (*They*, referring to a specific antecedent? *Scientists? Biologists?*); and rewrite the sentence around the new subject-verb:

A *study* is being made of the *causes* for the *decline* in the *birthrate*.

They [Scientists/Biologists] are *studying* what has *caused* the *birthrate* to *decline*.

They are *studying* why fewer children have been *born*.

See *Guide*, pp. 343–44; *Subject and verb §§ 1 and 2; *Verbs §2. References: Roderick A. Jacobs, *CCC*, Oct. 1969, pp. 187–90; Rulon Wells, "Nominal and Verbal Style," in *Style in Language*, ed. Thomas A. Sebeok (Cambridge, Mass.: MIT Press, 1960), pp. 213–20; Sledd, pp. 300–01; Williams, pp. 311–21.

Nominative case

A noun or pronoun that is the subject of a finite verb, the complement of a linking verb, or an appositive to either is sometimes said to be in the nominative (or subjective) case. The form of the nominative singular is the common form of the noun, the form to which, typically, the endings for the genitive and for the plural are added. *I, you, he, she, it, we, you, they* are the nominative forms of the personal pronouns; *who, which,* and *that* are the nominative forms of the relative pronouns. These forms are the usual ones for the nominative functions; but see **It's me;* **who, whom.* See also **Case, *Subject and verb.*

Nonce words

Strictly, a nonce word is a word used only once, but practically it is a word that is coined for a special occasion and that does not attain general use—for example, *steakola*, used in 1961 to mean meat given by a butcher as a bribe to an inspector of weights and measures.

none

The use of *none* with a plural verb has often been condemned, usually on the grounds that *none* means "no one" or "not one" and so must be singular. Some writers observe the rule where others would ignore it: "But it is safe to say that none of his books is so widely and genuinely admired as this short novel" (Alfred Kazin, *New York Review of Books*, March 28, 1968). Plural *none* would be ungrammatical as a substitute for an uncountable (He talks nonsense, but none of it matters), but when the reference is to countables, *none* has long been used as a plural in the most reputable writing:

. . . almost none [of the letters] are either thoughtful in their approach or deliberative in their style. — Louis J. Halle, *New Republic*, Nov. 23, 1969

None have been older than this sacramental alliance. — Sidney Hook, *New York Times Book Review*, April 9, 1961

None of these documents afford any solid support for those historians who have viewed Pike as a tool or accomplice in the Wilkinson-Burr schemes. — Harvey L. Carter, *American Historical Review*, Jan. 1967

References: Bryant, p. 8; Fries, *AEG*, p. 56.

Nonrestrictive

See **Restrictive and nonrestrictive.*

Nonstandard English

NS

Revision: Change the Nonstandard word, form, or idiom to one appropriate to Standard usage.

He do, they is, theirself, nobody ain't got nothing: these are Nonstandard. For other illustrations and discussion, see *Guide*, pp. 8–9. Among the articles that treat Nonstandard words or forms are

*Adverbs; *Double negative; *lay, lie; *learn, teach; *Principal parts of verbs; *Subject and verb § 4. See also *English language § 3.

no place

Although *anyplace, everyplace,* and *someplace* for "anywhere," "everywhere," and "somewhere" have become common in General writing, *no place* for "nowhere" is still mainly Informal and is spelled as two words.

nor

By itself, *nor* is an emphatic negative conjunction, most commonly used at the beginning of a sentence in the sense "and . . . not": *Nor was Paris the only place he visited.* Before the last member of a negative series, *nor* gives an added distinctness and emphasis: "I did not see him or hear him" is less emphatic than "I did not see him nor hear him."

As a correlative conjunction, *nor* is paired with *neither.* See *Correlative conjunctions.

not about to

Not about to is not the simple negative of *about to* but an idiom that stresses the remoteness of the suggested possibility: I'm not about to go along with their weird schemes. It occurs mainly in speech but sometimes in General writing. Overuse deadens its tone of lively determination.

not hardly, not scarcely

See *Double negative § 2.

Noun clauses

A noun clause has a subject and *finite verb and functions in a sentence as an abstract noun: *What I can do in society* [subject] depends on *what my neighbors will tolerate* [object of a preposition]. Many noun clauses are introduced by *that,* some by *what, who, whoever, whatever, why, when,* and other interrogative and indefinite relatives.

Subject: That anyone could raise his grades by studying has never occurred to him. *Whether or not he should go* had bothered him for days. *Why sociology has been growing so rapidly* is a complicated question. (A noun clause as subject suggests a Formal style.)

Object: He knew *that it would never happen again.* (In General writing, *that* would often be omitted.)

Predicate noun: His favorites were *whoever flattered him.*

Appositive: The doctrine *that we must avoid entangling alliances* was first stated by Washington.

See *Clauses § 2a, *reason is because.

Nouns

1. *Forms*. English nouns may be inflected for number and case. Many have a plural with an /s/ or /z/ sound, spelled *s* or *es: hats, kindnesses, lecturers*. These and other forms of the plural are discussed in *Plurals of nouns.

The same sound marks the genitive singular, though the ending is written with an apostrophe and an *s: boy's, manufacturer's*. In writing, the genitive plural adds an apostrophe to the regular plural spelling: *boys', manufacturers'*. Words with some of the other plural forms add *'s: men's, sheep's*. See *Genitive.

There are a few distinctive endings which make nouns from other parts of speech. They include *-er* or *-or, -ness, -th, -tion*.

A very few nouns in English have different forms for masculine and feminine: *actor – actress, confidant – confidante, executor – executrix*. See *Gender.

Nouns may be single words or compound words written solid, as two words, or hyphened: *bathroom, bookcase, stickup, hub cap, go-getter*. See *Group words, *Hyphen.

Linguists sometimes debate whether *stone* in "stone wall" is an adjective or a noun, and whether *days* in "He works days" is an adverb or a noun. The simplest solution is to define parts of speech both formally and functionally. *Stone* and *day* are nouns by their forms: they occur with plural and genitive inflections (a stone's throw, two days' work). But since they can occur in positions normally filled by adjectives and adverbs, they can be called, in context only, adjectivals or adverbials. Thus if we call them *nouns*, we define them by formal characteristics; if *adjectivals* or *adverbials*, by syntactic function. If they also function as nouns syntactically, as in "*Home* is where the heart is" or in "*Day* will come eventually," then they are nouns in nominal function.

2. *Principal uses in sentences (syntax)*. Noun phrases typically stand in certain positions and relationships in sentences: after prepositions, in the predicate after linking verbs like *be*, etc. Within noun phrases, nouns are typically preceded by determiners and adjectives and followed by prepositional phrases and relative clauses. The principal syntactic uses of noun phrases and hence of nouns may be illustrated as follows:

Subject of a verb: A high wind from the east blew for three days. See *Subject and verb.

Object of a verb: The wind damaged *the trees, which were loaded with ice*. See *Objects.

Object of a preposition: In *the night*, on *a frozen pond*, fishing is no sport for *a feeble spirit*. See *Prepositions.

Predicate noun: He has become *president of the firm*. See *Linking verbs.

Attributive: The young man's partner had the grace of a *baby* hippo. See *Attributive, *Genitive.

Apposition: The first settler, *Thomas Sanborn*, came in 1780. See *Apposition, appositives.

Modifiers of verbs: He came *two months ago.*

3. *Classes of nouns.* The common traditional groupings of nouns are as follows (many nouns would fall into more than one group):
a—Proper nouns, names of particular people and places, written with capitals and usually without *the* or *a:* Anne, George W. Loomis, London, Georgia, France, the Bay of Naples. See *Proper names.

In contrast with proper nouns, all other nouns are called common.
b—Concrete nouns, names of things that can be perceived by the senses: *leaf, leaves, road, trousers, intellectuals.* Concrete nouns are opposed to abstract nouns, names of qualities, actions, types, ideas, and so on: *goodness, theft, beauty, heroism.* The great majority of these nouns are related to verbs or adjectives: *intention (intend), goodness (good), refusal (refuse), stupidity (stupid), response (respond).* Given a choice between representing an action in an abstract noun or in a full verb, you will generally write a livelier, clearer sentence if you choose the verb:

The achievement of clarity of thought has a clear dependence on the correctness of the formulation of the problem.

To think clearly, formulate your problem correctly.

See *Nominalization.
c—Mass nouns, names of material aggregates, masses, or other units not defined by their discrete parts and their shape: *food, money, health, water, chaos, intelligence.* Mass nouns are syntactically distinguished by the fact that their indefinite meaning requires the absence of an indefinite article: *Intelligence* depends on *environment* and *heredity.* Mass nouns are opposed to count nouns, which refer to things that are conceived of as discrete units: *car, book, street, machine, horse.* Count nouns require *a/an* to mark their indefiniteness: a car, a book, a street, a machine, a horse. Some words can be either mass or count nouns: Wood is used in building—Mahogany is a valuable wood; Steak is expensive—I ate a steak.
d—Collective nouns, names of a group of things regarded as a unit: *fleet, army, committee, trio.* See *Collective nouns.

For additional information, see *Capital letters, *Case. References: Curme, *Parts of Speech*, Chs. 1 and 9, *Syntax*, Chs. 2, 4, 26; Francis, pp. 237–52, 298–312; Fries, *Structure*, pp. 65–79; Sledd, pp. 68–73; Williams, pp. 70–79.

nowhere near

Though in General use, *nowhere near* has an Informal tone: It was a good score but nowhere near as large as we'd hoped for. Formal usage would substitute "not nearly so large as." Reference: Bryant, pp. 148–49.

Number

Number in English grammar is the singular and plural aspect of nouns and pronouns and verbs. Number in nouns is most important, since it controls the number of verbs and pronouns. In verbs, overt indication of number is limited to the present tense and the single pair *was – were*. See *Plurals of nouns, *Reference of pronouns, *Subject and verb.

number

Number is a collective noun, taking a singular verb when the group as a group is meant and a plural verb when the individual units are the concern. A rule says that "a number of" takes the plural (A number of tickets have been sold) and "the number of" takes the singular (The number of tickets left to sell is discouraging); but a singular verb with "a number of" is not unusual: "A number of immunizations is . . . recommended for world travelers . . ." (*Journal of the American Medical Association*, Jan. 4, 1965).

Numbers

1. *Uses.* Figures are conventionally used for:

a — Dates (June 29, 1918), except in Formal social correspondence and some ceremonial contexts.

b — Hours with *a.m. or p.m.: 5 p.m. (but five o'clock).

c — Street addresses and highway numbers: 2841 Washington Avenue, Route 99.

d — Pages and other references: p. 761; Act III, scene iv, line 28 (III.iv.28) or act 3, scene 4, line 28 (3.4.28).

e — Exact sums of money: $4.98, 75¢.

f — Measures expressed in the conventional abbreviations: 15 cc., 6", 10 lbs., 32° F.

g — All members of a series of numbers applying to the same units and including one or more numbers that must conventionally be written in figures (from 9 to 125 days). That is, mixed series of figures and words should be avoided.

The plural of a figure is formed by adding either -s or, somewhat more formally, -'s (six 5s or six 5's; the 1970s or the 1970's). For the genitive, no apostrophe is usual with figures: They imported $12,000 worth of equipment.

2. *Figures or words.* Words are conventionally used for round numbers and indefinite numbers: ten million, hundreds, a dozen, a score. Words are also customary for numbers that begin sentences ("Nineteen-eighteen did not usher in the millennium. . . ." — Henry Steele Commager, *Saturday Review*, Nov. 9, 1968) and for ordinal numbers (*first, second, third*), except in routine technical enumeration where *1st, 2nd, 3rd* are used.

In general, newspapers and Informal writing have figures for numbers over ten, words for smaller numbers; magazine and book styles (most General writing) ordinarily have figures for numbers over one hundred except when the numbers can be written in two words: *four, ten, ninety-two, two thousand.*

This passage illustrates a typical book style in handling numbers:

Stage coaches reached new top speeds as their horses galloped over the improved roads. It had taken four and a half days to travel the 160 miles from London to Manchester in 1754; thirty-four years later the journey had been shortened to twenty-eight hours. — T. Walter Wallbank and others, *Civilization Past and Present*

Large numbers are increasingly written in a combination of figures and words: "$3 billion" is quicker to grasp than "$3,000,000,000."

Except in dates, street numbers, telephone numbers, and a few other regular series, a comma is used to separate thousands, millions, etc., though it may be omitted in four-digit numbers: 1952 (the year); 1,952 (or 1952) bushels; $4,682,981.

Numbers in two words between twenty-one and ninety-nine are usually hyphened, though the practice is declining: *forty-two* or *forty two.* A hyphen (set by compositors as an en dash) is used between figures to indicate a range: The prediction was based on 40–50 personal interviews and 200–300 telephone calls. It should not be used if the numbers are preceded by *from* or *between: from 40 to 50* (not: from 40–50).

3. *Arabic and roman numerals.* Arabic numerals (1, 2, 146 . . .) are used in almost all places where numbers are not expressed in words. Roman numerals, either lower case (i, ii, cxlvi . . .) or capitals (I, II, CXLVI . . .), are occasionally used to number units in a rather short series, as in outlines, chapters of a book, acts of a play, though now less often than formerly. The preliminary pages of books are almost always numbered with roman numerals; the body of a book begins a new pagination with arabic numerals. Sometimes roman numerals are used for the date on title pages and in formal inscriptions.

See also *Fractions, *Hyphen, *Money. References: *Chicago Manual; U.S. Style Manual.*

Objects

1. *Direct objects.* In the simplest kind of sentence, the direct object is a noun phrase that follows a transitive verb, to which the object is related as one of the primary elements of the predicate: Grammar puzzles *normal people;* Alice saw *the white rabbit;* The man was building *a fence.* In more complicated sentences a variety of elements can stand as direct objects, which do not always follow their verbs; and, of course, pronouns can replace noun phrases in the object relation: Everybody enjoys *eating steak;* Somebody said *that porpoises are smart; What he meant* I never knew; John met *them* earlier.

Often the direct object of an active verb can be made the subject of a synonymous sentence in the passive: *Normal people* are puzzled by grammar; *The white rabbit* was seen by Alice.

Traditionally, direct objects are said to name what is affected or effected by the actions of their verbs, but this appears incorrect for "He received a wound in the war" or "They experienced many humiliations." On a deeper level, however, what appear to be subjects (*He* and *They*) may be objects. See *Guide*, p. 273.

2. *Indirect objects.* The indirect object is said to name the person or thing to which something is given, said, or shown—the person or thing affected, but indirectly, by the verbal action: He gave *the church* a memorial window; She showed *him* the snapshot. Like direct objects, indirect objects are noun phrases or equivalents for noun phrases. They follow a special set of transitive verbs, precede direct objects, and are synonymous, in the appropriate sentences, with prepositional phrases introduced by *to* or *for:* He gave a memorial window *to the church.* Some transformational grammarians make the structure behind the prepositional phrase basic and derive the double noun-phrase pattern from the prepositional phrase:

```
NP    V     NP     to   NP
He    gave  money  to   Bill.
```

```
NP    V     NP    NP
He    gave  Bill  money.
```

3. *Objects of prepositions.* The object of a preposition is the noun phrase, or noun-phrase equivalent, that follows the preposition and bears to some other element in the sentence a relation which the preposition indicates: here, "some other element in the sentence" is the object of *to*. A relative or interrogative pronoun sometimes precedes the preposition: *What* are you talking *about?*

4. *Other objects.* Different grammarians use *object* in different ways. Noun phrases or adjectives that follow direct objects after a special set of transitive verbs and are related to the direct objects as if they were joined to them by the verb *to be* are sometimes called object complements: They considered his behavior a *threat to the school's welfare.*

When a direct or indirect object is made the subject of a passive sentence and the other object or object complement remains after the verb, that remaining object is called a retained object: His behavior was considered a *threat.*

Cognate objects are formally and semantically related to their verbs: He slept the sleep of *the just.* An adverbial object is a noun phrase in adverbial function after a verb: He ran *three blocks.*

Many linguists reject as direct objects words in a sentence that cannot be made the subject of a passive version of the same sentence: He resembles his father—His father is resembled by him; I have a cold—A cold is had by me; It cost a nickel—A nickel was cost by it.

References: Sledd, pp. 126–36; Jacobs and Rosenbaum, Ch. 18.

Obscenity

The words traditionally considered obscene are rarely appropriate in college writing. See *Profanity.

of

The double prepositions *inside of, outside of, off of* are heard regularly and are in General use in writing. Many Formal stylists reject the *of*, particularly with *off*.

of course

Of course should be used sparingly and fairly. It should not be used as a substitute for evidence: Of course, we all know the administration is corrupt. Nor should it be used to suggest that, for the writer, the esoteric is the everyday: Old English had, of course, no inflected passive.

OK, O.K.

OK or *O.K.* is Informal and commercial English for "approval" (The foreman put his OK on the shipment), "all right, correct" (It's OK with me), and "endorse, approve" (If you'll OK my time sheet, I can get paid). Occasionally it is spelled *okay*. As a verb the forms are *OK, OK'ed* or *OK'd, OK'ing* and *okay, okayed, okaying. Oke* and *okey-doke* are slang. Reference: For the most extensive treatment of the history of *OK*, see the series of studies by Allen Walker Read, *AS*, 1963–1964. Mencken, pp. 169–71, summarizes some of Read's findings.

Old English

See *English language.

one

1. The use of the impersonal *one*, referring to people in general or to an average or typical person, is Formal, especially if it is repeated: One can't be too careful, can one? Many writers consider a series of *one*'s pretentious and refer back to *one* with forms of *he:*

One can determine his own life. — J. A. Ward, *Journal of English*, Dec. 1967

One is left with the feeling that it doesn't matter what he thinks. . . . — Loudon Wainwright, *Life*, July 26, 1968

A shift from *one* to impersonal *they* is avoided in writing, and while a shift from *one* to impersonal *you* is not rare, it would be inappropriate in Formal contexts and disapproved by many readers. The *you . . . you* pattern is most common in General English. See *they, *you.

2. *One* may be used to avoid repeating a noun in the second of two compound elements: Fred took the new copy, and I took the old one. The plural *ones* is often so used, and logically enough, since *one* is not only a number but an indefinite pronoun: She had a yellow pon-

cho and two red ones. But *one* as a noun substitute is often
*deadwood, taking emphasis away from the adjective that carries the
real meaning: The plan was certainly [an] original [one].

Reference: Jespersen, *EEG*, pp. 83–85.

one another

See *Pronouns § I.

one of those who

In Formal English the clause following *one of those who* and similar
locutions is usually plural because the relative pronoun refers to a
plural antecedent:

He is one of those people who believe in the perfectibility of man. (*Who* refers to *people*.)

This is one of the books that make you change your ideas. (*That* refers to
books.)

But there is a strong tendency to regard *one* as the antecedent, and in
General writing a singular verb is common:

. . . Mills is one of an elite handful who has served more than half his lifetime in the House. — Murray Seeger, *Atlantic*, Aug. 1971

. . . one of those crucial questions that comes up again and again. . . .
— David Garnett, *American Scholar*, Summer 1965

The more Formal your context, the more appropriate a plural verb.
See also *Subject and verb § 3d. Reference: Jespersen, *MEG*, II, 181,
499; VII, 140.

only

To quibble about the position of *only* when meaning is not at stake is
to waste time. "Logically," perhaps, a single-word modifier should
stand immediately before the element modified: I need only six more
to have a full hundred. But usage often favors placing *only* before the
verb of the statement: I only need six more to have a full hundred.
The meaning is equally clear.

So while the placing of *only* can produce a rather ludicrous
statement (He only has a face a mother could love), putting it with
the verb is a characteristic and reputable English idiom:

The sentencing judge only learned his background a week or two before he
was to be officially murdered. — Arthur Miller, *Harper's*, Nov. 1962

On the strength of the historic record, one can only say that they knew that
there was a promised land and that it wasn't the one we were living in.
— Hans J. Morgenthau, *New York Review of Books*, Aug. 1, 1968

In this respect, *even, ever, nearly, just, exactly,* and other such
limiting adverbs are similar to *only*. But since they are used much
less and some of them only in Formal English, the idiom is not so

common. Like *only*, they can be placed so that they spoil the emphasis: I'm tolerant about such things, but his conduct even surprises me [for: surprises even me].

References: Gladys Haase, *CE*, April 1951, pp. 400–02; John S. Kenyon, *CE*, Nov. 1951, pp. 116–17; Bryant, pp. 155–56.

Onomatopoeia

See *Imitative words.

on, onto, on to

When *on* is an adverb and *to* a preposition in a separate phrase, they should be written as two words: The rest of us drove on to the city. The test is that *city* cannot be the object of *on*. Used as a preposition, they are written solid: The team trotted onto the floor; They looked out onto the park. Both *floor* and *park* are objects of the compound *onto*.

In the sense "to a place on" (The team trotted onto the floor), *onto* and *on* are sometimes used interchangeably: The band finally dashed on(to) the stage. Some readers and writers prefer *on* alone when it is not ambiguous. Reference: Bryant, p. 152.

on the part of

On the part of is often a clumsy way of saying "by," "among," "for," or the like: The new law resulted in less wild driving on the part of [by] young people; There has been a growing awareness of political change on the part of [among] scholars.

O, oh

In ordinary direct address, *oh* is the more common spelling: Oh, waitress; Oh, be quiet! *O* is used in solemn (or mock-solemn) invocations: "By the waters of Babylon we sat down and wept, when we remembered thee, O Sion" (*The Book of Common Prayer*, Psalm 137:1).

In emotional exclamation both *O* and *oh* are used (O dear, I suppose so; Oh well, I didn't need it anyway); but while *O* is not followed by punctuation unless it stands alone, *oh* is usually followed by a comma or an exclamation mark. *O* is always capitalized; *oh* is not unless it begins a sentence.

or

Or is a coordinating conjunction and, like *and, but,* and *for*, should connect words, phrases, or clauses of equal value. (See *Coordinating conjunctions, *Compound sentence, *Series.) According to conventional rules, two subjects joined by *or* take a singular verb if each is singular, a plural verb if both are plural or if the one nearer the verb is plural:

Cod liver oil or halibut oil is often prescribed.
Cod liver oil or cod liver oil capsules are often prescribed.
Cod liver oil capsules or cod liver oil is often prescribed.

In fact, writers sometimes use a plural verb after singular subjects joined by *or*, suggesting "either and perhaps both" rather than "not both but one or the other": "There is no evidence that Mao or Castro are taking advantage of their young fans" (Andrew Kopkind, *New Republic*, April 10, 1965). See *Correlative conjunctions. References: Curme, *Syntax*, p. 57; Jespersen, *MEG*, II, 176–77.

oral, verbal

Literally, *verbal* means "pertaining to words" and *oral* means "pertaining to the mouth." Insisting on the etymological distinction, some writers maintain that *oral* is the one true opposite of *written;* but *verbal* is used in the sense "unwritten" in all varieties of English: ". . . though written contracts were fairly often produced, a large proportion of the agreements seem to have been verbal . . ." (Robert Sabatino Lopez, *Speculum*, April 1967).

-or, -er

See *-er, -or.

Organization

Org

Revision: Improve the organization of your essay by arranging the parts in an orderly sequence or by making the movement clear through the use of appropriate signals and transitions, or both.

The main cause of poor organization is failure to get clear in your own mind the natural or logical divisions of your subject and the right relation of the parts of your discourse. Every essay should have a definable structure. In writing your paper, you should be able to see your material as a sequence of parts or stages; you should arrange the parts in an order that makes sense in terms of your purpose; and as you develop each part, you should take into account its place and importance in the whole scheme.

A poorly organized essay lacks direction—a logical movement from beginning to end. Or it lacks shape—proportions that do justice to the relative significance of the ideas. Or it lacks unity, with irrelevant material diverting attention from the main thread of the discussion. The best way to pinpoint such structural weaknesses is to outline your essay, reducing it to a skeleton of key statements. Then set about reorganizing and rewriting.

If rereading your essay and studying your outline leaves you convinced that the organization is basically sound, examine the ways you have introduced topics and linked up paragraph sequences. Although the sections of the essay are in the right order, you may have neglected to give the reader guidance in seeing the relationships you intend. If this is the case, relatively simple repair work—improving connections and supplying transitions—should give the essay the direction, shape, and unity it *seems* to lack. The remedy is not drastic reworking of the entire structure but adding or rewriting sentences, particularly those at the structural joints that divide the main blocks of material. See *Transition; *Guide*, Ch. Eight, and pp. 255–62.

Originality

Original is applied to writing in two somewhat different senses. The first refers to material. Material is original when it is gathered by the writer from his experience, from his observation of people, events, or places, or from documents like letters and newspapers. Most college papers should contain some original material. The content may come entirely or in large part from the writer's experience and thought. Or at least the central idea, the purpose, and the point of view can represent his thinking, and some of the examples, details, or applications can come from his observation. Merely rewriting a magazine article is not a profitable exercise in composition. Putting together material from several such secondary sources is more useful, since it requires selection and comparison of material. But the most useful work for growth in writing is composing papers in which a good deal of the material is original. The writing is a little harder, but it is more fun, and the gain is much greater than in simply working over what others have done. (See *Plagiarism.)

Originality in expression, in style, is a different matter. The English language has been used a long time, and absolutely new words and phrases are rare. The most threadbare figures and locutions can be avoided, and an honest attempt to tell exactly what you see and believe will ordinarily result in straightforward, readable writing, which is much more valuable than mere novelty. The one sure fact is that striving too hard for originality is almost certain to result in strained writing or *fine writing, uncomfortable to writer and reader alike. When a style deserving the label *original* appears, it is usually the by-product of an active and independent mind, not the result of trying to be different.

Origin of words

1. *The study of word origins.* Every word has a history. Some words, like *chauffeur, mores, television, parapsychology,* are relatively new in English; some, like *home, candle, go, kitchen,* have been in the language for centuries; others have recently acquired new meanings, like *satellite* (from a Latin word for "attendant," a term in astronomy which probably now means for most people either a dependent nation or a man-made object which orbits the earth, moon, or other celestial body). Etymology, the study of word origins, traces the changes of forms and combinations of word elements (as in *dis/service, wild/ness, bath/room, room/mate*) and pursues the word or its component parts to Old English, or to the foreign language from which it came into English, and so on back to the earliest discoverable forms. Of some words, especially Informal words like *dude, stooge, rumpus,* earlier forms are unknown; of others, like *OK or blizzard,* the sources are debated. But the efforts of generations of scholars have discovered fairly full histories for most words. These are given briefly in most dictionaries and more fully in the *Oxford English Dictionary* and in special works.

Many of our everyday words come down directly from Old English *(brother, go, house, tell)* or, if they are of foreign origin, were borrowed many centuries ago *(candle, debt, pay, travel)*. Many French words, of both early and recent borrowing, entered the vocabulary by way of high society *(debutante, fiancée)*. The vocabulary of philosophy and abstract thought has a large Latin element *(concept, fallacy, rational, idealism)*, and the vocabulary of science has many Greek elements *(atom, hemoglobin, seismograph)*.

The sources of words will often reveal something about our history, as the many Norman French and Latin words in law *(fine, tort, certiorari, subpoena)* remind us of the time, following 1066, when the government of England was in the hands of the Norman French. But it is more interesting to discover what meanings the words have had in their earlier career in English and in the foreign languages from which they have come. *Supercilium* in Latin meant "eyebrow"; *rehearse* is from a French word meaning to "harrow again"; *sarcophagus* is, according to its Greek originals, "a flesh eater," referring to the limestone coffins that hastened the disintegration of bodies; *profane* (Latin) meant "outside the temple" and gathered the meaning of "against religion, the opposite of sacred"; *alcohol* goes back to an Arabic word for a finely ground powder, used for painting eyelids, and came to be applied, in Spanish, to specially distilled spirits, and so to our alcohol. See *English language.

This article chiefly presents the various ways in which words have arrived and are still arriving in English. There are two general processes — making new words, by either creating or borrowing them, and compounding or clipping words and parts of words that are already in the language. Then this stock of words is increased in usefulness by changes in the meanings of the forms which are established.

2. *New words.*
a — Creation of words. Outright creation, "coinage," of words is rare. Even *gas*, first used by Van Helmont (1578–1644), a Belgian scientist, probably had the Greek *chaos* as well as a Dutch or Flemish word behind it. *Kodak* is probably an actual creation, as are a good many other trade names, some familiar from advertising. Informal words like *dud* and *burble* were also creations, good-sounding words someone made up. F. Gelett Burgess invented *blurb*, defining it as "self-praise; to make a noise like a publisher." *Imitative words like *buzz, honk, swish, whiz* are attempts to translate the sounds of nature into the sounds of language. Various exclamations of surprise, pain, scorn, may have started as emotional noises — *ow, ouch, fie, phooey* — and then became regular words. A word that is coined for a special occasion is a *nonce word. As a rule arbitrary coinages do not stick. Outright creation is a very minor source of new words.
b — Borrowed words. English has always borrowed words freely, from Latin, German, French and from other languages with which English-

speaking people have come in contact. It has assimilated words of quite un-English form: *khaki* (Hindustani), *seersucker* (Persian, Hindustani), *tycoon* (Japanese), *ski* (Norwegian), *hors d'oeuvres* (French), *intelligentsia* (Russian). The various words for *porch*, itself Norman French but the oldest and the most English-seeming of the group, come from various languages: *piazza* (Italian), *portico* (Italian), *stoop* (Dutch), *veranda* (Anglo-Indian).

Borrowing is still going on, though perhaps more slowly than at some periods. Some words come into Formal English and remain Formal words: *intelligentsia, bourgeois, chef-d'oeuvre, objet d'art, Zeitgeist,* and many others of political, philosophical, scientific, or literary bearing. *Sphygmograph* and many other scientific words are recent compoundings of Latin and especially of Greek words which are not otherwise in English usage, so that they may be regarded as borrowings as well as compounds. Others come in as General words, especially when large numbers of people go abroad, as during a war (*blitzkrieg, camouflage*) or when a foreign invention becomes suddenly popular, as in *chauffeur, garage, chassis* of the automobile vocabulary. Some words brought by immigrants have stuck: *sauerkraut, kohlrabi, pronto, pizza, kosher, goulash.*

Many borrowed words are dropped before they gain any general currency. The useful words are more or less adapted to English spelling and pronunciation and become true English words. (See *English language and, for suggestions about the use of recently borrowed words, *Foreign words in English.)

3.   *Changes in form of words.*
a—Word composition. Most new words are made by putting together two or more elements to create a different meaning or function, as *un-* added to *interesting* gives a word of the opposite meaning, *uninteresting,* or *-ize* added to the noun *canal* gives a verb, *canalize.* The fact that dictionaries separate words formed with prefixes into two groups, those that need to be defined and those that are self-explanatory, shows how deceptive affixes can be. The elements may be a prefix placed before the root word *(mis-related),* or a suffix added *(foolish-ness),* or a combining element like *mono- (mono-syllable, mono-rail),* or two independent words built together *(book-case, basket-ball, gentle-man).* *Group words like *high school, out of town,* though not written as single words, could be included as a type of word composition.

A list of prefixes and suffixes that are still active in English would take several pages. Here are a few of the more common prefixes:

a- (not): asymmetrical, amoral, atypical
ante- (before): anteprohibition era
anti- (against): antiprohibition
bi- (two): bivalve, biplane, bicycle
dis- (not): disinterested, dispraise
in- (in): income, impart, instill

in- (not): inelegant, impractical
mis- (wrong): mistake, misnomer
pre- (before): preview, prenatal, preempt
re- (again): revise, redecorate
up- (up): upend (verb), upswirl (noun)

A few suffixes are:

-en (to form a verb): heighten, lighten, weaken
-ful (full): playful, spoonful
-fy (to make): electrify, horrify
-ish (to form an adjective): dryish, foolish, smallish
-ize (to form a verb): circularize

Combining elements include a number of words or roots, many of them Greek:

-graph- (writing): biography, photograph
micro- (small): microcosm, micrometer, microphone, microbiology
mono- (one): monotone, monorail
-phil- (loving): philanthropy, philately, Anglophile
-side-: sidewall, sideswipe, ringside
-smith: locksmith, silversmith, gunsmith
tele- (distant): television, telemeter
-trop- (turning): geotropic, heliotropic

At first a compound has no more than the meaning to be expected from its elements: *unable = not able.* But often it will develop an independent sense which can hardly be guessed at from the meanings of its elements: *cupboard, loudspeaker.*

Several pairs of prefixes and suffixes have the same meaning, and often two words with the same meaning but somewhat different forms exist side by side, especially words with *in-* (not) and *un-* and nouns with *-ness, -ity,* or *-tion:*

aridness, aridity	indistinguishable, undistinguishable
completeness, completion	precocity, precociousness
corruption, corruptness	torridness, torridity
ferociousness, ferocity	unobliging, disobliging

b — Phonetic alterations. For a variety of reasons, one word may have two or more developments in its pronunciation, each form emphasizing a different shade of the older word's meaning. Here are four Anglo-Saxon words which have had such double developments: from *ān* we get *one* and *a, an;* from *of* come *off* and *of;* from *thurh, through* and *thorough;* and from *ūtera, utter* and *outer.* There are, of course, many more, especially if we go further back. Many such doublets are not so obvious because the spellings do not differ, though the pronunciations, functions, and meanings do: *con' duct,* noun; *con duct',* verb, etc.

c—Blends. Informal English has a number of words that show the liberties that the users of language have always taken with their words and always will take. Some of their experiments have been added to the main English vocabulary.

One common type is blends, or portmanteau words, made by telescoping two words into one, often making a letter or syllable do double duty. *Squish* is probably a blend of *squirt* and *swish; electrocute*, of *electro-* and *execute; smog*, of *smoke* and *fog*. Blends are common in the names of many firms and products. Other examples include *motel, paratroops, cinemactress* (*Time* magazine was once obsessed with such blends), and a good many folksy efforts like *absogoshdarnlutely*.

d—Clipped words. One of the commonest types of word change is clipping, dropping one or more syllables to make a briefer form: *ad* from *advertisement, bus* from *omnibus, taxi* from *taxicab* (earlier, from *taximeter cabriolet*), *quote* from *quotation, mob* (an eighteenth-century clip from *mobile vulgus*), *auto, movie, plane, phone*, and so on. *Shoptalk has many clips—*mike* for *microphone* or *micrometer*. The speech of any closely related group is full of clips; campus vocabulary shows a full line: *econ, home ec, phys ed, grad, dorm, ad building, lab, exam, gym, prof, premed*, and scores more. Clipped words are written (when they are appropriate to the context) without apostrophe or period.

e—Back formations. *Back formation* refers to the derivation of a new word (for example, *orate*) from an older word assumed to be its derivative (*oration*). The new word usually serves as a different part of speech, like *babysit* from *baby-sitter, peddle* from *peddler, typewrite* from *typewriter*. Some back formations are long established (*beg, diagnose, browse, edit*); some are still avoided by conservative writers (*emote, enthuse, sculpt*); some are mostly for fun (*buttle, revolute*).

f—Common nouns from proper names. A number of words have come into general use because of some association with a person or place: *boycott*, from the name of an Irish land agent, Captain Boycott, who was so treated; *macadam*, from the inventor of the road surface, John L. MacAdam; *sandwich*, from the Earl of Sandwich; *jersey*, from the island of Jersey; *pasteurize*, from Louis Pasteur, who developed the process.

g—Playful formations. Blends and back formations are likely to have a playful note, and so do some other word shifts that can't be classified. Some become quite generally used: *dingus, doodad, beanery, jalopy*.

References: The great authority on the origin of English words is the *Oxford English Dictionary;* the *Dictionary of American English* and the *Dictionary of Americanisms* supplement it for words peculiar to the United States. Besides general books on English, the following pay special attention to origin of words: Bolinger; W. Nelson Francis, *The English Language* (New York: Norton, 1963); J. B. Greenough and G. L. Kittredge, *Words and Their Ways in English Speech* (New York: Macmillan, 1961); Otto Jespersen, *Growth and Structure of the English Language*, 9th ed. (New York: Free Press, 1968); George H.

McKnight, *English Words and Their Backgrounds* (New York: Appleton, 1923); Pyles; Robertson; Margaret Schlauch, *The English Language in Modern Times*, 2nd ed. (London: Oxford Univ. Press, 1964).

-or, -our
> American spelling prefers *-or* in such words as *color, favor, honor*. Two familiar exceptions are *Saviour*, in reference to Jesus Christ, and *glamour* in advertisements. British usage is divided, though to an American reader the words in *-our* are conspicuous. In quoting directly from British writings and in referring to British institutions (like the Labour party), use British spellings. Otherwise follow American practice. Reference: Fowler, "-our & -or."

other
> See *any § 1.

ought
> See *should, would; *want.

-our, -or
> See *-or, -our.

Outline form

Outl

Revision: Revise the form of your outline to observe the conventions given below.

1. *The title.* The title of the essay should stand three spaces above the outline. It is not part of the outline and should not be numbered. The heads should carry their full meaning and not refer back to the title by pronouns. See *Titles of essays.

2. *Thesis statement.* An optional practice—but a good one—is to put a sentence stating the subject and scope of the whole paper between the title and the first main head.

3. *Numbering systems.* The most widely used numbering alternates letters and figures, as shown in the examples in the *Guide*, pp. 216, 218. Avoid intricate or confusing schemes of numbering.

4. *Indention.* Write the main heads flush with the left margin and indent subheads two or three spaces from the left—enough to place them clearly in a different column. Heads that run over a single line should be further indented, as in the sentence outline on p. 216.

5. *Punctuation and capitalization.* No punctuation is needed at the ends of lines in a topic outline. In a sentence outline the punctuation should follow regular sentence practice. Only the first word of a head and proper names are capitalized; an outline head is not a title.

6. *Heads.*

a—Meaningful heads. Each head should be understandable by itself, especially if the outline is to be shown to someone for criticism or is to be submitted with the essay. The following would do as a scratch outline but would not be satisfactory for other purposes:

> My Vocation
> I. The work I am interested in
> II. Why I prefer this type of work
> III. What my responsibilities would be
> IV. The chances for success

b—Heads of equal importance. The main heads of an outline, those usually marked by roman numerals, should show the several main divisions of the material. Similarly, the immediate subdivisions of these heads, those usually marked by capital letters, should designate logical divisions of one phase of the subject. The same principle applies to further divisions under any subhead.

Unequal headings	*Equal headings*
Books I Have Enjoyed	Books I Have Enjoyed
I. Adventure stories	I. Adventure stories
II. Historical novels	II. Historical novels
III. *The Sotweed Factor*	III. Character studies
IV. Autobiographies	IV. Autobiographies
V. What I like most	V. Books on mysticism

c—Headings in parallel form. Parallel heads or subheads are expressed in parallel grammatical form. A sentence outline should use complete sentences throughout; a topic outline should use phrase heads only. There should be parallel phrasing for all heads of the same rank; that is, the heads in one series should be all nouns or all adjectives or all phrases, or whatever is most appropriate.

Heads not parallel	*Parallel heads*
The Art of Putting	The Art of Putting
I. The stance is fundamental	I. The stance
II. The grip	II. The grip
III. Watch the backswing	III. The backswing
IV. Stroking the ball	IV. The stroke
V. Follow through with care	V. The follow-through

7. *Division of main points.* Since a topic is not "divided" unless there are at least two parts, a formal outline should have at least two subheads under any main head—or none at all. For every heading marked *I* there should be at least a *II*, for every *A* there should be a *B*, and so on.

Illogical single heads	*Proper subdivision*
The Tripartite System	The Tripartite System
I. The executive branch	I. The executive branch
A. President and Cabinet	A. President
	B. Cabinet
II. The legislative branch	II. The legislative branch
A. The House	A. The House of Representatives
B. The Senate	B. The Senate
1. Functions	1. Special functions
	2. Special privileges
III. The judicial branch	III. The judicial branch
A. The Supreme Court	A. The Supreme Court
	B. Lower courts

If there is a single detail, it may be included in the heading. For example, for an organization in which the whole executive power lay in the president the head might be:

I. The executive branch (the president)

8. *Introductions and conclusions.* Ordinarily an essay has a beginning, a middle, and an ending (or an introduction, a body, and a conclusion), but you should not use such labels in the outline. For one thing, they are too general to reflect specific content. For another, the beginning and ending can rarely be represented by heads that are coordinate with the others. The first and last topics in the outline are from the main body of material, chosen with a special view to their fitness for meeting and for taking leave of a reader.

Oxymoron

An oxymoron is a contradiction in terms used as a figure of speech — for example, "sweet bitterness," "loving hate," "mildly fatal," "making haste slowly." *Oxymoron* is occasionally used with the extended meaning "a compound of incongruous elements": "He was that religious oxymoron, a gentle Calvinist . . ." (George P. Elliott, *Commentary*, May 1963).

pair

When not preceded by a number or other plural indicator, *pairs* is the preferred plural of *pair:* Pairs of figures were common in the design. Otherwise, usage is divided:

. . . these hypotheses are confounded in two pairs. — Roselle and Campbell, *Psychological Bulletin*, Jan. 1969

. . . he found a car with one too many pair of skis. — *Time*, Feb. 18, 1966

Paradox

See *Epigrams and aphorisms.

Paragraph indention, No paragraph indention

¶   No ¶

Revision: Indent here for new paragraph; or join this paragraph to the preceding one.

For a discussion of paragraph division, see *Guide*, pp. 219–27.

Paragraphs

Par

Revision: Revise or rewrite this unsatisfactory paragraph.

A paragraph is a group of related statements that a writer presents as a unit in the development of his subject. It strikes the eye as a unit because it is physically set off by indention or spacing. It should also strike the mind as a unit because the statements in it are closely related, representing a stage in the flow of the writer's thought.

The most common faults in paragraphs are:

1. *Lack of development.* The paragraph lacks the particulars that will lead the reader to understand and accept its central point.

2. *Lack of unity.* Some of the sentences fail to contribute to the core of meaning that is the focus of the paragraph and that justifies its inclusion in the paper.

3. *Lack of continuity.* The relation between the statements that make up the paragraph is not clear.

4. *Lack of transition.* The paragraph is not sufficiently tied to what precedes and what follows to be integrated with the rest of the paper.

Guide, Chapter Nine, discusses paragraphs in detail.

Parallelism

When two or more words or groups of words are alike in grammatical rank and structure, they are said to be parallel. See *Guide*, pp. 321–27. For faulty parallelism, see *Shifted constructions and *Guide*, pp. 322–23.

Paraphrase

A paraphrase is a restatement of a writer's ideas in different words. The term *paraphrasing* is now usually applied to digesting the contents of a passage in one's own words, as in note-taking. See *Guide*, pp. 412–13.

Parentheses

Like commas and dashes, parentheses are used to enclose words and word groups that break away from the main structure of the sentence.

Of the three types of enclosing marks, parentheses indicate the greatest degree of removal, particularly in Formal writing.

1. *For additions.* Parentheses are used to enclose words and word groups that add facts to a statement without essentially altering its meaning. They allow such additions to stand outside the frame of the principal sentence. The additions may be illustrations, definitions, or information thrown in for good measure:

The few verb endings that English now retains (*-s, -ed, -ing*) are being still further reduced in ordinary speech.

Gresham's Law (that bad money drives out good) applies as usual in this case.

His concerts were well received in most cities (Chicago was particularly enthusiastic), but he was still dissatisfied.

2. *To enclose numbers or letters in an enumeration.* Parentheses are sometimes used to enclose the letters or figures used to mark items in an enumeration: The additions may be (1) illustrations, (2) definitions, or (3) information thrown in for good measure. They make the listed items more conspicuous.

3. *With other marks.* When a complete sentence in parentheses comes within a sentence (notice the punctuation of this one), it needs neither a capital letter nor a period, though exclamation marks and question marks are retained. Commas and other marks of punctuation in the main sentence always *follow* the parenthesis (as here and in the preceding sentence). (Parenthesized sentences, like this one, that do not stand within other sentences have the period before the closing parenthesis.)

See *Brackets, *Dash.

Participles

1. *Forms of participles.*

	Active	Passive
Present:	asking; singing	being asked; being sung
Past:	having asked; having sung	asked, having been asked; sung, having been sung

The participle forms are used in various verb phrases: I am asking, I am being asked, I have asked, I have been asked. Although participles are referred to as present and past, they do not themselves indicate definite time but time in relation to the context in which they are used. See *Tenses of verbs.

2. *As modifiers.* When not part of verb phrases, participles are most commonly used like adjectives. They are like adjectives in that they modify nouns: a *coming* era, a *frightened* cat. They are like verbs in that they may take an object (*Following these clues*, he soon found her) and may be modified by adverbs (The car, *rolling crazily* . . .). In fact, transformational grammars derive them from full underlying clauses:

The car [the car was rolling crazily] crashed into a bus.
⇒ The car, rolling crazily, crashed into a bus.

When used as an adjective, a participle should refer clearly to some particular noun or pronoun: Having opened the envelope, he began to read the letter (*Having opened* modifies *he*). A modifying participle is said to dangle when it seems to refer to a word the writer does not mean it to refer to: Kissing his wife good-by, the door slammed behind him. These errors occur when the subject of the participle and the subject of the main clause differ. In "[*He* was] kissing his wife good-by, *the door* slammed behind him," *He* and *the door* are not the same. Compare a correct modifier: [*He* was] kissing his wife good-by, *he* let the door slam behind him. *He* in "[He was] kissing" and *he* in "he let the door slam" are the same. The first subject can be deleted. See *Dangling modifiers; *Guide*, pp. 290–92.

3. *In absolute phrases.* The participle-as-adjective should not be confused with the participle in a phrase which relates to the whole sentence — to the situation — rather than to a particular word. Some such phrases have become *formulas: Judging from her looks, she isn't under fifty.

4. *Stylistically objectionable participles.* Unskilled writers sometimes use a participle or a gerund where a subordinate clause would sound better: The train was on time, necessitating our hurrying. Better: . . . so we had to hurry. Clumsy "nominative absolutes" should especially be avoided: She arriving then, I departed.

For *very* with participles, see *very § 2. Compare *Gerunds. References: Curme, *Syntax*, Ch. 22; Donald W. Emery and R. W. Pence, *Grammar of Present-Day English*, 2nd ed. (New York: Macmillan, 1963), pp. 305–15; Roberts, pp. 345–55.

Particles

Of the eight traditional parts of speech, four have no inflected forms in English—*adverbs, *prepositions, *conjunctions, interjections—and appear never to have been inflected in the Indo-European languages. They are sometimes lumped together under the term *particles*. To the grammarian they cause some discomfort. In the classical languages, nouns, adjectives, and pronouns have elaborate declensions, and verbs have elaborate conjugations. And even in English there are at least remnants of inflection for all these words. But for the particles, descriptive comment — aside from listing them — must be entirely about their syntax, their use in utterances. And since syntax is the most elusive part of descriptive grammar, discussion of the use of particles is especially difficult.

In a transformational grammar the term *particle* is usually limited to the second word in such idiomatic compound verbs as *look over* (examine), *hold up* (rob), *take after* (resemble), *run off* (print), and so on. See *Idiom.

Parts of speech

Parts of speech are the categories a linguist sets up in order to describe larger structures in sentences and finally sentences themselves. Since it would be pointless to list all the words in English, indicating for each one whether it can serve as a subject or object or modifier, linguists group words into categories and subcategories and then describe where these categories may occur in various patterns and how they form larger structures. The "correctness" of these categories, however, depends on how the linguist wants to describe sentence structure — even on what his notion of "structure" is. Linguists working with different grammatical theories will create different sets of definitions. Thus one linguist will classify a word like *some* as an indefinite pronoun and another will classify it as a prearticle. The different names are not just terminological quibbles. They may reflect different theories that determine the definitions. See *Grammar.

1. *Three approaches.* Traditional schoolroom grammarians, using a system much like that developed for describing classical languages, cite eight parts of speech: nouns, verbs, adjectives, adverbs, pronouns, prepositions, conjunctions, and interjections (or exclamations). Nouns and verbs are defined semantically: a noun is the name of a person, place, or thing, verbs show action, and so on. The others are defined functionally: adjectives modify nouns; adverbs modify verbs, adjectives, and other adverbs; pronouns replace nouns; and prepositions relate a noun to another word.

Because semantic definitions are very weak (what does the noun *lack* refer to in "There is a lack of time"?) and because the functional definitions are much too vague (the definition of *preposition* would, for example, cover *is* in "John is a friend"), structural linguists reject them in favor of purely formal definitions: Nouns are those words that can occur with plural and genitive endings or after *the* and before a verb; verbs are those words that can occur with third-person singular *-s* endings, with past-tense inflections, with perfect inflections, and with progressive *-ing* endings; adjectives are those words that can occur with comparative or superlative endings, after *more* or *most*, and in the position "The [noun] is very _____"; adverbs are those words made up of an adjective and an *-ly* ending. The residue of words such as *in, can, very, the, not, all, therefore, because, and, please, hello,* and so on are put into a large category of "indeclinable words" or function words, which is subcategorized according to where these words occur in a sentence relative to the parts of speech already identified.

Describing how transformational grammarians classify parts of speech would require more space than we can allot the subject here. Briefly, transformational grammarians are much less concerned than structuralists are with devising formal tests to classify parts of speech and more concerned with the most economical and general overall description. The labels for individual words are judged "correct" only if they are necessary to describe how the words behave in the context of a sentence. Transformationalists assume that one part of speech may derive from another, as the verb *discover* in a *deep structure like [[Tom *discovered* gold] elated us] becomes, in the *surface structure, a noun through a nominalization transformation: [[Tom's *discovery* of gold] elated us]. For transformational grammarians, it is impossible to talk about parts of speech without explaining the whole grammar of a language and without distinguishing between deep and surface structures.

Because structural grammars emphasize the careful and logical classification of parts of speech, we will generally rely on their methods here.

2. *Form-class words and function words.* The structuralist approach suggests that English words are of two general types: (1) form-class words, words that express the primary lexical or semantic meaning of a sentence and that can usually be inflected for number, tense, or comparison; and (2) function words, words that perform the grammatical or structural function of connecting, relating, and qualifying the form-class words. These function words usually cannot be inflected. The form-class words are commonly called nouns, verbs, adjectives, and adverbs, with certain pronouns fitting into subgroups under the category *noun*. All other words are function (or structure) words.

a—Form-class words. In addition to expressing lexical meaning, form-class words share other characteristics. As we have said, they can be inflected to indicate specific semantic meanings and grammatical relationships. Nouns (and the personal pronouns) inflect to show plural number and possession: *girl, girls, girl's, girls'; I, we, my, mine; she, her, hers; they, their, theirs.* Verbs inflect to indicate present third-person singular, past tense, present participle, and past participle: *walks, walked, walking, walked; sings, sang, singing, sung.* Adjectives and most adverbs add -*er* or -*est* (or *more, most; less, least*) to indicate comparison: *tall, taller, tallest; more fully, most fully; less difficult, least difficult.*

Form-class words are also an "open" class. Borrowed words and coined words, such as *astronaut, hippie, telecast, video, stereo*, are still being added.

b—Function words. Function words (also called structure words) have less specific lexical meanings than form-class words. (Consider the various meanings of *green* or *run* in comparison with the meaning of *by* or *the*.) Only a few groups of function words (if we choose to so classify them) can be inflected: the demonstrative, relative, and interrogative pronouns and the modal-auxiliary verbs. In contrast to form-class groups, which include hundreds of thousands of different words, most function-word groups contain only a very small number; some, like *not* and *do*, contain only one. And function words are members of closed groups. The idiomatic use of certain prepositions may vary or change, but English has borrowed or developed very few new prepositions or conjunctions over the seven hundred years since English was interpenetrated by French borrowings after the Norman Conquest. In that time it has lost pronouns and has added no articles.

The most detailed description of function words from a structural point of view is that by Fries in *The Structure of English*. Fries points out that such words as *yes—no* (or their colloquial equivalents), *please, not*, and *let's* are used in limited contexts. He also shows that such words as *very, extremely, considerably*, and others are quite different from such words as *quietly, thoroughly, angrily*. For example, the sentence "He collected the materials quickly" is meaningful; the sentence "He collected the materials very" is not. A structural linguist is thus forced to classify these two groups of words in two different categories—the first, qualifiers; the second, adverbs (or, in Fries' more esoteric terminology, Class 4 words).

c—Words in context. The respective grammatical roles of form-class words—to express the primary lexical meaning of communication—and of function words—to relate and give understandable structure to combinations of form-class words—can be illustrated either with regular English sentences or with nonsense sentences. Consider, for example, the sentence used by Fries: The mother of the boy will arrive tomorrow. The basic lexical information can be expressed telegraphically with the four form-class words: Boy's mother arrives tomorrow. The function words, *the* and *of*, signal the grammar of the message; *will* indicates that the arriving will occur in the future.

Or consider the nonsense sentence "The slithy toves will gyre and gimble very gluggily in the wabes." The sentence possesses only such meaning as grammatical structure (that is, word order, word forms, and function words) gives to it. The "nouns" *toves* and *wabes*, the "verbs" *gyre* and *gimble*, the "adjective" *slithy*, and the "adverb" *gluggily* can be replaced with meaningful words or with other nonsense words. But the function words *the, will, very, in* cannot be replaced if this is to be an English "sentence."

Both sentences indicate the distinctive features of the two general types of words. Form-class words can be inflected and are members of open classes: we recognize them by their forms and their position in the sentence and by the function words used to connect and relate them. Function words have almost no inflected forms (except for *will—would, this—these*, etc.); they are in closed groups; they occupy regular positions or slots in syntactic structures.

As the two illustrative sentences also indicate, we classify parts of speech according to their context in a sentence or according to their inflections. Certain words, like *walk, burn, run*, are used as either nouns or verbs. Other words, like *bomb, radio, dust*, are used not just as nouns or verbs but also, without change in form, as modifiers: bomb shelter, radio station, dust belt. The conjunction *after* (We will leave after we have eaten) may also serve as a preposition: After dinner, the group dispersed. How a word is classified in a specific instance depends upon the context in which it is used. That is why, in the chart of form-class words, we list the usual function of each part of speech.

The function-word chart lists the most frequently used types along with examples and usual functions. Identical words may either serve as different kinds of function words or (like some prearticles, *some, many, all*) appear to serve as both form-class words (nouns) and function words (prearticles). See *Determiners.

FORM-CLASS WORDS

PART OF SPEECH	INFLECTED FORMS	USUAL FUNCTIONS
*Nouns *(boy, house, city, truth)*	Plural: *-s (boys)* and a few anomalous forms: *oxen, deer, teeth,* etc. Genitive (or possessive): *-'s, -s'* *(boy's, boys')*	Serve as subject; complement; object of verbs, of verbals, of prepositions.
Personal *pronouns *(I, you, he, she, it)*	Plural: *we, they* Genitive: *my, mine, his, her, its* Objective: *me, him, them* (Note that personal pronouns have a special form when used as objects.)	Same function as nouns.
Indefinite nouns *(everybody, everything, everyone, no one)*		Serve in many but not all positions as nouns.
	(Other pronouns, such as *who* and *that,* are listed under function words, because they do not possess a full set of noun inflections and cannot be used in all the positions filled by nouns or personal pronouns.)	
*Verbs *(walk, play, breathe)*	Present participle: *-ing* Past participle: *-ed* Third-person singular, present tense: *-s* past tense: *-ed* (For irregular verbs, see *be, *Principal parts of verbs.)	Assert an action or express a state or condition.
*Adjectives *(tall, black, poor)*	Comparative: *-er* (or *more, less*) Superlative: *-est* (or *most, least*)	Modify nouns or pronouns.
*Adverbs *(slow, quickly)*	Comparative: *-er* (or *more, less*) Superlative: *est* (or *most, least*) (Some adverbs — like *here, tomorrow, everywhere* — are not compared.)	Modify verbs, adverbs, phrases, and clauses, usually indicating place, time, or manner.

PART OF SPEECH	USUAL FUNCTIONS
Auxiliaries (usually called *modal auxiliaries): *can, could, will, shall, may, must, get, used (to)*, etc.	Precede, point to, and qualify predicating verbs or serve as substitutes for verbs.
*Determiners (also called noun determiners) are subdivided into prearticles, articles, and postarticles.	Precede and enumerate nouns; they may be left when the nouns are transformationally deleted: Several boys were here ⇒ Several were here.
Prearticles: *some, few, several, much, many, each, both, all, neither, half, two*, etc.	
*Articles: *a/an, the, some; this, that, these, those*	Specify definiteness of reference. The words traditionally defined as demonstrative pronouns—*this, that, these, those*—can be classed as a variety of article. The absence of an article indicates indefiniteness before noncount nouns and plurals: Food is expensive; Carrots are cheap.
Postarticles: *several, many, few; first, second, third*, etc.; *one, two, three*, etc.; *former, latter, next, first, last*, etc.	Follow articles and precede adjectives: the few old men, the second young woman, the three pretty girls, *Several, few,* and *many* are identical to the prearticles *some, few,* and *many:* Few of the several sick children, several of the many brave soldiers. Postarticles usually quantify or indicate an order to the head noun.
*Qualifiers: *very, rather, fairly, mighty, less, least, more, most, too, quite, much*, etc.	Qualify or limit adjectives, usually by indicating degree or extent.
*Conjunctions or connectors	
*Coordinating conjunctions: *and, but, nor, yet, for, or, so,* and sometimes *not, rather*, etc.	Connect like or equal grammatical components (words, phrases, clauses, sentences).
*Correlative conjunctions: *both . . . and, either . . . or, so . . . as, not only . . . but (also)*, etc.	Used in pairs to connect clauses within a sentence.

*Conjunctive adverbs (also called sentence connectors): *accordingly, also, consequently, hence, however, therefore,* etc.

Connect either independent clauses within a sentence or sentences within or between paragraphs.

*Subordinating conjunctions: *after, as, if, since, when, until,* etc.

Join and subordinate, as a structure expressing modification or qualification, a dependent clause to another clause in the sentence. Usually the dependent clause modifies a verb, a clause, or an entire sentence.

Noun substitutes

Interrogative pronouns: *who, which, what, whoever,* etc.

Serve as subjects, objects, or single-word modifiers in interrogative sentences or dependent noun clauses.

*Relative pronouns: *who, whose, whom, which, that, when,* and also *where, wherever,* etc.

Serve as subjects, complements, objects, or single-word modifiers to link independent noun and adjective clauses to other clauses within a sentence.

*Prepositions: *at, about, by, in, on, under, underneath, back of, due to, in front of, on account of,* etc.

Precede and connect object, consisting of a noun or pronoun, with or without modifiers, to other constituents of the sentence. Usually the phrase can be identified as either an adjectival or an adverbial modifier.

Miscellaneous

do (did, does, done)

Used to form *yes — no* questions, to give emphasis, and as a substitute verb.

*Exclamations (or interjections): *oh, ouch, no, yes, hey, never, really,* etc.

Used to show feeling or — in some instances — to indicate that the speaker is listening.

Interrogators: *when, why, where, how,* etc.

Used alone or as introductory word for a phrase or clause asking a question.

Negatives: *no, not, never*

Show negation.

Yes — no words: *yes, yeah, uh-huh; no, not at all, maybe,* etc.

Give responses or — in some instances — indicate that the speaker is listening.

References: Fries, *Structure,* Ch. 5; Francis, Ch. 5; Sledd, Ch. 2.

Passive verbs

Pass

Revision: Change the passive verb or verbs to active.

Some writers seem attracted to the passive under a misapprehension that it is immodest to use *I* or *we* ("The music was enjoyed by us" instead of "We enjoyed the music"). Overuse of the passive inevitably creates wordiness:

The Auto Show is here. With it comes the usual host of new-model automobiles. Most of these cars were heralded in during the closing months of last year. They have been awaited with anxious curiosity by the buying public. In many instances, they have been looked forward to with too much anticipation.

Although "were heralded in" is a legitimate passive because the "heralders" need not be named, and although "have been awaited" throws "the buying public" to the end of the sentence for emphasis, the use of the passive becomes definitely objectionable with "have been looked forward to." The fourth and fifth sentences might better read: The buyers have awaited them with anxious curiosity, often with too much anticipation.

For the formation of the passive voice and its profitable use, see *Voice.

Past tense

See *Tenses of verbs.

Pathetic fallacy

Crediting places and things with human qualities and emotions is known as the pathetic fallacy. Today it is likely to suggest pretense or juvenile ineptitude: Vexed into foam, the purifying waves hissed their indignation among the beer cans.

people, persons

People has long been used as a collective noun referring to a group, but as recently as the early part of this century, it was regarded as Nonstandard when used with numerical quantifiers as the plural of *person*, as in "Five people are here." Though Formal usage still tends to prefer *persons*, *people* is now thoroughly established in such contexts.

per

Per (Latin, "through, by, among," etc.) is most appropriate in phrases that are still close to their Latin originals (per capita, per diem), in commercial expressions ($125 per week, $3.00 per yard), and in some technical phrases (revolutions per minute). In less specialized contexts, *a* or *every* usually replaces *per* (a dime a dozen, a thousand words every day).

percent

Percent is not followed by a period; sometimes it is written as two words. In Informal and General writing (but not Formal) it is often used instead of *percentage* or even *proportion:* Only a small percent of the class was [or were] present. With figures, *percent* (97.6 percent) is preferred to the percent sign (97.6%) except in technical and statistical material.

Perfect tense

See *Tenses of verbs.

Period

1. *At the end of statements.* The main use of the period is to mark the end of every completed sentence that is not a question or an exclamation. Sometimes even a sentence in the form of a question or an exclamation is ended with a period if the writer wants to suggest a meaning closer to that of statement: Would you be so good as to return the book at your earliest convenience. See *Rhetorical questions.

2. *Miscellaneous conventional uses.*
a—After *abbreviations: Oct.; etc.; Mr. W. Fraser, Jr.
b—Between dollars and cents: $5.66; $0.66 (but 66 cents/66¢)
c—Before decimals: .6, 3.14159, 44.6 percent
d—Sometimes between hours and minutes in giving precise time, though a colon is more usual: 2.36 p.m.
e—Three spaced periods are used as *ellipses to mark the omission of words. A series of spaced periods called leaders may be used to guide a reader's eye across a page, as in a table of contents.

3. *With quotation marks.* When a quotation ends a sentence, most American publishers place the period inside the quotation marks whether the quotation is a complete sentence or a single word:

"The longer you put it off," he said, "the harder it's going to be." He glared at me as he said "harder."

See *Quotation marks § 4b.

Periodic sentence

See *Guide*, pp. 331–33.

Periphrastic verbs

See *Phrasal verbs.

Person

Person as a grammatical term refers to both pronoun classification and verb inflection. Personal pronouns are of three classes: first person, the one(s) speaking (*I, my, me, we, our, us*); second person, the one(s) spoken to (*you, your, yours*); third person, anyone or anything else (*he, his, him, she, her, hers, it, its, they, their, them*). Nouns are regarded as third person, as are most other pronouns (the relative *who* and its derivatives take their persons from their antecedents).

Except in the verb *be* (I am, you are, he is . . .), English verbs indicate person only for the third singular of the present and perfect tenses: I see, you see, he *sees;* we, you, they see; I have seen, you have seen, he *has* seen; etc.

person

See *people, persons.

Personal pronouns

See *Person, *Pronouns § 1. See also *Apostrophe § 5.

Personification

Personification is a *figure of speech in which an object or animal or quality or ideal is given some attributes of a human being:

There has been, after all, something in the talk of American innocence. No doubt it is a false innocence, fabricated by a myth-charged education: the lady who was "once a beauty of magnificence unparalleled" nourished her complexion on genocide and slavery. Yet her beauty existed in the eyes of her children, especially her adopted, immigrant children. . . . —Conor Cruise O'Brien, *New York Review of Books*, June 20, 1968

It is less common today than formerly, and less common in prose than in verse. Flat and unnecessary personification is likely to sound amateurish: No steam engine can brag of such efficiency. See *Gender, *Pathetic fallacy.

phenomenon, phenomena

Phenomenon is the singular and *phenomena* (sometimes *phenomenons*) the plural: phenomena of the mind. Originally, *phenomenon* meant "any observable event," but now it also means "something remarkable," and *phenomenal* is almost always used in that sense. A shorter or more exact word is often preferable.

phone

Phone is a clipped word for *telephone*, in General use as a noun, verb, and modifier: on the phone, phone me later, the phone book (but telephone operator, telephone pole). It is written without an apostrophe.

Phonology

See *Linguistics § 1a.

Phrasal verbs

A main verb preceded by one or more auxiliaries (will go, has left, was thinking, is considered, must have been punished) is called a phrasal verb or a periphrastic verb. See *Verbs.

Phrases

A phrase is a group of words which functions as a unit in a sentence, a clause, or another phrase. In "The man in the car under the tree yelled," "the man in the car under the tree" is a noun phrase made up of an article, "the," a noun, "man," and a prepositional phrase, "in the car under the tree." The prepositional phrase, in turn, is made up of the preposition "in" and another phrase, "the car under the tree." This noun phrase is made up of the article "the" and the noun "car" and the prepositional phrase "under the tree," which, in turn, is made up of the preposition "under" and the noun phrase "the tree." Thus phrases can be contained in phrases ad infinitum.

Noun phrase: the *plumber*
Verb phrase: have *gone* to the store
Adjective phrase: old enough to be my father
Adverbial phrase: more *quickly* than usual
Prepositional phrase: in the house
Participial phrase: walking down the street

They may be further classified by their function in a sentence. "The plumber" is an adjectival noun phrase in the larger noun phrase, "my friend the plumber." "Walking down the street" is a nominal participial phrase (traditionally called a gerund) in "Walking down the street was dangerous." "In the morning" is an adverbial prepositional phrase in "He left in the morning," an adjectival prepositional phrase in "Breakfast in the morning," a nominal prepositional phrase in "In the morning will be soon enough."

The style of a passage depends in part on how a writer combines and coordinates these phrases:

His ideas
    about the need
        for intellectual renewal
          and
        spiritual reform
indicate the crisis
    faced not only
        by those
        in places
          of power
        but
        by those
        in all walks
          of life.

In this sentence, the phrases are balanced and coordinated to create a rhythm that carries the reader along smoothly to the end. In this next sentence, the phrases are merely strung out one after the other, creating a heavy, bumping kind of movement that interferes with the writer's idea:

Our situation
>in this century
>>of turmoil
>>>in the cities
>can only be alleviated
>>by improving the living conditions
>>>in ghettoes
>in the central cities
>>which have decayed
>>>beyond the livability
>>>>of most people
>who live
>>in them.

See *Absolute phrases, *Gerunds, *Infinitives, *Participles, *Prepositional phrases. See also *Dangling modifiers.

Plagiarism

Plagiarize is defined in *Webster's Seventh New Collegiate Dictionary* as "to steal and pass off as one's own (the ideas or words of another)." *Steal* is an ugly word, but plagiarism is an ugly thing. It occurs in college courses for several different reasons, including panic, dishonesty, and ignorance of what plagiarism is. Whatever the cause, the penalty—a failing mark in the paper and, if the cheating is chronic, a failing mark in the course—is justified. Copying someone else's work is the most complete failure possible.

The student who has not learned how to handle material obtained from reading needs guidance in the fundamentals of scholarship. Anyone using published material has a twofold responsibility: first, of making the ideas part of his own thinking and, second, of giving credit to the sources. No one is *composing* when he is merely copying. A student should read and digest the material, get it into his own words (except for the brief passages he intends to present as quotations). He should be able to talk about what he has read before he writes about it, and when he does write, he should name the sources of his ideas and facts. This is not only courtesy but a sign of good workmanship, part of the morality of writing. It is also part of the legality of writing, since the plagiarist who uses copyrighted material is liable to prosecution.

In an informal essay, credit can be given informally, perhaps in a preliminary note saying "This essay is based on. . . ." Or a source may be acknowledged in the body of the essay: "Professor Martin said in a lecture . . .," "According to an editorial in . . .," or "Here is Jackson's position as presented in last night's debate." Or credit may be given more formally in footnotes, as described in the *Guide*, pp. 418–24. Footnotes are a conventional part of a research paper.

Plagiarizing is stealing. By being careful to give credit where credit is due, you gain free and legitimate access to everything in print (though if what you write is to be printed, you must secure permission to quote copyrighted material directly); and you learn to integrate the ideas of others with your own ideas. Finally, you learn to express what you have to say in your own words, not copying but composing. See *Originality.

plenty

As an adverb (I was plenty worried; The car is plenty fast) *plenty* is used by some General writers but is avoided entirely by others, in favor of better-established adverbs like *extremely, amply*, and *quite*. In General use, an *of* is expected between *plenty* and the following noun: We had plenty of time.

plurality, majority

See *majority, plurality.

Plurals of nouns

The plural of the great majority of English nouns is made by adding the /s/ or /z/ sound to the singular form: *buckets, cups, days, rooms, trees*. In writing, this ending is usually spelled -s, as in these examples, and dictionaries do not give such plurals special treatment.

1. *Special groups in -s or -es.*
a—In English the /s/ or /z/ sound cannot be added to nouns ending with the sounds /ch/, /j/, /s/, /sh/, or /z/: *birch, edge, miss, dish, maze*. To make the plural of such words, a full syllable is added. The spelling is -s if the noun already ends in silent -e, otherwise -es: *birches, edges, misses, dishes, mazes*.
b—Common nouns ending in -y preceded by a consonant letter or the letters *qu* change y to *i* and add -es: *beauties, bodies, caddies, cherries, soliloquies*. Exceptions to this rule are proper nouns (*Henrys*) and a few common nouns: *stand-bys, emptys* (bottles). Words ending in -y preceded by a vowel letter add -s: *bays, boys, moneys* (but *monies* in the technical economic sense).
c—Nouns ending in -o preceded by a vowel letter make regular plurals with -s: *cameos, folios, radios, studios*. Words ending in -o preceded by a consonant letter vary individually between -s and -es. Some always or nearly always take -s: *dynamos, eskimos* (or *Eskimo*), *Filipinos, pianos, solos, sopranos*. Some always or nearly always take -es: *echoes, heroes, Negroes, potatoes, tomatoes, vetoes*. Some take either, now one and now the other being favored: *banjos, banjoes; cargoes, cargos; dominoes, dominos; mementos, mementoes; mottoes, mottos; tornadoes, tornados; torpedos, torpedoes; zeros, zeroes*.
d—Some common nouns ending in -f or -fe (*calf, half, knife, leaf, loaf, self, shelf, thief*) use -ves (*calves, halves, knives*, and so on). Some have two plurals: *elf, elves—elfs; hoof, hoofs—hooves; scarf, scarfs—scarves*. But many nouns ending in -f, -fe, and -ff form regular plurals with -s: *beliefs, fifes, rebuffs*.

2. *Same form for both singular and plural.* Nouns with the same form for singular and plural include names for some living creatures (*fowl, sheep, fish*—but *fishes* for varieties of fish), all words in -ics (*athletics, politics, civics*), and some common measurements (*foot,* *pair, ton*). A number of words are rarely or never singular in their form:

barracks	goods	odds (betting)	smallpox
bellows	headquarters	pants	species
billiards	measles	pincers	tactics
gallows	morals	scissors	trousers

3. *Survivals of older English plural forms.* Survivals include plurals in *-en* (in church use, *brother, brethren; child, children* — actually a double plural, since both the *-r-* and the *-en* are plural endings; *ox, oxen*) and plurals with changed vowels (*foot, feet; goose, geese; louse, lice; man, men; mouse, mice; tooth, teeth; woman, women*).

4. *Foreign language plurals.* Many nouns taken into English from other languages keep their foreign plurals, at least for a time. Words used chiefly in scientific or Formal writing tend to keep the foreign form longer. *Antenna*, for instance, has the plural *antennae* in biology but *antennas* in discussions of radio and TV. When the word is in transition, both forms will be found in the same context.

A few borrowed words that now regularly have plurals in *-s* or *-es* will suggest the extent of the change in English forms:

area	campus	dogma	museum
arena	census	encyclopedia	panacea
asylum	circus	era	panorama
bonus	dilemma	forum	plateau
bureau	diploma	metropolis	quota

Some common words have two plurals — the foreign (*appendices, media, nuclei*) and the English forms (*appendixes, mediums, nucleuses*).

5. *Compound and group words.* Most compound words and group words add *-s* to the end of the group, whether written as one word or as several: *bookcases, high schools, cross-examinations*. In a few the plural sign is added to the first element: *daughters-in-law* (and other *in-law* words), *passersby, poets laureate* (also *poet laureates*), *courts-martial* (also *court-martials*).

6. *Plurals of figures, words, letters.* Usually the plural of a letter of the alphabet, of a word as a word, or of a figure is written with *-'s:* There are two *c*'s and two *m*'s in *accommodate*; Don't use several *that*'s in a row; three *2*'s. But usage is divided; the plural of figures especially is often made with *-s*: three 2s; no *ifs, ands,* or *buts*.

7. *Plural substitutes.* A plural notion is sometimes expressed by a phrase that remains grammatically singular: College after college has gone in for intramural sports; Many a paleface has bitten the dust.

Other *Index* articles dealing with the formation of plurals include *Apostrophe § 3; *Genitive § 1a; *-ful, full*. Singular and plural constructions are treated in *Subject and verb, *Reference of pronouns.

References: Curme, *Parts of Speech*, pp. 112–27, *Syntax*, pp. 539–48; Fries, *AEG*, pp. 40–59; Jespersen, *EEG*, pp. 198–203; Long, pp. 203–27.

plus

Traditionally and by the description of all current dictionaries, *plus* is a preposition having the sense "with the addition of." A phrase introduced by *plus* would not therefore affect the number of the verb: His record, plus the magic of his family name, suggests that he will win by a large margin. Yet *plus* is often felt to be a conjunction with the sense "and"; as such, the *plus* phrase is allowed to affect the number of the verb in some General writing: "The Smyth Report, plus an idea and some knowledge of bureaucracy, were all I needed . . ." (Pat Frank, *Saturday Review*, Dec. 24, 1960). In more formal writing, the *plus* would be changed to *and,* or the verb would be made singular.

p.m.

See *a.m. and p.m.

Poetry

When verse is quoted, it should be lined off (as well as capitalized and punctuated) as written. If possible, the quoted lines should be approximately centered on the page, indented according to the scheme of the original. When so spaced, lines of verse quoted in a prose passage do not need quotation marks.

politics

Politics can be treated as either a singular or a plural but should not be both in the same passage: Republican politics were offensive to the Federalists; In almost any group, politics is a controversial subject.

position, job

See *job, position.

Positive degree

The positive degree of adjectives and adverbs is the simple adjective form (*poor, high, golden*) or adverb form (*slow, slowly, bitterly*). See *Comparison of adjectives and adverbs.

Possessive adjectives

See *Possessive pronouns.

Possessive case

See *Genitive.

Possessive pronouns

The personal pronouns have the following possessive forms: *my, mine; your, yours; his; her, hers; our, ours; their, theirs;* and the relative *who* has *whose*. *Its* is the only one that tempts writers to use an apostrophe, through confusion with *it's*, the contraction for "it is."

My, *your, her, his, our, their* are used as adjectives (and sometimes called possessive adjectives) in the attributive position: my car. *Mine, yours, his, hers, its, ours, theirs* are used without a noun: Ours is better than yours.

Précis

See *Guide*, p. 444.

Predicate

Almost all English sentences divide into two main elements—subject and predicate. The predicate of a clause or sentence is the verb with its modifiers and objects or complements. The predicate may be a single verb (The bell *tolled*), a transitive verb and its object (He *landed the big fish*), or a linking verb and its complement (The oldest member of the family *is usually the first to go*). Two verbs depending on one subject are known as a *compound predicate: The three of them *washed* and *wiped* the whole lot in fifteen minutes. See *Subject and verb; *Compound subject; *Objects; *Verbs; *Guide*, pp. 269–70.

Predicate adjectives

P Adj

Revision: Use an adjective here, since the verb is a linking verb.

Loudly in "The music sounds loudly" should be revised to *loud*.

The use of an adverb instead of a predicate adjective results from the habit of thinking that only adverbs belong in postverbal position. But adjectives fill that position whenever the verb is a linking verb. In addition to *be, about sixty verbs (*become, feel, turn, look, taste,* and so on) can perform this linking function. What follows the verb relates to or qualifies the subject, not the verb. Accordingly, an adjective—known as a predicate adjective or predicative—is required, even though in its other functions the same verb is followed by an adverb: He felt *tired* (adjective, relates to subject). Compare: He felt the edge of the knife *carefully* (adverb, relates to verb).

She acts *tired.* She acts *brilliantly.*
She looks *cold.* She looked at him *coldly.*

The test for a linking verb is that the appropriate form of *be* can replace it: "The story rings true" is structurally the same as "The story is true." When you have identified the verb as linking, use an adjective after it. In very rare cases, when adjective and adverb have the same form, ambiguity can occur: The cat looked longer than the dog. Such a sentence should be rewritten. See *Linking verbs; *bad, badly; *look. See also *Adjectives § 2.

Predicate nominative

Words and word groups that follow linking verbs and function as nouns are called *predicate nominatives*. They include nouns, pronouns, phrases, and clauses. See *Linking verbs, *Nouns § 2.

predominant, predominate

Predominant is the adjective: a predominant sentiment, a sentiment predominant in the state. Although increasingly common, the spelling *predominate* for the adjective is offensive to many readers. The present participle *predominating* is often used adjectivally.

prefer

To is ordinarily used with *prefer:* I prefer Ireland to Spain; He preferred going by train to flying. When an infinitive is used instead of a noun or gerund, however, *to* is impossible and *than* or *rather than* is used: He preferred to take the train rather than to fly [or: rather than a plane]. At times the *prefer . . . than* idiom turns up where *prefer . . . to* would be expected: "I would prefer the risk of revolutionary troubles . . . than the horror of drifting calmly into 1984 . . . (Paul Goodman, *New York Review of Books,* June 3, 1965).

Prefix

A prefix is a form that can be placed before a word or root to change its meaning or function: un*tie,* im*mobilize.* See *Origin of words § 3a. See also *Hyphen, *Latin and English, *Long variants.

Prepositional phrase

A prepositional phrase is a phrase made up of a preposition and its object: without hope, in a hurry, toward a more abundant life. Prepositional phrases are modifiers, used in the functions of adverbs or adjectives:

Adverbial modifier: She arrived *at just the right time.*
Adjectival modifier: The man *in the black coat* has left.

Prepositions

Prep

Revision: Change the preposition, making it more exact or idiomatic (§ 2a) or less conspicuous (§ 2b) or making the expression less informal (§ 2c).

1. *Definitions.* A preposition connects a noun phrase or a pronoun or a clause to some other part of the sentence. The whole phrase is usually adverbial or adjectival in its function: He showed her *to her room;* He was old *in experience;* the click *of flying wheels.* The noun or pronoun following a preposition is called its object. Prepositions may be word groups (in regard to, according to) as well as single words. And many words serve variously as prepositions, adverbs, conjunctions: *after, but, since* (preposition: This is the hottest summer *since* the drought; conjunction: *Since* the price was low, we bought three; adverb: She bawled him out, and he hasn't spoken *since*). Because of their variability, these words are grouped by some grammarians as particles or function words with different functions.

In some contexts, prepositions signal purely grammatical functions. *By* can signal the agent of an action: The window was broken by Mike. *Of* can signal either agent or object: The destruction of the city shocked everyone; The discussions of the committee were kept secret. *With* can signal instrumentality: He cut the bread with a knife. But *by, with,* and *of* can also indicate a meaning very close to lexical reference. *By* can be paraphrased as "in a space adjacent to" in "He sat by the river"; *with* means "in the company of" in "I left with Tom"; *of* means "belonging to" in "He is a citizen of France." Even in abstract contexts (under a cloud, with ease) prepositions have meaning.

Of the many prepositions in English, Fries estimates that nine—*at, by, for, from, in, of, on, to,* and *with*—account for 92 percent of prepositional use.

2. *Use of prepositions.*

a—Exact or idiomatic prepositions. A number of words are accompanied by certain prepositions, as "contented *with* conditions," "*in* my estimation." Some words have various meanings with different prepositions: agree *with* (a person), agree *to* (a suggestion), agree *in* (principle).

Getting the right preposition does not give much trouble with words that we use often, because we learn the words by hearing or seeing them in their usual constructions. When learning new words, we should learn their usage as well as their meaning: *acquiesce in* (acquiesce in a decision) rather than just *acquiesce.* A person uses an unidiomatic preposition because he is not at home with the word or because he is confused where usage is divided (as with *different from* or *than* or *to*). Dictionaries usually give the preposition appropriate to particular words. This book treats a few idioms that are likely to raise questions: *ability to; *agree to, agree with; *all of; *compare, contrast; *different. See also *Idiom.

When two words that take different prepositions are used together, both prepositions should be included: The first lesson he learned was obedience to and respect for others besides his parents. Not: . . . obedience and respect for others. When both words call for the same preposition, it need not be repeated: The box office refused to make any allowance [ ] or refund for tickets purchased from an agent.

b—Prepositions bulking too large. English has a number of group prepositions that sometimes become conspicuous because they take up too much space for the work they do, creating a flat-footed style. A reference to "recent demonstrations on the part of dissatisfied students" is weighed down by "on the part of" where *by* would do the job. Prepositions sometimes bulk too large in writing because we carry over from speech the tendency to use double prepositions: *in* *back (of), outside (of), off (of).* For further examples and discussion, see the articles *as to; *of; *on, onto; and so on.

c — Omission of prepositions. Sometimes prepositions are dropped:

. . . one of the best pieces written about the United States [in] this century.
—Arthur Schlesinger, *New Republic,* Oct. 9, 1961

. . . the mysterious command center beneath the Pentagon [from] where [or: from which] the ultimate orders go to distant area commanders. . . .
—Mark S. Watson, *New York Times Book Review,* April 26, 1964

Although such omissions as these are increasingly common in General writing, expressions like "a couple [of] days later" and "a different type [of] girl" remain conspicuously Informal.

d — Preposition at end of sentence. Some purists have said that prepositions should not stand at the end of their constructions (What did I do it for?), but postponing the preposition has been a characteristic English idiom for a long time. Idiom and rhythm often demand the preposition at the end, particularly with compound verbs like *dispose of* and in relative clauses with *that* or with no relative expressed. Attempts to avoid the postponed preposition are often clumsy or ungrammatical: Tell me what it is to which you object [better: what you object to]. Reference: Bryant, pp. 162–64.

Placing the preposition at the end is such a firmly fixed habit that sometimes care must be taken not to repeat one that has already been expressed: He brightened the life of everyone with whom he came in contact [with].

In addition to *Index* articles already referred to in this discussion, see *Parts of speech, *Objects § 3. References: Curme, *Syntax,* pp. 566–69; Fowler, "preposition at end"; Hall, pp. 213–17.

Present tense
See *Tenses of verbs.

Prewriting
The term *prewriting* refers to the thinking that a writer must do before he can produce even the rough draft of an essay. It applies to that part of rhetoric traditionally known as invention or discovery, the part that deals with the problem of finding something to say. See *Guide,* pp. 31–35. References: D. Gordon Rohman and Albert O. Wlecke, *Pre-Writing: The Construction and Application of Models for Concept Formation in Writing,* U.S. Office of Education Cooperative Research Project Number 2174, East Lansing, Mich., 1964. A brief discussion can be found in D. Gordon Rohman, *CCC,* May 1965, pp. 106–12.

Principal parts of verbs

Prin

Revision: Change the verb form to one in Standard use.

The principal parts of a verb are the base form or infinitive (*ask*), the past-tense form (*asked*), the past participle (*asked*). Most English verbs are "regular" — that is, their past tense and past participle are formed by adding *-ed* to the base form. A number, most of them descended from Old English strong verbs, make their past-tense and past-participle forms by a change in vowel (*strike, struck, struck*). Some (*let, cost*) remain unchanged; some (*bend, make*) change the final consonant; some have less common irregularities (past forms of *teach: taught, taught*).

The trend has been chiefly toward regularity. A few verbs (*broadcast, shine, speed, weave*) have acquired regular forms in addition to their old ones: *broadcasted, shined, speeded, weaved*. A few others (*dive, fit, prove, sew*) have reversed the general trend, acquiring irregularities that are either new or a revival of archaic forms: *dove, fit* (past tense), *proven, sewn*. For some verbs (*dream, plead, show, strive, thrive*) variant pairs have long existed side by side: *dreamed, dreamt; pleaded, pled; showed, shown; strived, strove; thrived, throve*.

The following list includes a number of verbs with irregular past-tense or past-participle forms. Forms in parentheses are decidedly less common in writing, and those labeled NS (Nonstandard) would not ordinarily be written. When doubts arise, a recent dictionary should be consulted for verbs not listed here; but usage is by no means uniform, even among speakers and writers of Standard English, and neither this list nor the dictionaries record all variations.

Infinitive	Past tense	Past participle
arise	arose	arisen
bear	bore	borne
bear	bore	*born (given birth to)
begin	began (NS: begun)	begun (NS: began)
bid (to offer)	bid	bid
bid (to order)	bade	bidden, bid
bite	bit	bitten, bit
blow	blew (NS: blowed)	blown (NS: blowed)
break	broke	broken (Inf. or NS: broke)
bring	brought (NS: brung)	brought (NS: brung)
catch	caught	caught
choose	chose	chosen
come	came (NS: come)	come
dig	dug (Archaic: digged)	dug
dive	dove, dived	dived
*do	did	done
draw	drew	drawn (NS: drawed)
dream	dreamed, dreamt	dreamed, dreamt
drink	drank (NS: drunk)	*drunk (drank, drunken)
eat	ate (chiefly NS: /et/)	eaten (chiefly NS: /et/)
fall	fell	fallen
find	found	found
flee	fled	fled

fly	flew	flown
forget	forgot	forgotten, forgot
freeze	froze	frozen (NS: froze)
*get	got	got, gotten
give	gave (NS: give)	given
go	went	gone (NS: went)
grow	grew (NS: growed)	grown
hang	hung	hung
hang (to execute)	hung, *hanged	hung, hanged
hear	heard	heard
knit	knitted, knit	knitted, knit
know	knew (NS: knowed)	known
*lay	laid	laid
lead	led	led
lend (*loan)	lent	lent
let	let	let
lie (see *lay)	*lay	lain
light	*lighted, lit	lighted, lit
lose	lost	lost
pay	paid (of ropes: payed)	paid (payed)
plead	pleaded, plead, pled	pleaded, plead /pled/, pled /pled/
prove	proved	*proved, proven
ride	rode	ridden
ring	rang, rung	rung
run	ran (NS: run)	run
say	said	said
see	saw (NS: seen)	seen
set	set	set
shine	shone, shined	shone, shined
show	showed	showed, shown
shrink	shrunk, shrank	shrunk
sing	sang, sung	sung
sink	sank, sunk	sunk
sit	sat (NS: *set)	sat (NS: set)
slide	slid	slid (slidden)
sow	sowed	sown, sowed
speak	spoke	spoken
spit	spit, spat	spit, spat
spring	sprang, sprung	sprung
stand	stood	stood
steal	stole	stolen
stink	stunk, stank	stunk
sweat	sweated, sweat	sweated, sweat
swim	swam, swum	swum
take	took	taken
tear	tore	torn
throw	threw (NS: throwed)	thrown
tread	trod	trodden, trod

wake	waked, woke	waked, woke (woken)
wear	wore	worn
weave	wove (of boxing and driving: weaved)	woven, wove
win	won	won
wind	wound (Nautical: winded)	wound
wring	wrung	wrung
write	wrote (Archaic: writ)	written (NS: wrote; Archaic: writ)

The evidence of *The Linguistic Atlas of the United States* continues to provide for revision of some of these descriptions. References: E. Bagby Atwood, *A Survey of Verb Forms in the Eastern United States* (Ann Arbor: Univ. of Michigan Press, 1953); Fries, *AEG*, pp. 59–71; Mencken, pp. 527–28; Pyles, pp. 124–30, 194–205.

principal, principle

Principal is either an adjective or a noun, *principle* only a noun. Associate the adjective *principal* (principal reason, the principal man of the town, the principal force involved) with other adjectives ending in *-al: historical, political, musical.*

Principal as a noun is probably an abbreviation of a phrase in which it was originally an adjective: the principal that draws interest was once the principal sum; the principal of a school, the principal teacher; the principal in a legal action, the principal party; the principals in a play, the principal actors. These are the only common uses of *principal* as a noun.

The noun meaning "a general truth or rule of conduct" is *principle:* the principles of science, a man of high principles.

prior to

In most contexts, particularly in General writing, *before* is the better word. *Prior to,* a rather formal preposition, is most appropriate when it adds to the notion of "before" that of "in anticipation of": "He urged reform leaders to work prior to the convention so as to minimize the influence of Greeley's supporters . . ." (Matthew T. Downey, *Journal of American History*, March 1967).

Profanity

Cursing is primarily oral, a matter of muscular release more than of meaning, and in print profanity often attracts more attention to itself than it deserves. Use the language the subject seriously calls for, compromising as little or as much as your temperament and the circumstances demand. See *Obscenity.

Professor

Write: Professor Moore; Prof. E. W. Moore; E. W. Moore, a professor of chemistry; or (Formal) E. W. Moore, Professor of Chemistry.

The slang *prof* (my math prof) is a clipped word, not an abbreviation, and is written without a period.

Strictly speaking, the title *Professor* should be given only to assistant professors, associate professors, and full professors, not to those who have not reached professorial rank. When the title follows the name in an *of* phrase, exact rank is usually indicated: Professor A. B. Plant, but A. B. Plant, Assistant Professor of English.

Progressive verb forms

Progressive verb forms are verb phrases made with *to be* and the present participle to show continuing action: I *am asking*, he *was asking*, they *have been asking*. See *Tenses of verbs, *Verbs.

Pronominal adjectives

Several types of pronouns, used also like adjectives, are sometimes called pronominal adjectives:

Interrogative: which way?
Demonstrative: that way, *this* book, *those* boys
Possessive: my hat, *his* idea, *your* dog, *their* seats
Indefinite: some people, *each* person, *all* men

Pronouns

Pron

Revision: Change the form of the pronoun marked to the one expected in the grammatical construction in which it stands.

Pronouns are difficult to define because traditionally the members of this category have included many different kinds of words. Almost all of them are used like words we usually define as nouns: they serve as subjects and objects; many have genitive form, and a few have separate plural forms. But while one kind of *grammar will define some words as pronouns, another grammar, using different criteria, will not. If we use a transformational-generative grammar to describe those words that traditional grammars have called pronouns, we may be able to define more clearly what groups of words to include in that category. (The uses of pronouns are described in *Reference of pronouns. In that article and in articles on the different kinds of pronouns, traditional classifications are generally followed.)

1. *The personal pronouns.* The personal pronouns are those words which specifically indicate first, second, or third person, number, and, in the third-person singular, gender. Some of the most common grammatical problems come from the fact that separate nominative and accusative *case forms survive for personal pronouns and for some *relative pronouns, though not for nouns (see *Person; *between you and me; *It's me; *who, whom).

		Nominative	Genitive	Accusative
1st person	singular	I	my, mine	me
	plural	we	our, ours	us
2nd person	singular	you	your, yours	you
	plural	you	your, yours	you
3rd person	singular			
	masculine	he	his, his	him
	feminine	she	its, its	her
	neuter	it	one's, one's	it
	genderless	one	their, theirs	one
	plural	they		them, 'em

Archaic forms of the second-person singular, *thou, thy, thee*, are used in some religious services and occasionally in poetry. Except for the relative pronoun *who (who, whose, whom)*, only the personal pronouns, and not all of them, occur in nominative, genitive, and accusative form.

Reflexive pronouns are variants of these personal pronouns. They are ordinarily used when a referent in the predicate of a sentence refers to another noun in the same simple sentence:

He shot *himself*. They sent the letters to *themselves*. I twisted the rope back on *itself*.

Compare: I asked them to help *me*. The *me* is not in the same simple sentence as *I: I* asked them [they help *me*] ⇒ I asked them to help me.

When used as intensives, these reflexive forms are usually construed as pronouns in apposition: The man *himself* sold the car.

Standard usage requires various forms of the pronoun preceding *self/selves: myself, yourself, himself, herself, itself, ourselves, yourselves, themselves*. Regardless of their logic, *hisself* and *theirselves* are Nonstandard.

Reciprocal pronouns appear to be quite different in form from personal pronouns. Historically, *each other* and *one another* are not related to *I, you, me*, etc. But they might be considered as special variants of objective forms. They are used when a plural noun in a predicate refers to a plural subject and the action of the verb is directed by each member of the plural subject toward the other members: Tom and Bill saw each other. Compare: Tom and Bill saw themselves. If we let form determine how we define pronouns, then these would not be personal pronouns. But if we let meaning define personal pronouns—a word that substitutes for a specifically referred-to noun in the discourse—then these reciprocals would fit the definition. The meaning of "Tom and Bill looked at each other" can be roughly paraphrased as a transformational sequence:

Tom looked at Bill and Bill looked at Tom.
⇒ Tom and Bill looked at Bill and Tom.
⇒ Tom and Bill looked at each other.

"Each other" specifically substitutes for the nouns "Bill" and "Tom." See *each other, one another.

2. *Relative pronouns.* A relative pronoun replaces the noun in an embedded sentence when the noun is identical to its referent in a main sentence:

I met the man [*the man* left] ⇒ I met the man [*who* left].

Like the personal pronouns, *who* has three forms. The other two relatives, *which* and *that*, do not:

Nominative	Genitive	Accusative
who	whose	whom
which	whose	which
that		that

These relative pronouns have an optional variant form when there is no apparent referent for the pronoun in the sentence: *whoever, whomever, whichever, whatever* (*Whoever* receives this will be pleased; I will accept *whomever* you choose; They will believe *whatever* he says).

Closely related to these are the adverbial relatives *when, where, why,* and their parallel forms, *whenever* and *wherever:* He arrived on the day *when* you left; The reason *why* I study is that my courses are hard; I know a place *where* you will be happy. Some transformational linguists have speculated that these relative adverbs are derived in the same way as relative pronouns, from identical noun phrases in embedded sentences:

I he arrived *on the day* [you left *on the day*]
⇒ He arrived *on the day when* you left.

I know *a place* [you will be happy *in the place*]
⇒ I know *a place where* you will be happy.

When the relative pronoun is not the subject of its clause, it can be deleted. The resulting clause has been called a *contact clause:

I know the man *whom* you met ⇒ I know the man you met.
He arrived on the day *when* you left ⇒ He arrived the day you left.
I read the book *which* you sent me ⇒ I read the book you sent me.

3. *Interrogative pronouns.* The interrogative pronouns are *who, whom, whose, *which, *what,* occasionally *whoever, whosoever, whomever, whatever, whichever.* The interrogative adverbials *where, when, why,* and *how* (with their parallel forms *wherever, whenever, however*) resemble them, as the relative adverbials resemble the relative pronouns. Some transformational linguists have speculated that all these interrogative pronouns, in fact, are related to a more basic kind of interrogative structure:

In what place do you live	⇒ Where do you live?
At what time did you leave	⇒ When did you leave?
In what manner does he work	⇒ How does he work?
For what reason did you stop	⇒ Why did you stop?
What thing do you want	⇒ What do you want?
What one do you want	⇒ Who do you want?

Thus in their deep structures the interrogatives with *what + place/ time/manner/reason/thing/one* are similar to *when, where, how, why, who,* and *what.* In a traditional grammar, *when, where, how,* and *why* seem to refer to adverbs of time, place, manner, and reason; and so they are classed as adverbials. But a transformational grammar might not make that distinction since they are all "derived from" a structure which may underlie a noun phrase in a prepositional phrase: *in what place* ⇒ *where.*

4. *Indefinite nouns.* In a traditional grammar, words like *someone, anyone, everyone* are called indefinite pronouns. But these words have no specific referent either in the immediate environment of the speaker or in the written discourse:

Personal: He should repair the road.
Indefinite: Someone should repair the road.

On that basis, the category *pronoun* does not seem entirely justified. These indefinite nouns form a partial pattern with what have traditionally been called indefinite adverbs:

someone	anyone	no one	everyone
something	anything	nothing	everything
somebody	anybody	nobody	everybody
somewhere	anywhere	nowhere	everywhere
sometime	anytime		
somehow	anyhow		

In casual speech *they* is also used for indefinite reference: They ought to do something about these roads.

5. *Prearticles, demonstrative articles, possessives, and postarticles.* In transformational grammars, words that in certain contexts traditional grammars have called indefinite pronouns, demonstrative pronouns, and numeral pronouns have been classed under the general term *determiners and divided into prearticles, articles, and postarticles. (See *Parts of speech.*) The italicized words in the following sentences, for example, have traditionally been called pronouns of one kind or another:

A *few* were found. *All* suffered. *Several* were lost.
This will fix it. *Those* are too large. *These* will help.
Yours is enough. *Hers* impressed me. *Ours* should be examined.
One remained. *Four* were paid for. The *first* was identified.

In a transformational grammar, these are respectively prearticles, demonstrative articles, possessives, and postarticles. They are the same parts of speech in "A *few* books were found," "*This* tool will fix it," "*Your* help is enough," "*One* man remained." It happens that in the examples below, a transformation has deleted a following noun that was identical to another noun previously mentioned:

We lost several books. A few of the books were found.
⇒ We lost several books. A few   were found.

I have some tools here. This tool will fix it.
⇒ I have some tools here. This   will fix it.

A lot of people gave their help. Your help is enough.
⇒ A lot of people gave their help. Yours   is enough.

Almost all the men left. One of the men remained.
⇒ Almost all the men left. One   remained.

If they are analyzed this way, such words are not, strictly speaking, pronouns. They remain after a repeated noun has been deleted and are still prearticles, demonstrative articles, possessives, and postarticles.

6. *So.* One pronoun form which does not fit any category is the *so* that replaces an entire clause: I think *I will win;* at least I hope *so.*

7. *Defining the pronoun.* If we exclude from the category *pronoun* those forms that remain after a noun has been deleted, they will not be labeled one part of speech in one context and another part of speech in a slightly different context. A traditional grammar would label *few* in "A few men left" as an adjective of some sort and the *few* in "A few stayed" as an indefinite pronoun. But a transformational grammar would define both as prearticles. In the second sentence, the fact that the following noun has been deleted does not change the category to which *few* belongs. This logic would exclude prearticles, postarticles, demonstrative articles, and possessives from the class *pronoun.* Because indefinite pronouns do not really replace words, perhaps they should not be classed with pronouns either.

Relative pronouns definitely replace a repeated noun phrase: I know *the man* [*the man* left] ⇒ I know *the man* who left. Because interrogative words are so much like these relatives and because they also "replace" something potentially more definite than themselves — the answer to the question — they too might be classed as pronouns. Thus we might classify as pronouns those forms which actually replace or stand for a particular referent. It is coincidental that among these forms are the only words in English that have three distinct case forms: *I, my, me; who, whose, whom.* The other words we can call indefinite nouns (*someone, anyone,* etc.), prearticles (*some, all, each,* etc.), demonstrative articles (*this, that, these, those*), postarticles (*one, two, three . . .; first, second, third . . .; first, last, former, latter . . .*).

Under any circumstances, our definitions depend on the linguistic theory we have chosen to describe English grammar. Words we would call pronouns in a traditional grammar are not pronouns in a transformational grammar, because each "theory" of language sets up different criteria for answering different questions.

References: Archibald A. Hill, *Introduction to Linguistic Structures* (New York: Harcourt, 1958), pp. 145–52; Jacobs and Rosenbaum, Chs. 12 and 26; John Ross, "On the Cyclic Nature of English Pronominalization," in *Modern Studies in English*, ed. David A. Reibel and Sanford A. Schane (Englewood Cliffs, N.J.: Prentice, 1969), pp. 187–200.

Pronunciation

The pronunciation of words is indicated in this *Guide* and *Index* by respelling them as follows:

a	apple /ap′ l/, fact /fakt/
ā	age /āj/, say /sā/, inflate /in flāt′/
ã	care /kãr/, air /ãr/
ä	far /fär/, father /fä′ ᴛʜ ər/
b	back /bak/, robber /rob′ ər/
ch	child /chīld/, question /kwes′ chən/, literature /lit′ ər ə chùr/
d	do /dü/, did /did/
e	bet /bet/, effect /ə fekt′/
ėr	urge /ėrj/, bird /bėrd/, term /tėrm/
ē	equal /ē′ kwəl/, see /sē/, police /pə lēs′/
f	fat /fat/, stuff /stuf/, cough /kôf/, photo /fō′ tō/
g	go /gō/, baggage /bag′ ij/
h	hotel /hō tel′/, boyhood /boi′ hùd/
hw	wheel /hwēl/, whether /hweᴛʜ′ ər/
i	if /if/, pithy /pith′ ē/
ī	ice /īs/, buy /bī/
j	jam /jam/, edge /ej/, age /āj/
k	king /king/, back /bak/, cocoa /kō′ kō/
l	life /līf/, silly /sil′ ē/, fill /fil/
m	am /am/, meet /mēt/, sample /sam′ pl/
n	note /nōt/, inner /in′ ər/
ng	sing /sing/, song /sông/, rank /rangk/
o	rock /rok/, stop /stop/
ō	open /ō′ pən/, hope /hōp/, go /gō/
ô	bought /bôt/, ball /bôl/, caught /kôt/, four /fôr/
oi	voice /vois/, boil /boil/
ou	house /hous/, out /out/, cow /kou/
p	paper /pā′ pər/, cap /kap/
r	reach /rēch/, try /trī/
s	say /sā/, listen /lis′ ṇ/, yes /yes/
sh	she /shē/, rush /rush/, cushion /kùsh′ ən/, nation /nā′ shən/
t	tie /tī/, sit /sit/, kitten /kit′ ṇ/
th	thin /thin/, both /bōth/, bath /bath/
ᴛʜ	that /ᴛʜat/, bother /boᴛʜ′ ər/, bathe /bāᴛʜ/, thee /ᴛʜē/
u	cup /kup/, butter /but′ ər/

u̇   book /bu̇k/, put /pu̇t/
ü   tool /tül/, rule /rül/, move /müv/
ū   useful /ūs′ fəl/, music /mū′ zik/
v   very /ver′ ē/, salve /sav/ or /säv/, save /sāv/
w   will /wil/, with /wiᴛʜ/ or /with/, won't /wōnt/
y   young /yung/, yellow /yel′ ō/
z   zero /zir′ ō/, breeze /brēz/
zh   measure /mezh′ ər/, rouge /rüzh/

ə   Schwa /shwä/ represents the neutral vowel sound of many unstressed syllables. It is variously spelled: a in *sofa* /sō′ fəl/, e in *secretary* /sek′ rə ter′ ē/, and by the other vowels and combinations of vowels.

/l̩, m̩, n̩, r̩/ Syllabic consonants, used in unstressed syllables when no vowel sound can be distinguished: little /lit′ l̩/, wooden /wood′ n̩/. When spoken slowly these syllables have /ə/, and are sometimes so respelled.

The stress of syllables is represented by ′ for a main stress and ′ for a lighter stress, placed after the stressed syllable: /ag′ rə kul′ chər/.
    A vowel sound in a stressed syllable will be more fully sounded than one without stress. Contrast the *o* of *below* /bi lō′/ and of *obey*, which ranges from /ō bā′/ to /ə bā′/. In unstressed syllables they tend to become the neutral vowel /ə/, as in the italicized vowels in a*g*ain, acade*m*y, dorm*i*tory, cur*s*ory, cir*c*us.
    An *r* following a vowel alters the vowel's sound, as in *care, sere, core, sure,* but a separate symbol is not used to represent the change (except for /èr/ as in *term* /tèrm/): /kār/, /sēr/, /kôr/, /shu̇r/.
    References: Edward Artin, ''Guide to Pronunciation,'' in *Webster's Third New International Dictionary;* John S. Kenyon, *American Pronunciation,* 10th ed. (Ann Arbor: Wahr, 1958); John S. Kenyon and Thomas A. Knott, *A Pronouncing Dictionary of American English,* 2nd ed. (Springfield, Mass.: Merriam, 1953); Hans Kurath and Raven I. McDavid, Jr., *Pronunciation of English in the Atlantic States* (Ann Arbor: Univ. of Michigan Press, 1961).

Proofreading
Checking the final copy of an essay for mechanical mistakes that may have slipped into the last draft is an essential part of preparing a manuscript. In making corrections, you may find it helpful to use some of the abbreviations and symbols used by professional proofreaders. Proofreaders place instructions to typesetters in the margins of galleys, but you will ordinarily make your corrections in the body of your manuscript. See *Caret, *Manuscript form, *Typewritten copy.

Insert period	St⊙Paul
comma	St. Paul‸Minn.
colon	Dear Sir ⊙
semicolon	today‸therefore, we must
apostrophe	Its late

superior figure	according to Hoyle.
quotation marks	Hello, he said
Paragraph	for mathematics. Psychology is
No paragraph	that year. Next fall I went back to
Transpose	Nor they did the following day
Close up	on April 4, 1860
Lowercase	that Nader is the last Crusader
Capital letter	the year of the first Crusade
Italics	Read his Symposium first

Proper adjectives

Proper nouns that are used like adjectives are capitalized, and so are adjectives that are directly derived from proper names if they still refer to the place or person. After proper adjectives lose the reference to their origins, they become simple adjectives and are no longer capitalized: the Indian service, india ink; a Paris (or Parisian) cafe, paris green; the Roman forum, roman type. See *Capital letters.

Proper names

Considerable care needs to be taken to spell the names of people, places, companies, institutions as the people most concerned with them wish to have them spelled. Often pronunciation is no guide: Thames /temz/; Worcester /wŭs'ter/; San Joaquin /san' wô kēn'/; Waco /wā' kō/, Texas, but Saco /sô' kō/, Maine; Cairo /kī' rō/ for the Egyptian city, /kā' rō/ or /ke' rō/ for the one in Illinois.

Many fairly common names occur in various forms: Burns, Byrnes; Harvey, Hervey; Cohen, Cohn, Kohen; Mac, Mc, M'; and so on. Special care is needed with names having silent letters or some peculiarity of spelling or phrasing: Pittsburgh (but Gettysburg), the Johns Hopkins University.

Dictionaries and encyclopedias give the spelling of the names of the best-known people and places. See particularly *Webster's Biographical Dictionary* and *Webster's Geographical Dictionary*, both published by Merriam-Webster. See *Capital letters § 2, *Course names.

proved, proven

Prove is a regular verb, forming a past tense and past participle with *-ed: proved. Proven,* originally the past participle of a Scots verb, *preve,* meaning "prove," has been used for centuries in English as an alternative past participle of *prove* and is now established in all varieties of usage. References: Bryant, pp. 165–66; Hall, pp. 227–29.

provided, providing

Both are in Standard use as connectives. Formal writing strongly prefers *provided;* in General writing usage is divided:

You can't even argue, much, with the picture, providing you look at it only as a clever Western. — David R. Slavitt, *Yale Review*, Winter 1965

Anyone who can get into M.S.U. can get into Justin Morrill, provided he is willing to work. — Duncan Norton, *Fortune*, May 1967

Provincialisms

See *Localisms.

Psychologese

Psychologese is a jargon made up of words from the technical vocabulary of psychology used repeatedly and inexactly by outsiders: *instinctual* for *instinctive, operant* for *operating, motorical* for *motor*. A great many other terms from psychology (*empathy, relate, neurotic, traumatic, motivational*) have entered the general language, become *vogue words, and lost much of their technical meaning.

public

Meaning "the people as a whole," *public* is a collective noun and can be treated either as a singular or as a plural. A plural construction is more common: The public depend on TV newscasts for most of their information. But in the sense "a group of people with a common interest," *public* is more often singular: ". . . there is a foreign policy public that is considerably smaller than the general public . . ." (Carl N. Degler, *American Historical Review*, Feb. 1969).

Punctuation, No punctuation

Pn   No Pn

Revision: Correct the error in punctuation either by inserting appropriate punctuation or by deleting punctuation that is unnecessary or confusing. If the change to be made is not clear to you, consult the Index *article on the particular mark.*

For a discussion of the function and general uses of the punctuation marks and of different styles of punctuation, see *Guide*, pp. 294 – 303. For details of the uses of the individual marks, see *Apostrophe, *Brackets, *Colon, *Comma, *Dash, *Ellipsis, *Exclamation mark, *Hyphen, *Italics, *Parentheses, *Period, *Question mark, *Quotation marks, *Semicolon. See also *Division of words, *Restrictive and nonrestrictive, *Series. References: Summey; Whitehall, Ch. 10.

Puns

A pun is a *figure of speech in which a word is simultaneously used in two senses (the nut that holds the wheel = automobile driver) or in which a word is substituted for another word of similar sound but different meaning (hire education). Deliberate punning may serve serious purposes as well as humorous ones, but unconscious puns should be weeded out in revision. See *Guide*, pp. 372 – 73.

purist

A purist is one who believes in and tries to practice nicety of choice in the use of materials of expression. The term is also used disparagingly of a person who wishes all writers to follow traditional "rules"—whether or not they are or ever were followed consistently by anyone—and who tries to hold words to narrower and older meanings.

Qualifiers

Qualifiers are words used not to convey meaning in themselves but to qualify—usually by intensifying—the meaning of adjectives. Such words are classed as adverbs in traditional grammars, but they share scarcely any of the characteristics of such words as *quickly, carefully, usually*, etc. Qualifiers include the first words in the phrases "much older," "very quiet," "too old," "somewhat sick," "rather careless," "quite intelligent." Degree adverbs can be included in this group; they are based on adjectives that fit in the frame [adjective] to a _____ degree (cold to a slight degree): *slightly, extremely, highly, mildly, fairly, terrifically, tremendously*, etc. Though sometimes effective in speech, qualifiers are seldom convincing in writing. They are more likely to weaken by overstating than to strengthen the passages in which they appear.

Question mark

1. The principal use of the question mark is as the end stop of a direct question: What was the real reason?

2. A question mark is not used after an indirect question: He wanted to know what the real reason was.

3. A request that is phrased as a question may or may not be followed by a question mark, depending on the formality of the style:

Formal: Will you please return the book at your earliest convenience?
General: Will you please get the book back as soon as you can.

4. Usage is divided over a question built into a sentence: Should I quit school now [ ] I ask myself. A question mark after *now* would emphasize the question; a comma would make it less emphatic. If quotation marks were used around the question, a question mark would be stylistically appropriate.

5. A question mark is used to show that dates are approximate or uncertain: Geoffrey Chaucer 1340?–1400 or Geoffrey Chaucer 1340(?)–1400.

6. A question mark in parentheses to indicate humor or sarcasm is usually distasteful: her fashionable (?) outfit.

7. When a question mark and a closing quotation mark fall together, the question mark belongs outside the quotation mark if the quoting sentence is the question (Did you really say, "I thought you were older than that"?), inside if the quotation is the question (He asked, "Did you really say that?"). If both are questions, only the inside question mark is used: Did she ask, "How many are coming?"

Questions

1. The intonation patterns for questions are complex; some questions end with the voice rising, others with it falling. Since in writing these patterns must all be suggested by one final mark, written questions are best described in terms of interrogative words and word order.

A question may be introduced by a pronoun (*Who* was that? *What* can be done?), an adjective (*Which* way did he go?) or an adverb (*Where* shall we eat?). A question may be indicated by inverted word order, with the verb or part of the verb coming before the subject. This order is now found only with such verbs as *be, have, shall, will, can, may, must, need,* and *ought* (Was he there?) and in Informal, usually spoken, subjectless sentences (Want this one?). Ordinarily a verb phrase is used, with part of it coming before the subject as a sort of compromise inversion: *Do you think* he can do it? (Here the auxiliary *do* is meaningless but allows us to begin the question with one verb while keeping the main verb, *think*, in its normal position after the subject.) A statement may also be turned into a question by adding an inverted clause at the end: He didn't try, *did he?*

2. A direct question is a question as it is actually asked, not just reported. It begins with a capital and with a question mark: Who killed Cock Robin? But if a direct question is introduced parenthetically into another sentence, it begins with a lowercase letter: "He felt a strong urge—as indeed who doesn't?—to write a really good modern novel" (Noel Coward, *To Step Aside*).

An indirect question is not a question as it is actually asked but a question reported as a subordinate element of another sentence. An indirect question does not begin with a capital or end with a question mark, and it is not set off by quotation marks. The tense of the direct question may be changed to match the verb of the sentence in which the indirect question is reported, and often a subordinating conjunction is introduced:

Direct: "What are our plans for tomorrow?"

Indirect: He asked what our plans for tomorrow were.

Direct: He asked, "Do you really understand what you have read?"

Indirect: He asked us if we really understood what we had read. He always asks us whether we understand what we have read.

3. A leading question is one phrased to suggest the answer desired, like "You wouldn't do that, would you?" (contrasted with "Would you do that?").

4. Stylistically, questions provide variety and, if used sparingly, may have a good effect. See *Rhetorical questions; *Guide*, p. 203.

Quotation marks

Quot

Revision: Make the quotation marks conform to conventional usage.

1. *Methods of indicating quotations.*
a—Double quotes are the usual marks, though single quotes are common in Britain and were once fairly common in the United States.
b—For quotations within quotations, double and single quotes are alternated; single quotes are used inside double quotes and so on: " 'Perry's instinct,' he says, 'soundly chose the point at which to halt the extension of the term "formula" ' " (Joseph Russo, *Yale Classical Studies*, Vol. XX, 1966).
c—When a quotation is longer than a paragraph, marks are used at the beginning of each paragraph but at the end of the last paragraph only.
d—When long quotations or a series of quotations are indented or are set in smaller type, as in this book, no quotation marks are used. In double-spaced typewritten copy, such quotations are usually indented and single spaced.

2. *Principal uses of quotation marks.*
a—Quotation marks are used to indicate all passages taken from another writer, whether a phrase or a page or more (except when the quotation is indented). Any change of language within the quotation should be indicated—omissions by *ellipses, additions by *brackets. The quoted matter may stand by itself or may be worked into the writer's own sentence:

The most that could be said for Haig was said by Churchill: he "was unequal to the prodigious scale of events, but no one else was discerned as his equal or better." (Lloyd George, more succinctly, said he was "brilliant to the top of his army boots.")—Geoffrey Barraclough, *New York Review of Books*, May 14, 1964

When speeches or a short conversation are used not for their own sake but to illustrate a point, they are usually incorporated in a paragraph:

La Patriote is a dimly lighted room over a tavern on St. Catherine Street East. There are fishnets all over the place. The washroom doors are marked "Québécois" and "Québécoise." I am having a drink with the manager, Yves Blais. "You don't speak French," he starts off by saying, "but that is all right because you are from Ontario, which is another country. I will speak English with you. But I have no British accent. I have a pea-soup accent."

Blais volunteers the obvious—that he is a separatist. "I'm glad to be. I don't care. I refused to accept a Canada Council grant of $8,000. But it has nothing to do with my shows." English-speaking people, he says, make up 10 percent of his audiences. He does not cater to them though.—Jon Ruddy, *Maclean's*, June 1969

b—There are no half quotes. A sentence is either an exact quotation and therefore in quotation marks, or else it isn't and so is not quoted. By paying scrupulous attention to the exact language of the material to be quoted, you can avoid using quotation marks with pronouns and verb tenses appropriate only to indirect statements: He boasted that he "could do twice as much work as me." The boast must have been, "I can do twice as much work as you." The choice is between—but not halfway between—direct and indirect quotation: He boasted, "I can do twice as much work as you"; or: He boasted that he could do twice as much work as me.

3. *Miscellaneous uses of quotation marks.*
a—Quotation marks enclose titles of poems, articles, stories, chapters of books, and, in most newspapers and many magazines, the titles of books themselves:

Until he began stumping for Willi Brandt during the 1965 election . . ., Grass was widely known only as a poet, playwright ("The Plebians Rehearse the Uprising") and novelist ("The Tin Drum," "Cat and Mouse," "Dog Years") of the first rank.—*Newsweek*, May 26, 1969

See *Titles of books, articles, etc. See also *Ships' names.
b—In Formal writing, words that are used as words rather than for their meaning are usually put in italics (as they are in this book); in General writing they are ordinarily put in quotes:

"Capitalism" is thus a shape, a form, which speaks, commands, fights, runs away. Asked to define it, the debater on the left introduces more abstractions: "Absentee ownership," "surplus value," "class struggle." . . . The great words roll.—Stuart Chase, *The Tyranny of Words*

c—In Formal writing a word from a conspicuously different variety of speech may be put in quotation marks, but the practice is less common than it was. Many stylists dislike this use of quotation marks in any variety of writing. If the word is appropriate, use it without apology:

. . . he spurns aspirants not of his clique, thereby creating a tyranny of taste that soon will have every center of imaginative expression . . . under its cheesy [not "cheesy"] thrall.—Benjamin DeMott, *New American Review #1*

d—A word may be put in quotation marks to show that the writer is using it derisively (The "cute" Great Dane had torn the upholstery to shreds) or that he refuses to accept its conventional sense in the particular context:

In numerous cases it is impossible to maintain on any solid ground that one pronunciation given is "better" than another, as, for example, that one pronunciation of *swamp* is better than the others given. . . .—John S. Kenyon and Thomas A. Knott, *A Pronouncing Dictionary of American English*

e—Directly quoted *yes* and *no* frequently appear without quotation marks when they are built into the sentence in which they appear: Steve said Yes, so we went to work at once. When they are not actually spoken, they should not be quoted: If he said no, I was prepared to resign.

4. *Quotation marks and other marks.*
a—When a question mark or an exclamation mark ends a quotation, it is placed inside the quotes:

"Don't go near that wire!" he shouted.

Later he said, "Aren't you wondering what would have happened?"

When a question mark or exclamation mark belongs to the construction that includes the quotation, it is placed after the quotes:

This rude revision of their image (no "community of scholars" engaged in the "disinterested pursuit of truth"?) is hard for the faculty to bear. . . . —Michael Miles, *New Republic*, April 12, 1969

b—In British usage, periods and commas are often treated as question marks and exclamation marks are, but American practice is to place periods and commas within the quotation marks. Colons and semicolons are placed after the closing quotes.
c—"He said" and all its variations are normally set off by commas from the quotations they introduce:

"History," it is said, "does not repeat itself. The historians repeat one another." — Max Beerbohm, *Works*

But the quoted phrase may be so closely built into the sentence that no comma is wanted:

Any moron can say "I don't know who done it." — Francis Christensen, *Notes Toward a New Rhetoric*

5. *In foreign languages.* Other languages have different methods of indicating quotations. If you have occasion to quote a passage in another language that includes a quotation, consult a stylebook.

raise, rear

Raise in the sense of bringing up a child has become suitable in all varieties of usage. *Rear* is becoming somewhat formal. See also *bring up.

reaction

Reaction has drifted from the scientific vocabulary into General usage and become a *counter word for nearly any response, whether emotional or mental, general or specific. With a little effort, a writer can usually find a more appropriate, more exact word.

Reading and writing

See *Guide*, pp. 26–27.

real, really

Ordinarily *real* is an adjective (a real difficulty, in real life), and *really* is the adverb (a really significant improvement; I really thought so). Both are overused as *qualifiers. Adverbial *real*, as in sentences like "Write real soon" and "It's real pretty," is avoided in General and Formal writing.

rear, raise

See *raise, rear.

reason is because

In Formal writing there is an overwhelming preference for *reason . . . is that;* but in General usage, particularly when a clause with a separate subject comes between the two parts of the expression, *reason . . . is because* is frequently seen in print:

One reason why music can stand repetition so much more sturdily than correspondingly good prose is because music, of all the arts, is by its nature least suited to the psychology of information, and has remained closer to the psychology of form.—Kenneth Burke, *Psychology and Form*

The major reason, finally, why the war may not be such a major handicap to the President is because the terms of this debate are unusually subject to control. . . .—Theodore Sorenson, *New York Times Magazine*, March 17, 1968

Nevertheless, many people regard *because* in such contexts as redundant, and even in General writing *that* is much more common when there are no intervening words (My only reason is that I have to work tonight) or when the intervening words do not constitute a clause with a subject of its own: "The reason usually given for Palmer's doldrums is that his great wealth and many business concerns . . . weigh too heavily on his spirit" (John Skow, *Holiday*, June 1969). So despite the long history of *reason . . . is because* in literature and its regular use by educated speakers, writers should remind themselves that *reason . . . is that* will make no one unhappy. References: Bryant, pp. 170–71; Jespersen, *MEG*, V, 391; Marckwardt and Walcott, pp. 31, 112; Roberts, pp. 237–38, 337.

Reciprocal pronouns

See *each other, *Pronouns § 1.

reckon

　　See *calculate, reckon.

Reduced clauses

　　See *Clauses § 3; *Guide*, pp. 279–83.

Redundancy

　　See *Deadwood, *Repetition, *Wordiness.

Reference of pronouns

Ref

Revision: Change the pronoun marked (or revise the sentence) so that the reference will be exact and obvious and the pronoun itself will be in the conventional form.

Because it takes the place of a noun phrase, a pronoun usually points to another word, not to a thing, so that its meaning must be completed by the word that it replaces, its antecedent. For this reason the use of pronouns is sometimes troublesome. In conversation they are inconspicuous words, casually serving various grammatical functions. In writing they can be scrutinized for form and reference, and a careful writer will conform to the expectations of educated readers.

1. *Clear reference.* If the meaning of a pronoun is completed by reference to an antecedent, the reference should be exact and obvious. Clear reference is a matter of meaning, not just of the presence or position of certain words. Confusion may arise when the pronoun seems to refer to a nearby noun to which it cannot sensibly refer or when there is no noun nearby; when it refers to a noun used subordinately in the preceding construction, perhaps to one used as a possessive or as an adjective; and when two or more pronouns are crossed so that the exact reference cannot be readily determined. Usually to improve such reference, the sentence must be revised:

He isn't married and doesn't plan on *it*. Revision: . . . and doesn't plan to marry.

The next year he had an attack of acute appendicitis. *It* burst before the doctors had a chance to operate. Revision: . . . His appendix burst. . . . (*It* cannot refer to *appendicitis*. Slips in reference are common when a sentence boundary separates a pronoun and its antecedent.)

A legislator should be a man who knows a little about law and government, and he should know how to apply *them* to the best interests of his people. Revision: . . . should know how to apply his knowledge. . . .

Bill provided more excitement one afternoon when he was skipping rocks across the swimming hole and cut open a young girl's head *who* was swimming under water. Revision: . . . and cut open the head of a young girl who. . . .

To many of us the word *geology* means little. Yet *it* deals with materials used to build our homes and factories, the metals for our cars, the fuel that enables us to drive them. Revision: To many of us the science of geology means little. . . . (It's the science, not the word, that deals with these things.)

Businessmen without regard for anyone else have exploited the mass of workers at every point, not caring whether *they* were earning a decent living wage but only whether *they* were getting a lot of money. Revision: . . . whether they paid a decent living wage but only whether they were getting. . . . (The sentence needs a complete rewriting, but this revision at least makes both *they*'s refer to the same thing.)

General English uses *which, that, this*, and sometimes *it* to refer to the idea of a previous clause. Formal usage tends to avoid this type of reference or to limit it to *this*.

General: Her friend was jealous of her clothes and money and had taken this way of showing it.
Formal: . . . and had taken this way of showing her feeling.

General: . . . Kunen went on filling up his spiral notebook while he hung around Columbia and the Movement for the rest of the summer, fell in love, went on the Merv Griffin show, hitchhiked home to Massachusetts, and drove up to Canada with his girl to look into the draft resister scene, which he did for about ten minutes. — Ted Solotaroff, *New Republic*, May 10, 1969
Formal: . . . the draft resister scene. This he did. . . . (But "draft resister scene" is Informal.)

General: He never seemed to realize when academic tempests were brewing, which was probably a good thing. — J. R. Parker, *Academic Procession*
Formal: . . . were brewing. His innocence was probably a good thing.

2. *Agreement.* Pronouns referring to antecedents usually agree with them in number, gender, and person. When the antecedent is singular, the pronoun should be singular: Hugh tried to go quietly, but *he* couldn't keep from whistling. When the antecedent is plural, the pronoun should be plural: The boys had tried to go quietly, but *they* couldn't keep from whistling.

In Formal English, *each, every, everyone* are generally referred to by singular pronouns (see *every and its compounds): Almost everyone has some little superstitions which *he* would not violate consciously. But in General and Informal English these words are treated as collectives and often take plural pronouns: Almost everyone has some little superstitions which they. . . . See also *they and the articles on the individual indefinite pronouns.

A *collective noun is referred to by either a singular or a plural pronoun: When a gang of rabbit hunters spreads out over a field, it doesn't [or: they don't] lose any time.

The agreement of pronouns in person and gender presents little difficulty:

First person: I wish the dean had told *me* before.

Second person: You should have thought of that *yourself.*
Third person, feminine gender: The woman said *she* was lost.

It is worth observing that relative pronouns agree with their antecedents in gender, number, and person — all three — though the agreement may not appear in the relatives themselves. *Who,* for example, can refer only to masculine or feminine antecedents; accompanying verbs and reflexive pronouns show its number and person: He is one of those people [third-person plural] who always get [plural] themselves [third-person plural] in trouble. See *one of those who.

The case of a pronoun depends upon the construction in which it stands, not upon its antecedent. See *Case; *It's me; *who, whom.

3. *Indefinite reference.* Often pronouns are used to refer to the readers or to people in general instead of to specifically mentioned people. English has no such convenient indefinite pronoun as the German *man* or the French *on.* Our *one* has a severe and Formal connotation. *We* and *you* seem to be slightly more personal, more expressive; both are very generally used. Whether to choose *you, *they, *we, *one,* or *people* or some other noun is a question of style, not grammar.

Indefinite pronouns should be kept consistent:

When you have worked a day here, you have earned your money. Or: When one has worked a day here, he has earned his money. Not: When one has worked a day here, you have. . . .

An indefinite pronoun should not be substituted for a definite personal pronoun: For me there is no fun in reading unless I can put myself in the position of the characters and feel that I am really in the scene. Not: For me there is no fun in reading unless you can put yourself in the position of the characters. . . .

Since English has no single pronoun to mean "*he or she," the masculine *he* is conventionally used: The time comes to every worker when he [not: he or she] anxiously awaits retirement. Less formally, *they* is often used to mean "he or she."

4. *Avoiding pronouns.* Because pronouns can lead to inconsistency or vagueness, writers sometimes try to avoid them, using nouns instead. The result may be unidiomatic or clumsy English: Arrest of the woman yesterday followed several days of observation of the woman's [better: her] activities by the agents.

5. *Omission of pronouns.* In Informal writing, as in conversation, pronouns — especially *I* — are often omitted, and all varieties of English frequently omit a relative pronoun used as an object: The people [that] I questioned had never heard of him.

For a transformational analysis of the classes and forms of pronouns, see *Pronouns. See also the articles on particular pronouns. References: All grammars treat the use of pronouns. Curme and Jespersen discuss many special uses.

Referent

The referent of a word is the thing it refers to: my feet—the things themselves—are the referents of the expression "my pedal extremities." Words without referents are called noise by semanticists.

Reflexive pronouns

See *myself, *Pronouns § 1.

relate

In the *shoptalk of psychology the verb *relate* is a convenient term meaning to "have a realistic social or intimate relationship," as in "the patient's inability to relate." This sense of *relate* has passed into General usage, but the relationship is usually—and preferably—specified by a *to* phrase: They find it almost impossible to relate to adults. *Relate* is a *vogue word.

Relative clauses

The most familiar kind of relative clause functions as an adjective and is introduced by a relative pronoun (*that, which,* or *who*) or a relative adverb (*where, when, why*). In General usage the adverb, or the pronoun when it is not a subject, is often omitted. A relative clause stands after the noun it modifies:

The rain *that began in the morning* kept on all night.

The coach was abused by alumni *who two years before had cheered him*.

The road to the left, *which looked almost impassable*, was ours.

The first place *where they camped* turned out to be a swamp.

The man *I met that afternoon* became my closest friend. Formal: The man *whom I met*. . . .

He will never forget the time *you tried to cheat him*. Formal: . . . the time *when you tried*. . . .

Several relative clauses in succession make for an awkward house-that-Jack-built sentence: People *who* buy houses *that* have been built in times *which* had conspicuous traits of architecture *which* have been since abandoned often have to remodel their purchases completely.

Indefinite relative clauses are less familiar than adjectival relatives. They are commonly introduced by *who, what,* and the compounds in *-ever* and function as nouns or adverbs:

The stranger at the door wasn't *who we thought he was*.
What actually happens is very different from *what the newspapers report*.
Whoever put the guppies in the bathtub, I want you to remove them.

See *that; *who, whom; *which; *Restrictive and nonrestrictive; *Guide,* pp. 312–16. Compare *Noun clauses. Reference: Jacobs and Rosenbaum, pp. 45–50, 199–213, 258–62.

Relative pronouns

The relative pronouns are *who (whose, whom), which (of which, whose), that, what, whatever, whoever (whomever),* and occasionally *as:*

Somebody *who* was sitting on the other side shouted, "Put 'em out."
The Senator, *whose* term expires next year, is already worrying.
I haven't read the same book *that* [*as*] you have.

That refers to persons and things, *who* to persons. *Which* in Standard English now refers to animals or objects or situations, but also to collective nouns, even if they refer to persons:

The army *which* mobilizes first has the advantage.
The Board of Directors, *which* met on Saturday. . . .
The Board of Directors, *who* are all bankers. . . .

In older English — and still in Nonstandard — *which* applies also to persons: "Our Father which art in heaven. . . ."

Particular points in the use of these relatives are discussed in separate entries, especially those on *that; *which; *who, whom. See also *Subordinating conjunctions, *Restrictive and nonrestrictive.

relevant

See *Vogue words.

Repetition

Rep

Revision: Remove the ineffective repetition of word, meaning, or sound.

Repetition of word, meaning, or sound may be an effective trait of style, contributing especially to emphasis. Successful repetition is discussed in the *Guide*, pp. 341–42. This article reviews some kinds of repetition that ordinarily require revision:

1. *Of words and phrases.* An attentive reading should have led the writer to remove the obvious repetition in this sentence: From here on there was no trail, and if there had been it would have been snowed under [by the snow of] the night before. Especially conspicuous is repetition of a word used in a different sense: No one in our commune belongs to a fraternity, but our unity and fraternity [substitute: brotherhood] have brought us real satisfaction and much success.

2. *Of meaning.* Meaning may be needlessly repeated through redundant modifiers or through deadwood:

It's a [true] *fact* that they're offering [free] *gifts.*
In *many* books the setting [very often] is in some foreign country.
At eight-thirty [in the morning] you punch the time clock *to start the day.*

3. *Of sound.* Jingles and rhyming words (hesitate to take the bait) are distracting in prose, and so are noticeable repetitions of unstressed syllables, especially the *-ly* of adverbs and the endings of some abstract nouns, like *-tion.* See *Adverbs § 4.

Requests
See *Commands and requests.

researcher
Researcher is shorter than *research worker* and not exactly replaceable by *scientist, investigator, editor, student,* or *scholar;* but some readers still do not accept it.

Research papers
See *Guide*, Chapter Fourteen.

Resolutions
A resolution is a formal record of the will or intent of an organization. It is typically used to express sympathy, to state opinion, or to recommend action. The style is Formal, and the clauses are arranged by a standardized formula:

WHEREAS, The experiences of the past year have shown . . .; and

WHEREAS, Our expectations of a more favorable attitude on the part of . . .; therefore be it

RESOLVED, That this body feels it its duty to inform . . .; and be it further

RESOLVED, That a copy of these resolutions be sent. . . .

John J. Smith, Secretary

Restrictive and nonrestrictive

Rest

Revision: If the modifier marked is restrictive, it should not be separated from the word it modifies by a comma. If it is nonrestrictive, it should be set off by a comma or by two commas.

1. *Restrictive and nonrestrictive modifiers.* A restrictive, or bound, modifier defines, limits, identifies the word or phrase it is attached to, in order to distinguish it from all the other referents that the word might name. The modifier and the *headword together are necessary to identify the referent:

Educational reform is now being brought about by undergraduates *who are concerned more with the value of their education than with getting a piece of paper at the end of four years.*

Without the italicized restrictive modifier, the sentence would refer to all undergraduates, not just those concerned about their education.

A nonrestrictive, or free, modifier, provides additional and often necessary information about the word or phrase it is attached to, but it does not identify a subcategory of that word or phrase:

Educational reform is now being brought about by undergraduates, who are concerned more with the value of their education than with getting a piece of paper at the end of four years.

The italicized nonrestrictive modifier, signaled in writing by a comma, does not identify a subcategory of undergraduates. The sentence claims that all undergraduates are bringing about educational reform. The fact that they are concerned about the value of their education is necessary to understand the idea but not necessary to identify the referent of *undergraduates.*

As a rule, the nonrestrictive modifier can be omitted or even put into a separate sentence without altering what the headword refers to:

Educational reform is now being brought about by undergraduates. They are concerned more with. . . .

After a proper noun, the modifier is usually nonrestrictive since a name ordinarily specifies a single member of a category: Just below Poughkeepsie, *which we reached in a little over an hour,* we had another lunch at a roadside diner. Occasionally, though, restrictive modifiers are required, as when we imagine a series of referents through time for a proper name: The Cleveland *that I was born in* is not the Cleveland that I know today.

In speaking or in reading aloud there is little pause before the restrictive modifier, and the voice is usually sustained. There is usually a slight pause before and after a nonrestrictive modifier and a slight drop in tone during the modifier.

Traditionally, the restrictive/nonrestrictive distinction has applied to relative clauses. Francis Christensen urged that the principle be extended to all adjectival modifiers, to appositives, and to some adverbial modifiers, including final adverbial clauses. Reference: Christensen, pp. 95 – 110.

2. *Optional punctuation.* Not all modifiers are clearly restrictive or nonrestrictive. Commas emphasize a slight relationship, their absence a closer relationship. Some modifiers, particularly adverbial elements, can be spoken or read with or without pause and drop in tone, with slight change in emphasis. The italicized modifiers in these sentences might or might not be set off by commas:

They had *of course* more experience by then.

The vibrations of the acid rock pounded against me from the room on the third floor *even before I heard the music that went with it.*

See *Guide,* p. 300.

3. *In transformational grammar.* In a transformational-generative grammar, a restrictive modifier is generated as part of the noun phrase that the headword occurs in:

I know   the man   [the man left]
⇒   I know   the man   who left.

Nonrestrictive modifiers are more puzzling. But because they can be paraphrased as a compound sentence, some linguists have suggested that they are originally generated in coordinate constructions and then transformed into nonrestrictive clauses:

John left and John is my friend.
⇒   John, and John is my friend, left.
⇒   John, who is my friend, left.
⇒   John,   my friend, left.

The last sentence contains what is traditionally called an appositive—demonstrating how a transformational grammar relates apparently unrelated structures through transformations (see *Apposition, appositives).
Reference: Jacobs and Rosenbaum, pp. 258–62.

rhetoric

In its classical, neutral sense of "the art of persuasion," *rhetoric* is now used mainly in Formal contexts. In textbooks like this one, it is broadened to mean "the study of the making, the qualities, and the effects of verbal discourse." But *rhetoric* has a wide range of other interpretations, some of which stress its baser uses, some its more dignified:

. . . the great Swiss writer, Ferdinand Ramuz, whom no one has ever accused of rhetoric.—Robert Speaight, *Shakespeare Quarterly*, Autumn 1967

A lucid, chaste Virgilian rhetoric. . . .—Howard Felperin, ibid.

In General usage, where derogatory senses of the word seem to prevail, *rhetoric* frequently suggests flamboyant insincerity, unprincipled manipulation of emotion, or ornamental verbiage. Currently a writer can assume that most audiences will regard *rhetoric* as a term of abuse. See *Guide*, pp. 117–18.

Rhetoric

For the history and theory of rhetoric, see Joseph Schwartz and John A. Rycenga, eds., *The Province of Rhetoric* (New York: Ronald, 1965), with bibliography; W. Ross Winterowd, *Rhetoric: A Synthesis* (New York: Holt, 1968), with bibliography; and many articles in *Quarterly Journal of Speech*. For current applications of rhetorical theory to writing, the best source is the journal *CCC*. For discussion of the elements that enter into the rhetorical situation, see *Guide*, pp. 19–25 and 123–27. Reference: Porter G. Perrin, "Freshman Composition and the Tradition of Rhetoric," in *Perspectives on English*, ed. Robert C. Pooley (New York: Appleton, 1960), pp. 121–32.

Rhetorical questions

Rhetorical questions are really statements in the form of questions, since no direct answer is expected and the writer does not intend to give one. In conversation they often carry some special accent—of accusation, for example:

Could you have done any better?

Did not Henry James, in using the family letters, perversely alter William's Old Abe into President Lincoln?—Lewis Mumford, *New York Review of Books,* Jan. 18, 1968

right

In the sense of "very," *right* is a *localism, in good standing in the South: We'll be right glad to see you. The use of *right* before phrases of place and time (right across the street, right after the show) is avoided in most Formal writing but is established in General usage.

Phrases like *right here, right there, right now,* and *right then* are similarly avoided in Formal contexts though commonplace in General. Idioms like *right away* and *right off* ("at once" or "now") and *right along* ("continuously" or "all the time") are slightly more Informal.

rise, arise, get up

In referring to standing up or getting out of bed, *arise* is Formal and poetic; *rise* is somewhat less formal; the General idiom is *get up.*

Roman numerals

See *Numbers § 3.

round, around

An occasional writer, mistaking prepositional or adverbial *round* for a clipped form of *around,* will spell it with an initial apostrophe; but *'round* has no claim to status. *Round* is a preposition and adverb in its own right, often interchangeable with *around:* ". . . an easy irony, good for a laugh the first two or three times round" (Stanley Kaufmann, *New Republic,* Jan. 18, 1969).

Around for "approximately" (around 1920, a cast of around forty) is now found in all varieties of usage.

All-round and *all-around* (an all-round flour, an all-around athlete) are overused General adjectives.

Run-on sentence

See *Comma fault, *Fused sentence.

said

As a modifier (the said person, the said idea) *said* is legal language. In General writing, *that* or *this* or some other word of demonstrative force is more natural.

saint

The abbreviation *St.* is commonly used in names of places (St. Albans, St. Louis); as part of a personal name *Saint* is often written out (Saint John, Saint Anthony of Padua). The plural of the abbreviation is *SS.* (SS. Peter and Paul). Occasionally the French feminine form, *Sainte*, is used (Sault Sainte Marie); the abbreviation is *Ste.* Spanish forms are common in the West: San Diego, Santa Barbara.

same

Besides being used as an adjective (the same color), *same* is used as a pronoun, ordinarily preceded by *the:* The same can be said of Republicans. *Same* without *the* was once identified with commercial jargon (We enclose payment for same), and though it now appears in General contexts, most writers avoid it.

say

Say is the usual word for "speaking" and can also be used for what is written (In his journal, Gide says . . .). *State* implies a formal "saying" and is better kept for this meaning.

Say in the sense of "approximately," "for instance," "let us say," is used in all varieties of writing: ". . . the specialist in the literature of, say, the English eighteenth century . . ." (Howard Mumford Jones, *Journal of the History of Ideas*, April-June 1967).

scarcely

See *Double negative § 2.

Schoolgirl style

A schoolgirl style—a highly emotional writing style by no means restricted to women, in or out of school—is characterized by sentimental *counter words (*lovely, cute*), by exaggeration, and by reliance on all sorts of mechanical forms of emphasis: exclamation marks, dashes, capitals, and one, two, even three underlinings. These may serve as a satisfying release for the writer but should be confined to personal correspondence between very close friends.

Schwa

Schwa is the name for the neutral vowel sound /ə/ which frequently occurs in unstressed syllables: ahead, angel, definite, occur, suggest.

Seasons

Winter, spring, summer, fall, autumn, midsummer, and so on are not capitalized except for stylistic emphasis or personification, as sometimes in poetry or nature essays.

seem

Seem is often used as a counter verb, needlessly qualifying a statement: They [seem to] run with a gang that can't [seem to] tell the difference between veracity and vandalism (see *Counter words). So used, it loses its power to distinguish between appearance and reality. Use *seem* only when you must be tentative; don't say something *seems to be* when you mean something *is*. See *cannot help but, cannot seem to.

self

Self as a suffix forms the reflexive and intensive pronouns: *myself, yourself, himself, herself, itself, oneself, ourselves, yourselves, themselves*. These are used chiefly for emphasis (I can do that myself) or as objects identical to the subjects of their verbs (I couldn't help myself). See *himself, herself; *myself.

As a prefix, *self* is joined to the root word by a hyphen: *self-control, self-explanatory, self-made, self-respect*. When *self* is the root word, there is no hyphen: *selfhood, selfish, selfless, selfsame*.

semi-

Semi- is a prefix meaning "half or approximately half" (*semicylindrical*), "twice within a certain period" (*semiweekly, semiannual*), or "partially, imperfectly" (*semicivilized, semiprofessional*). It is a live element for forming new words.

Semicolon

Semi

Revision: Use a semicolon as the link between these sentence elements.

1. *To link coordinate clauses.*
a—Between clauses without connectives. A semicolon is used, especially in Formal writing, to link two independent clauses whose relatedness the writer wishes to emphasize:

The auto industry has become a state within a state; its activities cannot and should not escape continuing public scrutiny.—*Consumer Reports*, April 1969

Some years ago, a learned colleague who was old and ill complained to me that he could no longer read German; it made his legs feel queer. I know that feeling well; I have had it while trying to read Henry James.—P. B. Ballard, *Thought and Language*

b—With conjunctive adverbs. A semicolon is ordinarily used between clauses connected by a conjunctive adverb (*however, moreover, therefore* . . .):

His popularity was undiminished; however, he no longer enjoyed the work.

Finally, despite the hopes and prophecies described before, we do not really agree on philosophical and political values; therefore the conference, moved by the same desire for survival and development as the world at large, carefully avoided exposing the ideological differences that remain. . . . —Stanley Hoffman, *Daedalus*, Spring 1966

A comma before *however* or *therefore* would have produced a *comma fault. See *Conjunctive adverbs.

c—With coordinating conjunctions. A semicolon may be used between clauses connected by a coordinating conjunction (*and, but, for, or* . . .) if the clauses are long, if they contain commas, or if for some reason—often for contrast—the writer wants a more definite break than he could show with a comma:

Words that are beautifully written by a scribe seemed to address his eye and mind in a personal way that was obliterated by mechanical type; and a manuscript illuminated by hand-painted miniatures gave him a pleasure that no woodcut could equal. —Edgar Wind, *Harper's*, Feb. 1964

I do *not* suggest that as English teachers we stop talking about planning and organization; nor am I saying that logical thought has nothing to do with the organizational process. —Robert Zoellner, *College English*, Jan. 1969

2. *To separate units with internal commas.* The units may be figures, scores, verbal items in series, or internally punctuated clauses:

Three things which a social system can provide or withhold are helpful to mental creation: first, technical training; second, liberty to follow the creative impulse; third, at least the possibility of ultimate appreciation of some public, whether large or small. —Bertrand Russell, *Proposed Roads to Freedom*

3. *Semicolon and colon.* The semicolon should not be used to introduce a quotation or a listing or to perform conventional functions of the colon (see *Colon § 3). In linking clauses, however, either mark can sometimes be used. The colon is somewhat more formal and carries some suggestion that the second clause will explain or illustrate the first; but often the choice seems to be chiefly if not solely stylistic.

4. *Semicolons and other traits of style.* Semicolons are more appropriate, more necessary, in Formal styles and in long, aggregating sentences than in General and Informal writing. They tend to slow the pace and are therefore more common in exposition than in narrative. In General styles commas are ordinarily used where semicolons might appear in Formal writing, or clauses that could be linked by semicolons are written as separate sentences.

Since in most places where a semicolon can be used, a period or a comma is also possible, the use of a semicolon is often as much a matter of style as of correct punctuation. When you can choose between using a semicolon and using some other mark, you should consider the appropriateness of the semicolon to your style of writing. If you decide that it is appropriate, use it to serve a purpose, for you and for your reader.

Compare *Comma, *Colon. References: Summey, pp. 97–101; Whitehall, pp. 121–22.

Sentences

S

Revision: Correct the fault in the sentence marked.

This general correction symbol requires you to first identify the weakness and then to improve the sentence. Problems in writing sentences are discussed in many *Index* articles, including *Agreement, *Comma fault, *Conjunctions, *Coordination, *Dangling modifiers, *Emphasis, *Fragment, *Fused sentence, *Idiom, *Reference of pronouns, *Shifted constructions, *Split infinitive, *Subject and verb, *Subordination, *Wordiness, *Word order.

seq.

See *Abbreviations § 2.

Sequence of tenses

See *Tenses of verbs § 5.

Series

Commas are ordinarily used between the items of a series of three or more: "How may a learning institution best be organized to express its commitment to reason, to pursue its search for basic knowledge, and to select and honor those cultural values which deserve continuity and preservation?" (William Birenbaum, *Overlive*).

Usage is divided over the insertion of a comma before the conjunction in a series. A comma helps to prevent ambiguity, especially if one member is compound. But many writers, especially in General and Informal styles, do not use one, particularly when the series is short: "A rash of red, white [] and blue has broken out in the good old U.S.A." (*Newsweek*, June 30, 1969).

If the members of the series are long or not closely connected, or if the members have commas within them, they may be separated by semicolons (see *Semicolon § 2). For further discussion, see *Guide*, pp. 301–02; *Comma § 5.

Reference: For the rhetorical effect of series, see Winston Weathers, *CCC*, Dec. 1966, pp. 217–21.

set, sit

In Standard English, people and things *sit* (past: *sat*) or they are *set* (past: *set*)—that is, are "placed":

I like to sit in a hotel lobby.
I have sat in this same seat for three semesters.
She set the soup down with a flourish.
The post was set three feet in the ground.

A hen, however, sets (on her eggs), cement sets, and the sun sets. A table sits eight, and few city people know how to sit a horse.

shall, will

Because distinctions between these auxiliaries have been regarded as important in reputable usage, it is necessary to discuss them in more detail than they deserve. Since the eighteenth century some grammarians have insisted that in expressing determination, obligation, or prohibition in statements about the future, *will* should be used with first-person subjects and *shall* with second and third; but usage has never been uniform. *Shall* is freely used with the first person (*I shall return*), and *will* is freely used with the second and third persons:

And as we walk, we must make the pledge that we shall always march ahead. — Martin Luther King, Jr., Address to the March on Washington Assembly

The United States cannot — and will not — ever permit itself to get into that position. — Robert S. McNamara, *Bulletin of the Atomic Scientists*, Dec. 1967

The great promise of Christ, that all will be one, cannot be made false. — Peter Chirico, *Theological Studies*, Dec. 1967

Standard American usage, then, is divided between *shall* and *will* when these auxiliaries have the double function of pointing to the future and expressing determination, prohibition, or obligation. Either auxiliary can be used with all three persons; *will* is more common.

The same grammarians have sought to keep the single function of indicating the future distinct by urging that *shall* be used with first-person subjects and *will* with second and third; but most writers use *will* freely with the first person for simple future:

What I will outline is not wholly my own speculation. . . . — Glenn T. Seaborg, *Bulletin of the Atomic Scientists*, Jan. 1968

We will also need a political process that is both open and coherent. — McGeorge Bundy, *Saturday Review*, April 4, 1970

In Standard American usage, *will* is much more common than *shall* for the single-function auxiliary, though *shall* finds some use in the first person.

In questions with these auxiliaries, *shall* is common only in the first person: Shall I go first?

See *should, would. References: Bryant, pp. 182–83; Fries, *AEG*, pp. 150–67; Jespersen, *MEG*, IV, 237–300; Pooley, pp. 49–55.

Shifted constructions

Shift

Revision: *Make the constructions marked consistent (parallel) in form.*

Shifted constructions are needless changes in grammatical form or point of view within a sentence. In speech and in much Informal writing, shifted constructions are common, but in General and Formal prose they are avoided because they trouble a careful reader. The many types of needless shift include the following:

Between adjective and noun: This book is interesting and an informative piece of work. Revised: . . . interesting and informative.

Between noun and clause: The most important factors are time and temperature, careful control at every point, and the mechanical equipment must be in perfect operating condition. Revised: . . . and perfect operating condition of the mechanical equipment.

Between adverb and adjective: Along these walks are the cottages, some of which have stood since the founding [adverb phrase] but others quite recent [adjective phrase]. Revised: . . . but others for only a short time.

Between gerund and infinitive: Associating with these fellows and to adapt myself to live with them will either make me more flexible or kill me. Revised: Associating with these fellows and adapting myself. . . .

Between gerund and finite verb: I have heard complaints about the plot being weak and that the setting is played up too much. Revised: . . . and the setting being played up. . . .

Between participle and finite verb: You often see a fisherman trying to get quietly to his favorite spot but instead he broadcasts warnings with his rhythmical squeak-splash, squeak-splash. Revised: . . . but instead broadcasting warnings. . . .

Between transitive verb and copula: Anyone who has persistence or is desperate enough can get a job on a ship. Revised: . . . who is persistent or who is desperate enough. . . .

Between past and present: The tanks bullied their way through the makeshift barricades and fan out across the enormous plaza. Revised: . . . and fanned out. . . .

Between active and passive: The committee members disliked each other heartily, and their time was wasted in wrangling. Revised: . . . heartily and wasted their time in wrangling.

Between personal and impersonal: When one is sick, you make few plans. Revised: When one is sick, one [or he] makes. . . .

No enumeration of shifted constructions could be complete: there are too many constructions to shift. See *Balanced sentences; *Reference of pronouns; *Tenses of verbs; *Guide,* pp. 321–23.

Ships' names

In most books and ordinarily in Formal writing the names of ships are italicized: "A more important incident was the explosion on (or next to) the United States battleship *Maine*" (Carl N. Degler, *The Age of the Economic Revolution, 1876–1900*). In newspapers and news magazines and in General writing, the names of ships are increasingly treated simply as proper nouns, capitalized but not otherwise set off: "Lashed to the Tawasa's side was the hulk of what had once been a sleek, 2,200-ton destroyer: the U.S.S. Frank E. Evans" (*Newsweek*, June 23, 1969).

Shoptalk

Shoptalk is the words and meanings that people in the same occupation use among themselves to refer to the things that specially concern them in their work: *mud* among bricklayers to mean "mortar," *docket* among lawyers to mean making an abstract.

No occupation gets along without shoptalk; all have everyday terms that are mostly unintelligible to outsiders but very useful to practitioners. Especially convenient are short, informal substitutes for long technical terms. So a *mike* may be a microphone in a broadcasting studio, a microscope in a laboratory, a micrometer in a shop; a *hypo* is a fixing bath to a photographer, a hypodermic injection to a nurse. Many such words, and some longer ones, are metaphoric, like *eggs* for "bombs" in the vocabulary of military aviation, *bandit* for "enemy fighter," *brain bucket* for "crash helmet." Others seem imitative, like *wump* for "a sudden flare of light on a television screen." Much shoptalk, though old and useful in its place, is so specialized and colorless that it has never spread to the General vocabulary— printshop words, for example, like *chase, em, pi, quoins*.

Many words and meanings from shoptalk are given in general dictionaries with the names of the occupations they belong to, but most of them are listed and adequately defined only in more specialized books. Indeed, so long as they remain narrowly specialized, they are inappropriate in writing for general audiences (see *Jargon). See also *Academic writing, *Gobbledygook, *Psychologese, *Slang. References: James Bradstreet Greenough and George Lyman Kittredge, *Words and Their Ways in English Speech* (New York: Macmillan, 1961), Ch. 5; Mencken, pp. 709–61; and many articles in *American Speech*.

should, would

In indirect discourse, *should* and *would* can function as the past tenses of *shall* and *will*. "We will go" can be reported as "He announced that we would go," and "We shall go" as "He announced that we should go." Since *should* has a connotation of obligation or propriety that may not be intended, the construction with *would* is preferred. The past-tense *should* of the following example would most likely—in American usage—be rendered as *would:*

The interview, however, took about five minutes. Was this scheme all right? Should we get enough men?—C. P. Snow, *Science and Government*

Should and *would* are used interchangeably as auxiliaries in the polite idiom "I _____ like to [say/repeat/take the opportunity]." *Would* is more common in American usage: ". . . I would like to indicate . . ." (Robert Langbaum, *Yale Review*, Winter 1965). See *shall, will; *Tenses of verbs § 5.

sic

See *Brackets.

sick, ill

Ill is the more formal, less common word. In the United States they mean the same thing. In British usage *sick* is usually restricted to mean "nauseated": "The mere touch of the thing would make me sick or ill, or both" (Richard Jones, *The Three Suitors*). In American usage *sick* in that sense is made clear by adding a phrase: It made me sick to [at/in] my stomach.

Silent letters

Written English is full of silent letters—that is, letters that represent no sound. A few of them are the result of mistaken analogies, like the *s* of *island*, which is there from confusion with Old French *isle*, though it comes from Old English *igland* and never has a sounded *s*. Renaissance scholars inserted a number of letters that corresponded to those in Greek and Latin words from which the English ones derived but that had never been pronounced in English: Chaucer could write *dette* without a *b*, but we must write *debt* because old scholars thought less of the French intermediary than of the original Latin *debitum*.

But most of our silent letters do represent older pronunciations. Because the pronounciations have changed but the spellings have not kept pace, the silent letters remain to mark the resting places of dead sounds—the final *b* in *bomb, comb, climb*, the initial *g* and *k* in *gnarl, gnash, knack, knave*, the *gh* for a lost Germanic consonant in *through* and *night* and *caught*.

Silent letters are sometimes defended as guides to etymology, though they can also be misleading: *delight* is from French *delite* but was reshaped in the sixteenth century by false analogy with *light*, with which it did not rhyme in Middle English. Some people think these spellings have an aesthetic value, that *night* has a beauty not found in *nite* or that the superfluous *h* gives *ghost* a special weirdness. A stronger argument for at least some silent letters is that they show deeper relations than appear on the surface of speech: *bomb* is related to *bombard, phlegm* to *phlegmatic*.

Some silent letters are gradually being dropped. *Through* has lost its *gh* at least in the new compound *thruway*, and *ph* has recently vanished from the more learned *apophthegm*. Other silent letters cease to be silent when people who know a word only from the printed page give it a spelling pronunciation, like *comptroller* with /komp/ for its first syllable or /in dikt'/ instead of /in dit'/ for *indict*. *Hypercorrectness may be involved in pronunciation of the *l* in *calm, palm, almond*, and *salmon*.

similar to

Similar to is often a pompously wordy way of saying *like:* It was my first wreck, and I hope I may never have another similar to that one [like it].

Simile

See *Figures of speech; *Guide*, pp. 367–73.

Simple sentence

See *Clauses § 1; *Guide*, pp. 276–83.

since

See *because.

sit, set

See *set, sit.

situated

Situated is often *deadwood: I visited the town of Picton, [situated] in the province of Ontario.

-size

Size is typical of a class of nouns (*age, color, height, shape, width, weight* . . .) that also function as apparent modifiers: *medium-size, standard-size, life-size, outsize, oversize.* The *-size* words are redundant in compound modifiers with adjectives that might modify the head nouns directly: not "small-size box" but "small box" (and similarly with "round-shape table," "younger-age students," "dark-color hair," and so on). See *Deadwood.

Slang

It is hard to draw a line between slang and other sorts of Informal English. Many people use the term too broadly—for almost any Informal word—and dictionaries have been too generous with the label, marking as "slang" many words that simply suggest spoken rather than written style. In fact, there is no fully accepted criterion for marking off the segment of the vocabulary that constitutes slang.

Though some of the words labeled slang in current dictionaries—*lulu, corker, egg* (for a person)—have been around for generations, the central characteristic of slang comes from the motive in using it: a desire for novelty, for vivid emphasis, for being in the know, up with the times or a little ahead. These are essentially qualities of style, and the tone and connotation are as important as the meaning of the words. Other varieties of language have ways of expressing the ideas of slang words, but their tone is more conventional. Young people like novelty, as do grown-ups with youthful ideas, and entertainers need it in their trade. Slang is especially common in talking about sports and amusements and all sorts of everyday activities for which the ordinary terms have worn thin. In-groups, both legal and illegal, have their slang vocabularies, which often spill over into General English: some of the slang of the drug culture has wide circulation among nonusers.

Slang is made by natural linguistic processes. It abounds in clipped words (*marvy, natch, hood*) and in compounds and derivatives of ordinary words (*screwball, sourpuss, cockeyed*). Many are borrowed from the *shoptalk of sports and the popular arts, especially jazz (*square, cool, funky*). And a great many are figurative extensions of General words (*nut, dope, egg* applied to people; *heavy, hung up, spaced out, trash*). In the desire for novelty and emphasis one word leads to another, as *square* led to *cube*. Sound is often an important factor, as in *goof, booboo, barf, zonk, zap*.

Since many slang words have short lives, any discussion of slang in print is bound to be out of date. *Twenty-three skidoo, vamoose, beat it, scram, hit the trail, take a powder, drag out, shag out, cut out, split* succeeded each other almost within a generation. Words for being drunk (*soused, plastered, bombed*), for girls (*baby, doll, chick, bird, sister*), and words of approval (*tops, neat, the most, cool, groovy, out of sight*) and disapproval (*all wet, cruddy; a fink, a bummer*) change from year to year—though some survive and some recur. Many slang words prove permanently useful and become a part of the Informal vocabulary (*blind date, boy friend, go steady*) or the General (*highbrow, lowbrow*).

Slang belongs primarily to familiar speech, to which it can give a note of freshness. This freshness wears off after some hundreds of repetitions so that the prime virtue of the words is lost. The chief objections to slang, aside from its possible conspicuousness, are to its overuse and to its use in place of more exact expressions. In writing, slang is often a liability, partly because it is likely to be trite or dated and partly because many of the words name general impressions instead of specific ones, so that they rank with *nice* and *good*. If slang expressions are appropriate to the subject matter and the audience and come naturally to the writer, they should be used without apology (that is, without quotation marks). If they are not appropriate, they should not be used, with or without quotation marks.

Notice that many of the illustrative words in this discussion look like items in the General vocabulary. Their slang quality results from the context in which they appear. That is why few words can be labeled slang solely on the basis of their form.

References: Mencken, Ch. 11; Harold Wentworth and Stuart Berg Flexner, eds. and comps., *Dictionary of American Slang* (New York: Crowell, 1967).

slow, slowly

Both *slow* and *slowly* are used as adverbs in Modern English, each representing in this use a possible or recorded Old English adverb (*slawe* and *slawlice*, respectively). *Slow* is more vigorous and is widely used in speech and in Informal writing in place of *slowly*, but in General usage it is restricted to limited contexts: He drove slow; but: He drove away slowly. There is some prejudice against adverbial *slow* in any context. See *Adverbs § 1, *Divided usage. Compare *bad, badly.

so

To introduce clauses of purpose, *so that* is ordinarily expected in Formal contexts, but *so* by itself is respectable in General use:

[The ghost of] Patroclus comes to ask Achilles to bury him quickly so that he may pass into the realm of Hades. . . . —Anne Amory, *Yale Classical Studies*, Vol. XX, 1966

I might have tried . . . to give a clearer idea of the rest of the contents, so readers could gather some notion of whether or not this kind of material might interest them. . . .—John Thompson, *New York Review of Books*, Nov. 9, 1967

To express consequence or result, both *so* alone and *so that* are found in all varieties of usage:

Neville Forbes died tragically and prematurely, so he did not live to bring his grammar up to date.—Edmund Wilson, *New Yorker*, April 20, 1963

. . . the Viet Cong overran the camp, blasting positions, bunkers, and buildings with explosives so that it looked as if a tornado had struck the area.—*Los Angeles Times*, May 7, 1967

Some objection may be made to the *so* of consequence, which is easily overworked; but the old injunction to replace it with the more consequential *so that* or *and so* has lost its force, at least when *so* introduces a full clause.

As an intensive, *so* is Informal: He's so handsome!

References: Fries, *AEG*, pp. 226–27; Russell Thomas, *CE*, May 1951, pp. 453–54; Bryant, pp. 190–93.

so . . . as

See *as . . . as.

so-called

If you have to use *so-called*, don't duplicate the idea by putting the name of the so-called object in quotes: the so-called champion; not: the so-called "champion."

Solecism

Solecism is a Formal word for a blunder in grammatical structure or idiom.

some, and compounds with some

1. In written English, *some* is normally used as what would traditionally be called an indefinite pronoun (Some travel and some don't) or an indefinite adjective (some people, some ideas).

2. As an adverb, qualifying *some* is Informal; more formal usage would have *somewhat*. Informally, *some* is also used to modify verbs (The springs were squeaking some).

3. The compounds *somebody, someway, somewhat, somewhere* are written as one word. *Someone* is one word (Someone is coming) unless *one* is stressed (some one of them). *Someday* is written as one word or two.

4. The adverb *someplace* is still avoided in Formal writing in favor of *somewhere*, but in the last generation or so *someplace* has moved from Informal to General usage: "Information that is put into the computer must be stored someplace until the machine is ready to make use of it" (Robert Campbell, *Life*, Oct. 27, 1967). *Somewheres* is Nonstandard. Compare *any.

sort [of a]

See *kind of a, sort of a; *kind of, sort of; *kind, sort.

Sound

See *Alliteration, *Assonance, *Homonyms, *Repetition.

Spelling

Sp

Revision: Correct the spelling of the word marked, referring to a dictionary if necessary.

Use your dictionary, and when alternative spellings are listed, choose the first. The following *Index* articles deal with spelling:

*-able, -ible	*en-, in-	*-ize, -ise
*-ally	*-er, -or	*-or, -our
*Apostrophe	*-er, -re	*Plurals of nouns
*Capital letters	*Foreign words in English	*Principal parts of verbs
*-ce, -ge	*Homonyms, homophones	*Pronunciation
*Contractions	*Hyphen	*Schwa
*-ed	*in-, un-	*Silent letters

See also *American and British usage, *Analogy in language, *Change in language, *Divided usage. Reference: Donald W. Emery, *Variant Spelling in Modern English Dictionaries* (Champaign, Ill.: NCTE, 1958).

Split infinitive

An infinitive is said to be split when an adverb or an adverbial element separates the *to* from its following verb: The receptionist asked them to kindly sit down.

The split infinitive gets more attention than it deserves. Many people have been taught to avoid it scrupulously; and sometimes there is good reason to do so. Certainly, long intervening elements are awkward and should be moved, often to the end of the sentence: After a while he was able to, although not very accurately, distinguish good customers from disloyal ones.

On principle, moreover, Formal writing does rather consistently avoid the split infinitive, even when the adverb cannot be placed at the end of the clause:

. . . we must have sufficient foresight and vision patiently to guide the peoples of the world along the road they have chosen to follow. . . . —Bernard Kiernan, *American Scholar*, Spring 1962

The Chinese model . . . never eclipsed the local differences that made Japan always and Korea sometimes so distinct from China as properly to constitute a separate civilization. —William H. McNeill, *The Rise of the West*

In General writing, putting the adverb at the end of the clause that contains the infinitive is probably more common than splitting:

. . . if both parties tried to speak simultaneously, part of the conversation might be lost. —Charles E. Silberman, *Fortune*, Feb. 1967

. . . surrounded by a sandstone wall that was low enough on one side for a child to climb easily, but that on the other side offered a drop of twenty or thirty feet. . . . —John Updike, *Assorted Prose*

. . . Malamud still shares the traditional inability of American writers to imagine society intelligently. —Joseph Featherstone, *Atlantic*, March 1967

But if long intervening elements are awkward, short adverbs that modify the infinitive may fit most smoothly and clearly between the *to* and the verb; and for such reasons split infinitives often occur in unquestionably reputable General writing. The first of the following citations, for example, would be ambiguous if "really" were placed before "to" and awkward if it were placed after "hate." In the second, "precisely to locate" would be awkward and somewhat ambiguous, and "to locate precisely enough" would invite misreading:

To really hate the old ruling class we would have to live under it in its days of decay. —John K. Fairbank, *New Republic*, Feb. 25, 1967

The major mission of Apollo 10 was to precisely locate enough lunar landmarks to prevent the crewmen of Apollo 11 from dropping onto terrain for which they would be unprepared. —John Lear, *Saturday Review*, June 7, 1969

I can't be expected to indefinitely attend these orgies of piety and blood. —Dwight Macdonald, *Esquire*, Jan. 1963

When the prejudice against the split infinitive makes a writer bend over backwards to avoid it, his phrasing may be objectionably *hypercorrect:

. . . a delinquent woman who already has demonstrated her inability to rear properly numerous other children.

Myrdal replies that it should be the proper function of planning constantly to strengthen nongovernmental structures.

In the first sentence, the adverb "properly" can be read as if it modifies "numerous"; in the second, "constantly" might modify "planning." Both sentences can be improved by splitting the infinitives.

References: Bryant, pp. 194–97; Curme, *Syntax*, pp. 458–67; Fries, *AEG*, pp. 132, 144–45; Roberts, pp. 204–06.

Spoken and written English

1. *Speech and writing.* Though talking and writing are related, overlapping skills, they differ in several respects. Speech is peppered with expressions that seldom appear in writing other than recorded dialog: "OK," "y'know," "y'see," "Right?" and all the grunts and murmurs that ask for and provide feedback in conversation. When we talk, we pay less attention to the shape of our sentences than when we write. We are more casual about pronoun reference and agreement; we let *and* do most of the work of joining statements; we rarely make the effort to build phrases and clauses in parallel series; and we scarcely ever use the nonrestrictive clause. (We might write, "Picasso, who was born in Spain, never lost his fondness for Barcelona"; but we would probably say, "Picasso was born in Spain, and he always loved Barcelona.")

The number of significant differentiations in sound that all of us use is much larger than the number of symbols in our writing system. In talk, words are always part of a pattern involving pitch and stress, for which the marks of punctuation provide only the barest hints. Writing therefore blurs or overlooks a great many speech signals — including the stance, the gesture, even the slight rise of an eyebrow that may reinforce or modify the messages sent by speech. Whether "more" modifies "competent" or "competent men" in "more competent men" would be shown in speech by stress (heavier stress on the "more" that modifies "competent men"). To make the distinction in writing, rewording might be necessary: more men who are competent, more really competent men.

But if we can communicate some things more directly in talk than in writing, the reverse is also true. Punctuation indicates quotations efficiently, including quotations within quotations. Spelling distinguishes some homophones that would be ambiguous in speech: We'll halve it; We'll have it. Because writing can be reread, it is a surer means of communicating difficult material — detailed, complicated instructions, for instance. And because writing can be repeatedly revised, it can be more precise, better organized, more economical than talk.

Though language originated as speech and though writing came very late in its history (only some six thousand years ago), it is legitimate to speak of the written language (or at least of the *written styles* of a language) as an entity in itself. Most prose literature was written to be communicated through the eye, not the ear; and though reading aloud often increases its effectiveness, its survival depends mainly on its capacity for communicating without the direct use of sound.

But in spite of their differences, written English and spoken English have a close relationship, especially at the present time. When we say someone "talks like a book," we mean that his talk is uncomfortably elaborate or stiff; it is more often a compliment to say that he "writes the way he talks." For most purposes we value writing that has the colloquial flavor of good talk.

2. *Colloquial English.* Dictionaries sometimes mark words *Colloq.* to suggest that in the editors' judgment they are more common in speech than in writing. Many people mistakenly take the label to mean that the dictionary frowns upon their use, when in fact colloquial words are often accurate, expressive words that are used freely in good General writing. Because this misinterpretation of *colloquial* is so common, the label is less used in recent dictionaries and is used in this book only infrequently and cautiously. If a usage is more common in speech than in writing, that fact is stated; if the word or expression is Standard English but is rarely found in General or Formal writing, it is labeled Informal.

Spoonerisms

A spoonerism is an exchange of the initial sounds of two words, as in "a half-warmed fish" for "a half-formed wish"—either unintentional or for humorous effect. It takes its name from the Reverend William Spooner of Oxford, who is credited with such prizes as "kinquering congs."

spoonful, spoonfuls

See *-ful, full.

Squinting modifier

See *Ambiguity § 2.

St., Ste.

See *saint.

Staccato style

This label (a metaphor from music) is applied to writing characterized by jerkily emphatic sentences, often without expressed connectives. Like other descriptive labels for style—"chatty," "relaxed," "nervous," "salty," "sinewy," and so on—it is not very useful unless it is supported by a close analysis of the diction and syntax that create the effect.

Standard English

See *Guide,* pp. 9–19.

state

See *say.

still

Still is an adverb in the sentence "It's still raining" and a conjunction in "I can see your point of view; still I don't agree with you." See *Conjunctive adverbs.

strata

In Formal usage *stratum* is singular and *strata* plural. In General usage there is a growing tendency to construe *strata* as a singular:

Youthful delinquents and vandals come from every strata of society. — Joseph Wood Krutch, *Saturday Review*, Jan. 16, 1965

The word permafrost simply means an iron-hard strata of frozen earth. — Robert Brigham, *Life*, April 22, 1966

Strong verbs

See *Principal parts of verbs.

Style

See the *Guide*, Chapter Thirteen, for essays on style by Benjamin DeMott and Theodore Solotaroff. Particular aspects of style are treated in other chapters of the *Guide*, especially Chapters Eleven and Twelve, and in many *Index* articles, including *Adjectives § 6, *Adverbs § 4, *Mixed usage, *Nominalization, *Participles § 4, *Subject and verb, *Subordination, *Verbs § 2. References: Glen A. Love and Michael Payne, eds., *Contemporary Essays on Style* (Chicago: Scott, 1969), which includes a bibliography by Paul C. Doherty, reprinted from *The CEA Critic*, May 1966; Thomas A. Sebeok, ed., *Style in Language* (Cambridge, Mass.: MIT Press, 1960).

Stylebooks

For editors and printers, style means the method of handling various matters of mechanics such as capital letters, punctuation, forms of plurals, division of words, details of typography. Since usage is divided on many of these points, publishers specify the practices to be observed in their publications and describe these practices in stylebooks — documents ranging from a single page to a thick volume. *A Manual of Style*, published by the University of Chicago Press (and referred to in this *Index* as the *Chicago Manual*), is the most influential stylebook among book publishers. The *United States Government Printing Office Style Manual* (the *U.S. Style Manual*) is another excellent stylebook.

Subject

For subject of a gerund, see *Gerunds § 2. For subject of an infinitive, see *Infinitives § 5. For subject of a verb, see *Adjectives § 5, *Agreement § 1, *Compound subject, *Gerunds § 1, *Infinitives § 4, *Shifted constructions, *Subject and verb.

Subject and verb

1. *As sentence elements*. The subject of a sentence can be defined in at least four ways:

a — It performs an action or is in a particular state of being. But this does not explain such sentences as "These socks wear out too quickly" or "He received the condemnation of millions." Neither *socks* nor *he* is the performer of any action. On the contrary, they are the objects of an action.

b—It is the person, place, thing, etc., that a sentence is about. But this does not explain "I just heard that someone shot President Kennedy." The sentence is, quite clearly, not "about" the speaker or even "someone." It is about President Kennedy. Both these definitions could be correct for some sentences: President Kennedy defeated his opponent in the 1960 elections. This sentence is "about" President Kennedy, the performer of the action—*defeat*.

c—The subject is the word, phrase, or clause that usually stands before the verb and determines whether the verb will be singular or plural. Where the first two definitions are based on meaning, this one is based on formal criteria—on position in the sentence or on the relationship between inflections for number in the subject and the verb: The man is here; The men are here. When a sentence is transformed into an expletive *there* sentence, the subject is the noun following the *be* verb that the number of the verb agrees with: There *is* a *man* outside; There *are men* outside.

d—In one form of a transformational grammar, the subject in the *deep structure is the first noun phrase (NP) generated before the verb by the rule S → NP + VP. This deep-structure subject does not always occur as the surface-structure subject:

Deep-structure pattern		Surface-structure pattern
Someone witnessed the accident	⇒	*The accident* was witnessed.
Bees swarm in the garden	⇒	*The garden* swarms with bees.
Someone wears out socks fast	⇒	*Socks* wear out fast.
Someone opened the door with a key	⇒	*The key* opened the door.

In each case the deep-structure subject has been replaced by another noun phrase that becomes the surface-structure subject.

The difference between definitions *c* and *d* is now clear: *c* is a surface-structure definition; *d* is a deep-structure definition. And the similarity between *a* and *d* should also be clear. The semantic definition of a subject in *a* seems to correspond to the usual semantic function of the first noun phrase in the deep structure. It is usually an agent of some kind, an actor, a performer of an action. But in the examples a transformation has changed a deep structure into a surface structure in which the subject is not the actor. Very often, of course, the deep-structure subject and the surface-structure subject are the same: The boy saw the man.

Thus in defining elements in a sentence, it is important to know what grammatical theory we are working with. Different theories will define elements in different ways. One of the attractions of transformational grammars is that they can reconcile a semantic definition (a) and a formal definition (c) by postulating different subjects in deep and surface structures.

2. *As rhetorical elements.* Despite the qualification in definition *b*, the surface-structure subject is very important because the subject is often the *topic* of a paragraph. Using the same subject or closely related subjects through a sequence of sentences keeps the focus of the paragraph clear (see *Guide*, pp. 249–53). Further, in direct, vigorous writing, the subject and verb usually express the central action in a sentence. See *Nominalization.

3. *Agreement of subject and verb*. When the verb form permits it, a verb shows agreement with its subject in number and person. This usually means with the grammatical number of the subject. But since our verbs, except for *be*, have only one form for both numbers and for all persons except an *-s* in the third-singular present (and the *modal auxiliaries lack this *-s*), relatively few problems in agreement can arise. Users of English can rely very little on formal indications of relation between subject and verb, and therefore lack of agreement in form seldom causes ambiguity, though it may be felt by the hearer or reader to be a serious mistake. "I is," for example, is entirely intelligible, but it is also certainly Nonstandard.

Singular: I am more tired than usual. *A chair was placed* in the corner. *This job takes* four weeks. *The job took* four weeks.

Plural: We are more tired than usual. *Three chairs were placed* along the wall. *These jobs take* four weeks. *The jobs took* four weeks.

Problems in the agreement of subject and verb arise either from using a construction in which the grammatical number of the subject is uncertain or is blurred by other words or from using the meaning of the subject rather than its grammatical form as the basis for agreement.

a—Collective nouns. The contradictions between meaning and form are most clearly seen in collective nouns, which are semantically plural but ordinarily take singular verbs. Some collective nouns always take plural verbs: *The police were* ready; *The cattle were* sold; *The people are* waiting. For further discussion, see *Collective nouns.

b—Compound subjects. Ordinarily a compound subject has a plural verb:

Alice and Francis *were* the first to arrive.
The text of the poem and the commentary *make* good reading.

When the two elements of a compound subject refer to the same person or thing, or when the writer thinks of them as a unit, the verb is singular:

The best teacher and the best scholar here *is* Professor Bach.

The spirit and accomplishment of these men *speaks* for itself.

. . . a love of sculpture and considerable practice in it has made me conscious of the hidden structure of everything I see. . . .—Marya Mannes, *New York Times Magazine*, July 9, 1961

The verb is often singular when a compound subject follows:

There *is* both health and wealth in this way of life.
For the winner there *was* a cash prize and weeks of glory.

When a second part of the subject is connected with the first by *with, together with, as well as,* the agreement varies. In Formal English such a construction is kept singular. In General English a plural is often found if the expression is equivalent to a compound subject:

The rudder is the only essential control in taxiing, and this together with a regulative speed *keeps* the plane going in a relatively straight line.

The winner with the four runners-up *were* given a reception. (To make this more formal, *with* should be changed to *and,* rather than *were* to *was.*)

He is not a good speaker, since his hesitating manner with long sighs interspersed in the address *make* [Formal *makes*] him hard to listen to.

See *either . . . or, *or.
When the two elements of the subject are pronouns in different persons, the verb is usually plural:

You and I *are* sure to go, anyway.

Either you or he *are* likely to go. (It is possible here to emphasize the singleness of choice.)

Neither you nor I *are* fit for that job.

In questions, the plural is common: *Are* [or *Is*] Fred or Harry in?
c—Plural modifier of a singular subject. When a rather long plural modifier of a singular subject comes between it and the verb, Informal English often has a plural verb where more formal writing would have a singular:

This *group* of essays *is* [not *are*] concerned with problems in sociology and philosophy as they are related to biology.

The *form* of your bibliography and footnotes *is* not standard.

To a beginner on the organ, the *array* of stops and pistons, couplers, and pedals *seems* [Informal *seem*] bewildering.

Two thousand dollars' *worth* of painting *were* [Formal *was*] lost.

d—Relative pronouns. A relative pronoun referring to a singular noun has a singular verb (The person *who takes* enough pains can do it), and one referring to a plural noun has a plural verb (The people *who take* pains win in the long run). In idioms like "This is one of the most discouraging things that _____ come out of the situation," Formal usage requires "that have come," since the antecedent of "that" is "things." Informal and General often have "that has come," because the central idea (of *one*) is singular. See *one of those who.
e—Subject and complement of different number. The verb agrees with the subject:

A day's *work is* four trips. Four *trips make* a day's work.

What finally concerns Singer most is the possibilities for life that remain after the exhaustion of human effort. . . . —Irving Howe, *Decline of the New*

f — Plural subject with singular meaning. When the idea conveyed by a plural subject is singular in intent, the verb is usually singular: *Five years is* a long time.

References: Curme, *Syntax*, Ch. 4; Fries, *AEG*, pp. 188–90, 249–50, and index references; Pooley, pp. 78–88; Charles Fillmore, "The Case for Case," in *Universals in Linguistic Theory*, ed. Emmon Bach and Robert Harms (New York: Holt, 1968), pp. 1–88.

4. *Nonstandard verbs.* Linguists investigating the patterns of some Black English dialects have found a predictable and therefore *grammatical structure in sentences that have traditionally been called ungrammatical:

The teacher gone right now, but she be back soon.
He always be playing records late at night.

The lack of a *be* form in the first clause (the teacher [is] gone) and the apparently incorrect form of *be* in the second (she [will] be back) result from a deletion transformation. It regularly and predictably deletes a form of *be* and other auxiliary verbs such as *will, would, have,* etc., where Standard English speakers contract their form of *be*. (An exception is *'m,* as in "I'm going.") Transformationally, the sequence would look like this:

    The teacher is gone right now, but she will be back soon.
⇒ The teacher's gone right now, but she'll   be back soon.
⇒ The teacher [ ]gone right now, but she [ ]   be back soon. .

Where Standard English speakers cannot contract a form of *be*, neither can speakers of some dialects of Black English delete it:

Standard English: I don't know who he is. Not: I don't know who's.
Black English: I don't know who he is. Not: I don't know who he.

The form of *be* in "He always be playing records late at night" is a different problem. It is evidently an invariant verb form that always appears as *be* to indicate a repeated action. When the action is temporary, not repeated, the first variations on *be* are found, as in "He not here right now, but he be back in a minute."

Thus we cannot condemn some forms of Nonstandard English because they are illogical or internally inconsistent. Some might reject them because they represent a social class and background that has little economic or social power; but in view of their grammatical predictability, the judgment must be a social, not a linguistic one.

5. *Punctuation between subject and verb.* Since the subject and verb are part of one construction, they should normally be separated by a comma only to prevent misreading: "Let those who will, rear lion cubs; I'll plump for a baby giraffe . . ." (Martha Gellhorn, *Atlantic*, Feb. 1966). See *Comma §§ 7 and 8.

Subjective case
See *Nominative case.

Subjunctives
In Modern English very few forms can be surely identified as "subjunctives," and the use of those few is so irregular that definite syntactical criteria are hard to state. Generally, the subjunctive is optional, a means of setting one's language, consciously or unconsciously, a little apart from everyday usage. It is not always a trait of Formal style, though there are Formal contexts, such as *resolutions, that use the subjunctive regularly.

1. *Form of subjunctives.*
a — Simple subjunctive. The identifiable forms of the subjunctive are *be* throughout the present tense of that verb, *were* in its past-tense singular, and *s*-less forms of the third-person singular of the present tense of other verbs that normally have an *-s*. Some past-tense forms with present or future reference are also subjunctives.
b — Subjunctives with auxiliaries. Some grammarians include as subjunctives all the locutions that can be used in expressing ideas that may also be, or have at some time been, expressed by the subjunctive, and the forms that could be used in translating into English the subjunctives found in other languages. Under this system several auxiliaries — *may, might, should, would, let, have, to*, and others — become subjunctives (or signs of the subjunctive, subjunctive markers). Because this broad interpretation makes consideration of the subjunctive unnecessarily complicated, only the simple subjunctive is considered here.

2. *Uses of the subjunctive.* English makes much less use of the mood than most modern European languages do. There are a number of idioms — set formulas — in which the subjunctive may be used in English; and it is fairly common in wishes, in conditions, and in various *that* clauses. The following examples, some with more common alternative expressions, are typical of the English subjunctive.
a — Formulas. The subjunctive is found in numerous formulas, survivals from a time when the subjunctive was used freely. Today we do not make other sentences on the pattern of "Far be it from me."

Suffice it to say	Heaven forbid	As it were
Long live the king	God bless you	Be that as it may

Many mild oaths have this form: Confound it! Psychiatrists be hanged!

Some of these formulas are used in all levels of the language; some, like "Come what may," are rather formal; the oaths are chiefly Informal.

b—*That* clauses. The subjunctive is relatively frequent in demands, resolutions, recommendations, and the like, usually in Formal contexts. Ordinarily there are alternative expressions without the subjunctive.

Formal: We recommend that the commissioner *designate* for this use the land formerly belonging to Mr. Brewster.
General: . . . that the commissioner should designate. . . .

Formal: I ask that the interested citizen *watch* closely the movement of these troops.
General: I ask the interested citizen to watch the movement of these troops closely.

Formal: Who gave the order that he *be dropped*?
General: . . . the order to drop him?

Formal: It is necessary that every member *inform* himself of these rules.
General: . . . that every member should inform himself. . . . Or: . . . for every member to inform himself. . . . Or: Every member must [should] inform himself. . . .

c—Conditions. The subjunctive may be used in *if* clauses when the fulfillment of the condition is doubtful or impossible: "If one good were really as good as another, no good would be any good" (Irwin Edman, *Four Ways of Philosophy*). The subjunctive *were* is not necessary to convey the meaning, which the past indicative *was* would convey just as well by its contrast between past form and present or future sense.

A large proportion of the conditions with the subjunctive in Modern English are simple conditions, not contrary to fact:

We set up standards and then proceed to measure each judge against these standards whether he be a sixteenth or nineteenth or twentieth century judge. . . .—Louis L. Jaffe, *Harvard Law Review*, March 1967

Stunkard recorded each subject's stomach contractions for four hours, and at 15-minute intervals asked him if he were hungry.—Stanley Schachter, *Psychology Today,* April 1971

In such conditions a choice is open between the subjunctive and another verb form. Charles C. Fries found that in both Standard and Nonstandard English the subjunctive is used rather seldom, in less than one fifth of the locutions in which it might be. There is no special virtue in using the subjunctive, and it should be rejected when it gets in the way of natural, idiomatic expression.

References: Fowler, "subjunctives"; Fries, *AEG*, pp. 103–07; Hall, pp. 311–14; Jespersen, *EEG*, Ch. 27; Marckwardt and Walcott, pp. 30, 37, 88–89; Pooley, pp. 55–59; Curme, *Syntax*, pp. 390–430; Charles D. Cannon, *AS*, Feb. 1959, pp. 11–19; William M. Ryan, *AS*, Feb. 1961, pp. 48–53, and May 1962, pp. 114–22; Richard L. Tobin, *Saturday Review*, Aug. 8, 1970, pp. 45–46.

Subordinate clauses

See *Clauses, *Comma § 2.

Subordinating conjunctions

The most common subordinating conjunctions—words that relate subordinate clauses to the main clauses of sentences—are these:

after	before	since	until
*although	-er/more . . . than	*so that	*when (whenever)
*as	how	*that	*where (wherever)
*as . . . as	*if	though	*whether
*as if, as though	once	*till	*while
*because	*provided	unless	why

The *relative pronouns (*who, which, that, what*) function also as subordinating conjunctions. See also *for.

Subordination

Sub

Revision: Correct the faulty subordination.

Subordinate sentence elements are single words, phrases, or clauses that modify other elements in the sentence; but the term *faulty subordination* applies specifically to the handling of dependent clauses. Dependent clauses are introduced by connectives like those listed in *subordinating conjunctions or by *relative pronouns. The clauses are used in the grammatical functions of nouns, adjectives, and adverbs. Three types of faulty subordination are commonly distinguished:

1. Tandem or excessive subordination is the piling up of one dependent clause after another, each modifying an element in the preceding clause. The weakness is in style, not grammar:

Tandem: For his teachers, he had carefully selected those who taught classes that had a slant that was specifically directed toward students who intended to go into business.

Revised:. . . those who slanted their courses toward students intending to go into business [or: toward future businessmen].

2. Thwarted subordination occurs when *and* or *but* is added to a dependent clause that is already connected to the independent clause by its subordinating conjunction or relative pronoun. It is a grammatical lapse most commonly found in the form of *and which* · and *but which* (see *which § 4).

Thwarted: In the first semester of the course we used three textbooks, and which were continued for the second semester.

Revised: . . . three textbooks, which were continued for the second semester.

Compare the appropriate use of a coordinating conjunction to join two dependent clauses that are parallel: Tolerance is a virtue [which] all of us praise but [which] few of us practice.

3. Upside-down or inverted subordination is not a blunder in style or in grammar but a failure to use subordination in such a way as to make the relationship between statements sensible and logical. It is therefore harder to discuss in isolated sentences, for often it is only the context that determines whether subordination is upside-down. In one writing situation, "Pearl Harbor was attacked when Roosevelt was President" would be satisfactory; in another, "When Pearl Harbor was attacked, Roosevelt was President" might be much better. Without a context, we cannot make a choice as to which statement should be put in the independent clause and which in the dependent clause. But the nature of the statements may make the choice apparent. In most contexts this sentence would sound odd: When I was recovering from the accident, fighting broke out in the Middle East. The relationship of dependent to independent clause needs to be clarified: I was recovering from the accident during the week when reports of fighting in the Middle East filled the news. Ordinarily, upside-down subordination is corrected by turning the dependent clause into an independent clause and vice versa. Often, as in the example provided, some rewriting is advisable.

See *Coordination; *Guide*, pp. 313–17.

Substantive

Substantive refers to nouns and pronouns and other words or groups of words used in the functions of a noun.

such

As an intensifier, *such* is somewhat informal (It was such a hot day; I have never seen such energetic people). In Formal and most General writing, the construction would usually be completed by a *that* or an *as* clause (It was such a hot day that the tar melted; I have never seen such energetic people as I saw in Ballydavid), or the basis of the comparison would be indicated elsewhere in the text:

In spite of high winds and raging seas, they were out in their boats before dawn. I have never seen such energetic people.

As a pronoun (or pronominal adjective), *such* is used to refer to the idea of the preceding sentence or clause, particularly in Formal styles.

When the Illyrians did achieve victory on the frontier, an invasion followed. Such was the situation in 359 B.C. — Harry J. Dell, *Classical Philology*, April 1967

This or *that* commonly serves the purpose in General writing.

Formal usage often has *such as* to introduce examples, where General would have *like. Such as* is preferable when the example is only loosely or nonrestrictively connected to the preceding noun: "A number of big processors, such as Campbell and Heinz, still make their own cans" (*Fortune*, Feb. 1967).

When *such* is used to modify a singular, countable noun, an indefinite article precedes the noun: Such a man is needed. But in the negative the article should be omitted: No such man is needed.

Such is used with *that* to introduce result clauses. An additional *so* is not necessary: There was such a crowd that [not: so that] we couldn't even get to the door. When *such* comes immediately before the *that*, the form is distinctly Formal: . . . a crowd such that we couldn't. . . .

Reference: Bryant, pp. 199–201.

such . . . that

See *such.

Suffix

An element that can be placed after a word or root to make a new word of different meaning or function is called a suffix: *-ize (criticize), -ish (foolish), -ful (playful), -th (warmth)*. See *Adjectives § 1; *-ce, -ge; *Origin of words § 3a.

Superlative degree

See *Comparison of adjectives and adverbs § 3.

sure

Sure in Standard written English is primarily an adjective (sure footing; as sure as fate; Are you sure?). As an adverb meaning "certainly," *sure* is Informal to General, while *surely* is General to Formal:

It's a novel interpretation, but it sure saves oranges. — Horace Sutton, *Saturday Review*, Feb. 8, 1964

. . . the Art Commission said it surely did want to honor this splendid son of Italy. — Donovan Bess, *Harper's*, Feb. 1963

As an adverb modifying *enough, sure* (never *surely*) is in General use: "And sure enough, in all the fearful discussions about computers, the question that inevitably comes up . . ." (Robert Langbaum, *Yale Review*, Winter 1965).

Surface structure

After the *base rules generate a *deep structure, this deep structure is changed by a series of transformations into a surface structure. Strictly speaking, the surface structure of a sentence is not the sentence spelled out or pronounced but rather the sequence of grammatical elements and the way they are grouped. However, we will use spelled-out sentences to illustrate surface structure. A sentence like "The chicken is ready to eat" has the surface structure *article + noun + verb + adjective + to + verb*. The deep structure may be either [the chicken is ready [someone eats the chicken]] or [the chicken is ready [the chicken eats something]]. See *Guide*, pp. 271–76.

Syllabication

See *Division of words, *Monosyllables.

Syllogisms

See *Guide*, pp. 156–71.

Synecdoche

See *Figures of speech.

Synonyms

Broadly, synonyms are words that mean the same thing. More strictly, they are words that share at least one cognitive meaning. Very few words are completely interchangeable, since no two are likely to share all their meanings and to have the same connotations. At the very least, they will differ in sound and therefore in stylistic value.

Choosing among synonyms requires consideration of both sense and sound. The chosen word must be exact in meaning and in suggestions, and it must fit the sound pattern. Unwisely used, collections of synonyms result in a stilted, pretentious style. See *Guide*, pp. 357–59. Reference: Bolinger, pp. 113–14, 232–34.

Syntax

Though the meaning of the term varies from one theory of grammar to another, *syntax* refers in general to the order and relations of the elements of sentences. That the subject of a sentence, for example, ordinarily comes before the predicate is a feature of English syntax. Many *Index* articles discuss points of syntax—for example, *Adjectives, *Subject and verb, *Word order. See also *Verbs § 4.

Taboo in language

See *Euphemisms. Reference: Mencken, pp. 339–400.

Tandem subordination

See *Subordination § 1.

teach, learn

See *learn, teach.

Telegraphic style

See *Newspaper English.

Tenses of verbs

Tense

Revision: Make the tense of this verb conventional in form or consistent with others in the passage.

Different grammarians have used the term *tense* very differently in describing English verbs. Is there a future tense in "He is going to go"? Is *could* the past of *can*? How many tenses are there in English, and what do they mean? Can we equate the inflected tense of a verb with the time of its action?

1. *Tense and auxiliaries.* If we ignore a good many problems of detail, we can find tentative answers to at least some of these questions. Assuming that *could* is the past of *can*, we can say that every English verbal phrase will contain a main verb and that either this main verb (if no auxiliaries precede it) or the first preceding auxiliary will be marked for present or past tense: He drives [main verb, present tense]; He did [past tense] drive [main verb] then. The chief auxiliaries are *do, have*, and *be. Do* is used not only in the so-called emphatic tenses, as in the preceding example, but in questions and negatives in the present and the past: The blockade *didn't frighten* the natives; *Does* the air never *smell* good in the city? *Have* and *be* as auxiliaries are not used with auxiliary *do* (except in imperatives like "Do be working when she looks in"); but they are used together, with *have* first, then the *be* of the progressive, then the *be* of the passive: have been being threatened. The remaining *modal auxiliaries include at least *shall, will, can, may*, and *must*.

Since the modals precede all other verb forms within an English verbal phrase, the longest such phrase that we can make would be something like "should have been being mended." Observe that the verb form after a modal or *do* is uninflected (should have), that the form after *have* or the *be* of the passive is a past participle (has been, was mended), and that a present participle follows progressive *be* (are reading).

2. *Tense and forms.* Given these facts, one can see how some grammarians have found just two tenses in English, others six, others eight (and even more). Those who say there are only two tenses are thinking of inflection, the changing forms of verbs as individual words: if we use no auxiliaries, the only tenses we can form are present and past (*plays, played; playing* is a participle). With the auxiliaries, however, we can just as easily find six tenses, which roughly translate the six of Latin. To the present and past, *shall* and *will* add a future (shall argue, will reason); *have* in its present and past forms adds present perfect (has confused) and past perfect (had baffled); and *have* and *shall* or *will* together give the future perfect (will have vanished). The complete scheme of the schoolroom grammars emerges if we consider the uses of *do* (emphatic: does consider) and *be* (progressive: is sleeping), while if the past of *shall* and *will* is also taken into account, one can speak of a past future (would go) and even a past future perfect (would have gone).

3. *Tense and time.* The meanings of our verbal phrases are harder to describe than their forms. Sometimes *could*, for example, is indeed the past of *can* (He could swim better last year than he can now), but in other uses the difference between *can* and *could* has nothing to do with time or tense (Can /Could you lend me five dollars until tomorrow?). Again, the meaning of the progressive is certainly not purely temporal: one element of it seems to be something like "voluntary activity," so that we say "The baby is crying" or "The baby is being good" but not "The baby is being fat" or "The baby is knowing her mother."

For reasons like these, what is commonly assumed — that the function of tense is to show time and that the time shown is that suggested by the name of the tense — is only partly true. When we say, "He leaves for New York tomorrow," we are talking about future *time*, but the inflection -*s* on *leaves* shows we are using present *tense*. When we say, "He has left," we are talking about the past, but the inflection -*s* on *has* shows we are again using present *tense*. Because tense and time do not coincide in English, some linguists use *past* and *nonpast* instead of *present* and *past* to name the inflections.

4. *Problems with tense.* Luckily, a finished analysis of tense in English is not necessary to the use of English verbs. Practical problems involving tense include mainly the forms of irregular verbs (see *Principal parts of verbs), a few *Nonstandard phrases (might could, had ought, if he'd a gone), the sequence of tenses (see § 5), and unnecessary shifts. Careless shifts like these are distracting and annoying:

The observers unobtrusively *slipped* in the back door while the children *were* still getting settled at their desks. The class *begins* with the teacher reading a short passage from *Christopher Columbus, Mariner,* at the end of which she *asked* whether anyone *has* read any other books about Columbus.

5. *Sequence of tenses.* The term *tense sequence* applies to a pattern of adjustment between verbals and verbal phrases occurring in certain sequences. Even though a dependent clause reporting something said, thought, or believed might refer to a present state of affairs, it is ordinarily put in the past tense when it is the object of a verb in the past tense: What did you say your name *was*? They didn't tell me that you *looked* like this.

But when the dependent clause describes a timeless state of affairs, the present tense is often used:

. . . the idealism of the Renaissance . . . asserted that honor is the reward of virtue. . . . —Jean Gagen, *PMLA*, Sept. 1964

It was finally realized, as late as the 19th century, that the two views are contradictory. . . . —George Gaylord Simpson, *American Scientist*, June 1967

The formal sequence of past—past can sometimes be misleading. To report the statement "I am optimistic about the outcome of the election" as "He said he was optimistic . . ." invites doubt about whether the optimism persists. "He said he is optimistic . . ." removes the ambiguity.

In most expository writing, problems of this sort are not troublesome. Though the past tense of the subordinate clause may refer to present as well as to past time, the resolution of its ambiguity can be safely left to the context or dismissed as immaterial. But in daily newspaper reporting, where space does not allow for leisurely development of facts and where the question of present reference is very important, writers commonly disregard the formal sequence of tenses and fit the tense to the time. The use of the present tense is well established here: "Sanford said many of the conflicts . . . arise from policies . . ." (*Chicago Daily News*, April 7, 1970).

See *Verbs. References: Robert L. Allen, *The Verb System of Present-Day American English* (New York: Humanities, 1966); Noam Chomsky, *Syntactic Structures* (New York: Humanities, 1957); Curme, *Parts of Speech*, pp. 241–333, *Syntax*, Ch. 18; A. S. Hornby, *A Guide to Patterns and Usages in English* (London: Oxford Univ. Press, 1954); Jespersen, *EEG*, Chs. 23–24; Joos; F. R. Palmer, *A Linguistic Study of the English Verb* (Coral Gables: Univ. of Miami Press, 1968); W. F. Twaddell, *The English Verb Auxiliaries* (Providence: Brown Univ. Press, 1960).

than

At its simplest level, the choice of case after *than* can be illustrated by the sentences "He is taller than I" and "He is taller than me." Both are used in General writing. Conservatives favor the nominative after an intransitive or linking verb, but many writers use the objective.

When the verb before *than* takes an object, however, the nominative and objective cases after *than* may have different meanings: She likes him more than I [do]; She likes him more than [she likes] me. Hence in Standard English the case of the pronoun used with *than* after a transitive verb is the same as would be used if the subordinate clause were written out. Use of the nominative case where the objective case is called for, as in the following example, is considered *hypercorrect: Though the jury said we were both guilty, the judge gave my partner a lighter sentence than I.

References: Jespersen, *EEG*, pp. 132–33; Pooley, pp. 166–70.

that

1. That *or* which. Writers have often been urged to use *that* to introduce restrictive clauses and *which* to introduce nonrestrictive clauses; and the advice has value for those who use *which* everywhere, in the belief that it is more elegant than *that*. In general practice, however, the choice between *which* and *that* in restrictive clauses is more likely to depend on rhythm, sound, emphasis, personal taste, and a desire to avoid repetition than on any rule: "A light romantic entertainment like *The Thomas Crown Affair* . . . is the kind of chic crappy movie which (one would have thought) nobody could be fooled into thinking was art" (Pauline Kael, *Harper's*, Feb. 1969).

Nonrestrictive *that* is less common: "Nowadays, it is often said that the copula, that figures so prominently in traditional logic, is superfluous" (Max Black, *Models and Metaphors*).

2. *Redundant* that. When *that* introduces a noun clause in which a modifying phrase precedes the subject, *that* should not be repeated after the modifier: "It must seem to many outsiders that if there is room for honest argument [that] a reasonable doubt had to exist, but the America's Cup Committee hasn't given house room to a reasonable doubt in 119 years" (Red Smith, syndicated columnist, Sept. 27, 1970).

3. *Clauses without* that. A complex sentence like "The work [that] he does shows [that] he has talent" is perfectly correct without either *that*. The subordinate clauses "he does" and "he has talent" are related to the rest of the sentence clearly enough to need no explicit signs of subordination, like *that*. No writer should handicap himself by thinking that a *that* should be inserted wherever it will fit. *That*-less clauses are common in all varieties of usage:

He thinks that the Italians neither approved of Fascist terror nor were really terrorized by it. He thinks [   ] they became numb, resigned, apathetic, and cynical. . . .—Naomi Bliven, *New Yorker*, May 26, 1962

. . . the convention [   ] we accept unthinkingly had not as yet established itself.—William Nelson, *Journal of English Literary History*, March 1969

To use *that* to stress the subordination of short clauses is often to rob them of their force: He knows [that] I'm sorry; I'm glad [that] you're here; Take anything [that] you want.

But *that* is necessary in writing when the clause comes first (*That he might be hurt* never occurred to us) and when a clause has no other subject (There is a moral standard *that has long been accepted*). When a modifier stands between two clauses, *that* is sometimes needed to show which clause is being modified: Mr. Wrenn said [   ] after the guests were gone [   ] Mrs. Wrenn should pack her bags. Depending on the intended meaning, *that* is needed either after *said* or after *gone*.

See *this. References: Curme, *Syntax*, pp. 223–36; Jespersen, *EEG*, pp. 350–51, 360–65.

that is

That is introduces the equivalent of, or the explanation of, what it precedes. It is a rather formal connective and is best kept to introduce series or complete statements. It is usually preceded by a semicolon and followed by a comma: The men worked continuously for three whole weeks to complete the dam on time; that is, they worked twenty-four hours a day in three shifts, seven days a week.

In briefer constructions a comma or a dash would be adequate: They used the safest explosive for the purpose—that is, dynamite. Better yet, *that is* could be omitted: . . . explosive for the purpose, dynamite.

the

1. Repetition of the article before the various nouns of a series emphasizes their distinctness: The color, the fragrance, and the beautiful patterns of these flowers make them universal favorites.

2. In the idiom *the . . . the*, the second *the* has the sense "by so much, by that much." Ordinarily but not always, a comma separates the two parts:

The better the meat, the better the stew. — Elizabeth Alston, *Look*, April 1, 1969

The farther the novel moves in time from the enclosed circle of the Victorian family the more diffuse it becomes. — Charles G. Hoffman, *PMLA*, Jan. 1969

When well handled, the *the . . . the* construction has rhetorical virtues. Treated clumsily, it can be an embarrassment.
References: Curme, *Syntax*, pp. 296 – 98; Jespersen, *MEG*, V, 380 – 82.

their

Their is the genitive of *they*. *Theirs* is the absolute form: This table is exactly like theirs. Except in Formal usage, *their* is often used to refer to indefinite pronouns:

Almost nobody has the words to really talk about their lives. — *Time*, Jan. 5, 1962

It is necessary to make anyone on the streets think twice before attempting to vent their despair on you. — James Baldwin, *Show*, Oct. 1964

then

Then is an adverb of time, frequently used as a connective (conjunctive adverb). Often the connection between clauses is made closer by using *and* with the *then:*

The next three hours we spent in sightseeing; then we settled down to the business of being delegates to a convention.

He ate a good meal, and then he took a nap before starting home.

Adjectival *then* (the then President) is common in General writing, rare in Formal.

then, than

In writing, *then* the adverb of time and *than* the conjunction in clauses of comparison should not be confused: Then the whole crowd went to Louie's; It was better as a movie than as a novel.

there is, there are

When *there* is used as a quasi-subject, the verb ordinarily agrees in number with the "real" subject, which follows the verb: There *is a size* for every need; There *are several ways* in which this can be done. When the subject is compound and the first element is singu-

lar, usage is divided. Some writers follow the rules of formal agreement and use a plural verb; others find a plural verb awkward before
a singular noun:

. . . there are much good history, intelligent analysis of social problems,
and good writing.—David Fellman, *American Historical Review*, Jan. 1967

. . . there is no jargon, few footnotes, some repetition, few insights and little
analysis.—Lewis A. Froman, *American Political Science Review*, June 1967

Repeated use of *there is* . . ., *there are* . . . constructions has a
deadening effect on style. See *Guide*, pp. 273, 339. Compare *it.
References: Bryant, pp. 13–14; Fries, *AEG*, pp. 56–57; Jespersen,
MEG, II, 181–83; Marckwardt and Walcott, pp. 37, 89–90.

they

They occurs in all varieties of usage with no explicit antecedent:
"One thinks of Tolstoy, and the story that all day long they had to be
beating omelets for him in the kitchen" (Louis Kronenberger, *New
York Times Book Review*, Jan. 5, 1964). The indefinite reference is
troublesome, however, when the vague pronoun clashes with the
suggestion of particular individuals (Around campus they were saying
that they had a plan to boycott classes); and often impersonal *there* is
preferable: There have been [instead of: they have had] no serious
accidents at that crossing in years. Reference: Bryant, pp. 211–12.

thing

Thing is often *deadwood in writing: The first thing you do is to [First
you] get a few small twigs burning.

this

This, like *that*, is regularly used to refer to the idea of a preceding
clause or sentence: He had always had his own way at home, and
this made him a poor roommate. Current usage favors *this*—so much
so that it is overworked. References: Paul Roberts, *AS*, Oct. 1952,
pp. 171–78; Bryant, pp. 172–74; Long, pp. 290–93.

though

After a period of literary disuse, during which it was considered colloquial, *though* in the sense "however, nevertheless, for all that" now
appears in all varieties of writing:

Two things are clear, though.—James W. Fesler, *American Political Science
Review*, Sept. 1967

The fall of Umuahia, though, wouldn't mean the end of the war.—William
Hedgepeth, *Look*, April 1, 1969

thus

Present participles that introduce phrases are expected to modify
nouns or pronouns. A *thus* before the participle does not change the
expectation but has a tendency to encourage loose modifiers:

D. Eldred Rinehart's term on the racing commission also is expiring, thus opening up the chairmanship. . . . —*Washington Post*, Jan. 27, 1969

Westmoreland has not been given enough troops, thus making his job nearly impossible. —*Newsweek*, Feb. 19, 1968

See *Dangling modifiers.

Thwarted subordination
See *Subordination § 2.

Tilde
The tilde is the mark (˜) placed over the letter *n* in Spanish words to indicate a pronunciation regularly indicated in English by *ny*: Spanish *cañon*, English *canyon.*

till, until
In all varieties of writing, *till* and *until* are interchangeable both as prepositions (Wait till/until tomorrow) and as conjunctions (Wait till/until they get here). As a clipped form of *until*, *'til* is sometimes found in Informal contexts, but it is not recognized by most dictionaries.

Time
In subordinate clauses the various time relationships are indicated by the conjunctions *after*, **as*, *as long as*, *as often as*, *as soon as*, *before*, *since*, **till*, *until*, *when*, *whenever*, **while*. See also *as . . . as*, *Centuries, *Dates, *Hours, *Tenses of verbs.

Titles of books, articles, etc.
For most purposes, there is a simple rule of thumb: Italicize titles of big works (by underlining them once in manuscript) and quote titles of small works. Italics are usual for titles of books, long poems, periodicals, pamphlets, symphonies, operas, and legal cases. Quotation marks are usual for essays, short stories, short poems, chapters of books, lectures, paintings, statues.

General usage is to capitalize the first word of every title; all nouns, pronouns, verbs, adjectives, and adverbs; and prepositions or conjunctions if they stand last or contain more than five letters: *Wit and Its Relation to the Unconscious; The Sun Also Rises; The Atlantic Monthly; Parts of Speech and Accidence; The New York Times.* Capitals are similarly used, but without italics or quotation marks, in titles of unpublished works, of book series, of books of the Bible, and in the words *preface, introduction, table of contents*, and *index* when they are used as labels for parts of a manuscript or published work.

The (or *a*) is capitalized and italicized or set within quotation marks only if it is a part of the recognized title: *The Yale Law Journal* but the *Harvard Law Review, The American Historical Review* but the *American Sociological Review, The New York Times* but the *Los Angeles Times.*

Most writers feel free to standardize their references when a printed title page varies from the standard form, as with a book entitled *the story of a NOVEL*, or *The Education of H*Y*M*A*N* K*A*P*L*A*N*. Minor variations in recommended practices need not be disturbing if a writer chooses one of the acceptable forms and follows it consistently. For example, one may or may not italicize the name of the city in a newspaper title (the *Los Angeles Times*, the Los Angeles *Times*).

Many newspapers and magazines adopt their own rules for the treatment of titles and enforce them in their pages. *The Wall Street Journal*, for example, the *Chicago Tribune*, and the *Los Angeles Times*, among others, use quotation marks around book titles and merely capitalize the names of periodicals. *Newsweek* uses quotation marks around titles; *Time* italicizes them. For the more rigid and elaborate rules governing very formal writing, like dissertations and scholarly articles, writers should consult such detailed treatments as those in the *Chicago Manual* and the *MLA Style Sheet*. See *Guide*, Ch. Fourteen.

Titles of essays

Since it can help stir the reader's interest, a striking and easily remembered title is an advantage. But strained titles are often ludicrous, and if no good title comes to mind, it is better just to name the subject of the essay as exactly as possible in a few words and let it go at that. As a rule, titles that give no clue to the subject are better avoided. Don't postpone writing an essay (or handing one in) to hunt for a clever title.

The title is considered a separate part of the essay, and the first sentence should not refer to it by a pronoun ("This is an important issue today").

too

In the sense "also," *too* is sometimes set off by commas, sometimes not. Usage is about evenly divided. At times commas are necessary for clarity. Without them, the sentence "Bob, too, frequently interrupted rehearsals to give advice" could be taken to mean that Bob interrupted excessively often.

Though *too* is used to modify past participles after *linking verbs in all varieties of usage (She was too excited; He was too concerned), conservative stylists prefer another adverb of degree between *too* and the participle (too greatly excited, too much concerned). Objection is strongest when the participle could not be placed before the noun as a modifier: He is not too identified with the opposition; Priests are too removed from real life. In such cases, many writers would insist on intervening adverbs—"too closely identified," "too far removed"—particularly in Formal contexts.

toward, towards

These words are identical in meaning, and the choice of one or the other is a matter of taste. The first has been the preferred form in the

United States, but both appear in all varieties of usage. Reference: Bryant, p. 220.

Transformation

A transformation is a rule which changes a sentence diagram, or tree, generated by a *base rule into a new tree. It consists of two parts: a line of symbols that describes the section of the tree to be changed and a second line that indicates how the first line is to be rearranged, shortened, or added to. For example, the base rules might generate a *deep structure for an indirect-object sentence as specified by the first line and transform it into the second line:

NP   V   NP   to   NP
⇒   NP   V   NP   NP

This corresponds to the difference between

Tom gave   money to Bill.
⇒   Tom gave Bill money.

There are perhaps hundreds of transformations in a grammar. The one above both moves elements about and deletes an element. Some just shift elements:

I held up the man.
⇒   I held   the man up.

Some just delete:

I can read German and Bill can read German too.
⇒   I can read German and Bill can   too.

Some replace one item with another item, as when a pronoun replaces a noun:

Tom asked Bill to help Tom fix the car.
⇒   Tom asked Bill to help him fix the car.

Transition

Trans

Revision: Make the transition between these sentences (or paragraphs) clear and smooth.

Transitions are words or phrases or sentences that show the relation between one statement and another, one paragraph and another, one part of the essay and another. When a sentence or paragraph stands as an isolated unit (as if nothing had preceded it and nothing was to follow it), the reader is bound to be puzzled about its relevance. A lack of transition between one paragraph and another is sometimes a sign of faulty organization, sometimes simply neglect on the part of the writer to provide a signpost that will show the reader where he has been or where he is going. A lack of transition between sentences usually indicates that the writer has not thought through the relationship between consecutive statements.

The most familiar of the transitions that indicate relationships and knit a piece of prose together are conjunctions and adverbs — *and, but, still, yet, for, because, then, though, while, in order that, first, second, however, moreover, therefore,* and so on.

Some of the choices available to indicate the common logical relationships are these:

And. When the writer wishes to call attention to the fact that he is adding something, *and is the usual connector. Others that indicate coordinate, equivalent, or similar ideas are **also, again, once again,* **too, likewise, moreover, furthermore,* **then, in addition, by the same token, similarly, analogously.* Restatements are sometimes indicated by such phrases as **that is, to clarify, more simply* or by clauses like *what this means is.*

But. When the relation is one of contrast, ranging from direct contradiction through various degrees of opposition, qualification, restriction, and concession, some of the choices are **but,* **yet,* **however, nevertheless, nonetheless, by contrast, at the same time, instead, in place of, conversely,* **actually, in fact, to be sure, at any rate, anyway,* **still,* **of course, on the other hand, provided that, in case.*

Or. A writer may call attention to an alternative by using **or,* **nor,* **either,* **neither, alternatively, on the other hand* (often following *on the one hand*).

For. A causal relation may be indicated by **for,* **because, since,* **then,* **as.*

So. Result or consequence may be marked by various words and phrases, among them **so,* **then, therefore,* **thus, hence, accordingly, as a result, in consequence.*

For example. When the relation is inclusive — when what follows illustrates what has come before or particularizes it in some way — some of the choices are *for example, for instance,* **thus, to illustrate, in particular,* **namely.*

One, two, three. When the relation is sequential, the transitions may indicate temporal or spatial relations in the subject itself, or they may point up the organization of the essay. Sample time indicators are *then, soon, after, now, earlier, later, ten years ago.* Sample space indicators are *here, there, on top, in the middle, below, on the left, on the right, beyond.* Sequence in a paper may be marked by transitions like *for one thing, for another; first, second, third; to begin with; in short, in brief; finally, to summarize, in conclusion, as we have seen.* Other transitions bring out the relative importance of points — *more important, less important, above and beyond.*

A transition should give an accurate indication of the relationship that the writer intends. Beyond that, the transition should be in keeping with the style and tone of the essay. *Actually* and *incidentally* are overworked as transitions. Since *actually* often introduces a correction and *incidentally* a digression, both may be signs of the need for revision. An unwarranted transition (a *therefore* when the case has not been made) can be misleading. And overuse of the heavier connectives (*however, nevertheless, consequently*) can weigh down the style. Less obtrusive transitions can be made by repeating a key word from sentence to sentence, by using a synonym or a pronoun to echo or pick up the key word, and by binding sentences or parts of sentences through parallel structures. Whether the transitions are overt or subtle, they are the chief means of giving a piece of writing *coherence. See *Guide*, pp. 201–04 and 247–62. Reference: W. Ross Winterowd, *CE*, May 1970, pp. 828–35.

Transitive and intransitive verbs

A transitive verb is one that is used with a direct object; an intransitive verb is not so used: The janitor put [transitive] the books on the shelf, but they soon vanished [intransitive]. Some verbs may be transitive in one sense and intransitive in another (He grows corn; The corn grows well), and in the course of time intransitives may become transitives (as *answer* has done) or transitives may become intransitive (some senses of *withdraw*); but at any one time in the history of English, a given verb in a given sense may be classified according to its use with an object or without. We can disappear, but not disappear something, put something somewhere, but not just put. See *lay, lie; *set, sit.

transpire

Long objected to in the sense of "happen" or "occur" because of its literal meaning in botany and its related figurative meaning "to emerge or come to light," *transpire* is regularly used to mean "happen" in General and Formal writing and is understood by many people in no other sense.

Transpose

A change in the order of sentences or paragraphs in copy can be shown by using numbers in the margins opposite the elements to be changed or by circling the material to be shifted and drawing arrows. The transposition of letters, syllables, or words can be shown by a curved line:

Connecticut   recieve

Triads

Parallel *series of three units are so common in writing, especially in Formal writing, that they form a definite trait of style. Such a series is called a triad:

And who am I to talk? A Catholic who is no longer a Catholic, an Ulsterman who holds a Canadian passport and lives in California, an Irishman who has lived longer out of Ireland than he has lived in it. — Brian Moore, *Atlantic*, Sept. 1970

Trite

Trite

Revision: Replace the trite expression with one that is simpler and fresher.

The most troublesome trite words are worn-out figures of speech or phrases: the picture of health, the order of the day, reign supreme, from the face of the earth, crack of dawn, acid test. What was once fresh and striking has become stale and hackneyed from being used again and again with no sense of its figurativeness. This passage compresses a great number of trite expressions into small space:

The Blushing Bride

I suppose it is natural that I should have been asked to step into the breach on this happy day, if only because I have had the privilege of knowing Geraldine since she was so high. . . . Onlookers see most of the game, you know, and it is easy to be wise after the event, but I thought I could see which way the wind was blowing last August.

They say marriages are made in Heaven, well, be that as it may, these two look as happy as the day is long. It was a great pleasure to me to see Hubert give away his one ewe lamb to such a regular chip off the old block as our friend here. Like father like son, they say, and I think his father deserves a pat on the back. As for Geraldine, bless her, she is a real Trojan, and has been a tower of strength to her dear mother, who doesn't look a day older than when I first set eyes on her, far longer ago than either of us cares to remember.

At moments like this, when family ties are stronger than ever, these young things should remember how much they owe to their parents.

One last word, I must not fail to remind Geraldine that the way to a man's heart is his stomach, and to warn Bertrand that the hand that rocks the cradle rules the world.

Now, I mustn't take up any more of your valuable time, I feel sure you will all join me in drinking the health of the happy couple, and wishing that all their troubles may be little ones. — Georgina Coleridge, *I Know What I Like*

One way to guard against triteness is to recognize figurative language for what it is and to avoid using it unless you mean it — that is, unless the figure conveys an intended extension or nuance of meaning. Remember, too, that triteness is not a matter of age. Yesterday's *vogue expression can be as worn a cliché as one handed down for generations. See *Guide*, pp. 361–62, 388–89.

try and

Though the idiom *try and* (He flew to Cairo to try and ease tensions) appears regularly in General and Informal contexts, Formal style insists on *try to*. References: Hall, p. 309; Jespersen, *MEG*, V, 209–10; Marckwardt and Walcott, pp. 34, 92.

-type

The use of *-type* in compound modifiers (Polaris-type missile, new-type car, handsome-type man) has spread in all varieties of usage but arouses strong distaste in conservative stylists. Most writers prefer *type of* (Polaris type of missile) or, where it is unnecessary, the omission of *type* (new car, handsome man). The practice of shortening *type of* and *make of* to *type* (this type letter) and *make* (this make car) is rejected by conservative stylists.

Typewritten copy

Use only one side of the sheet, leave wide margins at both left and right, keep type clean, and change ribbons regularly. In first drafts, using triple space and leaving extra space between paragraphs will provide room for revision. The final draft should be double spaced.

Indent the first lines of paragraphs five spaces. Long quotations may be indicated in double-spaced copy by indenting the number of spaces used in paragraphs and single spacing the quoted matter. No quotation marks are used with this style.

For the figure 1, use the small *l*, not capital *I*. For a dash use two hyphens. Leave a space after all other punctuation marks except at the end of sentences, where two spaces should be used.

Transposed letters should be erased and retyped or corrected with a curved line (see *Transpose). Strikeovers are often hard to read. A few mistakes can be corrected in ink, but if there are many, the page should be retyped. See *Proofreading.

Umlaut

Umlaut is the name nineteenth-century German grammarians gave to a sound change by which a vowel becomes more like a sound in a following consonant. *Umlaut* is also the name for the diacritical mark (¨) that is placed over umlauted vowels in German.

Underlining

See *Italics.

Understatement

See *Negatives.

uninterested

See *disinterested, uninterested.

unique

In strict Formal usage *unique* means "single, sole, unequaled" and consequently is not compared. In General usage, *unique*, like so many other words of absolute meaning, has become somewhat extended. As an emphatic *rare*, it is often found compared with *more* or *most:*

. . . the more unique his nature, the more peculiarly his own will be the colouring of his language. — Otto Jespersen, *Mankind, Nation and Individual from a Linguistic Point of View*

. . . it makes the ancients appear startlingly modern and we, and our problems, perhaps less unique than we had thought. — Helen Nelson, *Saturday Review*, Feb. 6, 1965

See *Comparison of adjectives and adverbs § 4.

United States

Like many proper nouns, *United States* is often used as an attributive: "There are some who think that the United States attempt to overthrow the Castro government was an act of international immorality . . ." (Richard H. Rovere, *New Yorker*, May 6, 1961). No apostrophe is needed. Since *United States* has no adjectival form, the construction often sounds awkward; and in most contexts *American* — or, where confusion is possible, *of the United States* — would be preferable. See *American.

Unity

Genuine unity is to be judged in the light of the writer's purpose. The test of unity is found not in any general principles that can be applied in every situation but in appropriateness to the writer's view of his material and his consistency in carrying out his purpose. Even so, the reader must always be considered: he cannot be expected to discern a unity that is not apparent in the essay, however clear it is in the writer's mind. See *Coherence.

until, till

See *till, until.

up

Up is a member of many typical *verb – adverb combinations in general use (*give up, grow up, sit up, use up*). Because they have developed meanings which are not the sum of the meanings of their parts, they are usually entered separately in dictionaries, and they behave like independent verbs. *Up* also appears in a number of other combinations to which it contributes no new element of meaning (*divide up, fill up, raise up, join up*). These idioms occur frequently in General writing but are usually avoided in Formal.

Upside-down subordination

See *Subordination § 3.

Usage

The study of usage is based on an accumulation of specific instances and depends on wide observation of what people say and write in various situations to provide a basis for judging the standing of particular words, forms, and constructions. No one person can cover this vast field thoroughly, though he can amass a considerable body of data. Since many people make special studies of individual points and present them in articles — in *American Speech, College English, Word Study*, and other periodicals — a good deal of reliable information accumulates. Four important books on usage are worth studying for their method, data, and conclusions:

Albert H. Marckwardt and Fred G. Walcott in *Facts About Current English Usage* (1938) present not so much a record of actual usage as of attitudes toward it. They include the results of the Leonard questionnaire to editors, teachers, and businessmen asking their judgment of a number of proscribed items and add the record of scholarly studies of those items. They give recommendations based on this material.

C. C. Fries' *American English Grammar* (1940) presents systematically the language found in a large group of letters and considers it in relation to the education and social position of the writers. The study made clear that educated writers of Standard English show more variation in usage than was commonly thought.

George Summey's *American Punctuation* (revised 1949) discusses the practices in punctuation he discovered from studying a large body of printed material.

Margaret M. Bryant's *Current American Usage* (1962), a compilation of evidence on American usage, contains about 240 entries and is based on hundreds of individual investigations.

As a result of these and other studies — including *Computational Analysis of Present-Day American English* by Henry Kučera and W. Nelson Francis (Providence: Brown Univ. Press, 1967) — we now have a more accurate picture of what educated users of English say and, more especially, write. But recording usage by itself is not enough. Although relative frequency of occurrence is an important fact, it gives only the range of usage. Dictionaries may not adequately present actual practice. The history of a word or construction, in the *Oxford English Dictionary* or a history of the language, is often instructive, because such histories reveal that a good many strictures on usage are of relatively recent origin. Another source of information is the explicit or incidental comments of writers, defending their own preferences or lamenting those of others.

People's attitudes toward usages — which are not always consistent with their own usage — need to be taken into account. Most questions are concerned not with differences between Standard and Nonstandard English but with matters of *divided usage within Standard English. A student of usage, then, needs not only to observe widely what is said and written but also to note the attitudes of people toward particular items. Although the authors are predominantly conservative, a range of attitudes is represented in the better-known guides to usage, among them Theodore M. Bernstein, *The Careful Writer* (New York: Atheneum, 1965); Roy H. Copperud, *A Dictionary of Usage and Style* (New York: Hawthorne, 1964) and *American*

Usage: The Consensus (New York: Van Nostrand Reinhold, 1970); Bergen and Cornelia Evans, *A Dictionary of Contemporary American Usage* (New York: Random, 1957); Wilson Follett, *Modern American Usage: A Guide*, ed. and completed by Jacques Barzun (New York: Grosset, 1970); and H. W. Fowler, *A Dictionary of Modern English Usage*, 2nd ed., rev. by Sir Ernest Gowers (New York: Oxford Univ. Press, 1965).

Usage judgments vary. The hundred-member panel on usage that expressed opinions on some eight hundred locutions for *The American Heritage Dictionary* agreed unanimously on just one. Like every other writer, you must make your own choices. But they should be intelligent choices, based on sound information. The best safeguard against avoidable bias is awareness of some principles of selection; the principle proposed in this *Guide-Index* is appropriateness. And there is the intangible called taste. If, like most of us, you find some locutions too stuffy or too crude, you can simply not use them. No one can control the usage of others, but everyone can control his own. References: Paul Faris, *CE*, May 1970, pp. 836–44; Martin Joos, *The Five Clocks* (New York: Harcourt, 1961).

utilize

Utilize means specifically "put to use." The verb *use* is almost always preferable.

Verb-adverb combinations

In "I looked up at the top of the tree," the verb *look* is used in its ordinary sense and is modified by the adverb *up*. In "I looked up the word in the dictionary," *looked up* is a verb meaning "investigated," a meaning not explained by a literal use of the two words. Similarly a man may *break out* (literally) of jail, or *break out* with measles; he can *look after* a departing car, or *look after* the children. In each of these pairs of expressions, the first has a verb modified by an adverb in its ordinary meaning, and the second is really a different verb, with a meaning of its own, composed of two elements. These have become a single word, the parts of which can sometimes have more than one position in a sentence. Compare "I *looked up* the word in a dictionary" and "I *looked* the word *up* in a dictionary."

There are hundreds of such verb-adverb combinations in use, most of them one-syllable verbs with adverbs like *about, around, at, by, down, for, in, out, through, to, up, with*. They are widely used in General English and often give an emphatic rhythm differing from the more formal *investigate* (look into), *sacrifice* (give up), *surrender* (give up). This pattern is now the most active way of forming new verbs in English. When the combinations develop meanings beyond what their elements imply, they are separately entered in dictionaries.

verbal, oral

See *oral, verbal.

Verbals

The parts of a verb that function as nouns or adjectives are called verbals. For their various uses see *Gerunds, *Infinitives, *Participles.

Verbs

1. *Verbs as a part of speech.* If we exclude *be* and the modals, all verbs can be identified by their capacity to add to the base form (*ask, sing, tear*) the suffix -*ing* (*asking*), the suffix -*s* (*asks*), and the suffix -*ed* (*asked*)—but *have* + *s* = *has*; *have* + *ed* = *had.* Some verbs use other formal devices as the equivalent of the -*ed*—*sing, sings, singing, sang, sung; tear, tears, tearing, tore, torn;* and *hit, hits, hitting, hit. Be* has eight forms (*be, am, is, are, was, were, being, been*); *can, may, must,* and other *modal auxiliaries have only one or two forms. We recognize verbs by their form and sentence position even when we don't know their meaning. In "I am sure that his words will coruscate," we know that *am, will,* and *coruscate* are verbs—*am* and *will* because we have already learned their forms, functions, and meanings, and *coruscate* because it depends on *will,* even if we have no notion of its meaning. As suggested in the first sentence of this paragraph, verbs fall into two classes, a closed one (no new ones are added) whose function is primarily grammatical, and an open one (new ones are constantly added) whose *lexical meaning is important. In "He got hurt," *got* performs the grammatical function of showing past tense and passive voice, and *hurt* carries the lexical meaning.

2. *Typical function.* The syntactical function of verbs is typically to form the predicate of a clause or sentence—that is, to join with a subject, and perhaps an object, to form a single construction. For convenience we are using *verb* instead of some more specific word like *predicator* to indicate this function as well as to indicate the part of speech.

The rhetorical function of a verb is usually to comment on the topic of a sentence. Generally speaking, the important action in a sentence should be in the main verb after the topic-subject has been stated. In the sentence "The possibility of a decision in regard to an investigation of student protest exists," the only verb is *exists;* it states only that the very long and complicated topic-subject is there for the reader to consider. But the important action is not that a possibility exists; it is that someone may decide to investigate why students protest: [The President?] may decide to investigate why students protest. This sentence has three verbs: *decide, investigate,* and *protest.* Those are the crucial actions in the sentence and should be represented in verbs, not in the abstract nouns related to the verbs.

Too often the main verb of a sentence is a lexically empty verb like *make, have, give,* and *get,* and abstract nouns related to lexically full verbs are subjects or objects. Unless there is good reason to keep a sentence abstract and impersonal, it can and perhaps should be rewritten with the abstract nouns changed into lexically vivid verbs:

The *intention* of the teacher is to make a *selection* of the best papers.
Better: The teacher *intends* to *select* the best papers.

3. *Details of verb forms.* The following *Index* articles give details of the principal characteristics of verbs:

*Auxiliary verbs	*Phrasal verbs
*Commands and requests	*Principal parts of verbs
*Gerunds	*Progressive verb forms
*Infinitives	*Subjunctives
*Linking verbs	*Tenses of verbs
*Modal auxiliaries	*Transitive and intransitive verbs
*Mood	*Voice
*Participles	

4. *Syntax of verbs.* Besides articles on numerous particular verbs (such as *ain't; *be; *do; *can, may; *get; *need; *shall, will), the following articles are especially concerned with the use of verbs:

*Absolute phrases	*Clauses
*Agreement	*Collective nouns
*Commands and requests	*Passive verbs
*Conditions	*Predicate adjectives
*Dangling modifiers	*Split infinitive
*Finite verbs	*Subject and verb
*Fragment	*Subjunctives
*Gerunds	*Tenses of verbs
*Infinitives	*Verb-adverb combinations
*Objects	*Voice
*Participles	

References: All grammars treat verbs. See especially Fries, *AEG*, Ch. 8, and *Structure*, Chs. 5 – 7; Joos.

Vernacular

Vernacular once meant "the local language as opposed to Latin." In England the word was used to refer to natural spoken English as opposed to formal literary English, and this usage gained social and political overtones in the United States. Vernacular humor—that is, comic writing in the English of the farm and the frontier—often celebrated Jacksonian democracy, rural interests, and naturalness and ridiculed the East, city ways, and "fancy" language. Since Twain and Whitman, it has been impossible to flatly oppose the literary language to the vernacular language, for the vernacular has been more important to American literature than the Formal or academic. Thus while *vernacular* is still encountered as a term for Nonstandard English, it is also the term for a literary style derived from the speech of particular classes or regions. See *Colloquial English. Reference: Richard Bridgman, *The Colloquial Style in America* (New York: Oxford Univ. Press, 1967).

very

1. *As a qualifier. Very* is so much used as a qualifier that it may weaken the expression it is meant to emphasize. The *Emporia Gazette* once described its war upon *very* this way:

"If you feel you must write 'very,' write 'damn.' " So when the urge for emphasis is on him, the reporter writes "It was a damn fine victory. I am damn tired but damn well—and damn excited." Then, because it is the Emporia (Kan.) Gazette, the copy desk deletes the profanity and the quotation reads: "It was a fine victory. I am tired but well—and excited." That's how the Gazette attains its restrained, simple, and forceful style. Very simple.

2. *With past participles.* The argument against using *very* before a participle is that a participle is not an adjective but a verbal, conveying not a quality but an action, and therefore cannot be modified by *very* (extremely), which is indicative of a degree of quality. By this argument, an adverb of degree, such as *much* or *greatly*, must stand between *very* and the participle (not *very distressed* but *very much distressed*). But in General usage many participles, both present and past, have for a long time been compared like adjectives and freely modified by *very* and *too: disturbing, more disturbing, very disturbing, too disturbing.* With past participles a scale can be set up: some take *very* (very tired), some *much* (much improved), some either (very pleased, much pleased), some neither (brightly [but not: very/much] lighted). References: Bryant, pp. 222–23; Jespersen, *MEG*, V, 422–24, VII, 398–99; Long, pp. 58–59.

viable

Viable was originally used for newborn infants in the sense "capable of living" and then extended to ideas, institutions, and plans with the metaphysical senses "capable of growth," "capable of sustaining itself in existence," and "capable of being put into practice." As a *vogue word, viable has developed more new senses than the dictionaries can keep up with; but in many contexts it means no more than "workable": a viable program, a viable organization.

viewpoint

Viewpoint is a natural and economical substitute for *point of view*. Although some conservative stylists insist on the longer form, *viewpoint* is not stigmatized in dictionaries: "Before we condemn him for affectation and distortion, we must realize his viewpoint" (E. M. Forster, *Aspects of the Novel*).

Vogue words

Particular words and expressions are constantly enjoying great popularity in one social or professional group or another, but a true vogue word is one that has moved into General usage and there become a fad. Some begin in the slang of the black ghetto or the campus and find their way into the copy of advertising writers; others start in the academy or the bureaucracy and become clichés through the efforts of journalists and commentators.

Some vogue words and expressions had little specific meaning to begin with in the contexts in which they appeared (*like, you know, wow*) and remain mere fillers. Others lose what force and meaning they had (*actually, basically, beautiful, meaningful, relevant*) and become *counter words. Still others take on so many different meanings as to become almost meaningless (*ambience, Establishment, commitment, polarize, massive, viable*). The one thing that all vogue words have in common is that they have become a bore. Writers should make every effort to avoid them.

Voice

1. *Definition and forms. Voice* is a term borrowed from the grammars of the classical languages where it usually differentiates distinctive endings on verbs. In English the term *passive voice* refers to constructions made with the past participle and some form of the verb *be* (was killed); all other verb forms are *active*.

	Active	Passive
Present:	he (is asking) asks	he is asked (is being asked)
Future:	he will ask	he will be asked
Perfect:	he has asked	he has been asked
Infinitives:	to ask, to have asked	to be asked, to have been asked
Participles:	asking, having asked	being asked, asked, having been asked

Get and *become* are also used for the passive voice, especially in Informal English:

If he should get elected, we'd be lost.
Our house is getting painted.
They had become separated from their guide.

The traditional definition in terms of meaning is often a useful guide in identifying active and passive verbs, but there are many exceptions. When the subject of a verb is the doer of the action or is in the condition named by its verb (and predicate), the verb is traditionally said to be in the active voice: The congregation sang "Abide with Me"; They will go swimming; His father gave him a car. When the subject of a verb receives the action, the verb is said to be in the passive voice: "Abide with Me" was sung by the congregation; He was given a car by his father; They had been caught.

There are, however, patterns in English that are formally active but semantically passive to the degree that the subject actually "receives" the action: Your car drives easily; This wood doesn't burn as well as that wood; I received one rebuff after another. These patterns and the formal passive with a form of *be* and the past participle of the verb result from transformations of a *deep structure in which the noun phrase that moves into the subject position is in some sense originally an object. This is clearest in the passive, where a *transformation changes the structure of an active sentence into one for a passive sentence:

NP$_1$ V   NP$_2$
⇒ NP$_2$ be V-ed   by NP$_1$

The truck   pulls   the car.
⇒ The car   is pulled   by the truck.

Other transformations are responsible for the other illustrative sentences. In each case, somewhere in the deep structure, the apparent subject has been an object, a "receiver" of an action.

2. *Use of active verbs.* In most spoken and in much written General English, active verbs are more common than passive because we are accustomed to the actor-action-goal pattern of expression. Active verbs that are not just empty fillers in a sentence are usually more direct and lively than passive forms:

Passive: The idea that we should leave was suggested by Kevin.
Active: Kevin suggested that we should leave.

3. *Use of passive verbs.* Passive verbs occur less frequently, but they have several important uses. They are appropriate in at least three rhetorical contexts:
a — Passives can be used (as in this sentence) when the subject of the discourse would otherwise be the direct object of a sentence. Because passives are the subject of this entire section, it is appropriate that the noun phrase referring to them be made the subject-topic of most sentences in these paragraphs.
b — Passives are appropriate when the agent of the action is either unknown, unimportant, or better left unsaid:

The wheel was not invented to create today's traffic jams.
The well was drilled into solid rock.
It has been decided that male students may not wear long hair.

c — Passives also allow a writer to focus on the agent of an action by shifting the agent to the end of the sentence, where it will be stressed. This is particularly appropriate when the agent is represented by a fairly long and complicated noun phrase:

Active: A team bigger and tougher than anything you would find outside professional football defeated us.

Passive: We were defeated by a team bigger and tougher than anything you would find outside professional football.

Such a shift also allows a writer to build a tighter transition from one sentence to the next. The element ending one sentence leads into the subject of the next.

4. *Overuse of the passive.* See *Passive verbs.

References: Curme, *Syntax*, pp. 102–03; Fries, *AEG*, pp. 188–93; Jespersen, *EEG*, Ch. 12; Joos.

Vowels
See *Pronunciation, *Schwa.

Vulgate English
See *Nonstandard English.

wake
English is oversupplied with verbs for waking from sleep (intransitive) and waking someone else from sleep (transitive):

wake (woke or *waked; woke, waked,* or *woken)* Most common. *Up* is frequently added in General writing.

awaken (awakened, awakened) Almost as common. Somewhat more formal.

awake (awoke or *awaked; awoke, awaked,* or *awoken)* Rather formal.

waken (wakened, wakened) Least used.

want
In the sense "to desire (that a person do something)," *want* is normally followed by an infinitive without *for:* I want you to go. *Want for* is considered objectionable by many.

Want is Informal for "ought, had better": You want to review all the notes if you're going to pass the exam.

In the sense of "lack" or "need," *want* is more common in British than in American usage: The letter, though clear, wants correcting.

Want in, want out, without a complementary verb, is common in speech and is seen in General and Informal writing. Reference: Bryant, pp. 224–25.

way, ways
Way in the sense "far" is established in General writing, though not yet fully accepted in Formal:

A stock can be selling at two cents and be way overpriced. . . .—Thomas W. May, *Atlantic,* Aug. 1969

It goes way back to his red-baiting days. . . .—T.R.B., *New Republic,* March 29, 1969

Both *way* and *ways* are used to mean "distance" (a little way[s] down the road). There is some prejudice against the use of *ways* in writing.

we

We is frequently used as an indefinite pronoun in expressions like "we find" and "we feel," to avoid passive and impersonal constructions. (See *Reference of pronouns § 3.) It is also used to mean "I and others," as in writing for a group or institution; and there is the *we* of the newspaper editorial page, the royal *we* of kings and popes, and the corporate *we* of business letters. Particularly since the spread of radio-television interview and "talk" shows, there is also the *we* that can only mean "I," as in a singer's "We always draw well in Las Vegas."

We for *I* has been taken up by ordinary individuals, with no hint of publicity agents, teammates, or bureaucratic associates, on the peculiar grounds that it is more modest than *I*. But the ambiguity of *we* for *I* is even worse than the condescension of *we* for *you* as in the kindergarten *we* (We won't lose our mittens, will we?) and the hospital *we* (How are we feeling this morning?).

well, good

See *good, well.

what

When a predicate nominative connected to a *what* clause by a linking verb is singular, the verb is singular: What I wish to discuss is the responsibility of students. When the predicate nominative is plural, usage is divided:

What we are getting is old answers to old questions. — Daniel Boorstin, *Look*, Aug. 20, 1968

What he wanted were people who could stimulate. . . . — Anthony Storr, *Esquire*, Jan. 1969

When *what* is the subject of its clause and the *what* clause is the subject of the sentence, usage is consistent if the *what* clause, linking verb, and predicate nominative agree in number: What is needed is a change; What are needed are changes. But when the *what* clause is singular and the predicate nominative is plural, the linking verb may be either singular or plural:

What is required is neither military bases, pacts, nor conspiracies. . . . — Anatole Shub, *Foreign Affairs*, Jan. 1969

Still, what holds all his work together are stylistic qualities. . . . — Richard Kostelanetz, *New York Times Magazine*, Oct. 9, 1966

See *but that, but what.

when, where

When and *where* are traditionally criticized when they occur in definitions: Welding is when [or where] two pieces of metal are heated and made into one. The grammatical argument is that an adverbial clause may not serve as the predicate complement of a noun, which requires as its complement another noun or a noun phrase or clause. Despite the objection, however, the *when* or *where* clause is probably the Standard form for defining in Informal usage and occurs often in General (though not in Formal) contexts.

whether

Or is required after whether when whether introduces a complete or elliptical adverbial clause: Whether [he is] right or not, we owe him respect. In noun clauses, or or or not is not strictly necessary, though it may be used for emphasis:

Whether readers find him successful will depend on their patience. — Charles F. Mullet, American Historical Review, Jan. 1967

If the child at home wonders whether he is loved, the pupil in school wonders whether he is a worthwhile person. — Robert Dreeben, Harvard Educational Review, Spring 1967

When the intended alternatives are fully expressed, or not is redundant: Whether or not the move is good or bad is debatable.

Repeating whether after or can be usefully explicit when the alternatives are long and complex, as in some Formal contexts.

See *if, whether; *Conditions. Reference: Fries, AEG, p. 217.

which

1. The use of which to refer to the whole idea of a preceding clause (They plan to tear it down, which is a pity) is well established; but objections are properly raised when the reference is so loose that the which, at first reading, seems to refer only to the preceding word: She liked the book, which was puzzling. Similarly, a reader should not have to grapple with two which's, one of specific and one of broad reference, in a single short sentence: I worked Saturdays to earn money which was owed on the car, which pleased my parents.

2. Whose as the genitive of which is older and less cumbersome than of which and is preferred by most writers: "a pattern whose outlines are clearly visible" rather than "a pattern the outlines of which are. . . ."

3. For the choice between which and that as relative pronouns, see *that.

4. The coordinating conjunctions and and but connect equivalent which clauses having the same antecedent. Sometimes a writer omits the relative pronoun before the first clause only to find that he needs it before the second: He ignored the game [ ] I watched yesterday and which was rebroadcast last night. In such cases, insertion of which will provide balance.

Sometimes an adjective which clause, which is subordinate, is mistakenly attached to a main clause by and or but: "I took to my heart the memorable statement in Joseph Pulitzer's will, now reprinted every day on the editorial pages of the St. Louis Post-Dispatch, and which I subsequently tacked to the wall of my office . . ." (Willie Morris, North Toward Home). This sentence could be construed as another case of equivalent clauses, to be revised by inserting *which is* before *now;* but it seems more likely that the writer intended to have the single *which* clause ("the memorable statement in Joseph Pulitzer's will . . . which I . . . tacked to the wall") and inserted the *and* to provide some separation from "the editorial pages of the *St. Louis Post-Dispatch.*" In careful writing, a conjunction before a single adjective clause should be avoided, even at the cost of considerable revision.

References: Curme, *Syntax*, pp. 228–30; Hall, pp. 320–27; Pooley, pp. 170–72.

while

As a temporal conjunction, *while* means "during the time that": While the rest were playing cards, he was studying. In General English it is also used to mean "although" or "whereas" (While the cast is talented, the play is a bore) and to introduce the second of two clauses where *though* or *but* might stand (The beagle was a thoroughbred, while the rest of the pack were mongrels). There is some prejudice against *while* when no sense of time is involved. References: Bryant, pp. 231–32; Fries, *AEG*, pp. 236–37.

who, whom

Ideally, function determines form: *who* is used for subjects and *whom* for objects. In all varieties of English, subjects are consistently rendered as *who* except when they are immediately followed by the subjects of interspersed clauses. Then *whom* is common, as if the pronoun rather than its clause were the object of the interspersed clause:

. . . his most ardent supporters were precisely those members of the German *haute bourgeoisie* whom Cecil claims were excluded from political power. — Gerald D. Feldman, *Journal of Modern History*, Dec. 1968

. . . . a solemn old man whom American officials thought might just possibly make a decent guide. . . . — Theodore H. White, *Saturday Review*, Dec. 23, 1961

Formally, *who* is required in such constructions.

Where *whom* is called for, Formal usage observes the proprieties, but Informal and General deviate considerably from the ideal. General usage permits *who* in questions like these:

And who was the hard sell aimed at? — Mary McCarthy, *New York Review of Books*, April 20, 1967

Who are they trying to impress? — Bruce Price, *Washington Post*, April 12, 1970

General usage much prefers *whom* in the object function at the beginning of subordinate clauses, but it sometimes accepts Informal *who:*

. . . how [elections] come out depends on who the voters have to choose between. — James Q. Wilson, *Commentary*, May 1967

. . . who we all know a little and ought to know far better. — Carlos Baker, *New York Times Book Review*, Dec. 13, 1964

The reason educated writers accept *who* as object when they would recoil from objective *I, we, he, she,* and *they* is that *who* is so often in subject territory, preceding the verb. (See the Sapir excerpt, *Guide*, p. 263.) When the pronoun functions as subject, function and position are in harmony, and *who* is almost inevitable. When the pronoun functions as object, function and position are at odds. In Formal contexts most writers take the trouble to ignore position and to let function determine form. In casual conversation, position is allowed to determine form. General usage usually favors the demands of function except when the pronoun introduces the whole sentence (Who can we turn to?). In college writing, subject *who* and object *whom* are normally the appropriate choices.

See *one of those who. References: Bryant, pp. 232–34; Jespersen, *MEG*, III, 197–201; V, 481–85; VII, 241–44.

whose

See *which.

will, shall

See *shall, will.

-wise

This suffix has long had a limited currency in forming adverbs from nouns (*edgewise, lengthwise, slantwise*). Some years ago it increased in faddish use, especially in an abstract rather than a special sense (*average-wise, budget-wise, legislation-wise, tax-wise*) until new *-wise* words became a joke. Now both the overuse and the ridicule have died down. When a noun has no established adjectival form, a *-wise* coinage may serve a need and have the virtue of concision. But often the *-wise* word lacks precision (*production-wise*); sometimes it represents no saving (*economy-wise* versus *in economy*); and it may simply duplicate an existing word (*drama-wise* for *dramatically*). The connotation of jargon is a further liability.

with

A singular subject followed by a *with* phrase is expected to take a singular verb: The sheriff with his three deputies was [not were] the first to reach the scene.

Wordiness

Wdy

Revision: Compress this passage by replacing the wordy expressions with more compact and exact ones.

The use of unnecessary words in conveying ideas produces flabby writing. You can often improve a first draft greatly by reducing long-winded phrases and other circumlocutions to single words that are more direct, more emphatic, and just as clear:

Instead of in this day and age   today
          at this moment in time   now
          during the time that   while
          come in contact with   meet

When *deadwood is involved, no replacement is necessary: Some of the foreign cars were neat and graceful [in appearance]. But often rewriting is needed to correct loose, unfocused expression. See *Guide*, pp. 343–46.

Word order

WO

Revision: Change the order of words or other elements so that the meaning is clearer or the sentence is more natural or more effective.

The placing of words and word groups in a sentence is the most important means of showing their grammatical relationships. Word order plays a major role in style, particularly in achieving emphasis. The work done in many languages by inflections (endings) is performed in English largely by function words (prepositions, auxiliary verbs, and so on—whose functions are made clear by their position) and by word order. We pick up standard word order as we learn to talk. We use the subject-verb-object order of clauses and sentences; we put adjectives before their nouns and relative clauses after their nouns and in general place modifiers near the words they modify.

This article is intended to bring the fact of word order to your attention rather than to attempt to cover the subject in detail.

1. *Position changed for emphasis.* As a rule an element taken out of its usual position receives increased emphasis, as when the object is put before subject and verb:

Object first: That book I read when I was sixteen.
Predicate adjective first: Lucky are the ones who need no longer worry.

See *Guide*, pp. 339–40.

2. *Interrupted constructions.* When a word or words interrupt a construction, the effect is usually unhappy unless the interrupting word deserves special emphasis:

Between subject and verb: Newspaper headlines in these trying and confused times are continually intensifying our fears. More natural: In these trying and confused times, newspaper headlines are. . . .

Between verb and adverb: He took his hat from the peg and put it thoughtfully on. Better: . . . and thoughtfully put it on.

See *Guide*, pp. 334–36.

3. *Confusing word order.* English usually has a modifier close to the word modified. When modifiers are separated from their headwords, the result is frequently awkward, sometimes misleading:

The jury convicted the defendant of assault and battery after deliberating two hours. Better: After deliberating two hours, the jury. . . .

Her uncle, King Leopold, was even unable to influence her. Better: Even her uncle. . . .

Until recently the chains have been able to get special prices on the goods they buy with little opposition. Better: Until recently the ability of the chains to get special prices on the goods they buy has met little opposition.

See *Ambiguity. References: Fries, *AEG*, Ch. 10; Curme, *Syntax*, Ch. 17.

Words
The framework for the treatment of words and word usage in this book is provided in the opening chapter of the *Guide*, pp. 1–26. For general discussion of the use of words, see *Guide*, pp. 349–73. Many specific words that are likely to raise questions have *Index* articles of their own—for example, *black, *comprise, *contact, *factor, *field, *finalize. *Index* articles containing general discussions of words and their uses include:

*Abstract and concrete words	*Gobbledygook	*Origin of words
*Antonyms	*Group words	*Phrases
*Compound words	*Headword	*Repetition
*Context	*Homonyms	*Shoptalk
*Contractions	*Hyphen	*Slang
*Counter words	*Idiom	*Synonyms
*Double negative	*Linguistics	*Usage
*Euphemisms	*Localisms	*Vogue words
*Foreign words in English	*Meaning	*Wordiness

world
Inflated phrases with *world*—"the business world," "the fashion world," "the publishing world," "the world of science (economics, finance, politics . . .)"—can usually be collapsed: After graduation he went into [the world of] advertising.

would, should
See *should, would.

would have, would of
See *have § 3.

Wrong word

WW

Revision: Replace the word marked with one that says what you mean.

No word is right or wrong in itself. As used here, *wrong word* means that the word does not convey a meaning that makes sense in the context. In the sentence "What he said showed real comprehensibility of the problems of Asia," *comprehensibility* does not make sense; it is the wrong word. *Comprehension* would be the right word. Errors like this occur when the writer is attempting to use an unfamiliar vocabulary, when he confuses words of similar sound, or when he simply writes too hurriedly and fails to proofread his work. See *Careless mistakes.

X

X

Revision: Correct the obvious error.

See *Careless mistakes.

Xmas

X is the first letter of the Greek word for Christ. It has been used for centuries as an abbreviation in the word *Xmas*, pronounced exactly like *Christmas*. Today, however, *Xmas* is most likely to be pronounced /ek′ sməs/, and for many its popularity with advertisers has given it unpleasant commercial connotations. Except for purposes of irony, *Xmas* is inappropriate in serious writing.

yet

Yet is both an adverb (The books haven't come yet) and a coordinating conjunction, equivalent to *but:* His speech was almost unintelligible, yet I found that I enjoyed it.

you

As an impersonal pronoun, *you* is more common than *one* in General usage and not at all rare in Formal:

In a sense, Richard III, as Shakespeare sees him, is the little boy who has found out that God does not strike you dead when you tell a lie. — Arnold Edinborough, *Shakespeare Quarterly*, Autumn 1967

. . . there are at least three ways to treat any philosophical work: (1) You may inquire into its background, its history. . . . —Frederick Sontag, *Journal of Religion*, Oct. 1967

Some care should be taken to avoid giving offense by seeming to indicate an invidious distinction between writer and reader: "Your parents depend on alcohol and pills to get them through the day" might better be "Our parents. . . ."

See *one, *they. References: Bryant, pp. 238 – 39; Jespersen, *MEG*, VII, 153 – 54, 156; Marckwardt and Walcott, pp. 30, 72.

youth

As a *collective noun, *youth* meaning "young people in general" can be followed by either singular or plural verbs and pronouns. In American usage the singular construction is much the more common: "Russian youth wants to avoid military confrontation as sincerely as American youth does" (George Feifer, *New York Times Magazine*, April 28, 1963). But when *the* precedes *youth*, a plural verb is often desirable to show clearly that more than a single person is meant: "Such a telecast would not only attract admirers of Mrs. King, but also the youth who identify with Carmichael" (Jack Gould, *New York Times*, June 2, 1968).

Though the collective use includes both sexes, *youth* meaning "a young person" ordinarily refers to a young man, and the ordinary plural is *youths*.

Youth has been so overused by journalists and commentators that sometimes almost any alternative —*young man* (or *men*), *boy(s)*, *adolescent(s), young people, boys and girls* —would be welcome. See *kid.

&

See *Ampersand.

✓   A correction symbol indicating approval: "good idea," "well expressed," and so on.

INDEX TO WRITER'S GUIDE

For additional references, see the alphabetically arranged *Index to English*.

punctuation with, 277, 295–302
restrictive, 300, 329
transformed and reduced, 279–83
Cleft-sentence shifting, 272
Clichés, 31, 37, 72, 361–63, 366, 368, 388
Climax
in essay, 200, 206, 213
in paragraph, 239–41, 251
in sentence, 340
Close (restrictive) modifier, 300, 329, 333
Close punctuation, 297–98, 301
Coherence, 247–62, 380–81
in description, 258–59
grammatical, 248–61
in narration, 54, 70, 92, 257–58
rhetorical, 247
Exercises, 247–48, 254–55, 257, 262–65
See also Transition.
Cohesion. See Coherence.
Coinages, 13
Collective noun, 364
College dictionaries, 350
Colloquial
as dictionary label, 353
style, 25, 283, 385, 390
Colon, 257, 295–99, 302, 317
Combining sentences, 273–76, 313–18
Comma, 294–302
for clarity, 299, 301, 302
in compound sentence, 277, 297, 299–300, 317
with dependent clauses and phrases, 299–300
with nonrestrictive modifiers, 300
with quotation marks, 302
in series,11, 301–02
Comma fault, 288–89
Exercise, 289–90
Comparison and contrast, 47, 76, 80–87, 114, 387
and analogy, 88–90
in argument, 81, 139–43
and balanced sentence, 325
organization of, 83–87, 197
Exercises, 82, 83–85, 88
Complement, 278, 334–35
Complex (false) question, 172
Complex sentence, 276–79, 312–17

Compound-complex sentence, 276, 279, 309
Compound object, 280
Compound sentence, 276–77, 314, 317
punctuation of, 277, 297, 299, 317
Compound subject, 280
Compound verb, 280, 299
Conclusion
of essay, 207–12, 417–18, 450
of paragraph, 239–41
of sentence, 339–40
of syllogism, 157–68
Concreteness
of description, 54–55, 71–72, 388–89
of diction, 13, 28, 55, 309, 363–64, 367–68
Conjoining, 273–76, 313–18
Exercise, 319–20
Conjunction, 13, 255–56, 274, 277–79, 339
coordinating, 255, 277, 300, 314, 317
correlative, 277
subordinating, 255, 278–79, 314–17
Conjunctive adverb, 13, 255, 277, 299
Connective. See Conjunction; Transition.
Connotation, 7–8, 13, 172–73, 213, 357–59, 365, 372
in definition, 112, 115, 352
and denotation, 357–58
Exercise, 359–60
Consequences, argument from, 96–97, 137
Consequent, in logic, 157–60, 168
Construction, shifted, 253, 322
Exercise, 322–23
Constructive definition, 115
Contact clauses, 288–89
Context, 8, 11, 273, 349, 357–60, 364
and allusion, 374
and conjunction, 317
and metaphor, 367, 369–73
See also Rhetorical situation.
Continuity. See Coherence.
Contractions, 9, 13
Contrast. See Comparison and contrast.
Coordination, 299, 313–17
Exercise, 319–20
Coordinating conjunction, 13, 255, 277, 300, 314, 317

Copula, 269–70
Core of meaning, 227–28, 232–33
Correctness, 1, 19, 385–87
Correlative conjunction, 277
Counter-thesis, 126, 173–76, 382
Counter words, 341
Critical essay, 448–54
    audience for, 453
    organization of, 449–50
    quotations in, 452
    voice in, 453
Cumulative sentence, 328–33
    Exercise, 333–34
Cutback in narration, 51

Damning the source, 172
Dangling modifier, 290–91, 331
    Exercise, 290–92
Dash, 294–96, 299–302, 335
Deadwood, 346
Deduction, 156–68
    and induction, 147, 156
    Exercises, 160, 168–71
Deductive order
    in essay, 189–90, 196–98
    in paragraph, 238–41, 243
Deep structure, 271–72
Definition, 47, 107–16, 130–34, 139
    analytic, 115
    circular, 113
    by connotation, 112, 115, 352
    constructive, 115
    dictionary, 351–52, 358
    enumerative, 115
    by etymology, 111–12, 351
    by example, 112, 352
    extended, 109–16, 197
    by function, 115
    genetic, 115
    genus + differentia, 113–15
    lexical and real, 111
    by negation, 113–15
    ostensive, 115
    stipulative, 108, 132
    by synonym, 112
    of technical terms, 20–21, 108
    Exercises, 110–11, 113, 117–18, 134–37
Deletion transformation, 9, 13, 273, 280

Denotation, 113, 357, 367
Dependent clause, 274–79, 312–16, 330
    punctuation with, 299–300
Derived sentence, 269, 271–76
Description, 46, 54–55, 64–65, 71–75, 388–89
    coherence in, 258–59
    cumulative sentence in, 328–29, 331
    and definition, 65
    dominant impression in, 74–75, 259
    objective, 71–72
    organization of, 74, 183–84
    scale of, 74
    subjective, 71–72
    Exercises, 72–74, 75–76, 359–60
Details, 36, 42–43, 87, 95, 105, 364
    in description, 46, 54–55, 71–75, 259, 388–89
    and examples, 76, 78
    and generalizations, 42–43, 54–55, 231, 237
    and sentence length, 308–09, 312
    Exercises, 44–45, 56–57, 72–74, 237
Determiner, 252
Devil-term, 134
Diagramming
    in logic, 163–65
    of structure of essay, 198, 220–21
Dialect dictionaries, 354
Dialects, American, 5–7, 9
Dialog, 50, 298
Dichotomy, 101
    false, 161–62
Diction, 349–77
    abstract and concrete, 13, 54–55, 79, 89, 309, 343, 363–64, 367–68, 385
    archaic, 4, 352
    big words, 360–61, 363
    circumlocution, 344–45
    clichés, 31, 37, 72, 361–63, 366, 368, 388
    colloquial, 283, 355, 385, 390
    connotation of words, 7–8, 13, 172–73, 213, 357–59, 365, 372
    counter words, 341
    deadwood, 346
    denotation of words, 113, 357, 367
    devil-terms and God-terms, 134
    euphemisms, 365–66
    figurative, 89, 367–73, 379

F., ff., in footnotes, 423
Fallacies, 121, 148
  arguing in a circle, 172
  argumentum ad hominem, 172, 174
  argumentum ad populum, 172
  bandwagon, 144
  begging the question, 134, 171–72, 174
  card-stacking, 150, 174
  complex (false) question, 172
  damning the source, 172
  equivocation, 134, 166
  false analogy, 142, 152–53
  false cause, 151–52
  false dichotomy, 161–62
  false dilemma, 139, 162
  faulty generalizing, 134, 149–50
  formal, 158, 161, 166–68
  of four terms, 167
  hypostatization, 144
  ignoring the question, 172
  incomplete enumeration, 161
  irrelevant emotional appeal, 125–26, 134, 172–73
  name-calling, 172
  non sequitur, 167–68
  part-whole (composition), 133–34, 166, 231
  poisoning the well (spring), 172
  post hoc, ergo propter hoc, 151
  prodigious, 139
  red herring, 172
  shifting the burden, 173
  special pleading, 150
  stereotyping, 134, 150
  straw man, 172, 176–77
  undistributed middle term, 166–68, 174
  Exercises, 153–55, 168–71
False dichotomy, 161–62
False question in argument, 172
Faulty generalizing, 134, 149–50
Faulty parallelism, 321–23
Figurative analogy, 90, 152–53, 368–69
Figures of speech, 89, 367–73, 379
  Exercise, 374–77
Flashback in narrative, 51, 183
Footnotes, 395, 415–24, 442
  abbreviations in, 423–24
  form of, 420–22, 438
  ibid. in, 422–23, 434
  informational, 422, 436

  placing, 432
  split, 422
  Exercise, 434–36
Formal English, 10–13, 21–24, 297, 360, 385
  punctuation in, 295, 299
  syntax in, 12–13, 22, 324, 345
  Exercise, 14–18
Formal fallacies, 148, 158, 161, 166–68
Form-class word, 250
Fragment, 284–85
  Exercise, 285–88
Free modifier, 329–30

General English, 10–14, 23–24, 359–60, 369
  allusions in, 374
  punctuation in, 297, 299
  syntax in, 13–14, 324, 345
  Exercise, 14–18
Generalizations, 42–43, 54–55, 237, 388
  in argument, 134, 148–50
  development of, 45–48, 80, 231–33
  and organization, 189–97, 230–31
  Exercises, 44–45, 56–57
Generalized narrative, 50–51, 67, 257–58
Generative-transformational grammar, 268–76, 279–82
Genetic definition, 115
Genus
  in argument, 131–32, 134
  and differentia, 113–15
Gerund, 274, 280
God-term, 134
Grammar, 9, 268–84
Grammatical constructions, long and short, 345
Grammatical means of coherence, 248–61

Hasty generalization, 149–50
Headword, 300, 316
Historical dictionaries, 354
Homonyms, 357
Hyphen, 296
Hypostatization, 144
Hypothesis, 94–95, 148, 150–51, 189, 208, 261

Hypothetical syllogism, 157–60, 174
  Exercise, 160

"I." *See* Voice of writer.
Ibid. in footnotes, 422–23, 434
Identification in argument, 124
Idioms, 6, 380, 385, 390
Ignoring the question, 172
Illicit major, 167
Illicit minor, 167
Illicit process, 167
Illogical argument, 122. *See also* Fallacies.
Illustration as functional unit in paragraph, 238–40. *See also* Example.
Images, 28, 42, 59, 184, 367, 388–90
  as organizing device, 32, 74, 386
Impersonal construction, 363
Incoherence
  in paragraph, 247
  in sentence, 311–12
Incomplete sentence, 283–85
  Exercise, 285–88
Indention
  in footnotes and bibliography, 420, 425
  for paragraph, 219, 222, 225–27, 243
  for quotation, 438
Independent clause, 276, 279, 314, 321
  punctuation of, 277, 295–99, 302
Indexes to periodicals, 398–401
Indirect question, punctuation of, 298
Induction, 78, 148–53
  and deduction, 147, 156
  Exercise, 153–55
Inductive leap, 149, 153
Inductive order
  in essay, 190–91, 196–98
  in paragraph, 241–43
Inference, 79, 147, 157–58, 165, 168, 230, 241
Infinitive, 274, 280–81, 334
Informal English, 9–14, 21–25
  Exercise, 14–18
Informal fallacies, 148, 171–73
Informational footnote, 422, 436
Infra in footnotes, 424
Intentional words. *See* Connotation.
Internal sources of argument, 130–43, 148
Interrupted sentence structure, 334–36
Interrupter, punctuation of, 297, 300–01

Intransitive verb, 270
Introduction to essay, 35, 199, 201, 205–13, 236, 416–18
Invention in argument, 34, 46, 130
Inversion, 336–37
Irony, 284, 337, 372
Italics, 423, 442
It is as sentence opener, 273, 339

Jargon, 363–64, 385, 388
  Exercise, 365
Journal-writing, 33, 49, 390

Kernel meaning, 352
Key passage, 451

Labeling, tactic in argument, 132
Labels in dictionary, 352–53
  Exercises, 8, 354–56
Levels of usage. *See* Varieties of English.
Lexical repetition for coherence, 250–53
  Exercise, 254–55
Library research, 28, 394, 397–406
Likeness-difference, 80–82, 88–89
  in argument, 139–43, 152–53
  organization of, 83–87
Linguistic Atlas of the United States and Canada, 3 n., 5
Literal analogy, 90, 152
Loaded words. *See* Connotation.
Localisms, 5–7
Loc. cit. in footnotes, 424
Logic, 122, 147–77
  and classification, 100–05
  and definition, 113–15
  and paragraphing, 225
  and proof, 122, 124
  Exercises, 153–55, 160, 168–71
  See also Deduction; Distribution of terms; Fallacies; Induction; Validity.
Loose sentence, 328

Magazines
  bibliography card for, 408
  footnote form for citing, 421–22
  indexes to, 398–401
Main (independent) clause, 276–77, 279, 314
  punctuation of, 277, 295–99, 302
Major premise, 157–68

unity, 311–12
and variety of English, 9, 12–14, 22, 324, 345
Exercises, 284–93, 310–11, 319–20, 322–23, 327–28, 333–34, 347–48
Sentence outline, 216–17
Sequence, 380. See also Coherence; Transition.
Series, 260, 323–24, 340, 412, 444
punctuation of, 301–02
Shifted construction, 253, 322
Exercise, 322–23
Shifting the burden, 173
Shoptalk, 13–14, 21
Sic, 411, 423
Simile, 370, 379. See also Metaphor.
Simple sentence, 276, 283, 318
Slang, 4, 13–14, 354, 358
Slanted words, 358
Exercise, 359–60
Slug, 407–10
Sources for research paper, 397–406
acknowledgment of, 418–26
primary and secondary, 414, 427
Sources of argument
external, 143–45, 148
internal, 130–43, 148
Spatial distance, 51–52, 67
Spatial order of description, 74, 183–84
Special pleading, 150
Speech areas of the United States, 5–7
Spelling, in dictionary, 351
Standard English, 8–14
Statement of intention, 33–34, 37, 46–48, 50
Statistics in argument, 144
Stereotyping, 106, 134, 150
Exercise, 107
Stipulative definition, 108, 132
Stock phrase, 362
Strategies of ordering, 199–202
Straw man, 172, 176–77
Stringy sentence, 312–13
Structure
of essay, 183–201, 220–21
of paragraph, 235–46
of sentence, 268–82
Style, 20–25, 378–90, 417
and character, 378–80, 389–90
and figurative language, 363–73, 379

and imagination, 386–90
and paragraphing, 222, 243
and sentences, 283–84, 315, 324–27, 330–37
Exercises, 14–17, 56–57, 390–91
Subject, grammatical, 269–73, 278, 336
and coherence, 249–51, 253, 257, 270
compound, 280
Subject of essay, 20, 33–34, 37
Exercises, 48–49, 128–29, 145–46, 396–97
Subjective description, 71–72
Exercise, 72–74
Subject term in syllogism, 163–67
Subordinate (dependent) clause, 274–79, 312–16, 330
punctuation of, 299–300
Subordinating conjunction, 255, 278–79, 314–17
Subordination, 312–17
tandem, 312
Exercise, 319–20
Summarized narrative, 50–51, 67, 257–58
Summary
of essay, 208, 417–18
notes, 409, 411–13, 419, 440, 444
Superlative for emphasis, 341
Support structure
in essay, 189–90, 196–98
in paragraph, 238–41, 243
Supra in footnotes, 424
Surface structure, 271–72
Suspension in sentence, 334–36
Syllogism, 156–57, 261
categorical, 163–68
either-or, 161–62
hypothetical, 157–60, 174
Exercises, 160, 162, 168–71
Synonyms, 24, 341, 357
as aid to coherence, 214, 252
in defining, 112, 353
Exercise, 354–56

Tandem subordination, 312
Technical terms in writing, 12, 20–21, 108, 172
Temporal distance, 51, 67, 184
Testimony in argument, 143–45
There is as sentence opener, 273, 339

Additional Symbols for Marking Essays